ECONOMIC AND SOCIAL PROGRESS
IN LATIN AMERICA
1996 REPORT

Special Section
Making Social Services Work

DISTRIBUTED BY THE JOHNS HOPKINS UNIVERSITY PRESS FOR
THE INTER-AMERICAN DEVELOPMENT BANK

NOVEMBER 1996
WASHINGTON, D.C.

The Office of the Chief Economist was responsible for the preparation of this report, under the supervision of Ricardo Hausmann and Eduardo Lora.

Part One was written by Michael Gavin and Eduardo Lora with the collaboration of Eduardo Fernández-Arias, Karnit Flug, Antonio Spilimbergo, Ernesto Stein and Ernesto Talvi from the Office of the Chief Economist, based on information, analysis and comments provided by Willy Van Ryckeghem, Bertus J. Meins and Neville O. Beharie and from Country Economists Marcello Averbug, Caroline Beetz, Ladislao Brachowicz, Gabriel Castillo, Gilberto Chona, Justino de la Cruz, James Dinsmoor, Roberto García Lopez, Gonzalo Giraldo, Badrul Haque, Ronan Le Berre, Dougal Martin, Ricardo Martínez, Alberto Melo, Paul Moreno, Ximena Morey, Carlos Oliva, Fernando Quevedo, Jorge Requena, Inder Ruprah, José Seligman and Rafaela Varela Duprat.

Part Two was coordinated by Eduardo Lora. Chapter One was written by Eduardo Lora and Ernesto Talvi. The chapter on trade was written by Florencio Ballestero and Antoni Estevadeordal with contributions from Claudio Ansorena, Martín Arocena, Rafael Cornejo, Tracey Herpen, Claudio Montenegro, Glenn Sheriff and Brenda Simonen. The chapter on tax reform was written by Martín Bes and the chapter on labor reform by Carmen Pagés. The social security reform chapter was written by Eduardo Lora and Carmen Pagés. Glenn Westley wrote the chapters on financial reform and privatization. All the chapters of Part Two substantially benefited from information and analysis provided by the Country Economists mentioned in the previous paragraph, sometimes in collaboration with the IDB's Representatives in the countries and with external consultants.

The Special Section was written by a team from the Office of the Chief Economist led by William Savedoff. The team included Juan Luis Londoño, Daniel Maceira, Claudia Piras and Mónica Rubio, with contributions by Karnit Flug, Guiomar de Mello and Antonio Spilimbergo.

The Statistical Appendix was prepared under the direction of Michael McPeak, and with the participation of Glenn Guymon, Jeremy Harris, Rajindra Lalchan, Fergus McCormick, José Antonio Mejía, and Fernando Orrego.

Research assistance for the production of the first two parts was provided by Alejandro Grisanti, Iván Sergio Guerra, Yoshiaki Hisamatsu, Martin Loser, Marco Rodríguez and Erik Wachtenheim. Extremely valuable secretarial assistance was provided by Cecilia Coder, Leticia Cuevas and Nathan Shattuck and administrative coordination by Cristina Echavarren.

Comments on earlier drafts of the Report were received from William Armstrong, Nancy Birdsall, Neville Beharie, José Luis Bobadilla, Luis René Cáceres, Ernesto Castagnino, Claudio Castro, Guillermo Collich, Xavier Comas, Dora Currea, Edgardo Demaestri, Ruthanne Deutsch, Robert Devlin, Stephen Doherty, Viola Espinola, Carlos Alberto Herrán, Hunt Howell, Enrique Iglesias, Gerard La Forgia, Esperanza Lasagabaster, Elio Londero, Ezequiel Machado, Andre Medici, Karen Mokate, Carlos Gerardo Molina, Samuel Morley, Lillian Quintero, Silvia Raw, Luisa Rains, Liliana Rojas-Suárez, Silvia Sagari, Ernesto Schiefelbein, Hans Schulz, Víctor Traverso, Waldo Vergara, Steve Weisbrod, Jesse Wright, María Eugenia Zavala and Elaine Zuckerman.

We are grateful to the World Bank for providing the data base on privatization and to Andrés Velasco, Amalia Anaya and María Victoria Murillo for background material. Numerous experts and directives of the social sectors of the countries and from the World Bank contributed valuable information and insights on social policies in the region.

The opinions expressed in this report are those of the authors and do not necessarily represent the views of the Inter-American Development Bank or its Board of Executive Directors.

ECONOMIC AND SOCIAL PROGRESS IN LATIN AMERICA

Distributed by
The Johns Hopkins University Press
2715 North Charles Street
Baltimore, Maryland 21218-4319

Library of Congress Card No.: 74-648164
ISBN: 1-886938-06-7
ISSN: 0095-2850

*Dedicated to the memory of
our esteemed colleague and friend,
José Luis Bobadilla,
who devoted his life to improving
health in the world.*

FOREWORD

The Inter-American Development Bank's Report on Economic and Social Progress is 34 years old. It has evolved with the different challenges faced by Latin America and the Caribbean, and has reflected the changes in the institutional and analytical context of the times. This year's Report is much changed from previous volumes. Given the wider availability of information on macroeconomic events in the region, the greater importance of structural aspects of development, and the new means of disseminating information, we thought that this was a propitious time to rethink the structure of our own Report.

The most fundamental change concerns our treatment of recent economic developments in the region. We have eliminated the 26 chapters on individual countries that detailed the previous year's macroeconomic and policy developments. These chapters are still produced twice a year and offered to our readership over the Internet, a medium better suited for efficiently providing information that must be frequently updated.

Instead, we have decided to move the

Report in a direction that capitalizes on the strength and credibility of an established publication and draws on the Bank as a long-term regional development institution. This new direction emphasizes four aspects:

• Cross-country comparison and regional patterns instead of single country analysis;

• Longer-term trends rather than annual fluctuations;

• More information about structural variables in addition to national accounts;

• Structural policies as well as macroeconomic policy management.

The traditional core of the Economic and Social Progress Report has been divided into two parts. Part One covers macroeconomic developments in the region during the previous year, but now in the context of longer-term trends. Part Two assesses the region's structural changes and progress in policy reform. This is of course a broad area, and rather than attempt to cover all of its aspects each year, we plan to analyze different dimensions of reform each time. This year, Part Two covers six areas: international trade and regional integration, tax reform, financial reform, privatization, labor market regimes, and pension reform. We expect this section to become a principal source of information on structural policies that to date have seldom been covered systematically by other organizations. Since these policies change little over the course of a single year, we expect to cover different areas in future issues, so that over time we will accumulate and make available to the public a significant base of comparative information on salient structural aspects of development policy.

The Report continues to provide the very useful country statistical profiles and the statistical appendix that have appeared in previous editions. We have also maintained the special section, which covers a topic of particular importance for development policy in the region. This year, we have chosen to discuss the organization of the social services, focusing mainly on education and health, two areas where the region has reasons not to be satisfied with current performance. Perhaps because they are very often publicly provided, these "industries" do not always capture the attention that they deserve in light of their enormous importance for human capital accumulation, and thus growth, poverty and income distribution. An analysis of their structure and organization permits us to distill lessons for making more effective use of the public role in these sectors.

This Report has benefited from its new structure in a very important and immediate way. Studying the structural reforms led us to analyze issues of timing, sequencing, speed and sustainability from a purely empirical point of view: who did what, when and how. This led to the realization that stabilization and reform programs were in many respects rather similar across countries, typically bundling an exchange rate based stabilization with tax, financial and trade reforms. Not surprisingly, these programs have represented a major policy shock with powerful macroeconomic effects, not just on long-run outcomes, but also on short-run fluctuations. Reviewing the history of these reforms enabled us to identify typical phases that countries go through during the adjustment to the new policy regime, which can include somewhat

counter-intuitive macroeconomic responses. These phases, although not intended to represent universally valid regularities, exemplify tendencies that help in analyzing the stages of change in the reform process, within a medium-term perspective that is supported by the experience accumulated in the majority of countries to date.

The adjustment process thus provided a useful device for organizing our discussion of recent macroeconomic developments in Part One. Focusing on the varying degrees of progress that many countries of the region have been making with stabilization and reform helps to make sense of an otherwise confusing year, during which some countries found themselves in major economic crisis, while others exhibited strong economic growth. It also sheds light on overall economic developments in the 1990s and on likely developments in the region over the short term, and has important policy implications for countries either just beginning or already in the process of major reform programs.

A historical perspective on 1995 highlights two relevant results. First, the reform process continues, even though there remains much ground to cover and many areas to deepen. The banking sector is one of the most visible. The Mexican financial crisis—with repercussions largely limited to Argentina—put to the test the political will of the respective governments to keep the reform process on course. However, the crisis shows that the adjustment process has not yet produced the effects expected by the large majority of the population. In some cases, the adjustment process has even exacerbated existing social problems, cutting personal incomes and strongly raising open and disguised unemployment. Even though the reform process requires time to mature, the increasing fatigue of many social groups requires that governments focus on social problems, with explicit policies to improve the quality of social services delivered with the resources available. For that reason, this Report has presented the subject in the special section.

Part Two of the Report documents progress in some structural reforms. This section starts with an analysis of timing, shifting the focus away from recent economic outcomes and toward the sequencing, speed and sustainability of reform. The analysis shows that countries have made very significant progress in trade, tax and financial reform, in which at least 22 countries in the region have made important changes. These reforms were typically adopted in a "big bang" at the time of inflation stabilization. In general, reforms were adopted in bad times and followed by recovery. These reforms tended to be implemented rapidly, and have survived economic recessions and elections. Privatization has typically lagged behind stabilization, while much less progress has been made on the labor and social security fronts. Only six countries have implemented pension reform and only five have introduced modest changes in their labor codes. In future Reports we will cover other areas of macroeconomics, particularly social areas.

This year's special section argues that, in spite of a very significant political and fiscal commitment to education and health, Latin American social service delivery systems underperform relative to the amount of resources they have managed and the level of per capita income of the populations they serve. It argues that many of the failures of the systems are related to their organizational structure, which it documents with institutional information previously not available. It finds that highly centralized command structures have removed decision-making authority from the schools and hospitals where the services are delivered, limiting providers' abilities to react to the needs of clients and to innovate. These centralized structures have created large bureaucracies typically characterized by conflictual labor relations and difficult governance problems. They have weakened consumer voice and choice, and reduced incentives for local community involvement. Declining quality has caused the middle class to leave the public systems, reducing their willingness to pay taxes for services they no longer demand, and threatening the long-term fiscal commitment to health and education.

The region is starting to deal with these challenges through important and innovative reforms, some of which are documented in this sec-

tion. The implications for policy are presented in the form of recommendations in tune with the complexity of the social service delivery systems. Simple solutions such as decentralization to municipal governments or voucher programs per se are no panacea. Instead, the section calls for coherent systems that clearly differentiate the roles of national governments, specialized purchasing organizations, providers and consumers. The public role in financing and regulating these services can assure equitable distributive outcomes. Allocation mechanisms in which resources follow outputs and not inputs can create incentives to improve the efficiency of services. Delegating greater authority to autonomous providers—such as schools and integrated medical practices—and holding them accountable through both public regulation and empowered consumers can simultaneously provide the scope of decision-making authority with adequate feedback and governance to assure that services perform.

The three parts of the Economic and Social Progress Report are thus very much related to each other. Part Two documents progress in six major areas of structural reform, while Part One analyzes the macroeconomic implications of those reforms to explain the otherwise confusing pattern of outcomes observed in 1995. The special section endeavors to put the reorganization of education and health on the region's reform agenda by providing a framework for the difficult issues involved and presenting the salient information and problems in this emerging area of reform.

In short, assessing progress on well-established areas of reform, analyzing their macroeconomic impact, and contributing an agenda for new areas of reform in education and health is all carried out in the context of a reformed Economic and Social Progress Report. We think this will make the Report more useful. We hope you will agree.

Ricardo Hausmann
Chief Economist

CONTENTS

PART ONE

MACROECONOMIC
DYNAMICS THROUGH
THE ADJUSTMENT
AND REFORM PROCESS

MACROECONOMIC DYNAMICS THROUGH THE ADJUSTMENT AND REFORM PROCESS

MAJOR DEVELOPMENTS IN 1995

After four years of steady growth and an increase in GDP of more than 5 percent in 1994, the average annual rate of economic growth in Latin America and the Caribbean fell to 0.7 percent in 1995. This deceleration was attributable to the fact that Argentina and Mexico, two of the region's largest economies, fell into deep recession in the aftermath of the international financial crisis that followed the Mexican devaluation of December 1994. In the rest of the region, growth in 1995 was, on balance, similar to that recorded in 1994.

The recovery of investment that has supported economic growth in the region continued in 1995, despite recession-related declines in investment in Argentina and Mexico. During 1995, the average rate of growth of real investment was 5.3 percent in the entire region and 14 percent in the region excluding Mexico and Argentina. Real investment grew at double-digit rates in half of the region's economies.

FIGURE 1

GDP Growth

(In percent)

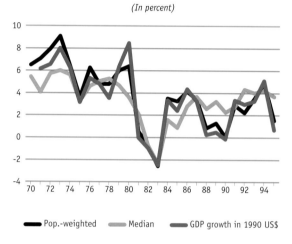

— Pop.-weighted   — Median   — GDP growth in 1990 US$

Table 1.	Major Economic Developments in 1995		

(In percent)

	1994	1995
Real GDP growth		
Regional average (GDP weighted)	5.1	0.7
Regional average (population weighted)	4.9	1.5
Argentina	7.4	-4.4
Mexico	3.5	-6.9
Other countries	5.0	4.4
Growth in real demand (population-weighted average)		
Consumption	5.3	2.8
Investment	5.3	5.3
Exports of goods and nonfactor services	6.1	9.1
Imports of goods and nonfactor services	8.9	13.8
Consumer price inflation (Dec.-Dec. percent change)		
Median	17.6	16.7
Average (population-weighted)	446.2	27.6
International payments (billions of U.S. dollars)		
Current account surplus	-47.5	-32.1
Net capital inflows	44.7	53.0
Change in international reserves (increase=-)	2.8	-20.9

As investment in productive capacity has recovered, so has public investment in people. Social investment in Latin America increased from about 13.5 percent of GDP in the late 1980s to roughly 15 percent in 1993 and 1994.[1] Despite the reduction in economic growth and the impo-

---

[1] Social investment as defined here includes spending on education and culture, health and sanitation, employment, welfare and social assistance, housing, and social security.

FIGURE 2

Median Annual Inflation

(In percent)

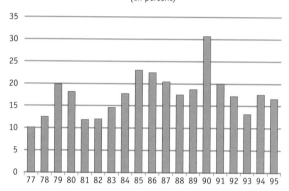

sition of continued fiscal discipline, this recovery of social spending continued in 1995, with increases in spending on education and health both in real terms and as a share of GDP.

Real exports of goods and nonfactor services rose by about 9 percent in 1995, continuing the strong growth recorded during the first years of the decade. This increase in exports reflected in part the very strong response of Mexican and Argentine exporters to the crises in their countries. But this is only part of the story; robust export growth was in fact widespread in the region, exceeding 6 percent in 17 of 24 countries.

At the same time, inflation continued to abate in the region as a whole, either declining or remaining roughly constant in 18 of 23 countries. The median rate of inflation, which represents the inflation experienced by the typical country in the region, fell from 18 percent in 1994 to 17 percent in 1995. With the 1994 stabilization in Brazil and the 1995 stabilization in Suriname, very high inflation has disappeared from the continent. During 1995, inflation rose in Mexico and Venezuela, but by the middle of 1996 Mexico had brought inflation down considerably, and there is good reason to believe that Venezuela will succeed in doing the same as part of its own 1996 stabilization program. The fiscal consolidation that underpins this inflation decline was strengthened during 1995; the average deficit of the region's economies fell to 1.2 percent of GDP, its lowest level in 20 years.

Capital flows to the region remained strong in most countries, despite a brief but sharp interruption in the first quarter of 1995. Capital flows to countries other than Argentina and Mexico during the year as a whole were in fact larger than they had been in 1994. And as the year progressed, even Argentina and Mexico—in whose short-term prospects international investors' confidence had been most severely shaken during 1995—were able to return to international financial markets, albeit at reduced quantities and higher interest rate spreads.

The region's rate of saving increased for the second consecutive year in 1995, although it remained low. Meanwhile, the current account deficit of the region shrank from about 3 percent of GDP to roughly 2 percent.

Economic Reforms

Despite the economic turbulence that affected much of the region during 1995, economic reforms continued to progress in a number of countries. As noted earlier, Suriname implemented a major inflation stabilization program. At the same time, important reforms of financial markets were implemented in Barbados, Belize and Haiti, while Bolivia made important progress in its privatization efforts.

As will be described in substantially more detail in Part Two of this Report, these are only the most recent of a wave of reforms that have been implemented across the region during the past decade and a half. Since the mid 1980s, 18 countries have controlled their inflation, 25 have liberalized trade, 12 have implemented important tax reforms, 24 have reformed the financial sector, 12 have engaged in major privatization efforts, five have reformed their labor market, and five have reformed their pension system.

During 1995, support for these reforms was put to the test, as economic growth slowed

Table 2. Number of Countries Implementing Economic Policy Reforms		
	1994 and before	1995
Inflation stabilization	17	1
Trade liberalization	25	
Tax reform	12	
Financial reform	21	3
Privatization	10	1
Labor market reform	5	
Pension reform	4	

and unemployment rose in several economies. Remarkably, however, the structural reforms undertaken by the region's economies have proven quite durable. Economic reforms were not reversed in 1995, and in several countries, most notably Argentina and Mexico, economic crisis was actually met with a deepening and broadening of reform efforts. Throughout the 1990s, economic stabilization efforts may have suffered a few setbacks, but the region's structural reforms have survived the test of elections and economic crisis in every case except that of Venezuela, where the economic crisis of 1994 was accompanied by reversal of some important reforms.

A Mixed Picture

On a regional level, economic developments during 1995 thus present a mixed picture: progress in many important dimensions was accompanied by various more worrisome trends. On the one hand, inflation generally continued to fall, investment maintained its recovery, fiscal consolidation continued, the region's access to international financial markets was for the most part protected, and there appeared to be no tendency for economic reforms to be rolled back. On the other hand, after a half-decade of increasing financial stability and improving international creditworthiness, the region found itself at the center of an international financial crisis that, at its height, affected many countries. Over the year as a whole, it contributed to the deep and painful recessions now being experienced in Argentina and Mexico. Although the worst effects of the so-called Tequila shock were limited to those two countries, economic recovery in a few others felt a certain stress as growth slowed, currencies came under pressure, and resultant high real interest rates threatened to destabilize the financial system and curtail the investment recovery upon which long-run growth depends.[2]

The picture is mixed, too, in the sense that individual country experiences were tremendously diverse in 1995. On the one hand, Chile, Brazil, Peru and a number of smaller countries experienced very rapid growth, while at the same time Argentina and Mexico fell into very deep recessions.

How do we interpret these developments? Looking forward, what do they tell us about medium-term prospects for the region? Was the 1995 slowdown a harbinger of slower growth to come, after a brief period of unsustainable growth facilitated by recovery from the deeply depressed 1980s and fueled by a burst of capital flows? Or was slower growth in 1995 a transitory interruption of recovery in a region that through its reforms has attained a path of higher long-run levels of growth?

These questions are not easy to answer. Over short periods, economic growth in the region has been influenced by many temporary factors largely unrelated to the economies' underlying longer-term growth potential. During 1995, as in previous years, many countries were hit by important shocks, including sudden variations in the international terms of trade and abrupt, perhaps election-related changes in monetary and fiscal policy. These shocks have been important causes of macroeconomic fluctuations throughout the region, and they are among the factors that make each country's economic history unique.

Adjustment to Economic Stabilization and Reform

As important as many of these shocks were for individual countries, they have been to a large extent country-specific, thus tending to average out over the region. As a result, a focus on such shocks is not very helpful in understanding recent macroeconomic developments in the region as a whole. Recent economic developments can be better understood if the focus is placed instead on the continuing impact of the major shock that actually was common to almost all countries of the region: the major stabilization and economic reforms of the past decade.

These stabilization and reform programs have wrought enormous changes in economic structure and in long-term prospects for growth in the region, and have therefore been an important influence on the trend rate of economic growth that countries can expect to achieve. The reforms in themselves have also constituted an economic shock that has exerted a major, though temporary, influence over economic growth and other important outcomes in the short run.

The response to reform has differed across countries, but certain adjustment patterns or tendencies are frequently observed. In the early phases of adjustment to new policy regimes, economies often experience a boom in spending and production. Economic stabilization often leads to a recovery in the demand for domestic money, which stimulates capital inflows and helps provide banks with financial resources to lend to investors and consumers. The increased bank lending tends to amplify the increase in domestic spending, which in turn often leads to substantial current account deficits and real appreciation of the currency.

The spending boom may involve an element of overshooting, thus setting the stage for a

---

[2] The direct effects of the international financial turbulence generated by the Tequila shock were confined largely to Mexico and Argentina, but some other countries were indirectly affected. Because Argentina is such an important trading partner for Uruguay, the Argentine recession contributed to Uruguay's sharp downturn in 1995. Similarly, there is some evidence that the drastic Mexican devaluation reduced the ability of exporters in some Central American and Caribbean economies to compete with Mexican exporters, thus creating an adverse spillover of the Tequila shock to those countries.

period of slower growth in the latter phases of the adjustment process. And as the boom proceeds, it often generates economic and financial vulnerabilities, as the banking system becomes overextended and external imbalances accumulate. These imbalances can make the economy vulnerable, and they often require a period of correction. In some cases, they can even precipitate an economic crisis.

The period of correction or crisis often associated with the adjustment process is painful in itself and also carries with it the danger that hard-won stabilization and reform measures will, at least temporarily, be reversed. Such reversals are not inevitable, however, and in fact a review of the Latin American experience suggests that the region's structural reforms have been very durable in surviving periods of economic stress and crisis. This message is an optimistic one because it means that even if a major crisis does occur, it need not mark a return to the pre-reform status quo but rather merely a transitory setback on the way to a future in which the benefits of economic reform will be realized.

These tendencies, which we shall later describe in more detail, are general patterns, not fixed and immutable laws of economic motion. The responses of the region's different economies to reform have exhibited substantial variation, depending upon the accompanying policy framework, the external environment at the time the reforms were undertaken, the structure and history of the reforming economy, and the various shocks that the economy may have the good or bad fortune to receive over the course of its adjustment to major reform programs.

Even so, the general patterns that we describe have been observed often enough to make them useful guideposts. The economic developments of recent years can be better understood if fuller account is taken of the process of adjustment to the various stabilization and reform programs—and in particular, of the actual progress that various countries in the region have been

making during this difficult adjustment process. We suggest that the diversity of the Latin American growth experience during 1995 has much to do with the fact that different countries were in different phases of the adjustment to economic stabilization and reform. Some countries, such as Brazil and Peru, were in an early, boom phase of the adjustment process, while others, notably Argentina and Mexico, were in latter phases often characterized by a slowdown in the growth rate, the appearance of economic and financial stress, and sometimes a crisis. Underlying the apparent diversity of country experience is, then, an element of commonality, obscured by the fact that the region's economies are making the adjustment to their reforms in a desynchronized manner.

Understanding the various phases of adjustment that often characterize the reform process not only provides a perspective on recent economic developments but also has policy implications for economies undertaking or still in the process of adjustment to reform. These policy implications stem from the following observation: the periods of economic and financial stress that often characterize the latter stages of the adjustment process stem in large part from fiscal, financial and external vulnerabilities that frequently develop during the earlier phases of the process. These vulnerabilities can be minimized if policymakers take appropriate actions in the earlier stages of adjustment, but because such actions must be taken before obvious signs of trouble emerge, they require a substantial degree of foresight.

What does all this have to do with the questions that are raised by economic outcomes in 1995? It suggests, first, that the more rapid growth of the early 1990s was attributable, in part, to the fact that several of the region's large economies were in the early or boom phase of the adjustment to their stabilization and economic reform programs, although it is also true that some important countries, particularly Brazil, had not yet stabilized. This more rapid growth, therefore, in part reflected transitory elements and was not an indication of the underlying rate of growth in the region.

By the same token, the much slower growth observed in 1995 is a reflection of the fact that, in part for reasons largely related to the adjustment process itself (we shall later examine these reasons), two of the region's largest economies fell into deep crisis. Such crises have been overcome in previous reform episodes, after which the reforming economy has reaped considerable benefits. Such crises thus have little to do with prospects for economic growth over the longer term; lower growth in 1995 is not a harbinger of slower growth in Latin America over the medium term.

Looking to the immediate future, it seems likely that economic developments in the region will continue to be significantly affected by the short-term impact of economic stabilization and reform. In 1996, three major economies—Brazil, Colombia and Peru—display signs that economic recovery is subsiding. In the case of Brazil, financial stresses are likely to have adverse implications for growth in the short run. By the same token, Argentina and Mexico are showing signs of recovery from the very deep recession that they entered in 1995, while Venezuela is restarting a process of stabilization and reform that had been interrupted by macroeconomic and political stresses.

These short-term fluctuations, however, have little to do with the major payoff of economic reform, which lies instead in the effect of reform on economic growth over the longer term, after the economy has undergone short-term adjustments to the new policy regime. On this the jury remains out, because in most countries the reform programs are still relatively young. Even so, the experience of major reformers such as Chile, the continuing recovery of domestic investment in Latin America, and the maintenance of macroeconomic stability in most of the region all give grounds for cautious optimism.

This part of the Economic and Social Progress Report examines recent macroeconomic developments in the region within the context actually created by the reform process itself. (Part Two of the Report looks in more substantial detail at progress in the region in making several key structural reforms.) We begin by describing the phases of adjustment to stabilization and reform as it has often played out in Latin America. We then use this description to shed light on recent economic developments in the region. The focus is on developments during 1995, but our goal is to put these developments into a medium-term perspective. In the concluding section, we draw out in more detail some implications that the discussion has for policy and for near- and medium-term prospects for the region.

TENDENCIES IN THE ADJUSTMENT TO MAJOR REFORM

No two reform programs undertaken in the different countries of the region have been identical, but enough similarities exist in their structure and in the subsequent economic response to be able to describe patterns that are frequently, although not universally, observed. These patterns can be divided into five periods: (i) stabilization and adoption of major reforms; (ii) economic recovery or boom; (iii) recovery comes under stress; (iv) correction or crisis; and (v) post-reform growth. Although this sequence of events is often observed, there is nothing inevitable about it, and it may be altered by economic policy or by major external shocks that arrive during the course of the adjustment.

Stabilization and the Adoption of Reforms

Most of the reform programs have been products of the 1980s, when countries in the region were faced with high inflation, debt crisis and stagnation. The broad stabilization and reform programs that were designed to address these problems have

Table 3. Country Experiences with Adjustment to Major Stabilization and Reform

	Stabilization and adoption of major reforms	Recovery	Stress	Correction or crisis	Post-reform
Argentina	1991	1991-93	1994	1995-96	
Chile	1975	1976-80	1981	1982-85	1986-96
Mexico	1988	1990-93	1994	1995-96	
Uruguay	1990	1991-94		1995	
Venezuela	1989	1990-92	1993	1994-95	

Source: Study calculations as described in text.

typically encompassed inflation stabilization supported by a major fiscal consolidation and a restructuring of external debt; privatization; liberalization of domestic markets, international trade and sometimes capital flows; tax reform; and liberalization and reform of domestic financial markets. These programs were generally successful in bringing down high inflation, reestablishing access to international financial markets, and establishing an environment more conducive to economic growth.

The characteristics of these reform programs are described in more detail in Part Two of this Report, and a lengthy discussion would be out of place at this point. But in order to make the upcoming discussion of the dynamics of reform adjustment more meaningful, we provide in Table 3 some examples of countries whose experience illustrates the process described here.[3]

The first column of the table gives the years when major reform programs were first adopted. These dates signify, of course, only a starting point; in no country were all reforms done at once. In addition, important differences exist among countries in the timing of the reforms and in the speed and scope of implementation. Furthermore, in many countries important reforms still remain on the policy agenda. More generally, reforms on the scale of those recently undertaken in the region necessarily constitute a process, not an event. Reforms have often continued to be implemented and deepened

well after the initial reform phase ends and throughout subsequent phases of the reform process.

The earliest reformer, Chile, began its reforms with the well-documented liberalization and stabilization episode of the mid-1970s. Argentina and Uruguay, too, implemented ambitious programs at about the same time, although these failed to achieve a lasting stabilization, as economic crises in the early 1980s were followed by a prolonged period of macroeconomic instability.

In most countries, however, major economic reforms were children of the debt crisis. Bolivia began its reforms by confronting hyperinflation around 1985, and in the majority of the other countries reforms began between 1988 and 1990, although some have only recently initiated major stabilization and reform programs. In Brazil, there was some privatization in the early 1990s, but the major Brazilian reforms began with the mid-1994 inflation stabilization and the supporting program of fiscal and other reforms that is still being implemented. In Venezuela, the government is in the process of implementing a major stabilization and reform program in the aftermath of the failure of stabilization efforts in 1994.

Admittedly, in a few countries the reform dynamics described here have not been the most important force behind economic developments in the 1990s.[4] Nevertheless, such reform dynamics have indeed been relevant for most countries, affecting roughly 97 percent of the region's GDP.

---

[3] The categorizations in Table 3 necessarily involve an element of judgment about the economic history of the countries in question, and thus should be viewed as a descriptive device for organizing recent economic developments of the many countries in the region rather than as a set of scientifically generated data.

[4] This does not imply that countries have not undertaken important reforms, but merely that other shocks appear to have been more important determinants of macroeconomic outcomes. For instance, Costa Rica did in fact engage in important liberalizations and reforms in the early 1990s, but these reforms appear to have been dominated by the impact of fluctuations in fiscal policy associated with the very pronounced political and business cycle in that country.

FIGURE 3
Macroeconomic Outcomes Before and After Major Reforms
(In percent)

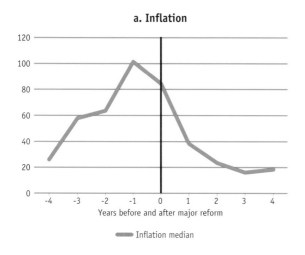

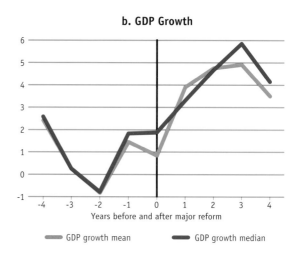

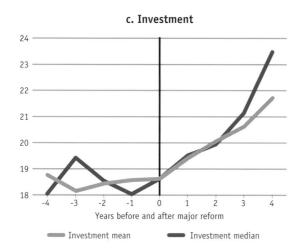

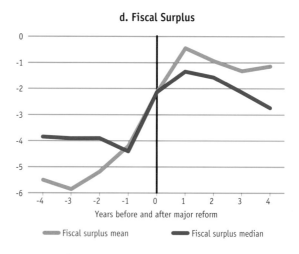

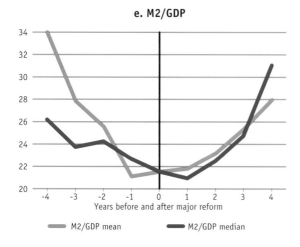

Figure 3 illustrates some characteristics of the years surrounding implementation of economic stabilization. It presents cross-country averages of inflation, GDP growth and other important quantities in the years just before, during and after implementation of stabilization.

In the years leading up to stabilization, inflation tends to rise dramatically to a peak of roughly 100 percent just before stabilization is implemented. By two years after stabilization, inflation has fallen on average to a rate of about 20 percent. The years preceding stabilization are also characterized by low GDP growth, low investment, high fiscal deficits, and declining demand for domestic money. These facts provide a vivid reminder of the conditions motivating the reforms that are documented more fully in Part Two of this Report; as is discussed there, these facts suggest the possibility that bad times are good times for reform.

After stabilization, countries in the region have on average experienced higher rates of economic growth, a recovery of domestic investment, an improvement in fiscal outcomes, and a substantial increase in real money demand, as can be seen in Figure 3.

Recovery, Boom and Vulnerability

A program of stabilization and reform generally triggers a recovery of economic activity; that is its primary purpose. It does so because a reduction of macroeconomic and financial instability raises confidence and removes a serious impediment to private activity. Recovery is also promoted because the programs generally include specific reforms that facilitate private spending, such as inflation stabilization and the liberalization of financial markets and international trade; indeed, a spending boom is a more constant feature of the recovery phase than is recovery of production.

The Latin American countries have experienced a lag between initiation of major stabilization and reform programs and the actual onset of recovery. In some cases recovery arrived slowly. The delay between adoption of major reforms and recovery was three years in Bolivia, Guatemala, Nicaragua and Peru. In Bolivia and Peru, a major element of the reforms was a money-based stabilization of inflation; as we later explain, such stabilizations tend to create a recession in the short run, with recovery beginning only after a delay.

In most cases, however, the recovery arrived more rapidly; the average delay between adoption of major reforms and recovery is about one and one-half years. Recovery tends to arrive most rapidly in the aftermath of major stabilization programs based on exchange rates, as in Argentina (1991), Brazil (1994), and Uruguay (1991). Where other reforms were the main shock or when the stabilization was based on a monetary anchor rather than on an exchange rate anchor, the recovery has tended to be more delayed. Once it begins, the period of recovery has generally lasted about three years, although booms lasting four to five years are fairly common, and in other cases the period of recovery has been much shorter than this three-year average.

The recovery that follows a successful stabilization and reform program typically involves growth in spending, output and other important quantities—growth that cannot be sustained indefinitely. This unsustainability is not itself pathological but arises naturally from a number of factors. Output can often grow rapidly, albeit temporarily, because there exists substantial excess capacity at the beginning of the reform program. The improvement in profitability generated by the reforms may lead to a burst of investment, as investors seek to increase their stock of capital to take advantage of the improved business environment. Consumer spending on durable goods may follow a similar pattern. Consumers increase their stock of durable goods in response to the expectation of higher incomes, and to the increase in availability and the decrease in cost of imported consumption goods as a result of trade liberalization or of the real appreciation of the currency that often form part of the recovery.[5]

What is the Latin American experience? Figure 4 illustrates the typical response of real output and spending to the phases of the stabilization and reform process. The figure presents the average growth rates of real GDP, real con-

---

[5] Fears that stabilization or liberalization will prove to be temporary may, somewhat ironically, reinforce the spending boom, as consumers and investors rush to purchase imported goods before the reversal of reform makes such goods more expensive once again.

Box 1. Theory and Evidence on the Economic Response to Stabilization and Reform

The macroeconomic fluctuations associated with major episodes of economic reform described here have not escaped the attention of professional economists. There is a substantial body of economic research devoted to documenting and explaining the macroeconomic dynamics of adjustment to economic reform. Much of the interest in this topic stems from a desire to understand the typical economic response to inflation stabilization. Experience has shown that programs based upon monetary targets in a context of flexible exchange rates generally lead to a recession in the short run, followed by economic recovery. But stabilization programs based upon a nominal exchange rate commitment instead generate a strong economic expansion in the short run, which is often followed by recession. (For an overview of the evidence, see Kiguel and Liviatan, 1992, and Reinhart and Végh, 1994.) During the boom that typically accompanies an exchange rate based stabilization, domestic investment and consumption spending increase strongly, the current account moves into deficit, and the real exchange rate appreciates.

A number of theories have been developed to explain these facts. Some, such as Dornbush (1982) and Rodriguez (1982), emphasize the idea that domestic wage and price inflation adjust only gradually to the new policy environment. The nominal interest rate, however, declines quickly when the rate of exchange rate devaluation declines. The real interest rate thus declines in the early stage of the

adjustment, contributing to a boom in domestic demand. Over time, the real exchange rate appreciation that is caused by the fact that domestic inflation is higher than the rate of exchange rate devaluation tends to create a recession.

Another set of theories focuses on limited credibility, the idea that individuals are typically unsure whether an inflation stabilization will be permanent. Because inflation is a tax on the monetary balances that must be held to finance consumption or investment spending, an inflation stabilization that is perceived to be temporary creates incentives to spend more during the period of low inflation, thus contributing to the early spending boom and current account deficits. Later in the adjustment process, spending must fall so that consumers can finance the debt that was accumulated during the period of high spending.

Yet other explanations focus on wealth effects associated with fiscal and supply-side aspects of an inflation stabilization. For example, Helpman and Razin (1987) maintain that inflation stabilization increases private wealth because the inflation tax has declined; in other words, lifetime tax burdens are reduced because the stabilization is associated with a future reduction in government spending. In a number of studies, such as DeGregorio, Guidotti and Végh (1994) and Roldós (1995), wealth effects are shown to arise because lower inflation increases the efficiency of the domestic economy.

---

sumption, and real investment during the five phases of the reform process, relative to the rates typically recorded during years unaffected by adjustment to a major stabilization and reform program.[6]

We see that during the period of recovery, output growth is typically about 4 percent higher than during a nonrecovery period. And the boom in spending, especially investment spending, is even more pronounced than the output boom; during the recovery phase, consumption typically grows more than 4 percent faster and

investment nearly 12 percent faster than either tends to grow in normal years.

The recovery also involves important changes in the demand for financial assets. As confidence in domestic financial stability increases, the demand for domestic financial assets rises, leading to higher money demand and capital inflows. The response of capital inflows will be particularly important in an international environment like that of the 1990s, when relatively low interest rates in the industrial countries create vast pools of wealth seeking higher returns in emerging market economies.

The capital inflows and the increase in demand for money and other domestic financial

---

[6] The methodology used to compute the estimates displayed in Figures 4 through 6 is described in more detail in Box 2.

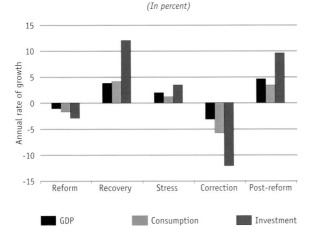

FIGURE 4

Growth Rates of Real GDP and Spending

(In percent)

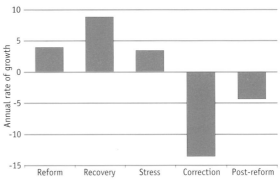

FIGURE 5

Real Bank Claims on the Private Sector

(In percent)

assets accompanying the return of financial stability help provide the domestic financial system with resources to lend to domestic individuals and firms. Thus, the boom in private spending is often accompanied—and amplified—by a boom in bank lending (which is also promoted by reduced public sector use of bank credit as a result of fiscal consolidation) and by the financial liberalization that is often a part of the reform package.

The increase in money demand and in capital inflows thus promotes the spending boom experienced during the recovery by helping to provide liquidity to support domestic financial intermediation and by providing the international credit required to finance the external deficits generated by the spending boom. This credit boom is necessarily a transitory phenomenon, however. When money demand stabilizes at its new, higher level, the growth of bank credit must decline to more sustainable levels.

Figure 5 illustrates the Latin American experience. During the period of recovery, real domestic credit to the private sector has grown about 9 percent per year more rapidly than during a normal year. This rate of growth is clearly a temporary phenomenon, and the rate of credit growth slows sharply in subsequent phases of the adjustment.

As the boom phase of adjustment to stabilization and reform proceeds, it often leaves the economy in an increasingly vulnerable position. A vulnerable economy is one in which even small disturbances can trigger highly disruptive reactions. This vulnerability emerges during the boom phase for three main reasons.

First, domestic financial systems often become vulnerable because an extended period of very rapid bank lending leaves banks holding a large stock of loans to increasingly leveraged individuals and firms, who may have difficulty servicing the loans if economic growth slows or interest rates rise.[7] The difficulty will be compounded if a drop in domestic money demand unexpectedly forces banks to curtail their lending sharply, creating demands for borrowers to repay their loans more rapidly than they are able to do.

Second, vulnerability often results because the spending boom leads to a transitory

---

[7] Because of well-known distortions and information problems associated with financial intermediation, there is good reason to worry that lenders will be less than optimally concerned about the vulnerability that their lending generates, essentially because the costs of a financial collapse are likely to be borne in substantial part by taxpayers rather than by those responsible for making the risky loans.

Box 2. Economic Outcomes Through the Adjustment and Reform Process

No two reform episodes are alike, but there are patterns that can be identified. To describe these patterns, we first identified the years when countries entered the various stages of the adjustment process. Then, using a panel of data on 26 countries in Latin America and the Caribbean over the period 1970-95, we regressed a number of key economic variables—including the real interest rate, and rates of growth of real consumption, real investment, real GDP, and real bank lending to the private sector—on dummy variables representing the stage of the cycle, on country dummy variables, and on a dummy variable for each year of the time period.

Typical Economic Outcomes During Stages of the Stabilization and Reform Cycle

(In percent)

	Real consump-tion growth	Real investment growth	Real GDP growth	Real bank credit growth	Real interest rate
Reform	-1.71	-2.93	-1.09	3.91	0.61
Boom	4.13	12.03	3.83	8.8	3.42
Stress	1.21	3.47	2.02	3.41	8.8
Correction	-5.79	-12.1	-3.15	-13.56	-2.32
Post-reform	3.43	9.59	4.64	-4.39	-4.98

Source: Study calculations as described in the text.

The coefficients on the dummy variables representing the stages of the cycle can be interpreted as the average realization of the variable in question during that stage of the cycle, after accounting for long-run differences in behavior across countries, and for variations over time that are common to the countries of the region, such as might be generated by a surge in capital flows or some other external shock to the region. Thus, for example, the results suggest that when a country is in the period of boom, consumption growth tends to be about 4 percentage points higher than would be typical for that country, taking into account shocks that appear to have affected the entire region during the year in question.

increase in government revenue, since most Latin American governments depend upon taxes based upon private spending. This fiscal revenue boom masks underlying fiscal disequilibrium that may be politically difficult to correct promptly and efficiently when the spending boom subsides.

Third, vulnerability often emerges because the boom in domestic spending tends to lead to real appreciation of the currency and to large current account deficits. If the external debt was manageable in the early stages of the recovery, these deficits will pose few problems in the short run. But as the boom continues and the stock of external debt becomes large, investors may begin to contemplate the need for a major adjustment. Knowing that such an adjustment may impose costs on owners of the country's debt, investors are likely to begin to demand short-term debt. If this demand is accommodated by policymakers, it can create a dangerous debt structure that exposes the economy to the danger of a self-fueling panic by international investors.

Stress

During the recovery phase the economy develops imbalances that will eventually require correction: current account deficits are typically larger than can be financed indefinitely, credit growth must slow from the rapid rates observed during recovery, and the required adjustment in private spending may lead to fiscal imbalances. It is possible to imagine this correction taking place in a smooth and easy manner, and in some instances in which the economic and political environment has been benign and the vulnerabilities generated by the boom modest, such soft landings have in fact occurred. But the process has typically been more complicated and has occasionally involved a major macroeconomic and financial crisis.

As this correction or crisis approaches, there often arises a preliminary period when the economy comes under stress. One source of stress

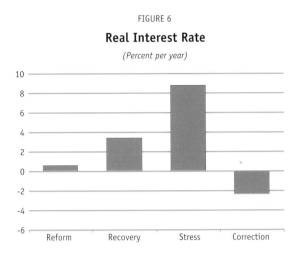

FIGURE 6

Real Interest Rate

(Percent per year)

is the natural reduction in the growth of domestic spending and production as the adjustment in the economy's stock of durable goods comes to an end and the economy's reservoir of underutilized capacity is exhausted. Figure 4 illustrates the typical dimension of this slowdown. During periods when countries of the region have been in the stress phase, the rate of economic growth has fallen by about 2 percentage points below that recorded during the boom, while consumption growth and investment growth have declined much more dramatically.

Similarly, when money demand stabilizes at its new higher level, growth in bank lending slows to more sustainable rates, as can be seen in Figure 5. As economies move from the recovery to the stress phase of the adjustment process, the growth rate of real credit to the private sector declines by more than 5 percentage points per year.

This lower rate of credit growth contributes to an increase in real interest rates. As Figure 6 illustrates, higher interest rates are in fact a common feature of the stress phase of the adjustment process. Before recovery arrives, real interest rates have typically been roughly in line with the historical norm for the country in question. Then, during the boom phase of the adjustment, real interest rates tend to rise to about 3.5 percentage points above the country's historical norm. During the stress phase of the process, however, interest rates

rise sharply, to about 9 percentage points above the levels that typified the pre-reform period.

Higher interest rates and slower growth in output, in domestic demand, and in bank lending put pressure on borrowers, bringing to the surface certain problems of credit quality that had been less visible during the boom and rendering the banking system increasingly fragile. In a similar way, higher interest rates and slower growth may uncover underlying fiscal disequilibriums that had been masked by the fiscal revenue boom experienced in the recovery phase. As the fiscal situation deteriorates, investors may lose confidence in the ability of the political system to generate the fiscal adjustment required to maintain public solvency, putting additional pressure on interest rates.

The natural deceleration of a temporarily booming economy thus contributes to overall economic stress. A second important source of stress is market participants' gradually increasing awareness that a correction of spending imbalances will sooner or later be required. Individuals may become concerned that a sharp devaluation will be part of the correction, leading to reserve losses, a weaker currency, and higher interest rates. Stress may also be triggered or amplified by important upcoming elections, which necessarily create at least mild doubts about the continuity of national exchange rate and fiscal policies, and which may also generate election-related fiscal slippage. Some observers emphasize upcoming elections as a source of uncertainty and therefore economic stress in Mexico (1994), Argentina (1994), and Ecuador (1996). In Venezuela, economic stress was greatly amplified by political tension in 1993.

Correction or Crisis

If dealt with promptly and effectively, the fiscal and financial vulnerabilities that result from the boom and become apparent during the period of stress may not generate a major crisis. Unfortu-

Box 3.   Adjustment to Stabilization and Reform: Considerations for Policy

A prompt, effective policy response can minimize the economic and financial vulnerabilities that tend to emerge during recovery. This reduces the probability of a painful correction or crisis and minimizes the costs associated with any crisis that does emerge. Although the required policy response will depend upon the phase of the adjustment and a host of country-specific considerations, some general lessons can be drawn from our analysis of the adjustment process to stabilization and reform.

Managing the Boom

The most productive interventions are those that prevent rather than respond to potential economic and financial vulnerabilities. These are also the most difficult policies to implement because they require the foresight to act before obvious problems arise. Some guidelines for policy are to:
- *Recognize that balancing the budget is not by itself sufficient.* Fiscal targets should be adjusted for the stage of the adjustment process, but fiscal resources generated during the largely transitory "recovery" should not be used to expand hard-to-reverse spending commitments. During the boom, precautionary fiscal surpluses should be run to strengthen the fiscal position and to provide the flexibility needed to permit a counter-cyclical fiscal response to the eventual downturn. A restrictive fiscal policy will also offset the boom in domestic spending and reduce the resulting current account deficits and exchange rate appreciation. (For more detailed discussion of these issues, see Gavin, Hausmann, Perotti and Talvi, 1996, and Talvi, 1996.)
- *Manage public debt with care.* The key consideration here is to avoid an excessive overhang of short-maturity debt, even if it seems much cheaper to issue than longer-term debt. In most countries, the distinction between "domestic" and "foreign" debt has become less meaningful. Public debt is not necessarily safer just because it was sold at home. Authorities should monitor the position of their international reserves net of short-term debt obligations, particularly debt issued for the purpose of sterilizing capital inflows.
- *Protect the domestic financial system.* A capable regulatory and supervisory apparatus is fundamental, and never more so than during the boom, when the fragilities that cause banking crises can be generated and are most difficult to detect. It should be recognized that the more volatile economic environment faced by most Latin American

economies requires more conservative financial regulation; there is a good case to be made for more conservative capital and liquidity requirements than in the Basle framework. Because such regulation will never be a panacea, monetary authorities should do their best to prevent bank lending booms. (See Gavin and Hausmann, 1996, and Rojas-Suárez and Weisbrod, 1996b, for further discussion).

Coping with Economic and Financial Stress

By the time significant economic and financial stresses have emerged, the scope for avoiding major economic problems is considerably more restricted. But there remain constructive policy responses that can reduce the likelihood of a hard landing.
- *Address fiscal shortfalls.* The slowdown in output and spending will undermine the budget. If the country enters a period of economic stress with relatively low public debt, a substantial fiscal surplus and high perceived creditworthiness, then it will be feasible and desirable to allow the surplus to turn into a deficit. But if the public debt is initially large, the budgetary position precarious, and perceived creditworthiness low, the downturn may generate a deficit large enough to raise the risk of a confidence crisis. In this case, prompt and convincing action to prevent a fiscal deterioration may be necessary to avoid the collapse of confidence that generates major economic crises.
- *Scrutinize domestic banks.* If during the boom supervision was inadequate and the credit boom large, the slowdown in economic activity and credit growth is likely to bring to the surface problems of credit quality, leading bankers and the public to understand the fragility of at least some banks. Bank supervisors should scrutinize banks with special care, and intervene early to prevent weak banks from gambling for resurrection, thus magnifying the likelihood and costs of a banking crisis.
- *Examine the role of exchange rate depreciation.* An exchange rate realignment can address some of the imbalances that contribute to economic and financial stress by assisting in the correction of external deficits, reducing the real value of nonindexed public debt, and—if the financial system is not fully indexed or dollarized—reducing in real terms the value of the commercial bank debt overhang that lies at the heart of a banking crisis. By addressing these imbalances, a realignment may reduce the destabilizing expectation that another devaluation is on

the way. The danger, however, is that one devaluation may create the highly destabilizing expectation of further devaluation and inflation. Much depends upon the credibility of the promise that the exchange rate realignment does not signal a loss of monetary and fiscal discipline.

Responding to Economic Crisis

By the time a crisis has erupted, the goal is to minimize the economic costs, shield the most vulnerable members of society, protect the structural reforms, and reestablish economic and financial stability as quickly as possible. The details of crisis management will vary with the nature of the crisis, but in all cases there is an urgent need to reestablish confidence in the currency, public debt and domestic banks. The following measures will likely be in order:

•   Despite the short-term pain it causes, a fiscal contraction is probably necessary to reestablish confidence in the currency and public debt. It is essential that the fiscal adjustment be timely and credible.

•   If the crisis requires a revision in the policy framework, it should be comprehensive and credible. Financial markets need assurance that the crisis is being addressed with an effective and coherent set of policies. It is particularly important to communicate the strategy for overcoming the crisis if an important element of the previous policy framework, such as the exchange rate regime, needs to be changed.

•   If a banking crisis erupts, prompt action to prevent problem banks from engaging in highly risky behavior is essential. When dealing with a problem bank, steps must be taken to ensure that shareholders and creditors of the bank who have benefited from risk bear a large part of the cost of its restructuring. A plan that imposes insufficient costs on the owners and major creditors of the bank risks amplifying the cost of the crisis, and promotes the expectation of future bailouts (see Rojas-Suárez and Weisbrod, 1996a). It must be recognized that bank crises are expensive, and fiscal resources need to be allocated to resolve the problem without a sharp increase in inflation.

•   Within the context of overall fiscal discipline, it is possible to design targeted extensions of the social safety net that protect the most vulnerable elements of society. These should be given high priority, even if the most vulnerable are not likely to be the most influential claimants on public spending.

nately, these vulnerabilities make the economy highly sensitive to external or domestic shocks and leave little room for policy correction and maneuvering. Foreign investors, already nervously contemplating the need for an eventual correction, are being asked to finance large external deficits, even as governments must rely on the investment market to finance deficits while they attempt to make a potentially large fiscal adjustment in an orderly fashion. Meanwhile, in an environment of slower growth and higher interest rates, the banking system must try to overcome the excesses generated during the boom. In such an environment, even a small shock can be severely disruptive if it leads to a self-fueling panic by international investors or if it pushes the domestic banking system into crisis.

Figure 4 shows that in Latin America the correction phase has tended to be traumatic; output growth falls nearly 5 percentage points below the rate typically recorded during the preceding periods of stress, consumption growth drops by nearly 7 percentage points, and investment growth declines by more than 16 percentage points. The recent experiences of Argentina and Mexico were even more extreme. Fortunately, neither country had to face a very large shock in 1994, although both found themselves in an extremely vulnerable state because of the fiscal and financial fault lines that had developed during the strong and extended boom phase of their adjustment to the very deep stabilization and reform efforts undertaken in the 1980s and 1990s. The result in both countries was a major crisis in 1995 in which output growth fell by more than 10 percentage points from the rate recorded in 1994, twice the typical decline.

The vulnerabilities that typically develop during the recovery phase of the stabilization and reform cycle thus have often led to stress and crisis, but in fact there is nothing inevitable about this scenario. A major crisis involving sharp correction is, of course, less likely if the basic reforms are relatively minor and the recovery correspondingly modest. And even during a major reform program it is possible to lean against the wind during the resultant boom stage, thus reducing the magnitude of the vulnerabilities eventually generated (see Box 3 for some policy implications of the adjustment process described here). This understanding was important in the latter part of 1995, when Peru and Brazil took action to reduce the imbalances generated by private spending booms associated with their stabilization and reform programs. In both countries growth slowed as a result, but by acting before the boom phase generated really major stresses, policymakers were able to reduce the likelihood that a major correction would be required in the years to come.

Post-reform

What comes after the correction or crisis? Not many countries in the region have yet reached the post-correction or post-reform stage, but enough experience has accumulated to allow us to describe a few possible scenarios. In one, the social and economic stresses generated by the crisis may lead to a prolonged period of macroeconomic and financial instability, eliminating or postponing for a long time the gains achieved by the stabilization effort. Such was the fate of the Argentine and Uruguayan stabilizations of the early 1980s and of the more recent Venezuelan stabilization, which collapsed in 1994.

Such an outcome is not inevitable, however. For instance, Chile emerged from its 1982-85 collapse with its earlier reforms largely intact. The country dealt with the difficulties created by the crisis and managed to reestablish macroeconomic and financial stability fairly quickly. The Chilean economy then entered a phase of strong and sustained post-reform growth in which the dynamics of adjustment to the country's considerable reform no longer play a major role. Bolivia, too, now appears to have arrived at a stage where the adjustment to the inflation stabilization and reforms of the mid-1980s has played itself out.

Even when an economic crisis leads to renewed macroeconomic instability, the structural reforms that accompanied the failed stabilization effort have generally been maintained. This continuity of reforms places the economy in a stronger position to recover from the macroeconomic instability and to reestablish economic growth. And once macroeconomic stability and growth are reestablished, the economy will continue to benefit from the structural reforms so painfully implemented in the preceding stabilization and reform episode. In this important sense, the crisis that may interrupt the process of adjustment to stabilization and reform could well be viewed as a bump in the road, not as a dead end in the reform process. Such continuity of structural reforms is likely to benefit Argentina and Mexico, where the current crises have not threatened the far-reaching structural reforms implemented over the past decade. Both countries appear to be overcoming the macroeconomic and financial instabilities created by the 1995 crisis, and thus the stage for recovery is likely already to have been set.

In Latin American countries, economic growth in the post-reform stage has been about 5 percentage points above the growth recorded during the pre-reform stage (Figure 4). This growth rate is to some degree related to recovery from the correction phase of the adjustment. It nevertheless provides some ground for optimism that the crisis often associated with the latter stages of adjustment to a major reform program need not be much more than a temporary, albeit painful, stage of the cycle, after which the economy stands poised to take advantage of the greater efficiencies and improved climate for economic growth that have been created by the economic reform programs of the past decade.

Bearing in mind this general overview of the dynamics of adjustment to stabilization and reform, we turn now to an examination of recent economic developments in Latin America and the Caribbean. We begin with the external and policy

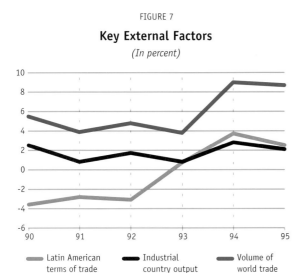

FIGURE 7
Key External Factors
(In percent)

Latin American terms of trade   Industrial country output   Volume of world trade

environment in 1995 and then review key economic outcomes, including growth, inflation, and international trade and payments. In the concluding section we discuss policy implications and some aspects of the regional economic outlook as suggested by the perspective on recent economic developments that is offered by examining the phases of the adjustment process.

THE EXTERNAL ENVIRONMENT

In 1995, the external environment was in most respects benign for Latin America. Modest but steady growth in the industrial economies provided for a substantial expansion of world trade, and the terms of trade improved for most countries in the region. Over the course of the year, world interest rates declined, reversing most of the increase that had taken place in the previous year. And after a sharp curtailment in the first quarter, capital flows to most countries of the region resumed at levels similar to those of preceding years. The crisis that followed the Mexican devaluation of December 1994 signaled a sharp reassessment by international investors of the risks of investing in Latin America. In most countries, however, the effects were transitory, and Mexico and Argentina—the two countries hardest hit by the crisis—

have rapidly reestablished access to international financial markets, although in substantially smaller quantities and at higher interest rates than in the years before the crisis.

World Trade and International Prices

The economies of the industrial countries grew by a modest but steady 2 percent in 1995, helping to propel an 8 percent increase in the volume of world trade that provided an opportunity for the Latin American countries to increase their exports. The growth in the volume of world trade was the same as in 1994, and substantially more rapid than in the earlier years of the 1990s (Figure 7). Latin America's terms of trade improved by about 1 percent in 1995, following a somewhat larger increase in 1994. These two years of improvement have partially offset the declines in the terms of trade experienced in the 1990-92 period.

Worldwide, the dollar price of tradable commodities generally rose during 1995, the result primarily of the weakening of the U.S. dollar that took place during the year. Even so, the prices of commodities important to the region had an uneven trajectory. During the course of the year, coffee prices retreated from the abnormally high level attained in 1994, although they remained high on average for the year. Oil prices rose only marginally in 1995 (but more strongly in the early months of 1996), while grain prices and the prices of copper and various other minerals rose more significantly.

As a result of these divergent developments, changes in the terms of trade varied widely across countries. Figure 8 shows the direct effect that changes in the terms of trade had on different countries' national income during 1995, expressed as percentages of 1995 GDP. The income of Trinidad and Tobago, for instance, was favorably affected by higher prices for ammonia and urea; the associated improvement in the terms of trade raised that country's national income by more than 7 percent of GDP. Suriname benefited

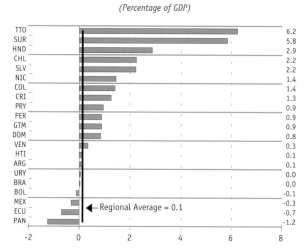

FIGURE 8

**Income Effect of the Change
in Terms of Trade, 1995**

(Percentage of GDP)

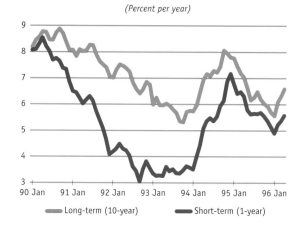

FIGURE 9

**U.S. Dollar Interest Rates
(U.S. Treasury Obligations)**

(Percent per year)

from much higher international prices for bauxite and alumina, which led to an income increase of more than 5 percent of GDP. Chile, Colombia, Costa Rica, El Salvador, Honduras and Nicaragua experienced increases of between 1 and 2 percent of GDP, while most other countries experienced smaller changes. Only four countries registered declines in their terms of trade, and only in Panama was the decline larger than 1 percent of GDP.

World Interest Rates and Capital Flows

After a sharp increase in 1994, U.S. interest rates declined by about 2 percentage points during 1995, bringing long-term rates to roughly the trough reached in late 1993. Short-term interest rates, however, remained higher in 1995 than the low levels reached during 1993 and early 1994. (During the first half of 1996, interest rates have risen somewhat, although they remain below the levels reached in late 1994.)

Lower world interest rates have in the past been associated with higher capital flows to Latin America, and despite the international financial turbulence associated with the Mexican devaluation, net capital flows did remain relatively high in 1995, amounting to slightly more than 3 per-

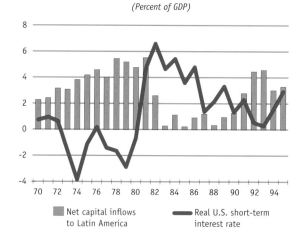

FIGURE 10

Capital Inflows to Latin America, 1970-95

(Percent of GDP)

cent of the region's GDP. This amount was slightly higher than the inflows received in 1994, but was well below the peak flows reached during 1992 and 1993.

The aggregate figures for 1995 include large official flows to Argentina and Mexico as part of the international response to the Mexican crisis. Private flows to those countries became negative in 1995. Venezuela also experienced large outflows of private capital in the context of high

FIGURE 11

Brady Bond Prices, 1993-95

(Collateral stripped par bond, in U.S. dollars)

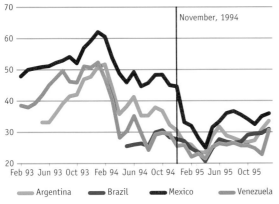

Note: Data represent the value of the Brady bond after subtracting the value of the collateralized principal and interest payments.

inflation, negative real interest rates, and substantial uncertainty about the macroeconomic outlook. Nevertheless, private capital flows to the rest of the region were, in aggregate, higher than in 1994.

Temporary Disruption of International Capital Flows by the Tequila Crisis

The most dramatic Latin American economic event of 1995 was actually initiated in December 1994, when Mexico unexpectedly devalued the peso. The devaluation was not received calmly by international financial markets, and investors' disappointment in Mexico was soon transformed into fears about the prospects for economic stability in other emerging market economies that seemed to be similarly situated—most notably Argentina, but also a number of other countries both within and outside Latin America. In the first two months of the year, investors remained unconvinced of the adequacy of the response by the international community and by domestic authorities in the affected economies, and the sell-off in emerging markets began to resemble a full-blown panic. This situation was reflected in the prices of Argentine and Mexican Brady bonds,

which fell by nearly 30 percent between December 1994 and March 1995. Not only these countries but also a wide range of other emerging market economies in Latin America, Asia and Central Europe faced intense pressure from international financial markets in the first months of the year. Countries such as Chile and Colombia, which were largely unaffected by the crisis, were the exception rather than the rule.

The epicenter of the Mexican crisis in early 1995 was the stock of tesobonos, about $30 billion of short-term, dollar-indexed government debt that was coming due in large amounts just as panicked financial markets were least willing to roll them over. In the first two months of the year, it became increasingly clear that in the absence of an intensified policy response, this unwillingness to roll over Mexican short-term debt would create an unmanageable situation, raising the possibility that the country would be forced into default, despite its capacity to service its debt over the medium term.

The crisis created uncertainty in Argentina about the viability of the macroeconomic policy regime, and particularly of the convertibility system that ties the peso to the U.S. dollar. The uncertainty led to substantial capital outflows that, combined with a current account deficit, generated substantial balance of payment deficits. Under the Convertibility Plan, these payment deficits could be sterilized only to a very limited extent, so the deficits were translated into an abrupt decline in the domestic money supply, which in turn led to a sharp increase in domestic interest rates and a contraction of bank lending, putting enormous stress on the nonfinancial economy.

In response to the growing crisis, the international financial community dramatically increased the financial support made available to Mexico to a level sufficient to ensure that the country's short-term debt could be honored even if private investors refused to roll it over. This response alone was insufficient to calm markets, but in early March both Mexico and Argentina announced redoubled efforts to adjust their economies to the reduced availability of foreign capital, including in particular very strong fiscal contraction. These adjustment programs were favorably received, and the panic gradually subsided, as reflected in a recovery of Brady bond and domestic equity markets, a substantial reduction in domestic interest rates, and somewhat reduced pressure in the foreign exchange market.

The end of the panic set the stage for an orderly adjustment but did not make the adjustment painless. Both Mexico and Argentina fell into a deep recession in 1995, with real output declining about 7 percent in Mexico and 4.4 percent in Argentina, and with consumption and investment falling even more sharply. But both countries have largely eliminated their current account imbalances and are now showing signs of economic recovery.

As Argentina and Mexico settled into the painful process of adjustment, international financial markets returned to a more normal state, and the Tequila effect on other economies in Latin America largely vanished. In the second half of the year, international capital flows to the region recovered as turbulence in international financial markets subsided and international interest rates fell. And, as noted earlier, for the year as a whole, capital flows to countries in the region other than Argentina and Mexico recovered strongly, while both Argentina and Mexico have reestablished access to international financial markets, albeit in greatly reduced quantities and at higher interest rates. As we later discuss in more detail, over the year as a whole, capital flows to most countries in the region remained sizable.

Progress in Debt Restructuring

Several countries of the region made progress during 1995 in restructuring their external debt. In December, Bolivia completed a Paris Club restructuring of its official source debt on so-called Na-

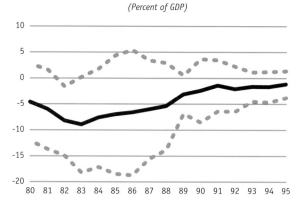

FIGURE 12

Average Central Government Budget Surplus

(Percent of GDP)

Note: Dotted lines are one standard deviation from the mean.

ples terms. Naples terms are designed as an exit strategy; they allow for a 67 percent reduction in the debt stock or in future debt service (on a present-value basis) on debt subject to restructuring. For Bolivia this applied to almost $880 million of debt stock. Nicaragua (March 1995) and Haiti (May 1995) also received 67 percent conditionality applying to amounts totaling $850 million (Nicaragua) and $120 million (Haiti).

In February 1995, Ecuador rescheduled $7.8 billion of commercial bank debt (of which $3.3 billion consisted of past-due interest) in a Brady style agreement. In October 1995, Panama completed its own Brady operation, restructuring about $3.5 billion in commercial debt, including $1.5 billion in past-due interest. Peru reached an agreement in principle to restructure about $8.6 billion, of which $4.2 billion is past-due interest.

In December 1995, Nicaragua bought back $1.1 billion of commercial bank debt, or 80 percent of the outstanding stock, at a price of 8 cents on the dollar. The cost was financed by a $40 million loan from the Inter-American Development Bank, a $40 million loan from the World Bank, and a grant of $8 million from European bilateral donors.

The World Bank and the International Monetary Fund unveiled an initiative for the com-

FIGURE 13

Central Government Fiscal Outcome

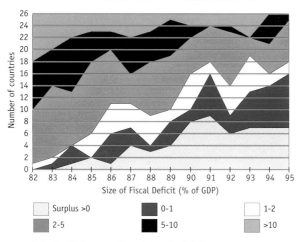

Size of Fiscal Deficit (% of GDP)

| | Surplus >0 | | 0-1 | | 1-2 |
| | 2-5 | | 5-10 | | >10 |

Note: Brazil's figures are for public sector deficit.

prehensive assessment of the debt relief needs of 41 heavily indebted poor countries. The list includes Bolivia, Honduras and Nicaragua. For countries found to hold an unsustainable level of debt obligations even after commercial bank debt relief and bilateral debt relief are implemented under existing programs, the initiative will explore additional means of extending relief, including official multilateral debt, under policy conditions that ensure a sustainable outcome.

THE POLICY ENVIRONMENT

Economic policy challenges and the strategies to address them were heavily influenced in 1995 by the stage of the stabilization and recovery process in which each country found itself, and by the exchange rate arrangements that were in place. Although country experience was diverse, a few common themes did emerge.

One important trend was that most countries continued the fiscal consolidation that has been pursued in the region for nearly a decade. A second trend was that changes in fiscal policy were procyclical in nature; all four of the countries in the correction or crisis stage of the adjustment implemented contractionary fiscal policy in 1995,

and several of the countries in the recovery phase implemented expansionary policies that amplified the magnitude of the boom.

In most countries, monetary conditions were tight. Monetary policy was preoccupied with the task of securing a reduction in the inflation rate or with the related task of maintaining a fixed exchange rate. In a number of countries this task was complicated by fiscal policies not fully supportive of the anti-inflationary monetary stance, by capital flows, and by fragile domestic financial systems.

Continuation of Fiscal Consolidation Despite Slowdown in Growth

Fiscal performance improved in most countries of the region during 1995, continuing the consolidation that has been under way since the mid-1980s. The average fiscal deficit fell to slightly more than 1 percent of GDP, somewhat smaller than in 1994 and substantially smaller than the large deficits recorded during the 1980s. A part of this improvement is attributable to the substantial reduction in inflation, and therefore in nominal interest payments, that has taken place in most countries during the past 15 years. But primary fiscal balances, which do not include interest payments, have also improved dramatically in the region.

The improvement in fiscal performance has been widespread and has been largest in the countries with the largest fiscal imbalances. This development means that very large fiscal deficits are increasingly rare in the region, as illustrated in Figure 13, which provides information on the fiscal outcomes of the countries in the region. As the figure illustrates, the number of countries with a fiscal surplus has risen from none in the early 1980s to seven in 1995, up from six in 1994. In 1995, there were 17 countries in which fiscal deficits were smaller than 2 percent of GDP, up from 15 in 1994. And in 1995 only one country (Guyana) had a deficit larger than 5 percent of GDP,

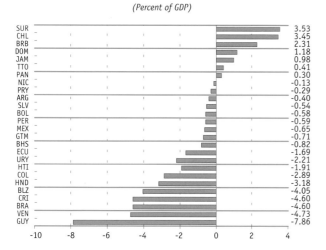

FIGURE 14

Overall Budget Surplus for 1995

(Percent of GDP)

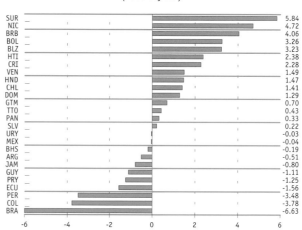

FIGURE 15

Change in Central Government Surplus, 1994 to 1995

(Percent of GDP)

compared with five such countries in 1993 and 1994.

Nevertheless, there remains substantial variation across countries in terms of fiscal outcomes. Figure 14 shows that in 1995 fiscal balances ranged from a deficit of nearly 8 percent of GDP (Guyana) to surpluses of more than 3.5 percent (Chile and Suriname). Central government fiscal balances improved in 15 of 25 countries. Another five experienced deteriorations of less than 1 percent of GDP. But in six countries (Brazil, Colombia, Ecuador, Guyana, Paraguay and Peru) the fiscal balance deteriorated by more than 1 percent of GDP; this fiscal deterioration was particularly notable in Brazil, Colombia and Peru.

Macroeconomic and Policy Determinants of Fiscal Outcomes

Fiscal outcomes are influenced both by the fiscal policy decisions and by broad macroeconomic developments that affect the tax base, the profits from public enterprises, and other similar determinants of public revenue, public spending and the fiscal balance. Such macroeconomic developments were especially important in shaping fiscal outcomes in several Latin American economies

during 1995. Figure 16 presents estimates of the impact that three important influences on budgetary outcomes—namely, real GDP growth, real consumption growth, and changes in the international terms of trade—had on central government fiscal outcomes in Latin America.[8] Box 4 provides a more detailed explanation of what these estimates mean and how they were constructed.

In Chile and Guyana, a favorable macroeconomic environment had a major positive effect on fiscal outcomes. In both countries, real GDP and consumption grew rapidly, giving a strong boost to taxes based upon income and spending. Additionally, in Chile the terms of trade improved dramatically, which raised fiscal revenue in a number of ways, including in particular the income from the state-owned copper company, CODELCO. We estimate that these factors would have led to an increase in the overall fiscal surplus of roughly 2 percent of GDP in both countries, fully accounting for the improvement actually recorded in Chile. In Guyana, however, the fiscal deficit actually increased, despite the favorable macroeconomic environment; the main rea-

---

[8] Data for Brazil refer to the operational balance of the nonfinancial public sector.

Box 4. Measuring the Impact of the Economy on the Budget

Budgetary outcomes are affected both by fiscal policy decisions and by changes in the underlying macroeconomic environment. In Latin America, fiscal revenues are the most important mechanism through which the economy affects the budget, and the most important influences on revenue are the level of real economic activity (GDP), the level of private spending, and the terms of trade. Real output affects revenue because income is an important tax base; private spending because Latin American governments are typically highly reliant upon value-added taxes, import duties and other taxes that are levied upon private spending; and the terms of trade through its effect on private income, and therefore on income taxes, and in some countries through its effects on the profitability of public enterprises.

The estimated impact of these factors on Latin American budgets is discussed in Gavin, Hausmann, Perotti and Talvi (1996). The most important determinant is real economic activity, but the other factors are important as well. For this document, we estimated the impact of these macroeconomic factors on fiscal revenue by taking the difference between the actual growth rate and the "normal" rate of growth, and multiplying it by the statistically-derived estimates of budgetary impact, to derive the effect that this "abnormally" high or low growth had on actual budgetary outcomes. This is the estimate described in the text. The "fiscal impulse" is defined as those changes in the actual fiscal position that are caused by all other factors. This methodology required that we estimate "normal" growth rates, which we somewhat arbitrarily assumed to be 2 percent per capita. The estimates that we discuss here are not very sensitive to variations in this assumption of a percentage point or two in either direction.

FIGURE 16

Impact of Selected Economic Factors on the Fiscal Balance

(Percent of GDP)

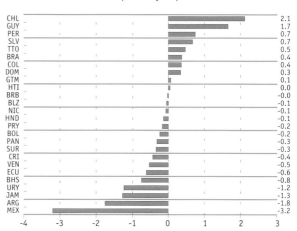

CHL	2.1
GUY	1.7
PER	0.7
SLV	0.7
TTO	0.5
BRA	0.4
COL	0.4
DOM	0.3
GTM	0.1
HTI	0.0
BRB	-0.0
BLZ	-0.1
NIC	-0.1
HND	-0.1
PRY	-0.2
BOL	-0.2
PAN	-0.3
SUR	-0.3
CRI	-0.4
VEN	-0.5
ECU	-0.6
BHS	-0.8
URY	-1.2
JAM	-1.3
ARG	-1.8
MEX	-3.2

son for this was a very large increase in public investment, amounting to about 4 percent of GDP.

In contrast, fiscal outcomes in Argentina, Jamaica, Mexico and Uruguay were adversely affected by macroeconomic developments. All four countries fell into recession in 1995, which lowered domestic income and consequently fiscal rev-

enue as well. We estimate that the recession in Mexico raised the fiscal deficit by about 3 percent of GDP, while the rather less severe recession in Argentina had an impact on the fiscal balance of nearly 2 percent of GDP. In Jamaica and Uruguay, fiscal outcomes were adversely affected by roughly 1 percent of GDP. In all four countries, the impact of recession on fiscal outcomes was offset by contractionary fiscal policy. As a result, in all four of them, the increase in the actual fiscal deficit was small, despite the adverse effects of recession. As we discuss later in somewhat more detail, this procyclical fiscal response was characteristic of most of the region again in 1995, as it has tended to be in recent decades.

In other countries, economic factors apparently played a smaller role, accounting for swings in the overall balance of less than 1 percent of GDP. In these countries, large changes in the fiscal stance were caused primarily by policy changes or, in a few cases, by shocks other than the ones considered here. Figure 17 provides an estimate of the 1995 fiscal impulse, which is the impact on the fiscal balance by factors other than the macroeconomic ones just presented. (The fiscal impulse is simply equal to the observed change in the fiscal surplus minus the estimated impact of macroeconomic factors.)

According to these estimates, fiscal policy was particularly expansionary during 1995 in Brazil, Colombia, Guyana and Peru. More moderate but nevertheless macroeconomically significant fiscal expansions were recorded in Ecuador and Paraguay. These fiscal expansions had a variety of causes. In Brazil, for instance, the fiscal expansion resulted from high real interest rates and increased real wages, both associated with the mid-1994 stabilization program. In Colombia, the deterioration of the central government fiscal balance was in large part associated with an increase in fiscal transfers to subnational levels of government—transfers not accompanied by commensurate reductions in central government spending. (The balance of the nonfinancial public sector, however, was more favorable than that of the central government.) The increase in Peru's deficit was associated with the border conflict with Ecuador, setbacks in efforts to reduce tax evasion, and some relaxation of spending discipline in the first half of the year; in the second half of 1995 measures were taken in Peru to reestablish fiscal discipline.

In several countries, fiscal policy (as measured by the fiscal impulse) was strongly contractionary, including in particular Barbados, Belize, Bolivia, Mexico, Nicaragua and Suriname. In Bolivia, the sharp move toward fiscal surplus was associated with transitorily high privatization revenue generated by the country's successful capitalization program. But in several other countries, the positive fiscal impulse involved important and more lasting fiscal adjustments.

Macroeconomic factors have importantly influenced budgetary outcomes in some countries, but the dominant cause of changes in the fiscal balance has been changes in fiscal policy. In most cases the actual change in the fiscal surplus is very close to the fiscal impulse, and in only a few countries (notably Argentina, Chile, Guyana, Jamaica, Mexico and Uruguay) were changes in the fiscal balance importantly affected by economic factors (Figure 18).

FIGURE 17

Fiscal Impulse, 1995

(Percent of GDP)

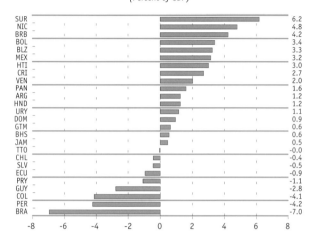

Procyclical Fiscal Policy

Changes in policy, as measured by the fiscal impulse, tended to be procyclical in 1995. This procyclicality is clearly visible in Figure 19. Countries in the recovery phase of the adjustment process, when economic growth was relatively rapid, tended to implement more expansionary fiscal policies. In this regard, Brazil, Colombia, Guyana, and Peru were notable. In contrast, the four countries that were in the correction stage of the adjustment process and experienced recession in 1995—Argentina, Jamaica, Mexico and Uruguay—implemented contractionary fiscal policy, as estimated by the fiscal impulse. In each of those four countries, the deep recession was met with contractionary fiscal measures designed to keep the recession from creating large fiscal deficits. In Mexico and Argentina in particular, those contractionary measures were required not only to adjust to the reduced availability of noninflationary financing of fiscal deficits but also to bolster confidence in the countries' medium-run macroeconomic management, thus preventing even larger capital outflows than actually occurred. We estimate that the contractionary fiscal impulse amounted to more than 3 percent of GDP in Mexico and to more than 1 percent of GDP in Argentina—large adjustments of fiscal policy by any measure. [9]

Generally Stable Exchange Arrangements

With the exception of Mexico (which moved from a narrow and slowly moving exchange rate band to a freely floating exchange rate in the aftermath of its December 1994 devaluation), exchange rate arrangements in the region were essentially the same in 1995 as they had been in the previous year. Eight countries—Argentina, the Bahamas, Barbados, Belize, the Dominican Republic, El Salvador, Panama and Venezuela—were operating under fixed exchange rates in 1995. In Argentina, commitment to this peg was buttressed with limitations on discretionary Central Bank action that were designed to ensure, among other things, that reserve outflows would generate the monetary contraction required to protect the exchange rate. The strengths and costs of this approach were on vivid display in 1995, as the Argentine economy adjusted to large capital outflows associated with the Tequila shock.

In most of the other countries operating under fixed exchange rates, inflation was at or below industrial country levels, and fiscal and monetary fundamentals were largely consistent with the requirements of maintaining the exchange rate; doing so does impose important medium-term discipline on macroeconomic management in these countries, but it did not pose great difficulties in 1995.

In Venezuela, however, the pegged exchange rate was not consistent with underlying fiscal and monetary fundamentals in 1995 and was maintained through the imposition of exchange controls; these controls were eliminated in the first half of 1996 and the exchange rate was allowed to float, in the context of a major stabilization program.

In most countries of the region, exchange arrangements were more flexible and provided more room for discretionary monetary policy. Sev-

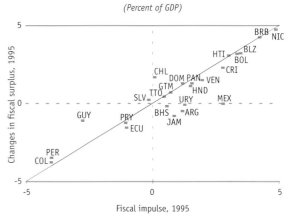

FIGURE 18

Fiscal Impulse and Outcome

(Percent of GDP)

eral countries (such as Bolivia, Jamaica, Mexico and Peru) operate under a regime of freely floating exchange rates, in which the monetary authority announces no exchange rate target. Other countries operate in an intermediate framework, in which the authorities permit the exchange rate to move within a band but intervene as required to keep the exchange rate within that band.

In Chile, the midpoint of the band is adjusted frequently to compensate for differences between Chilean inflation and that of the country's trading partners, with an eye toward maintaining a competitive real exchange rate. The band can also be adjusted in response to changes in the economic environment, but this happens less frequently and only when the authorities consider such changes permanent enough to warrant a corresponding adjustment in the real exchange rate.

In other countries, changes in the midpoint of the band are announced beforehand, with the aim of providing an expectational anchor in

---

[9] Such procyclicality is typical of fiscal outcomes in Latin America. In sharp contrast to the industrial economies, where fiscal outcomes are countercyclical (and strongly so in economic downturns), fiscal policy has tended to be procyclical in Latin America, particularly during recessions (see Gavin, Hausmann, Perotti and Talvi, 1996).

FIGURE 19

Procyclical Fiscal Policy in 1995

(In percent)

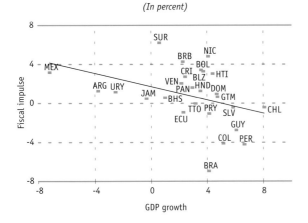

the context of a gradual inflation stabilization. This is the system followed, for example, by Colombia, Costa Rica, Ecuador and Uruguay.

Tight Monetary Conditions

Attempts to reduce inflation further were a key component of 1995 monetary policy in a number of countries, including Brazil, Colombia, Ecuador, Jamaica, Mexico, Peru and Uruguay (we shall later report on their progress). In this task, countries of the region followed different strategies and faced different constraints.

In several countries (notably Jamaica, Mexico and Peru), attempts to reduce inflation were pursued within the context of a regimen of a floating exchange rate. Many other countries (including Brazil, Colombia, Ecuador and Uruguay) based their disinflation strategy in large part upon the use of the exchange rate as a nominal anchor, typically in the context of a crawling-band arrangement.

High Real Interest Rates

The monetary policies designed to reduce inflation have contributed to the elevation of interest rates in much of the region. Real interest rates on bank deposits were nearly 20 percent in Brazil and

Table 4.	Exchange Rate Arrangements in Latin America, 1995		
Fixed	Crawling peg	Sliding band	Flexible
Argentina, Bahamas, Barbados, Belize, Dominican Republic, El Salvador, Panama, Venezuela	Bolivia, Costa Rica, Honduras, Nicaragua	Brazil, Chile, Colombia, Ecuador, Uruguay	Guatemala, Guyana, Haiti, Jamaica, Mexico, Paraguay, Peru, Suriname, Trinidad and Tobago

Ecuador and in the vicinity of 10 percent in Argentina, Bolivia, Colombia, and Jamaica. Lending rates were, of course, substantially higher.

In Brazil, high interest rates (especially at the beginning of 1995) and other measures were used to curb the growth in domestic demand in order to achieve the desired reduction in inflation under the Real Plan, and to halt the rapid deterioration of the current account and the real appreciation of the currency. In Ecuador, political uncertainty—coupled with the worsening of the public sector deficit and the decision by the Central Bank to use interest rates as a means to defend the ceiling of the exchange rate band—forced the monetary authorities to maintain a high level of real interest rates. The situation was similar in Colombia, where monetary conditions were tight because political uncertainty and a deteriorating fiscal situation left the exchange rate hovering near the ceiling of the exchange rate band in the latter part of the year, leaving very little space for the monetary authorities to attempt a reduction in interest rates. The persistence of high levels of real interest rates in Brazil, Colombia and Ecuador has contributed to deterioration of banks' loan portfolios and to tensions in the financial system.

The origins of tight monetary conditions in Argentina were not the same as in Brazil, Colombia and Ecuador. The banking panic of the early months of 1995 following the Mexican devaluation resulted in a loss of 18 percent of the deposits at commercial banks in Argentina in a period of three months. Interest rates skyrocketed as liquidity tightened because of the drain on bank

FIGURE 20

Real Interest Rates on Deposits

(Percent change from 1995 vs. 1994)

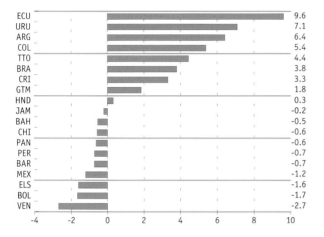

ECU	9.6
URU	7.1
ARG	6.4
COL	5.4
TTO	4.4
BRA	3.8
CRI	3.3
GTM	1.8
HND	0.3
JAM	-0.2
BAH	-0.5
CHI	-0.6
PAN	-0.6
PER	-0.7
BAR	-0.7
MEX	-1.2
ELS	-1.6
BOL	-1.7
VEN	-2.7

deposits, reaching levels of 70 percent in the interbank market at the height of the crisis. The Argentine Central Bank reacted immediately by providing liquidity to the banking system through reserve requirement reductions, swap operations and rediscounts, which allowed the banks to respond to the run without a significant decline in outstanding credit. These measures of the Central Bank were taken within the limitations imposed by the Convertibility Plan. The rapid response of the authorities—who announced a package of austerity measures designed to buttress confidence in the continuation of the Convertibility Plan and to ensure the continued support of international organizations—managed to turn the financial crisis around, and by the end of 1995 bank deposits and interest rates had returned to normal levels. Nevertheless, growth in bank credit has remained subdued.

In Venezuela, on the other hand, real deposit interest rates were strongly negative in 1995. These negative real interest rates stemmed from a very expansionary monetary policy, with its roots in the country's large fiscal deficit and the hangover from the financing of the banking crisis (which resulted both in large losses for the Central Bank of Venezuela and in continued concern that high real interest rates would further endan-

ger the banking system). Venezuela had capital and exchange controls in 1995, and so the excess liquidity led to high inflation, negative real interest rates, and a growing disparity between the parallel and the official exchange rate, despite the fact that the official rate went from 170 to 290 bolivares per U.S. dollar.

Monetary Management Complicated by Fiscal Policy

In some countries (including Brazil, Colombia, Peru, and to a lesser extent Ecuador), attempts to reduce inflation have been complicated by fiscal policies not fully supportive of the anti-inflationary monetary stance. A notable example was Brazil, where the mid-1994 stabilization unleashed a large spending boom, supported by large capital inflows and a rapid expansion of credit by the domestic financial system. This boom threatened to overheat the economy and to generate potentially destabilizing external sector imbalances. Fiscal policy turned sharply expansionary in 1995, and thus it fell to monetary policy to try to slow the economy. The result was very high interest rates, which have controlled the domestic spending boom but created an obstacle to domestic investment and major difficulties for the domestic financial system.

Peru, too, experienced fiscal expansion in the first half of the year, meaning that the monetary policy necessary for inflation reduction would have to entail high real interest rates. These high interest rates have complicated monetary policy by attracting large capital inflows (to be described later in more detail). In Colombia as well, fiscal slippage at the beginning of the year was met with higher interest rates, as the Central Bank attempted to reduce domestic demand and achieve its inflation targets. In mid-year, an agreement was reached by which the government agreed to scale back its spending plans while the monetary authorities acted to promote lower interest rates. At about that time, however, a political shock occurred that reduced confidence in the continuity of the economic policy regime, causing important changes in Colombia's monetary and financial environment.

Monetary Management Complicated by Volatility of Capital Flows

As we have noted, in a number of countries contractionary monetary policies designed to bring down inflation led to high interest rates. In several such countries, these high interest rates led to large capital inflows. A case in point is Jamaica, where the authorities attempted to sterilize the inflows, but at high fiscal cost.

In Ecuador, and in Colombia as well during the second part of the year, the context was somewhat different. These countries were at a more advanced stage of the stabilization and reform process, with Ecuador showing symptoms typical of the stress phase throughout the year and Colombia toward the end of the year. Political shocks in both countries—combined with economic shocks in the case of Ecuador—contributed to a loss of confidence that quickly made itself felt in financial markets. The problem was not overheating or excessive capital inflows, but rather a weakening currency that threatened to depreciate past the upper limit of the established band, thereby compromising inflation targets. In response, Ecuador devalued the central parity of its exchange rate band over the course of the year but nevertheless (like Colombia) had to maintain high interest rates to defend the band.

In Mexico and Argentina, the major problem for monetary policy was how to deal with a sharp decline in international capital flows. For Mexico, operating under flexible exchange rates and having faced a massive and highly inflationary depreciation, the first objective of monetary policy was to reduce inflation, which it did through very restrictive limits on growth of domestic credit. As we later discuss, this policy was successful in securing a rapid reduction in infla-

tion, at the cost of very high interest rates during 1995. In Argentina, on the other hand, monetary policy was largely out of the hands of the Central Bank, which faced important limitations on its actions under the Convertibility Plan designed to ensure the viability of the fixed exchange rate. The Central Bank of Argentina used the limited flexibility it had to minimize the disruptive impact of the decline in bank deposits on bank lending, with the aim of forestalling the bank crisis that might otherwise have occurred and somewhat reducing the adverse impact of the situation on the real economy.

Fiscal and Monetary Difficulties Caused by the Fragility of Domestic Financial Systems

Domestic financial systems complicated macroeconomic policy in much of the region. Failures of private banks and losses by state-owned banks created important fiscal problems in Bolivia, Brazil, Mexico, Paraguay and Venezuela, and threatened to do so in a number of other countries. In most countries, difficulties in the domestic banking system were compounded by high interest rates.

Authorities in Argentina, too, were faced with a major threat to their banking system when, in the first part of 1995, demand for domestic bank deposits shrank dramatically. The need to pay cash to their depositors depleted commercial bank reserves and made it difficult for the banks to finance their outstanding loans to individuals and firms. This situation threatened to produce a highly disruptive contraction of bank credit. Fortunately, the Central Bank was, within the limits created by the Convertibility Plan, able to provide enough liquidity to the commercial banks to prevent a catastrophic contraction of bank credit. As the year progressed and the financial panic subsided, bank deposits began to increase once again, relaxing the pressure on the domestic banking system. Although the event was highly disruptive, in the end a major banking crisis was avoided.

GROWTH, DOMESTIC DEMAND AND EMPLOYMENT

The growth rate of real GDP for the entire region was only 0.7 percent in 1995, considerably lower than the previous year's 5.1 percent, which had been the highest rate since 1980. The regionwide slowdown was very reflective of the performance of Mexico and Argentina, which suffered economic contractions of 6.9 percent (Mexico) and 4.4 percent (Argentina) during the year.

This aggregate rate of growth, which is based on the GDP amounts (in 1990 U.S. dollars) of all the countries, gives a pessimistic view of growth in the region. If weighted by population, however, the average growth rate was somewhat stronger at 1.5 percent, and the median growth rate, which is a measure of growth in the typical country in the region, was 3.7 percent in 1995, not far below the 4.2 percent rate of the previous year.

There occurred notable differences in performance among countries in 1995. In contrast with the sharp declines in Mexico and Argentina, four countries achieved growth rates greater than 6 percent (Chile, El Salvador, Guyana and Peru), and eight others experienced increases of between 4 and 6 percent (Brazil, Colombia, the Dominican Republic, Guatemala, Haiti, Nicaragua, Paraguay and Suriname). Contrary to what might have been expected when the crisis was unleashed in Mexico in December 1994, only three countries in the region experienced negative growth, one fewer than in the two previous years. Besides Mexico and Argentina, only Uruguay fell into recession in 1995.

For most countries in the region, the rate of growth in 1995 was similar to that recorded in the preceding four years. In addition to the three countries that entered into recession, only Barbados, Costa Rica, Guyana, Panama, and Trinidad and Tobago slowed down notably, and despite the deceleration Guyana still had a growth rate greater than 6 percent. By contrast, growth picked up

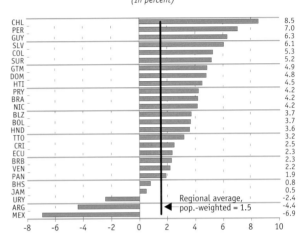

FIGURE 21

GDP Growth in 1995

(In percent)

CHL	8.5
PER	7.0
GUY	6.3
SLV	6.1
COL	5.3
SUR	5.2
GTM	4.9
DOM	4.8
HTI	4.5
PRY	4.2
BRA	4.2
NIC	4.2
BLZ	3.7
BOL	3.7
HND	3.6
TTO	3.2
CRI	2.5
ECU	2.3
BRB	2.3
VEN	2.2
PAN	1.9
BHS	0.8
JAM	0.5
URY	-2.4
ARG	-4.4
MEX	-6.9

Regional average, pop.-weighted = 1.5

considerably in the Bahamas, Haiti, Nicaragua and Suriname.

From a longer-range perspective, the region's recent growth trends have been favorable but not entirely satisfactory. For the region as a whole, growth has been more rapid than during the 1980s but substantially lower than during earlier decades. This pattern is very much influenced by the three largest economies. In Mexico, the long-run trends have been continually downward, with an average growth rate in the 1990s of a meager 0.7 percent, a far cry from rates of more than 6 percent achieved in the 1960s and 1970s. Over the course of the 1990s, Brazil has had an average growth rate of 2.7 percent, which is higher than the 1.7 percent of the 1980s but, as in the case of Mexico, far lower than the county's rapid growth of earlier decades.

Argentina, on the other hand, has achieved a remarkable recovery in the 1990s, the 1995 recession notwithstanding. Argentina's average growth rate of 5.2 percent during the 1990s exceeds the -0.8 percent of the 1980s and even the averages of earlier decades. For the remaining countries as a group, the average growth rate of the 1990s has meant a return to those of the 1960s and 1970s, after the low-growth period of

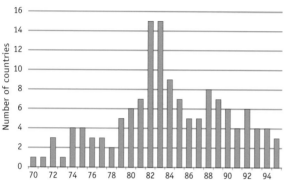

FIGURE 22

Latin America: Countries in Recession

FIGURE 23

GDP Growth: 1995 vs 1990-94

(In percent)

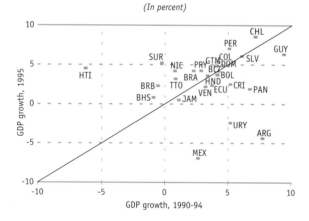

FIGURE 24

Historical Perspective of Latin American Growth

(In percent)

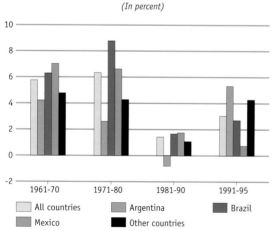

the 1980s. Indeed, in the 1990s several countries have surpassed their average pre-1980s growth rates.

The growth rates during the 1990s of Guyana and El Salvador (close to 9 and 6 percent, respectively) contrast quite favorably with the 2.5 percent rate that both averaged in the 1960s and 1970s. Argentina, Chile, Peru and Uruguay also have had more vigorous growth rates in the 1990s than in previous decades, while the most notable slowdowns by comparison with the 1960s and 1970s have occurred in the Bahamas, Barbados, Ecuador, Jamaica, Mexico, Paraguay and Suriname.

*The Reform Process
and Economic Growth*

Economic growth during 1995 can be better understood in the context of the dynamics of stabilization and reform discussed earlier. Table 5 characterizes the countries of the region in terms of the particular stage of the adjustment process in which each one found itself during 1995.

During 1995, only two countries—Suriname and Haiti—were in the adoption phase of the adjustment. Six countries—Brazil, Colombia, El Salvador, Guyana, Nicaragua and Peru—were in the recovery or boom phase of the process, continuing booms that had begun as early as 1992 (Colombia and El Salvador) and as recently as 1994 (Brazil and Nicaragua). Three countries—Ecuador, Guatemala and Trinidad and Tobago—were in the stress phase of the adjustment process. Ecuador illustrates well this phase of the dynamics of stabilization and reform. In that country the recovery phase of preceding years had been characterized by a spending boom, rapid growth in bank lending to the private sector, substantial current account deficits, and currency appreciation. Anticipation that a correction might involve a depreciation then combined with two major shocks (the war with Peru and the weather-related disruption in power supplies) to put pressure on the currency, which required increased in-

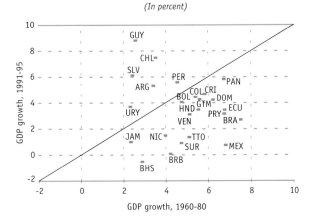

FIGURE 25

GDP Growth: 1991-95 vs. 1960-80

(In percent)

ses in Argentina and Mexico were much larger than the typical correction; in both of these countries the 1995 rate of GDP growth fell by more than 10 percentage points from the 1994 growth rate, while the typical correction involves a growth rate decline of only about 5 percent. If one uses the actual slowdown registered in these economies, the transitions between stages explain nearly all of the slowdown experienced by the region as a whole.

Economic Growth in the 1990s: Recuperation from the 1980s?

The 1980s were a period of economic crisis and depression in many countries of the region. As a result, many countries entered the 1990s with substantial reserves of unemployed workers and underutilized productive capacity. The question aris-

terest rates for its defense. These higher real interest rates in turn have put pressure on Ecuador's banking system and slowed economic activity. Meanwhile, four other countries of the region—Argentina, Mexico, Uruguay and Venezuela—were in the correction or crisis stage of the adjustment process. Venezuela continued in a crisis that had begun in 1994, and the other countries followed a period of stress (Argentina, Mexico) or recovery (Uruguay) in 1994.

Eight countries moved from one phase of the process to another in 1995. These transitions were key factors underlying the slowdown in economic growth. The third column of Table 5 gives the change in the rate of economic growth that is typically associated with the particular transition actually observed in each economy in 1995. Much of the 3.4 percentage point decline in the region's (population-weighted) average rate of growth can be attributed to these transitions between stages of the stabilization and reform process. Even so, these transitions explain only part of the slowdown, because the actual cri-

Table 5. The Stabilization-Reform Process and Economic Growth: Examples of Country Experience

(In percent)

	Situation in 1995	Typical change in GDP growth	Actual change in GDP growth
Countries that have not initiated the process of reforms in 1994			
Suriname	Adoption	-0.4	8.6
Countries in the phase of recovery in 1994			
Brazil	Recovery	—	-1.5
Colombia	Recovery	—	-0.5
Ecuador	Stress	-1.9	-2.0
Peru	Recovery	—	-6.3
El Salvador	Recovery	—	0.1
Uruguay	Correction	-6.7	-7.6
Countries in the phase of stress in 1994			
Argentina	Correction	-4.9	-11.8
Mexico	Correction	-4.9	-10.5
Countries in the phase of correction in 1994			
Venezuela	Correction	—	4.9
Regional Average *		-1.3	-3.4

* Regional average is population-weighted and includes all countries in the region.

FIGURE 26

Is Growth Recovery?

(In percent)

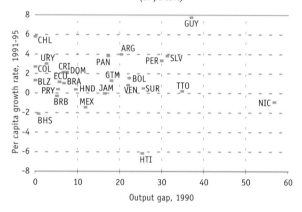

Output gap, 1990

es, therefore, whether the region's acceleration of growth in the 1990s was primarily the result of making greater use of existing underutilized capacity or whether it instead reflected an expansion in the economies' productive capacity. The question is worth asking because growth based on such recuperation has clear limits and will be exhausted when capacity is once again fully utilized. To be sustained, growth must eventually be based upon an expansion of productive capacity through investment.

Direct measures of capacity utilization not being available, we use the 1990 output gap as an indirect measure of spare capacity at the beginning of the decade. This measures the difference between the maximum level of per capita output ever achieved in the years up to 1990 and output's actual level in that year. In countries where the 1990 level of per capita output was much below previously achieved levels, there is likely to have existed substantial excess capacity.

Except for Nicaragua (a special case we shall examine later), a positive relationship exists between the output gap in 1990 and the rate of economic growth achieved in the subsequent five years (Figure 26). This outcome is consistent with the idea that in some countries growth was at least in part associated with increased use of existing capacity that was apparently unuti-

lized at the end of the 1980s. The figure highlights groups of countries whose experience in this context is noteworthy.

The first group started the 1990s with a large output gap and grew rapidly, suggesting that growth was at least to some extent drawing upon spare capacity. This scenario appears to have been part of the story behind rapid rates of economic growth in El Salvador, Guyana and Peru, where the 1990 output gap was more than 30 percent of GDP. Argentina and Panama fit this pattern as well, although to a lesser extent.

Spare capacity can facilitate a rapid output response when economic conditions become favorable for growth, but it is of course no guarantee of rapid economic growth. Therefore, it is not surprising to find a second set of countries in which economic growth was very slow during the 1990s, despite the apparent existence of substantial excess capacity at the beginning of the decade. Nicaragua, Suriname, and Trinidad and Tobago fit into this category. The most plausible explanation for Suriname's slow growth during the 1990s is the macroeconomic environment, which was unstable and deteriorating until the 1995 stabilization, after which the rate of economic growth in Suriname rose to more than 5 percent. In Nicaragua, on the other hand, the calculated output gap probably overestimates the amount of spare capacity available in that economy at the beginning of the 1990s, because the extreme macroeconomic instability and civil disturbances of previous years almost certainly destroyed productive capacity rather than simply leaving it idle. (Economic recovery in Nicaragua may also have been undermined by uncertainties related to a substantial debt overhang, until the country's debt rescheduling was completed.)

There exists a third group of countries with a small output gap at the beginning of the decade but that have nevertheless experienced healthy growth in the 1990s. This group includes most notably Chile and also Belize, Colombia, Costa Rica and the Dominican Republic, all of

FIGURE 27

Investment and Growth in the 1990s

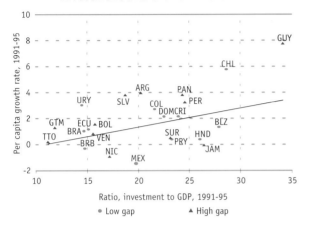

Ratio, investment to GDP, 1991-95
● Low gap   ▲ High gap

which combined low output gaps in 1990 with relatively rapid growth in the 1990s. In this group of countries, economic growth was driven primarily by factor accumulation and productivity growth.

The Role of Investment

In some countries, then, recuperation based upon more complete utilization of existing capacity is apparently one element of the improved growth performance during the 1990s. But this aspect is only part of the story; the improved growth record of the 1990s is also associated with a major recovery of investment, both at the regional and country levels. The actual dimensions of this investment recovery will be discussed in more detail later, but first let us examine the links between improved investment performance and economic growth.

Figure 27 shows the relationship between average rates of investment and economic growth in the 1990s. Countries with initial output gaps of greater than 15 percent are graphed with a triangle, and those with smaller output gaps are graphed with a circle. The upward-sloping line is the statistical relationship indicated by the observations in the figure; countries above the line grew more rapidly than would have been predicted on

the basis of their investment performance alone, and countries below it grew more slowly than we would have predicted on the basis of their investment performance.

The figure suggests several inferences about the relationship between investment, recuperation and growth in the 1990s. As one would expect, higher investment is associated with higher economic growth. In addition, most of the countries that lie substantially above the line are those where the output gap in 1990 was large. The figure thus suggests, for example, that growth was quite rapid in Guyana both because of high rates of investment and because the initially high level of spare capacity permitted a period of catch-up. Such a mix of relatively high investment and spare capacity recuperation also appears to underlie the fairly strong growth recorded in Argentina, El Salvador, Panama and Peru.

In Chile and Uruguay, growth was significantly more rapid than would be predicted by investment rates, which were very high in Chile and low in Uruguay, despite the apparent absence of substantial spare capacity at the beginning of the decade, suggesting that productivity growth has been an important element of growth in these countries. And in Honduras, Jamaica, Mexico, Nicaragua and Suriname, output growth was quite low relative to what would have been predicted on the basis of their investment rates. In some of these countries, persistent macroeconomic instability is a possible explanation for the disappointing growth record in the 1990s to date.

Continued Rapid Growth of Domestic Consumption and Investment

In 1995, as in the previous several years, both consumption and investment grew more rapidly than production. Consumption rose almost 3 percent, and investment by more than 5 percent.

Consumption did grow more rapidly than output in 1995 but nevertheless more slowly than it had during the previous four years. This relative regionwide slowdown is attributable largely to the performance of Argentina and Mexico, the only two countries where consumption fell in 1995. In Uruguay as well, the rate of expansion of consumption slowed sharply, although it did remain positive. Meanwhile, consumption recovered remarkably in Haiti after the trade embargo was lifted, and in Chile and Guyana the trends toward increased consumption that had been noteworthy since 1991 gathered even greater momentum.

In the region as a whole, investment rose by 5.3 percent—below the 7.1 percent average of the previous four years but substantially above the rate of growth of real GDP. This overall investment rise was notable, in view of the fact that investment fell almost 40 percent in Mexico and 13 percent in Argentina. By contrast, investment rose by approximately 20 percent (or even more) in Bolivia, Brazil, Colombia, Haiti, Peru, Suriname and Venezuela. Indeed, investment growth in 1995 exceeded that recorded during the 1991-94 period in a greater number of countries than the number of countries that suffered declines.

The relatively rapid growth in consumption and investment vis-à-vis GDP growth was largely consistent with the stages of the stabilization and recovery process in which countries of the region found themselves in 1995. The country in the adoption phase of the adjustment process, Suriname, had moderately high rates of growth in output and domestic demand in 1995.[10] The six countries of the region in the recovery stage had an average GDP growth rate of 5.5 percent, with very rapidly growing consumption (9.4 percent) and (especially) investment (15.2 percent). The three countries in the stress phase of the adjustment had slower but still positive growth; this outcome conforms to the pattern described earlier, but in contrast with the normal pattern, investment growth remained high, on average, in the economies experiencing stress. Real GDP in the

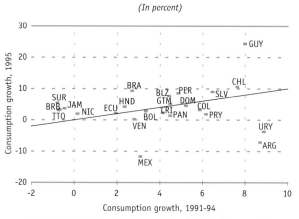

FIGURE 28

Consumption Growth: 1995 vs. 1991-94

(In percent)

Note: Excludes Haiti, where consumption declined -8.6 percent in 1991-94 and increased 44.5 percent in 1995.

Table 6. Sources of Demand in Latin America		
(Percent change per year)		
	1991-94	1995
Latin America		
Gross domestic product	3.4	1.5
Consumption	3.8	2.8
Domestic investment	7.1	5.3
Exports	7.2	9.1
Imports	15.5	13.8
Excl. Argentina and Mexico		
Gross domestic product	3.2	4.4
Consumption	2.6	5.6
Domestic investment	4.2	14.0
Exports	6.2	1.4
Imports	10.0	20.0

Note: All variables are measured at constant prices. The regional average is population-weighted.

four countries that in 1995 found themselves in the correction phase of the adjustment process fell by about 3 percent, and as is typically the case, consumption and investment fell even more. The four countries in the post-reform stage of the process experienced average GDP growth of a strong 5.2 percent, consumption growth at roughly the same rate, and very strong investment growth. Finally, in the seven countries in which the stabilization and reform adjustment process appears not to have been a key determinant of recent macro-

FIGURE 29

Investment Growth in 1995

(In percent)

HTI	82.6
SUR	25.0
VEN	23.6
COL	21.8
BOL	21.4
BRA	20.0
PER	19.9
CHL	19.0
TTO	18.0
SLV	13.7
DOM	11.9
NIC	10.8
ECU	8.5
BRB	7.0
GTM	6.0
HND	5.7
GUY	5.0
PRY	4.9
PAN	3.3
URY	1.7
JAM	0.3
BLZ	-1.3
CRI	-4.7
ARG	-12.8
MEX	-39.5

◄— Regional average, pop.-weighted = 5.3

FIGURE 30

Investment Growth: 1995 vs. 1991-94

(In percent)

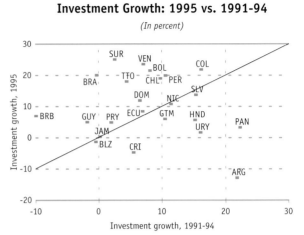

Note: Excludes Haiti and Mexico.

Table 7.	Growth of Domestic Output and Spending in 1995		
(Percent change)			
	Consumption	Investment	GDP
Adoption (1)	5.4	25.0	4.8
Recovery (6)	9.4	15.2	5.5
Stress (3)	3.5	10.3	3.3
Correction (4)	-5.6	-6.8	-2.9
Post-reform (4)	5.5	14.5	5.2
Other (7)	2.8	1.3	2.3

Note: Growth rates are simple averages of data for countries in each category. Numbers in parentheses give the number of countries in each phase of the cycle. Two countries, Suriname and Haiti, were in the adoption phase of the cycle in 1995, but data were available only for Suriname.

economic outcomes, growth in GDP, investment, and consumption was relatively sluggish.

Consumption growth has been strong during the 1990s, but investment and exports have been the most dynamic sources of aggregate demand. This fact is illustrated in Table 8, which provides information on the components of aggregate demand, with countries organized according to whether consumption, investment or export growth has been most rapid during the 1990s. Although many economies in the region have experienced major consumption booms at some

point in the 1990s, investment and exports appear to have been the most important sustained components of demand growth in most of them, as measured by the changes in the ratio of real spending to real GDP. In fact, only in Belize, Brazil, Haiti and Uruguay has consumption been the component of demand that has risen most in relation to GDP. Investment has been the most important component in 13 countries; in Colombia, Honduras and Panama investment coefficients rose more than 10 percentage points between 1990 and 1995, thereby contributing at least twice as much to demand as did consumption. In another six countries, investment coefficients rose between 5 percentage points and 10 percentage points. Exports, in turn, have been the main factor in the expansion of demand in seven countries; in Costa Rica, Guyana, Jamaica and Paraguay, export coefficients rose by more than 10 percent of GDP during the 1990s.

The Investment Recovery of the 1990s

The 1990s have been a period of investment recovery in the region. Real investment rose from a low of 16.5 of percent of real GDP in 1990 to 18.5 percent in 1995. Most countries participated in this recovery, and a few were particularly

Table 8.	Dynamics of Growth by Leading Demand Source

(In percent)

	Change of the leading demand source in GDP	Growth rates, 1991-95					Growth rates, 1995				
		GDP	Consumption	Investment	Exports	Imports	GDP	Consumption	Investment	Exports	Imports
Consumption											
Haiti	25.0	-4.2	0.1	-18.4	9.5	9.4	4.5	44.5	82.6	74.1	248.8
Uruguay	11.3	3.6	6.2	13.1	3.6	14.7	-2.4	-3.7	1.7	-4.8	-5.5
Brazil	5.3	2.7	4.0	3.5	6.3	17.0	4.2	9.4	20.0	-8.0	30.0
Belize	3.7	4.1	5.1	-0.6	3.0	2.4	3.7	7.6	-1.3	-5.6	-2.4
Investment											
Panama	12.4	5.8	3.8	18.3	5.5	9.3	1.9	1.3	3.3	3.9	4.6
Colombia	12.4	4.4	5.3	17.3	6.4	20.5	5.3	3.2	21.8	12.4	17.6
Honduras	11.0	3.4	2.7	13.3	1.2	6.9	3.6	4.2	5.7	9.4	12.0
Nicaragua	7.9	1.5	0.5	11.4	4.7	6.4	4.2	1.9	10.8	8.4	6.2
Peru	7.8	5.5	5.6	12.4	8.4	16.6	7.0	8.5	19.9	8.1	25.9
Argentina	7.0	5.2	5.3	14.0	7.1	27.1	-4.4	-7.1	-12.8	29.0	-9.8
Suriname	6.9	0.8	0.4	6.7	-14.3	-8.1	5.2	5.4	25.0	6.2	45.0
El Salvador	6.9	6.1	7.0	15.1	12.1	15.7	6.1	9.0	13.7	17.1	22.6
Chile	5.5	7.4	8.2	11.6	9.6	13.9	8.5	10.6	19.0	11.4	22.2
Venezuela	3.9	3.0	2.3	10.2	4.4	9.0	2.2	0.2	23.6	2.2	9.3
Dominican Republic	3.7	4.2	5.1	7.6	4.4	12.1	4.8	4.5	11.9	8.8	16.0
Trinidad and Tobago	3.3	1.3	0.0	7.1	2.2	1.9	3.2	3.0	18.0	18.0	47.0
Guatemala	2.6	4.3	4.6	9.6	5.1	12.5	4.9	5.1	6.0	8.1	11.0
Exports											
Guyana	16.4	8.8	11.1	-0.5	13.6	10.2	6.3	24.3	5.0	6.1	19.6
Paraguay	14.0	3.1	5.3	2.6	12.5	15.0	4.2	1.8	4.9	9.4	4.1
Costa Rica	12.8	4.6	3.7	3.4	9.4	8.1	2.5	2.2	-4.7	5.6	2.5
Jamaica	11.3	1.0	0.4	0.3	5.2	3.6	0.5	3.6	0.3	7.3	10.8
Mexico	8.6	0.7	-0.0	-4.9	8.7	2.7	-6.9	-11.7	-39.5	28.4	-27.6
Bolivia	6.4	4.0	3.2	10.7	9.3	9.9	3.7	2.8	21.4	5.5	11.7
Ecuador	6.1	3.4	2.0	7.3	7.6	6.6	2.3	2.2	8.5	5.0	9.8
Barbados	1.2	0.0	0.1	-6.8	0.4	-1.4	2.3	3.3	7.0	1.5	4.0
Bahamas		-0.6					0.8				

influential in the regional averages presented in Figure 31.

The first such case pertains to Brazil. Until the mid-1994 stabilization, investment in Brazil was declining steadily, while in other countries the investment recovery was even more robust than suggested by the figure for the region as a whole. In countries other than Brazil, the ratio of investment to GDP averaged about 21 percent in 1994, similar to the rates recorded during the 1960s, although not as high as the peaks reached during the late 1970s. In 1995, the situation became very different. In response to the 1994 stabilization, real investment in Brazil grew very rapidly, from about 14 percent of real GDP to more than 16 percent. At the same time, investment plummeted in Mexico and Argentina, as these two countries entered their major economic crises.

The overall recovery of investment during the 1990s has been quite widespread. In 15 countries the average annual growth rates of investment have been higher than 7 percent , and only in Belize, Guyana, Jamaica and Mexico has investment been stagnant or fallen during the 1990-95 period. This recovery is remarkable in terms of the contrast between the current investment coefficients and the averages of the 1982-90 period, when the halt in foreign financing and the insufficient rates of domestic saving led to severe declines in investment coefficients.

FIGURE 31

**Ratio of Investment to GDP
(Population-weighted Average)**

(In percent)

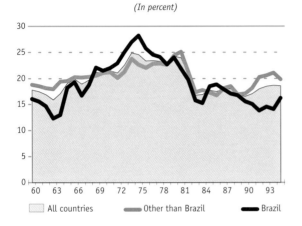

FIGURE 32

Investment Growth, 1991-95

(In percent)

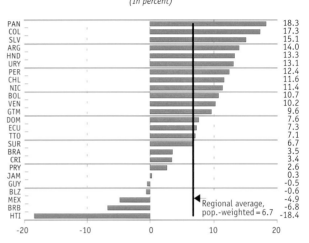

Indeed, investment has grown rapidly in most countries of the region over the past five years, but investment rates in most of them nevertheless remain modest by international standards and even in comparison with the rates of investment recorded in Latin America itself during the 1970s. One reason is the fact that major stabilization and reform programs are relatively recent in several of the countries, and investment is still in the process of responding to the more favorable environment. Another reason may be the longer-term or structural barriers to investment that remain in many of the countries despite the reforms undertaken thus far.

According to the responses to a survey of IDB country economists, various factors currently constrain investment in the region, the most common of which are insufficient public infrastructure, flaws in the countries' supporting legal framework (property rights, functioning of the judicial system, and so forth), and labor force deficiencies.

Consumption Booms in the 1990s

The rapid growth in consumption during the 1990s is related to the phenomenon of consump-

tion booms—that is, periods of rapid but temporary growth in domestic consumption—that has been observed in most countries of the region during the 1990s. Such consumption booms became more common as the 1990s progressed. In 1990 itself, only three countries experienced a "boom," defined as a year in which consumption growth per capita is at least 4.3 percent, or twice the (unweighted) regional annual average for the 1990s. Since 1991, six to nine countries have been in a consumption boom in any given year. The booms have been temporary; indeed, in most cases they have lasted no more than one or two years, while only five countries have had sustained booms of three years or longer. Not only have the booms been temporary but they also have begun suddenly and ended abruptly. At the beginning of the boom, the per capita growth rate has on average shot up from negative figures to more than 8 percent, and when the boom ends, the growth rate has typically dropped to below zero, as is illustrated in Figure 35.

Programs to cut inflation have been one of the factors most clearly associated with the consumption booms of the 1990s. Argentina (1991), Brazil (1994), Nicaragua (1991), Peru (1990), and Suriname (1995) brought inflation down from

FIGURE 33

Investment Ratios: 1991-95 vs 1982-90

(Percent of GDP)

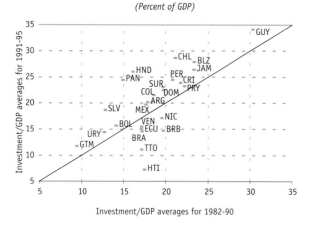

FIGURE 34

Per Capita Consumption Growth and Consumption Booms

(In percent)

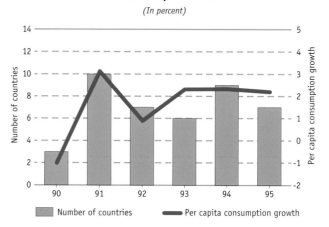

levels greater than 500 percent. With the exception of the Peruvian program, the anti-inflation efforts in these countries were based on the utilization of the exchange rate as a tool for anchoring nominal prices, which led almost immediately to consumption booms. In Peru, where stabilization was instead based on monetary control, consumption gained momentum only after a period of three years and did not begin to take on the features of a boom until the fourth year. Inflation stabilization in the group of countries that had experienced levels ranging from 60 percent to 150 percent brought about consumption effects that were more mixed.

Capital inflows have also been associated with consumption booms, most often in conjunction with inflation reduction. Capital inflows during the boom years were higher by at least 2 percent of GDP than were capital inflows the year before inflation reduction was initiated in Argentina, Barbados, Belize, Brazil, Colombia, Costa Rica, Panama, Paraguay, Peru, Suriname, Uruguay and Venezuela.

In addition, trade reforms have been associated with consumption booms in the 1990s. In the cases of Argentina, Colombia, the Dominican Republic, El Salvador, Nicaragua, Paraguay, Peru and Venezuela, the lowering of tariffs and

other restrictions that had hindered the import of consumption goods predated or coincided with the booms. In El Salvador, fears that some of these controls might be reimposed in 1995 may have helped prolong the boom that began in 1992.

Finally, the adoption of expansive public spending policies has been associated with the consumption boom in a number of countries. This was most notably the case in Argentina, Belize, Panama, Peru and Venezuela, where during the boom years central government spending on average rose by 2 percent of GDP or more.

National Saving in the 1990s

Concomitant with the rapid growth in consumption that has been observed in much of the region during the 1990s has been a decline in national saving. The (population-weighted) average rate of saving in Latin America declined by more than 3 percent of GDP, from roughly 20 percent in the late 1980s to a low of less than 17 percent in 1993.

Over the course of 1994 and 1995, the savings rate rose by about 1 percentage point, but it nevertheless remains low by comparison with rates recorded in the 1970s, especially by compar-

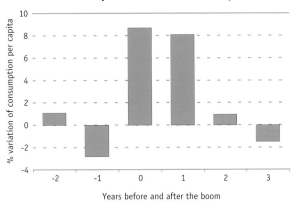

FIGURE 35

**Anatomy of Consumption Booms:
Per Capita Growth of Consumption**

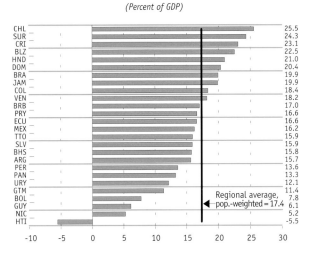

FIGURE 36

National Saving in Latin America, 1991-95

(Percent of GDP)

ison with the rapidly growing developing economies of Asia. This decline in saving has been in
almost all cases the result of sharp declines in private saving, since the 1990s have been a period of
increased public sector saving in most of the continent, as already noted in our discussion of fiscal
policy.

The experience with saving has been very
diverse from country to country. In seven countries of the region, saving has averaged more than
20 percent of GDP in the 1990s, while in eight
countries it has averaged less than 15 percent.
Chile stands out as the country with the highest
saving rate in the region, at more than 25 percent
during the 1991-95 period.

The current situation of saving can be
described as solid in only a small group of countries in the region: Chile, Costa Rica, the Dominican Republic, Honduras and Jamaica. In this
group the average rates of saving for the 1994-95
period were more than 20 percent, and they were
higher than they had been in the 1989-90 period.
In eight countries, saving has recovered in the
1990s but has not risen above 20 percent. In Belize and Brazil the situation may be described as
uncertain, since saving has fallen during the 1990s,
although its level is still higher than 20 percent.
In nine countries in the region, the situation of

saving is weak, because it is under 20 percent of
GDP and has declined during the 1990s. Countries with solid or recovering saving tend to have
higher growth rates, while fragile savings rates are
associated with low economic growth (Table 9).
As we shall later discuss in more detail, this finding is consistent with the idea that economic recovery promotes higher domestic saving.

Saving, Investment and the Current Account

One consequence of the region's low and declining saving rates, combined as they have been with
increasing rates of domestic investment, has been
the widening of current account deficits. Foreign
investors have been called upon to finance the widening gap between national saving and domestic
investment, a gap that is visible in Figure 37.[11]

During the 1990s, investment exceeded
domestic saving in almost every country of the

---

[11]   The investment data in Figure 37 differ from those presented in Figure
31 because the former are measured in current prices while the latter are
measured in constant prices. The constant price data in Figure 31 are more
informative about the speed of capital accumulation, while the current
price data in Figure 37 are relevant for questions surrounding the financing
of domestic investment.

Saving position	Per capita GDP growth			
	High (>3% annual)	Medium (1.5-3%)	Low (0-1.5%)	Negative (<0%)
Solid[1]	Chile	Costa Rica, Dominican Republic	Honduras	Jamaica
Recovery[2]	Argentina, Guyana, Panama, Peru, El Salvador	Bolivia	Ecuador, Guatemala	
Uncertain[3]		Belize	Brazil	
Fragile[4]		Colombia, Uruguay	Paraguay, Trinidad and Tobago, Venezuela	Bahamas, Haiti, Mexico, Nicaragua

Table 9.   Saving and GDP Growth in the 1990s

[1] Average saving coefficient, 1994-95, greater than 20 percent and greater than that of 1989-90.
[2] Average saving coefficient, 1994-95, greater than that of 1989-90, but below 20 percent.
[3] Average saving coefficient, 1994-95, less than that of 1989-90, but above 20 percent.
[4] Average saving coefficient, 1994-95, less than that of 1989-90 and lower than 20 percent.

FIGURE 37

Saving and Investment in Latin America

(Percent of GDP)

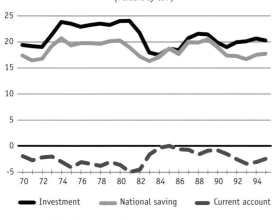

Note: Weighted by 1995 population.

region, so that nearly all countries ran current account deficits. This situation is made visible in Figure 38, which summarizes the saving-investment relationship in the countries of the region. Saving is measured on the vertical axis and investment on the horizontal axis. The vertical distance between each country's observation and the 45-degree line drawn in the figure are a measure of the current account surplus: countries above the line experienced current account surpluses and countries below experienced deficits.

Only Trinidad and Tobago has run large current account surpluses in the first half of the 1990s, the consequence of a very low rate of domestic investment. Barbados and Suriname had smaller surpluses. Five countries—Belize, Chile, Costa Rica, the Dominican Republic and Honduras—have had current account deficits during the 1990s despite having rates of saving higher than 20 percent of GDP. These countries' deficits have thus been driven largely by strong investment performance rather than by very low rates of saving. In a number of other countries—including the Bahamas, Bolivia, Guatemala, Nicaragua, Panama and Peru—substantial current account deficits have emerged despite relatively low rates of investment; in these cases, current account deficits have been attributable to low domestic savings rather than to high investment.

Saving, Investment and Economic Growth: The Virtuous Circle

Substantial historical and international evidence supports the idea that high and stable rates of economic growth are good for saving. At the same time, by helping to finance the investment required for sustainable growth, high rates of domestic saving support economic growth. Indeed, a key objective of the stabilization and reform programs implemented in the region has been to activate a virtuous circle in which the economic growth made possible by the efficiency-raising reform measures will lead, over time, to the increased saving and investment required for sustained economic development. The link between economic growth and saving is illustrated in Figure 39, which plots the average saving rate over the 1991-95 period against the average economic

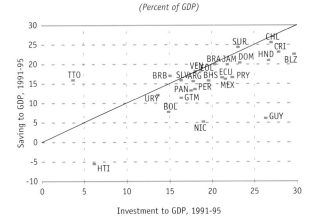

FIGURE 38

Saving and Investment, 1991-95

(Percent of GDP)

FIGURE 39

Economic Growth and National Saving

(In percent)

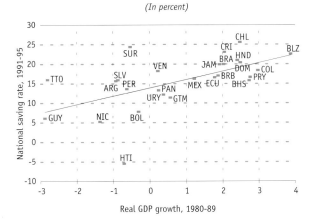

growth rate during the preceding 10 years.[12] It suggests that one important explanation of saving behavior in Latin America is the recent history of economic growth.

Table 10 illustrates the situation of the countries in the region by connecting the saving situation, the degree of success in the process of capital recovery, and the per capita growth rate during the 1990s. Chile stands out as the case in which complementarities among these three variables have unfolded most "virtuously" in a sustained way since the 1980s, but the Chilean case is not the only instance. Several other countries—

including Argentina, Costa Rica, the Dominican Republic, El Salvador, Guyana, Panama and Peru—have managed to recover saving, raise investment rates in a sustained way, and keep per capita economic growth rates at above 1.5 percent. At the other extreme, Brazil, Mexico, Nicaragua, Trinidad and Tobago and Venezuela have not yet managed in a sustained way to free themselves from the trap of weak saving, low investment rates, and low rates of economic growth.

The remaining countries present a mixed picture. Jamaica and Honduras display a good performance with regard to saving and investment, which does not square with their low economic growth; that situation could be connected with both the weight of excessive foreign debt and the insufficient consolidation of the structural reforms that they have undertaken. Paraguay is a unique case in which investment has remained high, the saving situation is weak, and economic growth is slow. Colombia faces a situation of weak saving that could be merely a temporary result of the recent consumption boom, inasmuch as it is performing well in investment and economic growth. In Bolivia, Ecuador and Guatemala, saving has shown signs of recovery, but investment has not—nor, in the latter two cases, has growth.

Rise of Unemployment

In 1995, rising unemployment was a reason for concern. For a group of 17 countries, representing more than 90 percent of the region's GDP and population, the unemployment rate rose from 6.6 percent to 7.8 percent, the largest rise since 1983. The unemployment rate of the region as a whole

---

12 We show the relationship between domestic saving and economic growth in the *previous* 10 years to emphasize the impact of growth on saving, it being more plausible that the lagged growth causes high saving than the reverse. This idea is explored more systematically in a number of recent studies of saving, many of which have argued that the impact of economic growth on saving is apparently at least as powerful as the impact of saving on growth.

Table 10. Saving and Investment in the 1990s

Saving position	Investment position			
	High since the 1980s	Recovery, sustained[1]	Recovery, not sustained[1]	No recovery[1]
Solid[2]	Chile,* Jamaica	Costa Rica,* Dominican Republic,* Honduras		
Recovery[3]	Guyana*	Argentina,* Panama,* Peru* El Salvador*		Bolivia,* Ecuador, Guatemala
Uncertain[4]			Belize	Brazil
Fragile[5]	Paraguay	Colombia*	Venezuela, Mexico	Nicaragua, Trinidad and Tobago, Uruguay*

[1] Recovery is defined as an investment coefficient above the 1983-90 average and above 20 percent.
[2] Average saving coefficient, 1994-95, greater than 20 percent and greater than that of 1989-90.
[3] Average saving coefficient, 1994-95, greater than that of 1989-90, but below 20 percent.
[4] Average saving coefficient, 1994-95, less than that of 1989-90, but above 20 percent.
[5] Average saving coefficient, 1994-95, less than that of 1989-90 and lower than 20 percent.
*Countries with a per capita GDP growth above 1.5 percent in the 1990s.

has in fact been rising almost uninterruptedly since 1989 despite the recovery of economic growth. The lower rate of GDP growth in 1995 further accentuated the unemployment trend.

Behind this behavior, however, lie important intercountry differences in the level and direction of unemployment rates. Five countries currently have unemployment rates higher than 15 percent (Argentina, Barbados, Jamaica, Nicaragua, and Trinidad and Tobago), and five others have rates of between 10 percent and 15 percent (the Bahamas, Belize, Panama, Uruguay and Venezuela). By contrast, unemployment rates are under 5 percent in Brazil, Costa Rica, Guatemala, Honduras and Paraguay.

These differences have been a constant feature during the 1990s and may reflect not only differences in structural conditions but also in the definition of unemployment. Nevertheless, unemployment rates in Argentina, Mexico, Uruguay and Venezuela are substantially higher than the averages for previous years, reflecting the economic difficulties in which these countries found themselves in 1995.

Indeed, rising unemployment in these countries, and particularly in Argentina, does much to explain the overall deterioration for the entire region. In most of the remaining countries, current unemployment rates are not really appreciably different from the rates prior to the 1990s, and in Guatemala, Honduras and Trinidad and Tobago, they are considerably lower.

Impact of Growth on Unemployment

The changes taking place in unemployment rates during the 1990s have been influenced by the economic growth rates of the countries. In the Bahamas, Barbados, Mexico and Nicaragua, where per capita production has fallen during the 1990s, unemployment rates have risen by 2 percentage points or more. Among the countries where economic growth has been negative in per capita terms, only Jamaica has avoided this tendency toward greater unemployment. At the other extreme, countries enjoying high economic growth—such as Chile, El Salvador and Panama—have been able to reduce unemployment. Nevertheless, it is significant that with the sole exception of Panama, such declines have been modest and that unemployment has risen in a number of countries with rapid economic growth. The most worrisome case is that of Argentina, where a per capita growth of more than 3 percent per year has been accompanied by an almost 7 percentage point rise in the unemployment rate. Peru and Uruguay also exhibit this apparent anomaly, although in a less pronounced way.

Recently, the inverse relationship between growth and unemployment has been somewhat tighter. Rising unemployment in Argentina, Mexico and Uruguay in 1995 clearly reflected the downward side of production. Nevertheless, the

FIGURE 40

Unemployment Rate, 1980-95

(Percentage of labor force)

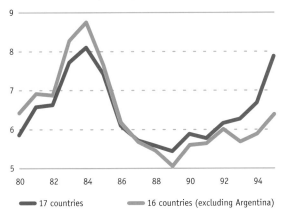

━━ 17 countries   ━━ 16 countries (excluding Argentina)

Note: Weighted by total population (1988), and based upon a sample of 17 countries that make up well above 90 percent of Latin American GDP (Argentina, Barbados, Brazil, Colombia, Costa Rica, Chile, Ecuador, Guatemala, Honduras, Mexico, Nicaragua, Panama, Paraguay, Peru, Trinidad and Tobago, Uruguay, and Venezuela). For the period 1981-84, Costa Rica, Peru and Paraguay are excluded because of the lack of data.

FIGURE 42

Unemployment, 1995 vs. 1991-94

(In percent)

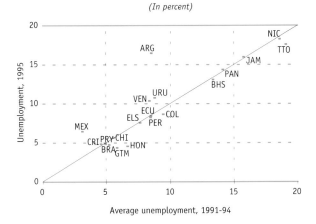

Average unemployment, 1991-94

greatest reductions in unemployment rates this year did not occur in the fastest-growing countries (such as Brazil, Chile, Colombia, El Salvador or Peru) but in a group of countries that in per capita terms grew much more modestly (including Barbados, Honduras and Nicaragua).

FIGURE 41

Unemployment, 1995

(Percentage of labor force)

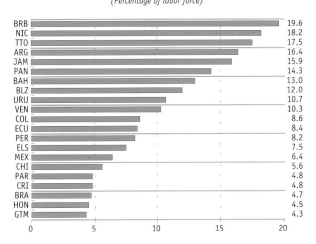

Impact of Macroeconomic Factors on Informal Labor Markets

Variations in formal unemployment rates, however interesting they may be, provide a very incomplete picture of the trends in the labor market in the region. One of the reasons is the existence of large undocumented sectors employed informally, including self-employed workers and family members, domestic service, and employees of small businesses (five workers or fewer). In the informal sector, labor contracts are flexible (or nonexistent) and standards of pay, job stability, and social security are partially or totally ignored.

The informal sector has grown significantly in most countries of the region during the 1990s, and with a few exceptions (such as Costa Rica, Panama and Venezuela), it represents more than half of nonfarm employment in the countries on which information is available. In Paraguay and Venezuela, increases of more than 6 percentage points in informal employment between 1989 and 1994 made it possible to raise the effective employment rate even though other sources of employment declined. In Argentina, Ecuador and Mexico, both unemployment and informal employment rose during this period, and only in Honduras and Panama did unemployment and

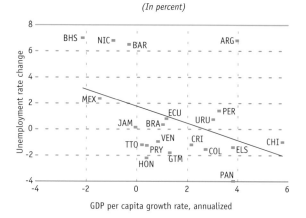

FIGURE 43

Unemployment and Growth, 1991-95

(In percent)

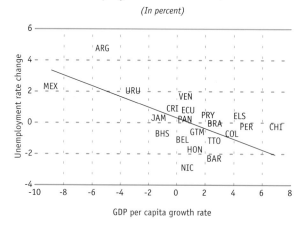

FIGURE 44

Unemployment and Growth, 1995

(In percent)

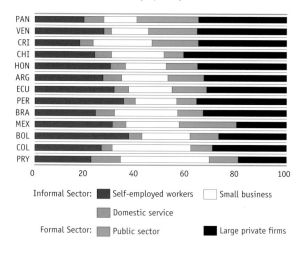

FIGURE 45

Nonagricultural Employment Structure, 1994

(In percent)

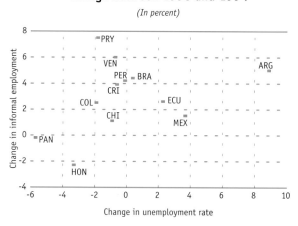

FIGURE 46

**Unemployment and Informality:
Change between 1990 and 1994**

(In percent)

informal employment decline simultaneously. According to ILO estimates for the region as a whole, 84 of every 100 jobs created during the 1990s have been in the informal sector.

Real Wages in the 1990s

Wages in the region have exhibited remarkably varied behavior in 1995. Average real wages experienced raises close to or above 5 percent in Brazil, Chile, the Dominican Republic, Ecuador and Peru, in every instance reinforcing trends appar-

ent since 1991. In Bolivia, Colombia and Nicaragua, the trend of rising wages also continued, although at a much slower pace. Elsewhere, however, real wages declined. In Argentina, Barbados, Trinidad and Tobago, and Venezuela, the decline was a continuation of previous trends, while in Costa Rica, Honduras, Mexico, Peru and Uruguay, some of the gains from previous years were lost. The most noteworthy reversal took place in Mexico, where real wages fell by around 15 percent , after having risen by an average of 7 percent a year since 1991. In the group of 14 countries on which

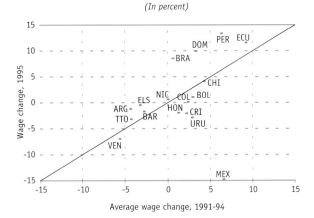

FIGURE 47

Real Wage Change, 1995 vs. 1991-94

(In percent)

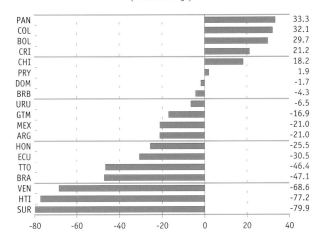

FIGURE 48

Real Wages, 1981-95

(Percent change)

PAN	33.3
COL	32.1
BOL	29.7
CRI	21.2
CHI	18.2
PRY	1.9
DOM	-1.7
BRB	-4.3
URU	-6.5
GTM	-16.9
MEX	-21.0
ARG	-21.0
HON	-25.5
ECU	-30.5
TTO	-46.4
BRA	-47.1
VEN	-68.6
HTI	-77.2
SUR	-79.9

there exist solid data on real wages, real pay (weighted by population) rose slightly, thus continuing the trend since 1991.

From a longer-range perspective, three groups of countries can be distinguished in accordance with their real wage trends. In Bolivia, Chile, Colombia, Costa Rica and Panama, real wages have risen from where they stood in the early 1980s; in all these countries the current level of real wages is at least 20 percent higher than it was in 1981. In contrast with this group, in Brazil, Ecuador, Haiti, Suriname, Trinidad and Tobago and Venezuela, real wages have tended to decline and

are currently at least 20 percent below where they stood at the beginning of the last decade. Within this group, Ecuador seems to be a special case, in that since 1992 real wages have tended to recover, rising from only 40 percent of their 1981 level in 1991 to about 70 percent of the 1981 level in 1995. Finally, in the remaining group of countries, wage levels are now at a level similar to where they stood in the early 1980s, although with significant instances of instability over time.

Differences in growth rates only partially explain this short- and long-range wage behavior. Figure 49 indicates a direct relationship between these two variables: in countries that have grown faster, real wages have tended to increase. But much of the change in real wages in 1995 remains unexplained by economic growth. In particular, the large increase in Ecuador and the decline in Trinidad and Tobago are not related to correspondingly large changes in real output.

Continued Recovery of Social Spending

One of the casualties of the lost decade of the 1980s was spending on social services, which plummeted in the aftermath of the debt crisis. Between 1982 and 1986, social spending per capita fell by 10 percent in real terms, because of a decline in national income per capita and a decline in the share of national income devoted to social spending.[13] By the end of the decade, the contraction in spending as a share of GDP had been reversed, but social spending per capita remained 6 percent lower than in the 1980-81 period, corresponding to a roughly equivalent decline in real per capita income. In 1991, per capita spending on health and education services—a crucial determinant of economic growth and a key force for social equity—was lower than it had been in the 1980-81 period.

---

[13] The primary source of data utilized in this subsection is Cominetti and Ruiz (1996). This work reconstructs social spending figures for each country of the region, using consistent definitions of spending and based on primary data sources for each country.

FIGURE 49

Real Wage and Growth, 1995

(In percent)

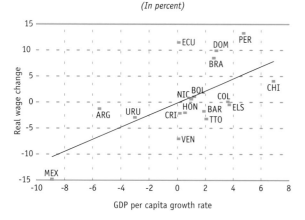

FIGURE 50

Social Spending in Latin America, 1989-95

(Percent of GDP)

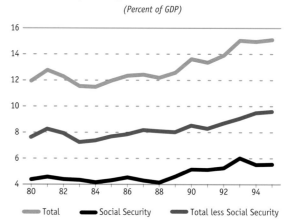

As Latin America began to recover in the late 1980s and early 1990s, however, social spending began to recover as well. This recovery gathered momentum in the 1990s, when such spending increased quite substantially. In the 1994-95 period, real spending on social services was 22 percent higher than it had been at the end of the 1980s, reflecting both a recovery of output and an increase in the share of output devoted to social spending.

As a share of GDP, spending on social security has increased the most dramatically, rising from a regional average of less than 4 percent of GDP in the late 1980s to about 5.5 percent in 1994 and 1995. In some countries, the increased demands that the social security system places on fiscal resources poses a threat to the viability of fiscal outcomes over the medium term and creates the danger that other desirable categories of spending will be crowded out. But in the 1990s, neither risk has thus far materialized, as most other categories of social spending have increased within a context of restraint over total government spending.

The recovery of spending on health and especially on education is a more recent phenomenon, beginning in 1993 and gathering force in 1994 and 1995, but it is an important development. By 1995, spending on education had risen to more

than 4 percent of GDP, substantially above the level of less than 3.5 percent of GDP recorded in the 1990-92 period. In 1995, real per capita spending on education was 18 percent higher than in 1992, and spending on health 22 percent higher.

The recovery of social spending in the 1990s has varied throughout the region. The recovery has been most rapid in Brazil and Mexico, two countries in which the social gap is most notable. But social spending in the Southern Cone has also risen to the share of GDP that prevailed before the debt crisis.

The recovery of education spending has also been notable in Brazil and Mexico. In Mexico, spending on education rose from less than 3 percent of GDP in 1990 to 4.5 percent in 1994.

Despite the 1995 crisis, overall social spending in Mexico as well as spending on education remained roughly constant as a share of GDP, although they fell in real terms. Similarly, in the Southern Cone, and particularly in Argentina, social spending rose as a share of GDP in 1995, as did spending on both education and health. This protection of spending on education and health— and the protection of all social spending more generally—contrasts sharply with the situation during the crisis at the beginning of the 1980s, when the share of national income devoted to social spending was slashed.

FIGURE 51

Social Spending by Sector

(Percent of GDP)

a. Social Security

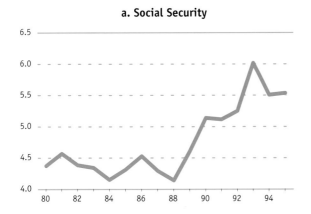

b. Education

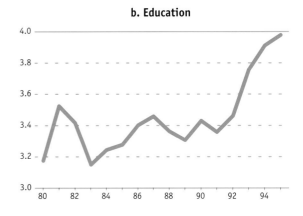

c. Housing and Labor

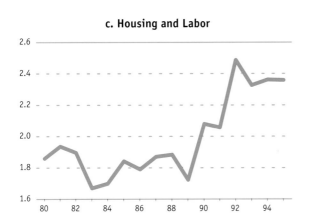

d. Health

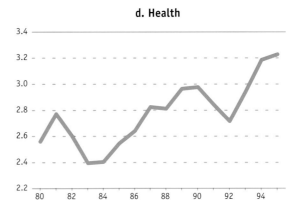

Even if social security spending is subtracted from the total, social spending has recovered from the low levels of the 1980s in many countries of the region. Spending on education and health has also recovered in most countries. The recovery has been particularly notable in Bolivia, Brazil, Colombia, Costa Rica, Mexico and Paraguay.

These developments indicate that governments in the region have been taking action to redress the region's social gap. Social spending has risen both as a percentage of GDP and in real terms, and since 1993 there has been a particularly notable increase in spending on health and educational services. This increase has taken place within a context of overall budgetary restraint, and thus the trend would appear to be sustainable. The region nevertheless has important strides to make in improving the efficiency with which social services are delivered. Part Three of this Report will take up this issue in detail.

INFLATION AND INTEREST RATES

Fears that the Mexican crisis would rekindle inflation in the region in 1995 were not borne out. The median inflation rate—which represents the rate of inflation of the "typical" Latin American country—declined in 1995 as inflation fell in all but five countries of in the region. With the drastic reduc-

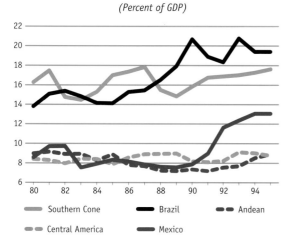

FIGURE 52

Social Spending by Region, 1980-95

(Percent of GDP)

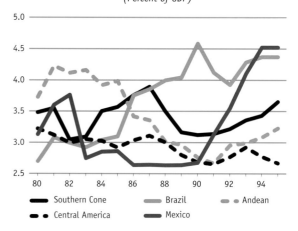

FIGURE 53

Spending in Education by Region, 1980-95

(Percent of GDP)

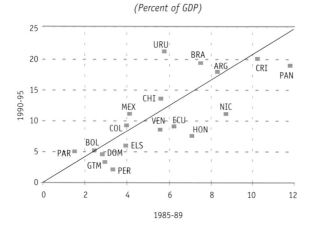

FIGURE 54

Non-Social Security Social Spending, 1990-95 vs. 1985-89

(Percent of GDP)

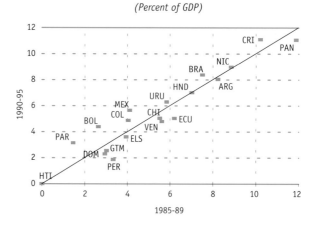

FIGURE 55

Spending in Health and Education, 1990-95 vs. 1985-89

(Percent of GDP)

tions in the inflation rates of Brazil and Suriname, extreme inflation (that is, in excess of 100 percent) has disappeared from the region in 1995.

Panama, the Bahamas and Argentina had the lowest inflation in 1995, with respective rates of 0.5 percent, 1.2 percent and 1.7 percent, which in all cases were below that of the United States. The low inflation rate in Argentina, a country with a highly inflationary past, bears special mention, coming as it did in the midst of a severe financial crisis. Venezuela and Mexico had the highest rates of inflation in 1995, with year-end inflation rates

of 57 and 52 percent, respectively. Figure 57 puts the year's inflationary outcomes into a recent historical context. In 1989, roughly one-third of the region's countries experienced either high (between 40 percent and 100 percent) or very high (above 100 percent) inflation; by 1995, only two countries had inflation this high.

The most notable declines in inflations were in Brazil and Suriname, which in 1994 had the highest and second-highest inflation rates in the region. In Brazil, the decline was the outcome of the continued success of the Real Plan launched

FIGURE 56

Inflation in 1995 (December over December)

(In percent)

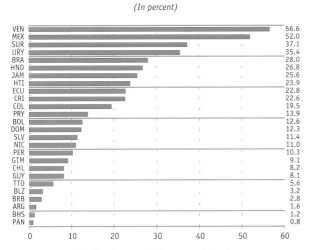

VEN	56.6
MEX	52.0
SUR	37.1
URY	35.4
BRA	28.0
HND	26.8
JAM	25.6
HTI	23.9
ECU	22.8
CRI	22.6
COL	19.5
PRY	13.9
BOL	12.6
DOM	12.3
SLV	11.4
NIC	11.0
PER	10.3
GTM	9.1
CHL	8.2
GUY	8.1
TTO	5.6
BLZ	3.2
BRB	2.8
ARG	1.6
BHS	1.2
PAN	0.8

Note: Data for Belize, Guyana and Nicaragua calculated year over year.

FIGURE 57

Classes of Inflation in the Region, 1989 and 1995

(In percent)

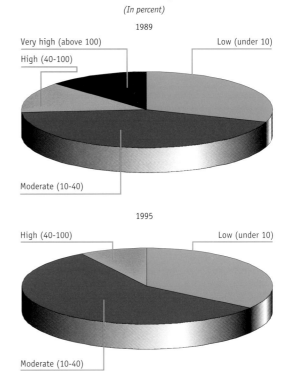

1989

Very high (above 100)   Low (under 10)

High (40-100)

Moderate (10-40)

1995

High (40-100)   Low (under 10)

Moderate (10-40)

in July 1994. In Suriname, inflation dropped sharply after the Central Bank was able to stabilize the parallel exchange rate in the first half of 1995 against the backdrop of substantial improvements in the fiscal accounts and a contractionary monetary policy. Inflation also registered significant declines in Colombia Haiti, Paraguay, Peru and Uruguay.

The notable exception to this trend was Mexico, where the steep devaluation at the end of 1994 created large inflationary pressures in 1995. Fortunately, a strong macroeconomic policy response and international support have secured a rapid stabilization of the Mexican economy, and inflation has abated considerably in 1996.

Although inflation declined in Venezuela during 1995, it accelerated dramatically in the first half of 1996. In mid-1996 Venezuela began to implement a major stabilization program, which is supported by the International Monetary Fund as well as the Inter-American Development Bank and the World Bank, and which contemplates a major reduction in the rate of inflation.

Contribution of Inflation Stabilization to Spending Booms

The Latin American disinflation of the 1990s has been the consequence of a large number of major stabilization and disinflation programs. These programs have contributed to the spending booms that have been an important factor in the stabilization and reform adjustment process that was outlined earlier. Let us now examine in greater detail the adjustment associated with inflation stabilization.

Table 11 describes the programs that have been implemented in the 1990s. For completeness, the table also reports the countries that suffered important setbacks in their fight against inflation, which we call reinflations; and those in which inflation was already at moderate levels in the late 1980s and either fluctuated within a nar-

Table 11. Stabilization, Disinflation and Reinflation in the 1990s		
	Date	Nominal anchor
Major stabilizations		
Argentina	April 91	Exchange rate
Brazil	July 94	Exchange rate
Nicaragua	March 91	Exchange rate
Peru	August 90	Money supply
Suriname	January 95	Exchange rate
Disinflations		
Dominican Republic	August 90	Money supply
Ecuador	September 92	Exchange rate
Guatemala	January 91	Exchange rate
Jamaica	February 92	Money supply
Uruguay	January 91	Exchange rate
Reinflations		
Mexico	December 94	
Venezuela	September 93	
Stable or moderate inflations		
Bahamas		
Barbados		
Bolivia		
Chile		
Colombia		
Costa Rica		
El Salvador		
Guyana		
Haiti		
Honduras		
Panama		
Trinidad and Tobago		

Note: Major stabilizations include countries that drastically reduced inflation from initial levels of 500 percent or more. In disinflations, inflation was substantially reduced from initial levels ranging between 60 percent and 150 percent. Reinflations include countries where there was an important acceleration of inflation. In stable and moderate inflations, inflation either fluctuated within a narrow range or declined from relatively moderate initial levels.

FIGURE 58

Change in Inflation, 1995 vs. 1994 (December over December)

(In percent)

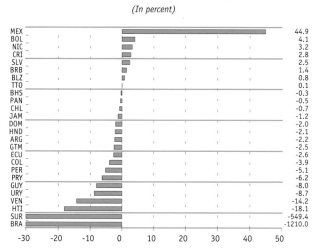

Note: Data for Belize, Guyana and Nicaragua calculated year over year.

of a stabilization policy in countries with chronic inflation, because this anchor affects important aspects of an economy's adjustment to stabilization. Money-based programs have tended to reduce inflation while generating short-term contraction in economic activity. In contrast, programs based on the exchange rate have tended to generate an initial boom in economic activity, with a contraction in economic activity emerging later in the adjustment process.

The major stabilization and disinflation of the 1990s appear to conform to this pattern. Figures 61a-f show the business cycle (as measured by the evolution of real private consumption) associated with the programs based on the exchange rate that were carried out in the 1990s. In the countries in which inflation fell most dramatically (such as Argentina, Brazil, Suriname and Uruguay), the rate of growth in consumption accelerated very substantially the year the program was launched and remained relatively high thereafter. In Argentina and Uruguay, which have the more mature stabilization programs, consumption recently entered a phase of contraction and has declined in both countries in 1995.

row range or declined from relatively low levels in the 1990s.

The stabilization programs were successful in securing major reductions in the rate of inflation. The stabilization was based largely on the exchange rate as the nominal anchor of the program, thus allowing the money supply to adjust in response to changes in money demand. Programs based on the control of the money supply, which therefore allowed the exchange rate to float, were more rare.

The nominal anchor is a critical element

FIGURE 59

Inflation Performance in Major Stabilizations of the 1990s

(12-month rate of change, CPI, in percent)

a. Argentina

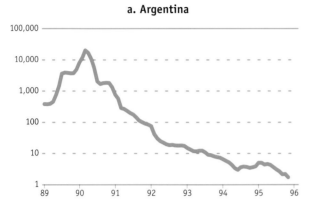

b. Brazil

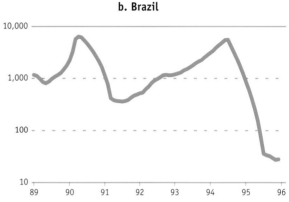

c. Nicaragua

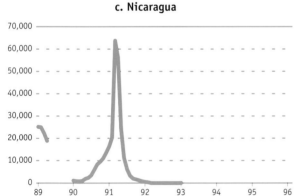

d. Peru

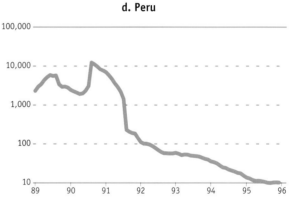

e. Suriname

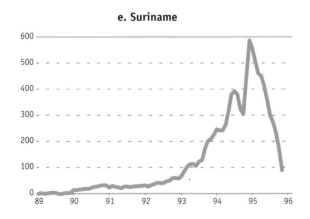

Similarly, Figures 62a-c show the economic fluctuations associated with the money-based stabilization of the early 1990s that were carried out in Peru, the Dominican Republic and Jamaica. As expected, these stabilizations generally began with a contraction of consumption spending, after which activity increased.

The cyclical characteristics of inflation stabilization programs have an important influence on the evolution of other important macroeconomic variables. Let us examine the typical patterns of response to those programs that are based on exchange rates and to the money-based programs.

FIGURE 60

Inflation Performance in Disinflations of the 1990s

(12-month rate of change, CPI, in percent)

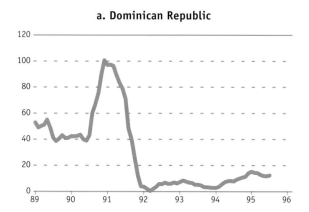

a. Dominican Republic

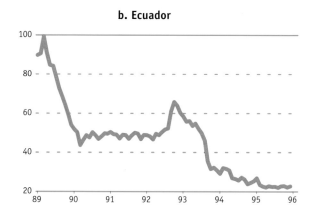

b. Ecuador

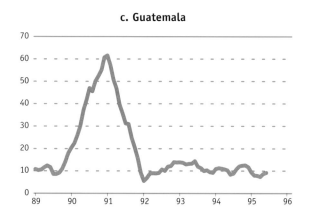

c. Guatemala

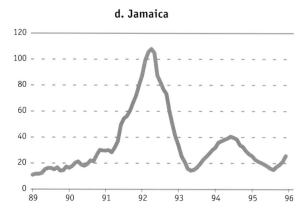

d. Jamaica

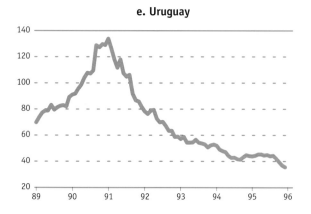

e. Uruguay

Responses to programs based on exchange rates include:

• Initial expansion in economic activity followed by a contraction.

• Deterioration in the trade balance and the current account, usually reflecting a large increase in imports of durable goods.

• Sustained rise in the relative price of nontraded goods (appreciation of the real exchange rate).

• Improvement in the fiscal accounts.

Responses to money-based programs include:

FIGURE 61

The Business Cycle Associated with Exchange
Rate-Based Stabilizations: Real Private Consumption in the 1990s

(In percent)

a. Argentina

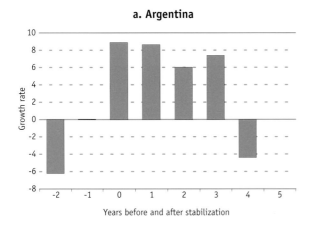

b. Brazil

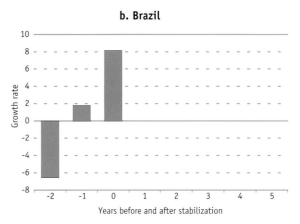

c. Suriname

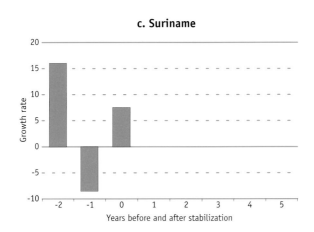

d. Ecuador

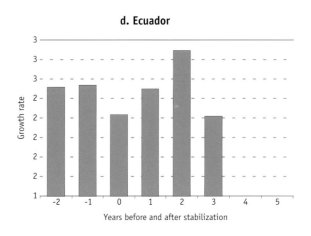

e. Guatemala

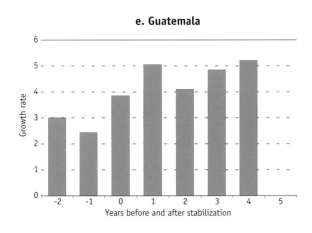

f. Uruguay

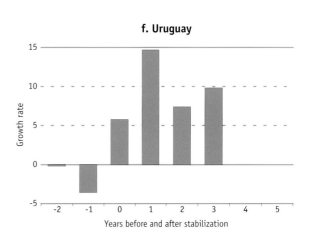

FIGURE 62

The Business Cycle Associated with Money-Based Stabilizations:
Real Private Consumption in the 1990s

(In percent)

a. Peru

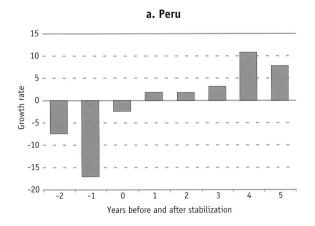

b. Dominican Republic

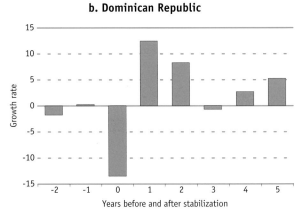

c. Jamaica

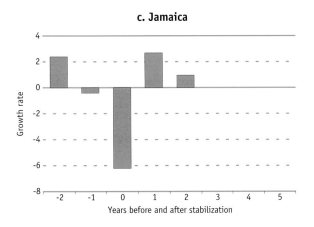

• Initial contraction in economic activity followed by recovery.

• Improvement in the trade balance and the current account.

• Rise in the relative price of nontraded goods (appreciation of the real exchange rate).

• Improvement in the fiscal accounts.

The behavior of the current account, the real exchange rate, and the fiscal deficit during the 1990s in the programs based on the exchange rate conforms to these observations, with only a few exceptions. In the initial stages of the program,

the current account deteriorated in all countries except Suriname, and the real exchange rate appreciated in all countries except Nicaragua. The money-based programs of the 1990s also conform to the expected patterns; in the early stages of the programs, the current account improved (except in Peru), the real exchange rate appreciated, and the fiscal deficit fell substantially.

INTERNATIONAL TRADE AND PAYMENTS

Decrease of the Current Account Deficit

The Latin American current account deficit of the balance of payments declined from $47.5 billion in 1994 (3.1 percent of GDP) to $32.1 billion in 1995 (2 percent of GDP). This was a result of a substantial increase in the value of exports, which grew by more than 20 percent in U.S. dollar terms, outpacing the growth rate of import value by a substantial margin. This decline in the region's overall current account deficit is attributable primarily to developments in Mexico and Argentina, where large current account deficits were virtually eliminated in 1995 in response to the financial crisis associated with the Tequila shock. In Brazil, on the other hand, the current account

Table 12. Balance of Payments Summary									
(In millions of U.S. dollars)									
	1986	1987	1988	1989	1990	1991	1992	1993	1994	1995
Exports of goods (fob)	87,389	99,868	115,443	128,510	141,675	141,754	150,743	161,956	187,692	227,047
Imports of goods (fob)	(69,627)	(78,415)	(90,539)	(99,065)	(111,295)	(129,475)	(156,818)	(171,815)	(203,146)	(227,753)
Trade balance	17,762	21,452	24,904	29,445	30,380	12,278	(6,075)	(9,860)	(15,454)	(706)
Investment income	(33,318)	(31,138)	(35,292)	(40,087)	(35,224)	(32,469)	(32,452)	(34,846)	(34,532)	(36,256)
Other services (net)	(5,939)	(4,653)	(5,752)	(4,672)	(6,783)	(7,846)	(9,068)	(10,895)	(10,105)	(10,114)
Unrequited transfers (net)	4,396	5,599	6,362	6,796	10,105	10,944	12,510	11,135	12,555	14,961
Current account balance	(17,180)	(8,740)	(9,779)	(8,518)	(1,522)	(17,093)	(35,086)	(44,466)	(47,536)	(32,116)
Total capital flows	12,072	14,092	7,972	7,029	16,099	29,414	59,032	66,864	44,103*	52,726*
Errors and omissions	(2,920)	(1,306)	(4,146)	4,168	(830)	6,852	1,578	(940)		
Change in reserves	7,949	(4,047)	5,951	(2,678)	(13,746)	(19,173)	(25,524)	(21,458)	2,833	(20,895)
Addendum (% GDP)										
Current account	-1.74	-0.83	-0.89	-0.74	-0.13	-1.32	-2.58	-3.09	-3.07	-2.01
Total capital flows	1.22	1.33	0.73	0.61	1.34	2.27	4.34	4.65	2.85	3.30
Reserve accumulation	0.80	-0.38	0.54	-0.23	-1.15	-1.48	-1.87	-1.49	0.18	-1.31

*Includes errors and omissions for Argentina in 1994; and for Argentina, Dominican Republic, El Salvador and Haiti in 1995.

swung from near-balance in 1994 to a deficit of almost $18 billion in 1995, nearly 3 percent of GDP, as a result of the spending boom and real appreciation that were associated with the country's mid-1994 inflation stabilization. The current account deficit of countries other than Argentina, Brazil and Mexico rose considerably, from $8.3 billion in 1994 to $11.483 billion in 1995.

Although the region's current account deficit declined, net payments of international interest and other investment income rose by nearly $2 billion. As a result, the net resource transfer to Latin America fell from positive $13 billion in 1994 to negative $4 billion in 1995, a swing of about 1 percent of the region's GDP.

Continuation of Large Capital Flows

Capital flows to most countries of the region remained large in 1995. In the region as a whole, total capital flows rose from about $44 billion in 1994 to $53 billion in 1995. These inflows were more than enough to finance the region's current account deficit, and the accumulation of international reserves reached $20 billion.

The increase in total capital flows masks important variations in individual country experiences. In Argentina, capital inflows were down sharply, and in Mexico they registered only a minor increase, and that only because of the large package of official support to the country. In Brazil, on the other hand, capital inflows more than tripled from $9 billion in 1994 to $29 billion in 1995. In countries other than Argentina, Brazil and Mexico, total capital inflows declined from $12.5 billion in 1994 to about $8 billion in 1995.

Despite this decline, flows remained large to most economies. Total capital inflows were more than 5 percent of GDP in 11 countries of the region and less than 1 percent of GDP in only five.

Private capital inflows were also large in most countries. Nevertheless, flows to the region as a whole were down because of sharp declines in Argentina and Mexico. Five countries—Argentina, the Dominican Republic, Mexico, Trinidad and Tobago and Venezuela—experienced outflows of private capital.

Private capital inflows increased by more than 3 percent of GDP in Bolivia, Brazil and El Salvador. In Bolivia, higher inflows resulted from

FIGURE 63

Net Capital Inflows in 1995

(Percent Of GDP)

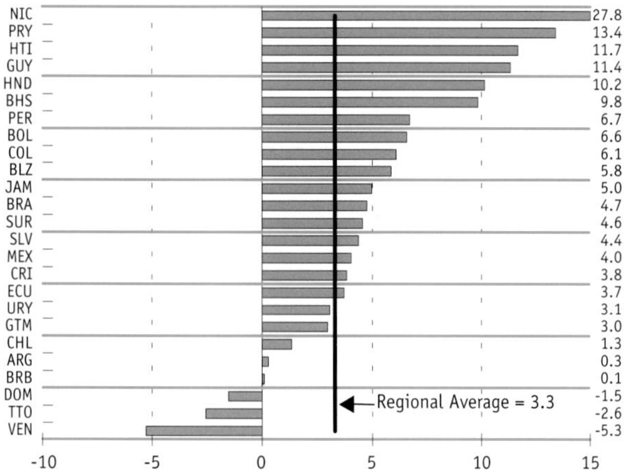

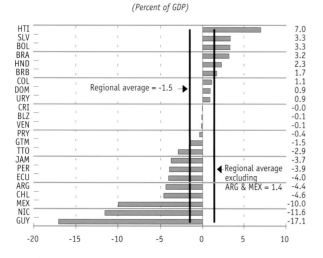

FIGURE 64

Net Private Capital Inflows in 1995

(Percent of GDP)

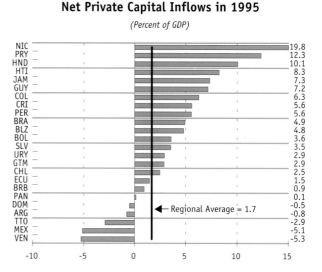

FIGURE 65

Change in Net Private Capital Inflows, 1995 vs. 1994

(Percent of GDP)

in the correction or crisis phase of the adjustment process. (Uruguay was the fourth country that entered the correction phase in 1995, but it nevertheless experienced an increase in private capital flows in 1995.)

Not all changes in capital flows reflected changes in perceived international creditworthiness. The sharp decline in capital flows to Chile reflected instead a large improvement in the terms of trade that pushed the current account sharply toward surplus, thereby reducing the country's external borrowing requirements. In Nicaragua, the very large inflows were associated with rescheduling of the country's international debt.

Moderate Increase in International Debt

The region's external debt rose from roughly $530 billion in 1994 to $574 billion in 1995. Mexico was the only country with a notable increase in international debt, from $128 billion in 1994 to $158 billion in 1995; this increase did not reflect an increase in Mexico's net indebtedness (the country's current account was roughly in balance in 1995) but served instead to finance a substantial accumulation of international reserves and to

the large privatization associated with the country's capitalization program, while in Brazil the inflows were associated with the mid-1994 inflation stabilization.

Private capital inflows declined significantly in 10 countries, including the three countries (Ecuador, Guatemala and Trinidad and Tobago) that entered the stress phase of the stabilization and reform process and three (Argentina, Mexico and Venezuela) of the four countries

FIGURE 66

Foreign Direct Investment

(Millions of U.S. dollars)

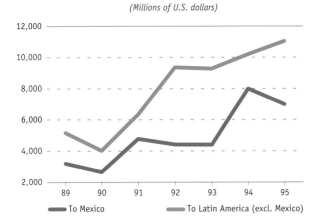

FIGURE 67

Foreign Direct Investment

(Share of GDP)

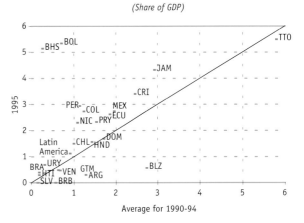

FIGURE 68

**Foreign Direct Investment and Privatization
(Total for the seven biggest countries)**

(Millions of U.S. dollars)

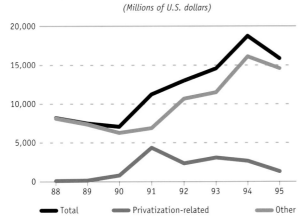

Note: The countries included here are Argentina, Brazil, Colombia, Chile, Mexico, Peru and Venezuela.

retire the stock of tesobonos.[14] In the countries other than Mexico, international debt rose from $401 billion in 1994 to $415 billion in 1995, increasing at a rate well below the rate of growth of exports.

Increase in Foreign Direct Investment

Foreign direct investment (FDI) in Latin America increased from $18.2 billion in 1994 to $19.2 billion in 1995, averaging about 1.5 percent of GDP.

Flows to Mexico slowed somewhat in 1995 from the exceptionally high rate of $8 billion achieved in 1994 (nearly half the regional total), but they still remained very high at $7 billion. FDI flows to the remainder of the region increased from roughly $10 billion in 1994 to slightly more than $11 billion in 1995.

FDI has been increasing strongly since 1991. In the first years of the decade, investments associated with privatization were important; in 1991, FDI associated with privatization accounted for nearly $5 billion, or roughly 40 percent of total FDI. But after 1991, privatization-related FDI began to decline in importance in both absolute and relative terms.

Even so, FDI associated with privatization remained important in some countries in 1995, most notably Bolivia, where, as noted, privatizations associated with the country's capitalization program were very important.

FDI was greater than 4 percent of GDP in the Bahamas, Bolivia, Jamaica and Trinidad and

---

[14] The tesobonos were categorized as domestic debt, even though a large fraction of the outstanding stock was held by foreign investors. When the government used loans from the IMF and the U.S. Treasury to retire this debt, the result was therefore an increase in the measured stock of international debt, even though there was no net change in the country's external indebtedness.

FIGURE 69

Latin America: The Real Exchange Rate

(Population-weighted average, 1990 = 100)

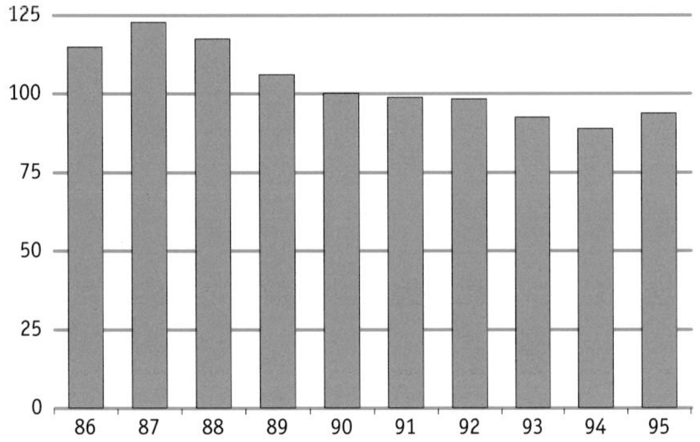

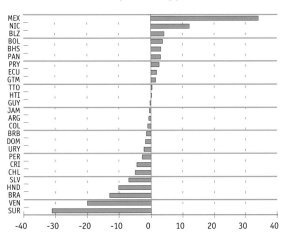

FIGURE 70

Real Exchange Rate Depreciation, 1994 to 1995

(Percent change)

FIGURE 71

Real Exchange Rate Depreciation, 1990 to 1995

(Percent change)

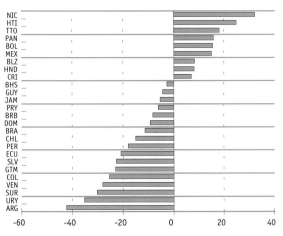

Tobago. In Bolivia and the Bahamas, the performance marked a sharp increase from the inflows recorded during the 1990-94 period. In Bolivia, this increase was attributable to major privatization, and in the Bahamas the surge of FDI was related to government divestment and large investments for hotel renovation. FDI in 1995 also increased sharply from the rates experienced in the 1990-94 period in Colombia, Jamaica and Peru.

The Real Exchange Rate

Taking the region as a whole, currencies depreciated in real terms during 1995, partially reversing the substantial appreciations that characterized the late 1980s and early 1990s. This regional average reflects highly diverse country experiences. In Mexico, the currency depreciated by about 35 percent in 1995, and Nicaragua experienced a large depreciation as well. On the other hand, large appreciations were recorded in Brazil, El Salvador, Honduras, Suriname and Venezuela, and in most countries the currency remained appreciated in 1995 relative to 1990. In eight countries, in fact, the real appreciation experienced between 1990 and 1995 exceeded 20 percent. In Argentina, the currency appreciated by more than 40 percent in real terms over the same period.

Continuation of the Trade Liberalization Process

A key objective and result of the reform programs implemented in Latin America has been to promote integration with the regional and world economy by liberalizing the countries' foreign trade regimes. These reforms have contributed to an important increase in the region's openness to international trade. The region's openness—defined here as the average of imports and exports divided by GDP—has increased dramatically during the past 10 years, and countries in the region continued to become more outward-oriented during 1995.

This increase in the region's trade open-

FIGURE 72

**Openness of Latin America:
Population-weighted Average**

(Percent of GDP)

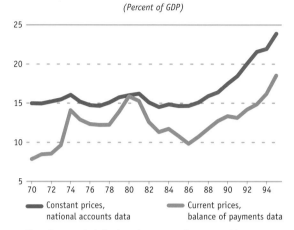

Note: Openness is defined as the average of exports and import divided by GDP.

FIGURE 73

Openness: 1995 vs 1990

(Percent of GDP)

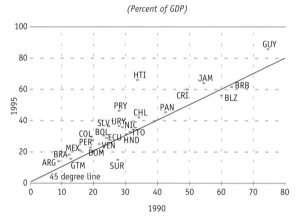

Note: Based on national account data in constant prices.

ness is quite widespread. Measured at constant prices, the region's international trade in goods and services increased between 1990 and 1995 in 22 countries and declined in only three.

Rapid Import Growth

One dimension of the region's increased openness to international trade has been rapid growth in its volume of imports. This rapid import vol-

ume growth continued in 1995, with purchases of foreign goods and services (in constant prices) rising 14 percent, only slightly less than the average in the 1991-94 period and substantially greater than the 1995 rise in exports volume.

Only Mexico and Argentina reduced their real purchases of goods and services from the rest of the world in 1995 (by 28 and 10 percent, respectively), as part of their adjustment. Contrary to what happened during the crisis of the 1980s, when many countries were forced to cut back their foreign sector deficits, in the more recent instance no new trade barriers were applied. Instead, the reduction of domestic demand (both countries) and a significant currency devaluation (Mexico) were the instruments used to achieve the desired effect.

In most of the remaining countries, imports rose by more than 9 percent. The increase was particularly high in Brazil, Haiti, Peru, Suriname and Trinidad and Tobago.

Continued Rapid Growth of Export Volumes

The average rate of growth of exports of goods and services in 1995 was 9.1 percent (in constant prices), nearly 2 percentage points above the average export growth rate recorded during the preceding four years. This result was importantly influenced by Mexico and Argentina, where the volume of exports grew by about 30 percent. Besides these two countries, real exports from Colombia, El Salvador, Honduras and Trinidad and Tobago also rose substantially from the previous year. In fact, all countries increased their exports, except for Uruguay (which was affected by falling Argentine demand) and Brazil (where the stabilization program prompted a sharp expansion of spending, together with an appreciation of the currency).

Exports have grown rapidly throughout the 1990s, and the ratio of export volumes to real GDP has notably increased in most countries of the region. With the exceptions of Barbados, Hon-

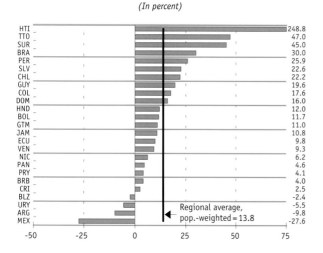

FIGURE 74

Import Growth in 1995

(In percent)

FIGURE 75

Export Growth in 1995

(In percent)

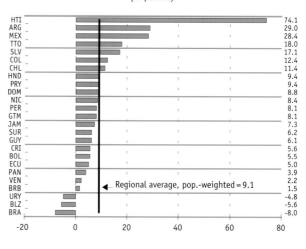

duras and Suriname, the ratio of real exports to real GDP in the 1994-95 period surpassed that at the end of the 1980s by large margins.

Export growth has also resulted in a greater diversification of the export base. Exports traditional to the different countries have been losing their share of total exports in most economies of the region. The countries in which this diversification has advanced most rapidly are, in order, Trinidad and Tobago, Paraguay, Panama, Bolivia, Mexico, Honduras and Argentina.

The strength of Latin American export growth during the 1990s is particularly notable in light of the fact that the domestic currency has tended to appreciate in many countries. Both at the regional and country levels, there has been a relatively low correlation between export growth and changes in the real exchange rate. This low correlation does not mean that a highly overvalued currency does not discourage exports, but it does suggest that factors other than the real exchange rate appear to have been more important to export growth during the 1990s.

Trade liberalization has apparently been one of those export-friendly factors. The countries with the most rapid export growth in the 1990s (again, with the exception of Haiti) all liberalized their trade policies at least five years ago.

FIGURE 76

Export Coefficient: 1994-95 vs 1989-90

(Percent of GDP)

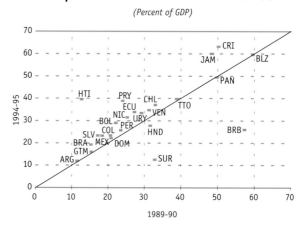

In contrast, those countries that have still not adopted trade liberalization programs or those where, as of 1995, trade liberalization had been in place for only four years or fewer, did tend to have substantially lower rates of export growth. Trade liberalization thus appears to have contributed to export growth, but it alone does not ensure export success. Indeed, a number of countries that have had such policies in place for some time have not yet achieved high rates of export growth.

FIGURE 77

Traditional Exports: 1989-90 vs. 1994-95

(Percent of total exports)

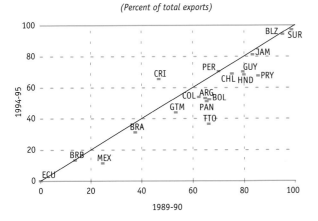

FIGURE 78

Export Growth and Domestic Demand, 1989-90 to 1994-95

(In percent)

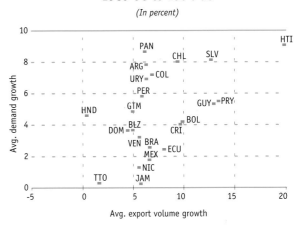

CONCLUSION: THE YEAR 1995 IN PERSPECTIVE

We have argued here that in 1995, as in the 1990s as a whole, a key influence over economic developments in Latin America has been the progress that different countries have been making through their adjustment to the major stabilization and reforms implemented during the past decade. This view has important implications for macroeconomic policy management in the region. It also provides a perspective on economic developments during 1995, with implications for medium-term economic prospects for the region.

Policy Implications: Manage the Boom, Protect the Reforms

For reasons developed earlier in some detail, the countries' economic response or adjustment to major reform programs tends not to be smooth, and is instead in many cases characterized by an initial boom during which vulnerabilities develop that eventually require a correction that may or may not involve a major crisis. The magnitude of the boom and the nature of the later correction are determined in large part by the response of policymakers to the very early phases of this ad-

justment. By acting to minimize the vulnerabilities that develop during the boom, policymakers can reduce the likelihood of a disruptive crisis requiring correction.

There exist three key vulnerabilities: fiscal, financial and external. To minimize fiscal vulnerabilities, authorities need to interpret budgetary outcomes in light of the current macroeconomic situation, bearing in mind that a transitory boom in income and spending will translate into an equally transitory boom in fiscal revenue, which may mask the fragility of the underlying fiscal situation. Authorities should be careful to run precautionary fiscal surpluses during periods of macroeconomic boom, which are likely to occur as the economy adjusts to major economic reforms, so that when the boom subsides the fiscal situation remains viable.[15]

To manage financial vulnerabilities, authorities need to recognize that bank lending booms can leave the financial system in a highly weakened state when the boom subsides, particularly in an environment of weakly capitalized and

---

[15] For a more complete discussion of issues surrounding the management of fiscal policy in Latin America, see Gavin, Hausmann, Perotti and Talvi (1996) and Talvi (1996).

poorly supervised banks. The danger of such financial vulnerabilities can be reduced if authorities maintain rigorous standards of capital adequacy, strictly supervised. And since such regulation will never be a panacea, policymakers should manage monetary policy so as to "lean against the wind" of bank lending booms.[16]

The main source of external vulnerability is the danger that a country will develop an excessive stock of short-term public debt, as investors become nervous about the need for a correction of external imbalances and begin to demand shorter maturities. This danger can be reduced if authorities minimize the external imbalances that develop during the boom phase by implementing more contractionary fiscal policies and maintaining a reasonably competitive real exchange rate. More importantly, authorities should resist the temptation to accommodate an increased demand for short-term public debt, despite its apparently lower cost.

These actions are politically and in some cases technically difficult to implement. It is therefore not entirely surprising that during macroeconomic booms, vulnerabilities have often developed that have required correction and occasionally even resulted in a crisis. An important lesson of the historical experience with stabilization and reform in Latin America is that such crises, even if they are severe, need not signal the failure of a reform program. The example of Chile is illuminating in this respect. That country fell into crisis in the early 1980s but protected its structural reforms and, after overcoming the macroeconomic instability generated by the crisis, entered a period of rapid, sustained growth. Indeed, as we have tried to make clear here, structural reforms in Latin America have been durable. Economic reforms have been maintained and even deepened in Argentina and Mexico, despite the crises into which the countries have fallen. Indeed,

the only example of a country in the region in which economic crisis has led to a reversal of important structural reforms is Venezuela; in the many other countries that have experienced a painful correction or crisis, the structural reforms of the recent past have been protected. This is an important consideration for medium-term prospects in the region.

Outlook: Will the Region's Reforms Pay Off?

The sharp slowdown of economic growth in the region raises the question of whether the reform programs of the past decade were oversold. Will there be a payoff to the reforms? An important message to come out of analyzing the effects of reform on recent economic developments is that there exists a need, first, to interpret the regional growth rate in light of the corresponding stage of the adjustment process in the various countries.

The relatively high growth rates of the early 1990s were generated in large part by countries that were in the boom phase of the adjustment process. Although they are very welcome, these high growth rates are not the ultimate payoff to economic reform; the payoff to reform lies instead in the higher rate of long-run growth that should be created by the more open and efficient economic environment after the economy has completed the adjustment to stabilization and reform.

The sharp reduction in the region's rate of growth during 1995 was attributable primarily to the fact that two large countries fell into very deep crises, in large part because of economic vulnerabilities that had developed during their earlier boom. Although these crises are very painful, they do not signify the failure of the reforms; many countries, including Chile and New Zealand, have overcome similar crises and appear to have reaped very considerable long-run benefits from their reforms.

Looking to the immediate future, it seems clear that the countries of the region will contin-

---

[16] For a more detailed discussion, see Gavin and Hausmann (1996) and Rojas-Suárez and Weisbrod (1996).

ue to be seriously affected by the economic adjustment to their stabilization and reform programs. Brazil, Colombia and Peru—which had been in the boom phase of the process in 1995—are experiencing stress and a degree of correction in 1996, as are some smaller economies. At the same time, Argentina and Mexico are clearly beginning to recover from the crises of 1995.

How these various effects will average out is not the main concern. The genuinely important question is how reforms have altered the region's long-run growth prospects, not what these reforms' transitory effects on short-run growth will be. What evidence do we have concerning the long-run implications of the region's reforms? If one looks at recent developments regarding the determinants of long-run growth, one finds reason for optimism.

First, the long-run rate of economic growth is determined largely by the rate at which physical and human capital is accumulated. The sustained recovery of physical investment that has taken place during the 1990s is therefore an indication that the region's trend rate of growth has increased. In addition, Part Three of this Report will describe the substantial improvement in the rate at which human capital has been accumulated in the region, a factor of no less importance for

long-run growth prospects. There also exists evidence that investment efficiency has increased in the 1990s; investment rates among the countries of Latin America have come to be positively correlated with economic growth, which was not the case in the 1970s, when a highly distorted policy environment undermined the efficiency of domestic investment. There also exists evidence that stabilization and policy reforms of the sort implemented by so many countries in the region are also associated with higher economic growth.[17]

These factors support a degree of optimism about longer-term prospects for the region, but at the same time, they should not be used to minimize the very real challenges that still face the economies of Latin America in the coming decades. Several countries will need to manage economic stress and overcome the macroeconomic instability generated by economic crisis. They will need to protect the reforms already implemented and push forward those elements of the reform agenda that remain incomplete. Much remains to be done to ensure that Latin America establishes rapid and sustained economic growth from which all elements of society can benefit. Nevertheless, there also exists reason to believe that the region will be building upon a solid economic foundation.

---

[17] See Easterly, Loayza and Montiel (1996).

REFERENCES

Calvo, Guillermo. 1986. Temporary Stabilization: Predetermined Exchange Rates. *Journal of Political Economy.*

Calvo, Guillermo, and Carlos A. Végh. 1993. Exchange Rate Based Stabilization under Imperfect Credibility. In *Open Economy Macroeconomics,* eds. Helmut Frisch and Andreas Wörgötter. London: MacMillan.

Cominetti, Rossela, and Gonzalo Ruiz. 1996. *Evolución del Gasto Público Social en América Latina: 1980-1995.* Santiago: ECLA/CEPAL.

De Gregorio, Jose, Pablo Guidotti, and Carlos Végh. 1994. Inflation Stabilization and the Consumption of Durable Goods. International Monetary Fund, Washington, D.C. Mimeo.

Dornbusch, Rudiger. 1982. Stabilization Policies in Developing Countries: What Have We Learned? *World Development.*

Easterly, William, Norman Loayza and Peter Montiel. 1996. Has Latin America's Post-Reform Growth Been Disappointing? World Bank and Williams College, Washington, D.C. Mimeo.

Gavin, Michael, Ricardo Hausmann, Roberto Perotti, and Ernesto Talvi. 1996. *Managing Fiscal Policy in Latin America: Volatility, Procyclicality, and Precarious Creditworthiness.* OCE Working Paper 326, Inter-American Development Bank, Washington, D.C.

Gavin, Michael, and Ricardo Hausmann. 1996. *The Roots of Banking Crisis: The Macroeconomic Context.* OCE Working Paper 313, Inter-American Development Bank, Washington, D.C.

Helpman, Elhanan, and Assaf Razin. 1987. Exchange Rate Management: Intertemporal Trade-offs. *American Economic Review.*

Kiguel, Miguel, and Nissan Liviatan. 1992. The Business Cycle Associated with Exchange Rate Based Stabilization. *World Bank Economic Review.*

Reinhart, Carmen, and Carlos Végh. 1994. Inflation Stabilization in Chronic Inflation Countries: The Empirical Evidence. International Monetary Fund, Washington, D.C. Mimeo.

Rodriguez, Carlos A. 1982. The Argentine Stabilization Plan of December 20th. *World Development.*

Rojas-Suárez, Liliana, and Steven Weisbrod. 1996a. *Managing Banking Crises in Latin America: The Dos and Don'ts of Successful Restructuring Programs.* OCE Working Paper 319, Inter-American Development Bank, Washington, D.C.

_____. 1996b. *Banking Crises in Latin America: Experience and Policy Issues.* OCE Working Paper 321, Inter-American Development Bank,Washington, D.C.

Roldós, Jorge. 1995. Supply Side Effects of Disinflation Programs. *IMF Staff Papers.*

Talvi, Ernesto. 1996. Exchange-Rate Based Stabilization with Endogenous Fiscal Response. *Journal of Development Economics.* Forthcoming.

PART TWO

THE STATE
OF STRUCTURAL
REFORM

THE SCOPE AND DEPTH OF STRUCTURAL REFORM

ABSTRACT

With varying depth and speed, all the countries of Latin America and the Caribbean have implemented structural reforms aimed at improving efficiency, spurring economic growth, increasing incomes, and improving the welfare of the population. This part of the Economic and Social Progress Report is devoted to examining the status of these reforms. This introductory chapter summarizes the progress and features of the reforms in six areas: trade liberalization, tax policy, financial opening and regulation, privatization, labor legislation, and pension systems. Subsequent chapters analyze the objectives, range and challenges in each of these six areas. Future editions of this Report will analyze other economic and social reforms.

Profound reforms have taken place in the areas of trade, exchange rate, tax and financial policy:

• Taking the region as a whole, average tariffs have declined from levels of 44.6 percent in the pre-reform years to 13.1 percent at present.

• Permits and other restrictions of a non-tariff nature, which affected 33.8 percent of imports in the pre-reform period, now cover 11.4 percent.

• Exchange rate unification and deregulation have lowered the average differential between market and official exchange rates to 2 percent, as opposed to 72 percent in 1989.

• Use of the value-added tax (VAT) has become widespread, replacing other more distorting taxes.

• Tax rates on firms have been reduced to international levels.

• Interest rate controls have been lifted, reserve requirements have been brought below 20 percent in most countries, and procedures for regulation and prudential supervision over financial systems have been modernized.

In other areas of reform, however, progress has been mixed:

• Latin America has led the world in privatization in the 1990s, but the process has been highly concentrated in a few countries and much remains to be done. While the 694 sales made represent more than half the value of privatization transactions in developing countries, only nine countries in the region have had privatizations totaling over 1 percent of GDP a year on average during the 1990s.

• Labor reforms have been few and superficial. It is still very costly to lay off workers and nonwage labor costs remain high, even though they do not adequately protect workers against the risk of unemployment or labor instability.

• In the area of social security, only six countries have begun to correct the administrative and financial flaws in their traditional pension systems by introducing individual capitalization systems.

The reforms have been adopted in times of crisis. This crisis has changed balances of power, making it possible to simultaneously adopt measures aimed at reducing inflation, liberalizing trade, modernizing the tax system, and making the financial system more flexible. The other structural reforms examined in this Report have followed separately.

The speed of the reforms has depended on the type of reform. Shock strategies have been well-suited for reducing inflation. The major advances in privatization in each country have been carried out in a few years. In the realm of trade and tax reforms, it has been just as common for deep reforms to be completed in a short period of time as it has for them to stretch out over time. Reforms affecting financial systems, labor legislation or pension systems, on the other hand, have generally been slow and often incomplete.

The process of structural reform has proven to be sustainable. In almost all countries of the region, the reforms have survived periods of economic crisis and changes of government.

REFORMS HAVE BEEN PROFOUND

Until the mid-1980s, the economies of Latin America and the Caribbean were plagued by structural problems. Trade policies were aimed at keeping some sectors protected through high tariffs and import restrictions. Multiple exchange rates and controls on capital outflows had become widespread as an administrative way of dealing with foreign exchange shortages. Tax systems were exasperating; they deeply distorted production decisions and encouraged evasion. Interest rates were controlled, credit was targeted at chosen sectors through a variety of devices, and the state was intensively involved in financial activities. However, the ability to regulate and monitor the financial sector was quite feeble. The private sector had practically no role in delivering public services, and government companies were involved in an array of unrelated economic activities ranging from agriculture to hotels. Restrictions on labor mobility and high nonwage costs for a wide range of items had become an obstacle to the creation of formal employment and labor stability. Pension systems were approaching bankruptcy because low contributions were out of step with rising pension payments.

The collapse of economic growth and the high inflation rates in the 1980s led to a shift of direction in many of these fields, complementing stabilization efforts in the fiscal and monetary realms. Almost all countries took up the task of opening up their economies and liberalizing and strengthening their financial structures, although the precise moment varied from country to country. Currently, trade and foreign exchange systems are more open than they have been for several decades; interest rates are being controlled administratively only in exceptional cases; and a growing number of countries have modern financial supervision systems. Tax systems have been simplified, and they are more neutral and better administered. Notable advances have also been made in privatization, although with major differences from one country to another. More slowly and in a more limited manner, some countries have corrected the more outstanding weaknesses of their labor systems. Lagging far behind Chile, only five other countries have begun to correct the weaknesses of their contribution-based pension systems and to encourage the development of private funds based on individual capitalization.

This chapter summarizes the progress made in the six areas examined in greater detail in the subsequent chapters of this report: trade liberalization, tax policy, finance reform, privatization of state-owned enterprises, labor legislation, and social security pension systems. In many countries the reform program has also included significant changes in other areas of structural policy that are not analyzed here. Those worth noting include reforms in market regulation procedures (price controls, regulation of monopolies), other kinds of privatization besides the sale of existing companies or assets, fiscal and administrative decentralization, and reforms of justice and property systems. Reforms of education and health service delivery are examined in a special section of this Report, and are not included in this summary.

More Open Trade Systems

For decades, the region's trade policies were characterized by high levels of protection and government involvement, resulting in systems with a range of tariffs and procedures to control imports administratively and to ration or postpone the use of foreign exchange. The external restrictions imposed by the debt crisis in the early 1980s aggravated these practices. However, the ensuing economic collapse created the conditions for a fundamental shift of direction, since it made it clear that the previous model was spent, and that becoming more involved in the world economy was necessary for recovering economic growth. Between 1985 and 1991, practically all countries

Table 1.1 Structural Policy Indicators: Openness and Exchange Rate Flexibility

	Average tariff[1]	Nontariff barriers to imports[2]	Market and official exchange rate differential[3]
Argentina	Low	Low	Low
Bahamas	High		Medium
Barbados	Low	Low	Low
Belize			Medium
Bolivia	Low	Low	Low
Brazil	Low	Medium	Low
Chile	Low	Low	Medium
Colombia	Low	Low	Low
Costa Rica	Low	Low	Low
Dominican Republic	Medium	Low	Medium
Ecuador	Low	Low	Low
El Salvador	Low	Medium	High
Guatemala	Low		Low
Guyana		Low	Low
Haiti	Low	Low	High
Honduras	Medium		Low
Jamaica	Low	Low	Medium
Mexico	Low	Medium	Low
Nicaragua	Medium	Medium	Low
Panama	High	Medium	Low
Paraguay	Low	Low	High
Peru	Medium	Low	Low
Suriname	Medium		High
Trinidad and Tobago	Low		Low
Uruguay	Low	Low	Low
Venezuela	Low	Low	High

[1] Low, up to 15 percent; medium, between 15 percent and 20 percent; high, 20 percent or above.

[2] Low, up to 5 percent of imports subject to nontariff barriers; medium, between 5 percent and 20 percent; high, 20 percent or above.

[3] Low, up to 3 percent; medium, between 4 percent and 10 percent; high, 11 percent or above.

initiated significant programs to open their trading systems.[1] The gradual decline of the burden of foreign debt and the renewal of net capital inflow into the region made it possible for most countries to liberalize their foreign exchange procedures by 1990-91. The region's trade and foreign exchange systems are currently freer than they have been since the period before the Great Depression of the 1930s.

---

[1] During the second half of the 1970s only Chile and Uruguay had begun significant advances, which were partly reversed during the debt crisis.

Trade reforms substantially reduced tariffs and practically eliminated procedures for administratively controlling imports. Taking the region as a whole, average tariffs fell from 44.6 percent in the pre-reform years to 13.1 percent in 1995; maximum tariffs fell from an average of 83.7 percent to 41 percent. Currently, only seven countries have average tariffs over 15 percent and only two apply maximum tariffs over 100 percent to a small number of articles. In most countries, tariff reductions took place rapidly over a two to three-year period and reductions were around 50 percent (Table 1.1).

During the pre-reform period, it was common practice in the region to require that permits or licenses first be obtained for certain groups of imports, and economic authorities could grant them at will. These and other restrictions of a nontariff nature, which affected 33.8 percent of import in the pre-reform period, today cover 11.4 percent (for the group of countries on which there is information). Only Brazil, Mexico and El Salvador have restrictions affecting over 5 percent of the value of imports.

The foreign debt crisis led to the adoption of foreign exchange controls and the imposition of controls on capital movements. Multiple exchange systems spread to most countries. All established some kind of restriction on capital outflows and repatriation requirements on export earnings. At times surcharges on imports and prepayment deposits were also imposed. These restrictions have been dismantled since the wave of exchange rate liberalizations of 1990-91. Multiple exchange systems are now the exception. Despite the problems that Argentina and Mexico experienced in 1995, they did not fall back on this device. The only country to retreat temporarily from the process of foreign exchange liberalization was Venezuela in 1994 and 1995. Today there is no kind of restriction on payment for current transactions in 14 countries, and in most the conditions for capital transactions have been removed or made notably easier. As evidence of the pro-

Table 1.2 Structural Policy Indicators: Tax Policies

	Corporate tax rate[1]	Personal tax rate[2]	VAT rate[2]	VAT productivity[3]
Argentina	Medium	Medium	High	Low
Barbados	High	High	na	
Belize	Medium	High	Medium	
Bolivia	Medium	Low	Medium	Medium
Brazil	Medium	Medium	High	
Chile	Low	High	Medium	Low
Colombia	Medium	Medium	Medium	High
Costa Rica	Medium	Medium	Low	Low
Dominican Republic	Medium	Medium	Low	Medium
Ecuador	Medium	Medium	Low	Medium
El Salvador	Medium	Medium	Low	Low
Guatemala	Medium	Medium	Low	Medium
Guyana	High	Medium	na	
Haiti	Medium	Medium	Low	
Honduras	High	High	Low	Low
Jamaica	Medium	Medium	Medium	
Mexico	Medium	Medium	Medium	High
Nicaragua	Medium	Medium	Medium	High
Panama	Medium	Medium	Low	Medium
Paraguay	Medium	na	Low	Low
Peru	Medium	Medium	Medium	Medium
Suriname	High	High	na	
Trinidad and Tobago	Medium	Medium	Medium	Medium
Uruguay	Medium	na	High	Medium
Venezuela	Medium	Medium	Medium	Medium

[1] Refers to the highest marginal rate: low, less than 25 percent; medium, between 25 percent and 40 percent; high, 40 percent or above.

[2] Refers to basic rate: low, up to but less than 12 percent; medium, between 12 percent and 20 percent; high, 20 percent or above..

[3] Ratio of total revenue to GDP and VAT rate: low, less than 25 percent; medium, between 25 percent and 40 percent; high, 40 percent or above.

cess of foreign exchange unification and deregulation, it may be noted that in 1995 the differential between the median market price of foreign exchange (including transaction costs and exchange taxes) and the official rate was on average only 2 percent, as opposed to 72 percent in 1989. In 16 countries, the exchange rate differential is zero or less than 3 percent, and in only five was it over 10 percent in 1995.

Tax Reforms: Neutrality and Simplification

In previous decades, the model of protectionism and discretionary government involvement gave rise to frustrating tax systems, with a multiplicity of taxes of questionable efficacy and diverse tax rates with high levels that distorted production decisions, discouraged work and penalized savings. It also created a host of exemptions intended to foster investment and the development of certain sectors, which became impossible to administer and control, given the weakness of tax agencies. The redesign of the development model in the 1980s led to a turnabout in this situation. Tax systems underwent profound reform in the pursuit of neutrality, legal and administrative simplification, and greater revenues.

Taxes on foreign trade, which represented 29.9 percent of tax revenues in the median country in the region in 1980, were partially replaced by higher domestic collection; currently they generate only 16.6 percent of revenue collected. To moderate the distorting effects of tax collection on production and saving decisions, 21 countries adopted the value-added tax (VAT) on consumption, and two others will do so by 1997. However, the revenue collection ratios of the VAT are much lower than their statutory rates, due to the exclusion of many final goods and services from the tax bases, and to problems of administration and control, all of which further limits the neutrality of this tax. The extreme marginal rates that were applied in the past to company profits have been lowered, and only in three countries are they higher than the highest marginal rate in the United States (39.6 percent). For reasons of equity, broader differential rates have been maintained on personal incomes , although they are still lower than those previously in effect. To improve collection, 14 countries have established special units for monitoring large taxpayers. Most tax administrations have abandoned the old division of functions based on taxes and have adopted more efficient forms of organization. Even so, evasion remains widespread throughout the region, and administration remains weak in crucial areas such as regular follow-up on the bulk of taxpayers, as well as monitoring, collection and enforcement.

Table 1.3 Structural Policy Indicators: Financial Liberalization and Deregulation

	Interest rates market determined?[1]	Quality of bank and capital markets regulation[2]	Quality of bank supervision
Argentina	Medium	High	Reasonable
Bahamas	High	High	Reasonable
Barbados	High	High	Reasonable
Belize	Medium	Medium	Reasonable
Bolivia	High	Medium	Medium
Brazil	Medium	Medium	Reasonable
Chile	Medium	High	Reasonable
Colombia	High	High	Reasonable
Costa Rica	Medium	Medium	Inadequate
Dominican Republic	High	Medium	Reasonable
Ecuador	High	High	Medium
El Salvador	High	High	Reasonable
Guatemala	High	Medium	Medium
Guyana	High	Medium	Medium
Haiti	High	Low	Inadequate
Honduras	High	Medium	Inadequate
Jamaica	Medium	Medium	Medium
Mexico	Medium	Medium	Medium
Nicaragua	High	High	Reasonable
Panama	High	Low	Inadequate
Paraguay	High	Low	Inadequate
Peru	High	High	Reasonable
Suriname	Low	Low	Inadequate
Trinidad and Tobago	High	High	Reasonable
Uruguay	High	Medium	Reasonable
Venezuela	High	Low	Inadequate

[1] Low, generalized controls; medium, specific controls on certain rates; high, total market determination of rates.

[2] Low, lack of modern regulations on the capital market and banking systems; medium, lack of modern regulations in either of the above mentioned; high, modern regulations on both.

Opening Financial Systems and Improving Supervision

Financial repression was common until the early 1980s and included such standard practices as controls on interest rates, various devices for allocating credit to specific sectors, and an intense direct participation by the state in financial activities. Given the lack of alternate tools, reserve requirements on deposits were used for monetary control. In the absence of a coherent regulatory framework, oversight and prudential rules based on reliable information and objective risk measurements, financial activities were controlled through poorly articulated administrative regula-

tions that hindered competition and the development of new financial activities. These circumstances began to change in the 1970s and reached a turnaround in the 1980s, when it came to be accepted that the financial sector plays a central role in the development process by channeling saving and making investment efficient. More recently, it has been recognized that the financial sector and capital markets also have a role in generating and processing information that is crucial for raising the quality of investments and hastening the adoption and spread of productive and administrative innovations.[2]

The financial reforms adopted since the late 1980s have focused on reducing or eliminating targeted credit programs, freeing interest rates, lowering reserve rate requirements, and establishing modern banking regulation systems. These reforms represent a notable advance toward freeing the operation of the financial market and shaping an adequate regulatory system, although they are still far from reducing the vulnerability of the financial markets to manageable levels in some countries.[3] The measure most commonly adopted to liberalize financial systems has been the reduction or elimination of targeted credit programs (19 countries). Two countries have eliminated these programs and most have cut them by at least half. The liberalization of interest rates has also been widely implemented. Fourteen countries have lifted administrative controls over some or all deposit rates, and 17 countries have freed lending rates. Currently in 18 countries all interest rates on deposits and loans are governed by the market, and only one country has broad controls on interest rates.[4] Reserve rate requirements have been lowered in 15 countries, and in seven of them reductions have been by 20 percentage points or more. Consequently, a total of 15 countries have

[2] Edwards (1995), chapter 7.

[3] In particular, cutting reserve rates may contribute to financial vulnerability in countries where money demand is quite unstable.

[4] In Argentina and Chile, restrictive procedures for some lending rates apply to very small segments of the credit market.

reserve rates on demand deposits no higher than 20 percent. The establishment of modern banking regulation and capital market systems has spread to most countries in this wave of financial reforms in the region. Currently, 14 countries have a regulatory and prudential oversight system that can be regarded as suited to the level of development of their financial activities (Table 1.3).

Privatization: Remarkable but Uneven

There has been substantial progress in the area of privatization in the region, although it varies from country to country. The number and significance of state-owned enterprises rose throughout Latin America from the 1950s to the early 1980s as part of a strategy to counteract the natural monopoly conditions of certain markets, and to bolster investment and the delivery of services in economically or socially important areas in which private sector involvement was regarded as limited by lack of financing or by risks inherent in certain projects. In the 1980s, however, it began to be recognized that the lack of market discipline by many state-owned enterprises had resulted in inefficient and lackluster operating practices and disastrous financial losses. Privatization aimed not only to improve efficiency and fiscal health, but also to enhance the balance of payments and stimulate foreign investment, lower the foreign debt, and generally increase competition and expand markets for goods, services and capital.

Latin America has been the worldwide leader in privatization during the 1990s. The 694 sales made between 1990 and 1994 represent more than half of the value of privatization transactions in developing countries. Mexico and Argentina have carried out the privatization transactions totaling the largest sums: $24 billion and $18 billion, respectively, representing 2 percent and 1.2 percent of their GDP in those years. When the size of their economies is taken into account, seven other countries have made similar privatization efforts. Of the total value of privatizations

in the region, 43.4 percent has involved the public service sectors, which have traditionally been closed to private participation, and where the potential for productivity and efficiency gains is greater. Another 23.4 percent has come from the sale of banks and financial institutions, bolstering financing reform trends. One of the most positive and tangible effects of privatization has been increased foreign investment in the region. Foreign investment directed at privatization on average has represented 21 percent of foreign direct investment. Privatization has also led to additional foreign investment seeking to capitalize the privatized companies or to invest in complementary activities that privatization has made more attractive.

Limited Labor Reforms

Reforms in the area of labor have been more limited than those in other areas and have focused on moderating layoff costs and making it easier to hire workers temporarily. The rules that have traditionally governed labor activity aimed to assure labor stability and protect the worker from unemployment, illness and old age. However, these aims have not always been achieved because high and uncertain layoff and termination costs have led to excessive worker turnover, and high nonwage costs have encouraged the spread of the informal sector.

In most countries in the region, the cost of dismissing a worker after a year of work is more than a month's pay, and in eight countries it is over two months' pay. If the worker has 10 years of seniority, the costs of firing are even greater; at least six months' pay in most countries, and over 12 months' in eight countries (Table 1.4). In Argentina, Colombia, Guatemala, Panama and Peru, reforms have recently been introduced to regulate dismissal costs. In Argentina and Panama, an upper limit was set for severance pay. In Colombia, Guatemala and Peru, annual payments were established to replace compensation payments

Table 1.4 Structural Policy Indicators: Labor Market Flexibility

	Layoff expenses after one year of work[1]	Layoff expenses after 10 years of work[2]	Social Security contributions[3]
Argentina	High	Medium	High
Bahamas	Low	Low	Low
Barbados	Low	Low	Low
Belize	Low	Low	Low
Bolivia	High	High	Medium
Brazil	High	High	High
Chile	Medium	Medium	Medium
Colombia	High	High	High
Costa Rica	Medium	Medium	Medium
Dominican Republic	Low	Medium	Low
Ecuador	High	High	Medium
El Salvador	Medium	Medium	Low
Guatemala	Low	Medium	Low
Guyana	Low	Medium	Low
Haiti	Low	Low	Low
Honduras	Medium	High	Low
Jamaica	Low	Low	Low
Mexico	High	Medium	Medium
Nicaragua	High	High	Low
Panama	Medium	Medium	Low
Paraguay	Medium	Medium	Medium
Peru	Medium	High	Medium
Suriname	Low	Low	na
Trinidad and Tobago	Medium	Medium	Low
Uruguay	Low	Low	High
Venezuela	High	High	Medium

[1] Low, up to one salary; medium, between one and two salaries; high, over two salaries.
[2] Low, up to six salaries; medium, between six and 12 salaries; high over 12 salaries.
[3] Low, up to 15 percent; medium, between 15 percent and 30 percent; high, over 30 percent.

made when labor contracts are terminated, calculated on the basis of the number of years worked and most recent wages. In Colombia, Panama and Peru, firms' obligation to reinstate workers with a certain amount of seniority when they could not prove justifiable cause for firing were lessened or eliminated. The new rules have thus sought to reduce uncertainty over dismissal costs for the company (and in some cases the actual sums). To counteract restrictions on dismissing workers, a number of countries have encouraged various procedures for temporary hiring of workers in order to increase flexibility around the edges of certain kinds of labor contracts.

In most countries in the region, the nonwage costs arising out of contributions charged to companies and workers for various social security, health, education and unemployment programs are very high (not to mention other nonwage benefits such as vacations, bonuses, maternity, etc.). In Argentina, Brazil, Colombia and Uruguay, the costs of contributions to such programs are over 30 percent of the direct wage cost; in eight more countries they are between 15 percent and 30 percent. No country has recently introduced measures to curbs such costs except Chile. As part of a social security reform in 1981, pension payments in Chile were lowered to 13 percent from previous levels ranging from 18.89 to 20.7 percent.

Social Security Reforms: Barely Beginning

High payments are merely a symptom of the difficulties of most pension security systems in the region. The benefits that public-managed systems offer have little relationship to individual contributions, giving rise to huge future pension payment obligations, low levels of financial reserves, and low coverage. To deal with this situation Argentina, Colombia, Mexico, Peru and Uruguay are implementing pension reforms whose common element is the creation of private pension funds based on a principle of individual capitalization. To respect pension obligations already acquired and guarantee basic or minimum pensions, these countries have chosen different ways to relate the new capitalization systems with the older public systems. These include competition in the cases of Peru and Colombia, complementarity between the two systems in Argentina and Uruguay, and the dismantling of the public system over the medium run in Mexico. These reforms envision reducing the imbalances between benefits and contributions in the public system, whether by raising retirement ages, adjusting contribution rates, or placing stricter conditions on access to pensions. In this manner the reforms have at least partially corrected the financial imbalances of the public system. In addition, by establishing the new pension funds, they have opened a new channel for increasing real and financial saving.

TIMING AND CHRONOLOGY OF REFORMS

The stabilization and structural reform process has encompassed enough countries and reforms, and has been applied for a sufficiently long time, that some of its main features may now be examined. This section concentrates on three elements of the reform process that are emphasized in the economic literature: opportunity, sequencing and speed.

Considerable analysis on the political economy of reform has aimed to find the political and social factors that condition structural reform processes.[5] In this section we use some of the theoretical models for interpreting the patterns actually characterizing the structural reform process in Latin America, explicitly leaving aside normative considerations—that is, what should have been done. The boxes accompanying this chapter provide theoretical frameworks that suggest alternative interpretations of what has happened with regard to stabilization and reform in Latin America, as well as arguments of a normative nature.

Reforms Initiated in Times of Crisis

Do crises facilitate reform? It is widely believed that economic crises facilitate the reform process. The evidence discussed in Part One of this report supports that belief. In most Latin American countries, the adoption of major reforms was preceded by deteriorating economic conditions that included declining investment rates, low or falling growth rates, large fiscal deficits, accelerating in-

flation, and a sharp contraction of financial intermediation activities.

The connection between crises and reform is related to the manner in which the politic-economic equilibrium is changed, setting the reform process in motion. Typically a crisis—whether generated by a prolonged period of poor economic performance or by an internal or external negative shock—makes the pre-reform phase so costly that the various conflicting groups in society more quickly reach an agreement on the reforms needed. A crisis can also prompt society to accumulate information on the mapping between economic policies and the performance of the economy, leading to a reassessment of the cost of maintaining the previous policies, thereby increasing popular support for reform.

However, although economic crises may have set off the reform process, it would be rash to say that they have been its cause. In the domestic realm, political and ideological factors have influenced the timing, intensity and direction of the reforms. External factors have also played a decisive role in leading countries to unite around the reform process. The growing importance of trade blocs, the globalization of the international economy, and the need to improve international competitiveness may have forced countries to rule out any other option.

Major Initial Reforms Followed by Other Measures

In analyzing sequencing, we use the expressions bundling and unbundling to refer to situations in which reforms are introduced all at once, as opposed to those in which they are introduced sequentially. Figure 1.1 and Tables 1.5 and 1.6 present the stylized facts on the sequencing of reform. The evidence indicates that inflation stabilization and financial and trade liberalization tend to occur at the same time. All the countries that have stabilized inflation also began trade liberalization measures, and all but one applied finan-

---

Box 1.1   The Political Economy of Reform

The literature on the political economy of reforms has focused on three points:

- *Timing*. When and why do reforms occur?
- *Sequencing*. Why are reforms on different fronts sometimes implemented simultaneously and sometimes one at a time?
- *Speed*. Why do some countries go "cold turkey" while others apply each reform gradually?

Each one of these positive questions has a normative equivalent: what should reformers do in these three areas to maximize the chances of achieving successful reform? Issues of speed and sequencing, in particular, have given rise to much controversy. Sachs (1994), among others, has passionately argued that going full speed on all fronts is often not just the best, but also the only strategy available to reformers. Skeptics, such as Desai (1995), have argued that shock therapy imposes unbearably high transitional costs and hence weakens political support for reform.

Latin America has witnessed an avalanche of reforms in the 1980s and 1990s. Why did they happen then, after many years of deteriorating economic performance? Why are reforms more often delayed? The political economy literature offers two explanations.

One stresses the role of distributive struggles among interest groups (Alesina and Drazen, 1991; Labán and Sturzenegger, 1992 and 1994; Mondino, Sturzenegger and Tommasi, 1993; Perotti, 1993; Velasco, 1993 and 1995; and Tornell, 1995). In these accounts, economic deterioration comes about through the endogenous evolution of an economic variable (public or external debt, degree of financial adaptation, information about other groups'

preferences) that determines the cost to each group of further delaying reform. When the situation deteriorates to the extent that the present value of a no-reform scenario falls below that of a reform policy, groups agree (or at least withhold veto) and changes in economic policy are implemented.

On the other hand, economic deterioration can come about because an exogenous adverse shock (for instance, a terms of trade shock) triggers a crisis that hastens the change in groups' payoffs, and thus leads to a sudden reform (see Drazen and Grilli, 1993; Velasco 1993; and Tornell, 1995).

An alternative view stresses that periods of economic disarray convey information about the mapping between outcomes and policies and may lead to a reassessment of the cost of previous policies. In this view, laid out by Harberger (1993) and formalized, in part, by Perktold and Tommasi (1994), dynamics evolve in the following way. At first the world changes—trade grows, technology is modified—in such a way that the older model of development becomes less and less adequate. As the world evolves, perceptions change, but very sluggishly, since people only observe economic outcomes, and cannot readily ascertain whether bad outcomes result from bad policies or simply from adverse random shocks. Learning can only take place over time as a process of gradual updating of beliefs. As a result, "bad" policies can rationally remain in place for long periods of time, allowing for a gradual but nonetheless painful deterioration of economic performance. Only when enough learning has taken place does reform successfully occur.

---

cial liberalization programs. Moreover, 67 percent of trade liberalization programs and 45 percent of financial reforms began the same year or during the months immediately following inflation stabilization.[6] In those instances when stabilization, trade liberalization, and financial reform were not applied together, trade liberalization preceded stabilization in all countries, and financial liberalization preceded stabilization in most of them.

A loosely-defined tax reform has been a common element of all stabilization or reform programs in the region in the 1990s.[7] However, even if tax reform is more narrowly defined as an overall reform of the tax system, or at least, of a

---

[6] The short-lived stabilization programs based on income policies adopted by Argentina, Brazil and Peru in 1985 and 1986 are not included. It is interesting to note that none of these programs was complemented by financial or trade reforms.

[7] This study does not document pre-1990 tax reforms.

FIGURE 1.1

Sequence of Reforms Before and After Stabilization

(In percent)

a. Trade Liberalization

b. Tax Reform

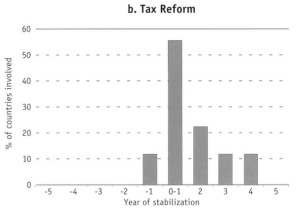

c. Financial Liberalization

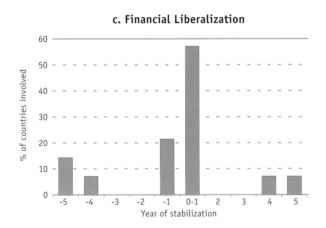

d. Privatization

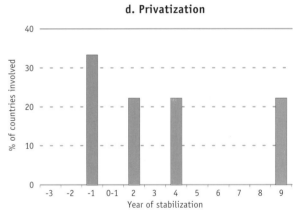

e. Labor Market Reform

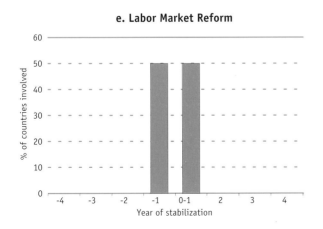

f. Pension Reform

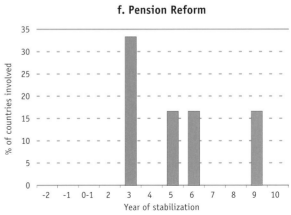

	1985 (or before)	1986	1987	1988	1989	1990	1991	1992	1993	1994	1995	1996
Table 1.5 Timing of Reforms												
Stabilization	Argentina (1978 and 1985); Bolivia, Chile (1975 and 1985); Costa Rica, Peru, Uruguay (1978)	Brazil Dominican Republic	Guatemala Jamaica	Mexico	Venezuela	Dominican Republic Peru	Argentina Colombia Guatemala Nicaragua Uruguay	Ecuador Guyana Honduras Jamaica		Brazil	Suriname	
Trade liberalization	Argentina (1978); Chile (1975 and 1985); Mexico, Uruguay (1978)	Bolivia Costa Rica	Jamaica	Guatemala Guyana	Argentina Paraguay El Salvador Trinidad and Tobago Venezuela	Brazil Dominican Republic Ecuador Honduras Peru	Colombia Nicaragua Uruguay	Barbados		Belize Haiti Suriname	Panama	Bahamas
Tax reform	na	na	na	na	na	Argentina	Nicaragua Peru	El Salvador	Ecuador Guatemala Honduras Jamaica Paraguay Venezuela	Belize Bolivia		
Financial reform	Argentina (1978); Chile (1975); Uruguay (1974 and 1985)	Mexico		Costa Rica Brazil Paraguay Guyana	Chile Venezuela	Bolivia Colombia El Salvador Nicaragua Peru Trinidad and Tobago	Dominican Republic Honduras Guatemala	Argentina Jamaica	Ecuador	Bahamas	Barbados Belize Haiti	
Privatization	Chile (1974-78)		Jamaica	Chile (circa 1988)		Argentina	Belize Jamaica Guyana Venezuela	Barbados Mexico	Nicaragua	Chile Peru Trinidad and Tobago	Bolivia	
Labor reform	Chile (1979)					Colombia Guatemala	Argentina Peru				Panama	
Pension reform	Chile (1981)								Peru	Argentina Colombia		Uruguay Mexico

major tax, it turns out that 69 percent of stabilizations since 1989 (of which there are 13) have been complemented either simultaneously or within a few years by tax reform.

By contrast, a smaller percentage of countries that stabilized inflation implemented other structural reforms, such as privatization (53 percent), labor market reform (29 percent), and so-cial security reform (35 percent). Moreover, privatization and social security reform were only applied at a later stage in the reform process.[8] In most countries, major privatization efforts were

---

[8] In those cases in which labor market reform was attempted, efforts were made in conjunction with stabilization programs. Very few countries in the region have carried out labor market reforms, however.

Table 1.6 Sequencing of Reforms					
	Trade Liberalization	Tax Reform	Financial Reform	Privatization	Labor Reform	Pension Reform
Argentina (nineties)	1	2	4	2	3	5
Argentina (seventies)	1		1			
Bahamas	2		1			
Barbados	1		2	1		
Belize	2	2	3	1		
Bolivia	2	3-5	3	4		
Brazil (nineties)	2		1			
Chile (eighties, nineties)	2		4	3		
Chile (seventies)	1		1		2	3
Colombia	3		2		1	4
Costa Rica			1	2		
Dominican Republic	1		2			
Ecuador	1	3	3			
El Salvador	1	3	2			
Guatemala	2	5	4		3	
Guyana	1		1	2		
Haiti	1		2			
Honduras	1	4	2			
Jamaica (eighties)	1			1		
Jamaica (nineties)		3	2	1		
Mexico	1		2	4		5
Nicaragua	2	2	1	3		
Panama	1				1	
Paraguay	2	3	1			
Peru	1	2	1	4	2	3
Suriname	1					
Trinidad and Tobago	1		2	3		
Uruguay (nineties)	2		1			3
Uruguay (seventies)						
Venezuela	1	3	1	2		

Note: Numbers represent the order of adoption of reforms. When numbers repeat, it is because reforms have been implemented in the same year.

only undertaken two years following stabilization, while pension system reform was implemented at least three years after stabilization.

This evidence suggests that in the stabilization and reform process in Latin America, the norm has been neither a complete bundling nor unbundling of reforms. Rather, a mixed strategy has been adopted in which a partial application was followed by a further set of reforms. Initial reforms tended to be applied together (stabilization, financial liberalization, trade opening, tax reform, and to a much lesser extent, labor market reform), while the other reforms (privatization and social security reform) tended to be unbundled and applied later. This evidence is consistent with Naim's (1994) description of the stabilization and reform process in two stages.

While the sequencing of stabilization and reform programs has not been identical in all countries, the similarities are sufficiently large to allow for the description of a typical pattern. After a prolonged period of unsatisfactory economic performance or the emergence of a crisis, the status quo is broken. The urgency generated by this situation prompts the government to take advantage of the opportunity and set in motion a reform process (whether out of conviction or because there is no feasible alternative). The tasks tackled immediately are stabilizing inflation, liberalizing trade, and eliminating financial repression. The common feature of these reforms is that they do not require a lengthy process of consensus building, since most of the measures can be applied rapidly by means of executive order.

Nevertheless, partial reforms can be inherently unstable in the sense that the full benefit of the initial reforms can be obtained only if complementary reforms are applied. Hence, it is likely that partial reforms initiate a dynamic process whose nature is as follows: the initial reforms increase the benefits of adopting further reforms and therefore the cost of applying reforms falls in relation to the cost of not applying them. Consequently, society will be more willing to accept less popular reforms so as not to lose the benefits derived from the initial reforms. For example, fiscal consolidation—rationalizing and cutting public spending or raising tax rates—will be more acceptable if society runs the risk of losing the price stability recently attained. Trade liberalization exposes local producers to foreign competition and increases the benefits of the reforms that improve the efficiency of the tax system and the opera-

Box 1.2   Sequencing and the Bundling and Unbundling of Reforms

The early literature on the sequencing of economic reforms was spurred by the experience of the Southern Cone in the late 1970s and early 1980s. Debate centered on the order of liberalization of the trade and capital accounts, with the majority of authors in favor of opening the former before the latter in order to avoid destabilizing capital flows (Edwards, 1984; McKinnon, 1991).

Subsequent research has been more precise in identifying potential welfare gains or losses associated with different sequences. One possible argument for unbundling is the presence of preexisting distortions (policy-induced or otherwise) in one or several markets that cannot be removed at the time the reform plan is announced. Potential candidates are labor market interventions, domestic capital market imperfections, and limits to foreign indebtedness that are not perceived as binding by individual agents (Edwards and Van Wijnbergen, 1986; Edwards, 1992). A related argument by Calvo (1989) emphasizes that imperfect credibility is equivalent to a distortion in the intertemporal price of imported goods. If the public wrongly believes that trade liberalization will be reverted in the future, quantitative control of the capital account may be called for. In addition, if imperfect credibility arises because the public is unsure about the true preferences of the government, overshooting can act as a signaling device (Rodrik 1989).

In this literature, exogenous political constraints have sometimes been invoked to claim that a certain distortion cannot be removed, but beyond that, political economy plays no role in determining the optimal sequence. Dewatripont and Roland (1994) provide a political economy case for unbundling in the implementation of economic reforms. Their basic point is that, if partial reforms are unstable (in the sense they cannot yield full results unless complemented by other reforms), at each stage of the transition the choice is between accepting the next set of reforms or reversing the previous one. If the initial reforms have been a success, people are more willing to accept less popular reforms so as not to lose the gains of the first reforms and to save on reversal costs. A related argument is presented by Wei (1993): he argues that sequencing may allow the building of constituencies for reform. A package of reforms that would have been rejected by majority voting may gain approval if submitted piecemeal, thus allowing information about costs to flow and alliances to form. Unbundling in this case is equivalent to a divide-to-reign strategy, pitching current majorities against future ones (see also Fernández and Rodrik, 1991).

On the other side of the debate, Martinelli and Tommasi (1993) argue that in societies with powerful interest groups and characterized by a cobweb of redistributive and distortionary policies, optimal unbundled plans will be time inconsistent. Winners of early reforms who are hurt by later reforms have an incentive to stop the gradual path in its later stages. Knowing that, losers from early reforms will oppose the earlier measures. In such an environment, a big bang is the only way of cutting through the Gordian knot of rents implicit in previous policies.

tion of factor markets, and that reduce the cost of nontradable intermediate inputs such as public services. Therefore, tax reform, social security reform and privatization constitute the natural result of the process begun by the first set of partial reforms. The second set of reforms, however, generally requires parliamentary approval and support by interest groups, which explains why this phase of the reform process begins later.

One noteworthy exception to this pattern is Colombia, a country with a solid macro-economic performance, which was not facing an imminent crisis when the government elected in 1990 began a significant process of combined reforms. The approach taken by Colombia can be understood better when one considers that in societies where powerful interest groups have in practice a veto power, and where there is a cobweb of redistributive policies, reforms are politically feasible only if combined in a way that offers something for everyone, and consequently cuts the Gordian knot of rents implicit in previous policies.

Speed Depends on the Reform

In analyzing speed, we use the terms "gradual" and "shock treatment" to describe a situation in which the reforms—whether introduced sequentially or all at once—are implemented slowly or rapidly.

The criteria for defining when a reform is considered gradual or a shock are by their nature controversial. The criteria proposed here nevertheless have the virtue of being simple and relatively strict: for a reform to be considered a shock, it must be large and rapid. In the case of trade reforms, a shock reform is defined as one that cuts average tariff levels by at least 50 percent in a two-year period, provided that the level goes below 20 percent and that during the same period the bulk of nontariff restrictions on imports has been removed. Of the 21 countries on which there is information on trade reforms since the early 1980s, 11 fit neatly into this definition.

With regard to tax reforms, we have defined a shock reform to be one that modifies the entire tax system in terms of neutrality, legal rationality, and horizontal equity. Although this is not a quantitative criterion, it is clear that during the 1990s, the reforms in Argentina (1990), El Salvador (1992), Jamaica (1993), Nicaragua (1991), Paraguay (1993), and Peru (1991) were of this type. Another six countries carried out significant reforms that can be regarded as gradual, or more precisely, partial, since they applied the same criteria to only one of the more important taxes. In this count we did not consider instances of minor reforms that could be called incremental in the sense that they introduced adjustments in tax rates or in tax bases into a tax system that was already sufficiently consolidated.

In the area of financial reform, a shock reform is defined as one that in no more than two years frees the interest rates that were subject to controls, cuts credit mechanisms by at least half, and introduces substantial reforms in one or several of the following areas: privatization of finan-cial institutions, independence of the central bank, and modernization of the capital market or of banking regulation and supervision systems. Of the 24 countries on which reforms have been documented since the mid-1980s, only seven fall into the shock reform category: Bolivia, El Salvador, Guatemala, Nicaragua, Peru, the Dominican Republic and Venezuela.

Although practically all countries in the region have carried out some kinds of privatization during the 1990s, we regard as active privatizers only those that in some year had privatization revenues of over 1 percent of GDP (12 countries).[9] Within these, rapid privatizations are defined only as those cases where in one year 40 percent or more of total privatizations during the 1990s took place (up to 1994 or 1995, depending on the availability of information). Although this criterion may seem extreme, in 10 of the 12 cases privatizations were rapid in nature (the exceptions are Jamaica and Argentina). In other words, when the privatization reform is large, it is also carried out quickly.

There are too few labor and social security reforms in the region to draw conclusions claiming to be generally valid. Under no reasonable standard can any of the five labor reforms documented in this study be considered to have been rapid. Nor have there been any rapid reforms related to termination costs or nonwage labor costs, which are the most significant labor restrictions. Making hiring conditions more flexible has been marginal and may even have introduced greater distortions in some countries.

Social security reforms are by their nature slow, because pension obligations are fulfilled gradually. To overcome this bias, a rapid pension reform may be defined as one that establishes the elimination or modification of the contribution

---

[9] Prior to the 1990s, at their peak, privatizations in Chile (1974-1979) and Jamaica (1987) were over 1 percent of GDP, and the latter would be classified as rapid. However, the fragmentary information available on the second round of privatizations in Chile (1985-89) and the first round in Mexico (1983-88) suggests that they were of a lesser amount.

FIGURE 1.2

Speed of Reforms

(Numbers of countries)

a. Stabilization

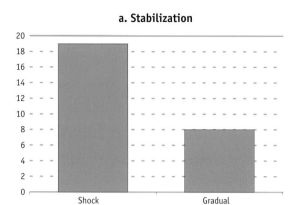

b. Tax Reform

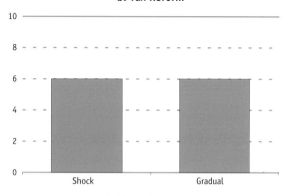

c. Trade Liberalization

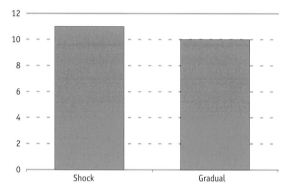

d. Financial Reform

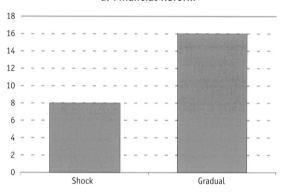

e. Privatization

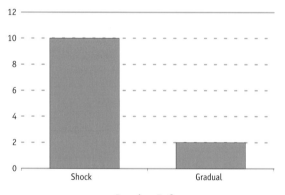

f. Labor Reform

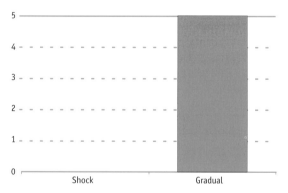

g. Pension Reform

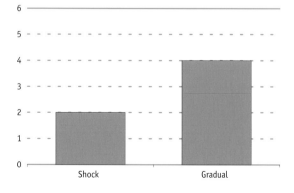

Table 1.7	Speed of Reforms	
	Shock	Gradual
Stabilization[1]	Argentina (1991); Bolivia, Brazil, Dominican Republic (1986 and 1990); Guatemala (1987 and 1991); Guyana, Honduras, Jamaica (1987 and 1992); Mexico, Nicaragua, Peru, Suriname, Venezuela	Chile (1975 and 1985); Colombia, Costa Rica, Ecuador, Uruguay (1978 and 1991)
Tax reform	Argentina, El Salvador, Jamaica, Nicaragua, Paraguay, Peru	Belize, Bolivia, Ecuador, Guatemala, Honduras, Venezuela
Trade liberalization	Argentina, Bolivia, Barbados, Chile, Colombia, El Salvador, Haiti, Mexico, Peru, Uruguay, Venezuela	Brazil, Costa Rica, Ecuador, Guatemala, Guyana, Honduras, Jamaica, Nicaragua, Paraguay, Trinidad and Tobago
Financial reform	Bolivia, Dominican Republic, El Salvador, Guatemala, Nicaragua, Peru, Venezuela	Argentina, Bahamas, Belize, Barbados, Brazil, Chile, Colombia, Costa Rica, Ecuador, Guyana, Haiti, Honduras, Jamaica, Mexico, Paraguay, Trinidad and Tobago, Uruguay
Privatization	Barbados, Belize, Bolivia, Chile, Guyana, Mexico, Nicaragua, Peru, Trinidad and Tobago, Venezuela	Argentina, Jamaica
Labor reform		Argentina, Colombia, Guatemala, Panama, Peru
Pension reform	Chile, Mexico	Argentina, Colombia, Peru, Uruguay

[1]The heterodox shocks of Argentina (June 1985 and December 1986), Brazil (February and December 1986) and Peru (August 1985 and August 1986), which were short-lived and based on price freezes, are not included.

pension system in a set period and establishes a time limit for the definitive transfer of workers from one pension system to the other. The 1981 reform in Chile clearly is in this category, as is also the reform planned for Mexico in 1997, even though in this latter case some benefit conditions and previous institutional arrangements that do not entirely fit into the new system based on individual capitalization remain in effect. The reforms

in Peru, Colombia, Argentina and Uruguay, on the other hand, are gradual in nature.

Due to the interplay between structural reforms and stabilization efforts, it is also relevant to distinguish between slow and rapid inflation reductions. When the starting point is inflation rates of over 500 percent, a rapid reduction consists of reaching inflation rates of under 100 percent in less than a year. For lower initial inflation rates, we are considering a reduction by half within one year to be a shock treatment. By this standard, 70 percent of the 24 stabilizations were shocks (the exceptions are Chile, Colombia, Costa Rica, Ecuador and Uruguay).[10]

Figure 1.2 and Table 1.7 sum up the previous evidence. They suggest that no specific speed is typical of all reforms (gradual or shock), but rather that the speed seems to be specific to each reform. Typically, stabilization and privatization tend to be implemented rapidly, while financial, labor market and social security reforms are implemented gradually. Trade liberalization and tax reform are intermediate cases in which neither gradual approaches nor shock treatment are the rule.

The traditional argument against gradual reforms is that they introduce intertemporal distortions into the decision-making process of firms and individuals that can lead to potentially large efficiency losses when compared to the shock strategy. Moreover, the dynamics of a gradual strategy may have major political economy implications. Those groups affected by the reforms will vehemently oppose them: import-competing industries in the case of trade liberalization; export and import-competing industries in the case of stabilization programs, which normally lead to an appreciation of the real exchange rate; beneficiaries of subsidized credit; and unions and workers facing privatization. However, if reforms are carried

[10] The stabilizations based on income policy in Argentina, Brazil and Peru in 1985 and 1986 are not included, but they would be classified as shock treatments.

Box 1.3   Speed: Tortoise or Hare?

The neoclassical benchmark in this area provided by Mussa (1982) is clear: the mere presence of adjustment costs does not imply that policy should adjust gradually. If the private cost of adjustment reflects the true social costs, the optimal policy is to set the distorting policy instruments to zero at the beginning of the planning horizon (the definition of shock therapy in this context) and let rational agents adjust their behavior optimally. Economic arguments for deviating from this benchmark must therefore rely on the presence of distortions. The cleanest case for gradualism along these lines is provided by Gavin (1993), who argues that congestion externalities create too much transitional unemployment (relative to the market optimum) after a big bang.

More explicit political economy arguments for gradualism have been made by Dewatripont and Roland (1992a,b), who focus on budgetary considerations. Consider a reform-minded government facing an inefficient sector with a work force that is heterogeneous in outside opportunities. A move towards allocative efficiency requires a major shift to higher productivity activities and massive layoffs. In order to make shock therapy politically acceptable, all workers have to be paid the same compensation, which will be determined by the income loss of the less productive worker and will therefore maximize the fiscal cost. Hence, shock therapy will be costly, and if raising revenue is distortionary, it may be dominated by a gradual reform, which generates less of a budgetary burden (see Rodrik, 1996).

out gradually, the groups benefitting from them will only slowly receive the benefits. This combination may weaken political support for the reform program, frustrating the process. In short, efficiency as well as political economy considerations can help us understand the reasons why certain reforms are applied by means of a shock treatment rather than being carried out gradually.

In most cases, however, labor and pension system reforms are applied gradually. This has to do with the fact that the beneficiaries have acquired contingent benefits from the old systems. A com-

plete transfer of the beneficiaries from the previous to the new system would entail fully assessing the value of the contingent benefits acquired by current workers. Designing adequate compensation schemes for inducing such transfers may turn out to be very complicated and will certainly be plagued with adverse selection problems.

REFORMS HAVE WITHSTOOD ECONOMIC CRISES AND POLITICAL CHANGES

Part One of this Report described the typical macroeconomic response to the adoption of a major stabilization and reform program: a recovery or an initial boom of economic activity and domestic demand, followed by a period in which the economy cools off and comes under stress, leading to a correction or crisis period when economic activity and internal demand fall, at times sharply. This economic cycle may give rise to an initial cycle of popular support and subsequent disenchantment with the reform program.

Most stabilization and reform programs begin after a long period of poor economic performance or in the midst of a crisis. Hence, they initially unleash a recovery or boom of economic activity and domestic demand, while at the same time inflation is sharply reduced. Under these circumstances, during the early years, stabilization and reform programs may enjoy broad popular support, because in comparison to the pre-reform situation, economic performance improves on almost all fronts. This does not necessarily happen in all cases. Many reforms are applied to prevent a drastic collapse of domestic demand. Although the adjustment required in the program is less severe than what would have been necessary had there been a collapse, in comparison with the period prior to the program the economy may be going through a painful adjustment that will provoke popular opposition to the reforms.

Nevertheless, even if the program enjoys popular support either during the recovery stage or at the height of the stabilization and reform

Table 1.8 Sustainability of Stabilization and Reforms						
	Adoption of major reform or stabilization	Years of stress, correction and crisis	Election years (after reforms)	Reforms continued	Reforms slowed down or stopped	Reforms were reversed	Stabilization was reversed
Argentina	1978	1981	1983		X		X
Argentina	1985[a]	1985					X
Argentina	1991	1994-96	1995	X			
Bolivia	1985	1992	1989/1993	X			
Brazil	1986[a]	1986					X
Brazil	1994	1996			X		
Chile	1975	1982-85			X		
Chile	1985	na	1990/1994				
Colombia	1991	1996	1994		X		
Dominican Republic	1990	1993-94	1994/1996		X		
Ecuador	1992	1995-96	1992/1996		X		
El Salvador	1988	1996	1994	X			
Guatemala	1988	1993-95	1991/93/96	X			
Guyana	1992	na	1992	X			
Haiti	1995	na					
Honduras	1990	1993-94	1994	X			
Mexico	1988	1994-1996	1988/1994	X			X
Nicaragua	1991	na	1996				
Paraguay	1989		1993		X		
Peru	1985[a]	1985					X
Peru	1990	1996	1995	X			
Suriname	1995	na	1996				
Trinidad and Tobago	1993	1995-96	1995	X			
Uruguay	1974-78	1982-84	1984/1989		X		X
Uruguay	1991	1995	1994	X			
Venezuela	1989	1993-95	1994			X	X

[a]Stabilization programs based on income policies which were not accompanied by structural reforms.

cycle, when the economy slows down and then moves into a correction or crisis period, the stabilization and reform program will be put to the test. During the period of tension, correction or crisis, the initial popular support enjoyed by the program may give way to skepticism about the benefits of reform. Popular and political support for the program may begin to dissipate, and the sustainability of the reforms may consequently be called into question.

Does the cycle of an initial boom and subsequent correction or crisis that is inherent in stabilization and reform programs work against the sustainability of the reforms? In other words, does the dynamic macroeconomic adjustment brought about by stabilization and reform programs bear within it the very seeds of its own destruction?

Table 1.8 presents the fate of the 21 epi-

sodes of inflation stabilization or structural reform carried out in Latin America during the 1970s, 1980s and 1990s that have experienced or are experiencing periods of tension, correction or crisis.

The results emerging from this sample are quite surprising. Among the 18 episodes of stabilization carried out in 12 countries, the gains of stabilization were reversed in seven programs (Argentina, 1981 and 1985; Brazil, 1986; Peru, 1985; Uruguay, 1982; Venezuela, 1993; and Mexico, 1995).

On the other hand, among the 18 structural reform programs carried out in 15 countries, structural reforms continued in 10, were halted or slowed in eight, and in only one case (Venezuela, 1993) were definitively reversed. In the cases of Argentina, Chile and Uruguay, which in the mid-1970s were the first to undertake reform, the structural reform process slowed down considerably after the severe crises in the early 1980s. Nevertheless, the three countries subsequently set in motion a second round of stabilization and reform: Chile in 1985, Argentina in 1990, and Uruguay in 1991. The rapid restarting of the reform process in Chile after the 1982 crisis may help explain why the country's economic performance during the 1980s was substantially better than that of Argentina and Uruguay.

Table 1.8 also shows the fate that stabilization and reform programs have had in conjunction with political changes. The picture that emerges is completely consistent with earlier studies of Latin American countries and other regions, and suggests that structural reforms are resistant to changes of government or to political circumstances even in those cases when the opposition to the government that initiated the reform takes office.

What does this evidence on the sustainability of stabilization and structural reform suggest? Although in many cases it is still too early to evaluate their sustainability—since many Latin American countries that have undertaken reforms have only recently entered into the period of tension, correction or crisis—some general patterns seem to emerge. With regard to stabilization, the evidence is not conclusive: around 40 percent of the stabilization episodes examined eventually failed. Nevertheless, the resilience of structural reforms to economic crises and political changes suggests that once the reform process is set in motion, it is very difficult to reverse. Based on this evidence, it can be said that there is a great deal of room for optimism about the sustainability of reforms in Latin America, despite the economic and political complexities inherent in this process.

Appendix. Economic Structural Indicators

	See chapter:	Argentina	Bahamas	Barbados	Belize	Bolivia	Brazil	Chile	Colombia	Costa Rica	Dom. Rep.	Ecuador	El Salvador	Guatemala
External sector	Trade													
Exchange rate premium, end of 1995[a]		0	5	1	5	0	1	6	2	2	4	2	11	0
Average tariff (simple average), 1995 (%)		13.9	30	11.8	na	9.7	12.7	11.4	11.4	11.7	17.8	11.2	9.2	10.8
Imports subject to nontariff barriers (% of value), post-reform, circa 1994		3.1	na	5	na	3.5	14.3	0.4	2.3	0	5	0	11	na
Membership in trade agreements, 1995		Mercosur, WTO	None	Caricom, WTO	Caricom, WTO	Andean Community, WTO	Mercosur, WTO	WTO	Andean Community, Group of Three, WTO	Central American Common Market, WTO	WTO	Andean Community	Central American Common Market, WTO	Central American Common Market, WTO
Tax policies, 1995 (%)	Tax													
Corporate income tax rate		30	na	40	35	25	25	15	30/35	30	30	25	25	30(1996)
Personal income tax rate		11/30	na	25/40	15-45	13	15/35	5/45	30/35	10/25	15/30	10/25	10/30	15/30(1996)
Value-added tax rate		21	na	None	15	13	7/25	18	16	10	8	10	13	10(1996)
Financial policies, 1996	Financial													
Are interest rates market determined? (deposit rate/loan rate)		All/Some	All/All	All/All	Some/All	All/All	All/Some	All/Some	All/All	All/Some	All/All	All/All	All/All	All/All
Reserve requirements on local currency demand deposits (%)		15	5	29	7	10	83	9	21	34	20	10	30	33.5
Reserve requirements on local currency time deposits(%)		15/10/5/0 (depending on maturity)	5	29	7	4	40/5/0 (depending on maturity)	3.6-0 (depending on maturity)	3	30	20	10	20	33.5
Reserve requirements on foreign currency time deposits (%)		15/10/5/0 (depending on maturity)	0	0	0	4	None[d]	0-30 (depending on maturity)	None[d]	10	20	10	30	None[d]
Status of commercial bank supervision		Reasonable	Reasonable	Reasonable	Reasonable	Needs some overhaul	Reasonable	Reasonable	Reasonable	Needs major overhaul	Reasonable	Needs some overhaul	Reasonable	Needs some overhaul
Privatization efforts	Privatization													
Number of transactions (total 1990-94)		123	6	6	4	28	45	14	16	4	0	9	11	0
Privatization revenues (total 1990-94, millions of US$)		17,119.7	25	51	58.7	21.7	8748.8	1,258.7	734.5	45.6	0	96.3	na	0
Privatization revenues (% of GDP, average 1990-94)		1.4	0.3	0.7	2.6	0.1	0.3	0.5	0.2	0.1	0	0.1	na	0
Labor market regulations, 1996	Labor													
Layoff expenses (after one year of work) (monthly wages)		3	0.5	1	0.75	4	2.4	2	2.5	2	0.5	5.25	1.25	1
Layoff expenses (after 10 years of work) (monthly wages)		12	1	5.8	3.5	13	15	11	25	9	6.9	23.5	10.25	10
Social security related contributions (% of wages)[b]		33.2	10.8	10.9	7.7	23.5	31	22	31.5	29	12.5	18.6	13.5	14.5
Pension system, 1995	Social security													
Retirement age, private sector (men/women)[c]		(60)62/(55)57	65/65	65/65	62/62	55/50	65/60	65/60	(60)62/(55)57	61/59	60/60	55/55	60/55	60/60
Social security contribution rate (employee/employer) (%)		11/16	2.55/6.25	3.15/3.15	na	6/6	9/20	13/none	3.37/10.12	2.5/4.75	2.5/7.5	7/2.39	1/2	1.5/3
Role for private pension funds		Complement public pillar	None	None	None	None	None	Mandatory	Compete with public system	None	None	None	None	None

Appendix. Economic Structural Indicators (Cont.)

	See chapter:	Guyana	Haiti	Honduras	Jamaica	Mexico	Nicaragua	Panama	Paraguay	Peru	Suriname	Trin. and Tob.	Uruguay	Venezuela
External sector	Trade													
Exchange rate premium, end of 1995[a]		3	36	0	4	1 (1996.I)	0	0	12	2	14	0	1	12
Average tariff (simple average), 1995 (%)		na	10	17.9	12.5	14.2	17.4	na	9.4	16.3	20	15	9.6	11.8
Imports subject to nontariff barriers (% of value), post-reform, circa 1994		3.9	0	na	0	19	0	na	4.6	na	na	na	na	2.8
Membership in trade agreements, 1995		Caricom, WTO	WTO	Central American Common Market, WTO	Caricom, WTO	NAFTA, Group of Three	Central American Common Market, WTO	None	Mercosur, WTO	Andean Community, WTO	Caricom	Caricom, WTO	Mercosur	Andean Community, Group of Three
Tax policies, 1995 (%)	Tax													
Corporate income tax rate		45	10/30	15/35/45/60	33.3	34	30	30/34	30	30	35/45	38	30	15/22/34
Personal income tax rate		33.3	10/30	9/40	25	3/35	7/30	3/30	0	15/30	14/50	5/38	0	6/34
Value-added tax rate		None	10	7	0/12.5	15	15	5	10	16	None	15	22	12.5
Financial policies, 1996	Financial													
Are interest rates market determined? (deposit rate/loan rate)		All/all	All/Some	All/All	Some/Some	All/Some	All/All	All/All	All/All	All/All	None/None	All/All	All/All	All/All
Reserve requirements on local currency demand deposits (%)		16	51	34	25	0	10	10	18	9	100	20	20	12
Reserve requirements on local currency time deposits (%)		14	51	34	22	0	10	5-0 (depending on maturity)	18	9	25-0 (depending on maturity)	20	20	12
Reserve requirements on foreign currency time deposits (%)		0	0	0	20	0	25	0	30	43.5	0	0	20	None[d]
Status of commercial bank supervision		Needs some overhaul	Needs major overhaul	Needs major overhaul	Needs some overhaul	Needs some overhaul	Reasonable	Needs major overhaul	Needs major overhaul	Reasonable	Needs major overhaul	Reasonable	Reasonable	Needs major overhaul
Privatization efforts	Privatization													
Number of transactions (total 1990-94)		19 (1989-95)	0	32	26	174	75	9	1	72	0	17	7	29
Privatization revenues (total 1990-94, millions of US$)		49.8	0	74.1	316	24,270.5	126.3	99.8	22	3,181.8	0	420.1	17	2,471
Privatization revenues (% of GDP, average 1990-94)		2.3	0	0.4	1.5	2.1	1.2	0.3	0.1	1.2	0	1.8	0	0.7
Labor market regulations, 1996	Labor													
Layoff expenses (after one year of work) (monthly wages)		1	1	2	0.5	4.2	3	1.85	1.5	2	0.5	2.5	1	3
Layoff expenses (after 10 years of work) (monthly wages)		6.9	3	13	1.5	10.7	22	8.5	8	20	5	6.25	6	23
Social security related contributions (% of wages)[b]		12.5	12	10.5	5	30	15	11.7	22.5	25	na	10.4	39	25.5
Pension system, 1995	Social security													
Retirement age, private sector (men/women)[c]		55/55	65/60	65/60	65/60	65/65	60/60	62/57	60/60	(60)65/(55)60		60/60	60/(55)60	60/55
Social security contribution rate (employee/employer) (%)		4.4/6	4/4	1/2	2.6/2.5	2.08/13	1.75/3.5	6.75/2.75	9.5/13	13.5/none	None	2.8/5.6	11.5/14.5	4/10
Role for private pension funds		None	None	None	None	Mandatory (since 1997)	None	None	None	Compete with public system		None	Complement public pillar	None

[a] Average of market (unofficial) exchange reates, including transaction costs, compared with the IMF official rate (rf).
[b] Comprises old age, disability, death, sickness, maternity, work injury, unemployment and family allowances.
[c] Numbers in parentheses are pre-reform.
[d] Foreign currency time deposits not allowed.

TRADE

LIBERALIZATION

ABSTRACT

In order to reduce price system distortions and improve efficiency, the countries of Latin America and the Caribbean have opened their economies to international trade, liberalized their foreign exchange systems, and entered into numerous integration agreements.

Trade and exchange rate liberalization in Latin America has been profound and swift:

• In one decade average tariffs have dropped from rates of 44.6 percent to 13.1 percent, and maximum rates have declined from 83.7 percent to 41 percent.

• Nontariff restrictions that affected 33.8 percent of imports now cover 11.4 percent.

• Multiple exchange rate systems common in the 1980s are now the exception, and constraints on international payments have been eliminated or greatly reduced. As a result, the price differential between the multiple foreign exchange markets has fallen on average from 72 percent in 1989 to only 2 percent.

The creation and deepening of trade agreements has been a key part of the liberalization process during the last decade, which has seen the following developments:

• MERCOSUR was created, while the Andean Community, the Central American Common Market and CARICOM were revitalized and are at different stages of consolidation as customs unions.

• Since 1990, some 20 bilateral agreements have been signed, some for universal and automatic liberalization (between Chile and Mexico and between Venezuela, Colombia and Ecuador), as well as free trade treaties whose scope includes trade in services in the Group of Three (Colombia, Mexico and Venezuela) and in the agreements between Mexico, Costa Rica and Bolivia.

• The North American Free Trade Agreement between the United States, Canada and Mexico was signed in 1992.

The main challenges for the integration process will be to extend it to trade in services and to guide it toward a transparent and effective institutional framework compatible with the rules of the World Trade Organization. Developing a Free Trade Area of the Americas will challenge the willingness and ability of the parties to negotiate, especially in view of the differing levels of development of the participating countries.

Advances in trade liberalization between countries and between groups of countries is moving ahead swiftly based on a strong commitment by political leaders. Preparatory work for the Trade Conference of the Americas is also continuing, but at a more measured pace than was foreseen at the meeting of heads of state in Miami. The European Union has also begun to work with groups of countries to hasten cooperation and establish free trade agreements. Taken together, these agreements stand to be mutually reinforcing, moving the region toward the goals established in the Uruguay Round.

INTRODUCTION

During the past ten years, the countries of Latin America and the Caribbean have profoundly reformed their foreign trade policy. Tariff and non-tariff trade restrictions have been reduced and controls on foreign exchange markets lifted. Although the extent of liberalization has varied from country to country, the foreign trade system of the region overall is now more free than it has been since the period before the Great Depression of the 1930s. Although this process has been primarily the result of unilateral decisions by countries of the region, the multilateral Uruguay Round negotiations and the wave of regional trade agreements during the 1990s have also played a role. The various forms of trade liberalization have fostered rapid growth of intraregional trade in recent years.

Although some countries in the region began their liberalization efforts earlier, the process has become widespread during the present decade. During the 1990s, the region's imports have risen rapidly while exports have increased much more slowly. This phenomenon is due largely to the reestablishment of capital flows and the revaluation of exchange rates, especially in the larger economies. Had this not occurred, liberalization would have brought about a much faster rise in exports. In any case, sustained export success will depend on productivity gains. Productivity, in turn, can be enhanced by microeconomic reforms that give stability and transparency to the regulatory framework, improve the formation of human capital and the functioning of the labor market, build up transportation infrastructure, extend financing and export support mechanisms, facilitate foreign investment and technology transfer, and allow markets to develop freely.

Regional integration offers conditions under which countries can deepen their commitments to trade liberalization, and creates an initial learning stage for new exports. In this manner, regional efforts can lay the groundwork for future liberalization toward external markets.

However, this process requires that integration move toward areas other than trade in goods, and that the institutional framework adopted include rules that are increasingly transparent, effective and compatible with those of the World Trade Organization. Furthermore, integration must be developed in a more global framework, making the most of future multilateral trade rounds.

The ambitious goal of building the Free Trade Area of the Americas (FTAA) before 2005, agreed upon by the hemisphere's heads of state at the Summit of the Americas in Miami in December 1994, will direct the integration process toward the principles set forth above. Nevertheless, the FTAA also entails challenges for countries in areas of negotiation, identification of trade opportunities, and capacity to adjust to changes in the productive structure involved in the integration process. This is a formidable challenge, especially given the different levels of development between the participants.

The region has made remarkable progress in liberalization of trade and economic integration. However, it is still too early to render judgment on the effects of liberalization across the spectrum of economic and social areas. The benefits of these processes can be assessed only in the medium and long run and will ultimately depend on the interaction between trade reform and other structural reforms.

OBJECTIVES

Trade liberalization seeks to eliminate or reduce policies that distort a country's price system and have a negative impact on the efficiency of resource allocation and productivity, and hence impair the country's economic growth and welfare. Trade reform processes generally include liberalizing constraints on trade in goods and liberalizing foreign exchange markets. Reducing constraints on trade includes lowering tariff levels on imports and exports, as well as reducing their dispersion by converting specific tariffs to ad valorem tariffs and substantially lowering or eliminating nontariff barriers. Exchange rate reform involves deregulating the foreign exchange market, unifying the exchange rate for all transactions, and allowing free access for all trade in goods and services. This process entails eliminating surcharges on the foreign exchange rate for imports and dismantling requirements for repatriating the proceeds of exports, differential taxes on dividends, and all other such measures that create differential costs for some trade activities and therefore entail multiple foreign exchange markets. Naturally, the scope and mix of liberalization policies adopted depend on a country's specific circumstances and objectives.

Reducing distortions through trade liberalization enables a developing country to become more efficient and productive by taking advantage of economies of scale through production for the world market; by attracting foreign investment in order to complement national factors of production; by better incorporating worldwide technological advances; and by improving the quality and selection of goods and services for consumers. Strictly from an administrative point of view, liberalization lowers transaction costs and makes the external sector more transparent by simplifying rules and procedures.

Naturally, the effect of trade liberalization in practice depends on the existence and behavior of many other domestic factors—including the initial conditions of the country and the nature of public policies in other areas of the economy—as well as external factors that affect the level and composition of a country's international trade. It is especially difficult to isolate the effects of trade liberalization in Latin America due to natural lags and to the fact that it has been combined both with other extensive structural reforms that affect the regional economy and with major changes in the international context. Hence, the direction and size of the changes in foreign trade that have taken place following the trade liberalization period in the region are only a partial result of trade reforms. Ultimately, they cannot provide the basis for a final verdict on the policies introduced by the countries of the region. However, the analysis in this chapter makes it clear that a profound change in the relationship of the region to the world economy has taken place.

CHRONOLOGY

For many decades, the region's trade policies were typified by high levels of protection and government involvement. This orientation, partly the legacy of reactions to the external crisis of the Great Depression and the subsequent slow recovery, emphasized the use of high import tariffs, a large number of tariff levels with a wide dispersion, tariff exceptions, and a great variety of devices for restricting and prohibiting the entry of goods. The foreign exchange system included multiple exchange rates, rationing of foreign exchange and other exchange restrictions to discriminate by type of import or export, and restriction on the movement of capital or payment for its services.

By the 1970s there was a tendency toward relaxing trade policy restrictions in some countries in the region, with liberalization experiments that were radical for the time in the Southern Cone countries, starting with Chile in the middle of decade and followed by Argentina and Uruguay. However, the burden of servicing the foreign debt and the profound crisis of the early 1980s were the principal factors that unleashed a dramatic redefinition of the region's trade policies.

At first the effects of the crisis ran counter to liberalization because of the reaction to balance of payments disequilibrium. Low availability of foreign exchange triggered higher import tariffs, greater discrimination in the way tariffs were set (turning to concepts such as the degree of economic needs), and especially a greater use of nontariff barriers. Increased use of multiple foreign exchange markets and restrictions on the movement of capital and factor payments characterized the exchange rate system.

Table 2.1 Chronology of Trade Liberalization, 1985-95								
1985	1986	1987	1988	1989	1990	1991	1992	1995
Chile Mexico	Bolivia Costa Rica	Jamaica	Guatemala Guyana	Argentina El Salvador Paraguay Trinidad and Tobago Venezuela	Brazil Dominican Republic Ecuador Honduras Peru	Uruguay Colombia	Barbados	Panama

Source: IDB Integration and Regional Programs Department.

Nevertheless, the economic collapse of the 1980s laid the foundation for a fundamental change of direction in the region's trade policy. The protectionist model, already seriously questioned, now lost credibility. This allowed for emergence of a consensus around alternative liberal approaches aimed at making greater involvement in the world market possible. This change in approach was reinforced by major pressures through the 1980s by creditor nations to generate foreign exchange for debt service. Most countries then began a new phase of economic expansion between 1984 and 1986. This economic reactivation, though modest, was an important stimulus to initiate the liberalization of trade, just as the earlier crisis had prompted the restrictions. Indeed, practically all the countries began significant programs to liberalize their trade regimes between 1985 and 1991, with 1989 marking the beginning of trade reforms for the region as a whole (weighted by the GDP of the countries) (Table 2.1).

The gradual decline of the foreign debt burden and the return to net capital inflows into the region enabled most countries to liberalize their exchange rate systems during the 1990-91 period, thereby completing the liberalization of trade restrictions. In general, the countries of the region currently have the most liberalized trade and foreign exchange system that they have had since the 1920s.

Liberalizing trade has also been pursued by means of regional integration initiatives. Latin America has a long tradition of promoting integration. In fact, the first formal integration schemes appeared shortly after World War II. However, these initiatives enjoyed only limited success, partly because high trade restrictions predominated when they were created. During the crisis of the 1980s, imports fell sharply and simultaneously across the region, reflected by the collapse of intraregional trade and institutional deterioration within the integration groups. However, the gradual recovery of the regional economy since 1984, along with major unilateral trade liberalization efforts by all the countries, stimulated a recovery of intraregional trade. Moreover, during the 1990s, there has been renewed interest in integration, with the emergence of many new trade agreements and an extraordinary expansion of intraregional trade. In contrast to past integration agreements, which were used as tools to isolate economies from international competition, these new initiatives have served as an instrument to augment trade liberalization and prepare countries for the challenges of growing economic globalization.

The countries of Latin America are now practicing what has been called "open regionalism." Within the bounds of what is permitted by the WTO, a gradual opening of unilateral trade is combined with a more radical opening of intraregional trade. When countries sign an intraregional free trade agreement, they are also indicating their commitment to continue to move ahead with overall trade liberalization. The reciprocal treatment and institutional guarantee of market access gained with free trade agreements often makes it politically possible to make decisions in favor of general trade liberalization which otherwise would have met resistance. In fact, some of the recent free trade agreements constitute an effort to go beyond WTO standards not only in the traditional area of market access but also on other trade issues, such as services, investment and intellectual property rights. On the other hand, the proliferation of free trade agreements runs the risk of reducing the transparency of trade relations, increasing overall administrative costs, and particularly, differentiating costs on the basis of the merchandise's country of origin. Nevertheless, to the extent that regional agreements stimulate trade liberalization efforts in each country, as the WTO has said, "regional and multilateral trade liberalization efforts are complements rather than alternatives within the objective of achieving freer and more open trade." In any case, the desired outcome would be the multilateral elimination of tariffs around the world within the WTO process. Indeed, there are proposals to reach that objective for the WTO in 2015.

DISMANTLING TRADE BARRIERS

From 1985-95, the vast majority of Latin American countries carried out significant reforms by dismantling import barriers and adopting export promotion policies. Import liberalization has been carried out on various levels: first, as a result of the multilateral commitments of the Uruguay Round of the GATT; second, in unilateral or "autonomous" reform programs; and finally, through the signing of numerous bilateral or subregional free trade agreements, culminating in the recent effort to fashion the FTAA.

Liberalization of Trade Restrictions in the Multilateral Realm

The Uruguay Round negotiations, which began at the Punta del Este Conference in 1986 and concluded with the signing of the Morocco Final

Document in December 1993, were concerned with two basic aims. The first was to assure better access to markets by reducing or eliminating obstacles to trade through such measures as reducing import tariffs, lowering nontariff assistance for agriculture, eliminating quantitative bilateral restrictions, and lowering obstacles to trade in services.[1] The second was to make the new levels of access to markets more legally secure by establishing standards, procedures and institutions with a wider scope of authority.

The result of these ambitious multilateral negotiations with regard to tariffs was an average reduction in industrialized countries of 38 percent weighted by trade. The effect of these tariff reductions will be to considerably increase the percentage of imports coming from developing countries. Once the concessions agreed upon are applied, tariff-free access for developing countries, including those of Latin America, will rise from 12 to 37 percent for imports into the United States, from 24 to 36 percent into the European Union, from 26 to 43 percent into Canada, and from 25 to 48 percent into Japan. Nevertheless, the average post-Uruguay Round tariffs affecting the most important export products for Latin America—such as farm products, textiles and clothing, and leather goods and shoes—remained at levels considerably higher than average tariffs for the entire range of products, since tariffs were set very high as a result of the conversion of quantitative restrictions into tariffs. The case of agricultural products is especially significant, as some farm products subject to specific or mixed tariffs involve equivalent ad valorem rates of around 500 percent.

From the standpoint of the region's contribution to the commitments to dismantle import barriers, the following points should be highlighted: quantitative restrictions and nontariff

---

[1] The Uruguay Round was unusual in that it also incorporated new issues into trade liberalization negotiation: trade in services, investments and intellectual property.

Table 2.2 Tariff Consolidation at the Uruguay Round

(In percent)

Country groups	Industrial goods				Agricultural goods			
	Number of consolidated tariff items		Value of imports in consolidated items		Number of consolidated tariff items		Value of imports in consolidated items	
	Before	After	Before	After	Before	After	Before	After
Developed countries	78	99	94	99	58	100	81	100
North America	99	100	99	100	92	100	94	100
Western Europe	79	82	98	98	45	100	87	100
Developing economies	21	73	13	61	17	100	22	100
Latin America	38	100	57	100	36	100	74	100
Africa	13	69	26	90	12	100	8	100
Asia	16	68	32	70	15	100	36	100
Transition economies	73	98	74	96	57	100	59	100
Central Europe	63	98	68	97	49	100	54	100
Total	43	83	68	87	35	100	63	100

Source: IDB Integration and Regional Programs Department, based on data from the World Trade Organization.

measures have been almost completely eliminated; the tariffs actually applied have relatively low averages; and especially important, practically all tariff lines have been bound (Table 2.2).[2] Thus, Jamaica, Uruguay and Venezuela bound 100 percent of their tariff items; Argentina, Brazil, Chile, Colombia and Peru, 99 percent; and Mexico, over 95 percent. Tariff bindings established tariffs below 30 percent in Chile, and below 40 percent in the other countries mentioned. These levels are especially significant when compared to the tariff bindings existing before the Uruguay Round began. For Latin America as a whole, industrial products had only consolidated 38 percent of their tariff lines, equivalent to 57 percent of imports. For agricultural products, the percentages were 36 and 74 percent, respectively. GATT tariff bindings are a key element for eliminating uncertainty for producers and exporters. Tariff binding also play a key role in lending credibility nationally and internationally to unilateral reform programs carried out by countries individually.[3]

Finally, it is important to highlight the inclusion of 25 countries of the region into the recently created WTO, one of the main results of the negotiations. The WTO will facilitate the application of those negotiations, compliance, and procedures for resolving disputes.

Unilateral Trade Liberalization

Reduction of levels of tariff protection. Until the early 1980s, the levels of tariff protection in Latin America were characterized by high averages, a high proportion of products subject to the maximum tariffs (some of them reaching 300 percent), high indices of tariff dispersion, and tariffs staggered according to the degree of processing in production. One of the most important elements of the reform process has been the sharp reduction in the levels of tariff protection on imports. Such protection, in conjunction with other trade restriction measures, constitutes one of the main sources of distortion between domestic prices and international prices, leading to significant inefficiencies in the allocation of resources. Reforms have almost completely replaced specific or mixed tariffs with ad valorem tariffs, which has resulted in more stable percentage levels of protection. Currently, only Argentina, and to a lesser extent Venezuela, maintain specific tariffs for some

[2] With the tariff binding at a particular level, the country agrees not to raise that tariff above the limit established (except by negotiation with the affected trading partners).
[3] One effect of tariff binding was observed in Brazil. In 1995, a transitory rise in some tariffs led to problems with the WTO because it exceeded the levels bound in the Uruguay Round.

products. Taking the region as a whole, average tariffs declined from 44.6 percent in the pre-reform years to 13.1 percent in 1995 (Figure 2.1). Only Honduras, Nicaragua, Peru and the Dominican Republic have tariffs higher than 15 percent, although none has tariffs over 20 percent (Figure 2.2).

While liberalization has taken place worldwide, there are still major differences among regions both in terms of the depth of reform and protection levels. Latin America is one of the regions where this process has been most substantial (Figure 2.3). The average maximum tariffs applied in the region have fallen from 83.7 percent to 41 percent. In the pre-reform period, the maximum tariffs in more than half of the countries in the region were over 100 percent; currently only two countries apply those levels, and only on a small number of products. This process of gradually eliminating tariff barriers was especially intense from 1985-90, when the average regional tariff fell from 40 to 15 percent (Figure 2.1). For most of the countries being considered, tariff reduction took place over a two to three-year period, and reductions were on the order of 50 percent.

Another important feature of the liberalization process has been the gradual adoption of more uniform tariff structures, which reduces tariff layers and, consequently, offers flatter real protection levels. Uniform tariff systems offer important advantages in terms of administration and transparency, preventing tariff policy from being manipulated by certain sectors capable of applying pressure. It was precisely this type of pressure that led in the past to high protection levels and widely dispersed tariff structures, resulting in an overall welfare loss and uncertainty in production and investment decisions. On average, the levels of tariff dispersion in absolute terms declined from 20.9 percent in the pre-reform years to 7.1 percent at present. Furthermore, a good portion of the significant lists of ex-

ceptions that traditionally existed in most countries of the region has been eliminated, and hence nominal levels more closely reflect duties actually collected on imports. Despite this process of lowering and leveling tariff structures, however, there are still significant differences in protection levels by sectors of production (Figure 2.4).

The dismantling of nontariff barriers. As previously mentioned, the Latin American countries traditionally used extensive nontariff measures to control imports. These included setting minimum

FIGURE 2.1

Tariff Liberalization in Latin America, 1985-95

(In percent)

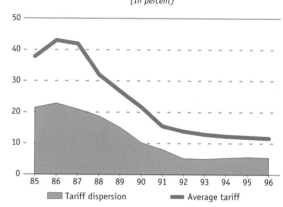

Source: IDB Integration and Regional Programs Department, based on official data from ALADI countries, weighted by imports.

FIGURE 2.2

Tariff Reduction in Latin America

(In percent)

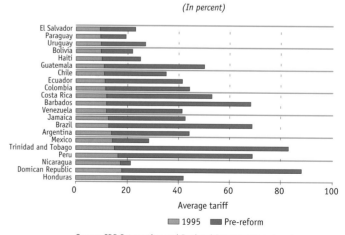

Source: IDB Integration and Regional Programs Department.

prices, automatic license arrangements, nonauto-matic licenses, use of quotas, import prohibitions, monopolistic measures in the administration of imports, and other technical measures. The next section wil look at financial measures commonly used as nontariff barriers, such as advanced payment obligations, multiple exchange rates, and restrictive allocation of foreign exchange.

During the pre-reform period, most countries required (for practically all import transactions) prior licenses in order to assure that imports did not surpass pre-set quotas. These levels could be modified by the authorities throughout the course of the year in response to foreign exchange availability. Thus, license systems were an effective instrument for administrative control to deal with balance of payment problems.

Quantitative limits on imports were gradually eliminated both unilaterally and within the framework of multilateral commitments assumed during the Uruguay Round. The gradual elimination of quota systems on imports, and their conversion into tariffs prior to their reduction, had the initial effect of raising revenues from custom duties and therefore limiting opposition to tariff reform. Nevertheless, when both instruments were simultaneously reduced, problems arose in the fiscal domain, even though the reform had greater credibility. In Argentina, Bolivia, Colombia, Ecuador, Honduras and Peru, quotas were reduced at the same time as tariffs were lowered. In Brazil, Jamaica and Mexico, quotas were lowered before tariffs. The opposite took place in Costa Rica and Venezuela. Taking a regional average for those countries for which there is information, nontariff measures that affected 33.8 percent of imports in the pre-reform period subsequently declined to

cover 11.4 percent (Figure 2.5a). The number of tariff lines affected by these measures fell from 29.6 to 1.6 percent (Figure 2.5b). While it is true that there has been a clear tendency to use control measures based more on prices than on quantities, there are still areas of trade regulation that may be potential sources of trade restriction, such as government purchasing arrangements, or the inappropriate use of anti-dumping measures, technical standards, or certain policies on competition.

FIGURE 2.3

Average Tariff, 1985-90 and 1990-93

(In percent)

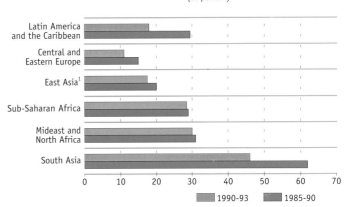

[1] Excludes China.
Source: World Bank, *Global Economic Prospects and the Developing Countries* (1996).

FIGURE 2.4

Average Tariff by Type of Good, 1995

(In percent)

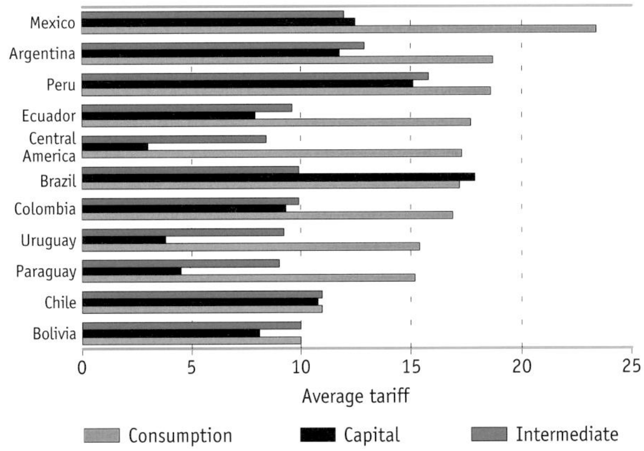

Source: IDB Integration and Regional Programs Department.

Export promotion policies: Chile and Costa Rica. Export promotion is an integral part of trade reform, and is one of its medium- and long-term objectives. The economic opening sought by trade reforms encompasses several measures for promoting exports, including (i) market measures, such as tariff reductions; (ii) fiscal incentives; and (iii) institutional measures, such as technical assistance and personnel training at the various levels (production, sales, and marketing of exports), support for innovation and technology transfer, establishment of appropriate legal frameworks, and measures to orient the business culture toward exporting to new markets.

Among the most successful export promotion programs have been those of Chile and Costa Rica. The exports of these two countries, which have open economies, have displayed high growth rates and diversification both in terms of their products and destination markets. Both have combined "implicit" export-promotion policies (i.e., exchange policy) with imaginative selective and institutional promotion policies.

Chile and Costa Rica have used fiscal incentives to increase exports. In Chile, a system of returning a percentage of the FOB value of exports, according to different exports value for each firm, is especially beneficial for small and medium exporters. Three export incentive arrangements have been utilized in Costa Rica (two of which are still in effect): export contracts, which involve granting exemptions from tariffs on a proportional percentage of the FOB value of exports that have a minimum of value added in the country (this incentive was eliminated in 1996; see Box 2.1); the temporary admission regime *(maquila),* which exempts inputs necessary for manufacturing products for export to other markets from all tariffs and taxes; and free trade zones, with the same benefits as those of the temporary admission regime plus 100 percent exemption for repatriated profits, and authorization to sell up to 40 percent of production on the local market.

In addition to trade liberalization and fis-

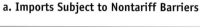

FIGURE 2.5

Nontariff Barrier Reduction in Latin America

(In percent)

a. Imports Subject to Nontariff Barriers

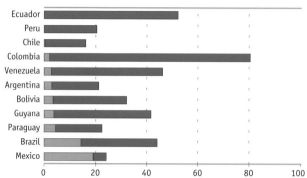

b. Items Subject to Nontariff Barriers

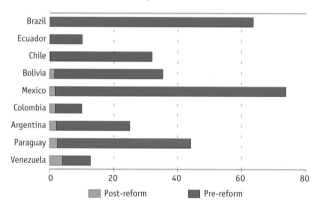

Source: IDB Integration and Regional Programs Department.

cal incentives, export promotion has included an institutional component, without which market conditions and fiscal incentives would not be utilized efficiently. Public and private institutions have played a fundamental role in export promotion through programs to identify markets and to provide technical assistance in the production, sales and marketing of goods. In Chile, these institutions have included the Chile Foundation, CORFO (Corporación de Fomento—Chilean Development Corporation), and Pro Chile. In Costa Rica, an example is the Coalition for Development Incentives and the Export Promotion Center for Costa Rica.

LIBERALIZATION OF EXCHANGE RATE SYSTEMS

In order to understand the circumstances under which exchange rate liberalization is taking place in Latin America, it is useful to distinguish between three periods of exchange rate systems operation: (i) the sporadic balance of payment problems and protectionist policies before 1980; (ii) the critical balance of payments situation resulting from the foreign debt crisis of the 1980s; and (iii) the return to external capital flows and liberalization of the exchange rate market from 1990 to the present. Table 2.3 presents the foreign exchange markets of each country in the region in 1979, 1984 and 1995 as representative moments for each of those periods.

Period of sporadic balance of payments problems and protectionist policies (pre-1980). Exchange rate systems during this period were influenced by the balance of payments situation, inflationary conditions, and prevailing economic policies. The predominant exchange rate system, because most countries had manageable inflation situations, was a fixed exchange rate vis-à-vis the dollar (see Table 2.3, 1979). The exchange rate only suffered sporadic although often quite sharp devaluation. A smaller number of countries, including the largest (Argentina, Brazil, Colombia and Peru), which were experiencing high inflation rates, already had more flexible systems.

Given the abundant supply of external financing, most countries did not have multiple exchange rate systems. However, the prevailing protectionist philosophy in the 1970s and, in some cases, worsening terms of trade due to oil price increases, prompted some countries to establish multiple exchange rates that made distinctions for both the type of import and export, between exports and imports, and whether or not they were for exchange rate transactions related to movements of capital or payment for its services (Figure 2.6). Given that this philosophy was opposed to the free movement of capital, most countries maintained restrictions on the capital transactions of their residents and required exporters to repatriate foreign exchange resulting from their exports. The obligation to pay a surcharge on imports was widespread, and some countries required deposits in advance for importers.

In 1979, the exchange rate premium, which reflects the distortions that the exchange rate imposes on a country's price system, was only 4 percent on average for the region, although some countries (such as Nicaragua, Guyana and El Salvador) had large premiums (between 50 and 100 percent, see Figure 2.7 and Table 2.4).[4]

Period of critical balance of payments problems resulting from foreign debt problems (the 1980s). Initially during the foreign debt crisis, an attempt was made to deal with the foreign exchange shortage by setting up multiple exchange rate systems that favored certain imports and sought to promote certain exports. The multiple exchange rate system spread to most countries (Figure 2.6) and was carried out in a more complex manner than during the previous period. All countries except Panama established restrictions on payments for capital movement and requirements for the repatriation of the value of exports. In many cases surcharges on imports and pre-payment deposits were also set up.

During this crisis-ridden period, inflation problems spread to almost all countries in the region, so the nominal dollar-parity exchange rate system ceased being practical and was replaced by various forms that made the exchange rate more flexible, enabling it to respond quickly to the na-

---

[4] The exchange rate premium is calculated on the basis of the free or black market exchange rates published by Currency Data and Intelligence, Inc. This premium reflects the difference between the average of the multiple exchange rates (including the black market rate if there is one, plus the exchange transaction costs to which they give rise) vis-à-vis the official exchange rate (which may coincide with that of the market). An index of 100 signifies that there is no difference. An index over 100 indicates distortions in the exchange rate market, which in turn generate other distortions in the country's price system; in this sense it is widely used in economic literature. The exchange rate premium of Latin America and the Caribbean is the weighted (by the value of foreign trade) average of the premiums of each country.

Table 2.3 Exchange Rate Arrangements and Currency Restrictions

(End of year)

1979

	CARICOM							Andean Community					MERCOSUR				CACM					Other				
	Bhs	Brb	Blz	Guy	Jam	Sur	Tto	Bol	Col	Ecu	Per	Ven	Arg	Bra	Pry	Ury	Cri	Els	Gtm	Hnd	Nic	Chi	Do	Hti	Mex	Pan
Exchange rate arrangement																										
Pegged to the U.S. dollar	X	X	na	X	X	X	X	-	-	X	-	X	-	-	X	-	X	X	X	X	X	X	X	X	-	X
More flexible																										
Adjusted according to a set of indicators	-	-	na	-	-	-	-	-	X	-	-	-	-	X	-	-	-	-	-	-	-	-	-	-	-	-
Other managed floating	-	-	na	-	X	-	-	X	-	-	X	-	X	-	-	X	X	X	-	-	-	X	-	-	X	-
Independently floating	-	-	na	-	-	-	-	X	-	-	-	-	-	-	-	-	-	-	-	-	-	-	-	-	-	-
Multiple exchange rates																										
Different for capital or nonvisible transactions	X	-	na	-	-	-	-	X	X	X	X	-	X	X	X	X	-	-	-	-	X	-	X	X	-	-
More than one rate for imports	-	-	na	-	-	-	-	-	X	-	X	-	X	X	X	X	X	X	-	-	X	X	X	X	-	-
More than one rate for exports	-	-	na	-	-	-	-	X	X	-	-	-	X	X	X	X	-	-	-	-	X	-	X	-	-	-
Different import and export rates	-	-	na	-	-	-	X	X	X	X	X	-	X	X	X	X	X	-	-	X	X	X	X	-	-	-
Payment restrictions																										
For current transactions	-	X	na	X	X	-	-	X	X	X	-	-	X	X	-	-	X	X	-	-	X	X	X	-	-	-
For capital transactions[1]	X	X	na	X	X	X	X	X	X	X	-	-	X	X	X	-	X	X	-	-	X	X	X	…	-	-
Extra charges on imports																										
Import surcharges	-	-	na	X	X	X	-	X	X	X	-	-	X	-	X	X	X	X	-	X	X	X	X	X	X	X
Deposit prior to import	-	-	na	-	X	-	-	X	X	X	-	-	-	-	-	X	X	X	-	-	X	X	X	-	-	-
Mandatory foreign exchange repatriation for exports	X	X	na	X	X	X	X	X	X	X	X	X	X	X	X	X	X	X	X	X	X	X	X	X	X	X

1984[a]

	CARICOM							Andean Community					MERCOSUR				CACM					Other				
	Bhs	Brb	Blz	Guy	Jam	Sur	Tto	Bol	Col	Ecu	Per	Ven	Arg	Bra	Pry	Ury	Cri	Els	Gtm	Hnd	Nic	Chi	Do	Hti	Mex	Pan
Exchange rate arrangement																										
Pegged to the U.S. dollar	X	X	X	X	-	X	X	-	-	-	-	X	-	-	X	-	-	X	X	X	X	-	X	X	-	X
More flexible																										
Adjusted according to a set of indicators	-	-	-	-	-	-	-	-	X	-	X	-	-	X	-	-	X	-	-	-	-	X	-	-	-	-
Other managed floating	-	-	-	X	X	-	-	-	-	X	-	-	X	-	-	X	-	-	-	-	-	-	-	-	X	-
Independently floating	-	-	-	-	-	-	-	X	-	-	-	-	-	-	-	-	-	-	-	-	-	-	-	-	-	-
Multiple exchange rates																										
Different for capital or nonvisible transactions	X	-	-	X	-	X	-	X	X	X	X	X	X	X	X	X	X	X	-	X	X	X	X	-	X	-
More than one rate for imports	-	-	-	X	X	X	X	X	X	X	X	X	X	X	X	X	X	-	-	X	X	X	X	X	X	-
More than one rate for exports	-	-	-	X	X	X	X	X	X	X	X	X	X	X	X	X	X	X	-	X	X	X	X	X	X	-
Different import and export rates	-	-	-	X	X	X	X	X	X	X	X	X	X	X	X	X	X	X	-	X	X	X	X	X	X	-
Payment restrictions																										
For current transactions	-	X	-	X	X	X	X	X	X	X	X	-	X	X	X	X	X	X	-	X	X	X	X	-	X	-
For capital transactions[1]	X	X	-	X	X	X	X	X	X	X	X	-	X	X	X	X	X	X	-	X	X	X	X	X	X	-
Extra charges on imports																										
Import surcharges	-	-	X	X	-	X	X	X	X	X	X	-	X	-	X	-	X	X	-	-	X	X	X	-	X	X
Deposit prior to import	-	-	X	-	-	X	X	X	X	X	X	-	X	-	X	X	-	-	-	X	-	X	X	-	X	-
Mandatory foreign exchange repatriation for exports	X	X	X	X	X	X	X	X	X	X	X	X	X	X	X	X	X	X	X	X	X	X	X	X	X	X

Table 2.3 Exchange Rate Arrangements and Currency Restrictions (continued)

(End of year)

1995[b]

	CARICOM							Andean Community					MERCOSUR				CACM					Other				
	Bhs	Brb	Blz	Guy	Jam	Sur	Tto	Bol	Col	Ecu	Per	Ven	Arg	Bra	Pry	Ury	Cri	Els	Gtm	Hnd	Nic	Chi	Do	Hti	Mex	Pan
Exchange rate arrangement																										
Pegged to the U.S. dollar	X	X	X	-	-	-	-	-	-	-	-	X	X	-	-	-	-	-	-	-	-	-	-	-	-	X
More flexible																										
Adjusted according to a set of indicators	-	-	-	-	-	-	-	-	-	-	-	-	-	-	-	-	X	-	-	-	X	X	-	-	-	-
Other managed floating	-	-	-	-	-	-	-	-	X	X	-	-	-	X	-	X	X	X	-	X	-	-	X	-	-	-
Independently floating	-	-	-	X	X	X	X	X	-	-	X	-	-	-	X	-	-	-	X	-	-	-	-	X	X	-
Multiple exchange rates																										
Different for capital or nonvisible transactions	-	-	-	X	-	-	-	X	X	-	-	-	-	X	-	-	-	-	-	-	-	X	-	-	-	-
More than one rate for imports	-	-	-	X	-	-	-	X	-	-	-	-	-	X	-	-	-	-	-	-	-	-	-	-	-	-
More than one rate for exports	-	-	-	X	-	-	-	X	-	-	-	-	-	X	-	-	-	-	-	-	-	-	-	-	-	-
Different import and export rates	-	-	-	X	-	-	-	X	-	-	-	-	-	X	-	-	-	-	-	-	-	-	-	-	-	-
Payment restrictions																										
For current transactions	X	X	X	-	-	X	X	-	X	-	-	X	X	X	-	X	-	-	-	-	-	X	X	X	X	-
For capital transactions[1]	X	X	X	X	-	X	X	-	-	-	-	X	-	X	X	X	-	X	-	-	X	X	X	X	X	-
Extra charges on imports																										
Import surcharges	-	X	X	-	-	X	X	-	-	X	X	X	X	-	-	X	-	-	-	-	X	X	X	-	-	X
Deposit prior to import	-	-	-	-	-	-	-	-	-	-	-	-	-	-	-	-	-	-	-	-	-	-	-	-	-	-
Mandatory foreign exchange																										
repatriation for exports	X	X	X	X	-	X	-	X	X	X	-	X	X	X	X	X	X	X	-	X	X	X	X	X	-	X

X A feature of the exchange rate or trade arrangement.

- Not a feature of the exchange rate or trade arrangement.

[1] Funds owned by residents.

[a] Or the year of the greatest currency restrictions between 1980 and 1990. Exceptions are Bolivia (1985), Costa Rica (1985), Ecuador (1987), Guyana (1990), Haiti (1990), Honduras (1988), Jamaica (1987), Trinidad and Tobago (1985) and Uruguay (1985).

[b] 1994 IMF data projected on the basis of the Economist Intelligence Unit estimates.

Source: IDB Integration and Regional Programs Department, based on IMF data, *Exchange Arrangements and Exchange Restrictions Annual Report* and EIU Business Latin America.

FIGURE 2.6
Exchange Rate Arrangements and International Reserves, 1983-95

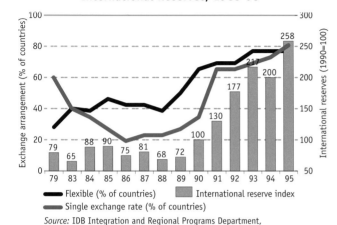

Source: IDB Integration and Regional Programs Department, based on IMF data.

FIGURE 2.7
Real Effective Exchange Rate and Exchange Rate Premium, 1975-95

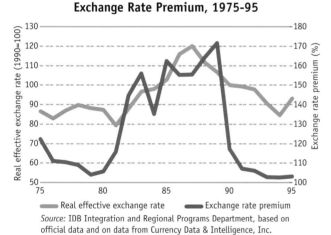

Source: IDB Integration and Regional Programs Department, based on official data and on data from Currency Data & Intelligence, Inc.

Table 2.4	Exchange Rate Premium[1]		
(In percent)			
	1979	1989	1995
Argentina	100	203	100
Bahamas	103	115	105
Barbados	104	114	101
Belize	116	124	105
Bolivia	102	101	100
Brazil	108	273	101
Chile	105	119	106
Colombia	102	114	102
Costa Rica	114	116	102
Dominican Republic	130	166	104
Ecuador	108	116	102
El Salvador	156	185	111
Guatemala	115	109	100
Guyana	182	188	103
Haiti	na	335	136
Honduras	na	220	100
Jamaica	122	128	104
Mexico	101	111	101[a]
Nicaragua	199	105	100
Panama	100	100	100
Paraguay	109	131	112
Peru	101	285	102
Suriname	120	852	114
Trinidad and Tobago	123	156	100
Uruguay	99	112	101
Venezuela	100	113	112
Latin America and the Caribbean[2]	**104**	**172**	**102**

[1] Market or black market rate of the U.S. dollar (official rate is equal to 100). Figures are for the end of the indicated year.
[2] Trade-weighted average. Does not include Nicaragua or Suriname.
[a] March 1996.
Source: IDB Integration and Regional Programs Department, based on data from Currency Data & Intelligence, Inc.

tional currency's continual loss of purchasing power. Countries that held the fixed dollar-parity exchange rate found themselves pressured to devalue their currency more frequently than during the previous decade and, in some instances, had to carry out large and traumatic devaluations. Many countries, including those with the largest economies, when faced with tremendous foreign exchange shortages, devalued their currency by huge amounts in real terms, such that the real average exchange rate of the region from 1983-92 was much greater than the rate prevailing between

1974 and 1982 (Figure 2.7).[5] The higher real average exchange rate stimulated export recovery and aided the economic expansion of the region that began in 1984. Nevertheless, despite the devaluation of the real effective exchange rate throughout the decade, there was an almost constant in-

[5] Figure 2.7 presents the movement of the effective real exchange rate in the region, which is calculated as the weighted (by the value of each country's foreign trade) average of the real effective exchange rate of each country. These are the average (weighted by trade) of the bilateral exchange rate of the country with its trading partners. These effective exchange rates are presented in units of national currency per unit of foreign currency, in such a way that a rise in its value represents a devaluation.

Table 2.5 Trade Performance in Three Periods

(In percent)

	Pre-crisis 1974-79	Transition 1984-88	Liberalization 1989-95
GDP average annual growth rate			
LAC	4.9	2.3	2.3
World	3.0	3.0	2.6
LAC/World	163.0	77.0	88.0
Average annual growth rate of exports			
LAC	4.1	5.2	6.1
World	4.7	6.9	6.5
LAC/World	87.2	73.3	93.8
Export/GDP ratio			
LAC	10.7	13.4	16.7
World	16.7	20.2	24.6
LAC/World	64.0	66.0	68.0
Average annual growth rate of imports			
LAC	7.5	5.7	10.3
World	4.7	6.9	6.5
LAC/World	159.6	82.6	158.5
Import/GDP ratio			
LAC	14.3	10.6	16.6
World	16.7	20.2	24.6
LAC/World	86.0	52.0	67.0
Average export/import ratio			
LAC	74.9	126.6	103.2
Trade balance/GDP			
LAC	-3.6	2.8	0.1
Total trade/GDP			
LAC	25.0	23.9	33.3
World	33.4	40.4	49.2
LAC/World	75.0	59.0	68.0
Real effective exchange rate (1990=100), annual average			
LAC	86.9	110.1	98.0
Real effective exchange rate change			
LAC	1.3	2.8	-2.6

Source: IDB Integration and Regional Programs Department and INTAL.

Table 2.6 Regional Distribution of Trade

(In percent)

	Average 1984-88		Average 1993-94	
	Exports	Imports	Exports	Imports
Intraregional				
Latin America and the Caribbean	12.3	16.8	19.5	16.9
Extraregional				
North America	41.3	39.5	48.2	47.4
Europe	24.8	22.2	17.6	19.2
East Asia	7.5	8.5	7.4	10.5
Rest of world	14.2	13.1	7.4	5.9
Total	100.0	100.0	100.0	100.0

Source: IDB Integration and Regional Programs Department and INTAL.

crease in the use of multiple exchange rates, which was reflected in a maximum exchange rate premium of 72 percent in 1989 (Table 2.4). By way of exception, only four countries had a premium that was lower than 10 percent.

Period of return to external capital flows and liberalization of the foreign exchange market (1990 to the present). An era of exchange rate systems began in 1991-92, based on an economic policy favoring liberalization. Liberalization was facilitated because of the easing of foreign debt problems, because the positive export experience stimulated the high exchange rate, and fundamentally, because of the renewed flow of foreign capital to the countries of the region. Currently, most countries have unified exchange rate systems (Table 2.3 and Figure 2.6). Especially noteworthy are the cases of Mexico and Argentina, which, despite balance of payments problems in 1995, maintained the progress they had achieved in liberalizing their foreign exchange markets.

The only instance of a notable regression in the process of freeing the exchange rate is Venezuela between 1994 and mid-1996. Even in the countries that in Table 2.3 exhibit multiple exchange rates in 1995 (or restrictions on capital movement payments, or import surcharges) the system is much more liberalized than it was in the previous decade. Such is the case, for exam-

Box 2.1   Two Cases of Export Success

Salmon breeding in Chile and the raising of nontraditional agricultural products in Costa Rica provide two concrete illustrations of the results of export promotion.

Practically unknown in Chile in 1980, salmon breeding has become one of the country's top export activities, making Chile one of the main salmon exporters worldwide. Between 1986 and 1993, Chilean salmon exports multiplied 58 times over, rising from $5 million to $291 million. At the same time, salmon species and destination markets were diversified. Of the 60,728 tons exported in 1993, 24,833 were Atlantic salmon, 17,960 Pacific salmon, and 16,670 were trout. Markets were diversified after 1989, as Japan moved ahead of the United States to become the main market, absorbing 56 percent of exports by 1993.

Salmon breeding became successful in Chile following the involvement of the Chile Foundation, a mixed government and private agency devoted to research and technology transfer. The Chile Foundation introduced intensive salmon raising in floating cages in the late 1970s, a technology that was then producing good results in the Northern Hemisphere. The Chile Foundation provided impetus with its own company, which had various production centers, and, at the same time, gave technical assistance for setting up other Chilean companies. In 1993, there were 120 national and foreign companies devoted to salmon and trout breeding, employing over 10,000 persons directly and indirectly.

The success was also attributable to the marketing support provided by the Salmon and Trout Breeders Association together with Pro Chile, a government export promotion agency. These institutions participated in fish product trade fairs and sent Chilean entrepreneurs on trade missions to present their products to potential clients and trade publications. Also important was the lobbying effort by Pro Chile to defuse threats against Chilean salmon for alleged dumping in the United States.

In Costa Rica, exports of nontraditional agricultural products (NTAP) to other markets outside Central America rose from $26 million in 1982 to $335 million in 1993, an average annual increase of 24 percent. NTAPs include products such as mangos, papayas, hearts of palm, guanabanas, flowers, ornamental plants, strawberries, melons, macadamia nuts, peppers, asparagus and pineapples. Export of these products received a great deal of support from government and private institutions such as the Coalition for Development Initiatives (CINDE), the Center for Export Promotion (CENPRO), the University of Costa Rica, the Center for Tropical Agriculture Research and Extension, and the Ministry of Agriculture.

To overcome obstacles associated with exporting NTAPs, measures were introduced to address storage and transportation infrastructure, chemical wastes, management and post-harvest processing, management in export marketing, and credit needs. Many of these problems were tackled through technical assistance programs to provide information, investment and training for the institutions involved. For example, in the area of research, new and more profitable species of flowers and new varieties of strawberries were introduced and developed, new hot water treatment technologies were developed for improved mango preservation, and the quality of the cacao seed and flowers was improved genetically. Other products, such as fruit pulp, juices and concentrates were developed as byproducts of tropical fruits. Extension services were set up to help small producers with post-harvest management and quality control up to the time of export. These services even involved organizing small farmers into cooperatives in order to obtain a multiplier effect and economies of scale. Transport problems were resolved through the use of new technologies for refrigeration and for keeping perishable fruit fresh. These new techniques made it possible to extend harvest periods to coincide with the periods of greatest demand in the main export markets. In the marketing realm, the packaging and presentation of a number of products was improved and participation in various international trade fairs was promoted.

In Costa Rica, one of the fiscal incentives for exports, the Tax Voucher Certificates *(CAT - Certificados de Abonos Tributarios)*, initially was flawed because it had a high fiscal cost and tended more to encourage dependence on the tax system than to make companies more competitive. Accordingly, these certificates were gradually reduced and then entirely phased out in 1996. It should be emphasized that the maneuvering room for using export promotion subsidies was reduced by the Uruguay Round agreement, which seeks to eliminate fiscal incentives that may distort trade.

Table 2.7   Western Hemisphere: Intraregional and World Exports, 1990-95

(Percent, current U.S. dollars)

	1990	1991	1992	1993	1994	Average 1990-94	1995ᵖ
Western Hemisphere[1]							
World (growth)	8	5	8	5	13	8	17
Within hemisphere (growth)	9	6	15	11	18	12	15
Within hemisphere/world	46	46	49	51	53	49	52
Latin America/Caribbean[1]							
World (growth)	10	-1	21	7	17	11	23
Within LAC	9	22	26	20	18	19	25
Within LAC/world	13	16	17	19	19	17	19
Andean Community							
World (growth)	26	-9	-1	5	16	6	15
Within Andean Group	25	31	27	28	21	27	33
Within Andean/world	4	6	8	10	10	8	12
CARICOM							
World (growth)	19	-5	-0	-5	14	4	na
Within CARICOM	10	-8	1	22	23	9	na
Within CARICOM/world	11	11	11	14	15	12	na
Central America[2]							
World (growth)	12	2	13	8	8	9	29
Within Central America	16	17	25	11	11	16	22
Within Central America/ world	18	20	22	23	24	22	19
MERCOSUR							
World (growth)	-0	-1	10	7	15	6	14
Within MERCOSUR	11	24	42	39	19	26	27
Within MERCOSUR/world	9	11	14	19	19	15	20
NAFTA							
World (growth)	8	7	8	5	13	8	16
Within NAFTA	9	7	14	11	19	12	13
Within NAFTA/world	41	41	43	45	48	44	46

ᵖ Preliminary estimates.

[1] Does not include the Caribbean or Panama in 1995.

[2] Does not include Panama in 1995.

Source: IDB Integration and Regional Programs Department, Caristat and INTAL.

ple, of Brazil. Foreign exchange markets in Chile, Uruguay and Colombia are quite liberalized. Chile maintains a system with two exchange rates and has restrictions on the payment of capital transactions; nevertheless, the first of those situations has only a minimal impact, and the second has been designed only as a device for restraining the entry of short-term capital. Restrictions on capital movements in Uruguay and royalty payments in Colombia are of little significance.

To maintain international competitiveness in the context of average or moderate inflation rates, most countries use flexible exchange systems: either exchange rates corrected for differential inflation rates, rates that are floating but controlled by the monetary authority within a band, or rates simply floating independent of the monetary authority. Of the five countries that have a fixed exchange rate, four (Bahamas, Barbados, Belize and Panama) have had them for decades and have traditionally had a liberal exchange system. The experience of the fifth country, Argentina, has been very different from the others. Argentina has used a fixed exchange rate as an anchor for reducing inflation, thus far with remarkable success. Venezuela established a fixed exchange rate system in 1994 but abandoned it in 1996.

Exchange rate liberalization has had an enormous impact on reducing the exchange rate premium and hence in moderating its distorting effects on the price system. The exchange rate premium has been reduced substantially in all countries, with the exception of Venezuela until 1996. At the end of 1995, only a fifth of the countries had premiums of 10 percent or more; in 1979 the proportion was twice that high. In 1995, almost 25 percent of the countries had no exchange rate premium, while in 1979 only 12 percent enjoyed that situation. In conclusion, it can be said that the exchange rate systems in the region are currently the most liberal that they have been since World War II.

Box 2.2   Institutional Framework of Integration Schemes

The institutional frameworks of current integration treaties in the Americas vary depending on their objectives and features, although there are also similarities between them. At one extreme are treaty-based agreements that carefully regulate commitments, dates and exceptions. These are true "treaty laws" in accordance with established legal doctrine. Such is the case of NAFTA, the Group of Three, and the bilateral agreements recently signed by Mexico. At the opposite extreme are the "framework treaties" that establish the fundamental guidelines of the agreement and delegate joint bodies to prepare what is legally necessary to support the integration process, granting those agencies specific powers. Such is the case of MERCOSUR and, outside the hemisphere, the European Union.

The institutional structure of traditional schemes that predate the foreign debt crisis (Andean Community, Central America Common Market and CARICOM), presents elements of both kinds of treaties and is now being revised to adapt to the new realities of each subregion. These agreements originally had institutions designed to attain ambitious objectives that were not compatible with the possibilities of the member countries. They were focused fundamentally on semi-autonomous development processes, such as import substitution. Today, these institutions are trying to adapt to the demands of economic opening, a process in which all their member countries are involved.

The Latin American Integration Association (LAIA) also displays the features of the "framework treaties," but inasmuch as it has temporarily taken to playing a passive role as a depository for free trade agreements signed among its member countries, it does not have much impact on integration processes, even though it has the juridical and technical tools necessary for helping to bring them together. The agreements being negotiated between MERCOSUR and the other LAIA members (that is, Chile, Mexico and the Andean countries) illustrate this point.

The most outstanding feature of the new institutional organization of subregional integration agreements is that they are being given maximum political support, with the presence of presidents or heads of state as members of the highest body in each agreement.

Present tendencies, with the exception of NAFTA and the Group of Three, indicate the desire to continue adapting the organic structure of agreements so that they can keep pace with the evolution of the integration process, while assuring that the agencies do not grow more than the process itself. A representative case of this tendency is MERCOSUR, whose institutional apparatus was strengthened once the objectives of the transition period had been attained, enabling MERCOSUR to then move on to meeting the objectives agreed upon for the following phase. In the current phase, both the Council, MERCOSUR's highest body made up of the Ministers of Foreign Relations and of Economy, and the Common Market Group, which is the executive body, have legal standing. However, both bodies retain their intergovernmental character and the system of voting by consensus, which have been in effect since the signing of the Treaty of Asunción. The attendance of the presidents of the four MERCOSUR countries at the Council's biannual meetings clearly demonstrates the political support that this subregional agreement has at the highest level.

The members of Andean Community, which will replace the Cartagena Agreement as soon as the new agreement is ratified by the Congress in each country, agreed to adopt an institutional structure that involves direct participation by the Presidents and Ministers of Foreign Relations in decision-making matters in order to spur subregional integration. Accordingly, the Andean Presidential Council and the Andean Council of Ministers of Foreign Relations were created as the highest bodies of what is known as the Andean System. Aspects of the Court of Justice also were changed to allow private citizens to present claims directly if they feel that they have been harmed by decisions made by the countries of the Community to present claims directly. In addition, a Technical Secretariat was created to support the integration process, replacing the Board of the Cartagena Agreement.

In the 1990s, substantial changes have been made in the legal and institutional framework for Central American integration. In 1991, the member countries agreed to create the Central American Integration System, which is responsible for subregional institutional coordination and for implementing the mandates of the presidential summits and the main political forums. The Central American Parliament and the Central American Court of Justice were also established. The Guatemala Protocol went into effect following ratification by three countries. It contains reforms to the General Treaty of Central American Economic Integration, thereby strengthening the framework for legal action on the part of the Secretariat of the General Treaty for Central American Economic Integration.

The new protocols and treaties have still not been legislatively ratified by some Congresses in the region. Moreover, the Central American Common Market has set new objectives, both regarding relations with other countries as a result of economic liberalization, trade negotiations and the Uruguay Round, as well as issues regarding subregional integration stemming from the Alliance for Sustainable Development. While the recent institutional development is in part a response to these new challenges, no evaluation of the existing agencies and mechanisms for coordination has been made on the basis of the reformulated objectives. At present, by mandate of the presidents of Central America, the IDB and ECLAC are jointly supporting a process to rationalize and strengthen subregional integration institutions.

CARICOM's main bodies for policy decisions are the Conference of Heads of State and the Common Market Council. The former issues common policies and reaches decisions by consensus. The main responsibility of the Council is to resolve differences between the members of the community. Both bodies are supported by ministerial committees in the following areas: health, education, labor, foreign affairs, finances, agriculture, industry, transportation, energy, mines and natural resources, and science and technology. The CARICOM Secretariat handles technical and administrative endeavors.

Membership in the Group of Three has been established through two bilateral free trade agreements, one between Colombia and Mexico and the other between Venezuela and Mexico. Thus far it has no secretariat. In general, these bilateral agreements and all others existing within the LAIA framework are administered by a simple binational commission.

Finally, it is important to point out that although a formal process for resolving disputes has been stipulated in practically all the agreements, in practice the countries have tended to resolve them diplomatically rather than judicially. This situation should change in the future in response to growing pressures that trade agreements move toward a transparent system based on compliance with established rules.

REGIONAL AND HEMISPHERIC INTEGRATION AND PREFERENTIAL TARIFF REDUCTION

The creation of new trade agreements and the deepening of existing ones has been an extremely important part of trade liberalization in Latin America. Descriptively, it is possible to distinguish between the free trade agreements and common markets established between the countries of the hemisphere.[6] The shaping of a genuine common market entails the full liberalization of trade in goods, services and factors within an integrated area. Reaching such a thorough degree of integration requires that the trade, protection and macroeconomic policies of the countries be strictly harmonized. There are four regional agreements that are seeking to become common markets: MERCOSUR, the Andean Community, the Central American Common Market, and CARICOM. These agreements, with the exception of MERCOSUR, date to the 1960s, though they have been reinvigorated in the 1990s and are now at different stages of consolidation as customs unions (see Box 2.2).

Free trade agreements or areas, on the other hand, constitute a less advanced stage of integration, since they involve trade liberalization among partners but not the adoption of a common protection policy toward competition of goods from third countries. Within the region, a distinction should be made between two kinds of free trade agreements on the basis of the scope and depth of liberalization: first, traditional agreements to selectively liberalize trade in goods, negotiated within the LAIA framework; and second, a set of what are known as "new generation" agree-

---

[6] This section does not examine nonreciprocal agreements, such as those under the Caribbean Basin Initiative (CBI), the U.S. Andean Tariff Preferences Act for Bolivia, Colombia, Ecuador and Peru, Canada's agreement with the Caribbean Community (Carbean), or some bilateral agreements of LAIA countries with CARICOM and Central America pursuant to Article 25 of the Montevideo Treaty. Agreements between countries of a strictly sectoral nature are also not included.

ments. These latter accords include bilateral agreements in which liberalization is universal and automatic under a relatively simple normative framework, as in agreements negotiated by Chile with Mexico, Venezuela, Colombia and Ecuador during the past few years. They also include those agreements that follow the model of the North American Free Trade Agreement, characterized by programs with automatic preferential tariff reduction, a more ambitious regulatory framework, and negotiated commitments that extend to other realms, such as services, investment, government procurement and intellectual property. This group includes the Group of Three Agreement (between Mexico, Colombia and Venezuela) and Mexico's recent bilateral agreements with Costa Rica and Bolivia.

Finally, at the December 1994 Summit of the Americas in Miami, the heads of state of 34 countries in the hemisphere announced a far-reaching proposal to negotiate a Free Trade Area of the Americas (FTAA) before the year 2005, with concrete advances expected before the year 2000. While the exact scope of the FTAA is still to be defined, its discussion agenda is ambitious and includes all the realms of trade that emerged in the Uruguay Round.

Building Common Markets

In practice, agreements that aspire to become genuine common markets are typically partial and imperfect customs unions. There are long lists of exceptions, including the kinds of goods excluded both from the common external tariff and from the full elimination of tariffs applied to intra-subregional trade. There is also varying compliance with common commitments on the part of the member countries, so much so that certain member countries have decided for the moment to cease participating fully in the customs union. Despite their imperfections, however, customs unions throughout the region in the last few years have been liberalized to such a degree that intraregional trade has been significantly boosted.

MERCOSUR began in 1991 with a tariff reduction program for reciprocal trade which culminated in 1994, followed by the inauguration of the Common External Tariff (CET) on January 1, 1995. At that time intra-subregional trade in goods was not yet fully liberalized because there were still nontariff barriers or temporary exclusion mechanisms established for certain goods, notably the automobile sector and sugar. The CET structure is staggered at intervals from 0 to 20 percent, with numerous exceptions scheduled to converge into the CET in 2001 for Argentina and Brazil and in 2006 for Paraguay and Uruguay.

MERCOSUR's vast market has aroused considerable interest in other countries in the region. Chile has already joined the group as an associate member country, participating in the free trade zone, although not in the CET arrangement. Bolivia is also continuing its discussions to become an associate member, while, Peru, Ecuador, Colombia and Venezuela have expressed interest in reaching an agreement with this market. These negotiations of individual countries with MERCOSUR are known as "4 + 1" agreements. In addition, MERCOSUR is holding negotiations as a group in order to establish a trade relationship with the European Union.

The Andean Community (formerly the Andean Group) was created in 1969 by Bolivia, Colombia, Chile, Ecuador and Peru; Venezuela joined in 1973 and Chile withdrew three years later. Few of its prior goals were reached in the 1980s, and reactivation of the agreement had to wait until the end of the decade. Currently, there is a free trade zone between the members (except for Peru), and a customs union between Venezuela, Colombia and Ecuador. The customs union took effect in February 1995 with a common external tariff structured in tiers of 5 percent for agricultural products, 10 percent for processed raw materials, 15 percent for semi-manufactured goods, and 20 percent for manufactured goods. Bolivia and Peru continue to maintain their own national tariffs. There are significant lists of exceptions and a margin of maneuverability for unilaterally lowering the tariff by 5 percent for goods not produced in the region.

The establishment of the Central American Common Market between Costa Rica, El Salvador, Guatemala, Honduras and Nicaragua also dates to the early 1960s. While it was one of the most advanced and successful arrangements during its early years, it experienced major problems during the 1970s and 1980s. The integration process in the region took on new life starting in the early 1990s as tariff structures began to converge. A common external tariff was adopted in 1993, with rates ranging from 5 to 20 percent. The schedule for adoption of the CET granted a longer period for Nicaragua to lower tariffs and for Honduras to lower surcharges. In 1995, the countries agreed to adopt a new CET structure that will lower the tariff applied to capital goods and raw materials to 1 percent and the maximum tariff to 15 percent. Different countries might approach this new structure at different speeds.

Finally, CARICOM was created in 1973 in order to eliminate restrictions on mutual trade and to establish an external tariff. Its antecedents are found in the Caribbean Free Trade Association, which was created in 1967. The external tariff was applied immediately only among the larger countries in the Community (Barbados, Guyana, Jamaica, and Trinidad and Tobago). The second phase of the CET now being implemented involves a maximum tariff level of 35 percent, with the objective to reach a structure of from 5 to 20 percent by 1998. The lists of exceptions for sensitive products are also significant in this arrangement, as are differential treatments given to some members.

Free Trade Agreements

Traditionally, and especially since the early 1980s, Latin American countries have negotiated a large number of trade treaties (not necessarily in order to establish free trade zones) under the legal framework of the Latin American Integration Association (LAIA). These agreements have typically been strictly trade-related and have had relatively simple preferential tariff concessions of a partial and transparent nature. Since 1990, some 20 agreements of this type have been signed. Among those that stand out for their economic significance are several negotiated by Argentina and Brazil with other countries of the region.

The 1990s have seen the emergence of what are called "new generation" agreements, which differ from traditional agreements in the depth of the trade commitments acquired. Some, such as the bilateral agreements signed by Chile, incorporate a good deal of the LAIA legal framework around key issues such as rules of origin or safeguard systems. Others have been negotiated under terms similar to the North American Free Trade Agreement, with explicit chapters on what are called "new issues" in trade such as investments, services and intellectual property. Examples of the latter include the Group of Three agreement between Mexico, Colombia and Venezuela, as well as Mexico's more recent bilateral agreements with Costa Rica and Bolivia.

The primary aim of Chile's bilateral agreements with Mexico (1992), Venezuela (1993), Colombia (1994), and Ecuador (1995) is to establish free trade zones by negotiating tariff reduction programs that are brief, automatic and practically universal in nature. The agreements cover high percentages of products with immediate free access and include special time periods for products regarded as "sensitive" (treatment of the automobile sector is especially noteworthy). They likewise envision the elimination of quasi-tariff restrictions at the beginning of the tariff reduction schedules. In the agreement with Mexico, the tariff reduction mechanism set a maximum tariff of 10 percent on reciprocal trade and a schedule of gradual tariff elimination that concluded at the beginning of this year. Agreement was reached with Venezuela on a schedule for simultaneously reducing each section of that country's tariff over

Box 2.3   Rules of Origin: Key Instrument in Free Trade Agreements in the Americas

Under agreements on rules of origin, the signatory countries set as a primary objective the elimination of trade barriers between them, while maintaining their own tariff structures for third countries. Since external tariffs generally vary, exporters from third countries would have an incentive to enter the more protected markets by way of the least protected market among the members of the area. That is what is known as "trade deflection." The purpose of origin requirements is to assure preferential access to markets by establishing criteria for distinguishing between goods coming from the free trade areas that are eligible for preferential access and those that have their origin outside the free trade zone and hence must pay the external or most favored nation tariff.

Rules of origin requirements are not free of controversy. Many experts often regard them as a form of protectionism and a source of trade diversion. Despite this criticism, however, in practice rules of origin requirements are an indispensable component for creating a free trade area. Furthermore, the degree of implicit protection as a result of rules of origin is essentially variable and hard to predict in practice. The level of implicit protection depends on a number of factors, including possibilities within domestic production of replacing inputs according to their geographic origin; technological changes and productive innovation; supply conditions in the national industries producing intermediate goods; the structure of the intermediate goods market in the integration zone; protection policies toward third countries; and the degree of economic integration existing between the participants in a free trade area before the agreement entered into effect.

When the final product incorporates inputs from other countries, or part of the production process takes place in one of the countries in the area and part takes place elsewhere, specific technical criteria are required to determine the "nationality" of the final product. Thus far, three basic criteria have been used alone or in combination: (i) whether or not there has been a change in tariff classification between the various stages of production; (ii) whether the value added incorporated reaches an established minimum; and (iii) whether a series of specific technical requirements having to do with the production process used in producing the item have been met.

The free trade agreements signed by the countries of the region use two basic regimes for determining the origin of merchandise. First, there is the general regime of the Latin American Integration Association (LAIA), whose generic requisite applicable to all products is based on whether there has been a change in the tariff item, or lacking that, on whether the value of content outside the region does not exceed 50 percent of the FOB export value. That regime is applied in most regionwide agreements made within the LAIA framework. Secondly, there is the NAFTA regime, which is more complex and specific. In NAFTA, the norms for judging origin are specific to each product level and combine the three criteria mentioned above. Another distinctive feature of the LAIA regime is the detailed regulation of the entire system for administering those requirements, that is, the tasks of documentation, certification and verification both by private parties and customs officials. That regime has served as a model for the new generation of free trade agreements established recently, such as the Group of Three Agreement and Mexico's bilateral agreements with Costa Rica and Bolivia.

The debate regarding the design of rules of origin in the shaping of free trade zones will be increasingly important as new initiatives for regional agreements continue to emerge around the world. Certainly, as they strive to shape the Free Trade Area of the Americas (FTAA), the countries of the hemisphere will have to deal with the challenge of specifying rules of origin that will allow the system of preferences agreed upon to operate effectively without becoming factors that distort the flow of trade.

a four-year period. Given the commitments of Colombia and Venezuela under the Andean Community, Chile negotiated a preferential program with Colombia under the same terms.

The signing of the North American Free Trade Agreement (NAFTA) in December 1992 between the United States, Canada and Mexico, which went into effect in January 1994, marked the beginning of a new stage in hemispheric free trade area negotiations. It was the first time that a Latin

FIGURE 2.8

Tariff Reduction Calendar in Trade Agreements

(In percent)

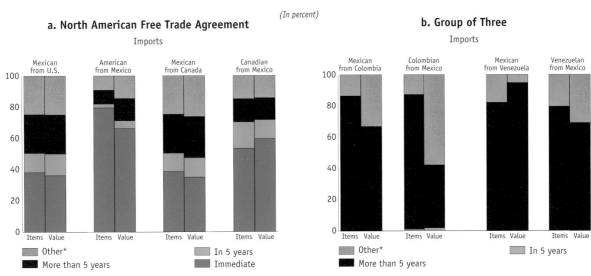

a. North American Free Trade Agreement
Imports

b. Group of Three
Imports

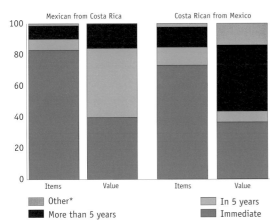

c. Costa Rica and Mexico
Imports

*Tariff reduction calendars that apply to specific goods
(i.e. textiles, cars) and sectors not included in the program.
Source: IDB Integration and Regional Programs Department.*

American country became formally integrated with the industrialized countries of North America, and it was remarkable because of the broad scope of the agreement and the way it fully incorporated new trade issues. Moreover, as will be noted below, NAFTA left its imprint on the other countries of the region. With regard to lowering tariffs, the sectors receiving special treatment are the automotive,

farming, textiles and apparel, energy, and basic petrochemical sectors. Negotiations in these areas included special time periods for tariff reduction, elimination of import quotas, and the opening of state-run companies to services provided by companies of other member countries.

In 1994, Mexico also began to extend the NAFTA concept southward, setting in motion three other agreements (Group of Three, Mexico-Costa Rica, and Mexico-Bolivia) with similar features. These programs generally contain more selective and longer tariff reduction schedules, with more specific sector treatments than other new generation agreements in the region. The schedule for preferential tariff reduction between markets for some of these agreements is shown in Figure 2.8 (a, b, and c), both in terms of the coverage of products and their importance in terms of exports to the preferential market. In the case of the Group of Three agreement, there is special treatment for the automotive sector and short lists of exceptions concentrated in agricultural products and foods; beverages and tobacco in the agreement between Colombia and Mexico; and for textiles and apparel in the case of Mexico and Venezuela.

A key element distinguishing these agreements from those signed by Chile is the rules of origin, the system for determining the source of goods so that they can benefit from the agreed upon preferences (see Box 2.3). Following the NAFTA model, arrangements in Mexico's agreements for investment, services and intellectual property are regulated comprehensively, and mechanisms and procedures for disputes settlement are established.

Toward a Hemispheric Free Trade Area

The integration process in the region clearly is very much on the upswing, with ambitious plans for future expansion. Furthermore, the process is not limited to Latin America and the Caribbean, since it extends to all countries in the hemisphere.

There are individual efforts to continue bilateral negotiations between countries or groups of countries. In this regard, the most prominent centers of negotiation are located in Chile, Mexico and MERCOSUR. After some efforts to enter NAFTA, halted by the lack of "fast track authority" in the United States, Chile is now engaged in bilateral negotiations with Canada on what may ultimately serve as a bridge for its entrance into NAFTA. Mexico has its agenda open to future negotiations, similar to its "new generation" agreements, with countries in Central America (Nicaragua; El Salvador-Guatemala-Honduras) and the Andean Community (Ecuador). As a group, MERCOSUR has been bilaterally negotiating free trade agreements with neighboring countries, beginning a process that could become a South American free trade area. While this network of crisscrossing treaties (Figure 2.9) could potentially become a major obstacle to transparency and the smooth functioning of trade relations between the countries of the region, it is at the same time a means for learning technical skills necessary to meet the challenge of competition and trade standards and regulations. In any case, the acceptance and compliance with WTO obligations may serve as a common denominator between the countries in their agreements with one another.

Another great challenge facing the hemisphere during the coming years lies in successfully concluding the process of building the FTAA. The 34 countries at the Miami Summit of the Americas have already set up 11 working groups with specific terms of reference for the areas of negotiation. At a meeting of trade ministers in Denver in June 1995, nine groups were launched (market access, customs procedures and rules of origin, investment, standards, technical barriers, sanitary and phytosanitary measures, subsidies, anti-dumping and countervailing duties, and smaller economies). Subsequently, four new working groups were established at a ministerial meeting in Cartagena in March 1996 (competition policies, services, government procurement, and intellectual property). The IDB is providing technical support to groups on market access, customs procedures and rules of origins, investment, and government procurement.

The successful process to date of building the FTAA represents a historic milestone in trade relations of the Americas. The FTAA reflects a convergence of interests between the region and its neighbors to the north that would have seemed impossible a decade ago. Indeed, North America, which traditionally defended free trade, moved toward an appreciation of regionalism, expressed in the free trade agreement between Canada and the United States and then in NAFTA. For their part, Latin America and the Caribbean, which have a long tradition of regionalism, switched their philosophy and moved toward a more outward oriented approach. If the FTAA project is judged by its own goals, expressed by the working plans issued by the countries in Miami, Denver and Cartagena, the process is meeting its expectations and the technical preparation and discussion in the FTAA framework is exposing the countries in the region to the huge challenges posed by trade liberalization.

FIGURE 2.9

Free Trade Agreements in the Americas, 1990-95

Andean Community
CARICOM
Central American Common Market
MERCOSUR
NAFTA

▲ Agreement with group

——— Free trade agreement
------ Free trade agreement (in negotiation)
········· Nonreciprocal preferential trade agreement

Source: IDB Integration and Regional Programs Department.

FIGURE 2.10

**Trade and GDP in
Latin America, 1973-95**

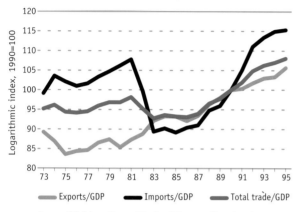

Source: IDB Integration and Regional Programs Department
and INTAL.

FIGURE 2.11

**Trade Index in
Latin America, 1973-94**

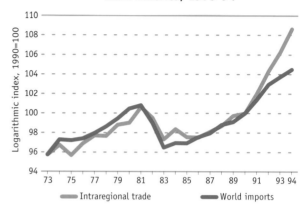

Source: IDB Integration and Regional Programs Department
and INTAL.

BEHAVIOR OF FOREIGN TRADE DURING THE LIBERALIZATION PERIOD

General Trends in International Trade

The process of trade liberalization in Latin America began comprehensively in 1989,[7] while liberalization of the exchange rate began in almost all countries in 1990-91. The period of trade liberalization (1989-95) includes both kinds of reforms. It is useful to compare it to two earlier periods: 1984-88, which was an expansionary period prior to the beginning of liberalization (which is called the "transition period"); and 1974-79, the pre-crisis period. This section examines the trade performance of Latin America using the evaluation of worldwide trade as a benchmark. For that purpose, the evaluation of the coefficient of trade openness, that is, exports and imports as a percent of GDP, is used. This coefficient is an indicator commonly used to measure the integration of a country or region into the world economy. In addition to observing the trend of the absolute

value of the regional coefficient, it is also important to observe how it evolves in comparison to that of the rest of the world. For example, if the relationship between this coefficient for a country and the worldwide coefficient rises, it can be said that such a country has had an integration process more rapid than that of the rest of the world.

Since the beginning of the post-World War II era, the coefficient of total world trade (exports plus imports over GDP) has been constantly rising (Table 2.5). During the 1970s, the coefficient for Latin America was growing at the same rate as the world figure. However, the crisis of the 1980s produced a dramatic reversal: a sharp fall in the figure in 1981 and 1982, followed by stagnation until 1986. However, during those years the world coefficient continued to grow. Thus the relative trade coefficient for Latin America fell dramatically from the pre-crisis period to that of transition, while in absolute terms the coefficient stood still.

During the period of trade liberalization, the total trade coefficient for Latin America and the Caribbean grew more rapidly than the world figure, and hence the relative coefficient rose substantially, but still without reaching its pre-crisis

---

[7] It is the average weighted for GDP on the date when it began in each country (see the above section on the chronology of reform).

FIGURE 2.12

Exports to the Region

(Percentage of total exports)

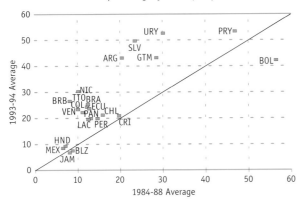

Source: IDB Integration and Regional Programs Department and INTAL.

period value. In conclusion, therefore, during the trade liberalization period the region was able to end the stagnation of its integration with the world economy observed in the 1980s, and it improved its relative position, although that figure has not yet returned to the value that it held in the 1970s.

Normally, coefficients of exports and imports with GDP tend to evolve in line with the total trade coefficient. That, however, is not the experience of Latin America through the phases of overindebtedness in the 1970s, the crisis and cutoff of external capital flows in the 1980s, and renewal of external financing in the 1990s. Hence, the conclusions that may be drawn about the integration of the regional economy into the world economy during the liberalization period are quite different depending on whether they are viewed from the standpoint of exports or of imports.

Indeed, it is clear that the variations in the coefficient of total trade resulted primarily from the behavior of imports, because growth of the export coefficient remained stable (Figure 2.10). The export coefficient, in contrast with that of imports, grew significantly during the critical 1981-83 years, and continued to grow from 1987 onward. Thus its value grew from the pre-crisis period to that of transition and from then to the liberalization period. Even more significant is the

fact that the relative coefficient of exports also grew continually through those periods, albeit slowly (Table 2.5). That is, exports displayed quite stable behavior over time (1975-95), and that behavior was determined by the growth of productive capacity in the region and the stability of the growth of demand from outside the region for imports from Latin America.

By contrast, the movement of imports was quite unstable, reflecting the instability of the economies in the region (Table 2.5 and Figure 2.10). During the 1970s, imports grew rapidly as a result of the growth of the region and major inflows of external capital. During the economic crisis of 1982 and 1983, imports fell sharply, so that by the end of 1983 they were almost as low as the 1973 levels. The reason for the phenomena was the abrupt cutoff of foreign capital inflows and the recession of the regional economy. In 1984, with the beginning of a new phase of economic expansion, there also began a slow expansion of imports based on their GDP growth. Owing to the lack of access to foreign capital, however, imports lagged behind GDP. Indeed, while regional GDP was below its 1981 level from 1982 to 1986, the value of imports remained lower than the 1981 figure from 1982 to 1990. The return of foreign capital since 1990 in a context of fewer trade barriers reversed that situation.

The trade liberalization period has been associated with a one percentage point rise in the growth rate of exports in real terms and with a 4.6 percentage point rise in imports, as compared with those observed during the transition period (see Table 2.5). The reduction of import tariffs and other trade barriers and the 11 percent revaluation of the real effective exchange rate (calculated between the average of the two periods) have contributed to this trend in trade flows. However, it should be emphasized that during the liberalization period the average exchange rate has been devalued by 13 percent in comparison to the average of the pre-crisis period. It is also worth noting that the expansion of exports and the contrac-

			Table 2.8 Exports from Trade Areas by Destination, 1995					
			(Composition in percent)					
				Destination				
Exporter	MERCOSUR	Andean Group	Central American Common Market	CARICOM	NAFTA	LAC	Hemisphere	Rest of world
MERCOSUR	20.3	4.9	0.4	0.3	16.9	31.0	46.9	53.1
Andean Group	3.7	12.0	1.3	0.5	41.7	21.8	62.3	37.7
CACM	2.0	1.5	18.8	0.4	41.8	24.7	65.7	34.3
NAFTA	2.3	1.7	0.8	0.5	46.1	12.1	52.6	47.4
LAC	8.8	4.9	1.4	0.3	48.3	18.4	66.1	33.9
Hemisphere	3.8	2.5	0.9	0.5	43.3	14.0	52.4	47.6

Source: IDB Integration and Regional Programs Department and INTAL.

Note: Estimates based on preliminary data as of December 30, 1995. Figures for CARICOM were not available.

tion of imports during the transition period was supported by a 27 percent devaluation vis-à-vis the pre-crisis period. The differential behavior of exports and imports during the trade liberalization period is consistent with the pattern of macroeconomic performance. During the first six years of the liberalization period the value of imports was greater than that of exports, with a tendency for the unfavorable trade balance to diminish over time. Also consistent with that pattern is the fact that the countries that experienced the greatest improvement in the growth rate of their exports between the period of transition and that of trade liberalization (an increase of from 5 to 10 percentage in points, as opposed to only one point for the regional average) are all among those countries that began their liberalization early: Chile, Costa Rica, Bolivia, Jamaica, Guyana, Argentina and El Salvador.

Geographic Distribution and Composition of Trade

Significant changes have taken place in the geographic distribution of the region's trade in the 1990s (Table 2.6 and Figures 2.12 and 2.13). The importance of the United States and Canada as trading partners for the region has risen in terms of both imports and exports.[8] In both cases, the joint participation of these countries is 48 percent, making them the main trading bloc for the region. By contrast, Europe has lost its shares of both exports and imports, which now stand at around 18 percent each.[9] East Asia's share in the market for the region's exports has remained unchanged at a little over 7 percent.[10] However, imports from Asia rose by two percentage points, and now represent a little over 10 percent. In most countries, the geographic distribution of imports changed in the same direction as the region; for exports, the changes were far more diverse (Figure 2.13).

Changes in the importance of intraregional trade have been very different when viewed from the side of imports, as opposed to exports. Intraregional imports as a percent of total imports remained constant at almost 17 percent. Intraregional exports have risen by 7 percentage points and now represent almost 20 percent of the total. From Table 2.7 it is clear that exports within the region and within subregional integration agreements in the hemisphere have been growing considerably more rapidly than total exports during the 1990s.

---

[8] These conclusions are drawn from comparing the 1993-94 average with that of 1984-88.

[9] European Union countries plus Norway, Switzerland, Turkey, Poland, Hungary, Bulgaria and the former Czechoslovakia and Yugoslavia (today Yugoslavia, Bosnia-Herzegovina, Croatia and Slovenia).

[10] Japan, Korea, Hong Kong, Singapore, Taiwan, Indonesia, Thailand and Malaysia.

FIGURE 2.13

Total Imports and Exports by Origin and Destination

(Percentage of total)

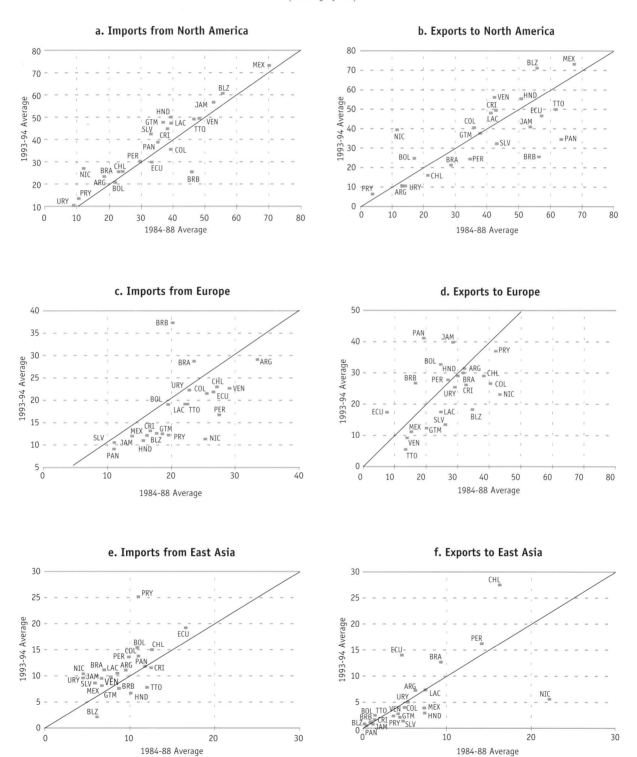

Source: IDB Integration and Regional Programs Department and INTAL.

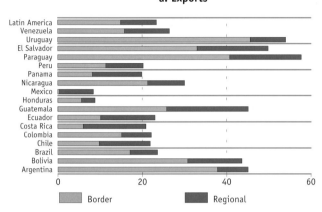

FIGURE 2.14

Intraregional and Border Trade, 1994

(Percentage of total)

a. Exytps

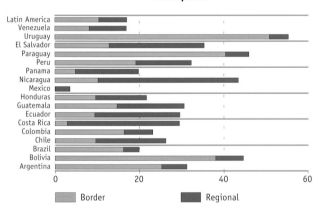

b. Imports

Note: The countries included are those that share borders and have available information. Mexican border trade does not include trade with the United States.
Source: IDB Integration and Regional Programs Department.

It should also be emphasized that most exports within Latin America take place between countries belonging to the same integration group, which, in turn, are made up of neighboring countries (the data along the diagonal in Table 2.8). Figure 2.14 also shows the great importance of border trade within regional trade for both imports and exports.[11] It is obvious that most intraregional trade takes place between neighbors and hence geographic proximity has been decisive in the expansion of commerce.

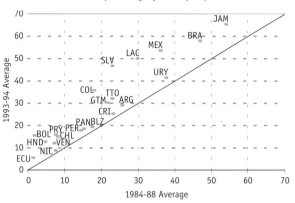

FIGURE 2.15

Exports of Manufactures

(Percentage of total exports)

Source: IDB Integration and Regional Program Department.

As noted above, there has been a marked difference in the behavior of the region's overall exports and imports. Exports have grown rather steadily since 1975, while the behavior of imports has been quite unstable. The trend of intraregional trade (it should be recalled that the value of intraregional exports and imports is always equal) from 1970 to 1995 has followed the trend of total imports very closely (Figure 2.11). In fact, the explanation for the behavior of trade within Latin America is largely the same as that applied to the region's total imports, namely the region's import capacity.[12] This correlation of trade within Latin America with total imports, together with the fact that imports have expanded more than exports, explains why the proportion of intra-Latin American trade in total imports has not grown, and yet it has grown in total exports.

---

[11] The obvious exception is Mexico, whose share of intraregional and border trade within Latin America is very low. The reason is that the bulk of its trade is with its hemispheric neighbor, the United States. The statistics used exclude Mexico's *maquiladora* trade with the United States.

[12] An approximate quantification of import capacity is the value of total imports. Based on that relationship, it has been estimated that the movement of total imports from 1970-95 explains over 90 percent of the behavior of intraregional trade, whether in constant 1990 dollars or in current dollars.

FIGURE 2.16

Share of Manufactures in Trade Within Each Bloc
and to the World, Except Latin America

(In percent)

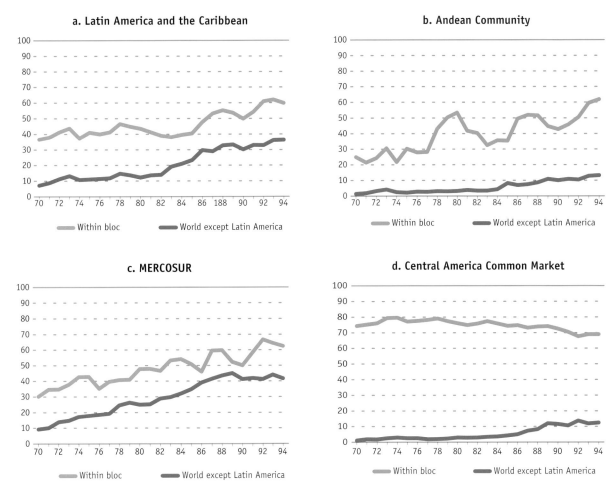

Source: IDB Integration and Regional Programs Department.

While trade within Latin America has followed the changes in total imports, it has done so more rapidly. Thus the increase in the growth rate of total imports tended to cause even greater acceleration in the growth of trade within the region, owing to the natural attraction of trading with neighboring countries, whether because of transportation costs, culture, similar per capita income or greater information. This natural factor was more forcefully at work during the 1990s because the liberalization of trade in subregions of Latin America was considerably deeper than that of imports from the rest of the world. This last fact is clearly part of the explanation of the greater growth of intraregional trade as opposed to total imports during these years.

The long-run trend of Latin American exports to change their structure from primary products toward manufacturing has continued in the 1990s. Manufacturer share in exports has increased in all countries during these years, especially in Colombia, El Salvador, Mexico, Brazil and Jamaica (Figure 2.15). During the period of trade liberalization, the trend of manufactures to account for a higher percentage of exports within the region than in those sent outside the region has continued. This is true of Latin America as a whole as well as within MERCOSUR, the Andean Community and the Central American Common Market (Figure 2.16). The more pronounced the orientation of manufactures toward regional markets, the lower the relative development level of the countries making up the integration agreement. These patterns are due to the greater effective protection that manufactures have in the region (on average), and to the fact that the lower levels of manufacturing sophistication often make products more suited for regional demand patterns. Thus, in practice regional markets operate as a platform for the learning process for producing and exporting more sophisticated goods .

CHAPTER 3

TAX
REFORM

ABSTRACT

Tax reforms initiated in the 1980s and deepened in the 1990s in Latin America and the Caribbean have aimed to make systems more neutral, simplify and streamline the number and structure of taxes, emphasize the horizontal dimension of equity in tax systems, and enhance revenues. Consequently, tax reforms have:

• Lessened the importance of taxes on foreign trade.

• Increased the share of taxes on consumption within total revenue collected.

• Eliminated less significant taxes.

• Broadened tax bases and level rates.

• Reduced income tax rates.

• Modernized and strengthened institutions involved in tax administration.

• Reengineered tax administration processes to facilitate voluntary compliance and detect noncompliance with tax obligations.

The average tax burden among Latin

American countries is 14.1 percent of GDP, somewhat less than that of the fast growing countries in Southeast Asia. However, there are major differences between the countries of the region. The tax system currently in effect in most countries is structured around value-added taxes (VAT), excise taxes and income taxes.

Although the design of the VAT eases collection, its effectiveness is limited because many products are not included in the base, and because of problems of evasion and administration. To increase VAT collection in the future, the list of goods and services covered by this tax will have to be expanded.

Income tax collection in Latin America is seriously flawed. Eliminating exemptions and lowering rates have facilitated administration and collection of this tax, but auditing efforts have produced very limited results.

The challenges facing tax systems in the region in the next few years are to:

• Increase collection of direct taxation, primarily the income tax.

• Streamline excise taxes.

• Improve administration of the VAT, extending the base and in some cases reducing rates.

• Reexamine the distribution of tax powers among the levels of government and revenue sharing systems, increasing tax assignments of the lower levels of government.

• Modernize tax administration management and strengthen auditing, collection and legal action.

• Adjust tax administration mechanisms to the economic integration process.

INTRODUCTION

The reorientation of the development strategy of Latin America and the Caribbean since the 1980s has been reflected in a new paradigm that places greater trust in the market's ability to allocate resources, in trade as the driving force of growth, and in the private sector, including the foreign private sector, as a provider of goods and services. Government economic activity has focused increasingly on regulation in order to assure smooth market functioning, and on the provision of basic social and collective services, such as justice, health care, education and security. Reformulating development strategies has made it necessary to revitalize economic policy tools and adjust them to new objectives. In the field of taxes, this revitalization has given rise to a relatively homogeneous tax system in the region.

In countries like Argentina, Bolivia, Nicaragua and Peru, the major reforms that produced this system were a centerpiece of the stabilization and fiscal adjustment programs implemented to defeat hyperinflation. In most other countries in the region, the circumstances were less traumatic. Nevertheless, tax reform was crucial to the economic policy agenda of the 1980s and early 1990s, and in most cases predated second generation economic reforms such as privatization and labor and social security reforms. In recent years, initiatives in the tax area have been incremental in nature, fine tuning a relatively well established system.

This chapter begins with a description of the elements of tax reform, examining the initiatives taken over the past five years and the resulting tax structure in the countries of the region. It then describes the questions pending in the tax field for the remainder of the decade. The analysis focuses primarily on the tax powers of the highest level of government, central or federal, as the case may be. Moreover, only taxes on domestic activity are examined, and even in this case those connected to financing the pension system are not counted because trade and social security reforms

are treated in other chapters in this Report. Finally, the concept of a tax system described here is not limited to policy decisions, but extends to the tax administration tools needed to implement it.

Elements of Tax Reform

Three features characterized the tax reforms of the 1980s: (i) the pursuit of neutrality; (ii) the streamlining of both policy and administration of tax systems; and (iii) the declining importance given to matters of equity, especially in vertical terms.[1] A fourth common element that must be mentioned separately is adequacy of resources, since as a result of the reform, revenue increased by between 2 percent and 4 percent of GDP.[2] Tax policy was thus implemented largely in order to sustain stabilization policies applied during the period.

As long as the closed economic model with strong state involvement was in place, the effects of tax policy on resource allocation were considered secondary to the objective of having enough resources. That essentially static vision of tax collection gave way with the reformulation of development policy, and microeconomic considerations emerged along with a greater concern for the effects of tax collection on economic growth.

The pursuit of neutrality sought to reduce both the distortions created in the economy by the preferential treatment received by some sectors, and the disincentives that the existing tax system created in economic agents, particularly with regard to work-leisure and consumption-saving decisions. This objective was met by reducing the importance of taxes on foreign trade; extending tax bases and flattening rates; reducing income tax rate levels; and increasing the proportion of taxes on consumption as opposed to direct taxation.

[1] See Pita (1993), Perry and Herrera (1994), IDB (1995), and Rains, Bes and Febres (1996).
[2] See Shome (1992).

Abandonment of the import-substitution model meant that import tariffs were lower and less dispersed, and that export fees in effect in many countries, which were basically imposed on primary good production, were suppressed. This change brought about a profound readjustment of public sector financing, with significant consequences for the functioning of the real sector in economies of the region, prompted by the resulting change in relative prices (Table 3.1).

The rationale for broadening tax bases and making rates more uniform was to minimize tax considerations in the decision-making process of economic agents, not only regarding the economic sectors but also the production factors employed in them.[3] At the same time, lowering the average rate of the income tax and its marginal values made it possible to counteract the incentives to avoid or evade taxes caused by the high rates.

While it is true that poor economic performance by Latin American economies was the main factor setting these changes in motion, international developments in taxation, and especially the 1986 tax reform in the United States, had significant influence in the design of these reforms.[4] The interdependence of national tax policies in the context of growing economic globalization tended to harmonize the tax systems of capital-exporting countries with countries receiving foreign investment.

The objective of neutrality has been addressed by thoroughly streamlining tax systems both in the realm of law and in tax administration. Literally hundreds of taxes whose contribution to tax collection was insignificant were eliminated. They were replaced with a small number of taxes, primarily through indirect taxation, that broadened the tax base and flattened rates. Most goods and services were taxed primarily through excise taxes. Tax revenue has been strongly concentrated on these excise taxes and on the income tax (Table 3.2).

The aim of simplicity in the reform has

Table 3.1	Share of Taxes on International Trade in Total Tax Revenue			
(In percent)				
	1980	1985	1990	1991-95[a]
Argentina	45.8	16.7	12.1	5.6
Bahamas	71.1	72.4	67.2	57.1
Barbados	23.1	16.1	12.9	15.7
Belize	56.2	60.6	61.5	58.1
Bolivia	39.2	22.4	11.8	10.1
Brazil	6.8	3.9	2.5	2.8
Chile	5.8	39.5	14.1	12.5
Colombia	27.2	19.7	33.7	15.0
Costa Rica	30.3	35.5	27.8	24.4
Dominican Republic	41.1	30.3	38.7	34.5
Ecuador	32.1	41.0	30.8	24.1
El Salvador	38.9	29.7	22.4	19.1
Guatemala	38.7	28.7	40.6	42.2
Guyana	12.4	12.2	15.0	13.4
Haiti	-	-	19.4	17.5
Honduras	39.9	41.5	38.6	19.7
Jamaica	5.5	20.9	21.0	20.6
Mexico	9.5	6.3	8.0	8.6
Nicaragua	15.2	5.9	15.8	12.5
Panama	18.0	18.8	22.0	23.9
Paraguay	32.3	16.1	25.5	20.0
Peru	29.9	24.9	17.3	14.8
Suriname	34.8	33.6	29.2	29.6
Trinidad and Tobago	8.0	11.6	9.9	9.7
Uruguay	21.4	15.0	15.3	9.5
Venezuela	9.5	20.4	7.6	12.8

[a] For Brazil, 1991-92; Panama and Chile, 1991-94.
Source: IDB calculations based on official figures.

been addressed through administrative modernization. That represented a change from what most countries had done in the past, when modernization emphasized reproducing the tax policy then in effect in developed countries with no comparable effort to implement it.

At the outset of the 1990s, most tax administrations in the region were organized functionally, after the abandonment of the prevailing

---

[3] An exception is that of payroll contributions to finance social security. Conceptually, this is a tax borne by the labor market through a specific allocation to the pension system. The reform of this system is still at an early stage in most countries and is examined in another chapter in this Report.

[4] Great Britain introduced reforms similar to those ultimately adopted in the United States in 1984. While both were very important in the realm of ideas in Latin America, the latter clearly went beyond analytical interest, since it created the immediate need to bring regional tax policies into line so as not to discourage U.S. investment (McLure, 1992).

Table 3.2 Share of Income Tax, Value-added Tax and Excises on Total Tax Revenue

(In percent)

	1980	1985	1990	1991-95[a]
Argentina	73.52	63.02	68.03	76.76
Bahamas	-	-	-	-
Barbados	60.83	79.61	79.46	75.62
Belize	56.86	48.44	-	33.63
Bolivia	35.18	34.16	32.09	36.91
Brazil	51.65	65.43	58.67	63.23
Chile	66.76	66.86	71.28	76.86
Colombia	54.57	59.26	73.54	84.26
Costa Rica	62.46	58.88	63.06	56.64
Dominican Republic	47.81	-	54.17	62.24
Ecuador	44.20	51.30	64.80	73.00
El Salvador	68.00	71.94	58.74	74.05
Guatemala	51.04	59.32	67.68	75.39
Guyana	39.27	64.49	67.51	69.91
Haiti	31.30	58.31	-	74.26
Honduras	71.14	69.89	-	64.29
Jamaica	56.53	53.25	55.48	63.57
Mexico	82.91	67.29	-	86.34
Nicaragua	64.01	59.45	71.57	86.00
Panama	15.43	56.44	59.72	66.02
Paraguay	34.34	44.19	36.20	56.16
Peru	48.37	47.91	67.70	65.40
Suriname	-	48.47	58.70	75.08
Trinidad and Tobago	89.39	83.48	79.04	81.04
Uruguay	68.92	79.60	68.99	58.03
Venezuela	83.94	77.86	90.50	80.21

[a] For Brazil, 1991-92; Panama and Chile, 1991-94.
Source: IDB calculations based on official figures.

Table 3.3 Special Taxpayer Units in the Region

Argentina	Yes
Bolivia	Yes
Brazil	No
Chile	No
Colombia	No
Costa Rica	Yes
Dominican Republic	Yes
Ecuador	Yes
El Salvador	Yes
Guatemala	No
Guyana	Yes
Haiti	Yes
Honduras	Yes
Jamaica	No
Mexico	No
Nicaragua	Yes
Panama	No
Paraguay	Yes
Peru	Yes
Uruguay	Yes
Venezuela	Yes

the taxes of the most significant taxpayers (Table 3.3). This opened the way to introduce new techniques and procedures on an experimental scale, making it possible to check how they worked before they were extended throughout the administration.

In practice, the modernization of the remainder of tax administration has been postponed because of the effectiveness of pursuing the economically most significant taxpayers, as well as because of fiscal constraints faced by many countries. The result is an undesirable discrimination among taxpayers, since the lack of resources for managing compliance with the tax obligations of the remaining 95 percent leads to unfair treatment of the small target group, who become the only ones whose obligations are actually monitored with some frequency.

To facilitate oversight over the obligations of the rest of the taxpayer universe, most administrations extended the use of withholding taxes, under which companies withhold personal income taxes of their employees and value-added taxes of their suppliers. At the same time, most countries used some alternative of presumptive taxation in order to estimate the obligations of taxpayers who are expensive to monitor. Applying such mechanisms requires the capacity to identify easily observable indicators tied to the activity in question or others of a more general nature, such as utility consumption.

The growing share of indirect taxes in revenue composition in comparison to direct taxation has been taken as an indication that equity (at least from a vertical standpoint) has been abandoned in tax reform. These criticisms, however, do not take into account two factors: (i) the worldwide trend in tax matters, which made it necessary to harmonize rates so as not to discourage

method of structuring by specific taxes. The basic functions of these agencies (taxpayer service, master files, collection, auditing, legal issues) were streamlined. Intense reengineering took place with a view to making it easier for taxpayers to voluntarily comply with their obligations and for the tax administration to quickly spot tax evasion.

Modernization also featured a strategy of dividing the taxpayer universe, since no more than 5 percent of taxpayers often represent around 80 percent of revenue collected. Most countries created special units and physical installations for monitoring and collecting foreign investment; and (ii) the meager revenues from the income tax during the pre-reform period, whether as a result of excessive exemptions and incentives or the widespread failure by taxpayers to meet their tax obligations, flowing from the weakness of tax administration.

Curiously, the criticism that there is little concern for issues of fairness does not extend horizontally. In economic literature, the idea that groups with similar abilities to pay should pay similar levels of taxes has not received attention comparable to that given to the principle of progressivity, even though ignoring it can give rise to serious distortions and inequality. On the other hand, emphasis on the vertical dimension of fairness often ignores the fact that very high inflation rates during the pre-reform period primarily hurt the poorest sectors through the inflation tax. Tax reform was one of the ingredients that made it possible to assure the sustainability of the anti-inflation policy, thereby correcting this major source of inequality.

The average tax burden of the countries of Latin America is 14.1 percent of GDP, an amount lower than, but comparable to, that collected by a group of rapidly growing countries in Southeast Asia. However, in contrast with what occurs in the Asian countries, this rate varied widely among the Latin American countries (Figure 3.1).

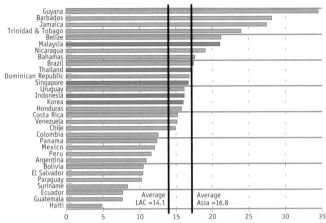

FIGURE 3.1

Total Tax Burden

(Average 1991-95, percent of GDP)

The Reforms of the 1990s and the Current Tax System

The process of tax reform initiated in the 1980s has extended into the first five years of the current decade. Initiatives in the tax field during this period may be classified into comprehensive, partial and incremental reforms. The first have been profound changes, directed along the lines of neutrality, legal and administrative streamlining, and horizontal fairness. The partial reforms are associated with the creation or restructuring of a single tax, typically the income tax. Incremental reforms, of which there have been many in the 1990s, have been limited to modifying rates or tax bases, usually in already established tax systems, in order to increase public sector resources (Table 3.4).

The tax system governing most countries of the region is structured around value-added taxes, excise taxes and the income tax. Brazil was one of the first countries

Table 3.4	Nature of Tax Reform since 1991			
Global	**Partial**		**Incremental**	
Argentina	Belize	Gross income	Barbados	Income
El Salvador	Bolivia	Profits	Brazil	Income
Jamaica	Ecuador	Presumptive (income)	Chile	Income
Nicaragua	Guatemala	Presumptive (income)	Colombia	VAT, income
Paraguay	Honduras	Presumptive (income)	Costa Rica	VAT, income
Peru	Venezuela	VAT	Guyana	Income
			Haiti	VAT
			Mexico	VAT
			Panama	VAT, income
			Suriname	Income
			Trinidad and Tobago	Income
			Uruguay	VAT, income

FIGURE 3.2

Productivity of the VAT, 1995

(In percent)

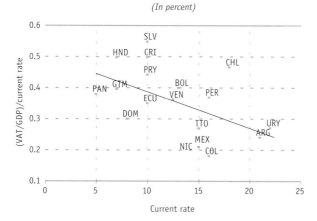

in the world to apply the VAT, which has become the primary tax tool in many Latin American countries. By 1995, 21 countries in the region used the VAT, and it was expected to go into effect in Belize in 1996 and in Barbados in 1997. Throughout the five-year period, with some exceptions, there has been a sharp tendency toward increasing VAT rates, while efforts to broaden the tax base have been relatively modest.

Under the system adopted in most countries, the VAT is a tax on consumption, since the tax obligation arises from the difference between taxes charged on sales (tax debit) and those paid on purchases, which includes capital goods (tax credit). The different treatment of the tax credit generated by purchases of consumable goods in Colombia, Haiti, Jamaica, Nicaragua, Panama, Paraguay and the Dominican Republic in some cases reduces, and in others eliminates, the incentive to save associated with this tax (Table 3.5).

Due to the multiphase character of the VAT, calculation of the tax is determined incrementally. From an analytical point of view, this way of determining the VAT enhances compliance, since it pits the interests of taxpayers in successive transactions against one another, insofar as the incentive to underestimate sales by one group is at odds with the interest of other groups to overestimate

purchases. Despite these design features, however, evasion is widespread in the region. To counteract it, the countries that have managed this tax most successfully have devoted a great deal of resources to analyzing documentation supporting transactions (invoicing systems), to computerized cross-checking of transactions declared by taxpayers, and to monitoring the tax by following the production cycle through the use of input-output coefficients.

However, evasion of the VAT is exacerbated by the reduction of the tax base because of the relatively large number of goods not covered by the tax in many countries, such as basic food baskets, agricultural production, and most services, including those of the financial sector. VAT productivity is measured by defining the ratio between tax collection in terms of GDP and the VAT rate. While this indicator does not take into account differences in taxable bases, the state of tax administration and other factors, simply correlating these variables indicates that for each percentage point that the tax rate increases, the productivity of the tax declines by approximately half a percentage point (Figure 3.2).

In keeping with international practice, it has become common to impose the VAT using the destination principle, by which goods and services are taxed in the country where they are consumed. Thus, imports are taxed when they enter the country, while exporters are reimbursed on their purchases of inputs. The characteristics of the tax make it suited to a centralized administration, an approach that has been adopted by all countries in the region except Brazil, where it is assigned to the states.[5]

Brazil adopted the VAT in 1967 as a subnational tax to encourage the states to raise their own revenues. In this instance, there is a combi-

---

[5] When the VAT was introduced in Mexico in 1980, it was also assigned to the subnational level. Subsequent problems in tax administration led to it being transferred to the federal domain in 1988.

		Treatment		Rate (%)	
Country	Main exemptions	Investment	Exports	General	Special
Argentina	Certain foodstuffs, education and health, publications	Generates tax credit	Zero tax rate levied	21	27
Bolivia			Zero tax rate levied	13	
Brazil	Food basket, varies by region	Generates tax credit	Tax levied	7/25	
Chile		Generates tax credit	Zero tax rate levied	18	
Colombia	Foodstuffs, agricultural prod., publications	Income tax credit	Zero tax rate levied	16	20 to 60 (autos)
Costa Rica	Agricultural products, food basket	Generates tax credit	Zero tax rate levied	10	
Dominican Rep.	Primary products, foodstuffs, publications, drugs	Does not generate tax credit	Zero tax rate levied	8	
Ecuador	Agricultural products, drugs, publications	Generates tax credit	Zero tax rate levied	10	
El Salvador	Foodstuffs, publications, education and health, public services	Generates tax credit	Zero tax rate levied	10	
Guatemala	Foodstuffs, merchandise, education	Generates tax credit	Zero tax rate levied	7	
Haiti	Education and health, sales threshold	Does not generate tax credit	Exempt	10	
Honduras	Food basket, petroleum derivatives, education and health, public services	Generates tax credit	Zero tax rate levied	7	
Jamaica		Generates conditional tax credit	Zero tax rate levied	0/12.5	8.1 to 176.9 (autos)
Mexico	Publications, education and health	Generates tax credit	Zero tax rate levied	15	0
Nicaragua	Foodstuffs, health, publications	Generates prorated tax credit	Zero tax rate levied	15	
Panama	Food supply, services	Does not generate tax credit	Zero tax rate levied	5	10
Paraguay	Cultural services, agricultural	Partial, primary installation	Zero tax rate levied	10	
Peru	Foodstuffs, some services	Generates tax credit	Zero tax rate levied	16	+2
Trinidad & Tobago	Services except education and medicines	Generates tax credit	Zero tax rate levied	15	0 (foodstuffs)
Uruguay	Agricultural, public services, tobacco products and fuels	Generates tax credit	Zero tax rate levied	22	12
Venezuela	Foodstuffs, agricultural, fuels, publications, education and health, residential public services		Zero tax rate levied	12.5	+10 to +20, luxury consumption goods

Note: The Bahamas, Barbados, Belize, Guyana and Suriname had no VAT in 1995.

Source: Estructura y administración de los impuestos sobre rentas y ventas en países miembros del CIAT, technical publication of the Inter-American Center for Tax Administrators (CIAT), May 1995.

nation of the origin principle and the destination principle, depending on whether transactions take place between states or between them and other countries. In practice, exports are taxed by the states, while treatment of imports is problematic because the customs stations fall under the federal government's jurisdiction. Major complications have arisen in the course of implementing this tax in Brazil as a result of the tax assignments, making it necessary to harmonize 27 bodies of tax legislation.

Differentiated tax treatment is often extended to goods whose consumption presents negative externalities, that have a low demand elasticity vis-à-vis price and a high elasticity vis-à-vis revenue, or that have a small supply structure. Ex-

amples are alcoholic beverages, soft drinks, tobacco products, vehicles, auto parts and fuels.

Most countries take advantage of their revenue-raising possibilities, and for that purpose they contribute high rates and a relatively simple administration due to the limited number of suppliers of such goods. Recently, several countries, including Argentina, Colombia and Costa Rica, have taken steps to streamline these taxes by limiting them to the products mentioned above in order to reduce the distortions that occur when such taxes are applied excessively.

Of the three taxes being examined, the income tax is the most difficult to administer because its base is spread among a variety of activities, the number of potential taxpayers is very large,

FIGURE 3.3

Income Tax Revenue

(Average 1991-95, percent of GDP)

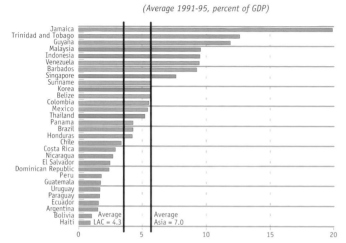

To improve administration of the income tax, a number of countries use taxpayers' assets as an indicator to establish income levels, allowing the taxes paid on assets to be credited to the income tax account. Withholding systems have also been applied with employers to facilitate collection of personal income tax. In addition, most countries have adopted some kind of a special treatment for remittances outside the country in connection with matters such as payment of royalties, trademarks, patents, and licensing agreements, which are becoming increasingly important in a context of economic globalization.

Challenges of the Next Five Years

Despite the growing involvement of the private sector in activities until quite recently carried out by the public sector and supported by public investment, the demands for the region's economies to develop will continue to put pressure on fiscal resources. Although there are benefits from more efficient spending, the main sources of an increase in revenues must come from taxation, since in most countries the portion from nontax resources, public spending and sale of assets is limited.

Increasing tax revenues requires ongoing improvement of the tax system in both policy and administrative areas. Due to the current high share of indirect taxes, the increased tax burden should be expected to come from direct taxation. Streamlining of excise taxes seems unavoidable in many countries because this instrument is better focused on more limited objectives connected with the negative externalities generated by consumption or other activities, such as deterioration of the environment.

At the same time, the list of products and activities outside the scope of the VAT must be reduced, because of the distortions generated by such differentiated treatments, including those affecting the administration of the tax. The rates in effect in Argentina and Uruguay, and to a lesser extent in Chile and Peru, do not offer much room

and the tax process does not create a paper trail comparable to that left by the VAT. Such being the case, administration of the income tax remains very flawed in most of the region, with the exception of the English-speaking countries. As a percentage of GDP, revenues from this tax in the group of previously mentioned Southeast Asian countries is 63 percent higher than it is in Latin America (Figure 3. 3).

Reducing exemptions and the levels of general and marginal rates has made it easier to administer this tax. Currently, the single rate for corporations in most countries of the region is lower than the highest marginal rate in the United States (39.6 percent). For individuals, however, most countries have maintained some kind of progressivity in the tax structure, albeit with intervals and marginal rates lower than they were in the past (Table 3.6).

Compensation for losses during fiscal periods is in effect in most countries, although with restrictions in time and scope. It has become widespread practice to take worldwide revenue as the basis for applying the income tax for residents and to take only domestic revenue for nonresidents. As a result, compensation affects only local losses for this latter group.

for increasing revenue. In such cases there should be a return to the strategy of extending the tax base and cutting rates, which would make administration less complex and reduce incentives for tax evasion.

Higher taxes from direct taxation basically comes from taxing income and wealth, which will bring renewed concern for its effects on saving.[6] While it will be necessary to devise mechanisms for moderating that effect, it must be kept in mind that a major advance associated with the tax reforms of the 1980s was the simplification of a vast array of tax exemptions that created problems of equity and efficiency in resource allocation and tax administration. Future exemptions to protect saving and investment for both individuals and companies will have to be strictly selective, focused and quantifiable. That will demand a great deal of transparency and an adequate incentive system, including sanctions for unmet commitments.[7]

Increasing the share of personal income tax within total revenue collection requires lowering the tax threshold. The reform of social security systems will make such a process easier, since the tax character that employer and worker pay-

Table 3.6	Main Features of the Income Tax in Latin America, 1995				
Country	Corporate General rates (%)	Individual rates (%)	Special tax rates for remittances	Special treatment for capital gains	Compensation for losses in previous tax periods
Argentina	30	11/30	Yes	No	Yes
Barbados	40	25 and 40	Yes	No	Yes
Bolivia	25	13	Yes	No	Yes
Brazil	25	15/35	Yes	Yes	Yes
Chile	15	5/45	Yes	No	Yes
Colombia	30/35	0/35	Yes	Yes	Yes
Costa Rica	30	10/25	Yes		Yes
Dominican Republic	30	15/30	Yes	Yes	Yes
Ecuador	25	10/25	No	Yes	Yes
El Salvador	25	10/30	No	No	No
Guatemala	25	15/25	Yes	Yes	Yes
Haiti	10/30	10/30	Yes	No	Yes
Honduras	15, 35, 45, 60	9/40	Yes	No	No, partial
Jamaica	33.3	25	No	Yes	Yes
Mexico	34	3/35	Yes	No	Yes
Nicaragua	30	7/30	Yes	Yes	Yes
Panama	30, 34	3/30	Yes	Yes, real estate	Yes
Paraguay	30	-	Yes	No	Yes
Peru	30	15/30	Yes	No	Yes
Suriname	35/45	14/50	No	No	Yes
Trinidad and Tobago	38	5/38	Yes	No	Yes
Uruguay	30	-	Yes	No	Yes
Venezuela	15, 22, 34	6/34	Yes	Yes, stock dividends	Yes

Source: Estructura y administración de los impuestos sobre rentas y ventas en países miembros del CIAT, technical publication of the Inter-American Center for Tax Administrators (CIAT), May 1995.

---

[6] Bolivia recently examined the alternative of a direct tax based on consumption, which would be implemented through a cash flow tax. A corporate income tax was finally adopted in late 1994 because of the limited international experience with consumption-based direct taxation, and especially given problems of harmonizing taxes with the United States.

[7] Tanzi and Shome (1992) examine tax incentives within the role played by tax policy in the development of the Southeast Asian economies. The authors link the effectiveness of incentives to the quality of the bureaucratic apparatus responsible for granting them. The decline of the public sector in most countries of the region indicates the need for major institutional strengthening, should the decision be made to move in this direction.

roll contributions have in traditional systems will be reduced as benefits are more closely tied to individual contributions. At the same time, the continuing importance of taxes on consumption makes it advisable to maintain a degree of progressivity in personal income tax rates. While economic integration places an upward limit on income tax rates on legal entities, there is no reason why they should be significantly lower than the rates in effect in capital exporting countries, given the principle of worldwide income that this group of countries applies.

The tax assignments of the various levels of government is another task facing tax policy during the next few years. As has been clear throughout this chapter, the taxes that are currently most elastic with respect to GDP, such as taxes on value added, specific consumer items, income and foreign trade, are within the central government sphere, while the taxes over which lower levels of government have authority are typically those on property, as well as some sales taxes. However, lower levels of government are increasingly being made responsible for spending in order to draw service providers and their beneficiaries closer together. To overcome the asymmetry arising from the delegation of powers to collect and to spend revenues, most countries have adopted tax revenue sharing systems implemented automatically in conjunction with tax collection.

This creates two kinds of problems. For the central government, the automatic transfer of resources makes fiscal management more rigid, because the resources transferred become current spending that is difficult to eliminate. Such a situation discourages the central government from increasing the tax load to deal with a possible future need to increase current saving. For lower levels, while this solution manages to compensate for the problem of revenues, it does not allow for adequately internalizing budgetary constraints, with the consequent loss of accountability. This issue needs careful discussion in many countries. One possible direction is to strengthen the link between central government transfers with tax collection efforts at lower levels of government and with the quality of service provided.

The process of regional and worldwide integration demands an enormous effort to harmonize tax legislation, which in turn places growing demands on administration. The most urgent tasks are the verification of requests for return of the VAT and the monitoring of transfer prices in conjunction with the income taxes of companies conducting business in different tax jurisdictions.

The need to increase the share of direct taxes, broaden the mass of taxpayers, design and administer fiscal incentives, and make tax administration fit the requirements of international administration are tasks that will demand further resources for the agencies responsible for tax collection. The tax burden of from 8 to 22 percent of GDP in the region has a cost of collection of between 1.5 to 2.5 percent of revenue collected.

However, it is to be expected that revenue increases will become smaller as coverage of the taxpayer universe is extended, while it is probable the opposite will occur with tax administration costs.

It is important to keep in mind that even without having taken on new activities, the tax administration of some countries is still in a highly precarious condition. While modernization has covered all areas of tax administration, the greatest advances have taken place in the special taxpayers units, and the functions of collection and taxpayers' service and master file.

In the coming years, tax administration in many countries must make progress in oversight functions, the collection process, and the legal area. Currently, the goals of the audit plan often refer exclusively to the tax administration's actions regarding not only both formal but also substantial fulfillment by taxpayers. Nevertheless, relatively little is known about the amount collected through the auditing activities, partly because of the complex appeal procedures that the taxpayer may invoke, aggravated by the slowness of judicial processes and by ineffective tax administration in the area of collection.

Special attention must be paid to organizational reform, moving forward to implement a tax administration management model that makes centralized regulation compatible with decentralized operation. The model to be adopted will require greater resources in the areas of management, planning, operational oversight and information systems. At the same time, local levels will need greater autonomy and more decentralized management of the operational resources that are currently concentrated at the central level. Institutional reform must also include a policy for strengthening and updating human resources. The complexity of problems to be faced and the technological resources required for solving them demand that tax administration officials be better trained than they have been in the past.

CHAPTER 4

FINANCIAL
REFORM

ABSTRACT

A great wave of financial reform has taken place in Latin America since the late 1980s. Countries across the region have adopted liberalization measures to eliminate interest rate controls, dismantle targeted credit programs, reduce reserve requirements, and privatize or liquidate state-owned commercial and development banks. Additional measures have enhanced prudential safeguards for banks and capital markets, and granted central banks greater de facto independence. This chapter summarizes, quantifies and dates the major financial reforms undertaken since 1988 by the countries of Latin America and the Caribbean. The genesis, salient features and current issues confronting each of the country's financial reforms are selectively capsulized.

The 26 countries are grouped into four groups reflecting the amount of financial reform each has undertaken since 1988. Seven countries (Argentina, Bolivia, Colombia, El Salvador, Nicaragua, Peru and Uruguay) are classed as major re-formers, having carried out the greatest amount of financial reform. The seven substantial reform countries (Dominican Republic, Ecuador, Guatemala, Guyana, Mexico, Trinidad and Tobago and Venezuela) have done only somewhat less reform than the first group. Nine countries have carried out some reform (the Bahamas, Barbados, Belize, Brazil, Chile, Costa Rica, Honduras, Jamaica and Paraguay), while three countries (Haiti, Panama and Suriname) have done little or no reform. Within this last group, Chile is a special case, having completed a comprehensive process of liberalization and strengthening of financial supervision before 1988. The larger countries (Mexico plus the countries of South America) have undertaken more financial reform as a group than the Central American countries, which in turn have been more active than the Caribbean countries.

The changes in the reform areas tracked here have been almost uniformly in the direction of more liberalization, enhanced prudential safeguards, and greater central bank independence. From the beginning of the post-1988 period of financial reforms until mid-1996, no countries increased the amount of their targeted credit programs in real (inflation-adjusted) terms, none allowed commercial bank supervision to deteriorate significantly, and none permitted their central banks to become less independent. Only five countries raised bank reserve requirements; in all others, reserve requirements were lowered or kept at about the same level. Impressively, in 23 of the 26 countries, all commercial bank deposit interest rates are presently market determined, while commercial bank lending rates are free in 19.

Our analysis indicates that undertaking financial liberalization in the absence of a reason-able level of prudential bank regulation and supervision appears to be associated with an increased likelihood of a banking crisis. Against the backdrop, the reform data collected here indicate that most countries in Latin America did not have sufficient prudential safeguards in place when they began to liberalize, a shortcoming that may help explain the substantial number of banking crises observed in the region. Many of the initially deficient countries, however, eventually improved banking safeguards in the course of their reforms, so that the situation today is one of much greater balance between liberalization and prudential controls.

Although many financial reforms were initiated in the late 1980s and early 1990s, even over the past year and a half many countries in Latin America continue to undertake the kinds of reforms discussed in this chapter—primarily those in the banking sector—at almost the same pace as in the preceding seven years. Eventually, this pace must slow much more, as more countries adopt these measures. While continued attention should and will be given to deepening bank reforms, another important future challenge lies with improving the longer-term segments of the financial system, which are comparatively underdeveloped in Latin America. These include stocks and bonds, insurance, pension funds, leasing, and venture capital. With the deceleration of inflation in the region over the past several years, attention has already begun to—and should increasingly—turn toward this task. Another great challenge confronting many countries that have closed their public development banks is to fill the vacuum these closures have left in rural financial markets, in lending to micro, small, and medium-scale firms, and in supplying longer-term finance.

INTRODUCTION

This chapter systematically describes—country by country and theme by theme—the major financial reforms undertaken since 1988 in Latin America and the Caribbean. An introductory section discusses the advantages and drawbacks of each of the financial reforms, and examines the issue of the sequencing of liberalization measures versus prudential safeguards. Subsequent sections provide data on the reforms themselves, examine current status indicators, analyze the relationship between financial reforms and banking crises, and take a brief look at trends and possible future directions for enhancing the development of financial systems in the region.

Although the impact of the sequence of reforms on the likelihood of bank crises is examined here, the chapter does not attempt to link financial reforms with various outcome measures such as financial depth, interest rate levels and spreads, and investment rates. However, as discussed in Part One of this Report, the adoption by many countries in Latin America of a comprehensive package of reforms—of which financial reform is often a component—has been associated with an increase in both financial depth and investment rates, and with a tendency for negative real interest rates to rise to positive levels. This chapter focuses almost entirely on banking system reforms. It touches only marginally on securities markets, and not at all on other financial market segments such as insurance, pensions, leasing, bonded warehouses and venture capital. This emphasis on banks reflects the preeminent role they have played and still play in the financial systems of most Latin American countries.

THE AREAS OF REFORM

The great wave of Latin American financial sector reforms that began in the late 1980s and grew to encompass nearly every country in the region during the 1990s was a reaction to serious problems that developed in the model of state control of the economy in general and of the financial sector in particular. Major state interventions in the banking sector that were common in previous decades included:

- Administrative controls on interest rates, such as ceilings and occasionally floors on loan and deposit rates.
- Targeted credit programs, which directed lending to certain sectors, usually at subsidized interest rates.
- A state banking sector, often covering a sizable segment of the market, which enhanced the state's ability to control financial transactions.
- Reserve requirements set well above the levels needed for prudential management of the banking system.

Most of these interventions have now been rolled back in the majority of Latin American countries, a liberalizing trend that has had many benefits, but which has also given rise in some cases to revisiting certain problems the interventions were initially intended to solve. In addition, two other interventions, not always considered essential in the past, have recently been strengthened in many countries:

- Prudential regulation and supervision of banking institutions and capital markets.
- Greater independence of the central bank.

Liberalization measures aimed at solving the first four problems generally have had the effect of increasing the size and scope of the private sector banking system, and of giving this system greater freedom to set prices and quantities. Acting as a counterweight, improved prudential regulation and supervision help control the increased moral hazard, potential fraud and mismanagement, and other problems associated with this expansion and liberalization. The next section shows that most countries that have undertaken a significant amount of financial reform have by now achieved a balanced program involving a great deal of liberalization as well as the improvement of bank regulation and supervision. However, it is also shown that almost all of these countries have undertaken these two reform blocks in a sequence that is the reverse of what is generally considered best, with a good deal of liberalization coming before prudential safeguards were strengthened. As will be discussed below, this may well have led in Latin America to serious banking system problems and even crises. In many cases, this suboptimal sequencing reflected political-economy constraints, as also discussed below.

In addition to this tension between greater liberalization on one hand and better regulation and supervision on the other, there is also a tension within each of the individual reform elements, particularly within each of the four liberalization elements. In order to set the stage for a discussion of Latin America's recent financial reforms, we now examine each of the six reforms, starting with the four areas of liberalization and the tension that exists between their major advantages and drawbacks.

Interest rate controls were often seen as a tool to increase investment and accelerate growth, particularly during the 1950s and 1960s, as a result of simplistic interpretations of Keynesian economics. By pushing interest rates down to low levels it was thought that the demand for investment goods (plant and equipment) would be stimulated, and that the resulting increase in investment levels would lead to faster economic growth. Since McKinnon (1973) and Shaw (1973), it has been widely discussed whether these objectives were ever attained, as reducing interest rates may restrict the supply of aggregate savings to finance aggregate investment. Governments also controlled interest rates in order to reduce the costs of public sector borrowing and thus relieve the pressures of budget deficits, to be able to easily and cheaply favor certain sectors with low-cost credit, and to help prevent or contain banking and economic crises that might be caused by real interest rates becoming very high and pushing bank

borrowers into default and aggregate investment down to recession-generating levels.

Primarily because controls reduce overall productivity levels by worsening the allocation of investment and working capital resources in the economy, it is now generally agreed that they have impacted negatively on economic growth. Low bank interest rates diminish the role of banks in mobilizing deposits, causing a concomitant decrease in their role in allocating credit to the highest and best economic uses. Loan rate ceilings also provide fertile soil for corruption, or at least for rent-seeking behavior, in which potential borrowers waste substantial time and economic resources vying for artificially-scarce credit. In some instances, controls also help spur capital flight, contributing to a reduction of investment and growth rates and a destabilization of the macroeconomy. Reflecting perhaps all of these factors, econometric studies have found that when interest rates are sufficiently controlled to reduce the level of deposit rates to five percentage points or more below the rate of inflation, the annual GDP growth rate is reduced by over one percentage point, a substantial loss.[1]

Targeted credit programs direct bank loans, usually at subsidized interest rates, to selected sectors or groups. These programs were intended to serve a number of purposes, including delivering credit to small borrowers and other groups that were not well served by the banking system, isolating selected sectors from monetary and financial swings, and increasing the supply of food and certain other goods. Targeted credit programs have operated through a number of mechanisms: (1) specialized development banks (in such areas as agriculture, industry, mining and housing) that channel funds to specific sectors; (2) direct central bank loans to the favored groups; (3) regulations mandating that commercial banks lend a certain share of their portfolio for the targeted

---

[1] For example, see Easterly and Wetzel (1989), Roubini and Sala-i-Martin (1992), and King and Levine (1992).

purposes; and (4) economic incentives such as preferential reserve requirements or special rediscount lines and rates for lending to the priority sectors.

While many targeted credit programs have no doubt delivered credit to the intended sectors and achieved other objectives as well, there is substantial literature discussing and documenting the many and often severely negative effects of these programs. One major drawback is that by disrupting the allocation of credit to the most productive activities, targeted credit programs reduce investment efficiency and economic growth. Financial and economic development may also be curtailed as banks are discouraged from mobilizing deposits when lower cost funds are available to them from rediscount lines at the central bank or other apex lenders. Targeted credit lines have also encouraged the acquisition of banks by nonfinancial firms seeking to secure ready access to low-cost loans. The resultant insider lending frequently has been a major source of bank portfolio weakness in many Latin American countries. Finally, while targeted credit programs have often increased the flow of credit to the intended sectors, because of the scarcity of this credit relative to the demand for it, these funds have normally gone disproportionately to the more powerful and well-connected within and outside the targeted sector. Consequently, these programs have often failed to reach the target group (usually the smaller producers and lower-income households) and have also tended to widen income and wealth disparities. For example, Vogel (1984) estimates that 80 percent of the agricultural loan subsidies in Costa Rica flowed to households in the top 10 percent of the income distribution, increasing their share of total household income from 30 to 34.4 percent.

Public commercial and development banks were often established to assist small, high-risk, rural and other types of borrowers who were underserved by private sector financial institutions. To this end, public banks frequently served as conduits for targeted credit programs. Public development banks have also been a major source of medium- and long-term credit, including mortgage and investment credit, which has not been generally available from private sector financial institutions. Finally, public banks have acted as control rods in financial panics, in the sense that they often lessened problems of bank runs since their deposits were generally seen as government guaranteed.

The major drawbacks of public banks in their role as conduits for targeted credit programs have already been discussed above. The public development banks have also been natural magnets for special interest lobbying and political favoritism. Consequently, targeted credit programs channeled through these institutions have often resulted in loans being granted on administrative or political grounds, with insufficient attention being given to the creditworthiness of the borrowers. The result has often been staggering loan losses and institutional insolvency. Public commercial banks frequently have been bloated with excess personnel and branches, and have generally been slow to pick up on financial innovations. While the public banks have often become a major source of financial system inefficiency and a drain on government fiscal resources, a great challenge now confronts many countries that have closed these banks: to fill the vacuum these closures have left in rural financial markets, in longer-term lending, in lending to micro, small, and medium-scale firms, and in other areas that were once predominantly served by public banks and now may be greatly underserved by the remaining financial entities.

Reserve requirements for financial institutions have frequently been set above the prudential levels (approximately 5-15 percent) generally required to manage bank runs. This has often been done to tighten money supply and reduce inflationary pressures, to reallocate some of the inflation tax revenues from the banks to the government, and, in the case of reserve requirements on foreign currency deposits, to help stem excessive capital inflows. While raising reserve requirements (sometimes to quite high levels) is often an important means for stabilizing the macroeconomy and accomplishing these other objectives, it generally results in lower deposit rates and higher loan rates, as banks increase their spreads to compensate for the larger tax on intermediation. These interest rate changes lead to less deposit mobilization and bank credit availability, with the latter further eroded by the increased reserve requirements themselves. This curtailment of financial intermediation, in turn, diminishes productivity levels and growth rates.[2] The reduced deposit rates may also exacerbate problems of capital flight.

Prudential banking regulations and their enforcement through supervision are needed because of the special nature of banking. First, there are major informational deficiencies in this industry. For example, banks do not know the true ability or willingness of their borrowing clients to repay loans, and depositors, in choosing a bank with which to entrust their funds, know even less about the portfolio quality of alternative financial institutions. Depositors generally also know very little about management weaknesses, fraudulent financial dealings, and other shortcomings of banks. Second, banks accept deposits from the public, leveraging bank capital many times over with these funds. This gives rise to an important moral hazard problem, generating incentives for bank owners (and bank managers acting on behalf of the shareholders) to hold excessively risky portfolios, since bank owners receive the full benefit of good outcomes while depositors and any deposit insurance scheme pay part of the price of outcomes sufficiently bad as to bankrupt the bank.[3]

Regulation attacks these information problems and moral hazards in two ways. First, it develops information about asset quality and fraudulent financial dealings and other shortcomings of the banks, so that depositors will shun poorly-managed institutions, at least to the extent that they are not covered by deposit insurance and thus would suffer losses from poor bank perfor-

mance. Thus, for example, regulations generally call for loans to be classified according to quality (based on each loan's delinquency status, borrower repayment capacity, etc.), and for qualified, independent auditors to regularly check each bank's financial health and disclose this information to the public. Second, regulation tries to limit the risky behavior of banks and its consequences for depositors and the overall economy by requiring, for example, that banks have a minimum of capital and liquidity, avoid the risks of excessive loan concentration and insider credits, set aside funds (provisions) to cover the possibility of loan default, avoid rollovers of bad loans so that credits of dubious quality are not redefined as current, and are intervened by the banking authority if their affairs begin to go badly so as to limit losses to depositors and the public, and the possibilities of a crisis that damages the macroeconomy.

Adequate bank supervision implies that there are sufficient resources to hire, train and retain qualified personnel, and acquire the necessary technology. It also requires that supervisors be free of political interference and have sufficient authority to enforce compliance with their decisions.

Capital markets regulation and supervision aims to protect and inform those investing in stocks and other securities. Thus, a good capi-

---

[2] There is much econometric evidence in support of this last point. For example, King and Levine (1993) find that a 10 percentage point rise in the ratio of private banking system credit to GDP (e.g., from 0.40 to 0.50) is associated with an increase in the annual GDP growth rate of about one-third of a percentage point. Ghani (1992) finds an even larger growth effect, approximately one-half of a percentage point.

[3] Even if explicit deposit insurance does not exist in the country, governments are often unwilling to let a major bank crisis develop unchecked because of the losses that would be suffered by so many depositors and because of the potential damage to the macroeconomy. Hence, it often happens that even in the absence of an explicit deposit insurance scheme, governments pay off depositors for some or all of their losses, at least in a large bank crisis. Like explicit deposit insurance, this implicit deposit insurance reduces the vigilance of depositors over bank affairs, and diminishes the need depositors feel to move away from or demand higher deposit rates from riskier banks. The presence of explicit or implicit deposit insurance makes banks different from other firms (even those that are highly leveraged and have uncertain prospects) and provides the rationale for government regulation of banks (but not of the other firms). For additional discussion of the rationale for bank regulation, see Hausmann and Gavin (1995, Sect. 2).

tal markets law would include such measures as setting up a supervisory system; creating licensing standards for brokers, dealers and investment banks, including minimum capital requirements; protecting against conflicts of interest, insider trading and other abuses of minority shareholders; and ensuring adequate auditing and information disclosure.

Independence of the central bank from the Finance Ministry and the rest of government (both the executive and legislative branches), as has been argued by Cukierman (1992) and others, is useful in establishing a more credible and less inflationary set of monetary and exchange rate policies. The lack of automatic deficit financing may also restrict fiscal imbalances. Hence, greater independence can help foster a commitment to sounder macroeconomic policies. Greater independence may also insulate the central bank from pressures to place administrative controls on interest rates, establish large targeted credit programs, or increase reserve requirements to obtain the resources needed for such directed credits or other programs.

A sequencing issue. The final section of this chapter presents empirical evidence that removing interest rate controls, dismantling targeted credit programs, and lowering reserve requirements before strengthening regulation and supervision can contribute materially to the likelihood of a banking crisis. As a prelude to that and to the presentation of data in the next section on the degree to which countries in Latin America followed this sequence, we briefly discuss at the conceptual level the problems that may arise from liberalizing before adequate prudential safeguards are in place.

A number of things may happen when the financial system is liberalized without adequate regulations or a superintendency that is able to properly perform its supervisory functions. One important impact may come about as a result of lifting interest rate controls and reducing reserve requirements, both of which enable the banks to expand—possibly by a large amount—their lending volume (since they can mobilize more deposits and lend a greater share of what is taken in). In such circumstances, a superintendency that cannot or does not properly monitor the existing volume of financial transactions and bank activities will fall even further behind. As a result, banks may engage in a greater volume of lending to insiders (which can often be disguised and made difficult to detect) and in other risky practices, which because of the moral hazard problem described earlier may be in the private interests of the banks but not in the more general interests of society. These practices include inadequate capitalization and provisioning, overly concentrated lending or lending to high-risk clients, fraudulent financial schemes, or simply practices that reflect management incompetencies or poor judgment. With the expansion of financial activity, the superintendency also may not be able to maintain a good early warning system for detecting bank problems based on timely, accurate and complete reports. Its capacity to close down banks at an early stage of crisis, before losses mount and problems spread to other financial institutions, may therefore be impaired.

In addition to these problems, which arise purely because of greater financial activity levels, bank crises may develop in other ways as the result of engaging in liberalization without adequate regulation and supervision. The general expansion of bank lending and the dismantling of targeted credit programs give banks the potential to move increasingly into lending areas in which they have not been very active before. This carries the risk that the rate of problem loans may rise dramatically, particularly if there is an adverse macroeconomic or other shock to the economy.[4] The fact

---

[4] It would be mainly in the shorter run (which may last some years) that the elimination of targeted credit programs may increase the rate of problem loans as a result of banks moving into new and unfamiliar lending areas. In the longer run, with the greater freedom banks have to choose their loan clients and the experience they gain with the new the client base, elimination of targeted credit programs may reduce problem loans.

that real lending rates are free to rise to potentially high levels may also add to these problems in another way. Higher lending rates attract a riskier portfolio of loans to the bank, since higher-risk/ higher-return activities are the only ones that yield enough to be worth undertaking with expensive bank financing. Serious problems may develop if the superintendency cannot or does not obtain feedback on how the loans to new clients are faring through an adequate loan classification system, does not enforce adequate provisioning and capital standards, does not find and challenge excessive insider lending, and does not intervene as banks begin to get into trouble. For all these reasons, then, financial liberalization without adequate regulation and supervision can increase the rate of banking system problems and the likelihood and severity of a banking crisis.[5]

Díaz-Alejandro (1985) and others have made much the same argument based on the experience of Argentina, Uruguay and Chile in removing interest rate and exchange controls, dramatically reducing targeted credit programs, progressively diminishing reserve requirements, and liberalizing other aspects of their financial systems in the mid- and early 1970s. The permissive regulatory environment that accompanied these changes contributed importantly to the financial crises that occurred in these Southern Cone countries in the early 1980s.

OVERVIEW OF THE REFORMS

In most of the countries of Latin America, financial reforms have been part of a broader package of macroeconomic, fiscal, trade, price, state enterprise and other reforms that were commonly introduced in varying degrees and mixes starting especially in the late 1980s and early 1990s. The years of recession, slow growth and inflation that followed the 1982 debt crisis, along with the success of liberalization policies and other reforms of East Asia and Chile, helped prompt many countries to liberalize their economies in several areas.

Peru provides a dramatic illustration of this. When the current government first assumed office in July 1990, it was faced with hyperinflation, real wages that had fallen by more than one-half over the preceding five years, depleted international reserves and a foreign debt largely in arrears, and a real GDP that had plunged 25 percent since 1987. Hyperinflation and macroeconomic instability were combatted with an orthodox stabilization program of fiscal and monetary discipline. A deep-seated reform program was implemented to restore efficiency and international competitiveness and to stimulate growth. Major reforms included unification and floating of the exchange rate, a dramatic reduction of import barriers and abolition of exchange controls, elimination of price controls and wage indexation, introduction of flexibility into a rigid labor code, and privatization of major state-owned enterprises.

Along with these measures, Peru adopted one of the most far-reaching programs of financial reform in Latin America. All interest rate controls were dropped by April 1991. By 1992, all subsidized, targeted lending was eliminated (though some marginal targeted credit at market rates has returned recently). Reserve requirements on local currency deposits were progressively reduced to prudential levels, and are currently 9 percent.[6] A bank law passed in March 1991 began to introduce regulatory discipline, and was further strengthened by a second law in 1993. Supervision and regulation, which were very weak at the

---

[5] The IMF (1993) gives a variant of this argument for developed countries, making the case that the recent spate of developed country bank failures— for example, in the United States, Japan and Scandinavia—are connected by the common thread of financial reform and the greater competitive pressures it has unleashed. For example, the removal of deposit rate controls and the increased competition for deposits (including from high-yielding money market funds) has driven up bank deposit rates. This, in turn, has pushed up loan rates and resulted in an increase in the riskiness of bank portfolios, including rapidly expanding participation in new areas of activity such as derivative markets.

[6] Foreign currency reserve requirements, now at 43.5 percent, have been kept high in an attempt to hold back the wave of short-term capital inflows that have been attracted to the country.

start of the reform program, were greatly improved over a period of several years, and the ratio of nonperforming to total outstanding loans dropped from over 20 percent in 1990 to 6 percent in 1995. The five public development banks, which had run up enormous losses in the past, were closed. All seven public commercial banks were also liquidated or divested. A new capital markets law was enacted in 1992. In December 1992, a law was passed to solidify the position of the central bank as an independent entity. Its new charter specified the central bank's sole objective as the preservation of the value of the currency, in contrast to the old charter which also specified the objective of a high growth rate of output and employment.

While Peru's far-reaching financial reforms eventually brought about reasonably effective bank regulation and supervision, prudential safeguards were not adequate in the early years of its wholesale financial liberalization program. As discussed in the previous section, this lack of sequencing between financial liberalization and prudential safeguards can lead to serious banking system problems, and, in the case of Peru, it may have contributed to the country's banking crisis in 1991-93, which mainly affected state-owned commercial banks which had been inadequately supervised.

In order to chart broadly and systematically the extent (and overall sequencing) of financial reforms in all 26 borrowing member countries of the IDB, data were gathered on financial reforms since 1988 in the following areas of reform:[7] liberalization of commercial bank deposit and loan rates of interest, change in reserve requirements on local currency (LC) and foreign currency (FC) bank deposits, change in the amount of targeted credit in real (i.e., inflation-adjusted) terms, share of the banking system loan market served by public banks that were privatized or liquidated, change in de facto central bank independence, adoption of modern laws or regulations on capital markets and banking, and a

change in the overall quality of commercial bank supervision. These data are presented in Tables 4.1a to 4.1d, with one column devoted to each of the 10 reform areas. Each of the 26 countries are placed in one of four categories describing the overall extent of its financial reforms: major reforms, substantial reforms, some reforms, and little or no reform.[8] Box 4.1 provides further explanations of the reform themes found in the columns of the tables. The sequencing of reforms is discussed once their nature and overall dimensions have been presented.

We find that there has indeed been a great wave of financial reform in Latin America in the late 1980s and first half of the 1990s, particularly in the 14 countries labeled as either major reformers or substantial reformers. Reforms have been generally strong in all 10 of the reform categories, though stronger in some than others. The reforms have tended to move almost uniformly in the direction of more liberalization, enhanced prudential safeguards, and greater central bank independence. From the beginning of each country's reform period until the time of the survey (May 1996), no countries increased the amount of their targeted credit programs in real (inflation-adjusted) terms, none allowed commercial bank supervision to deteriorate significantly, and none permitted their central banks to become less independent. Only five countries raised bank reserve requirements; in all others reserve requirements were lowered or kept at about the same level.

There is a great range in the scope of financial reforms carried out among the 26 coun-

---

[7] Data were gathered primarily by means of written country surveys completed during May 1996. The information provided was cross-checked against that obtained from a similar survey carried out in November 1994—which used the same survey instrument but a mostly different set of respondents—and against outside information to the extent possible. See Westley (1995) for the results of the earlier survey.

[8] The surveys provided the initial extent of reform rankings. These were checked for cross-country consistency using information on the number and depth of the individual reform elements for each country, with much of these reform data given in the 10 columns of Tables 4.1a to 4.1d. Only a few initial rankings had to be modified as a result of this review.

Table 4.1a What Did the Reforms Do? Class 1 (Major Reform) Countries

Country (and period of main reforms)	At least some commercial bank interest rates currently free, and this is due to reforms — Deposit	Loan	Change in reserve requirements (from before reforms until now) — Local currency	Foreign currency	Percent of targeted credit remaining (from before reforms until now)	Percent share of loan market privatized or liquidated (date)	Change in de facto central bank independence (from before reforms until now)	Reforms brought a new and modern capital markets law or set of regulations? (date)	Reforms brought a new and modern bank law or set of regulations? (date)	Change in commercial bank supervision (before reform → now)
Argentina (1992-on)	—*	—	Much lower	Much lower	1-49	15 (1992-on)	More independent (2)	Yes (1991-on, series of improvements)	Yes (1992-93)	3 → 1 (Needs major overhaul → reasonable)
Bolivia (1990-on)	Yes	Yes	Somewhat lower	Same	1-49	40 (1989-91)	Much more independent (1)	No	Yes (1993)	3 → 2 (Needs major overhaul → needs some overhaul)
Colombia (1990-94)	Yes	—*	Much lower	na[1]	1-20	30 (1991-95)	Much more independent (1)	Yes (1993)	Yes (1984, 1990, 1993)	1 → 1 (Reasonable → reasonable)
El Salvador (1990-92)	Yes	Yes	Somewhat lower	Much lower	1-49	95 (1990-93; 1996)	More independent (2)	Yes (1994)	Yes (late 1991)	3 → 1 (Needs major overhaul → reasonable)
Nicaragua (1990-on)	Yes	Yes	Much lower	Much lower	10-15	40 (1990-91; 1996)	Much more independent (1)	Yes (1993)	Yes (1993)	3 → 1 (Needs major overhaul → reasonable)
Peru (1990-on)	Yes	Yes	Much lower	Much lower	1-49	25 (1992-95)	Much more independent (1)	Yes (1992 or early 1993)	Yes (1991, 1993 — two new bank laws)	3 → 1 (Needs major overhaul → reasonable)
Uruguay (mostly 1985-92; also 1992-on)	—*	—*	Much lower	Much lower	0	10-15 (1991-on)	More independent (2)	No	Yes (1993)	2 → 1 (Needs some overhaul → reasonable)

[1] Foreign currency deposits not permitted at present.

* Indicates that all deposit or loan rates were already free-market determined prior to the financial reform period.

Table 4.1b What Did the Reforms Do? Class 2 (Substantial Reform) Countries

Country (and period of main reforms)	At least some commercial bank interest rates currently free, and this is due to reforms — Deposit	Loan	Change in reserve requirements (from before reforms until now) — Local currency	Foreign currency	Percent of targeted credit remaining (from before reforms until now)	Percent share of loan market privatized or liquidated (date)	Change in de facto central bank independence (from before reforms until now)	Reforms brought a new and modern capital markets law or set of regulations? (date)	Reforms brought a new and modern bank law or set of regulations? (date)	Change in commercial bank supervision (before reform → now)
Dominican Republic (1991-on)	Yes	Yes	Somewhat lower	na[1]	1-49	0	Same (4)	No	Yes (1993-95)	3 → 1 (Needs major overhaul → reasonable)
Ecuador (1985-94; mostly 1992-94)	Yes	Yes	Somewhat lower	Somewhat lower	100	0	Little more independent (3)	Yes (mid-1993)	Yes (May 1994)	3 → 2 (Needs major overhaul → needs some overhaul)
Guatemala (1991-94)	Yes	Yes	Somewhat lower	na[2]	1-49	0	Little more independent (3)	No	Yes (1992)	3 → 2 (Needs major overhaul → needs some overhaul)
Guyana (1988-92; 1995-on)	Yes	Yes	Somewhat lower	Same	1-49	50 (1991; 1994-on)	Little more independent (3)	No	Yes (1995)	3 → 2 (Needs major overhaul → needs some overhaul)
Mexico (1989-92; 1995-on)	—*	Yes	Much lower	Much lower	1-49	92 (1991-92)	Much more independent (1)	Yes (1989)	No	3 → 2 (Needs major overhaul → needs some overhaul)
Trinidad & Tobago (1990-on)	—*	—*	Same	Much lower	1-49	25 (1990-93)	More independent (2)	Yes (1996)	Yes (circa 1990-91)	2 → 1 (Needs some overhaul → reasonable)
Venezuela (1989-93; 1996)	Yes	Yes	Much lower	na[2]	1-49	5 (1989-92)	Same (4)	No	No	3 → 3 (Needs major overhaul → needs major overhaul)

[1] Foreign currency deposits were not permitted in the pre-reform period.
[2] Foreign currency deposits not permitted at present.
* Indicates that all deposit or loan rates were already free-market determined prior to the financial reform period.

Table 4.1c What Did the Reforms Do? Class 3 (Some Reform) Countries

Country (and period of main reforms)	At least some commercial bank interest rates currently free, and this is due to reforms — Deposit	Loan	Change in reserve requirements (from before reforms until now) — Local currency	Foreign currency	Percent of targeted credit remaining (from before reforms until now)	Percent share of loan market privatized or liquidated (date)	Change in de facto central bank independence (from before reforms until now)	Reforms brought a new and modern capital markets law or set of regulations? (date)	Reforms brought a new and modern bank law or set of regulations? (date)	Change in commercial bank supervision (before reform → now)
Bahamas (1994-95)	—*	—*	Somewhat lower	Same	Never was any	5 (1994-95)	Same (4)	Yes (1995-96)	No³	1 → 1 (Reasonable → reasonable)
Barbados (1995-on)	—*	Yes	Same	Much lower	0	35 (ongoing)	Same (4)	No³	Yes (late 1980s; ongoing)	2 → 1 (Needs some overhaul → reasonable)
Belize (1995)	Yes	Yes	Same	Same	100	0	Same (4)	No	Yes (late 1995)	1 → 1 (Reasonable → reasonable)
Brazil (1988-89)	Yes	Yes	Much higher	na¹	1-49	0	Same (4)	Yes (1989)	No	1 → 1 (Reasonable → reasonable)
Chile (1989 & 1993)	—*	—	Same	Much lower	100	0	Much more independent (1)	Yes (1994)	No³	1 → 1 (Reasonable → reasonable)
Costa Rica (1988, 1992, 1995)	Yes	Yes	Somewhat higher	Same	1-49	0	More independent (2)	No	Yes (1995)	3 → 3 (Needs major overhaul → needs major overhaul)
Honduras (1991-92; 1995)	—*	Yes	Somewhat higher	Same	1-49	0	Same (4)	No	Yes (1995)	3 → 3 (Needs major overhaul → needs major overhaul)
Jamaica (1992-94)	—	—	Somewhat higher	na²	2-3	0	More independent (2)	Yes (1993)	No	2 → 2 (Needs some overhaul → needs some overhaul)
Paraguay (1988-92)	Yes	Yes	Somewhat lower	Same	50-99	0	Same (4)	Yes⁴ (1991)	No	3 → 3 (Needs major overhaul → needs major overhaul)

1 Foreign currency deposits not permitted at present.
2 Foreign currency deposits were not permitted in the pre-reform period.
3 A modern capital markets or bank law (or set of regulations) was in effect prior to the financial reform period.
4 The law exists but is not in operation, since there is effectively no capital market (no equity in any company is listed or traded on the exchange). Exchange trading is generally in money market instruments and the like.
* Indicates that all deposit or loan rates were already free-market determined prior to the financial reform period.

Table 4.1d What Did the Reforms Do? Class 4 (Little or No Reform) Countries

Country (and period of main reforms)	At least some commercial bank interest rates currently free, and this is due to reforms Deposit	Loan	Change in reserve requirements (from before reforms until now) Local currency	Foreign currency	Percent of targeted credit remaining (from before reforms until now)	Percent share of loan market privatized or liquidated (date)	Change in de facto central bank independence (from before reforms until now)	Reforms brought a new and modern capital markets law or set of regulations? (date)	Reforms brought a new and modern bank law or set of regulations? (date)	Change in commercial bank supervision (before reform → now)
Haiti (1995)	—*	Yes	Somewhat higher	Same	Never was any	0	Same (4)	No	No	3 → 3 (Needs major overhaul → needs major overhaul)
Panama (no recent reforms)	—*	—*				0	There is no central bank[1]	No	No	Currently 3 (needs major overhaul)
Suriname (no recent reforms)	—	—				0		No	No	Currently 3 (needs major overhaul)

[1] The U.S. dollar is used as local currency.

* Indicates that all deposit or loan rates were already free-market determined prior to the financial reform period.

Box 4.1 Financial Reform Data

Interest rates. The first two data columns of Tables 4.1a to 4.1d tell whether any commercial bank deposit or loan rates were allowed to become market determined (instead of being administratively set). For this, we compare the present day to the point in time just before the period of main financial reforms given in the first column (that is, to the "pre-reform period" as it is called henceforth). For example, Table 4.1a gives Colombia's main financial reform period as 1990-94; the pre-reform period in this case is the point in time just before the reforms began in 1990. The basic data given in the interest rate columns is a yes or no answer, with a dash (—) used to indicate no for ease of identification. In a number of cases, *all* deposit or loan rates were already market determined prior to the reforms, and these cases are marked with an asterisk (*).

Reserve requirements. In assessing the change in marginal reserve requirements from the pre-reform period to the present, current marginal requirements are classified as much lower," "somewhat lower," "about the same," "somewhat higher," or "much higher," where "much" indicates a change of about 20 percentage points or more (e.g., a drop in reserve requirements from 45 percent to 25 percent or an increase from 15 percent to 35 percent).

Targeted credit. In describing how the size of targeted credit programs has changed from the pre-reform period to the present day in real (inflation-adjusted) terms, respondents selected from six categories: "None remains (0 percent)," "some remains (1-49 percent)," "most remains (50-99 percent)," "about same level (100 percent)," "more today than before (>100 percent)," and "never was any targeted credit (from just before reforms until now)." In a few cases, respondents wrote a more specific description, which is reproduced in the tables. For example, the Colombia response was given as 1-20 percent, as shown in Table 4.1a, meaning that the amount of targeted credit today is 1-20 percent of what it was in the pre-reform period, in real terms. One cannot necessarily conclude that there was a greater reduction of targeted credit in Colombia (with a response of 1-20 percent) than in Bolivia (with a response of 1-49 percent) since the ranges still overlap.

Privatization or liquidation of public banks. To understand this column, it is helpful to define the term "bank-

ing system" somewhat narrowly as referring to all state and all private or public commercial and development banks with first tier lending operations (that is, that lend to the private or public sectors, not just to other financial institutions). This column gives the share of total first tier banking system credit held by public banks that were privatized or liquidated since the beginning of the reform period given in the first column. This credit share is measured in the pre-reform period in order to show the importance of these banks at a single point in time prior to the privatization or liquidation of any of them. The approximate time period over which these activities were carried out is shown in parentheses. The percentages given in this column do not include private banks that failed, became public banks, and then were quickly liquidated or reprivatized (say, within a year or two). On the other hand, private banks that failed in the early or mid-1980s or before and were taken over and operated as public banks for five to 10 years before being liquidated or reprivatized are counted here.

Central bank independence. The change in de facto central bank independence from the pre-reform period to the present is measured on a seven-point scale: "1. Much more independent," "2. More independent," "3. A little more independent," "4. About the same," "5. A little less independent," "6. Less independent," and "7. Much less independent."

Capital market and bank laws. The next two columns show whether a modern law or set of regulations covering the capital markets or the banks came into operation during the reform period, and gives the approximate date when the new statutes or regulations took effect.

Supervision. The last column indicates the quality of commercial bank supervision at two points in time, the pre-reform period and the present. Supervision quality is rated as: "1. Reasonable (should detect most major instances of mismanagement and fraud)," "2. In need of some overhaul," and "3. In need of major overhaul."

In the interests of simplicity, the supervision as well as the interest rate questions were asked only in reference to commercial banks.

Reform	Class 1 (Major reform countries)	Class 2 (Substantial reform countries)	Class 3 (Some reform countries)	Class 4 (Little or no reform countries)	Total (All countries)
Liberalized deposit rates	5	5	4	0	14
Liberalized lending rates	4	6	6	1	17
Lowered reserve requirements - local currency deposits	7	6	2	0	15
Lowered reserve requirements - foreign currency deposits	5	3	2	0	10
Reduced targeted credit	7	6	6	0	19
Privatization/liquidation of public banks	7	4	2	0	13
Greater central bank independence	7	5	3	0	15
New capital markets law/regulations	5	3	5	0	13
New bank law/regulations	7	5	4	0	16
Better bank supervision	6	6	1	0	13

Table 4.2 Number of Countries Reporting Positive Changes

tries surveyed. At one end of the spectrum are Peru and Nicaragua, the only two countries to undertake reforms in all 10 of the categories, and generally rather deep reforms at that, completing a major overhaul of commercial bank supervision as well as making their central banks much more independent and their reserve requirements much lower. At the other end of the spectrum are the three countries in Table 4.1d, which have undertaken virtually no financial sector reform. Class averages are also revealing, with the mean number of reforms of the seven Class 1 (major reform) countries at 8.6 (out of 10), diminishing to 7, 3.9, and 0.3, respectively, for the seven Class 2 (substantial reform) countries, the nine Class 3 (some reform) countries, and the three Class 4 (little or no reform) countries.

Table 4.2 shows the number of countries reporting positive changes in each of the 10 reform categories.[9] As the table makes clear, financial reform activity has been widely distributed across categories. The most commonly adopted changes have been the reduction of targeted credit programs (19 countries), the liberalization of

lending rates (17 countries), and the institution of a new bank law or regulations (16 countries). The least common change was lower foreign currency reserve requirements (10 countries). All other reforms were adopted by about half the countries (13 to 15). A special caveat applies to the least commonly adopted reform. Changes in foreign currency reserve requirements cannot even be considered for six of the countries, reducing the universe of possible reform cases from 26 to 20, since Brazil, Colombia, Guatemala and Venezuela do not allow such deposits and the Dominican Republic and Jamaica did not permit them in their pre-reform periods.

Not only has the reduction of targeted credit programs been the single most common reform, but the reductions have almost always been quite substantial. Two countries abolished

[9] By a positive change we mean some or all commercial bank deposit and loan rates of interest liberalized, lower reserve requirements on local and foreign currency bank deposits, less targeted credit in real terms, at least some privatization or liquidation of public banks, at least a little more central bank independence, new and modern capital markets or bank laws, and better commercial bank supervision.

	Table 4.3 Who Did How Much Reform?			
Subregion	Class 1 (Major reform countries)	Class 2 (Substantial reform countries)	Class 3 (Some reform countries)	Class 4 (Little or no reform countries)
South America plus Mexico (11 countries)	Argentina (1988-89; 1995-on) Bolivia (1995-on) Colombia Peru (1991-93) Uruguay	Ecuador Mexico (Dec. 1994-on) Venezuela (Jan. 1994-on)	Brazil (1995-on) Chile Paraguay (1995-on)	
Central America (Seven countries, including Belize and Panama)	El Salvador Nicaragua	Guatemala	Belize Costa Rica (1994) Honduras	Panama (March 1988- March 1990)
Caribbean (Eight countries, including Guyana and Suriname)		Dominican Republic (1989-91) Guyana (1989-95) Trinidad and Tobago	Bahamas Barbados Jamaica (1995-on)	Haiti Suriname

Note: This table refers to financial reform over the period 1988-96. The starting and ending dates of any banking crises that began in 1988 or afterwards are shown in parentheses.

these programs entirely (Uruguay and Barbados), and 16 eliminated most targeted credit (leaving only 1-49 percent of the real, pre-reform targeted credit levels remaining). Only one reform country, Paraguay, reported having most of these credits (50-99 percent) still remaining.

Interest rate reform was quite far-reaching. Fourteen countries went from administrative to free market determination of some or all of their commercial bank deposit rates and 17 countries did so for some or all of their commercial bank loan rates. These totals would probably be even larger if it weren't for the fact that a number of the remaining countries already had free market determination of all commercial bank loan or deposit rates prior to their financial reforms. (This was the case for five and 10 countries, respectively, for loan and deposit rates.) As will be seen in Tables 4.6a to 4.6d later in this chapter, all commercial bank deposit rates are presently market determined in 23 of the 26 countries and all commercial bank loan rates in 19 of the 26 countries.

Marginal reserve requirement ratios were

often reduced quite sharply. Of the 15 countries reporting lower local currency reserve requirements, the requirements were made much lower in seven.[10] Of the 10 countries reporting lower foreign currency reserve requirements, the ratios went much lower in nine. These developments were not unmixed, however, as noted earlier. Of the five cases in which reserve requirements were increased, all were for local currency deposits, with one case of much higher ratios (Brazil) and four of somewhat higher ratios (Costa Rica, Haiti, Honduras and Jamaica).

Sixteen countries put a modern bank law or set of regulations into effect since 1988. In addition, Chile and the Bahamas already had a reasonable set of regulations prior to 1988, bringing to 18 the total number of countries with reasonable prudential norms at the present time. Commercial bank supervision improved significantly

---

[10] As noted in Box 4.1, much lower (much higher) indicates a decrease (increase) of about 20 percentage points or more in the marginal reserve requirement.

Table 4.4 Reform Sequencing: Amount of Liberalization vs. Quality of Prudential Safeguards at the Start of Liberalization		
	Intensive liberalization since 1988	Some or no liberalization since 1988
Had acceptable regulation and supervision at the start of liberalization	From Class 1: Colombia From Class 2: Trinidad & Tobago	From Class 3: Bahamas, Barbados, Belize, Chile
Did not have acceptable regulation and supervision at the start of liberalization	All of Class 1 except Colombia All of Class 2 except Trinidad & Tobago	From Class 3: Brazil, Costa Rica, Honduras, Jamaica, Paraguay All of Class 4

Table 4.5 Reform Balance: Amount of Liberalization vs. Current Quality of Prudential Safeguards		
	Intensive liberalization since 1988	Some or no liberalization since 1988
Have acceptable regulation and supervision now	All of Class 1 All of Class 2 except Mexico and Venezuela	From Class 3: Bahamas, Barbados, Belize, Chile
Do not have acceptable regulation and supervision now	From Class 2: Mexico and Venezuela	From Class 3: Brazil, Costa Rica, Honduras, Jamaica, Paraguay All of Class 4

in 13 countries—moving up by at least one category out of the three, a substantial change—and was completely transformed in five of these 13 cases (moving up from needing a major overhaul to being reasonable).

Finally, improvements in de facto central bank independence were also quite substantial. Of the 15 cases in which independence increased, six central banks were rated as becoming much more independent, six as more independent, and only three as a little more independent.

Table 4.3 cross-classifies the 26 countries by the four extent-of-reform categories and according to geographical location. This table shows that the larger countries (Mexico plus the countries of South America) have undertaken more financial reform as a group than the Central American countries, which in turn have been more active than the Caribbean countries. Table 4.3 also shows the starting and ending dates of any banking crises that began in 1988 or afterwards.

Reform Sequencing and Balance

Tables 4.4 and 4.5 demonstrate the following two propositions:

Sequencing: Most countries in Latin America have not sequenced their reforms well, in the sense of having had adequate bank regulation and supervision in place before undertaking financial liberalization.

Balance: Most countries in Latin America that had undertaken a significant amount of financial reform by May 1996 had also improved their bank regulation and supervision enough to be said to have a reform process balanced between liberalization and improving prudential safeguards.

To prepare Tables 4.4 and 4.5, the 26 countries were divided into the most intensive liberalizers during the 1988-96 period and those that did only some or no liberalization, where liberalization covers the first five or six out of 10 reform categories in Tables 4.1a to 4.1d (that is, the categories pertaining to deposit and loan interest rates, domestic and foreign currency reserve requirements, targeted credit, and perhaps privatization/liquidation of public banks[11]). As it turns out, the 14 major and substantial reform countries (Classes 1 and 2) are also the countries that were most intensive in their liberalization efforts. All nine countries that did some reform (Class 3) also did some liberalization, and the three countries that did little or no reform (Class 4) also did little or no liberalization.

In Table 4.4, countries are also divided between those that had acceptable regulation and supervision at the start of their financial liberalization period and those that did not. In Table 4.5, the same division is made, only based on the quality of regulation and supervision *at the present time*. By "acceptable" regulation and supervision, it is meant that the country has (1) a modern bank law or set of regulations, and (2) a level of supervision that is rated either as "reasonable" or "in need of some overhaul," but not "in need of major overhaul."[12]

While all but two countries in Latin America have done at least some financial liberalization, only six (Colombia, Trinidad and Tobago, Bahamas, Barbados, Belize, and Chile) had regulation and supervision that qualified as acceptable when liberalization began. In only four of these six (Colombia, Bahamas, Belize, and Chile) was supervision reasonable prior to the startup of financial liberalization. Of the 14 intensive liberalizers, only two (Colombia and Trinidad and Tobago) had acceptable prudential safeguards when liberalization began. In summary, most countries did not sequence their reforms well.

The good news comes in Table 4.5. While most countries did not have good regulation and supervision in place when they began to liberalize, many improved these safeguards along the way. All of the improvement came from the group of intensive liberalizers, with all but two of these countries now having achieved a balanced financial reform, meaning that in addition to being intensive liberalizers these countries have now

achieved at least acceptable regulation and supervision.

The Major Reform Countries

Like the Peruvian reforms discussed earlier, the financial reforms in Nicaragua and El Salvador were set in a dramatic landscape of political and economic change. It is at least partly as a result of those larger changes that these two countries achieved major financial reforms, the only two outside of South America to have done so.

In *Nicaragua*, a new administration came to power in April 1990, following years of civil war and economic mismanagement. As in Peru, the new government faced the formidable task of turning around a huge production decline and runaway inflation. From 1990-92, significant progress was made in macroeconomic stabilization and in the transformation to a market-based economy. In this context, legislation allowing the creation of private banks was passed in mid-1991, and a superintendency set up to oversee them. By the end of 1991, four private commercial banks were operating. These have since expanded to 12, which together account for about half of total banking system credit. The new administration also inherited four public development banks, all of them generating huge losses from nonperforming loans. Here, progress has been somewhat slower. While the Housing Bank was liquidated early

---

[11] While the privatization or liquidation of public banks is normally considered to be a liberalization, it is different from the other five categories in that it may not lead to banking system problems that the other five do. Arguments can, in fact, be made both ways about the direction of the effect privatization or liquidation of public banks has on banking problems. For example, privatizing a poorly-run public bank can help strengthen the banking system if the public bank is cleaned up prior to sale, and competent owners and managers are found. Transferring a weak public bank to private owners can, however, be a costly mistake, particularly if the new owners and managers are not competent. In any case, the country classification and the entire discussion in this chapter are unchanged by whether liberalization is defined as covering the first five or first six reform categories in Tables 4.1a to 4.1d.

[12] These regulation and supervision ratings are given in the last two columns of Tables 4.1a to 4.1d.

on, the Industry and Commerce Bank is only now being privatized. The National Development Bank and a bank for small enterprise credit will continue in the public sector, but are currently being reduced in scope and size. In addition to these important changes in property regime, Nicaragua has carried out financial reforms in all other areas that we have surveyed, with many of the reforms quite profound.

In *El Salvador*, the new government signed the Chapultepec peace accords soon after it took office in June 1989, ending 12 years of civil war and ushering in an era of economic reconstruction. With this came a deep reform of the financial system, highlighted by putting back into private hands over a period of several years nearly the entire banking system (which had been nationalized in 1980), the complete liberalization of interest rates in 1990-91, the elimination of most targeted credit, and the passage of a modern bank law in 1991.

As in El Salvador, the government in *Bolivia* has gotten out of banking (liquidating nearly all of its bank holdings) and undertaken a broad array of other reforms. In October 1995, Bolivia enacted a new central bank law that increased the independence of the central bank and established maintenance of the value of the currency as the institution's main objective. In addition, the new law mandates that commercial banks raise their capital-to-asset ratio from 8 to 10 percent over a three-year period and eliminate all loans to insiders. The widespread practice of lending to firms owned by important bank shareholders, together with the inadequate enforcement of other prudential controls over the preceding four years, played a major role in bringing about the 1995 Bolivian banking crisis. Supervision is also being strengthened, partly with the help of outside technical assistance. For the future, Bolivia must contend with the resolution of four problem banks, which together account for about one-quarter of total banking system assets. It must continue to strengthen its superintendency in order to prevent a recur-

rence of problems and to extend adequate supervision to all nonbank financial intermediaries (credit unions, mutual savings banks, etc.) as was mandated in 1993. Bolivia must also grapple with the vacuum left in rural financial markets by the closing of the Agricultural Bank.

Uruguay and *Colombia* both had major banking crises in the early 1980s, but compared to the preceding three countries and to Peru, both have had substantially less turbulent political economies from the mid-1980s on. This is particularly true in Colombia, with its long tradition of prudent economic management and steady growth. While both countries have carried out many financial and other reforms since these crises, they still confront today important inefficiencies in their banking systems. In Colombia, this is the result of a system of specialized banking in which a financial institution must have separate subsidiaries for its activities in housing, leasing, trusts, pensions and other areas. Together with limits on the types of deposit mobilization instruments that each subsidiary may utilize, this impedes competition and efficiency and has contributed to high bank spreads. In Uruguay, the major inefficiency in the banking system is associated with BROU, the enormous state commercial bank. In addition, the sizable public mortgage bank (Banco Hipotecario del Uruguay) operates with large currency and term mismatch risks, an important contingent liability for the taxpayer. These risks arise because the bank collects dollar deposits with a maturity averaging around eight months, and lends for 20-25 year mortgages in a unit of account based on local currency wages. With stability far from complete (for example, inflation rates averaged about 40-50 percent per annum in 1993-95), there is the potential for losses arising out of significant changes in the real exchange rate or from variations in U.S. dollar interest rates. While important measures have been taken since 1990 to reduce the extent of these mismatches and the associated risks, they remain considerable.

Argentina has substantially strengthened its traditionally weak superintendency in the past two years, accelerating its efforts as the tequila effect impacted the economy in 1995. This has facilitated the process of closing failed banks and helped smooth the transition from a banking system that still has substantial excesses of personnel and branches (a leftover from the 1989-90 hyperinflation) to a much leaner and more efficient structure. Argentina has also undertaken a broad range of other financial reforms. A very large public banking sector remains, however, though some of the smaller provincial banks are currently being divested or liquidated.

The Substantial Reform Countries

The countries in the substantial reform category have, in general, carried out only slightly less reform than those in the major reform category, and so the distinction between the two groups is occasionally blurry.

Following a major foreign exchange crisis in 1988, a new administration took office in *Venezuela* in early 1989 with an ambitious program of stabilization and reform. Monetary and fiscal policies were tightened, the exchange rate unified and floated, trade barriers reduced, and most price controls removed. In addition, significant financial sector reforms were undertaken. Interest rate controls were removed, targeted credit programs were substantially scaled back, reserve requirements were greatly reduced, and four small public commercial banks were liquidated or privatized. The economic situation began to deteriorate, however, with a marked weakening of oil revenues in 1992 amidst increasing public resistance to fiscal adjustment measures, two attempted military coups, also in 1992, and the removal of the President from office in mid-1993. A new elected administration took office in February 1994, inheriting a weak economy, a tenuous fiscal position, rising inflation, and a bank crisis that had erupted in mid-January with the closure of Banco

Latino, the second largest bank in the country. This crisis quickly spread to several other banks. The government responded to these problems with a reimposition of controls and a rolling back of reforms in a number of areas, including the reinstatement of interest rate ceilings (which were finally removed again in May 1996). The much-delayed new banking law, which took effect in January 1994, was never really implemented, since there was little political will to supervise banks very closely. The superintendency has been quite weak in any case, with inadequate human and information technology resources, though attention is now being focused on this issue.

The privatization in 1991-92 of the 18 commercial banks that *Mexico* nationalized in 1982 is easily the largest divestiture of bank assets in Latin America in dollar terms, and the second largest (after El Salvador) in terms of the percentage of the loan market privatized or liquidated (92 vs. 95 percent, respectively). Mexico's principal shortcoming at present is in supervision and regulation. While a sensible legal framework exists and supervision has been strengthened significantly since December 1994, further upgrading of the enforcement capabilities of the superintendency and of the asset classification standards is needed. These and other regulatory improvements are expected in the near future.

In the *Dominican Republic*, the number of banks and other formal and informal financial institutions increased rapidly in the last half of the 1980s as a result of a flexible entry policy, fiscal incentives for some types of financial activities, and controls on foreign exchange and interest rates under inflationary conditions, which brought about a large expansion in the number of informal financial institutions. The inability of the superintendency to enforce compliance with existing regulations led many of the intermediaries to operate recklessly. This and the recession of the period resulted in a banking crisis in 1989-91 in which several commercial banks and other financial institutions collapsed. Out of this banking and larger economic crisis came a reform program that included tightened fiscal and monetary policy, trade liberalization, the elimination of many price controls, and the freeing of all interest rates. Improvements in supervision and regulation came later, starting with the central bank's modification of major banking regulations in 1993 and continuing on after this as well. The consolidation and legitimization of many of these regulatory changes is to come with the passage of the new bank law, which is still awaiting congressional approval. Supervision, traditionally extremely weak, has been greatly strengthened since 1993, partly as the result of an ongoing financial sector reform operation with the IDB.

Like the financial reform program of the Dominican Republic, those of Guyana and Trinidad and Tobago are ongoing. In *Guyana*, a modern bank act was passed in 1995, and a new central bank law, now in the final drafting stages, should be approved in the near future. Both statutes increase central bank independence. The Guyanese government has interests in three banks, each of which has enjoyed about a 20 percent share of the loan market in recent years. GAIBANK, the insolvent public development bank with a long history of poor loan recovery, is being liquidated. The central government is also divesting its remaining 30 percent share of the commercial bank NBIC. The remaining public commercial bank, GNCB, which like GAIBANK has typically had only about a 50 percent loan recovery rate, requires serious restructuring prior to sale. This process has only just begun.

Along with other financial reforms, *Trinidad and Tobago* divested or liquidated its three public commercial banks in the early 1990s. This has left a modest-sized Agricultural Development Bank as the only remaining public financial institution, one that is likely to remain majority state owned in the future. More recently, a new Securities Industry Law passed in the first half of 1996 provides for setting up an independent oversight agency, which should permit better control over local stock market activity and help eliminate past abuses.

Guatemala and *Ecuador* undertook substantial reforms in the early 1990s but have done little since mid-1995, with the exception, perhaps, of the gradual strengthening of bank supervision in Guatemala. In 1995, Ecuador abandoned its program of fiscal adjustment under an IMF Stand-by Agreement and lost its momentum on financial sector and other economic reforms. While some of the precipitating events are now well past (such as the border conflict with Peru and the resignation of the Vice President, who was head of the economic team), it remains to be seen whether the July 1996 elections will result in a recommitment to the reform process.

Other Countries

The remaining countries have, in general, carried out far less financial reform since 1988 than the major and substantial reform countries. In the case of the highly liberalized and relatively well-functioning financial system of *Chile*, most of the reforms came before our 1988 cutoff date. Still, Chile passed a very important central bank law in 1989 that extricated the central bank from the traditional influence of the Finance Ministry and has given it great independence to set monetary and exchange rate policy. An important new capital markets law, with provisions affecting pension fund diversification, closed-end mutual funds and other second generation reform issues, took effect in 1994.

Panama and the *Bahamas* have been international financial centers for a long time, and more recently *Belize* is attempting to become one. Like Chile, though to a lesser extent, these economies instituted many of the reforms being discussed here before, and sometimes well before, 1988. For example, Panama has had a fully liberalized interest rate regime since 1970, as well as low reserve requirements and very limited credit targeting since at least the 1980s. In light of the growing importance of domestic banks servicing the domestic economy, and Panama's relative stagnation as an international banking center, interest has recently been rising in Panama to strengthen its traditionally weak bank superintendency.

While *Brazil* liberalized all deposit and most loan rates during 1988-89 and has eliminated most targeted credit programs, it has yet to carry out a comprehensive program of financial reforms. For example, it still has a very large public banking sector, which controls about half of all banking system credit and includes many state-level banks that are excessively staffed and heavily burdened by bad loans to their state governments. Further, its central bank is still far from independent of the Finance Ministry, and bank regulation is still deficient, although regulations were significantly strengthened in 1995 in such areas as loan quality, capital standards and reporting.

Barbados has recently undertaken a modest though important program of financial reform. With IDB assistance, it is closing down the Barbados Development Bank, its only public development bank, and is privatizing its only public commercial bank, the Barbados National Bank. Both of these banks have had a long history of inefficient operations and poor loan recovery. In addition, Barbados has an ongoing program to strengthen supervision and expects in the near future to pass the Financial Intermediaries Act, which will represent an incremental improvement of an already reasonable set of banking regulations.

Costa Rica and *Honduras* have also undertaken some partial reforms recently, with Costa Rica passing a new central bank law in November 1995, and Honduras a new banking law in the same month. In addition, Costa Rica has made a number of changes to its national bank law, the most important of which eliminates the monopoly previously enjoyed by the public banks to offer demand deposits.

In late 1995, *Jamaica* equalized the reserve ratios for commercial and merchant banks and

made other regulatory changes aimed at reducing severe problems of regulatory arbitrage, in which financial groups record transactions as belonging to one or another type of affiliate in order to take advantage of differing reserve ratios and unequal tax treatment.

Paraguay's reforms include liberalizing all deposit and loan rates in 1990, and reducing targeted credit and reserve requirements somewhat. Paraguay has continued to operate with strong deficiencies in its regulation and supervision, which contributed to a banking crisis that began in 1995. *Suriname* and *Haiti* have carried out little or no recent reform, the only exception being Haiti's removal of its 22 percent ceiling on interest rates on loans in the first half of 1995.

A FURTHER LOOK AT THE CURRENT STATUS OF REFORMS

Tables 4.6a to 4.6d present data for each of the 26 countries on the current commercial bank interest rate regime and marginal reserve requirements. These tables are organized in the same way as Tables 4.1a to 4.1d, with one table covering each of the Class 1 - 4 country groups.

Interest Rates

The interest rate columns of Tables 4.6a to 4.6d show whether all, some, or no commercial bank deposit and loan rates are market determined and since when the rates have been free of administrative controls.[13]

As has been alluded to earlier and can be seen in the tables, interest rate liberalization has usually come at an early stage of most countries' financial reform programs. Hence, perhaps it should not be so surprising to see how reformed the interest rate regime is in Latin America, with

---

[13] If all interest rates are free, the date shown is the time since this has been the case. If some interest rates are free, the date shown is the last time that interest rates were liberalized.

Country (and period of main reforms)	Commercial bank interest rates currently market determined? (Since when?)		Commercial bank marginal reserve requirements (%)			Different marginal reserve requirements by region or size of bank?
			Local currency		Foreign currency	
	Deposit	*Loan*	*Demand deposits*	*Time deposits*	*Time deposits*	
Argentina (1992-on)	All (before reform)	Some (before reform)	15	15 10 (90-180 days) 5 (180-360 days) 0 (>360 days)	15 10 (90-180 days) 5 (180-360 days) 0 (>360 days)	No
Bolivia (1990-on)	All (early 1990s)	All (early 1990s)	10	4	4	No
Colombia (1990-94)	All (1990; most since 1980)	All (mid-1970s)	21	3	Do not exist	No
El Salvador (1990-92)	All (1990-91)	All (1990)	30	20	30	No
Nicaragua (1990-on)	All (1990-91)	All (1990-91)	10	10 0 (>12 mos.)	25	No
Peru (1990-on)	All (1991)	All (1991)	9	9	43.5	No
Uruguay (mostly 1985-92; also 1992-on)	All (mid-1970s)	All (mid-1970s)	20	20 14 (30-180 days) 12 (>180 days)	20 14 (>180 days)	No

Table 4.6a Selected Current Status Indicators: Class 1 (Major Reform) Countries

all commercial bank deposit rates market determined in 23 countries and all commercial bank loan rates totally free in 19. Deposit rates are completely free in all major and substantial reform countries, and loan rates are totally free in all of these same countries except two.

Reserve Requirements

None of the 26 countries engage in the inefficient and discriminatory practice of having different reserve requirements by region of the country, and only in one case (Brazil) are there still varying reserve requirements based on the size of the financial institution.

As noted earlier, reserve requirements for both local and foreign currency deposits have dropped impressively and are now 30 percent or less for local currency deposits in all but six countries and for foreign currency time deposits in all but one (Peru). Eleven countries have no reserve requirements at all on foreign currency time deposits. These are mostly small Caribbean and Central American countries, many looking to stimulate foreign investment inflows. (Included in this group are the international financial centers of Panama and the Bahamas and the would-be international financial center of Belize.) Nine of the 26 countries have all three ratios shown in Tables 4.6a to 4.6d (for local and foreign currency time deposits and local currency demand deposits) at reasonable prudential levels of 15 percent or less.

Table 4.6b   Selected Current Status Indicators: Class 2 (Substantial Reform) Countries

Country (and period of main reforms)	Commercial bank interest rates currently market determined? (Since when?)		Commercial bank marginal reserve requirements (%)			Different marginal reserve requirements by region or size of bank?
			Local currency		Foreign currency	
	Deposit	Loan	Demand deposits	Time deposits	Time deposits	
Dominican Republic (1991-on)	All (1991)	All (1991)	20	20	20	No
Ecuador (1985-94; mostly 1992-94)	All (1992)	All (1992)	10	10	10	No
Guatemala (1991-94)	All (1991)	All (1991)	33.5	33.5	Do not exist	No
Guyana (1988-92; 1995-on)	All (circa 1990)	All (circa 1990)	16	14	0	No
Mexico (1989-92; 1995-on)	All (well before reform)	Some (1989)	0	0	0 (15 liquidity coefficient)	No
Trinidad & Tobago (1990-on)	All (Well before reform)	All (well before reform)	20	20	0	No
Venezuela (1989-93; 1996)	All (1989)	All (May 1996)	12	12	Do not exist	No

An additional seven countries have all three reserve ratios at 25 percent or less.

The decline in reserve requirements mirrors the stability that has increasingly returned to the region, with the need for high reserve requirements to combat macroeconomic imbalances and inflation having subsided in most countries. Because high reserve requirements have been needed less often for reasons of macroeconomic management, they have been lowered in many countries to increase the efficiency and international competitiveness of local banks. In addition, in some countries, open market sales of central bank or central government paper has increasingly been used as an instrument to tighten money supply, instead of higher reserve ratios.

There is some counterpoint to this trend toward lower reserve ratios, however. Brazil's 83 percent reserve requirement on demand deposits is a salient example, reflecting that country's use of tight monetary policy in lieu of an adequate fiscal adjustment. Brazil's 0 to 40 percent reserve ratios on time deposits are well below the demand deposit rate in order to encourage a lengthening of deposit maturities.

Some countries have maintained high reserve requirements on foreign currency deposits in order to help restrain capital inflows, and thus limit exchange rate appreciation and the expansion of the money supply. For example, Peru has experienced substantial inflows of short-term dollar deposits in recent years, and its 43.5 per-

Table 4.6c Selected Current Status Indicators: Class 3 (Some Reform) Countries						
Country (and period of main reforms)	Commercial bank interest rates currently market determined? (Since when?)		Commercial bank marginal reserve requirements (%)			Different marginal reserve requirements by region or size of bank?
			Local currency		Foreign currency	
	Deposit	*Loan*	*Demand deposits*	*Time deposits*	*Time deposits*	
Bahamas (1994-95)	All (long ago)	All (long ago)	5	5	0	No
Barbados (1995-on)	All (at least since mid-1960s)	All (1995)	29	29	0	No
Belize (1995)	Some (Jan., 1995)	All (Jan., 1995)	7 (26 liquidity coefficient)	7 (26 liquidity coefficient)	0	No
Brazil (1988-89)	All (± 1989)	Some (± 1988)	83	40 5 (30-60 days) 0 (> 60 days)	Do not exist	Size
Chile (1989, 1993)	All (circa 1985)	Some (circa 1984)	9	3.6 0 (> 1 year)	0 (30 for capital inflows of < 1 year)	No
Costa Rica (1988, 1992, 1995)	All (circa 1988)	Some (mostly 1992; also 1987)	34	30 10 (>6 mos.)	10	No
Honduras (1991-92; 1995)	All (before reform)	All (1992)	34	34	0 (50 liquidity coefficient)	No
Jamaica (1992-94)	Some (well before reform)	Some (well before reform)	25	22	20	No
Paraguay (1988-92)	All (1990)	All (1990)	18	18	30	No

cent reserve requirement on foreign currency deposits is aimed at reducing this flow. (In contrast, Peru's reserve requirement on domestic deposits is 9 percent.) Chile specifically targets foreign currency deposits that arise from foreign capital inflows, applying a 30 percent reserve requirement to all such deposits of one year duration or less. All other foreign currency deposits have no reserve requirement, and all domestic currency deposits have reserve requirements of 9 percent or less, reflecting Chile's stable, reformed economy.

Capital Markets in Transition

Capital markets have recently been or are soon expected to be reformed almost everywhere in Latin America. Twenty of the 26 countries either now have or are expected to enact in the next year and a half a modern capital markets law or set of regulations. Fourteen of these 20 presently have such laws or regulations and another eight plan to enact a new capital markets law in 1996-97. Two countries (Argentina and Jamaica) fall into both categories, indicating that they plan to fur-

Country (and period of main reforms)	Commercial bank interest rates currently market determined? (Since when?)		Commercial bank marginal reserve requirements (%)			Different marginal reserve requirements by region or size of bank?
			Local currency		Foreign currency	
	Deposit	Loan	Demand deposits	Time deposits	Time deposits	
Haiti (1995)	All (well before reform)	All (first half of 1995)	51	51	0	No
Panama (No recent reforms)	All (1970)	All (1970)	10	5 0 (> 1 year)	0[a]	No
Suriname (No recent reforms)	None	None	100	25 0 (> 12 mos.)	0	No

Table 4.6d Selected Current Status Indicators: Class 4 (Little or No Reform) Countries

[a] Refers to reserve requirements held against deposits of foreigners (not foreign currency). Panama uses the U.S. dollar as local currency.

ther improve or refine an already-reasonable existing set of laws or regulations (Table 4.7).

Capital markets reform is mostly a recent phenomenon. Of the 14 countries that currently have reasonably modern laws and regulations, the majority implemented them in the last three years (since 1993). Only in one case did the implementation of such laws and regulations come before 1988 (Barbados in the mid-1980s). The six countries that neither have nor are expected by the end of 1997 to enact a modern capital markets law or set of regulations are all small Central American or Caribbean countries: Belize, Honduras, Panama, Haiti, Guyana and Suriname. All of the larger countries (Mexico and those in South America) already have or expect in the near future to enact modern capital markets reform.

FINANCIAL REFORM AND BANKING CRISES

This section examines the possible role of out-of-sequence financial reforms as an important contributing factor to precipitating or exacerbating banking crises. Following along the lines of the conceptual discussion earlier in the chapter, we provide evidence taken from recent Latin

American experience that removing interest rate controls, dismantling targeted credit programs, and lowering reserve requirements before there is adequate bank regulation and supervision can contribute materially to the likelihood of a banking crisis.

We know from Table 4.4 that very few countries in Latin America have met the strict sequencing test of having had adequate regulation and supervision at the very outset of their liberalization programs, which often began in the early 1990s. In the context of explaining something as severe as a banking crisis, we may ask the further question: did the countries improve their regulations and strengthen their supervisory systems quickly enough, before serious banking system problems had time to develop and turn into a crisis? Accordingly, we turn the clock ahead and examine all banking crises over the past three years, three of which began in 1994 and five in 1995 (Table 4.8). We examine recent crises since a large amount of liberalization will likely have been undertaken in both crisis and noncrisis countries by 1994-95, permitting us to see if there are any differences in the adequacy of regulation and supervision in each group.

Class 1 Major reform countries		Class 2 Substantial reform countries		Class 3 Some reform countries		Class 4 Little or no reform countries
Argentina (1991-on)	Both[1]	Mexico (1989)	Already	Barbados (mid-1980s)	Already	Haiti
Peru (1992 or early 1993)	Already	Ecuador (mid-1993)	Already	Brazil (1989)	Already	Panama
Colombia (1993)	Already	Trinidad & Tobago (1996)	Already	Paraguay (1991)	Already	Suriname
Nicaragua (1993)	Already	Dominican Republic	Plan	Jamaica (1993)	Both[1]	
El Salvador (1994)	Already	Guatemala	Plan	Chile (1994)	Already	
Bolivia	Plan	Guyana		Bahamas (1995-96)	Already	
Uruguay	Plan	Venezuela	Plan	Belize		
				Costa Rica	Plan	
				Honduras		

Table 4.7 Countries that Have Enacted or Plan in 1996 to Enact a Modern Capital Markets Law or Set of Regulations

[1] Argentina and Jamaica fall into both groups, having already enacted a modern capital markets law or set of regulations which they plan to further improve or refine during 1996-97.

The eight crises that have occurred since 1994 are classified as smaller or larger according to the number and size of banks intervened and closed, and the likely bank losses and government rescue costs (all relative to the size of the overall banking system). While the classification is somewhat rough, it is sufficient for the purposes at hand. In any event, it certainly seems beyond question that Mexico and Venezuela have suffered very large crises, much larger than those in the remaining countries.

Table 4.8 also cross-classifies the crisis countries by the extent of their overall financial reforms. There have been four banking crises among the 14 countries that have been significant reformers (those in the major reform and substantial reform categories) and four among the remaining 12 countries (those in the some reform and little or no reform categories). Hence, the likelihood of crisis does not seem to vary much with the amount of overall reform. The significant reformers have, however, had more severe crises. Since the countries classified here as major and substantial reformers are the same ones that have

been intensive liberalizers (as discussed earlier), these results suggest that significant liberalization does have its dangers.

While we believe this conclusion has a certain element of truth to it, it is overly simple, as the remaining information in the table makes clear. The two sets of dates for each country show the period over which the full set of financial reforms in the country took place (from Tables 4.1a to 4.1d) and the time when the country's banking crisis occurred. This information tends to indicate (and a more detailed examination confirms) that in every case a substantial share of the country's financial liberalization had occurred prior to its banking crisis. Moreover, in four of the cases (Brazil, Jamaica, Mexico and Paraguay), all of the countries' liberalization-type reforms were essentially completed before the onset of the crisis. Since interest rate liberalization has usually been carried out early in the reform process, it should not be surprising that both deposit and loan rates of interest were all or almost all free before (and usually well before) the onset of the crisis in all eight countries. Targeted credit programs had also been reduced by over half (and sometimes by well over half) in all countries prior to their crises, except in Paraguay, where there were also reductions, but on a more modest scale.

To complete the picture, the two pieces of data just below the name of the country indicate the state of prudential regulation and supervision at the beginning of the banking crisis.[14] These ratings are taken from Westley (1995), which provides the same type of supervision and regulation ratings as those discussed in Tables 4.1a to 4.1d, only based on a survey conducted in November 1994.[15] With six of the eight countries entering their crises soon after that survey was completed (either in December 1994 or in 1995), these ratings are very well timed for present purposes. A further inquiry into whether regulation and supervision quality at the beginning of each country's crisis differed from these November 1994 ratings confirmed their appropriateness in all eight cases.

These regulation and supervision data suggest the importance of having adequate prudential safeguards, particularly if one is liberalizing. All eight of the crisis countries have done at least some financial liberalization, and four of the eight have been intensive liberalizers. While 16 of the remaining 18 noncrisis countries in Latin America have also done at least some financial liberalization (and 10 of these have been intensive liberalizers), what is special about the eight crisis countries is that they have done so poorly in regulation and supervision. The quality of the prudential regulations was judged to be reasonable in only two of the eight crisis countries, as compared to 15 out of 18 of the noncrisis countries (the 18 noncrisis countries serving as a con-

trol group). This difference in proportions is statistically significant at less than the 1 percent level, meaning that there is more than a 99 percent probability that the difference was not simply the result of chance. On the quality of supervision, five of the eight crisis countries received the worst rating ("in need of major overhaul"), compared to five out of 18 among the noncrisis, control group countries. Conversely, only one of the eight crisis countries received the best supervision rating ("reasonable"), compared to nine out of the 18 noncrisis countries. Again, these differences are highly significant. These results suggest that the combination of liberalization and weak regulation and supervision is associated much more often with banking crises than is the combination of liberalization and strong regulation and supervision (or than is the case of little or no liberalization at all, a relatively unimportant category in this analysis since it characterizes only two countries).

While this evidence suggests that improving supervision and regulation too late in the financial reform process appears to be a dangerous and potentially very costly sequencing error, we must also recognize the limits to this analysis. There are, of course, many other causes for bank crises (some, such as recessions, devaluations, and interest rate increases, are discussed in Part I of this Report), and it would be difficult to apportion blame among all of the possible factors. In addition, to some degree, some of the other causes for bank crises may themselves be partly the result of financial liberalization without adequate regulation and supervision, and so such liberalization may contribute indirectly as well as directly to the precipitation of banking crises.

The fact that the sequencing error under discussion appears to be a common one in Latin America may reflect the difficulty of achieving a better ordering of reforms. Strengthening superintendencies is a time-consuming process. It often takes years to produce a well-trained and equipped corps of supervisors. A new government

---

[14] While the ratings are given at the time of the onset of the crisis, in no country are the ratings any better in the two or three years leading up to the crisis (during which time the crisis may have been developing).

[15] That is, the regulation rating tells whether or not the country had a reasonably modern set of prudential regulations. Supervision is rated employing the usual three categories: reasonable (should detect most major instances of mismanagement and fraud), in need of some overhaul, and in need of major overhaul.

Table 4.8 Recent Banking Crises, by Size of Crisis and Degree of Financial Reform

Degree of overall financial reform	Characteristics	Countries with a recent banking crisis, by size of crisis		
		Larger crises	Smaller crises	
1. Major reform	Country		Argentina	Bolivia
	Reasonable regulations?		Yes	Yes
	Quality of supervision		In need of some overhaul	In need of major overhaul
	Reform years		1992-on	1990-on
	Crisis years		1995-on	1995-on
2. Substantial reform	Country	Mexico		
	Reasonable regulations?	No		
	Quality of supervision	In need of major overhaul		
	Reform years	1989-92; 1995-on		
	Crisis years	Dec., 1994-on		
	Country	Venezuela		
	Reasonable regulations?	No		
	Quality of supervision	In need of major overhaul		
	Reform years	1989-93; 1996		
	Crisis years	Jan., 1994-on		
3. Some reform	Country		Brazil	Costa Rica
	Reasonable regulations?		No	No
	Quality of supervision		Reasonable	In need of major overhaul
	Reform years		1988-89	1988, 1992, 1995, 1994
	Crisis years		1995-on	
	Country		Jamaica	Paraguay
	Reasonable regulations?		No	No
	Quality of supervision		In need of some overhaul	In need of major overhaul
	Reform years		1992-94	1988-92
	Crisis years		1995-on	1995-on
4. Little or no reform				

Note: Data on the quality of regulation and supervision were collected in a November 1994 survey, thus predating six of the eight crises shown here; see Westley (1995).

that comes to office with an ambitious and far-reaching program of financial and other reforms may be loath to wait years before removing interest rate controls, dismantling targeted credit programs, and engaging in other out-of-sequence reforms. Or a new government may find that it first achieves other (nonfinancial) reforms, such as those in the trade and fiscal areas, and that these other reforms then prompt or necessitate substan-

tial financial liberalization, with the whole package of reforms occurring before banking regulation and supervision can be significantly strengthened. For example, in Venezuela in the late 1980s and early 1990s, trade liberalization quickly led to liberalization of the international capital account, and this mandated the lifting of domestic interest rate controls (to prevent a massive exodus of capital occasioned by domestic interest rates that were out of line with world levels). Also, because of fiscal and other reforms, inflation fell and so bank reserve requirements were greatly reduced. Whatever the cause may be, however, the analysis in this section suggests that important risks may be incurred when financial liberalization is pursued without an adequate foundation of regulation and supervision.

LOOKING FORWARD

While a great deal of financial reform has been carried out in Latin America, there is still much that remains to be done. One indicator of this is that 12 of the 26 countries examined here are still classified as having done little, some or no financial reform since 1988 (though in the case of Chile, and to a lesser extent Panama and the Bahamas, this is because many of their reforms preceded our 1988 cutoff date). Viewed thematically, there is much room for progress in the region in all 10 reform areas discussed in this chapter, with two of great importance being the need to improve banking regulation and supervision. Eight countries still do not have a reasonably modern bank law or set of regulations. Supervisory systems are considered reasonably good in only half of the 26 countries, while they are judged to be in need of a major overhaul in seven countries and in need of some overhaul in six. It is to be hoped that regulation and supervision will be strengthened in the many countries where they are weak before substantial new liberalization initiatives are undertaken.

While a great deal of financial reform began in the late 1980s and early 1990s, countries in Latin America continue to undertake the kinds of reforms discussed in this chapter—primarily those related to the banking sector—at almost the same pace as before. Some indication of this, albeit very partial and imperfect, can be obtained by comparing the reform data developed in this chapter, which covers January 1988 to May 1996, to similar data in Westley (1995), which

covers January 1988 to November 1994. Both studies employ identical methodologies to catalogue the reforms carried out in the same 10 reform areas and 26 countries. The average number of reforms (out of 10) that have been carried out in the 26 countries over the seven years from January 1988 to November 1994 is 4.8, as compared to 5.6 when the period is extended one and a half years to May 1996. The recent reforms have been made across the board in all 10 areas, though with somewhat greater frequency in the areas of loan rate liberalization and improvement of banking regulation and supervision.

While the pace of the kind of banking reforms discussed in this chapter appears to have slowed only slightly in recent times, eventually it must decelerate further as more and more countries adopt these measures. The longer-term challenge then lies with giving greater attention to improving areas of the financial system that are comparatively underdeveloped in Latin America, such as stock and bond markets, insurance, pensions, leasing, venture capital, bonded warehouses, and the provision of financial services to smaller enterprises. With the deceleration of inflation in the region over the past several years, conditions are becoming even more propitious for many of the longer-term financial services to increase their market share relative to that of commercial banking, which has been dominant partly because of its short-term nature. An example of a salutary trend in this area is the flurry of recent capital markets laws and regulations noted earlier in this chapter, and the expectation that several more countries will make improvements to their securities regulation in the near future.

CHAPTER 5

PRIVATIZATION

ABSTRACT

A boom in privatizations began in the late 1980s in Latin America and accelerated sharply in the early 1990s. Frequently cited achievements include efficiency gains in the divested firms and an expansion in their range of services, a reduction in public sector borrowing requirements, and the promotion of foreign investment. Major difficulties have included opposition by political parties and labor unions, weak regulatory frameworks or institutions, lack of sufficient transparency, and controversial views on the destination of privatization revenues.

Latin America has been a leader in the developing world's efforts to privatize. Its public sector obtained $59 billion in revenue from 694 divestitures over the 1990-94 period, more than half of the $104 billion realized by all developing countries. Latin America's privatization revenues averaged nearly 1 percent of its GDP during each year of the period, more than double the ratio of the next nearest region.

Annual privatization revenues show a strong peak in 1991 for Latin America as a whole, reflecting the disposal of large state enterprises in some of the major countries of the region, particularly Mexico, Argentina and Venezuela. In the nineties, the countries with the largest privatization programs measured in terms of privatization revenue have been (in declining order) Mexico, Argentina, Brazil, Peru, Venezuela and Chile. Measured as a share of GDP, the leaders are (again in declining order) Belize, Bolivia, Mexico, Guyana, Trinidad and Tobago, Peru, Nicaragua, Jamaica and Argentina.

The bulk of divestitures has taken place in five sectors: telecommunications (25 percent), banking (22 percent), energy (14 percent), steel (11 percent), and petroleum (11 percent).

In choosing how to privatize, governments can either sell the company (direct sale, public offer, management/employee buyout, or joint venture), rent it out (concession or lease), or break up the enterprise and sell its assets. Direct sales have been the mainstay of Latin America's privatization programs, generating 60 percent of all privatization revenues and accounting for 80 percent of all transactions. Most of the remaining transactions have been carried out through public stock offerings, which have produced 34 percent of all privatization revenues and accounted for 10 percent of all transactions. Public offerings have mainly been used for very large transactions due to the high fixed costs of underwriting and marketing, and so have been little employed by the smaller countries.

For Latin America as a whole, the amount of revenues obtained from foreign buyers as a percentage of total privatization revenues has increased dramatically in recent years, from about 35 percent during 1990-93 to over 70 percent during 1994-95. This reflects the deepening of Latin America's reforms, the removal of barriers to equity participation from abroad, and the increase in foreign investor interest in the region. Privatization programs directly generated about 20 percent of Latin America's foreign direct investment (FDI) inflows over the 1990-95 period. Additional indirect FDI inflows have been estimated to be almost as large, and are obtained both by attracting further investments from the same buyers and by attracting completely new investors. Thus, privatization programs are not just one-time events. Rather, they can help to achieve a sustainable, higher level of capital inflows by enhancing the business climate and improving key infrastructural services.

INTRODUCTION

Privatization has marked a new chapter in Latin America's program of structural reforms, reversing decades of state intervention. This latter tradition, dating from the 1950s, called for governments to intervene in a number of key sectors such as infrastructure, finance, raw materials and manufacturing in an attempt to restrain monopoly power, allocate investment to priority areas of the economy, and accelerate development. In certain infrastructure sectors such as electricity and water, where the private sector had earlier played a more active role, the state often stepped in because of the unavailability of sufficient private capital to finance needed investments. For many state enterprises, however, political considerations interfered with economic management, budgets were overspent, and the market was not available to discipline behavior. The results were often disappointing, with many inefficient state-owned enterprises (SOEs) draining public finances.

The privatization movement was born and gathered momentum partly in reaction to these problems. Privatization programs have not been carried out, however, without important misgivings. Among them has been the fear that domestic markets will come to be excessively controlled by a small number of local families or by foreign capital. And because of the immediate infusion of revenue that privatization makes possible, some have also had the concern that divestiture programs would allow governments to more easily delay making needed fiscal adjustments, as occurred, for example, in Venezuela in 1992.

This chapter describes Latin America's privatization process, quantifies how much divestiture has been undertaken in the region, and compares these efforts to those of the other developing regions. Privatization is analyzed by country, sector, divestiture method, and by how much foreign participation was involved, thus yielding a detailed portrait of Latin America's privatization efforts in the first half of this decade.

While privatization is understood broadly to include both sale and rental arrangements, other methods for increasing private sector participation such as management contracts and outsourcing are not covered here. Neither does the chapter attempt to quantify the macro or microeconomic impacts of privatization, although some evidence is provided on the welfare gains from privatization, based on case studies. More detailed analysis on regulatory reforms that accompany the divestiture process and on best practices for managing privatization programs is available from other sources.[1]

AIMS AND DIFFICULTIES OF PRIVATIZATION

With the onset of the debt crisis came the lost decade of the 1980s and its fiscal and foreign exchange imbalances. A hangover of slow growth continued even into the 1990s. A privatization movement was sparked by these events, taking on important macroeconomic as well as microeconomic roles. While the aims of divestiture have varied from country to country, they have generally included:

• Improving firm-level efficiency.

• Reducing public sector borrowing requirements in the short run (from the privatization sales proceeds) and in the longer run (because the operating deficits and investment needs of SOEs need no longer be covered by the public sector, and because many privatized firms become profitable and pay taxes).

• Strengthening the balance of payments (through sales to foreign buyers).

• Promoting macroeconomic stability (especially as a result of the previous two effects).

• Increasing investment (because firms can escape from the public budget constraint and raise their own capital).

---

[1] Lucid discussions of these two issues are available in Edwards (1995, pp. 181-83) and Kikeri, Nellis and Shirley (1992), respectively.

• Promoting competition and deregulation.

• Expanding the range and quality of services offered.

• Developing capital markets.

In some specific cases such as Bolivia's capitalization program, the democratization of ownership has also been an important goal, with all Bolivian adult citizens receiving shares in the six capitalized enterprises. In other instances, such as the divestiture of Aeroméxico, privatization became the only way to wrest control of the SOE from its powerful employees, who enjoyed entitlements sustainable only through subsidies.

A wide variety of difficulties have been encountered by the different countries as they have undertaken privatization during the 1990s. The most common obstacle has been opposition by labor unions and political parties (Figure 5.1). This result is hardly surprising. Many SOEs have generated an enormous following among those who have benefited most from their policies, and this in turn has created large political constituencies. For example, bureaucrats and their unions have gained from relatively secure and high-wage public sector jobs. (The prospect of eliminating 100,000 state sector jobs has generated so much political opposition in Paraguay that the cur-

rent administration has been stymied in attempts at privatization since coming to power in May 1993.) Substantial benefits have also accrued to those consumers and firms who have benefited from low-cost government services (e.g., the recipients of targeted credit, telephone services, water and electric hookups). Other beneficiaries have included contractors and suppliers who have had cozy relationships with state enterprise managers, and private agents who have been able to "capture" regulators.

FIGURE 5.1

Latin America: Major Difficulties in Privatization

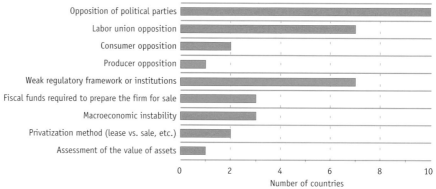

Source: IDB survey.
Note: Countries included in Figures 5.1 and 5.2 are the Bahamas, Barbados, Bolivia, Brazil, Colombia, Costa Rica, Dominican Republic, Ecuador, Guyana, Haiti, Honduras, Jamaica, Mexico, Paraguay, Peru, Trinidad and Tobago, and Uruguay. Responses were provided by IDB country economists often in consultation with sources in the country.

FIGURE 5.2

Latin America: Major Achievements of Privatization

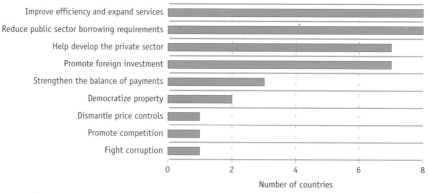

Source: IDB survey.

Table 5.1a Proceeds from Privatization by Region						
(In millions of U.S. dollars)						
Region	1990	1991	1992	1993	1994	1990-94
Latin America and the Caribbean	7,231	18,108	15,549	10,646	7,656	59,190
East Asia and Pacific	376	790	5,204	7,606	6,231	20,207
Europe and Central Asia	1,447	2,807	4,051	4,150	2,883	15,338
Middle East and North Africa	2	17	70	634	638	1,361
South Asia	29	996	1,557	974	2,666	6,222
Sub-Saharan Africa	71	50	178	648	792	1,739
All developing countries	**9,156**	**22,768**	**26,609**	**24,658**	**20,866**	**104,057**

The other major difficulty cited in our sample countries' privatization programs has been weak (or absent) regulatory frameworks or institutions. If purchasers fear regulatory expropriation, in which permissible selling prices for the enterprise's outputs are reduced by the government after completing the sale of the company, then they will either not be willing to bid or will only offer a low price.

As privatization proceeded in the 1990s, it gathered political support in many countries. As underscored in Figure 5.2, it has often improved efficiency. On a macroeconomic level, privatization has reduced public sector borrowing needs and thus in many cases improved prospects for macro stability and stimulated investment and growth.

There was little systematic privatization in Latin America prior to the late 1980s. Chile was an early exception, with the Pinochet military government divesting over 550 SOEs in the mid-1970s, including about 350 that the previous socialist government had nationalized. Additional privatizations followed in the mid-1980s after Chile's 1982-83 economic crisis. Mexico was another front-runner, with President de la Madrid selling about 150 smaller SOEs between 1983 and 1988 for approximately $500 million.[2] The Salinas administration, which came to power in December 1988 with a sweeping program of reform, sharply accelerated the process, addressing the task of selling the larger SOEs as well as the myriad of remaining smaller ones.

THE SCOPE OF PRIVATIZATION[3]

Along with the former East Bloc, Latin America has been a leader in the developing world's privatization movement. The $59 billion that Latin America realized from its 694 divestitures over the 1990-94 period is more than half the $104 billion realized by all developing countries (Table 5.1a). It far exceeds the $20 billion realized by East Asia and the $15 billion obtained by Europe and Central Asia.[4]

The large size of Latin America's privatization program is not simply because Latin Amer-

---

[2] Clutterbuck (1991).

[3] The divestiture data that appear in the tables in this chapter are based on the privatization database of the World Bank's International Economics Department. This database covers all types of divestitures, including both sales and rental arrangements, either of the entire enterprise or a part of it. Privatizations over $50,000 in value are tracked for 76 countries worldwide, including 19 nations in Latin America. The data for all of these countries were fairly complete through 1994 and very partial for 1995 at the time this report was prepared. (In Latin America the 1995 data cover only some transactions in six countries.) The database does not include the mass voucher privatizations employed in the former East Bloc countries, an omission which affects that region's reported performance in Tables 5.1a and 5.1b. Bolivia's capitalization program, however, is included in the database and tables. These World Bank data are supplemented with totals for the number of transactions and for total privatization proceeds in six of the seven IDB member countries which the World Bank database does not cover: the Bahamas, Dominican Republic, Guatemala, Guyana, Haiti and Suriname. These supplementary data are obtained from the IDB country economists survey and permit us to cover these two concepts for all 26 IDB member countries except El Salvador.

[4] It should be noted, however, that our database excludes the mass voucher privatizations commonly used in the former East Bloc countries, so our figure dramatically understates the true Europe and Central Asia total.

Table 5.1b Proceeds from Privatization by Region						
(Percent of regional GDP)						
Region	1990	1991	1992	1993	1994	1990-94
Latin America and the Caribbean	0.61	1.41	1.15	0.75	0.50	0.89
East Asia and Pacific	0.04	0.07	0.42	0.57	0.40	0.32
Europe and Central Asia	0.11	0.23	0.37	0.39	0.31	0.27
Middle East and North Africa	0.00	0.01	0.03	0.27	0.25	0.12
South Asia	0.01	0.30	0.47	0.29	0.69	0.35
Sub-Saharan Africa	0.04	0.03	0.09	0.35	0.39	0.18
All developing countries	**0.21**	**0.52**	**0.60**	**0.54**	**0.43**	**0.46**

ica has the largest economy of the regions shown. Table 5.1b shows the ratio of regional privatization revenue to regional GDP, and Latin America again stands well ahead of the other regions, with annual privatization revenues averaging almost 1 percent of GDP in the 1990-94 period.

The trend in privatization activity in Latin America differs from that in the other regions. Annual revenues peak in Latin America in 1991 and decline strongly thereafter, while revenues continue to increase in most of the other regions at least through 1993. The sharp decline in Latin America reflects the rapidity of the process in some of the major countries in the region; these countries had simply disposed of much of their public assets by the early nineties.

Mexico is a clear example of this, divesting an extraordinary $11 billion in 1991, half of the privatization revenues received that year by the entire developing world. In 1991, Mexico divested 20 percent of its national telephone company, TELMEX, for $2.7 billion, and much of its banking system, including the two largest banks, Bancomer and Banamex (the latter selling for $3.2 billion, the largest single sale in the developing world). By the end of 1994, the number of SOEs in Mexico had dwindled from 1,155 in 1982 to less than 80.[5] Important state enterprises remain,

such as the oil monopoly PEMEX, but clearly the transition to private sector ownership has been made in Mexico.

Argentina's privatization program is of a more recent vintage, but also dramatic in its scope and impact. It began with the start of the Menem administration in 1989, which undertook a program to stabilize the macroeconomy, then suffering from hyperinflation and deep recession. Privatization was an integral part of the program because of its salutary effects on public sector deficits in the short and longer runs (on the latter, SOE operating deficits had reached $4 billion by 1991) and on the balance of payments (as of 1994 the Menem privatization program had reduced the external debt by $18 billion through the use of debt/equity swaps, about one-quarter of the total debt in that year). It also responded to the need to improve the quality of key infrastructural services, including electricity, transportation, telecommunications and ports. Like Mexico, Argentina had sold much of its state-owned sector by the close of 1993.

Tables 5.1c and 5.1d show the total value and the number of privatization transactions, respectively, for individual Latin American countries and for the region as a whole. Mexico and Argentina clearly stand out by these measures as the regional leaders in privatization. Adjusting for size by comparing privatization revenue to GDP (Table 5.1e), however, other countries emerge as strong privatizers as well. For the 1990-

---

[5] Edwards (1995, p. 191).

Table 5.1c Privatization Revenues

(In millions of U.S. dollars)

	1990	1991	1992	1993	1994	1995	1990-95
Mexico	3,160	11,289	6,924	2,131	766	na	24,271
Argentina	3,841	2,091	5,567	4,732	890	1,326	18,446
Brazil	44	1,726	2,564	2,718	1,697	387	9,136
Peru	0	3	212	127	2,840	1,176	4,358
Venezuela	10	2,278	140	36	8	39	2,510
Chile	98	364	8	106	683	na	1,259
Colombia	0	168	5	391	170	na	735
Bolivia	0	0	9	13	0	615	637
Trinidad & Tobago	0	0	0	172	248	28	448
Jamaica	49	83	30	78	75	na	316
Nicaragua	1	32	11	66	16	na	126
Panama	1	2	17	21	60	na	100
Ecuador	0	0	0	1	96	na	96
Honduras	1	10	26	31	6	na	74
Belize	8	29	7	14	0	na	59
Barbados	0	3	28	0	20	na	51
Guyana	3	27	0	0	11	9	50
Costa Rica	0	3	0	10	32	na	46
Bahamas	0	0	0	0	15	10	25
Paraguay	0	0	0	0	22	na	22
Uruguay	15	0	0	0	2	na	17
Dominican Republic	0	0	0	0	0	0	0
Guatemala	0	0	0	0	0	0	0
Haiti	0	0	0	0	0	0	0
Suriname	0	0	0	0	0	0	0
Latin America	**7,231**	**18,108**	**15,549**	**10,646**	**7,656**	**3,590**	**62,780**

95 period, Belize and Bolivia rank ahead of Mexico, followed in order by Guyana, Trinidad and Tobago, Peru, Nicaragua, Jamaica and Argentina, though these last six countries are closely bunched. The remaining 16 countries in this table have been much less intensive privatizers than the first nine.

Since the beginning of the Fujimori government in July, 1990, Peru has been committed to making deep-seated structural reforms, including an ambitious program of privatization. The sale in 1994 of 35 percent of the two telecommunications companies, CPT and Entelperu, for $1.4 billion, has been the largest transaction, although the program has also stressed the divestiture of energy and mining companies. Bolivia's capitalization program, registering its first transactions only in 1995, has become one of the region's leaders in the nineties just on the strength of one year's activities (see Box 5.1). The sale of Belize Telecom-

munications Ltd. and Belize Electricity Ltd. in several tranches in 1990-93 gave Belize the highest ratio of privatization revenue to GDP of any country in the region. However, Belize does not have a large state enterprise sector and has not been active in privatization since these two large transactions. Guyana is another small country that has made a relatively sizable divestiture effort in the nineties, despite the virtual suspension of its privatization program in 1992-93 as a result of a re-evaluation by the then newly-elected government. Among its important divestitures have been the Guyana Telecommunications Corporation in 1991 (which alone accounts for about one-third of Guyana's total 1990-95 privatization revenue), the banks NBIC in 1991 and GBTI in 1994, and a number of other industry, infrastructure and primary sector firms. The strongest subregional privatizer has been the Caribbean, with impressive efforts by Jamaica (particularly in telecommunica-

Box 5.1   Bolivia's Capitalization Program

Bolivia's capitalization program was a cornerstone of the current government's platform in the May 1993 elections, and represents an ingenious solution to a number of problems that would have been encountered under a more traditional privatization scheme.

To illustrate how the program works, consider the capitalization of ENTEL, the national telecommunications company, by strategic investor STET in 1995. The book value of ENTEL prior to the start of the international competitive bidding was $130 million, which may be contrasted to STET's winning tender offer of $610 million (easily the highest multiple of book value received thus far in the capitalization program). With this bid, STET obligates itself to make $610 million in capital investments in ENTEL's telecommunications network. The government receives no funds. In return, STET retains half or slightly less than half of the equity shares in ENTEL and obtains management control. The other half of the shares are divided equally among the 3.8 million Bolivians of voting age (except for a small block reserved for ENTEL employee stock options, exercisable at the book value price). The shares going to the Bolivian people actually do not go directly to them but rather will be deposited with one of the several new private pension funds that are expected to emerge from the social security reform under discussion, along with the shares each individual receives in the other five companies being capitalized.

The capitalization program covers part or all of the six largest state-owned enterprises: ENDE (electricity), ENTEL (telecommunications), LAB (airline), ENFE (railways), YPFB (oil and gas), and EMV (minerals and smelting). Together these SOEs accounted for about 12 percent of GDP. Numerous other smaller companies are being privatized using traditional techniques such as concessions and direct sales. In 1995, the first four of the six SOEs were capitalized (at least in part), with capitalization tenders totaling $836 million. The program is scheduled to be completed in 1996 and should yield a total of around $1.5 billion or more in capital infusions. In addition, the legal and regulatory frameworks of all six sectors will have been modernized to allow for private participation and hopefully to encourage efficiency, profitability and additional future investments.

Why did Bolivia choose to capitalize rather than privatize? First, the country had achieved economic stability and had undertaken extensive reforms in the years following the 1985 hyperinflation. But it had not obtained a very strong growth performance; for example, the average annual GDP growth rate was 3.4 percent for the 1987-93 period. It was believed that higher investment levels were a key to accelerating growth. Capitalization was a mechanism to ensure that there would be a large injection of investment that could hopefully put Bolivia on a faster growth path. This would be reinforced by the fact that much of the new investment would be in key infrastructure sectors that could raise the productivity of investments throughout the economy. Second, capitalization was a way to keep the injection of new private sector money *in* the private sector, where it might be more efficiently used, rather than having it accrue to the government as would happen under a traditional privatization. Third, privatization had unpopular overtones in Bolivia. Capitalization had the political advantage of allowing the argument to be made that the national patrimony was not being sold to foreign interests (even though, as expected, all the partners have so far been foreign companies that enjoy strategic and managerial control). Rather, this patrimony would be transferred to the Bolivian people as their half of the new company. The foreign strategic investors would own the other half of the company, but only because of the new investments they themselves would make. Finally, the capitalization program involved a component of democratization of ownership and of capital markets development that has added to its appeal.

Table 5.1d	Number of Privatization Transactions						
	1990	1991	1992	1993	1994	1995	1990-95
Mexico	57	48	35	22	12	na	174
Argentina	11	10	39	37	24	2	123
Brazil	1	5	16	8	14	1	45
Peru	0	3	11	15	30	13	72
Venezuela	1	7	10	6	3	2	29
Chile	1	4	1	3	5	na	14
Colombia	0	5	4	4	3	na	16
Bolivia	0	0	8	18	0	2	28
Trinidad & Tobago	0	0	0	4	11	2	17
Jamaica	3	11	2	6	4	na	26
Nicaragua	1	7	22	26	19	na	75
Panama	1	1	2	4	1	na	9
Ecuador	0	0	0	1	8	na	9
Honduras	3	4	10	11	4	na	32
Belize	1	1	1	1	0	na	4
Barbados	0	1	3	0	2	na	6
Guyana	na	na	na	na	na	na	19
Costa Rica	0	1	0	1	2	na	4
Bahamas	0	0	0	0	na	na	6
Paraguay	0	0	0	0	1	na	1
Uruguay	1	0	0	3	3	na	7
Dominican Republic	0	0	0	0	0	0	0
Guatemala	0	0	0	0	0	0	0
Haiti	0	0	0	0	0	0	0
Suriname	0	0	0	0	0	0	0
Latin America	**81**	**108**	**164**	**170**	**146**	**22**	**716**

tions and hotels) and Trinidad and Tobago (electric power, chemicals and steel). The ratio of total privatization revenue to total GDP over the 1990-95 period for the Caribbean is 1.15 percent, vs. 0.8 percent for Latin America as a whole, and only 0.4 percent for Central America.

Brazil and Venezuela have been weaker privatizers, considering the size of their economies and the large SOE sector in each country. The reformist Pérez administration in Venezuela launched its privatization program in 1990, and by 1991 had sold the national telephone company (CANTV) for $1.9 billion, the major government-owned airline (VIASA) for $145 million, and several smaller companies. However, following two coup attempts in 1992 and Pérez's resignation in 1993, Venezuela's privatization program stalled and has yet to regain its momentum.

In Brazil, the Collor administration came into office offering a reform program that stressed trade liberalization, deregulation and a much smaller role for government in the economy. From the time Collor took power in March 1990 until his resignation in November 1992, the privatization program gathered steam. Vice President Itamar Franco assumed control with a much more hesitant approach to reform in general, including privatization. The Cardoso administration, which took power in January 1995, has proposed accelerating Brazil's privatization program despite strong political opposition. Legal and regulatory frameworks are being modernized in the telecommunications, electricity, coastal shipping and petroleum sectors, with a view toward facilitating divestiture and greater competition.

Colombia has also had a relatively small privatization program. Unlike Brazil and Venezuela, however, the state enterprise sector in Colombia has always been quite modest in size. Nonetheless, there is currently consideration being given to privatizing some natural resources enterprises, such as those producing coal and nickel, as well as SOEs in the financial sector and in other areas. Divestiture of all of the federal government's electricity generation plants (some 40 percent of the country's total installed capacity) is expected during 1996-97, adding to the 10 percent currently owned by private sector power producers. There has also been significant recent activity in awarding toll road concessions, and much more expected in the next few years.

Finally, Table 5.1f shows that the short-term fiscal impacts of privatization can be very substantial. For example, Argentina received annual privatization revenues of about 10 percent of central government expenditures in 1990, 1992 and 1993. Mexico obtained approximately 15 percent in 1991 and 1992. Even these fiscal windfalls are well short of Belize's 22 percent in 1991 and

Peru's 35 percent in 1994. For Latin America as a whole, privatization revenues were about 5 percent of central government expenditures in the 1990-95 period, though with enormous country-to-country and year-to-year variations. For example, the first nine countries in Table 5.1f generated privatization revenues that averaged some 5 to 10 percent of central government expenditures, while for the remaining 16 countries this share was generally 2 percent or less.[6]

SECTORAL DECOMPOSITION OF PRIVATIZATION

The sectoral breakdown of Latin America's privatization process is shown in broad terms in Table 5.2a and in detail in Table 5.2b. From the standpoint of total revenue generation, the privatization of infrastructure stands out, having produced 43 percent of Latin America's total revenue in the 1990-95 period. The divestiture of financial services, particularly banks, has also been important, with a 23 percent share. The industrial and primary sectors have each produced 16 percent of total revenue, while other (i.e., nonfinancial) services account for only 1 percent of total proceeds.

In terms of the number of transactions, there is a reversal, however, with the industrial and primary sectors the leaders. This reflects the relatively small average transaction size in these latter two areas ($55 and $49 million, respectively) as compared to infrastructure and finance ($163 and $277 million, respectively).

Table 5.2b subdivides each of these five broad sectors into a total of 24 subsectors, and shows that in terms of revenue generation, privatization has been dominated by only five of the 24 subsectors, which produced 82 percent of all privatization revenue during the 1990-95 period:

Table 5.1e Privatization Revenue as a Percentage of GDP							
	1990	1991	1992	1993	1994	1995	1990-95
Belize	2.06	6.64	1.41	2.74	0.00	na	2.45
Bolivia	0.00	0.00	0.17	0.24	0.00	10.19	2.03
Mexico	1.47	4.83	2.83	0.85	0.29	na	2.00
Guyana	0.89	6.81	0.07	0.01	1.93	1.39	1.73
Trinidad & Tobago	0.00	0.00	0.00	3.75	5.04	0.54	1.60
Peru	0.00	0.01	0.51	0.28	5.42	2.05	1.58
Nicaragua	0.07	0.19	0.68	3.92	0.92	na	1.52
Jamaica	1.25	2.01	0.71	1.76	1.64	na	1.48
Argentina	1.94	0.93	2.23	1.75	0.30	0.46	1.21
Barbados	0.00	0.18	1.88	0.00	1.19	na	0.65
Venezuela	0.02	3.47	0.20	0.05	0.01	0.05	0.61
Chile	0.24	0.81	0.02	0.19	1.18	na	0.51
Honduras	0.04	0.31	0.79	0.87	0.18	na	0.45
Panama	0.01	0.04	0.28	0.31	0.85	na	0.33
Brazil	0.01	0.33	0.48	0.48	0.28	0.06	0.27
Colombia	0.00	0.30	0.01	0.61	0.24	na	0.24
Bahamas	0.00	0.00	0.00	0.00	0.47	0.30	0.14
Ecuador	0.00	0.00	0.00	0.00	0.56	na	0.13
Costa Rica	0.00	0.05	0.00	0.13	0.39	na	0.13
Paraguay	0.00	0.00	0.00	0.00	0.26	na	0.06
Uruguay	0.12	0.00	0.00	0.00	0.01	na	0.02
Dominican Republic	0.00	0.00	0.00	0.00	0.00	0.00	0.00
Guatemala	0.00	0.00	0.00	0.00	0.00	0.00	0.00
Haiti	0.00	0.00	0.00	0.00	0.00	0.00	0.00
Suriname	0.00	0.00	0.00	0.00	0.00	0.00	0.00
Latin America	**0.61**	**1.41**	**1.15**	**0.75**	**0.50**	**0.32**	**0.79**

telecommunications and energy (the dominant areas within infrastructure), banking (which dominates the financial sector), petroleum (in the primary sector), and steel (in the industrial sector). These have yielded 25, 14, 22, 11, and 11 percent of total revenue, respectively.

Infrastructure sales not only have the potential to raise significant revenue given the large size of many of the companies involved, but

---

[6] Several caveats should be noted about the percentages in Table 5.1f. First, all of the figures are gross of sale preparation expenses (including such items as employee buyouts and capital investments); these reduce the net revenue received by the government from the privatization exercise. Second, none of Bolivia's spectacular 46 percent in 1995 accrues to the government under the workings of that country's unique capitalization program. Less spectacular but more commonly encountered is the fact that some of the privatization proceeds in some of the countries are not available to the central government to meet its general expenditures, but rather may accrue to certain autonomous agencies that were the owners of the divested assets. Finally, in some cases, not all privatization revenues are actually paid in the year shown but are received afterwards.

Table 5.1f   Privatization Revenue as a Percentage of Central Government Expenditure

	1990	1991	1992	1993	1994	1995	1990-95
Belize	7.62	22.39	4.71	8.57	0	na	8.07
Bolivia	0	0	1.05	1.37	0	46.39	11.39
Mexico	2.41	16.11	12.76	3.48	1.65	na	11.48
Guyana	1.24	13.4	0.13	0.01	4.12	2.99	3.31
Trinidad & Tobago	0	0	0	13.57	19.13	2.04	5.76
Peru	0	0.06	4.01	2.15	34.96	12.62	11.53
Nicaragua	0.21	7.24	2.4	14.29	3.05	na	5.18
Jamaica	4.31	6.93	2.68	6.17	5.55	na	5.18
Argentina	12.43	5.31	11.89	9.78	1.77	2.58	6.9
Barbados	0	0.56	5.84	0	3.88	na	2.04
Venezuela	0.07	14.34	0.94	0.26	0.05	0.25	2.75
Chile	0.99	3.22	0.07	0.81	4.98	na	2.1
Honduras	0.15	1.42	3.2	3.16	0.82	na	1.9
Panama	0.06	0.18	1.09	1.56	4.12	na	1.57
Brazil	0.02	1.18	1.51	na	na	na	0.84
Colombia	0	2.3	0.06	4.1	1.56	na	1.73
Bahamas	0	0	0	0	2.41	1.46	0.7
Ecuador	0	0	0	0.03	3.53	na	0.82
Costa Rica	0	0.28	0	0.72	1.76	na	0.67
Paraguay	0	0	0	0	1.92	na	0.47
Uruguay	0.65	0	0	0	0.05	na	0.12
Dominican Republic	0	0	0	0	0	0	0
Guatemala	0	0	0	0	0	0	0
Haiti	0	0	0	0	0	0	0
Suriname	0	0	0	0	0	0	0
Latin America	2.25	6.46	4.93	7.00	4.57	4.50	4.76

also hold out the promise of increasing the productivity of existing capital and new investments throughout the economy. Electricity, telephone services, water and transportation services are basic inputs that are relied on by producers economywide. If their quality is poor, prices high, queues long, and selection limited, as has often occurred with publicly-provided infrastructure services, then the potential gains from private sector ownership and operation of these services can be quite substantial.

Governments in Latin America have found themselves in the banking business for a variety of reasons, including as the result of bank takeovers during financial crises. Typically, government-run commercial banks are notably less efficient than their private sector counterparts, as has been the case, for example, with Peru's "bancas asociadas" (public commercial banks). The lending decisions of public development banks

have too often been guided by political considerations and favoritism instead of by the creditworthiness of the borrowers. This has all too often resulted in huge arrearage rates and staggering losses for the institutions, as for example the cases of Nicaragua's four and Peru's five state development banks in the 1990s. The state-owned commercial and development banks in Barbados (BNB and BDB, respectively), Guyana (GNCB and GAIBANK, respectively), and in numerous other countries also offer many clear examples of these problems. The evidence in Latin America firmly supports the premise that banking is best carried out by the private sector, and the large volume of bank privatizations is a testament to this hard-earned lesson.

Public sector involvement in the exploitation of primary commodities such as oil, coffee and minerals often occurred at an early stage in development, and represented an easy way for the government to obtain foreign exchange. Divestiture of such activities, therefore, can have a strong signaling effect that the investment climate in the country has changed and the economy is now much more open to private capital and initiative. Latin American countries are also divesting themselves of a large number and variety of industrial firms, often on the belief that such activities can be more efficiently carried out and effectively expanded by the private sector.

Sectoral privatization revenues by country are shown in Table 5.2c, and display some interesting differences across countries. For example, Argentina derived most of its revenue from infrastructure sales and secondarily from primary sector divestitures. The leading example of the former was the $3.2 billion it received from the privatization of telecommunications giant

Table 5.2a Privatization Revenue, Number of Transactions and Average Transaction Size, by Sector, 1990-95

	Privatization revenue		Transactions		Average transaction size
Sector	US$ millions	Percent of total	Number of transactions	Percent of total	(US$ millions)
Infrastructure	27,211	43	167	24	163
Financial services	14,682	23	53	8	277
Industry	9,858	16	180	26	55
Primary sector	10,283	16	210	30	49
Other services	669	1	81	12	8
Total	**62,703**	**100**	**691**	**100**	

Table 5.2b Privatization Revenue by Detailed Sector

(In millions of U.S. dollars)

	1990	1991	1992	1993	1994	1995	1990-95	% of the 1990-95 total
Infrastructure	5,739	6,366	6,199	2,574	3,394	2,940	27,211	43.4
Airlines & airports	1,914	237	45	25	61	31	2,313	3.7
Railroads	0	159	217	0	0	0	376	0.6
Road transport	300	2	11	1	0	0	314	0.5
Ports & shipping	10	0	19	28	19	0	76	0.1
Telecommunications	3,514	5,742	2,649	1,091	1,950	630	15,576	24.8
Energy (electricity & gas)	0	226	3,259	1,379	1,364	2,279	8,506	13.6
Water & sanitation	0	0	0	50	0	0	50	0.1
Financial services	25	7,624	4,930	1,125	468	511	14,682	23.4
Banking	25	7,428	4,929	408	460	511	13,760	21.9
Insurance	0	0	0	549	7	0	556	0.9
Real estate	0	0	1	163	0	0	164	0.3
Others	0	197	0	4	1	0	202	0.3
Primary sector	1,265	1,135	2,231	3,802	1,814	36	10,283	16.4
Agriculture & forestry	371	138	52	314	18	0	894	1.4
Fishing & livestock	35	6	3	2	10	9	64	0.1
Mining	482	235	271	82	1,338	25	2,432	3.9
Petroleum	378	756	1,905	3,404	448	2	6,893	11.0
Industry	177	2,760	2,089	2,927	1,867	39	9,858	15.7
Light manufacturing	28	680	209	183	300	39	1,439	2.3
Steel	109	1,998	1,310	2,266	1,115	0	6,798	10.8
Chemicals	39	74	554	467	68	0	1,202	1.9
Construction materials	0	8	15	11	384	0	419	0.7
Other services	22	197	100	219	88	43	669	1.1
Tourism	8	54	22	15	86	43	228	0.4
International trade	0	21	4	35	1	0	62	0.1
Retail trade	0	6	2	15	0	0	22	0.0
Other services	14	0	72	153	0	0	239	0.4
Not classified above	0	116	0	0	1	0	117	0.2
Total	**7,228**	**18,081**	**15,549**	**10,646**	**7,630**	**3,569**	**62,703**	**100.0**

Table 5.2c   Sectoral Privatization Revenue, 1990-95

(In millions of U.S. dollars)

Country	Infrastructure	Financial services	Primary sector	Industry	Other services	Total
Belize	59	0	0	0	0	59
Bolivia	615	0	11	10	1	637
Mexico	8,052	12,989	1,491	1,517	222	24,271
Trinidad and Tobago	138	0	8	302	1	448
Peru	2,437	583	989	282	64	4,356
Nicaragua	0	0	83	24	19	126
Jamaica	111	23	88	51	43	316
Argentina	12,498	263	4,976	618	91	18,446
Barbados	24	0	0	10	17	51
Venezuela	2,128	163	53	147	18	2,510
Chile	512	0	672	11	64	1,259
Honduras	12	0	25	33	4	74
Panama	18	0	19	61	3	100
Brazil	583	0	1,862	6,600	91	9,136
Colombia	0	645	6	56	27	734
Ecuador	0	1	0	96	0	96
Costa Rica	0	0	0	42	3	45
Paraguay	22	0	0	0	0	22
Uruguay	2	15	0	0	0	17
Latin America	**27,211**	**14,682**	**10,283**	**9,858**	**669**	**62,703**

ENTEL in tranches over the 1990-92 period. The sale of the flagship national airline Aerolíneas Argentinas in 1990 for $1.9 billion was another early indicator of the government's commitment to divesting its infrastructure holdings. Finally, petroleum companies are often important symbols of national patrimony and independence. So, when 45 percent of the national oil and gas company YPF was finally sold in 1993 for $3 billion, with 75 percent of the revenues coming from foreign investors, Argentina was seen by the international investment community as open to foreign capital.

Argentina has yet to privatize much of its huge public banking sector, however. In contrast, the cornerstone of Mexico's privatization program has been to put back into private hands the 18 banks that it nationalized in 1982. This alone yielded $12.1 billion in 1991-92, one-half of Mexico's total privatization proceeds for the nineties. Half of the remainder is accounted for by the privatization of TELMEX for $6.3 billion in several tranches over the 1990-92 period. Mexico still re-

tains the huge, vertically-integrated state electricity company, CFE, in contrast to Argentina, which sold all of its federally-owned electric power utilities for a total of $2.1 billion.

Brazil has been the region's leader in industrial privatizations, selling the huge steel companies Usiminas for $1.5 billion in 1991 and CSN for $1.3 billion in 1993. Altogether, the divestiture of industrial enterprises has accounted for three-quarters of Brazil's privatization revenues in the nineties.

In Venezuela, Bolivia and Belize the sale of the national telecommunications enterprise has been responsible for well over half of the revenues generated by each country's entire privatization program. This reflects the high book value of many of the national telephone companies, and their great potential for expansion given the low connection densities in the region.

FOREIGN PARTICIPATION IN PRIVATIZATION

Foreign participation in a country's privatization program can offer the divesting nation considerable economic advantage. First, there are the fiscal and economic benefits of widening the field of potential bidders: a better price and better terms of sale may be obtained, the latter including such things as future investment commitments and labor agreements.[7] Second, and particularly if they obtain a controlling interest in the company being sold, foreign firms may bring new technology, management methods, and capital to the enterprise, which may be keys to its revitalization. Despite these advantages, considerable political opposition can be aroused when a government sells off to foreign interests what many in the country regard as national treasures.

Foreign investors have participated in privatizations primarily as either direct or portfolio equity investors. Direct investors acquire sufficient shares in the enterprise to have control over operations and the strategic direction of the firm, and thus can be keys to upgrading the company's management and technological standards. For portfolio equity investors, share ownership is a purely financial transaction, with no significant control over day-to-day operations or future strategic direction. Industrial country institutional investors such as mutual funds and insurance companies, looking to increase their returns and their diversification by investing in developing

Table 5.3a Privatization Revenue From Abroad as a Percentage of Total Privatization Revenue

	1990	1991	1992	1993	1994	1995	1990-95
Belize	0	0	0	0	0	na	0
Bolivia	0	0	0	0	0	100.0	96.6
Mexico	31.6	36.6	18.7	0	71.8	na	28.7
Trinidad & Tobago	0	0	0	98.1	97.3	78.8	96.5
Peru	0	0	67.2	74.8	91.6	63.8	82.4
Nicaragua	0	0	0	0	28.7	na	3.7
Jamaica	85.7	66.8	0	0	5.3	na	32.2
Argentina	36.8	53.9	37.3	66.3	50.8	0	47.9
Barbados	0	100.0	99.4	0	100.0	na	99.7
Venezuela	0	66.7	80.8	0	0	100.0	66.6
Chile	100.0	0	0	0	81.3	na	51.9
Honduras	0	5.3	1.2	0	0	na	1.1
Panama	0	0	30.4	0	96.7	na	62.9
Brazil	0	11.7	10.7	2.6	42.6	0	14.5
Colombia	0	33.2	0	63.2	100.0	na	64.4
Ecuador	0	0	0	0	56.3	na	55.9
Costa Rica	0	0	0	0	0	na	0
Paraguay	0	0	0	0	50.0	na	50.0
Uruguay	100.0	0	0	0	50.0	na	94.1
Latin America	**35.5**	**39.2**	**25.3**	**34.9**	**71.4**	**76.7**	**39.7**

Table 5.3b FDI from Privatization as a Percentage of Privatization Revenue from Abroad

	1990	1991	1992	1993	1994	1995	1990-95
Belize	0	0	0	0	0	na	na
Bolivia	0	0	0	0	0	100.0	100.0
Mexico	99.4	19.7	7.0	0	0	na	27.2
Trinidad & Tobago	0	0	0	100.0	100.0	100.0	100.0
Peru	0	0	97.1	100.0	96.8	100.0	97.6
Nicaragua	0	0	0	0	100.0	na	100.0
Jamaica	100.0	100.0	0	0	100.0	0	100.0
Argentina	100.0	100.0	100.0	25.0	26.6	0	67.3
Barbados	0	100.0	100.0	0	100.0	na	100.0
Venezuela	0	100.0	2.50	0	0	100.0	93.4
Chile	100.0	0	0	0	100.0	na	100.0
Honduras	0	100.0	100.0	0	0	na	100.0
Panama	0	0	100.0	0	100.0	na	100.0
Brazil	0	27.4	31.0	37.1	32.2	0	31.5
Colombia	0	100.0	0	0	0	na	11.8
Ecuador	0	0	0	0	0	na	0
Costa Rica	0	0	0	0	0	na	na
Paraguay	0	0	0	0	100.0	na	100.0
Uruguay	100.0	0	0	0	100.0	na	100.0

---

[7] López-de-Silanes (1994), in an econometric evaluation of 346 privatizations in Mexico, shows that foreign participation resulted in significantly higher sales prices.

Table 5.3c FDI from Privatization as a Percentage of Total FDI

	1990	1991	1992	1993	1994	1995	1990-95
Belize	0.0	0.0	0.0	0.0	0.0	na	0.0
Bolivia	0.0	0.0	0.0	0.0	0.0	165.2[a]	103.6[a]
Mexico	37.7	17.1	2.1	0.0	0.0	na	7.9
Trinidad & Tobago	0.0	0.0	0.0	44.6	46.7	7.8	26.4
Peru	0.0	0.0	95.6	25.5	108.3[a]	44.3	76.7
Nicaragua	0.0	0.0	0.0	0.0	11.8	na	5.0
Jamaica	30.5	41.7	0.0	0.0	3.4	na	16.7
Argentina	76.9	46.3	49.6	12.4	9.4	0.0	30.4
Barbados	0.0	46.7	208.4[a]	0.0	199.0[a]	na	110.5[a]
Venezuela	0.0	87.9	0.6	0.0	0.0	10.7	66.0
Chile	16.8	0.0	0.0	0.0	63.8	na	25.3
Honduras	0.0	1.0	0.6	0.0	0.0	na	0.3
Panama	0.0	0.0	3.0	0.0	na	na	-0.9[a]
Brazil	0.0	62.0	4.4	3.3	11.5	0.0	5.2
Colombia	0.0	12.9	0.0	0.0	0.0	na	1.4
Ecuador	0.0	0.0	0.0	0.0	0.0	na	0.0
Costa Rica	0.0	0.0	0.0	0.0	0.0	na	0.0
Paraguay	0.0	0.0	0.0	0.0	6.1	na	1.9
Uruguay	na	na	na	0.0	0.6	na	0.4

[a] Privatization values may exceed FDI due to differences in the accounting methods of the two variables.

countries, are the main foreign portfolio equity investors.

The dramatic increase in foreign participation in Latin American privatizations is documented in Table 5.3a. For Latin America as a whole, revenues obtained from foreign buyers as a percentage of total privatization revenues jumped from about 35 percent in 1990-93 to over 70 percent in 1994-95. As Latin America has increasingly committed itself to a program of structural reforms, particularly since the late 1980s and early 1990s, foreign investors have become increasingly interested in taking equity positions in the region. Further, as Latin American countries have become more aware of the advantages of foreign investment to them, they have removed legal, regulatory and other obstacles to equity participation from abroad, spurring such participation in SOE divestitures as well as in other ventures.

The split between foreign direct investment (FDI) and the remainder of privatization revenue from abroad, which is overwhelmingly portfolio equity investment (PEI), is shown in Table 5.3b. For Latin America as a whole in the

nineties, about 60 percent of the privatization revenue received from abroad has been in the form of FDI.

While the larger Latin American countries have received considerable PEI inflows, the smaller countries of the region have received little or none. For example, the Caribbean and Central American countries have received all of their privatization revenues from abroad in the form of FDI, none in the form of PEI. This result reflects the high fixed costs of preparing an initial public stock offering, which makes this method uneconomical except in the case of large enterprises. The fact that the smaller countries have many fewer such enterprises, and much less well developed stock markets to facilitate initial offerings and subsequent trades, explains much of the dominance in these countries of FDI over PEI.

Latin America has received about $2-3 billion per year in FDI from privatization during the nineties. These inflows have averaged about 20 percent of total FDI inflows for the region, as shown in Table 5.3c.[8] The immediate FDI revenues obtained from a privatization program are only part of the story, however. Sader (1993) presents econometric evidence based on a worldwide sample of countries that each dollar of immediate FDI revenue obtained from privatization generates an additional 88 cents of FDI outside of the privatization transactions themselves. This is attributable to at least three factors. First, there may be a signaling effect, in which privatization serves to indicate that the country is a hospitable place for private investment. Second, many privatiza-

[8] Ratios in Table 5.3c that fall outside of the 0 to 100 percent range reflect the fact that the FDI inflow figures we have used, while gross of FDI outflows from residents investing abroad, are net of domestic purchases of foreign-owned firms in the country. It also reflects the fact that in some cases not all privatization revenues from abroad are actually paid in the year shown.

tions lead to additional FDI flows because of the need to undertake subsequent investments to modernize and improve the plant and equipment of the purchased companies. Third, infrastructure privatizations may stimulate significant additional FDI because of their capacity to improve the quality and availability of key services and thus raise the profitability of investments (foreign as well as domestic) throughout the economy. For all these reasons, privatizations are not just one-time events, with FDI flows returning to their original levels upon completion of the program. Rather, by enhancing the business climate and improving key infrastructural services, privatizations can have powerful and lasting effects on future capital inflows.

Table 5.4a Revenues from Different Methods of Privatization							
(In millions of U.S. dollars)							
	1990	1991	1992	1993	1994	1995	1990-95
Direct sale	6,534	9,308	9,656	3,767	4,876	3,569	37,711
Public offer	108	7,814	5,109	6,118	2,177	0	21,325
Concession	571	251	301	702	23	0	1,846
Lease	0	0	0	38	0	0	38
Joint venture	0	615	465	0	555	0	1,635
Management/Employee buyout	16	44	18	0	0	0	78
Liquidation plus asset sale	0	50	0	21	0	0	70
Total privatization revenue	**7,228**	**18,081**	**15,549**	**10,646**	**7,630**	**3,569**	**62,703**

Table 5.4b Transactions Using Different Privatization Methods							
	1990	1991	1992	1993	1994	1995	1990-95
Direct sale	70	82	130	131	116	22	551
Public offer	2	10	21	15	19	0	67
Concession	4	3	10	12	9	0	38
Lease	1	3	0	5	0	0	9
Joint venture	0	1	1	0	1	0	3
Management/Employee buyout	4	6	2	0	1	0	13
Liquidation plus asset sale	0	3	0	7	0	0	10
Total number of transactions	**81**	**108**	**164**	**170**	**146**	**22**	**691**

FORMS OF DIVESTITURE

Box 5.2 explains the major privatization techniques that have been used in Latin America. Basically, governments can choose either to sell the company (direct sale, public offer, management/ employee buyout, or joint venture), rent it out (concession or lease), or break up the enterprise and sell its assets.

Direct sales have been the most important technique used in Latin America, generating 60 percent of all privatization revenues and accounting for 80 percent of all transactions (Tables 5.4a and 5.4b). Most of the remaining transactions have been carried out through public stock offerings, which have produced 34 percent of all privatization revenues and accounted for 10 percent of all transactions. Thus, 90 percent or more of privatization has been carried out using these two sales techniques. The preference for sale over rental arrangements reflects the desire of governments to completely return most privatizable assets to the private sector, in hopes of realizing more

fully the potential benefits of divestiture. Among the available sales techniques, the use of management/employee buyouts is problematic, and the scope for joint ventures evidently quite limited in practice.

The average transaction size reflects the privatization technique used. Public offers have generated an average of $318 million each, while direct sales have yielded a mean revenue of only $68 million. As noted earlier, there are large fixed costs associated with public offers, such as those resulting from prospectus preparation, underwriting and marketing. The services of an investment bank must normally be retained, and all this is only justified for large transactions. In contrast, direct sales can be arranged more cheaply and easily, and so have proven to be the workhorse of Latin American privatization programs.

Box 5.2   Privatization Techniques

Direct Sale. This is the most straightforward privatization technique: the enterprise is simply sold to a private investor. The sale is normally carried out by means of a competitive bidding process in order to ensure a high price for the government and fairness to the prospective buyers.

Public Offering. Here, shares in the enterprise are sold in the domestic stock market and perhaps internationally as well. This is a particularly useful technique for large but financially-sound SOEs, where finding a single buyer capable of purchasing the entire enterprise could prove difficult. A public offering is often preceded by a direct sale of a controlling interest in the enterprise to a single investor. That investor then takes charge of the firm's future strategic direction and hopefully engenders interest in the company in the wider investment community. Public offerings can also be useful in creating a broad constituency for privatization, with some countries, such as Chile and Mexico, even selling shares at preferential prices to small investors. Finally, public offerings may help spur the development of local capital markets, both when the company is initially sold and when it subsequently seeks to raise additional capital through the further issue of shares.

Management/Employee Buyout. This is a direct sale to the workers or managers of an SOE. This method may be politically expedient because the potentially thorny issue of personnel reductions can be left to some or all of the affected parties. However, it has the disadvantage of not being a competitive process, so that the company is usually underpriced. Moreover, the efficiency gains often associated with direct foreign investment and sometimes even domestic investment by an outside party—especially from the infusion of new capital, tech-

nology and management know-how—are frequently lacking in these transactions. On the other hand, management/employee buyouts may allow the divestiture of poorly-performing state enterprises that otherwise might not attract a purchaser.

Joint Venture. This is a direct sale of a part of an SOE to a private investor, with the government retaining the remainder. The part that is sold generally becomes a new company. This can be an attractive way for an investor to become involved in a large, diversified SOE without having to buy the entire enterprise, some parts of which may be particularly problematic.

Concessions and Leases. In these arrangements, the private sector firm rents the assets and takes over the operation of an SOE for a specified period of time, often for as long as 15-30 years, and sometimes with an option to buy the enterprise at the end of the rental period. The private sector firm retains all profits from running the enterprise, after paying rent. A concession differs from a lease primarily in that the concessionaire takes responsibility for some or all new investment while the lessee simply operates what's there. Concession and lease arrangements are often used when the government decides against a complete transfer, for example because it would be politically difficult to sell certain mineral resource or infrastructure companies, particularly to foreigners. Rental arrangements may also be favored by purchasers fearing regulatory expropriation, in which permissible selling prices for the enterprise's outputs are reduced by the government after completing the sale of the company. Privatizing management can improve operating efficiency, but continued dependence on the government for investment may limit gains, particularly in lease arrangements.

INTO THE FUTURE

Regardless of whether the downward trend in privatization revenue continues in 1995 and beyond for Latin America as a whole, the fact remains that in many of the individual countries of the region there is still great potential for future priva-

tization that could substantially improve people's lives (see Box 5.3). Brazil is perhaps the most obvious example, with many large enterprises still in state hands. Venezuela also has ample state assets, but its privatization program has essentially remained dormant since 1992. A great deal also remains to be done in many of the smaller coun-

Box 5.3   Welfare Gains from Privatization

Does privatization really help? Do the gains to society outweigh the losses when a public enterprise is sold and then operated by the private sector? Unfortunately, there is a reasonably satisfactory answer to this question for only a small number of case studies, many of which refer to privatizations in the United Kingdom. Perhaps the best work on the subject is that by Galal, Jones, Tandon and Vogelsang (1994), who exhaustively studied nine developing country (plus three UK) privatizations, including six privatizations in Latin America. Of these 12 cases, the authors found that privatization yielded positive overall net benefits in all instances except one, supporting the hypothesis that divestiture is generally beneficial.

The chart accompanying this box summarizes some of the main results of this study for the six Latin American privatizations, including three in Chile and three in Mexico. All figures are the annual component of the

perpetuity equivalent of the welfare change, expressed as a percentage of annual sales in the last predivestiture year. The meaning of this rather complicated sounding concept can be most easily understood by way of an example. Consider TELMEX, which, let us say, earned revenues of $100 million in its last predivestiture year. The first two numbers in the TELMEX row of the chart tell us that the overall net gains to Mexicans are equivalent (in present value terms) to an annual sum of $6.6 million in perpetuity, while the overall net gains worldwide are equivalent to $49.5 million per year in perpetuity.

To obtain these net welfare changes, the authors compared the firm's performance as a privatized entity with what they believe would have been its performance had it continued in the public sector. In this way, they attempted to properly isolate the effects of the divestiture itself, avoiding the error of mixing in exogenous

Welfare Changes in Six Latin American Privatizations

(In percent)

Enterprise and year divested	Sector	Net welfare change		Selected sources of worldwide welfare changes		
		Domestic	Worldwide	Labor productivity	Investment	Output price
Chile						
CHILGENER (1987)	Electricity generation	0.7	2.1	2.1	0	0
ENERSIS (1987)	Electricity distribution	4.6	5.2	0	0	3.7
CTC (1988)	Telecommunications	145.0	155.0	9.6	97.3	0
Mexico						
TELMEX (1990)	Telecommunications	6.6	49.5	19.8	0	16.3
Aeroméxico (1988)	Airline	52.9	48.5	48.1	0	0.4
Mexicana (1989)	Airline	-2.4	-7.0	2.8	-8.9	-0.2

changes in product demand, increases in labor costs, and so forth. They claim to have been very conservative in attributing changes to divestiture, in which case, the figures in the table should be considered lower bound estimates of the effects of privatization.

Of the 12 cases studied, in only one, Mexicana Airlines, did welfare decline because of divestiture. The major cause for this decline was a series of mistaken business decisions, particularly the decision to expand capacity when demand was stagnant or declining. Private managers, just like public ones, are not infallible. It is hoped that they will make good decisions, but if they do not, the private market will likely be there to act as a disciplining device, something that is absent in the case of public firms. This is illustrated in the case of Mexicana by the fact that many of the mistakes and large losses of the first few years were subsequently turned around.

The major sources of the welfare changes are shown in the last three columns of the table. Labor productivity gains should follow the conversion of poorly managed parastatals into well-managed private firms. In the case of TELMEX, greater output was obtained from about the same size work force, while for Aeroméxico the bulk of the productivity gains came from maintaining output while shedding labor (dramatically reducing the bloated size of both ground and flight crews). The next column shows that the ability of the divested firm to relax the investment constraint had enormous benefits for the Chilean phone company CTC, but that it was not important in the other Latin American cases. The last column indicates that the output price movements were almost always welfare enhancing. This occurred even in the case of price increases because of movements toward efficiency prices.

tries in the region such as Ecuador, Paraguay, Uruguay and much of Central America. And even the leading privatizers in total revenue terms, Mexico and Argentina, still have significant state assets left. Examples are Mexico's near-monopoly state electricity enterprise and the nearly half of Argentina's banking sector still in public hands. In Bolivia's capitalization program, the largest of the six enterprises to be capitalized, YPFB, the state oil and gas company, has yet to be put out for bids.

As a further illustration of the great potential for future privatization, consider the electricity industry, one of the leading producers of privatization revenues in the 1990s.[9] While revenues have been large, electricity in fact is an area where the divestiture movement is just taking hold. Barbados, Trinidad and Tobago and Chile have put or soon will have put their entire generation/transmission/distribution systems in private hands. Argentina and Peru have divested significant state assets, Brazil a little, and Colombia is aiming to sell all federally- and some municipally-held generating plants in the next two years. Most other countries in the region have privatized very little of their extensive state-owned systems, illustrating that the possibilities for reaping the benefits of privatization are far from exhausted in Latin America.

---

[9] Almost all energy sector privatization revenue shown in Table 5.2b is from the divestiture of electricity, not gas, enterprises.

LABOR REFORM

ABSTRACT

Reforms in the realm of labor have been meager and partial in Latin America and the Caribbean. Opening to international competition and deregulating domestic markets has exposed workers to higher risk of unemployment and labor instability. Labor legislation has not adjusted as quickly to protect workers from these risks and to ease the adjustment processes for companies.

Labor legislation seeks to provide employment stability rather than offer adequate protection for the unemployed. At least 15 countries impose moderate or severe restrictions on terminating labor contracts, while only eight offer unemployment insurance, in very limited amounts and with limited coverage.

To prevent arbitrary treatment of workers, practically all countries have established compensation for dismissal without just cause. However, only seven countries provide special treatment for layoffs caused by bankruptcy or the economic troubles of companies. In 18 countries, compensation payments following termination rise with the worker's seniority in the company, with the potential risk of greater labor turnover rather than greater stability.

Four countries provide severance payments at the end of a labor contract, to be charged to funds that accrue in individual accounts. Under recent reforms in two countries, this procedure works as a compulsory saving system, making it possible to stabilize workers' incomes in the event of unemployment or retirement without distorting labor costs or making them uncertain.

To protect employment stability, 14 countries impose limitations on temporary contracts, in some cases quite severely. Nevertheless, in order to survive in the current changing economic environment, companies are increasingly turning to temporary contracts and other atypical forms of labor. The flexibility entailed in such contracts in at least four countries has made this process easier. However, labor is only becoming more flexible at the margin, and that entails a segmentation between groups of workers. The consequences are potentially adverse for negotiation processes and the setting of pay scales, decisions on investment in on-the-job training within companies, and productivity growth.

In nine countries in the region, social security programs require contributions of over 20 percent. Such rates are sometimes higher than in developed countries. Due to the lack of a connection between these contributions and the individual benefits that such programs offer workers, in practice they operate like a tax. The result is enormous evasion, which translates into informal labor and a lack of protection for workers. The recent pension reforms discussed in the next chapter have alleviated this problem in a few countries.

The minimum wage is a component of labor legislation in most countries in the region. This chapter does not find a relationship between this policy tool and the behavior of unemployment. That should be taken more as an indication that such policies have been used cautiously in recent years than as an argument for using them indiscriminately.

Modernization of labor legislation is a challenge in almost all countries in the region. Without ignoring the peculiar features of each country and the status of labor relations, it would be well to move toward:

• Accepting as justified a layoff that is due to the economic conditions of the company, and establishing unemployment insurance for such cases.

• Replacing formulas for calculating compensation for dismissal based on multiples of the most recent wages with contributions that can be built up in individual accounts.

• With regard to hiring, opting for comprehensive reforms instead of introducing measures to increase flexibility at the margin for certain kinds of contracts.

• Tightening the connection between contributions and benefits for each participant in social security programs.

INTRODUCTION

Only by way of exception has the extraordinary structural reform process that has taken place in the region during the past decade been accompanied by reforms to adjust the operation of the labor market and labor legislation to the new economic context. Labor legislation in most countries exhibits major problems that hinder hiring and labor mobility and drag rather than stimulate employment.

The labor market must function properly in its role in both production and allocation of resources if there is to be a sustained rise in productivity, income and quality of life. That does not mean deregulation at any cost, nor the disappearance of agencies responsible for labor policies. Labor relations are by their very nature complex. The information possessed by a company or a worker is always incomplete and asymmetrical, since it is impossible for one party to precisely determine the characteristics, history and degree of effort of the other party. It is impossible to establish clear property rights over investment in human capital and the parties cannot put a price on the stability of a worker's job. All this requires transparent legislation and solid institutions that define and sanction each party's rights without hindering efficient resource allocation.[1]

In most countries, however, labor legislation has been designed following motives and principles that hinder the productive sector from adapting to the new context of open economies, that encourage inefficient resource allocation, and that do not protect the worker from the risk associated with economic fluctuations. Excessive, unclear and often contradictory laws intended to protect the worker leave little leeway for companies and workers to negotiate contracts that could favor both parties. The inclination of labor legislation toward provisions to guarantee job stability

and hinder labor mobility generate extra costs that can limit job creation and cause excessive labor turnover. While hiring procedures for a particular time period can make the labor market more flexible, such greater flexibility "in the margin" may increase rigidities in setting wages and discourage the creation of human capital. In the area of social security, high rates of contribution and their weak connection to the benefits offered may cause major distortions in relative prices, lessen demand for labor, and encourage informal labor.

Although the degree of flexibility in labor legislation regarding hiring and firing, the work day and nonwage costs vary considerably, the overall trend is of great inflexibility in all these areas (Table 6.1). The lack of flexibility in hiring can be measured by the legal restrictions on "atypical" contracts, whether they are by the job, probatory period, or fixed-term contracts. The English-speaking countries of the Caribbean are among the more flexible in this area, since they generally do not impose restrictions on contracting under these formulas. At the opposite extreme are Bolivia, Guatemala, El Salvador and Paraguay, where labor legislation prohibits hiring under a fixed-term contract for any of the company's own permanent activities.

The amount of compensation that a company must pay the worker when it wishes to sever the labor relationship is a direct measurement of the degree of flexibility in dismissing workers. Again, the Caribbean countries, except Trinidad and Tobago, are outstanding in their flexibility, since they do not prescribe obligatory compensation in the event of dismissal prompted by economic conditions. In this group of countries the amount of compensation is determined by negotiation between workers and companies. At the opposite end of the scale are Colombia and Ecuador, where legislation sets payment for dismissal that can be as high as 25 months' pay, when workers have 10 years or more of seniority. While the legislation in the Caribbean countries may not adequately protect the

---

[1] Márquez (1995).

worker who loses his or her job, the excessive rigidity in Colombia and Ecuador certainly does not contribute to labor stability and it might entail high efficiency costs.

Flexibility with regard to the work day can be observed in the restrictions and extra costs that legislation imposes on companies for assigning other than the normal shifts and work days. Countries where overtime and work on holidays are less costly are Chile and Panama; at the opposite extreme are Mexico and Suriname. This aspect of legislation can reinforce or correct the lack of flexibility in other areas. Thus, although it is relatively expensive to sever the labor relationship in Chile, flexibility on shifts and hours worked can make up for that rigidity. Likewise, although it is relatively expensive to adjust the hours worked in Suriname, legislation on hiring and firing is sufficiently flexible that it can be used to adjust to changes in labor demand.

Finally, with regard to the cost of social security contributions, the Caribbean countries have the lowest contributions, while Uruguay, Argentina, Colombia and Brazil are the countries with the highest.

This chapter is devoted to analyzing the impact of labor legislation on the operation of the labor market by describing the reforms adopted in the last five years and indicating some guidelines for future reforms. A central implication of this analysis is that making one isolated aspect of legislation more flexible does not always produce greater efficiency or welfare, since the outcome depends on how it interacts with other aspects of legislation.

	Types of contracts[a]	Cost for dismissal after one year[b]	Cost for dismissal after 10 years[c]	Work day and extra charge for additional hours[d]	Social security[e] contributions
More flexible **F**	Bahamas Barbados Belize Guyana Jamaica Suriname Trin. and Tobago	Bahamas Barbados Belize Dominican Rep. Guatemala Guyana Haiti Jamaica Suriname Uruguay	Bahamas Barbados Belize Haiti Jamaica Suriname Uruguay	Argentina Barbados Brazil Chile Dominican Rep. Guyana Haiti Panama Paraguay Peru	Bahamas Barbados Belize El Salvador Dominican Rep. Guatemala Guyana Haiti Honduras Jamaica Nicaragua Panama Trin. and Tobago
Intermediate **I**	Argentina Brazil Chile Colombia Ecuador Nicaragua Peru	Chile Costa Rica El Salvador Honduras Panama Paraguay Peru Trin. and Tobago	Argentina Chile Costa Rica Dominican Rep. El Salvador Guatemala Guyana Mexico Panama Paraguay Trin. and Tobago	Bahamas El Salvador Venezuela	Bolivia Chile Costa Rica Ecuador Mexico Peru Paraguay Venezuela
More rigid **R**	Bolivia Dominican Rep. El Salvador Guatemala Honduras Mexico Uruguay Venezuela	Argentina Bolivia Brazil Colombia Ecuador Mexico Nicaragua Venezuela	Bolivia Brazil Colombia Ecuador Honduras Nicaragua Peru Venezuela	Bolivia Mexico Suriname Uruguay	Argentina Brazil Colombia Uruguay

Table heading: **Table 6.1   Flexibility of the Legal System**

[a]   F: without restrictions; I: contracts with limited duration and renewability;
R: only for temporary workers.
[b]   F: up to a monthly salary; I: between one and two salaries; R: more than two salaries.
[c]   F: up to six monthly salaries; I: between six and 12 monthly salaries; R: more than 12 salaries.
[d]   F: charges for extra hours at 50 percent, holidays 0-100 percent; I: additional, 100 percent, holidays more than 100 percent; R: additional hours more than 100 percent, holidays more than 100 percent.
[e]   F: up to 15 percent of salary; I: between 15 and 30 percent; R: more than 30 percent.

REGULATIONS ON DISMISSAL, HIRING AND WORK DAYS

In most countries in the region, labor legislation is shaped around two basic principles: labor stability and worker protection, under the implicit assumption that the worker has limited negotiating power vis-à-vis the company. The principle of labor stability implies that once a short probatory period is over, the worker acquires ownership rights over his or her job position. Thus, in the event that the company initiates separation, the worker has the right to compensation for the loss of his or her job, or in some cases, to be reinstated if there is no just cause for the separation. In most countries, legislation determines which causes for dismissal are just and which are not, the notification period for severing the labor relationship, and the formula for calculating compensation based on seniority and the reason for dismissal. As a rule, legislation favors hiring for an indefinite period of time and imposes many restrictions on atypical contracts. Finally, work hour regulations set a maximum work period and an obligatory extra charge for hours worked over that maximum.

Compensation for Dismissal

Although terminology varies from country to country, in this chapter severance pay is considered to be a payment that the company makes to the worker when it severs the labor relationship, regardless of which party initiated or caused the separation. A payment that the company has to make to the worker in the event of unjustified firing is called compensation for dismissal. However, because in most countries the economic difficulties of the company are not accepted as a just cause for dismissal, the law regards such dismissal to be just as arbitrary as dismissal resulting, for example, from the decision to fire a worker who joins a labor union. Severance pay is only established in a few countries in the region, such as Brazil, Colombia, Ecuador, Peru and Venezuela.

As a rule in the other countries, the law only stipulates compensation for unjustified dismissal.

Current Legislation

The principle of labor stability has weighed in on the side of severance pay and compensation for dismissal to be made by companies rather than unemployment payments financed through special taxes and administered by the government. Legislation in most countries sets a compensation payment for firing that often amounts to considerable sums, while only a small group of countries have systems of unemployment payments, which in all instances are limited in amounts and coverages (Tables 6.2 and 6.3).

Severance pay amounts are based on two components: first, the advance notification or the obligatory period between notification of the worker and the loss of the employment, which as a rule is paid but not worked;[2] and second, compensation that follows termination. The definition of just cause varies from country to country. In the English-speaking Caribbean countries, Chile, and recently in Argentina and Peru, just cause encompasses the needs of the company, including rationalization of labor, modernization, change in market conditions, and the unsuitability of the worker for the assigned job from a labor or technical standpoint. However, in Guatemala and El Salvador, the costs may be reduced in the specific case when the company declares bankruptcy. In El Salvador, a reduction of this type may entail being exempted from payment. With the exception of the countries previously mentioned, termination is considered unjust if the company cannot prove a breach of discipline or negligence.

Three groups of countries may be distinguished in terms of flexibility of compensation for termination. The first includes countries influenced by Great Britain—the Bahamas, Barbados, Belize and Jamaica—where labor legislation

[2] Márquez (1995).

Table 6.2 Legislation Concerning Conditions of Dismissal in 1990 and 1995

Country	Date of Reform	Period of Prior Notice 1990	Period of Prior Notice 1995	Payment for dismissal with just cause 1990	Payment for dismissal with just cause 1995	Payment for dismissal without just cause 1990	Payment for dismissal without just cause 1995	Payment for dismissal for economic reasons 1990	Payment for dismissal for economic reasons 1995	Limit to payment or dismissal	Compensation for termination by worker
Argentina	1991	1-2 months	1 month	0	No change	$x*N$	No changes	$x*N$	1/2 $x*N$; Min. 2 months	Max. limit to x	No
Bahamas	None	1/2-1 month	No change	0	No change	Min. 2 months	Min. 2 months	Min. 2 months	No change	No	No
Barbados	None	Negotiable. In practice, 1 month	No change	0	No change	Negotiable between employer and employee. Legislation doesn't establish a determined amount	Negotiable between employer and employee. Legislation doesn't establish a determined amount	Negotiable between employer and employee. Legislation doesn't establish a determined amount	No change	Max. limit to x	No
Belize	None	1/2-1 month	No change	0	No change	2 1/2 weeks if N>1 and N<=10; 3 wks. if N between 10 and 20; 3 1/2 weeks if N more 20	No change	2 1/2 weeks if N mon =10; 3 wks. if N between 10 and 20; 3 1/2 weeks if N more 20	No change	Max. 2 wks.	As of N =10 1/4*N
Bolivia	None	3 months	No change	0	No change	1 week pay per year of service after 5 years of service	No change	1 week per year of service after 5 years	No change	No	As of 5th year 1x*N
Brazil	None	1 month	No change	Fund	No change	1.4*Fund	No change	1.4*Fund	No change	No	
Chile	None	1 month	No change	0	No change	1.2 $x*N$[a]	No change	$x*N$	No change	Max. N =11	As of 7th year 1/2x*N[b]; Fund
Colombia	1990	45 days	No change	$x*N$ Double retroactivity given for lack of inflationary adjustment of withdrawals	Fund without withdrawals	$x*N$ + $x*4,2$ if N=5; $x*10,5$ if N=10; $x*15,5$ if N=15; $x*20,5$ if N=20	Fund + $x*4,2$ if N=5; $x*13,5$ if N=10; $x*20,2$ if N=15; $x*21,8$ if N=20	$x*N$ + $x*4,2$ if N=5; $x*10,5$ if N=10; $x*20,2$ if N=15; $x*20,5$ if N=20	Fund + $x*4,2$ if N=5; $x*13,5$ if N=10; $x*20,2$ if N=15; $x*21,8$ if N=20	No	Fund
Costa Rica	None	1 month	No change	0	No change	$x*N$	No change	$x*N$	No change	Max. N =8	No
Dominican Rep.	None	1/4-1 month	No change	0	No changes			1/3-1 $x*N$	No change	No	No
Ecuador	None	1 month	No change	Fund+ 1/4x*N	No changes	1/4 $x*N$+fund; More than $3*x$ if N is less than 3; $x*N$ if N is between 3 and 25 years; Pension if N is greater than 25	No change	1/4 $x*N$+fund; More than $3*x$ if N is between 3 and 25 years; Pension if N is greater than 25; 0 if loss of business, $x*N$ otherwise		No	Fund
El Salvador	1994	0-7 days	No change	0	No change	$x*N$	$x*N$; Change in the compensation; Upper limit	$x*N$	No change	Calcul. max. salary 4 sal. min.[d]	No
Guatemala	1991	No	No	0	No change	$x*N$	$x*N$	2 days to 4 months if loss of business, $x*N$ otherwise	2 days to 4 months if loss of business, Fund + interest otherwise	No	No
Guyana	None	1/2 month	No change	0	No change	Negotiated collectively. In practice, 2 1/2 weeks per year worked	1 month/per year of service; Fund + interest	Negotiable	No change	No	No
Haiti	None	2-12 weeks	No change	0	No change						No
Honduras	None	1 day-2 months	No change	0	No change						No
Jamaica	None	2-12 weeks	No change	0	No change						No
Mexico	None	0-1 month	No change	$x*3$	No change	2/3 $x*N$	No change	$x*N$	No change	Max. N =15	No
Nicaragua	None	1-2 months	No change	$x*N$	No change	2 $x*N$	No change	2 $x*N$	No change	No	No
Paraguay	None	1-2 months	No change	Determined by a judge after legal proceedings	No change	1/3 $x*N$	1/2 $x*N$[c]	1/3 $x*N$	1/2 $x*N$[c]	No	No
Peru	1995, 1991	No	No		Fund	Very difficult	Fund + $x*N$	Very difficult; 3 $x*N$	Fund + $x*N$	Max. N =12	Fund
Suriname	None	1/4-6 months	No change	0	No change	If judgment in favor of worker	Idem	Idem	Idem[e]		None
Trin. and Tobago	None	2 months	No change	0	No change	1/2 $x*N$ if N between 1 and 4 yrs; 3/4 $x*N$ if N greater than 5 yrs	Idem	1/2 $x*N$ if N between 1 and 4 years; 3/4 $x*N$ if N greater than 5 years	Idem	None	No
Uruguay	None	No	No	$x*N$	No change	$x*N$	No change	$x*N$	No change	Max. N =6	None
Venezuela	None	1/4-3 months	No change	1/3 -1 $x*N$	No change	2/3-2 $x*N$		2/3-2 $x*N$	No change	No	1/3 -1 $x*N$

Source: Ministries of Labor in the region; Cox-Edwards (1993); Márquez (1994).

x = monthly salary   N = tenure

[a] If the employee cannot prove an "economic cause" there is a surcharge of 20 percent. If worker cannot prove "just cause" the surcharge is 50 percent.

[b] Workers can choose one month per year in the case of dismissal or one-half month per year for whatever cause after the seventh year.

[c] Prohibited to dismiss employees with more than 10 years with a firm.

[d] Reforms of 1994 established a maximum calculation for the computation of dismissal payments of 60 colons to four minimum salaries = 120 colons.

[e] Payment only if it is determined in a legal proceeding. Economic condition is considered a just cause.

	Current Law	Financing	Rate of replacement[a]	Duration of benefits	Min/Max Benefits	Coverage	Requirements
Argentina	1991 reform of 1995	Worker: 1% sal. Employer: 1.5% payroll	60%	4-12 months	Min: 1 min. wage Max: 4 min. wage	Employees	1 (12), 2,3
Barbados	1982	Worker: 1.5% salary Employer: 1.5% payroll	60% 10 weeks 40% 16 weeks	26 wks. in 1 period of 52 wks.		Employees 16-64 years	1(6)
Brazil	1986 1990	Government	1-3 min. salary	4 months	Min: 1 min. wage	Employees	4(36, 4), 5,6
Chile	1981	Government	37 $ per month, 1st 6 months 18 $ last 6 months	Max. 1 year[b]		Employees	2, 4(12,2), 5,
Ecuador	1958, 1988	Worker: 2% salary Employer: 1% payroll	Subsidy paid once, with contributions deducted annually			Employees	1(24), 7
Mexico		Social Security	95% of pension	5 years, max.		Employees age 60-65	Age between 60-65
Uruguay	1981	Contributions to Social Security	Up to 50%	6 months	Min: 0.5 min. wage Max: 4 min. wage	Employees in commerce and industry	1(6), 5, 3, 8.
Venezuela	1989	Worker: .7% salary Employer: 1.5 % payroll	Up to 60%	13-26 weeks	Max: $44	Employees	1(12), 2

Table 6.3   Unemployment Insurance

Source: Social Security Programs throughout the World - 1995, U.S. Department of Health and Human Services.

[a]Percentage with respect to salary when employed.

[b]Subsidy payments to beneficiaries for family support, medical benefits and maternity.

Requirements:

1 (s) Be employed "s" months before receiving subsidy.

2 Available to work immediately.

3 Does not receive other social security benefits.

4 (s, j) Not have received more than "s" months of subsidy in the last "j" years.

5 Be unemployed for reasons outside the conduct or willingness of the worker.

6 Subsidy is conditional on the beneficiary demonstrating an economic need.

7 There is a period of "x" waiting days before receiving subsidy.

8 There has to be a lapse of 12 months between periods of receiving subsidies.

is not very specific about advance notification or compensation for firing for just cause, unjust cause, or voluntarily quitting, and where much leeway is left for contractual agreements. In Jamaica and the Bahamas, legislation establishes a minimum advance notification period but does not specify a minimum amount of compensation. That amount is either set during the collective bargaining process between companies and employees, or can be imposed by a judge in the event that the court's decision favors the worker. In Belize and Barbados, legislation specifies the amount of compensation, but it is much less than it is elsewhere in the region. Consequently, the countries in this group are among those where it is cheapest to dismiss a worker (Tables 6.1 and 6.2). In

this group, legislation cannot be considered to be distorting. However, because workers in some cases can appeal firing decisions to the courts, the legislation creates an element of uncertainty that makes it difficult to evaluate the cost of firing and make adequate provisions for that contingency. Moreover, with the exception of the Bahamas, a country that has a program of unemployment payments, the legislation does not protect the worker against the risk of unemployment.

The countries that have severance payments periodically deposited in accounts in the name of the workers can be classified in a second group. Such is the case of Brazil and Ecuador, and since the 1990 reforms, Colombia and Peru. The fund in Brazil is called FGTS (*Fundo de Garantia do Tempo de Serviço*—Time of Service Guarantee Fund), and in Peru, CTS (*Compensación por Tiempo de Servicios*—Compensation for Time of Service). In Colombia, it is simply called a severance fund. These funds build up a fraction of annual wages, which augmented with normal market yields, is available to the worker, if dismissed. In Colombia, Ecuador and Peru this sum is also available to the worker if he or she voluntary quits or is fired for cause. These programs have the advantage of making the link between contributions and payments transparent, thereby reducing or eliminating distortions in the labor market. However, in all these countries there is also a supplementary compensation that must be paid in the event that the company cannot prove just cause. Because the needs of the company are not considered to be just cause in any of the countries but Peru, any adjustment of the labor force prompted by a change in economic conditions falls in this category. In Brazil, the supplementary amount is established by multiplying the cumulative amount of the FGTS by 1.4. In Colombia, Ecuador and Peru, the supplementary amount is calculated by means of the traditional formula of multiples of the most recent wage. Once compensation for dismissal is added in, total payments to be made for initiating an unjustified dismissal of a worker are substantial, and places the countries in this group among those where firing is most costly. Even more serious, these compensations do not reflect a connection between contributions and payments, as there is in Brazil's FGTS or Peru's CTS. A pay raise in Colombia, Ecuador or Peru produces a final compensation sum that is proportionally greater than it is in Brazil, because any pay raise affects the entire amount owed, whereas in Brazil it rises by only 40 percent. In terms of both the size of compensations

FIGURE 6.1

Dismissal Pay to Workers with One Year of Seniority

(Multiples of last monthly wage)

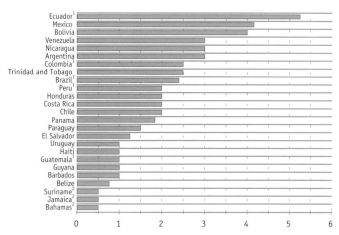

Note: Includes period of notice.
[1] The company deposits an annual amount in an account under the name of the employee.
[2] The pay for dismissal is part of the negotiation process between the worker and the company. The law does not mandate a particular arrangement.
Source: Ministries of Labor throughout the region; legislation in effect in 1995.

FIGURE 6.2

Dismissal Pay to Workers with 10 Years of Seniority

(Multiples of last monthly wage)

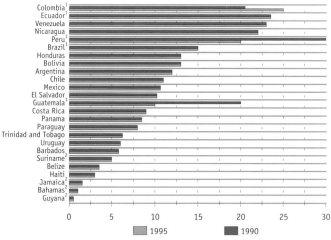

Note: Includes period of notice.
[1] The company deposits an annual amount in an account under the name of the employee.
[2] The pay for dismissal is part of the negotiation process between the worker and the company. The law does not mandate a particular arrengement.
Source: Ministries of Labor throughout the region; legislation in effect in 1995.

and the formula for calculating them, Colombia, Ecuador and Peru are among the countries whose legislation is most distorting in this regard.

The other countries on which there is information make up the third group. Except for Venezuela, these are cases in which legislation does not make provision for severance payment. Venezuela is included in this group because, although the legislation prescribes payment in any case, it is taken from funds accumulated in group accounts, and because the severance payment is not strictly speaking based on capital accumulated, but is calculated as a month of the last annual salary, and the interest on the accumulated funds is paid separately. In the remaining countries in this group, the legislation stipulates that compensation is to be paid only in the event of unjustified dismissal. The formula for calculating this compensation is based on multiples of the most recent wage, and it varies between a half month's pay per year worked in Paraguay to two months pay in Nicaragua. Except in Venezuela, there is no compensation in the event of firing for negligence or breach of discipline on the part of the worker, and only Bolivia and Chile prescribe payments when one quits of one's own accord. Bolivian legislation makes provision for payment in this case starting with the fifth year of tenure, while in Chile, as of the seventh year workers may choose between a month per year worked when firing is unjustified, or a half month per year regardless. Some countries set upper limits on the sums of compensation for dismissal. Thus, in Uruguay there is a six-month wage limit, in Costa Rica it is eight, in Chile, 11, in Peru, 12, and in Honduras, 15. In a variation, Argentina and El Salvador have upper limits on the base salary for calculating payments. Finally, only in the cases of Argentina and Chile are economic conditions a just cause for termination. That means that when a company can claim economic difficulties or the need to rationalize labor, the compensation for termination is less than in the case of unjustified dismissal.

Legislation in the countries in this latter group is problematic in a number of respects. The fact that payments are not transferable generates extra costs and restricts labor mobility, while the computation formula entails retroactive effects that also have the effect of breaking the connection between contributions and payments. However, except for Venezuela and Nicaragua, the legislation in these countries sets compensation lower than that specified in the countries of the previous group, thereby moderating the distorting impact of these policies.

In principle, there is no reason why the obligation to pay the worker a certain sum when the labor relationship ends should have distorting effects on the labor market. It can be argued that this transfer is a deferred remuneration for work, and hence any sum required by law can be compensated for by lower wages during the employment period. If, as is generally considered to be the case, workers prefer that their incomes be stable over time, such an arrangement between companies and workers would be neutral for the company and favorable for the worker. The company accordingly saves a sum taken from the base pay of the individual to provide insurance for potential unemployment. However, such a relationship between present and future income holds only if (i) the worker and the company are certain of how much is being transferred; (ii) the relationship between contributions and payments is transparent; and (iii) the saving performed by the company does not exceed what the worker would like to accumulate to provide for loss of employment.

The legislation in effect in most countries in the region, however, creates uncertainty over the final sum to be paid by the company, and clouds the relationship between contributions (the amount to be deducted somehow from pay), and income (the amount received when the labor contract is severed). The problem does not lie primarily in severance payments, which because they are payable in any event and can build up in funds in the worker's name, encourage transparency and minimize distortions, but rather in compensations for dismissal, which the company sees as an extra cost that makes the labor factor more expensive and limits demand for it. Among the characteristics of the law preventing such compensation from being perceived as deferred remuneration, the following should be noted:

• *Formula for calculating compensation based on most recent wage.* A problem arising in connection with the usual formula for calculating compensation is that companies make contributions based on current pay, although the compensation is calculated as a multiple of the most recent wage. The usual formula establishes a compensation of one month of the most recent wage per year of service in the company. As the wage increases with tenure, the debt rises proportionally more than the wage. This means that in order to maintain the link between contributions and payments, the company would have to contribute to the severance payment fund a proportion of the wage rising with the individual's seniority.

• *Compensation for dismissal as a penalty against the company.* As we have noted, legislation in most countries in the region does not distinguish between layoff due to economic conditions and arbitrary dismissal. The principle of labor stability grants the worker property rights to his or her job, which in the event of dismissal are translated in some countries into the right to be reinstated in the job if the company cannot prove serious fault, or in most countries, into compensation for the loss of that property. This penalty component is clearly reflected in legislation in Brazil, Ecuador, Colombia and Peru, where besides severance payments the law requires additional compensation for unjustified dismissal. This provision has the effect of obscuring the link between contributions and payments even in those countries where the existence of funds accrued in accounts in the workers' name should make the connection more transparent.

• *Failure to make provisions on the part of companies.* In many countries, the total amount of the dismissal cost is charged to company liabilities, without having set up an individual or group fund for that purpose. This means that companies can use such funds owed to the workers for their current activity. However, when the situation of the company turns bad, this policy can create an unwanted connection between low availability of funds and the need to rationalize labor.

• *Nontransportability of the compensation.* In many countries there is no obligation to pay if the worker quits of his or her own accord, and hence the connection between contributions and payments is lost. Any uncertainty in the perception of the payment for termination reduces the expected value of this sum in the minds of the workers, and hence reduces willingness to pay for it (through wage contributions). Besides obscuring the relationship between contributions and costs, nontransportability of the compensation limits the mobility of workers and encourages them to create conditions likely to lead to being fired if they want to change jobs. Nontransportability can generate considerable efficiency costs, especially in periods of economic restructuring, while the tendency to provoke firing strains relations between workers and companies, and means that companies have to pay an unjustified extra cost for worker mobility.

Hence, legislation on ending the labor contract suffers from serious design problems that limit its neutrality. Companies and workers accordingly modify their behavior in the following ways in order to minimize these costs and interferences:

• *Minimizing labor adjustments.* When the costs of dismissing workers are seen as adjustment costs, companies may react by minimizing movements in the labor force. Such behavior implies that labor is perceived as a quasi-fixed factor that is very difficult to adjust once it is inside the company. This means that when facing tough but transitory economic circumstances, companies will tend to keep more workers employed than they would if dismissal costs were cheaper. Such a response is not surprising and fits the original reason for the legislation, namely to preserve labor stability. Nevertheless, for the same reasons, the greater the adjustment costs, the less employment will respond to economic expansions, especially if they are temporary in nature. This employment pattern may help to explain why employment in the region responded so weakly to the economic growth of the first half of the 1990s. In Latin America, the employment response to an increase in GDP is weak when compared to what takes place in countries like the United States or Canada, which have flexible labor markets. Thus a 10 percent rise in production would reduce unemployment by 4 percentage points in Chile, around 3 points in Uruguay and Venezuela, 2 points in Argentina and Mexico, and 1.5 points in Peru and Brazil,[3] which is very similar to what happens in France or Germany, where legislation imposes substantial costs on terminating workers. The poor response of unemployment to changes in output (or output-unemployment elasticity) is connected to the cost of firing a worker with ten years of seniority (Figures 6.3 and 6.4).[4]

• *Greater labor force turnover.* We have seen that the legislation in effect prescribes some termination costs that increase with worker seniority. In extreme cases, it may be in the interest of companies not to allow workers to build up seniority. Thus, a body of legislation that aims to preserve labor stability may ultimately have the opposite effect. In Colombia, for example, where it is extremely expensive to fire workers with more than 10 years of seniority but relatively cheap to fire them when they have been working only a few years, labor turnover is very high, with average worker seniority of from 2.7 to 4.4 years.[5] The strategy of maximizing labor turnover can have very serious consequences for worker training, the acquisition of company-specific human capital, and labor productivity. Since specific human capital is of little worth in different occupations, workers have no incentives to improve their training on company-specific jobs. Something similar happens with the company,

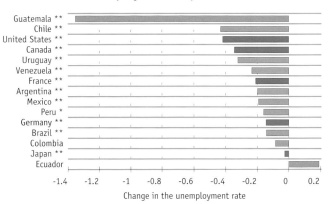

FIGURE 6.3
Unemployment Response to GDP Growth

Note: * or ** indicate the coefficient is significant at the 5 or 1 percent level, respectively. Only countries for which unemployment data is available for at least 10 years are included.

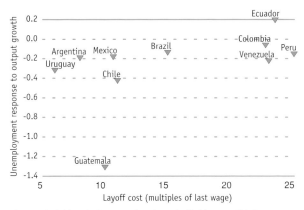

FIGURE 6.4
Unemployment Response and Layoff Cost

Sources: Social Security Programs throughout the World - 1995, U.S. Department of Health and Human Services; IDB data base.
Note: Layoff cost applies to workers with 10 years of tenure.

---

[3] Given the economic stability in Colombia and the number of available observations, the figure for this country is not significant. In the case of Ecuador, although the rate seems to be negative, the possibility of it being zero is conceivable.

[4] The correlation between the costs of firing and the employment response is .5. A regression of the production-unemployment elasticity depending on firing costs after 10 years of employment produces a positive and significant coefficient at the 15 percent level.

[5] Lora and Henao (1995).

which does not find it profitable to invest in the human capital of its workers.

● *Subcontracting workers in the informal sector or hiring under fixed-term contracts.* When firing costs are high, temporary contracts can be a way to avoid them. In many countries, deregulating these hiring formulas has meant making things more flexible "at the margin," applying only to new workers, without affecting those who have indefinite contracts. According to ILO data, the proportion of workers with temporary contracts in Argentina rose from 28.5 percent in 1985 to 34 percent in 1995. In Colombia, 20 percent of workers have such arrangements, while in Peru the figure rose from 30 percent in 1985 to 50 percent in 1995. In Bolivia, a country were there are many constraints on limited fixed-term contracts, and where there has been no major labor reform, the portion of workers employed under fixed-term contracts rose from 11 percent to 30 percent between 1985 and 1990. Temporary contracts have accordingly smoothed labor's adjustment to a changing economic environment. In Mexico, however, the portion of workers with temporary contracts has held steady at around 20 percent, because such contracts produce expensive obligations in the event of firing.

Another alternative for cutting labor adjustment costs is to subcontract a portion of the company's operation to the informal sector. In periods of economic expansion companies make use of this sector for delivery of certain goods and services, because it gives them flexibility in the event of an economic downturn. Although there is no documented evidence of such behavior, two observations lead to the suspicion that it is common in the region. In keeping with the tendency that began in the 1980s, and contrary to what might be expected, the proportion of informal employment within total employment has continued to rise during the 1990s. Thus, according to ILO data, between 1990 and 1994, which were years of remarkable economic buoyancy, the informal sector on average rose

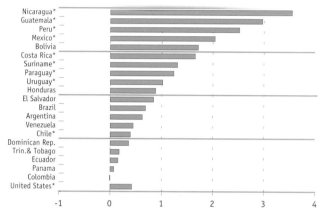

FIGURE 6.5
Responsiveness of Wages to Per Capita Output Variations

Note: * indicates significance at 10 percent level; regressions done correcting for possible AR1 error structure.
Source: IDB data base.

52 percent to 56 percent of total employment. On the other hand, it is consistent with this argument that wage flexibility is apparently greater in countries where the percentage of workers occupied in the informal sector is greater. Figure 6.5 shows the average response of real wages to variations in per capita output for different countries. These results indicate that a 1 percent decline in per capita output entails a fall in real wages of approximately 3 percent in Nicaragua and Guatemala, 2 percent in Mexico, 1 percent in Uruguay, and 0.5 percent in Venezuela. Although this observation is compatible with other not necessarily contradictory explanations, it suggests that the informal sector helps provide flexibility to formal sector remuneration because it widens supply options for companies and generates competition between groups of workers.

Finally, it is important to analyze what grade of protection current legislation gives workers who lose their jobs. In general, the risk and duration of unemployment depend both on the worker's personal characteristics, which make him or her more or less employable, and on the macroeconomic conditions which determine the level of aggregate unemployment. Under the assumption that the risk and duration of unemployment rise with the worker's seniority on the job and the specificity of his or her labor experience, the legislation offers protection that increases with the amount of time one has been on the job. However, compensation for dismissal has no relation to the risk associated with economic conditions. This problem is aggravated by the nontransferability of compensation, the low coverage of unemployment payments, and the labor turnover that the legislation itself may generate. Thus, workers who because of their characteristics, type of employment or bad luck find themselves forced to change jobs frequently, end up being more unprotected that those who may build up years of service in the same company. Likewise, depending on economic conditions, compensation after a year of service may be clearly insufficient for weathering a long period of unemployment.

Reforms in Legislation

There have been few legal reforms in the region in the area of severance payments and compensation for dismissal. During the first half of the 1990s, only Argentina, Colombia, Guatemala, Panama and Peru have implemented reforms that have made it possible to reduce the real or perceived costs of compensations. In Argentina, the law on dissolving labor contracts that established an upper limit on compensation sums was amended in 1991. This upper limit determines that the basis for calculation may not exceed the equivalent of triple the average monthly wage as found in the collective bargaining agreement applicable to the worker. This reform has made it possible to noticeably reduce the cost of compensations owed to employees with medium and high monthly incomes. Likewise, the law reduces the advance notification period to a month, regardless of a worker's tenure. It must also be pointed out that Argentine legislation has incorporated the presumptions of lack of work or diminished work as just cause for firing. In these cases, compensation

falls to half of what is provided under normal conditions. These reforms have made it possible to moderate the distorting effect of legislation by reducing the compensation sums. However, because the customary formula of multiples of the most recent year has been retained and the law on payments in the case of quitting of one's own accord has not been changed, Argentine legislation still imposes a number of distortions that obscure the connection between contributions and payments.

In Colombia, the 1990 reform changed the conditions for terminating the labor relationship in two ways. First, it established that unemployment funds were to be deposited in accounts in the workers' names in specialized finance agencies, where they were to receive a market remuneration and from which partial withdrawals might be made for some purposes. Uncertainty about such costs was thereby reduced, inasmuch as previously when the labor relationship was terminated workers had the right to receive from the company a sum equivalent to one month's pay, multiplied by the number of years worked, minus the nominal value of the withdrawals made in the past. Because withdrawals were calculated at their nominal value, the real termination costs of contracts rose with seniority and with the frequency of withdrawals, which were uncertain variables for the company. However, workers with contracts prior to its promulgation are not obliged to observe the new law, which limits its effectiveness and creates distortions between groups of workers. Second, the 1990 reform eliminated the right of workers with more than 10 years' seniority to be reinstated, and changed the formula that relates years of seniority and compensation, although it raised the number of monthly wages that the company has to pay in the event of unjustified dismissal. Thus the reform reduced uncertainty, but not necessarily the actual costs of terminating labor contracts.

In Panama, the 1995 reform changed the labor code in various ways. First, the formula to compute the compensation was changed. Under the new system, compensations for dismissal increase at a rate of 3.4 weeks' pay per year of service in the company, until the tenth year. From then on, each additional year of work adds two weeks' pay. This reforms seeks to reduce the incentives to rotate workers embedded in the old formula, which mandated compensations that were sharply increasing with workers' tenure. Second, to eliminate the lack of adequate provisioning of resources, firms are obliged to generate a fund, funded with workers' contributions and administered by private firms. Finally, the reforms decreased the payment of *salarios caidos* (foregone wages), that is, all wages since the dismissal until the judge gives a verdict. Also, the penalty for no reinstating a worker—in case this has been determined by a judge—for all workers hired after the reform was reduced from 50 percent to 25 percent with total exemption for firms that updated their contributions to the fund.

In the case of Peru, the Employment Stimulus Act that took effect in December 1991 made it possible to replace the obligatory reinstatement of the worker in the event of unjustified firing with a compensation payment. In 1995, absolute stability or the right to reinstatement was abolished, as was the constitutionally established right to job stability. Compensation per year of work was reduced to one month's pay and a maximum was set at 12 months. Recent years also saw modification of the law of compensation for time of service (CTS), or the capital accrued made up of one monthly wage per year of service to be received at the end of the labor relationship or in the form of periodic withdrawals. Prior to the reform the amount was continually adjusted to the most recent wage received by the worker and the loans and withdrawals from this fund were calculated at nominal value. Since the reform, the CTSs accumulate in a personal account in the name of the employee, who receives a market return on the funds accrued.

Finally, in the case of Guatemala, in November 1990 the Congress approved the annual

bonus law, which replaced the payment of the economic compensation of one month's pay per year of service to be paid at the time of separation for whatever reason with an annual bonus paid once a year. The law did not affect the compensation received in the event of unjustified dismissal, which increases by one month per year of service, and does not apply to workers who are fired for just cause or who quit their job of their own accord.

Unemployment Compensation

Only a minority of countries in the region have unemployment compensation programs. As is the case in OECD countries, these programs are administered by a government agency and are partly financed by the company or the worker through special or social security contributions, or they are charged to the general budget.

Such programs have a twofold purpose. On the one hand, they are intended to offer insurance against risk of job loss for reasons beyond the worker's will or activity. Since workers have limited access to capital markets, these programs provide an income source that reduces the instability of consumption and improves welfare. On the other hand, to the extent that they encourage mobility by reducing the costs incurred by workers from changes in technology or in demand for goods, such programs help make resource allocation more efficient.

Although their potential benefits are widely recognized, it has been suggested that such programs may amount to subsidizing idleness, since they lower the intensity and effort of the search for work and make unemployment last longer. Although that possibility has inspired a good number of studies, the evidence gathered thus far suggests that such effects are of little significance.

In the region, only Argentina, Barbados, Brazil, Chile, Ecuador, Mexico, Uruguay and Venezuela have some kind of special program for unemployment assistance. In most of them, workers have to meet a series of requirements to be eligible for assistance during unemployment. In Argentina, Barbados, Ecuador, Uruguay and Venezuela, workers have to have been paying into social security or the unemployment fund for a number of months before qualifying for the assistance, thereby reducing the incentive to find a job simply to requalify for unemployment compensation. Likewise in Brazil and Chile there is a minimum time period between periods of receiving benefits. In Argentina, Chile and Venezuela, the worker has to be actively looking for a job and be available to work immediately, while in Argentina, Brazil, Chile and Uruguay, the worker has to be unemployed for reasons other than his or her behavior or intention.

In most programs nominal coverage extends to all employees, but actual coverage tends to be quite limited. In some cases, such as Chile or Ecuador, benefits are set periodically and the amount is low. In Brazil, the program requires workers to demonstrate economic need in order to be eligible and provides payment of from one to three minimum wages. In Uruguay, the replacement ratio is 50 percent of average pay for the six months prior to being unemployed; however, figures from that country show that only around 15 percent of the unemployed receive a payment.[6] This low coverage is partly explained by the fact that a good proportion of the beneficiaries are workers who have been laid off only temporarily due to economic conditions in the company. Most do not look for a new job because they expect to be rehired at their old job, and hence they are not counted as unemployed. Finally, coverage in Argentina is limited by the newness of the program, which was established in permanent form only in 1992.

The duration of benefits depends on the country. They may last up to a year in Argentina, Barbados or Chile; up to four months in Brazil; or up to six months in Uruguay and Venezuela. Mexico is a special case, since it provides benefits only for those workers between 60 and 65 years old. In this latter case, the program supplies 95 percent of the old age pension as a maximum for five years.

Given the amount and current coverage of these programs, they are not likely to be distorting or to lead to disincentives in seeking work. Even in Argentina, where the expansion of the program has been accompanied by an unprecedented rise in unemployment, it is conceivable that these two phenomena are causally linked, but it does not seem likely. Given the magnitude and complexity of the reforms and structural changes that are taking place in Argentina, the major increase in unemployment may also be attributable to many other causes.

A potentially more problematic aspect is the overlapping of such programs with severance pay and compensation for dismissal. The expansion of unemployment payment programs, whether financed by payroll taxes, general taxes, or withholding from wages for individual accounts, must be carried out in conjunction with an overall reform of legislation on the severing of the labor contract. Otherwise, the lack of coordination and stratification of protection in different programs can lead to costs that make the system less efficient and disproportionately raise the cost of insurance.

Formulas for Hiring Workers

There are major differences between the legislation of Latin American countries and the English-speaking Caribbean with regard to hiring formulas. In the former, legislation favors formulas of hiring for an indefinite time period and sets significant restrictions on atypical contracts, whether they are part-time, probatory period or fixed-term contracts. By contrast, in the Bahamas, Belize, Barbados, Jamaica and Suriname, the law does not set restrictions on the duration or renewability of temporary contracts.

---

[6] Márquez (1995).

Table 6.4 Contractual Reform Formulas

	Reforms in the 90s	Probatory Period		Duration of temporary contracts	
		1990	1995	1990	1995
Argentina	Dec. 1991 Mar. 1995	3 months	3-6 months	2 years. NR[1]	New methods are created Dur. 6 mon - 2 years
Bahamas	None	3 months-1 yr	No change	Without restrictions	No change
Barbados	None	Negotiable	Negotiable	Without restrictions	No change
Belize	1991, 93, 95	2 weeks	No change	Without restrictions	No change
Bolivia	None	3 months	No change	Only for temporary workers	No change
Brazil	1988	3 months	No change	2 years. Renewal once a year	No change
Chile	None	None. In practice, 3-month contracts		1 year. NR	No change
Colombia	1990	2 months	Without limits	1 year maximum Renewable during the 1st year	Max. duration 3 years Renewable indefinitely
Costa Rica	None	3 months	No change		
Dom. Rep.	None	3 months	No change	Duration without restrictions but only for temporary jobs	No change
Ecuador	1991	3 months	No change	Virtually nonexistent	2 years. NR
El Salvador	None	1 month	No change	Only for temporary workers; if not, presumed indefinite	No change
Guatemala	None	2 months	No change	Only for temporary workers; if not, presumed indefinite	No change
Guyana		None	No change	Without restrictions	No change
Honduras	None	2 months	No change	Without restrictions[3]	No change
Jamaica	None	3 months	No change	Without restrictions	No change
Mexico	None	None	None	Without restrictions[3]	No change
Nicaragua		12 months	No change	2 years. NR	
Panama	1995, 1996			Prohibited by law	Max. duration 2 years
Paraguay	1993		1-2 months[1]	3 months	No change
Peru	Dec. 1991 July 1995	3 months	3 months, with exceptions Qualified workers, max: 6 months Employers, max: 12 months	Contracts only per job Virtually nonexistent	Different methods are created. Duration 6 months-5 years, depending on the case
Suriname	None	2 months[2]	No change	Without restrictions	No change
Trin. & Tobago	None	Negotiable	No change	Without restrictions, in practice, 6 months	
Uruguay	None	3 months	No change	5 months. Renewable once[3]	No change
Venezuela	None	3 months	No change	1 year. Renewable twice[3]	No change

Source: Ministries of Labor in the region; Cox-Edwards (1993); Márquez (1995).

NR = Not renewable

[1]Contract for training: one year duration with 60 percent of minimum legal salary. Technicians and professionals can negotiate longer periods.

[2]If both parties agree.

[3]Generate the same obligations as firms with indefinite contracts.

The regulatory framework for atypical hiring is consistent with the regulations governing the termination of the labor contract. Thus in those countries where the law places special emphasis on labor stability, compensations for dismissal are greater, and hiring for a fixed term is limited or prohibited. In the English-speaking Caribbean there is either no obligatory payment for dismissal or it is minimal, and hence the ter-mination of a fixed-term contract produces obligations very similar to those caused when a contract for an indefinite time period expires.

Until the early 1990s, in most countries legislation either directly prohibited temporary contracts for performing "permanent activities proper to the company," as in Bolivia, El Salvador, Guatemala and Peru, or the duration and number of renewals allowed was very much restricted, as was the case in Argentina, Brazil, Ecuador, Nicaragua and Venezuela. In all cases, when the maximum number of renewals had been reached the contract of necessity had to become of unlimited duration. Nevertheless, as we have seen, in recent years there has been an explosion in the number of those working under atypical hiring formulas, even in countries where there had been little in the way of formulas to make the use of such contracts more flexible. This phenomenon is attributable to the ease of hiring and firing that companies need in order to survive in a more competitive economic environment. The need to cut the costs of adjusting the labor force to respond to often unpredictable changes in economic conditions has produced a demand for flexibility by companies, both with regard to firing costs and new hiring formulas. In a few countries, such as Argentina and Peru, the reforms have moved in the direction of reducing the costs of dismissal in tandem with deregulation of hiring formulas. In other countries, such as Ecuador, the reforms have merely made hiring more flexible.

In Argentina, the reform in late 1991 introduced new formulas governing the hiring of young people in training or without professional experience, and also for hiring groups affected by a high unemployment rate. These contracts involve a lowering of payroll taxes or of compensations for dismissal.[7] In Peru, there is a shift from a system where there are virtually no temporary contracts to the creation of different arrangements according to activity, making it possible to extend the duration of these contracts from six months to five years, as the case may be. In Ecuador, as in Peru, there is a shift from a situation where virtually all atypical hiring was prohibited to a deregulation of one-time, occasional and seasonal hiring.

The increased importance of such hiring formulas in many countries makes it likely that this trend will continue until there are comprehensive reforms that lower hiring and dismissal costs. Nevertheless, although evidence is not yet available on the impact that the spreading use of fixed-term contracts will have on the countries of the region, studies carried out in European countries suggest that such "liberalization at the margin" increases the employment response to changes in economic conditions, but that it can have negative consequences on wage barganing, productivity, and company-specific human capital.[8]

Thus, when workers with indefinite contracts (generally those who were contracted prior to the reforms) and workers with fixed-term contracts (recently hired) exist alongside one another in the same company, there is a danger that the full weight of the adjustment in the future will fall on those whose stability is most precarious, thereby generating several unwanted effects. On the one hand, workers with indefinite contracts do not sufficiently realize that excessive pay raises can jeopardize employment, since workers with atypical contracts will be the first to be laid off. Thus, if fixed term workers are not properly represented by the unions, the latter will tend to negotiate excessive pay raises. On the other hand, if the adjustment to economic conditions is made at the cost of fixed-term workers, they will tend not to be in the company for very long, and hence the incentives for both workers and companies to invest in human capital will be lowered. This effect is especially worrisome when those likely to get such contracts are young people with little or no experience. Finally in situations with high compensation for being laid off, the clauses prescribing that temporary contracts must become indefinite contracts after a certain number of renewals lead companies not to renew contracts so as to prevent them from being turned into indefinite contracts. The upshot is an excessive turnover of the labor force and a less than optimum accumulation of human capital.

---

[7] Bour (1996).
[8] Bentolila and Dolado (1994), Jimeno-Toharia (1993), and Bentolila (1992) examine these effects in detail.

Table 6.5 Restrictions to Work Day and Charges for Additional Hours

(In percent)

	Maximum workday	Charges for additional hours	Charges for night work	Charges for work on holidays
Argentina	48 h. week	50	Nothing[b]	100
Bahamas	48 h. week	50	Nothing[b]	150-100[d]
Barbados	40 h. week[h]	50	Nothing	100
Belize	45 h. week	50	Nothing[b]	Nothing[be]
Bolivia	48 h. week	100	25 - 50	100-300[c]
Brazil	44 h. week	50-100[a]		
Chile	48 h. week	50	Nothing[b]	Nothing[b]
Colombia	48 h. week	25-75[a]	Nothing[b]	100-200[d]
Dom. Rep.	44 h. week	35-100[g]	15	100
Ecuador	40 h. week	50 -100	25	100
El Salvador	44 h. week	100	25	50
Guatemala	44 h. week			
Guyana	48 h. week	50	Nothing[b]	100
Haiti	48 h. week	50	50	50
Mexico	40 h. week	100[c]	Nothing[b]	100
Panama	48 h. week	25-50[a]	Nothing[b]	150
Paraguay	48 h. week	50 -100[a]	30	100
Peru		50	Nothing[b]	100
Suriname	48 h. week	50[f]	Nothing[b]	200
Uruguay	48 h. week	100	Nothing[b]	150
Venezuela	44 h. week	50-30[a]	Nothing[b]	150

Source: Ministries of Labor in the region.

[a]The first amount corresponds to extra daylight hours, and the second for extra evening hours.
[b]If an ordinary workday.
[c]200 percent as of nine additional hours.
[d]The first figure corresponds to holidays and the second to Sundays.
[e]100 percent on holidays such as Christmas or Good Friday.
[f]Extra hours are permitted only during certain periods (i.e., Christmas) or under very special circumstances, if and when the firm has permission from the Labor Ministry. The amount reported is a charge for hours worked in addition to the hours in the contract. This amount is below the legal minimum.
[g]The first amount corresponds to the charge for extra hours in addition to the 44 hours per week, but less than 68 hours per week. Hours above 68 per week have a charge of 100 percent.
[h]No law, but common practice.

Legislation on Hours Worked and Overtime

With the same purpose of protecting the worker vis-à-vis the company, the typical legislation in the region covers limits on working hours, overtime pay, night work, and holidays. As a general rule the maximum work period is 48 hours a week and eight hours a day, including Saturdays. However, Mexico has a 40-hour work week, and in Brazil, El Salvador, Guatemala and Venezuela, it is 44 hours. If the worker is needed for more hours than those set in the ordinary work period, he or she is entitled to receive overtime pay varying between 25 percent and 100 percent per hour according to

the country or whether it is a day or night shift. Bolivia, Mexico and Uruguay are the countries that set overtime pay highest, although, given the differences in the work period, it is likely that overtime pay is granted more often in Mexico. In Suriname, overtime is allowed only at certain times of the year (Christmas season, for example), and provided that the company has permission from the Ministry of Labor. Any hour worked above what has been agreed upon is counted as overtime in Suriname, even if it is below the ordinary maximum work period. In the case of Mexico, every hour over nine on a week day must be compensated with an extra 200 percent. The extra charge for work on holidays can vary between zero, as in Belize and Chile, to 300 percent, as in Bolivia. In all these cases, work on Sunday has to be paid at the holiday rate (Table 6.5).

Regulation of the work day is motivated by the desire to protect workers and companies from excessively long work days that jeopardize the worker's health and hinder his or her personal development. However, such legislation must be sufficiently flexible to make it possible for work hours to adjust to fluctuations in demand. That is all the more necessary the more rigid legislation is on temporary hiring and termination costs.

LEGISLATION ON MINIMUM WAGES AND WAGE COSTS

Most countries in the region set the minimum remuneration that a worker must receive. Except for Costa Rica, Colombia and Paraguay, however, the minimum wage in effect today is lower in real terms than it was in 1980. Between 1980 and 1985 the minimum wage fell by approximately 90 percent in Peru, 65 percent in El Salvador, 60 percent in Bolivia, Brazil, Guatemala and Mexico, 40 percent in Uruguay and Venezuela, 20 percent in Argentina, 18 percent in Chile, and 10 percent in the Dominican Republic and Honduras. Thus, the minimum wage fell more than the average wage. In Colombia, Mexico, Panama and Uruguay, the marked decline of the minimum wage vis-à-vis the average wage suggests that these countries have in practice given up having an active minimum wage policy, while in Bolivia since 1990 and Chile since 1988, minimum wages have stabilized at a much lower level than in 1980 when compared with average wages. In Ecuador, Guatemala, Peru and Venezuela, the behavior of the minimum wage in comparison to the average wage has been quite erratic, reflecting a pattern of setting minimum wages that consists of occasionally declaring large increases, very much above trends of average wages, which are then eroded by inflation. In other countries, minimum wages are stabilized at a level compared with average wages that is equal to or higher than where it stood in 1980.

The existence and setting of minimum wages has been and remains a very controversial issue. On the one hand, it is claimed that minimum wages are a classic example of intervention in the labor market that leads to higher unemployment among the very people that the policy seeks to defend, that is, low-paid workers with little training. On the other hand, it is claimed that minimum wages are redistribution tools whose viability depends on whether the benefits from modestly raising the wages of low-paid workers makes up for the losses of those who are displaced from the labor market.

The empirical evidence is not conclusive. In the case of Chile, for example, it has been argued that there is no causal relationship between changes in minimum wages and unemployment.[9] In the aggregate, minimum wages have appreciable effects only when they are used actively and decisively as a wage policy tool. Likewise, country-level analyses performed for this study show that in general there is no evidence that raising minimum wages leads to greater unemployment. An analysis of the determinants of unemployment indicates that only changes in GDP and average wages are relevant (but not the minimum wage or its relationship to the average wage).[10]

There are several reasons why minimum wages may have only a minor impact on unemployment or other aggregate variables. First, it is to be expected that when setting the minimum wage, those responsible for economic policy will take into account recent trends in production, wages and unemployment. If such is the case, minimum wages are set selectively in a way that promotes active policies during periods of economic growth and encourages moderation and even a decline of the minimum wage when the economy heads into recession or crisis.[11] This explanation is consistent with the sharp fall in minimum wages in most countries in the region and with the modest increases of the average wage in Chile after 1988 and in Bolivia after 1990. Second, if minimum wages are set at levels that the economy obviously cannot sustain, workers and companies will have incentives to sidestep the law by renegotiating agreements that allow the worker to stay on the job. This is all the more likely, the less the monitoring capability in an economy. Finally, if part or all of the labor demand can be characterized as a monopsony, raising minimum wages would entail a rise in employment and a decline in unemployment.

With regard to the effectiveness of minimum wages as a redistribution tool, there is evidence for both Latin America and other countries suggesting that higher minimum wages are associated with lower poverty levels.[12] However, even

---

[9] Paldam and Riveros (1987).

[10] Inasmuch as minimum wages can be set by the government in terms of either the unemployment situation or production, we tested the hypothesis that minimum wages are endogenous, using estimators in two stages. The results did not vary substantially.

[11] Freeman (1993).

[12] Lustig and McLeod (1996) and Morley (1994).

if active minimum wage policies have positive effects in reducing poverty, they are not necessarily an efficient tool for pursuing that objective.

Payroll Deductions

Payroll deductions began with obligatory contributions by companies and workers for different pension, family aid, occupational safety, and unemployment programs. Uruguay, Argentina, Colombia and Brazil are the countries where these extra costs are highest as a proportion of wages, followed by Costa Rica, Venezuela, Bolivia, Paraguay and Mexico. Among the countries with the lowest extra charges for labor are Jamaica, Trinidad and Tobago, Honduras, the Bahamas, and Barbados (Figure 6.6).

Labor costs are regarded as a significant source of distortions in the labor market. What type of distortion depends largely on whether they are perceived by companies and workers as payments in kind, deductible from the base salary, or as taxes on the labor factor that do not have a close and individual connection with the benefits that the worker can derive from them. As a rule, given the characteristics of social security programs in the region, it can be argued that contributions are perceived as a tax and benefits as an acquired right.[13] In this case, their ultimate impact on employment depends on the amount of the contributions and the elasticity of demand and the labor supply. The pension and social security system reforms carried out in recent years have sought precisely to establish a transparent connection between contributions and benefits with the aim of reducing these distortions and consequently moderating their effect on labor costs.[14]

Another distortion often associated with payroll deductions is the segmentation between the sectors that have to pay (formal sector) and the sectors that evade the legislation (informal sector). In countries where the monitoring level is low, high payroll deductions can lead to high

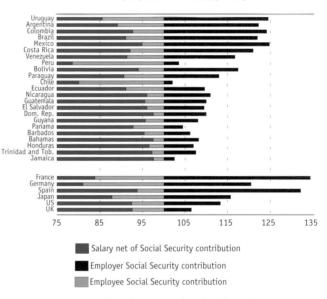

FIGURE 6.6
Payroll Taxes and Contributions
(Compared with base salary = 100)

Sources: *Social Security Programs Throughout the World - 1995*, U.S. Dept. Health and Human Services.
Note: Includes old age, disability, and death; sickness and maternity; work injury; family allowances; and unemployment.

levels of fiscal evasion and an increasingly informal economy. Figure 6.7 shows the relationship between the percentage of workers in the informal sector and payroll deductions—measured as the total amount of contributions from workers and companies as a percentage of the base wage. As can be seen, there is a positive and significant relationship between wage costs and informal employment.[15] Causality, however, might move in the other direction, that is, in countries with high levels of informal labor and few contributors, contribution systems may require higher rates.

The aspect related to payroll deductions that has been most controversial in the region is undoubtedly the possible loss of competitiveness associated with higher contributions. There are

---

[13] Cox-Edwards (1993).

[14] See the chapter on pension system reforms.

[15] This statement is based on a regression of the size of the informal sector on obligatory contributions (variables that appear in the figure) and income level.

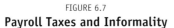

FIGURE 6.7
Payroll Taxes and Informality

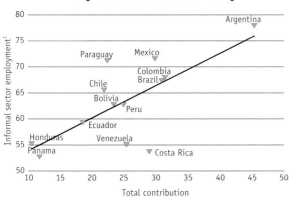

Sources: Social Security Programs Throughout the World - 1995, U.S. Dept. Health and Human Services; ILO.
Note: The slope of this relationship is 0.62 and is significant at the 5 percent level.
[1] This variable was transformed by controlling for real GDP per capita.

two variants to the argument. First, it is said that in the new context of globalized markets, companies cannot pass cost variations on to prices. Therefore, any cost increase above productivity has to be absorbed by companies, which makes if difficult for them to survive on the market and orients production toward nontradable sectors.[16] Second, it is argued that high extra costs for labor distort the relative prices of capital vis-à-vis labor by reducing the comparative advantage of having relatively cheap labor. However, the degree of distortion that these costs generate depends on the extent to which companies in the new context are able to negotiate wage settlements that make up for higher contributions and on the movement of the exchange rate. Thus, for example, according to ILO data, competitiveness between 1990 and 1995, measured as productivity growth minus growth of labor costs, rose in Argentina, Brazil, Mexico and Peru, and declined in Chile. After correcting for the movement of the exchange rate, only Argentina and Mexico showed greater competitiveness.

RECOMMENDATIONS FOR FUTURE REFORMS

This chapter has examined the characteristics of labor legislation and its impact on the operation of the labor market. Some conclusions should be emphasized for economic policy purposes.

• Excessive, contradictory, and unclear regulations leave little leeway for negotiating contracts that can serve both parties.

• Excessive compensation for dismissal leads to extra labor costs that can reduce labor demand, constrain the adjustment of the labor factor to changes in economic conditions, and reduce labor mobility. Besides the efficiency costs that such regulations may entail, current legislation in terms of compensations for dismissal may cause excessive work force turnover and discourage the formation of human capital. Finally, compensation for dismissal does not adequately protect the worker from the risk associated with loss of employment.

Hence, future reform programs must first distinguish clearly between arbitrary dismissal and layoff caused by adverse economic conditions. The legislation should punish unjust dismissal, but its actual text needs to be revised to cover all those cases in which continuing the labor relationship does not make economic sense, whether for the worker or for the company. Second, legislation must convert compensation for layoff due to economic conditions into unemployment insurance, and eliminate the component that penalizes the company. To that end and in order to increase as much as possible the connection between contributions and payments, reforms should move from formulas for calculating compensation consisting of multiples of the most recent wage to contributions that can be accrued in an account in the worker's name (as established in the CTSs). Such funds must yield a market interest rate and be available to the workers should they lose their jobs

---

[16] Cox-Edwards (1993).

involuntarily or quit of their own accord. The compensation portion, as covered in legislation in Brazil, Colombia and Ecuador, ought to be eliminated, and if considered necessary, the amount accrued in the CTSs should be raised. Third, the legislation must set a maximum limit to the funds accumulated in the CTSs by obligation, and that limit should be strictly related to the expected duration of unemployment. Doing so would prevent institutional saving from being higher than what individuals would want to do themselves. For the same reason, whatever additional contributions that a worker might wish to make would be acceptable. Fourth, it would be a good idea to set a lower limit for the amount received by the worker in the event of layoff due to economic conditions. The gap between the minimum severance payment and the amount accrued to the worker could be financed by drawing on the government budget or through low interest loans, payable from the time of returning to work.

• Making the labor market more flexible "at the margin," that is, preserving the rights of workers already hired and deregulating the hiring of new entrants into the job market may cause a segmentation of the market, with grave consequences for wage setting, investment in specific human capital, and productivity growth. Although such ways of increasing flexibility may be the only ones feasible for reasons of political economy, and may even be absolutely necessary in order to bring about the long-term benefits of economic restructuring, in the short run they may create serious distortions in the operation of the labor market, and insofar as possible they should be avoided in favor of labor reforms of a more all-encompassing nature.

• In the region, obligatory contributions to social security programs are high, and in some cases are at levels similar to those in countries like Germany, Japan, United States or the United Kingdom. In view of how little individual connection there is between these costs and the benefits they provide, the contributions are regarded as a tax, whose distortions become greater the larger the contributions. Although the evidence is not conclusive, it can be argued that greater social security contributions encourage the spread of the informal economy. Although the recent reforms in social security have not been accompanied by lower contributions, the fact that a greater connection has been established between contributions and payments will reduce the tax component and weaken distortions in the labor market.

• Finally, this chapter does not find evidence of any impact of minimum wages on unemployment. However, that finding should be taken as an indication that this tool has been used cautiously in recent years, and not as an argument in favor of using it actively and indiscriminately.

CHAPTER 7

PENSION
REFORM

ABSTRACT

Obligatory pension systems in Latin America and the Caribbean are seriously flawed, covering on average only 38 percent of the economically active population and providing pensions to no more than 31 percent of people over age 60. Protection levels are high among public sector workers and other stably employed, high-wage workers, but very low in rural areas and for those in the informal sector.

Financial weaknesses of these systems are mounting because they have little or no accumulated reserves, and most are dependent on government transfers, the proportions of which are likely to grow rapidly in the future as the ratio between contributors and pensioners falls due to the aging of the population and the maturing of the pension systems themselves.

Traditional pension systems have no means for responding to these challenges. Members' incentives for properly contributing to the system are weak or nonexistent because there is no strict relationship between contributions and benefits. Managers and governments do not have adequate incentives because their decisions are affected by political considerations and because there are no mechanisms of competition and social control that might assure sound financial management of government social security agencies.

Five countries have reformed their pension programs in the 1990s to resolve these problems. Although the reform in Chile in the early 1980s has been quite influential, recent reforms have moved away from exclusive reliance on the individual capitalization system. Peru and Colombia opted for an arrangement in which the government system and the new pension funds compete; Argentina and Uruguay adopted a system in which the two are complementary; and Mexico

has decided to maintain the public system solely as a guarantor of benefits for those currently enrolled. In all cases, reforms have entailed major if incomplete corrections of the imbalances between contributions and benefits in the government pension system.

The mixed solutions have provided an escape from the fiscal, financial and political constraints that result from replacing a government system with one based on individual capitalization. The difficulties lying ahead include the problem of adverse selection of affiliates of the public system, limited management ability to deal with the more complex responsibilities facing government agencies (such as issuing recognition bonds, and determining benefits based on labor history and contributions), and the problems of financial risk and insufficient alternatives for investing the resources of private funds.

INTRODUCTION

Most pension systems in Latin America and the Caribbean are contribution-based systems managed by the public sector. They operate either with a simple pay-as-you-go formula, in which pensions of retired workers are paid out of contributions from those still working, or with some graduated premium arrangement in which contributions also make it possible to build up a partial reserve for paying future pension obligations. At the outset of the 1990s, the only exception was Chile, which after the 1981 reform set up a fully-funded private pension management system based on individual capitalization accounts. Five countries have subsequently adopted systems partially inspired by the Chilean reform, under which, at least temporarily, a contribution-based system managed by the public sector exists side-by-side with a fully-funded individual capitalization account system that is primarily privately managed.

The reforms have been a response to the flaws and structural imbalances of traditional contribution-based systems, such as low coverage levels, large disparities between workers, sectors and regions, and growing financial imbalances.

This chapter examines current pension systems and analyzes the pension reforms of a structural nature recently or about to be introduced or implemented in Peru (1993), Colombia (1994), Argentina (1994), Uruguay (1996) and Mexico (1997). Some countries have made nonstructural reforms in social security systems, but they are not discussed here. Mexico in 1991 and Costa Rica from 1990-92 strengthened traditional contribution-based systems by setting stricter conditions for access to pensions, increasing contributions, and in the case of Mexico, introducing a compulsory savings or complementary pension program. At least nine countries in the region are also discussing the possibility of carrying out structural reforms in their pension systems: Bolivia, Brazil, Ecuador, El Salvador, Guatemala, Nicaragua, Panama, Paraguay and Venezuela.

TRADITIONAL PUBLIC PENSION SYSTEMS

The public pension systems in Latin America are disparate arrangements with low coverage, inequalities between sectors and regions, and growing financial weaknesses.

Although these public pension systems

Table 7.1   Pension System Coverage, 1995

	Employed	Self-employed Mandatory	Self-employed Voluntary	Main special programs and exclusions
Argentina	x	x		Military
Bahamas	x	x		
Barbados	x	x		
Bolivia	x		x	
Brazil	x	x		Public employees, military
Chile	x		x	
Colombia	x		x	Public employees, teachers petroleum workers, military
Costa Rica	x		x	
Dominican Republic	x		x	Public employees
Ecuador	x	x		
El Salvador	x	x		Public employees
Guatemala	x	x		Some public employees
Guyana	x	x		
Haiti	x	x		Public employees
Honduras	x	x		Teachers, public employees, doctors military
Jamaica	x	x		
Mexico	x		x	Petroleum, public employees, military
Nicaragua	x		x	Miners, indigents, service to country
Panama	x		x	
Paraguay	x			Railroad, banking, public employees
Peru	x	x		Many
Trinidad and Tobago	x	x		
Uruguay	x	x		Banks, notaries, university teachers, military police
Venezuela	x			

Source: *Social Security Programs throughout the World - 1995*, U.S. Department of Health and Human Services.

are by regulation managed by the public sector and cover both public and private sector workers, it often happens that arrangements for different groups separated by occupation exist side by side. Ten countries have special programs wholly or partially covering public sector workers, and at least six have special programs for the armed forces (Table 7.1). A number of countries provide special treatment for sectors as different as banking, railways, oil or mining, and the teaching and medical professions. Fragmentation causes inequalities in coverage and benefits, financial and fiscal imbalances, and hinders labor mobility, since there is little or no likelihood that one's contributions will be recognized under other arrangements.

Coverage of the systems is generally low. Only 38.3 percent of Latin America's economically active population make contributions, and only 30.8 percent of persons over age 60 receive pensions (Figures 7.1 and 7.2). At the outset of the 1990s, less than 25 percent of the economically active population was contributing, and fewer than 20 percent of persons over age 60 were receiving a pension in Colombia, El Salvador, Honduras, Nicaragua or Bolivia. The percentage of contributors within the entire economically active population was between 25 percent and 40 percent in Peru, Guatemala, Venezuela, Ecuador, Panama, Jamaica and Mexico. From 13 percent to 32 percent of persons over 60 were receiving a pension in this group of countries. Coverage is greater in more mature pension systems, such as those in Argentina, Brazil, Chile or Uruguay, or in younger ones like those in Costa Rica and Trinidad and Tobago, which made universal coverage their objective. In most of these countries, self-employed workers are obliged to join on

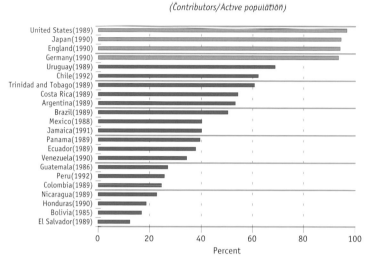

FIGURE 7.1
Coverage of Active Population
(Contributors/Active population)

Source: World Bank (1994).

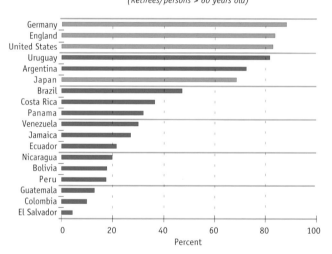

FIGURE 7.2
Coverage of Seniors
(Retirees/persons > 60 years old)

Source: World Bank (1994).

their own, and coverage for farmers and other workers in rural areas is greater than that of other countries in the region, although it is still lower than urban coverage.

Protection levels differ enormously by geographical zones or occupational sectors. In Colombia, where the recent reform seeks to broaden regional coverage, two-thirds of the persons covered by the system live in the largest cities, while coverage is practically nil in rural areas. Likewise, coverage tends to be very high in groups working in the public sector or manufacturing, while farmers are generally very much unprotected. In Belize, for example, pension spending is so concentrated that 92.2 percent of payments are made to public sector retirees. In Costa Rica that same indicator is 49.5 percent, and in Colombia and Mexico it is between 35 percent and 40 percent. (Figure 7.3).

From a financial viewpoint, pension systems in the region display major weaknesses. Programs in Central America and the Caribbean, with the exception of Costa Rica, are graduated premium systems and have considerable accumulated reserves. Thus in Guyana and Jamaica, over half of the revenue comes from returns on investments made with the reserves, while in the Bahamas, Belize, El Salvador, Honduras, Panama and Venezuela, that same revenue source ranges from 25 percent to 50 percent. In many of the remaining countries, however, the pension system is unable to finance itself completely with the contributions of those enrolled, and hence operates as a simple pay-as-you-go system in deficit. Hence many of the systems have had to turn to transfers from the national budget. In 1986, the pension systems of Bolivia and Guatemala obtained more than 30 percent of their revenues from contributions by the state, while that same figure was in the 20 percent to 30 percent range in Argentina, Colombia, the Dominican Republic, Ecuador and Mexico (Table 7.2). The more mature systems, such as those in Uruguay and Argentina prior to the reforms, displayed severe and growing financial difficulties, with spending patterns that would prob-

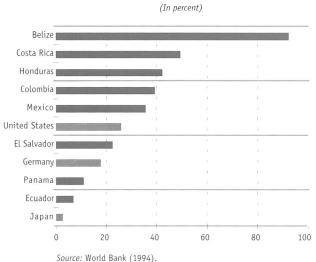

FIGURE 7.3

Proportion of Pension Expenditure on Public Sector Retirees, 1985-92

(In percent)

Source: World Bank (1994).

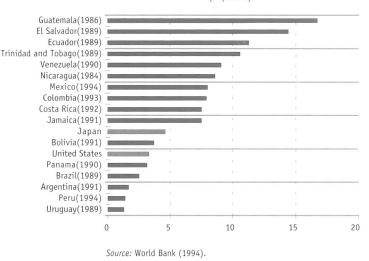

FIGURE 7.4

Contributor/Retiree Ratio

(In percent)

Source: World Bank (1994).

ably prove difficult to finance in the future. As a temporary solution, both countries decided that a portion of revenue from the value-added tax (VAT) would be allotted to financing the growing social security debt. Even then, the needs for further transfers from the public budget were growing. In 1994, more than 34 percent of total revenues in Uruguay came from direct transfers from the budget or were revenues from consumption taxes (Table 7.3). Looking toward the future, studies available on some countries show that financial imbalances will become greater unless reforms are carried out. Mexico is expected to have a deficit of over 3 percent of GDP starting in 2017 and for Colombia it has been estimated to reach 3.5 percent of GDP in 2025.[1]

REASONS FOR WEAKNESSES

Traditional public pension systems are weak principally because of demographic factors, imbalances between contributions and the benefits provided by the systems, evasion of contribution payments, and inadequate administrative and financial management of social security agencies. Aside from the demographic factors, it is plain that the other causes are largely the result of the lack of incentives for the system to function properly. From the viewpoint of participants, the incentives for fully meeting contribution obligations are weak because benefits and contributions are not closely enough connected. From the standpoint of the administrators and the government, there are not enough incentives for reducing these imbalances or for improving the best long-run financial management because the decisions of these officials are often affected by short-term political considerations, or the mechanisms of competition and public oversight for assuring good management of pension resources are nonexistent or flawed.

A major change has occurred in the age structure of those enrolled in social security systems, as seen in the decline of the ratio of contributors to pensioners. In Argentina in 1991, there were barely 1.66 contributors per pensioner;[2] in

Table 7.2 Pension System Financing, 1986

Investment income (%)	Countries	State financing (%)	Countries
More than 50	Guyana Jamaica	More than 30	Bolivia Guatemala
Between 25-50	Bahamas Belize El Salvador Honduras Panama Venezuela	Between 20-30	Argentina Colombia Dominican Republic Ecuador Mexico
Between 5-25	Bolivia Colombia Ecuador	Between 10-20	Costa Rica Venezuela
Less than 5	Dominican Republic Guatemala Mexico	Less than 10	Bahamas Honduras Jamaica Panama Uruguay
0	Argentina Peru Uruguay		Belize El Salvador Guyana Peru

Source: World Bank (1994).

Table 7.3 Social Security Revenues and Expenditures

Argentina	Millions of 1991 pesos				Percent of expenditure financed			
	1988	1989	1990	1991	1988	1989	1990	1991
Expenditures	11,012	7,801	9,963	9,668	100.00	100.00	100.00	100.00
Revenues	7,714	5,991	7,366	8,302	70.05	76.80	73.93	85.87
Deficit	3,299	1,810	2,596	1,366	29.96	23.20	26.06	14.13
Taxes	2,645	1,325	1,875	2,082	24.02	16.99	18.82	21.53
Transfers	654	485	721	-716	5.94	6.22	7.24	-7.41

Uruguay	Millions of 1994 pesos				Percent of expenditure financed			
	1991	1992	1993	1994	1991	1992	1993	1994
Expenditures	9,686	10,580	11,188	11,736	100.00	100.00	100.00	100.00
Revenues	7,340	8,034	7,557	7,654	75.78	75.93	67.55	65.22
Deficit	2,346	2,547	3,631	4,082	24.22	24.07	32.45	34.78
Taxes	1,180	1,272	1,729	1,818	12.18	12.03	15.45	15.49
Transfers	734	1,156	1,712	2,267	7.58	10.92	15.30	19.31

Source: Argentina: Cottabi and Demarco (1996); Uruguay: Márquez (1996).

[1] Schmidt-Hebbel (1995) and Márquez (1996).
[2] Cottani and Demarco (1996).

Peru, it went from 13 in 1980 to 1.4 in 1994;[3] and in Uruguay, it stands at 1.3. All these are very much below the Latin American average (5) or even that of the OECD countries, which is estimated to be 2.6 contributors per pensioner (Figure 7.4).[4] The fall in the ratio between pensioners and contributors is due partly to the gradual aging of the population associated with the development process and partly to the maturing of pension systems. In Argentina, for example, the relationship between the adult population (24-65 years) and persons over 65 went from 11.6 in 1950 to 5.2 in 1980. Demographic projections for the next few years indicate that the proportion of the population over 60 will rise rapidly, especially in those countries whose populations are relatively young, thus further diminishing the ratio of contributors to pensioners in contribution-based systems (Figure 7.5). But the maturing of the systems has had an even more significant influence on the decline in the ratio because during the early years of a program only a small portion of the participants is receiving benefits. The bulk of the contributions must then build up in a reserve fund whose returns will finance a portion of future pensions. As the program matures and more participants reach retirement age, the contributors-to-beneficiaries ratio drops. This would not be a problem if the system had developed with a view to reaching maturity in financial balance so that from that moment onward the yield from accumulated capitalization and contributions were equal to pension payments. This has not been the case, however, due to the other reasons causing weaknesses in contribution-based pension systems.

The most important reason is the imbalance between benefits and contributions. In practice, the benefits that have been established cannot be sustained in the long run, although they can be financed temporarily in the early stages in the life of the system. Due to the lack of effective mechanisms for public oversight over pension resources, it has often happened that such decisions

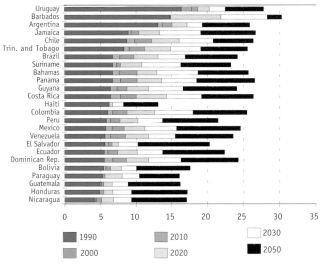

FIGURE 7.5
Population Over 60, 1990-2050
(Percent of total population)

Source: World Bank (1994).

are made in response to political convenience or pressure groups. Those who decide the access conditions and the amount of benefits operate within narrow decision-making confines dictated by electoral cycles, which is incompatible with the long-range nature of pension systems.

Pension benefits depend essentially on the retirement age and on the formula connecting the sum of the pension with the wage base for making payments. The retirement age or the minimum age at which a person can receive a pension is much lower in Latin America than in the OECD countries. In 1995, only the Bahamas, Barbados and Mexico had retirement ages of 65 for men and women, along the lines of those existing in France or the United States. The median retirement age in the region is 60 for men and 55 for women, although in Ecuador or Haiti both men and women can retire at 55. This difference is partly explained by the greater life expectancy in the OECD countries. However, given the retirement

[3] Mouchard Ramírez (1995).
[4] Márquez (1996).

Table 7.4 Qualifying Conditions, 1995								
	Retirement age		Life expectancy		Expected duration of retirement		Minimum contribution period (years)	Must retire?	Maximum benefits?
	Men	Women	Men	Women	Men	Women			
Argentina	(60) 62	(55) 57	69	76	16	24	20		x
Bahamas	65	65	69	78			14		
Barbados	65	65	73	78			10		
Bolivia	55	50	58	61			15		
Brazil	65	60	64	69			5		
Chile	65	60	71	78			20		
Colombia	(60) 62	(55) 57	67	73	17	19	10		
Costa Rica	61	59	74	79			20	x	
Dominican Republic	60	60	68	72			15	x	
Ecuador	55	55	67	72	21	23	30	x	
El Salvador	60	55	64	69			14	x	
Guatemala	60	60	63	68	17	18	15	x	
Guyana	60	60	63	68			14		x
Haiti	55	55	55	59			20		
Honduras	65	60	66	71			15	x	
Jamaica	65	60	72	76			7		
Mexico	65	65	68	74			10		
Nicaragua	60	60	65	69			14		
Panama	62	57	71	75	19	25	15	x	
Paraguay	60	60	68	72			15		
Peru	(60) 65	(55) 60	64	68	15	21	15		
Trinidad and Tobago	60	60	70	74	16	18	14	x	
Uruguay	60	(55) 60	69	76	17	25	30	x	
Venezuela	60	55	69	75	17	24	14		
France	65	65	73	81	19	24	38		
Spain	65	65	75	81	15	18	15	x	
United Kingdom	65	60	74	79	14	21	47		
United States	65	65	73	79	15	19			

Source: Social Security Programs throughout the World - 1995, U.S. Department of Health and Human Services. Expected duration of retirement taken from World Bank (1994).

Note: Pension ages in parentheses are pre-reform.

ages in the various countries, the expected retirement period is longer than it is in the OECD countries. The difference is sharper for women, due to their longer life expectancies and lower retirement ages (Table 7.4).[5]

In most countries, the pension amount at retirement age is set as a percentage of the wage base of contributions (or replacement rate), provided a minimum contribution period has been met. This percentage gradually rises as the years of payment exceed this minimum. The countries

in the region have high replacement rates, in many cases much higher than those guaranteed in OECD countries, and short contribution periods difficult to sustain in the long run. The minimum replacement rate is 33 percent in Haiti after 20 years of payments; 40 percent in the Bahamas, Barbados, the Dominican Republic, El Salvador, Guyana, Honduras, and Nicaragua, after a payment period of between 10 and 15 years; 50 percent in Guatemala after 15 years of contributions; and 60 percent in Costa Rica, Panama and Uruguay after 20, 15 and 30 years, respectively. Prominent among the countries with more generous replacement rates are 70 percent in Argentina (prior to the reform) and 75 percent in Ecuador, after 30 years of enrollment, and 70 percent in Brazil after only five

[5] The expected period of pension use is substantially longer than the difference between life expectancies at birth and retirement age, because life expectancy *at retirement age* is higher, inasmuch as it is affected solely by mortality rates from that age onward.

years of payment. These rates may rise substantially in many countries with further years of enrollment in the systems. For example, in Ecuador the replacement rate for an individual with a 40-year work life is 87.5 percent, in Costa Rica, 75 percent, and in El Salvador it can reach a maximum of 60 percent. By comparison, in France one needs 37.5 years of payment to obtain a 50 percent replacement rate (Table 7.5).

The value of the pension is also determined by the wage base used in the formulas for calculating the pension. In general, the wage base is defined as an average of the highest pay received during the final years up to the moment of retirement (not always adjusted for inflation). This procedure has an enormous disadvantage, namely because contributions during the early years of one's work life do not affect pensions, creating an incentive for workers and companies to underdeclare or avoid paying contributions. The system likewise generates incentives to overdeclare income during the final years so as to increase the amount of the pension to be received. However, many countries are forced to maintain such a definition of reference wages, based on the final years of contributions, because they do not have adequate records for calculating them on the basis of the entire work life of participants. Such flawed administration imposes an enormous cost on the entire system.

Most systems establish maximum and minimum pensions, the aim of which is to redistribute income between workers with different pay levels. Thus, the difference between the pension calculated according to the administrative formula and the minimum amount is generally covered by the system, while the maximum pension is set either as a monetary amount or as a limit in the replacement rate above which the pension does not rise. The upper limits to pensions also encourage evasion, but they have the virtue of preventing the subsidies granted by traditional pension systems from being concentrated in higher-income individuals.

The contributions made by workers and firms are currently the main, and in some cases the only, financing source of pensions in public pension systems. According to legislation in effect in 1995, the total contribution to pension programs is 29 percent, 27 percent, and 27.5 percent of the wage base in Brazil, Argentina, and Uruguay, respectively; 22.5 percent in Paraguay; and 10 percent to 20 percent in Bolivia, Colombia, Guyana, Peru and Venezuela (Table 7.6). In the other countries in the region, pension contributions are less than 10 percent of wages. However, the revenue actually generated by these contribution rates tends to be a good deal less than its potential due to evasion of the system; moreover, incomes are underdeclared and payments to the system are not made on a regular basis. It is estimated that in Argentina average evasion as a percentage of potential collection is as high as 49.1 percent. Evasion is even higher among the self-employed, where it represents 74.5 percent of total potential revenues.[6] In Brazil the sum of annual revenues lost through evasion is estimated to be around 1 percent of GDP, while in Peru revenues lost through evasion are 33 percent of total potential revenues.[7] In order to understand such high losses of potential revenue it should be emphasized that in many countries participation by the self-employed and domestic workers is voluntary. Such workers participate very little in pension systems because they do not share the cost of the contribution with their employers, their incomes are unstable and hence they do not tend to make regular contributions, and they have to hold their savings in more liquid forms. Coverage is also very limited for workers in small businesses, because there are few incentives for employers to make contributions and monitoring is very difficult. These are very severe problems given the high rates of informal employment in many countries in the region. Indeed, the combined total of the

---

[6] Cottani and Demarco (1996).
[7] Nitsch and Schwarzer (1995).

Table 7.5　Benefits

	Minimum replacement ratio	Replacement ratio adjustments	Relevant wage	Minimum pension	Old age allowance	Max?
Argentina	45% plus minimum pension	Public: 1.5% per year >30; 0.85% per year after 1994; Private: Determined by capitalization	Average of last 10 years	Fixed amount defined in the annual national budget		
Bahamas	40%	+1% per 50 weeks >750	Covered wage	B$43.85 (US$36)/week	B$36.92 (US$30)/week	x
Barbados	40%	+1% per 50 weeks >500	Average of best 3 in the last 15 years	B$76 (US$36)/week	Lump sum of 6 weeks earnings per 50 weeks contribution	
Bolivia	30% (basic); 40% (complementary)	+2% per 12 months >180; +1% per 12 months	Average of last 12 months wage base		One month per 24 months of contribution	
Brazil	70%	+1% of average income for contribution year (max. 100%)	Average earnings in last 36 months	100% of minimum wage	100% of minimum wage	x
Chile	Determined by capitalization			Guaranteed		
Colombia[1]	Public: 65%; Private: Determined by capitalization	+2% per 50 weeks >1000 <1200; +3% per 50 weeks >1200 <1400	Average over last 10 years	Minimum wage		x
Costa Rica	60%	+0.0835% per month >240	Highest earning 48 months of the last 5 years	16,000 colones (US$90)/month; 500 pesos (US$36)/month		x
Dominican Republic	40%	+2% per 100 weeks >800	Average earnings in the last 2 years	Minimum wage		x
Ecuador	75%	+1.25% per year >30	Average earnings in the highest 5 years			
El Salvador	40%	+1.25% per 50 weeks >150	Average monthly income	300 colones (US$34)/month	50% of monthly earnings per 50 weeks of contribution	x
Guatemala	50%	+0.5% per 6 months >120	Average income of the last 5 years of contribution	140 quetzales (US$24)/month	Contribution	x
Guyana	40%	+1.0% per 50 weeks >750	Average weekly income during the best 3 years in the past 5 years	50% of minimum wage	1/12 average annual covered earnings per 50 weeks contribution	
Haiti	33%		Average income during the past 5 years			
Honduras	40%	+1% per 12 months >60; +3% per year >age 60(65) female(male)	Monthly basic income	50% earnings		x
Jamaica	J$84 (US $2.39) per week	+J$0.06 per J$1 of contribution			J$360 (US$10) for 52 contributions+ +J$7.20 (US$0.20) for 13 weeks >52 +J$9.30 (US$0.26) for US$0.37 o[2] contribution	
Mexico[2]	1 to 6 times the minimum salary or 35%	+1.25% per year >500 weeks	Minimum wage of the Federal District; Average earnings during the last 250 weeks	Minimum wage of the Federal District		x
Nicaragua	40%	+1.365% for 50 weeks of contribution; +1% per year >60	Average earnings of last 5,4,3 years based on contributions of 15,20,25 years	66 2/3% of minimum wage		x
Panama	60%	+1.25 per 12 months >180	Average earnings during highest 7 years	175 balboas (US$175)/month	1 month pension per 6 months contribution	x
Paraguay	42.5%; +4.5% per year after retirement age	+1.5% per 50 weeks >750; +50% of average income	Average earnings during last 3 years			x
Peru[1]	Public: 50%; Private: Determined by capitalization	+4% per year >20	Indexed average earnings of last 36-60 months (depending inversely on years of contribution)	300% of minimum pension		x
Trinidad and Tobago	35%-75%	+1% for 25 weeks >750	Average weekly earnings according to 8 wage classes			
Uruguay[2]	60% male; 65% female	+5% per five years >30	Average earnings in last 3 years	100% minimum wage	T$ 426 (US$72)/month	x
Venezuela	9000 bolivares (US$22)/month+ 30%	+1% per week >750	Average earnings of 5 highest years in last 10 years	40% of earnings	10% of total covered earnings	x

Source: Social Security Programs throughout the World - 1995, U.S. Department of Health and Human Services.

[1] After reforms.

[2] Before reforms.

Table 7.6 Contributions to Pension Systems

(Percent of wage)

	Employee	Employer	Self-employed	Government	Additional Coverage Sick/Maternity Leave	Work Injury	Unemploy-ment	Family Allowance
Argentina	11.00	16.00	27.00	Helps to cover deficit				
Bahamas	2.55	6.25	7.80	None	x	x		
Barbados	3.15	3.15	6.30	None				
Bolivia	6.00	6.00		1.50				
Brazil	9.00	20.00	15.00	Helps to cover deficit	x			x
Chile	13.00	None		Subsidies				
Colombia[1]	3.37	10.12		Partial subsidy				
Costa Rica	2.50	4.75	5.88	0.25				
Dominican Republic	2.50	7.50		2.50	x			
Ecuador	7.00	2.39	8.39	4.00				
El Salvador	1.00	2.00		0.50				
Guatemala	1.50	3.00		3.00 and helps to cover deficits				
Guyana	4.40	6.60	9.55	Loans to cover deficits	x	x		
Haiti	4.00	4.00		Any deficit				
Honduras	1.00	2.00		1.00				
Jamaica	2.50	2.50	5.00	As an employer	x	x		
Mexico[2]	2.08	13.00		0.42				
Nicaragua	1.75	3.50		0.25				x
Panama	6.75	2.75		Revenues from alcohol tax				
Paraguay	9.50	13.00		1.50		x		
Peru[1]	13.50	None		None				
Trinidad and Tobago	2.80	5.60		Full cost of means tested benefits	x			
Uruguay[2]	11.50	14.50		Help to finance deficit			x	x
Venezuela	4.00	10.00		1.50				

Source: Social Security Programs throughout the World - 1995, U.S. Department of Health and Human Services.
[1] After reforms.
[2] Before reforms.

self-employed, domestic workers, and those employed in small businesses is over 60 percent in Bolivia, Colombia and Paraguay, and 50 to 60 percent in Argentina, Brazil, Chile, Ecuador, Honduras, Mexico and Peru.

Management flaws have been another factor financially undermining pension systems. The nature of the incentives and time horizons with which those in charge of social security agencies operate have not been conducive to maximizing financial yields, nor to properly controlling the costs of these agencies. In Peru, Venezuela and Ecuador, real annual yields on the investments of social security agencies during the 1980s were -37.4 percent, -15.3 percent, and -10 percent, respectively.[8] Inflation may be partly responsible for this phenomenon, especially in Peru, since it distorted financial yields and produced negative real returns. In a number of countries, inflation may have contributed to the loss of revenues mentioned in the previous paragraph, since it created incentives for businesses to delay their payments to the system as a way of reducing their social security obligations. These effects were nevertheless magnified by the failure of administrative bodies to make timely decisions and by the possibility that the funds of these agencies were used as a discretionary device for government financing.

Finally, flawed management has been reflected in high administrative costs. In Colombia and Peru before the reforms, these costs absorbed approximately 10 percent of revenues from contributions. In Costa Rica in 1992, administrative costs represented 7.2 percent,[9] and in Mexico in 1995 they accounted for 20 percent of contribu-

---

[8] World Bank (1994, p. 95).

[9] Costa Rica, *Indicadores de Seguridad Social, 1988-1992.*

tions. Compared with the OECD countries, World Bank figures indicate that as a percentage of per capita income, administrative costs per member are much higher in Latin America than in such countries as Germany, Japan and the United States (Figure 7.6).[10] Nevertheless, the figures for Chile, which are unquestionably the highest in the region, suggest that such costs could be even higher following structural reforms.

NATURE OF THE REFORMS

During the 1990s, five countries have introduced substantial reforms in their pension systems to resolve problems of disparate arrangements, low coverage, inequalities and financial imbalances. The centerpiece has been the establishment of incentives, such as a close connection between benefits and contributions, and the creation of various competition mechanisms to help cut down evasion, rationalize pension spending, and improve administrative and financial decision-making. Although the Chilean reform has been notably influential in all cases, the reforms have generally steered away from the type of system that is based solely on individual capitalization accounts. The mixed solutions that have been adopted have addressed the fiscal, financial and political constraints that ultimately lead to replacing the pay-as-you-go system with one of individual capitalization accounts.

In individual capitalization account systems, each worker contributes a fixed percentage of his or her income, most of which is set aside to form a capitalization fund that together with its financial yields will at retirement determine the value of the individual pension. The fraction of individual contributions that is not capitalized is set aside to cover administrative costs and premiums for group insurance policies to protect all the

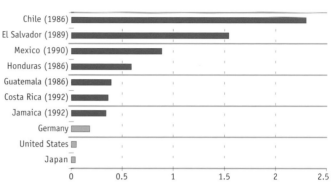

FIGURE 7.6

Administrative Costs by Contributor

(Percent of per capita income)

Source: World Bank (1994).

enrolled or their survivors against risks of disability or death before retirement. The amount of the pension is determined by the yield that the managing agencies are able to obtain for the mutual fund made up of all individual savings; those savings are invested in fixed yield securities, shares and other financial instruments within the limits set by the government. With real long-term yields of around 4 percent and contributions of 10 percent (net with administration and insurance), it is possible to achieve pensions equivalent to 65 percent of incomes at age 65 years and after 35 years of contributions. The pensions may adopt either the form of income for life purchased from insurance companies with the yield from the savings, or the form of collective insurance policies in the event of disability or survival. Additionally, there may be pensions with regular payments scheduled as agreed upon at retirement directly between the pensioner and the agency managing the pension fund.

Because this individual capitalization account system is a form of forced saving imposed by public decision, adopting it inevitably requires limiting the elements of risk. First, the administrative agencies and the funds that they manage should be separate entities in which the capitalization of the former operates as an initial guarantee in the event of bankruptcy or insufficient yield.

---

[10] World Bank (1994).

Second, the operations of fund management bodies must be carefully regulated and supervised so as to avoid excessive and systemic risks and guarantee participants a minimum yield. Finally, in some countries participants enjoy some further guarantee that they will receive a minimum pension once they complete a period of participation or that they will be able to return to the public pension system with defined benefits if they find them more attractive.

When the individual capitalization account system was introduced in Chile, it was anticipated that the old system of defined benefits would be dismantled except for the provision of minimal pensions welfare benefits. At the time of the reform, workers were obliged to definitively choose one system or the other, without any possibility of future enrollment in or return to the defined benefit system. In most of the countries that have established individual capitalization account systems in the 1990s, however, the intention has not been to definitively dismantle the old system. It has been maintained as one enrollment option, as the basis for a dual pension system, or as a means for guaranteeing previously existing benefits (Table 7.7).

Under the reforms in Peru (1993) and Colombia (1994), current workers, and new entrants into the labor market in the case of Colombia, have the option of choosing between the two systems. Furthermore, in Colombia they are allowed to transfer from one system to another during their work life (with a limit on the number of times or the frequency). In these two cases, there is thus a principle of competition rather than complementarity between the public and private pillars. In Argentina (1994) and Uruguay (1996), on the other hand, there is complementarity between the public system with defined benefits and the new private pension funds. The public system is responsible for providing a basic pension for all those enrolled and receives basic contributions from all workers. Above and beyond the basic contribution, workers in Argentina must make an ad-

ditional contribution that may be assigned to the public or private pillar, depending on one's preference. In Uruguay, the basic contribution rises to an upper income limit, above which additional contributions are assigned exclusively to the private pillar. However, workers with incomes below that upper limit have the option of making a portion of their contributions into the individual capitalization account system. In the case of Mexico (1997), the public system retains only a supplementary relationship to the private system. The public system stops receiving contributions but remains as a guarantor of current pension benefits for those who at retirement make that option. However, the entire contribution of those participating will not be apportioned to the new private funds, because there remains a public fund for financing housing which contributes to paying individual pensions.

One of the crucial problems in the transition from the old to the new systems is recognizing the contributions or the rights acquired by workers in the public system who want or must transfer to the individual account system. In Chile, recognition bonds reflecting approximately the value of past contributions were used, and they went on to become part of the individual capitalization funds in the Pension Fund Administrators (PFAs). Peru and Colombia chose similar options, but due to the lack of detailed information on contributions, Peru adopted a recognition formula based on how long the person had been participating and his or her salary during the final year. In Colombia, a complex formula was set up to calculate the actuarial value of the pension owed to each active contributor at the time of transfer to the new system. Although theoretically consistent with the principle of recognizing acquired rights (which are much greater than contributions made), this procedure has in practice been difficult to implement for individuals. This has slowed the transition process and weakened the conditions of competition between the new private pension funds and the former government social se-

Table 7.7   Comparison of Pension Reforms

	Chile 1981	Peru 1993	Colombia 1994	Argentina 1994	Uruguay 1996	Mexico 1997
Nature of the reform	Public defined benefit (PAYG) changed to private defined contribution (all workers)	Public PAYG changed to choice between public PAYG and private defined contribution	Public PAYG changed to choice between public PAYG and private defined contribution	Public split into public PAYG and private defined contribution	Public split into public PAYG and private defined contribution	Public defined benefit changed to private defined contribution (for private workers only)
What role for public pillar?	Minimum pension guarantee. Social assistance	Social assistance	Minimum pension guarantee. Social assistance	Flat and minimum pension	Basic pension for all	Minimum pension guarantee. Social assistance
Relation between pillars	Subsidiary public pillar	Competitive	Competitive	Complementary	Complementary	Subsidiary public pillar
Transition arrangements						
What happens to old system?	Phased out	Continues with changes	Continues with changes	Continues with changes	Continues with changes	Eliminated[j]
Is current labor force allowed to remain in old scheme?	Yes	Yes[b]	Yes	Yes	Yes	No
Is new system mandatory for new labor force entrants?	Yes	Yes	No	No	For high wage workers only	Yes
Can workers switch back to public system after entering AFP?	No	No	Yes, every three years	Yes, for two years	No	No[j]
Recognition bonds	Yes	Yes	Yes[d]	Yes[f]	No	No[j,k]
How are they calculated?	Based on contributions plus a real return	Based on contributions and last year's earnings	Complex formula reflecting present value of acquired rights	Compensatory pension is based on years of contribution and last 10 year's earnings		
Contributions (%)						
Total contribution						
Before reform	18.8 - 20.7[a]	9[c]	8	27	27.5	15.5
- paid by employer		6[c]	5.33	16	14.5	13
- paid by employee	18.8 - 20.7[a]	3[c]	2.67	11	13	2.1
- paid by government						0.4
After reform	13	13.3	13.5 - 14.5[e]	27	27.5[h] 15[i]	16.5 - 21.0[m]
- paid by employer			10.125	16	12.5[h] 0[i]	12
- paid by employee	13	13.3	3.375 - 4.375[e]	11	15	2.1
- paid by government						1.4 - 5.9
Total contribution rate for new system (%)						
Available for old age annuity	10	10	10	8	11.5[h]	6.5 + 5.0 - NP$1/day
Disability/survivors/administrative	3	2.3	3.5	3	3.5[h]	4
Public pillar and social assistance	General revenues	1	1	16[g]	27.5[i]	General revenues
Minimum period of contributions						
Before reform	10 years (salaried employees) or 800-520 weeks (men/women wage earners)	15/13 years (male/female), 5 years for minimum benefits	500 weeks	20 years (or 10 years for reduced pension)	30 years (or 10 years for reduced pension)	500 weeks
After reform (in the public system)		20 years for those in the public system	1000 weeks	30 years	35 years	25 years

	Chile 1981	Peru 1993	Colombia 1994	Argentina 1994	Uruguay 1996	Mexico 1997
Benefits						
Pension age -before reform		60-55 (men/women) or after 30 years of coverage (men) or at age 50 after 25 years of coverage (women)	60-55 (men/women)	60-55 (men/women)	60-55 (men/women), or 70-65 for reduced pension	65
- after reform	65-60 (men/women)	65-60 (men/women) for all (since 1995)	62-57 (effective in 2014) for the public system	62-57 (men/women) in 1995, 63-58 in 1996, 64-59 in 1998 and 65-60 in 2001	60 (men and women) in the first pillar, 65 in the second	65
Minimum pension						
Before reform		3 times the minimum wage	Yes, minimum wage	Yes	Yes, 85% of minimum wage	100% of current minimum wage, 2 times the nominal contributions to the housing fund and contributions and returns to the personal savings
After reform	Yes	Idem for those in the public system; no minimum in the new system	Yes, common for both systems	Flat benefit and higher minimum	Yes, Ur$550 (provided by the public pillar)	100% of real minimum wage as of the end of 1996
Wage base for pensions						
Before reform		Highest 3 of last 5 years	Last 3 years	Highest 3 of last 10 years (or last 5 years for a reduced pension)	Last 3 years	Last 250 weeks
After reform	Last 5 years	Indexed average earnings of last 36-60 months (depending inversely on years of contribution)	Last 10 years	Last 10 years	Last 10 years	Last 250 weeks
Replacement ratio (% of base wage)						
Before reform		50-80	45-90	70-82 (60 if reduced pension)	55-75 (50-80 if reduced pension)	35-100 or between 1 and 6 minimum wages
After reform in the public pillar	50-70	50-100	65-85 in the old system (after 23 years of contributions)	In the public pillar: 25.5 for 30 years of service + 25 as flat benefit. In the private pillar: 25 as flat benefit plus returns	50-52.5 at the age of 60, up to 75 for later retirement	35-100 or between 1 and 6 minimum wages
Financial regulations applying to private funds (%)						
Maximum percentage of portfolio allowed in:						
Domestic equities	37	30	30	35		To be decided
Foreign equities	9	5	10	10		Not currently permitted
Government bonds in 1994	45	25	50	50		To be decided
Minimum return?	Yes, relative to the system	Yes, relative to the system	Yes, relative to the system	Yes, relative to the system		To be decided

a Current contribution for those who stayed in the old system.
b Workers must decide by 1998.
c Also applies to those in the public system after the reform.
d Workers with fewer than 150 weeks of contributions are not eligible for a recognition bond.
e Additional point to be paid by workers earning more than four minimum wages. The rate shown is for 1996 and following years. The contribution rate will increase gradually between 1994 and 1996.
f Compensatory pension is paid upon retirement, not as a bond. The value is based on years of contribution and last 10 years' earnings.
g This is paid by the employer.
h For the first Ur$5,000 of wages (approx. US$728).
i For wages in excess of Ur$5,000.
j Contributions to the old system cease on December 31, 1996. Transition workers can choose at retirement between the benefits of the old PAYG scheme or the private pensions plan.
k Contributions to individual saving accounts at Central Bank and housing fund are portable at retirement.
m Including NP$1/day,which corresponds to between 1 and 5.5 percent of wages.

curity agency. In Argentina, instead of issuing bonds, the decision was made to guarantee a compensatory pension payable at retirement based on years of contribution and income during the most recent 10 years. In Uruguay, where the public and private pillars work together to pay pensions, the implicit acknowledgment of contributions and rights is the basic pension; the same is true in Argentina for payment of the basic benefit. Bonds will not be issued in Mexico either, but there is an acknowledgment of acquired rights by the fact that the workers can opt for their current benefits by returning to the public system at retirement. Furthermore, workers will also be credited for their individual funds accumulated in the public fund for financing housing and in their savings accounts in the Central Bank, which were complementary pension financing mechanisms dating from before the 1997 reform (the first of which will continue to operate and receive contributions).

CORRECTING IMBALANCES BETWEEN CONTRIBUTIONS AND BENEFITS

Since the main weakness of all earlier pension systems was the imbalance between contributions and benefits, major reforms have been introduced in both areas. Whereas reducing contributions in Chile gave rise to high fiscal costs that the government decided to assume, the previously existing contribution rates affected by the reforms of the 1990s have been raised or at the very least maintained. In Peru and Colombia, contributions rose from 9 percent and 8 percent, respectively, to 13.3 percent and 13.5 percent after the reform. In Peru, it was decided to maintain the previous contribution rate (and its distribution between worker and company) for those workers who decide to remain in the public system, whereas workers participating in the individual capitalization account system would be responsible for paying the entire new rate. To prevent that from affecting the real net income of workers, wages were adjusted by 13.5 percent for those workers who decide to trans-

fer to the individual capitalization account system. Nevertheless, the differential in contributions between the two systems until mid-1995 was a distortion that affected decisions to participate, since the costs between the two systems differed for both workers and the company. In Colombia, a single contribution rate was set for all workers, no matter which system they chose, and employers were made responsible for three-quarters of the contribution and the worker for the remainder. For distributional reasons, workers who receive over four times the minimum wage must pay an additional percentage point into the public system. For those choosing the private system, ten percentage points are set aside to build up the capitalization fund, and the remainder is designated for disability and survivor insurance and administrative expenses for the funds. In Peru, one percentage point of contributions by private system participants is assigned to the public pillar, 10 percent goes to capitalization, and 2.3 percent goes to insurance and administration.

In Argentina and Uruguay, the pre-reform basic contribution rates of 27 percent and 27.5 percent, respectively, did not allow any increase. These rates were maintained, along with their distribution between workers and employers in the case of Argentina, while in Uruguay a portion of the employer's contribution was passed to the worker. Due to the complementarity between the public and private pillars in these two countries, at least a portion of the contributions is allotted to the public sector: 16 percentage points in Argentina, and in principle the entire contribution up to a top salary of Ur$5,000 in Uruguay (approximately US$728). The 11 remaining percentage points of the contribution in Argentina can be assigned to the public or private pillar, whichever suits the worker in terms of benefits. If the choice is for the private plan, eight of the 11 points go into forming the individual capitalization amount and three points are assigned to insurance and administration. In Uruguay, the contributions on income above the previously mentioned upper limit have a rate of 15 percent, which is assigned entirely to private funds (11.5 percentage points of which go into capitalization). On the other hand, 7.5 percent of the contribution of workers earning less than the top salary can be placed in private funds, with the further incentive that for those who choose this option, the base salary for calculating the basic pension in the contribution-based system is raised by 50 percent.

In Mexico, the total contribution rose from 15.5 percent to a range of 16.5 to 21 percent, depending on pay level. Prior to pension reform, 8.5 percentage points went into the government system: 4.5 points were channeled into pension programs and the rest went to medical insurance for pensioners and to disability and life insurance. Another 5 points went to individual accounts in the government housing fund and the remaining 2 points went into individual savings accounts in the Central Bank, both in order to form an individual fund for future pension payments. In addition to already existing payments, the new system includes a government contribution of N$1 per day, which is equivalent to a contribution of from 1 percent to 5.5 percent, depending on the worker's income level. The individual capitalization accounts are to be sustained with the 4.5 percentage points that are used to finance public system pensions, plus the two points that go to individual capitalization accounts at the Central Bank, plus the government contribution of N$1 per day. The five points going into the housing fund will remain, and the four remaining points set aside for covering disability, survivors' benefits, and health care for pensioners.

Under previous arrangements, contributions were low and there were few incentives to make regular contributions, since the minimum payment periods required for receiving benefits were very short. To correct this situation, those minimum periods have been significantly increased in all the reforms for those workers who want to remain in the public system or become eligible for the government guaranteed basic or minimum pension. These periods were raised by approximately five years in Peru, Colombia and Uruguay, 10 years in Argentina, and 15 years in Mexico.

The parameters that determine the benefits in public systems have also been modified under the recent pension reforms in order to lessen the imbalance with contributions. Furthermore, in most reforms, limits have been introduced on survivor's benefits issued to the heirs of pensioners, on the minimum conditions required for enjoying disability pensions, and on arrangements for complementary assistance benefits.

With the exception of Mexico, where the retirement age prior to the reform had already been set at 65 years with no difference between men and women, the other countries had retirement ages of 60 years for men and 55 for women. Given life expectancies upon arrival at these ages, it would seem that people could enjoy pensions for periods close to, or even longer than, their work life, especially in the case of women. Nevertheless, for political reasons it has proven difficult to make the decision to raise the age and make it equal for men and women. Peru decided to raise retirement ages by five years, initially only for those who opted for the private pension system and since mid-1995 for all. In Colombia, only in the year 2014 would the ages for those enrolled in the public system be raised by two years, while in the private system the option of retiring at a younger age was left open, provided that the sums accrued would assure a pension of over 1.1 minimum wages. Argentina introduced gradual increases in ages in order to reach 65 years for men and 60 years for women in the year 2001. In Uruguay, retirement ages were brought into line for both sexes at 60 years in order to receive the benefits from the basic pillar.

As noted, one of the causes of imbalance between benefits and contributions in the traditional public systems in Latin America has been the wage base used to define what pensions are worth. Because usually only the most recent years count, there are incentives for underdeclaring wages, except during these final years, when the incentive runs the other way. Nevertheless, in some countries, wage bases during these years have been taken at their face values, without correcting for inflation, thereby arbitrarily reducing pension benefits. In order to thoroughly correct these flaws, the wage base should reflect real pay throughout the period of participation in the system. Unfortunately, the lack of accurate records undermines such a solution and has forced all countries to adopt partial solutions. In Peru and Colombia, an inflation correction was introduced into the calculation of wage bases, and in Colombia, Argentina and Uruguay the base period was extended. In order to reward remaining in the contribution-based system, Peru adopted shorter base periods for participants with more seniority in the system. In Mexico, because the Constitution protects rights acquired by the workers, no change was made in conditions for access to pensions in the public system for workers already enrolled.

The parameters determining the relationship between the pension amount and wage base have been modified under most reforms to reduce the financial imbalances of the contribution-based systems. The most notable change took place in Argentina, where replacement rates of between 70 percent and 82 percent were reduced to around 50 percent. However, in practice the change was less substantial, because prior to the reform the delays and difficulties in obtaining pensions meant that replacement rates were much lower.

Since replacement rates are very rarely 100 percent, the contribution-based systems always have provisions for assuring that pensions are above a minimum as a means for protecting very low-income workers (provided that they have contributed at least for a certain number of years). The minimum pensions may be extended to those enrolled in the individual capitalization account system, in which case the public pillar acts as a guarantee that it will be paid. This arrangement, which was originally adopted in Chile, has also been established in the recent reforms in Colombia and Mexico. Furthermore, workers in transition in Mexico are guaranteed that at retirement they will receive double the value of their contributions to the housing fund and their contributions to individual capitalization accounts in the Central Bank with a real yield of 2 percent. In both countries, the minimum pension has been maintained at its previous real value (equal to one minimum wage). In Peru, the minimum pension equivalent to three minimum wages was maintained but only for those enrolled in the public system. In Argentina and Uruguay, due to the complementarity between the public and private columns, minimum pensions are determined by the basic benefits granted by the public pillar.

PROBLEMS AND PROSPECTS

Above the government-guaranteed minimum, replacement rates in the individual capitalization account systems depend on the amounts accumulated in individual accounts up to the moment of retirement, and the life expectancy situation of the pensioner and his or her heirs. In the new pension systems in Peru, Colombia and Argentina, where the individual capitalization account systems are not obligatory, participation of workers in one system or the other depends crucially on which offers them a higher replacement rate. A comparison of the situations in Colombia and Argentina illustrates the complexities and implications of that choice. In Colombia, individual capitalization account system pensions tend to be attractive only for men who are under 25 at the time of decision, assuming that they have not contributed to the public system for more than five years and will have stable work lives, and based on real yields of 5 percent or more in the capitalization system. The public system is unquestionably more attractive for those currently participating who are over 40 (men) or 35 (women), because they still enjoy the earlier retirement ages. The public system is also more attractive to low-income workers because the guarantees of the minimum pension under this system require shorter contribution periods. Hence, choosing between the two systems inevitably leads to a problem of adverse selection, which will further weaken the financial situation of Colombia's public system. In Argentina, remaining exclusively with the public pillar tends to be more attractive to men starting at age 47 and for women at age 40, assuming a real yield in the funds of 5 percent and that the conditions for obtaining basic benefits are met. Thus, the individual capitalization account system in Argentina is more attractive for a broader range of young people than in Colombia. The public pillar grants some basic benefits for everyone, although the higher retirement ages as compared with Colombia and greater incentives for remaining in the contribution system also have a bearing. The Uruguayan system stands between the Colombian and the Argentine: men and women under 36 find it advantageous to be included in the individual capitalization account system, as will high-income people over 40.

The possibilities of choosing (wholly or partially) between the two systems offered by the new pension systems in Peru, Colombia, Argentina and Uruguay may also be affected by the perception that workers have of risks presented by one or the other. Although the public system in principle guarantees the benefits, workers may have good reasons for being skeptical of that guarantee, either from experience or because of a lack of confidence in the financial prospects of the guarantor agency. In saving systems, there is the risk of low or negative real yields and the possibility of bankruptcy stemming from wrong financial decisions, inefficiency or improper handling by the entities managing the funds. For these reasons, all the reforms have made certain that the capital of the management entities is independent of the funds capitalized by the workers and expert supervision systems have been set up. In addition, ceilings have been placed on the investments that can be made in different kinds of assets, and the minimum yields that must be achieved periodically have been set for the funds accumulated. Partly for reasons of risk, but primarily because of nationalistic political pressures, in Uruguay and Mexico the funds may not be invested outside the country.

Investment ceilings for stocks and other securities entailing risk have usually been set at very low levels, largely due to the small size of such financial markets and the fact that in some countries these markets are not very transparent. These requirements have been a problematic area in the process of implementing the reforms because they have entered into conflict with the aim of broadening the capital market.

Moreover, when investment ceilings are combined with the requirement of short-term minimum yields for the average of the funds, the effect has been that all the funds end up structuring their portfolios in a similar manner, with the risks of destabilizing the investment market for some securities, and creating common risks for the entire system. These problems have been mitigated by allowing the minimum yields to be calculated as averages over several fiscal periods, and in some countries by establishing procedures that allow the funds to compensate within certain limits for over- or underachievement of yields. This aims to correct the problem arising from the fact that minimum yield requirements are in principle asymmetrical, since they penalize the capital of the management agency when the required minimums are not met, but they do not allow it to make up those losses when extraordinary earnings are achieved.

On the other hand, the need to finance the fiscal cash deficit, which is sometimes increased by the pension reforms themselves, means that government securities tend to absorb a high proportion of the total investments of the funds. In Uruguay, from the beginning, 80 percent of the portfolio of capitalization funds is expected to go into government bonds. However, the experience of Chile shows that portfolio diversification, including the possibility of investing outside the country, can take place gradually. To the extent that the initial investment opportunities constrain the amount of capital built up by the funds, it becomes more likely that properly regulated new investments will be accepted, and that new investment alternatives will be created that take advantage of the stability and long periods of capital built up in the funds. Hence, there is a process of gradually adapting pension fund investment regulations, and extending, diversifying and strengthening the capital market. There is no need for previous markets to have existed in order for the funds begin to operate, although that can facilitate the process, especially since it can reduce the degree of uncertainty and instability of the regulations. Development of fund investment possibilities also depends on the solidity of other institutions in the financial market and on the quality of supervision. Under current conditions of the financial systems in Argentina, Mexico and Uruguay, this is one of the most difficult challenges facing the pension reform process.

Despite these difficulties, the pension funds offer great potential for financial saving over the medium run. With very conservative assumptions on the number of workers who will transfer to the funds, it is estimated that in Colombia the cumulative reserves of the funds will be over 3 percent of GDP by the year 2000, 11 percent ten years later, and 27 percent by 2025. In Mexico and Uruguay the process will be slower. In Mexico by the year 2000, the funds accumulated in individual accounts will barely be 0.7 percent of GDP, and of this sum only 0.5 percent will be in the retirement accounts of the funds. Ten years later, however, these indices will rise to 7.4 percent and 4.8 percent, respectively, and by 2025 they will be 27.3 percent and 18.5 percent. In Uruguay, it is estimated that the investment resources of the pension funds will be 2.5 percent of GDP in the year 2000, 10.5 percent by 2010, and 27.6 percent by the year 2025. The pace of the accumulation of reserves in all these cases is slower than it has been in Chile, where the cumulative reserves are already

40 percent of GDP, and it is estimated that they will reach their maximum of over 50 percent of GDP in the next decade. In the other countries, however, transition processes are slower and funds in individual capitalization accounts will not completely replace the contribution-based systems, since they will either compete with or complement one another (Table 7.8).

The fiscal costs of pension reforms have been the subject of considerable debate in all countries. In part the discussion has reflected a methodological confusion between the concepts of cash deficit and actuarial deficit. The reformed public systems were generating growing actuarial deficits that did not show up as cash deficits, because they were being covered by the contributions of future retirees. In some instances, when the reforms were made, there was a partial reduction in the rate of increase of the current actuarial deficits or those expected in the future, thanks to the lowering of the imbalance between benefits and contributions of the systems. In other instances, the decision was made to begin to actually pay those actuarial deficits and the debts caused by them, thereby increasing cash deficits.

Such being the case, what is usually regarded as the fiscal cost of the reforms is in fact the change in the cash deficit. In Chile, where the actuarial value of the pension debts represented 126 percent of GDP, a deficit arose starting at 3.2 percent of GDP in 1982 and reaching a maximum of 4.8 percent of GDP in 1991. In order to cover it, surpluses were created elsewhere in the public sector partly as a result of greater saving and partly thanks to large one-time revenues from privatizations. Once the reform had been carried out, the creation of new actuarial deficits halted, except for workers in transition who decided at that point to remain in the public system. In subsequent pension reforms, the starting point has been actuarial deficits similar to, or lower than, those of Chile: 141 percent of GDP for the Mexican social security agency, and 72.5 percent in the case of Colombia (including government workers cov-

Table 7.8	Projections of Savings Accumulated in Individual Accounts

(Percent of GDP)

Year of Reform	Chile 1981	Colombia 1994	Uruguay 1996	Mexico, 1997 Total	Mexico, 1997 Pension Funds
1981	0.9				
1985	10.9				
1990	26.5				
1995	41.5	0.4		0.1[a]	0.0[a]
2000	48.5	3.1	2.5	0.7	0.5
2005	52.5	6.9	6.0	3.2	2.1
2010	52.8	11.5	10.5	7.4	4.8
2015	51.6	16.6	15.7	13.0	8.6
2020	48.4	22.4	21.4	19.7	13.2
2025	44.7	27.1	27.6	27.3	18.5

[a]Estimate for 1997.
Sources: Chile: Mujica (1994, p. 138, alternative 1); Colombia: Lora and Helmsdorff (1995, p. 98, simulation 4); Uruguay: Márquez (1996); Mexico: World Bank estimates.

ered by the reform). Contrary to what happened in Chile, however, deficits have sometimes been allowed to continue to grow, and in all instances transition systems have been adopted in which deficits are paid over a more protracted period of time.

The fiscal (cash) costs arising from the recent reforms range from 1 percent to 3 percent of GDP. In Colombia, the deficit in the first year was calculated to be 0.9 percent of GDP and is expected to reach a maximum of 2.6 percent of GDP by 2013, and then to decline very gradually to 1.5 percent of GDP by 2025, disappearing around the year 2060. In Mexico, it is estimated that the fiscal cost of the reform will be around 1 percent of GDP for several decades at least, primarily as a result of benefits that will continued to be paid to workers in transition who stop contributing to the system. In Uruguay, thanks to the reform, the benefits paid by the contribution-based system will grow more slowly than under the old system. The short-term projections indicate that had there been no reform, total spending (excluding health and maternity benefits) by the year 2005 would have reached 11.4 percent of GDP, whereas with the reform that spending will be 10.9 percent of GDP. Nevertheless, the reform

further reduced the contributions that the contribution-based system will receive, and thus the deficit that will have to be covered with fiscal transfers will rise from 2.1 percent to 2.7 percent of GDP by the year 2000, and from 1.2 percent to 1.8 percent of GDP by 2005. Such being the case, the recent pension reforms have not completely resolved the medium-term financial imbalances of the contribution-based systems, so much so that in some countries the need for further reforms is beginning to be debated. Nevertheless, due to the accumulation of financial savings in the funds of the individual capitalization accounts, the fiscal costs of the reforms will be able to be partially or totally covered without generating macroeconomic imbalances. Indeed, as happened in Chile, the explicit financing of pension deficits will make public financing more disciplined, helping to strengthen overall savings rates.

Concern for the contribution-based systems is not limited to their financial viability but extends to their administrative viability as well. Indeed, in some cases the reforms have heightened management problems, because the public agencies of the contribution-based system have been assigned more complex tasks during the transition process. In particular, there is the problem of establishing the amounts of past contributions by participants in order to issue recognition bonds (Peru, Colombia), or in order to specify the benefits that they could receive in the contribution-based system as a complement or alternative to the private system (Uruguay and Argentina in the former case, Mexico in the latter). In Mexico, there also remains the problem of introducing changes into the housing financing agency that will continue to receive individual contributions in order to reach the yields required to make the new pension system viable. The transparency with which these tasks are performed will be decisive for the success of the reform. The reform could be undermined by the legacy of inadequate management practices that these agencies are inheriting and the additional pressures to which they will be subjected in some cases as a result of lower revenues from contributions.

Nor is there yet a solution to the financial and administrative problems of the special pension systems that various groups of public employees, teachers and members of the armed forces enjoy in almost all countries. These problems are especially serious in Peru, Colombia and Mexico. The problem is less severe in Uruguay, where the main public system agency covers public employees and teachers. In this case, nevertheless, it will be necessary to restructure the quasi-official funds that grant workers in certain professions very favorable pension conditions that are hard to fit into the overall pension framework and that are partly financed with specific taxes that cause distortions and are hard to justify. One problem still to be confronted in Mexico is that of occupational pension systems, which cover around 20 percent of the labor force, operate within a flawed regulatory environment, and offer their members only partial opportunities to transfer.

Alesina, Alberto, and Allen Drazen. 1991. Why Are Stabilizations Delayed? *American Economic Review* 81(5): 1170-88.

Bentolila, Samuel. 1992. The Macroeconomic Impact of Flexible Labor Contracts, with an Application to Spain. *European Economic Review* 36: 1013-53.

Bentolila, Samuel, and Juna J. Dolado. 1994. Labour Flexibility and Wages: Lessons from Spain. *Economic Policy* 18 (April): 55-97.

Bour, Juan Luis. 1996. Procesos de Reforma del Mercado de Trabajo en la Argentina. FIEL, Buenos Aires. Unpublished.

Calvo, Guillermo. 1989. Incredible Reforms. In *Debt, Stabilization and Development*, eds. J. Braga de Macedo, G. Calvo, P. Kouri, and R. Findlay. Oxford: Basil Blackwell.

Clutterbuck, David. 1991. *Going Private*. London: Mercury Books.

Cottani, Joaquin A., and Gustavo C. Demarco. 1996. The Shift to a Funded Social Security System: The Case of Argentina. NBER Social Security Project, Washington, D.C. Unpublished.

Cox-Edwards, Alejandra. 1993. *Labor Market Legislation in Latin America and the Caribbean*. Report No. 31, Latin America and the Caribbean Technical Department, Regional Studies Program, World Bank.

Cukierman, Alex. 1992. *Central Bank Strategy, Credibility, and Independence: Theory and Evidence*. Cambridge, Mass.: MIT Press.

Desai, P. 1995. Beyond Shock Therapy. *Journal of Democracy* 6 (no. 2, April).

Dewatripont, M., and G. Roland. 1992a. Economic Reform and Dynamic Political Constraints. *Review of Economic Studies* 59: 703-30.

——————. 1992b. The Virtues of Gradualism in the Transition to a Market Economy. *Economic Journal* 102: 291-300.

——————. 1994. The Design of Reform Packages under Uncertainty. ECARE, Brussels. Unpublished.

Díaz-Alejandro, Carlos. 1985. Good-Bye Financial Repression, Hello Financial Crash, *Journal of Development Economics* 18: 1-24.

Drazen, Allan and V. Grilli. 1993. The Benefits of Crises for Economic Reforms, *American Economic Review* 83 (June).

Easterly, William R., and Deborah L. Wetzel. 1989. *Policy Determinants of Growth: Survey of Theory and Evidence*. PPR Working Paper 343, World Bank, Washington, D.C.

Edwards, Sebastian. 1995. *Crisis and Reform in Latin America*. Oxford: Oxford University Press.

——————. 1992. *The Sequencing of Structural Adjustment and Stabilization*. International Center for Economic Growth Occasional Paper 34, San Francisco.

—————————. 1984. *The Order of Liberalization of the External Sector in Developing Countries*. Princeton Essays in International Finance (no. 156, December).

Edwards, Sebastian, and Sweder Van Wijnbergen. 1986. Welfare Effects of Trade and Capital Market Liberalization. *International Economic Review* (February).

Fernández, R., and D. Rodrik. 1991. Resistance to Reform: Status Quo Bias in the Presence of Individual-Specific Uncertainty. *American Economic Review* (December).

Freeman, Richard B. 1993. *Labor Market Institutions and Policies: Help or Hindrance to Economic Development*. World Bank Economic Review, Proceedings of 1992 Conference on Development Economics: 117-44.

Galal, Ahmed, Leroy Jones, Pankaj Tandon, and Ingo Vogelsang. 1994. *Welfare Consequences of Selling Public Enterprises*. Oxford: Oxford University Press.

Gavin, Michael. 1993. Unemployment and the Economics of Gradualist Reform. Columbia University. Unpublished.

Ghani, Ejaz. 1992. *How Financial Markets Affect Long-Run Growth: A Cross-Country Study*. PRE Working Paper 843, World Bank, Washington, D.C.

Harberger, A. 1993. Ely Lecture. *American Economic Review*.

Hausmann, Ricardo, and Michael Gavin. 1995. The Roots of Banking Crises: The Macroeconomic Context. Presented at the IDB Conference on Banking Crises in Latin America, October 6-7, 1995, Washington, D.C.

Ito, Takaoshi and Anne O. Krueger, eds. 1992. *The Political Economy of Tax Reform*. Chicago and London: The University of Chicago Press.

Inter-American Development Bank 1995. *Reforma de la Administración Tributaria en América Latina*. Washington, D.C.: Inter-American Development Bank.

International Monetary Fund. 1993. *International Capital Markets*. Washington, D.C.: International Monetary Fund.

Jimeno, Juan F., and Luis Toharia. 1993. The Effects of Fixed Term Employment on Wages: Theory and Evidence from Spain. *Investigaciones Económicas* 18 (no. 3, September): 475-94.

Kikeri, Sunita, John Nellis, and Mary Shirley. 1992. *Privatization: The Lessons of Experience*. Washington, D.C.: World Bank.

King, Robert, and Ross Levine. 1992. *Financial Indicators and Growth in A Cross Section of Countries*. PRE Working Paper 819, World Bank, Washington, D.C.

—————————.1993. Finance and Growth: Schumpeter Might be Right. *Quarterly Journal of Economics* 108 (3): 717-37.

Labán, Raúl, and Federico Sturzenegger. 1994. Fiscal Conservatism as a Response to the Debt Crisis. *Journal of Development of Economics* 45.

—————————.1992. Distributional Conflict, Financial Adaptation and Delayed Stabilization. UCLA. Unpublished.

López-de-Silanes, Florencio. 1994. Determinants of Privatization Prices. Harvard University. Unpublished.

Lora, Eduardo, and Loredana Helmsdorff. 1995. *El Futuro de la Reforma Pensional.* Bogota: Fedesarrollo-Asofondos.

Lora, Eduardo, and Marta Luz Henao. 1995. Efectos económicos y sociales de la legislación laboral. *Coyuntura Social* 13: 47-68.

Lustig, Nora, and Darryl McLeod. 1996. Minimum Wages and Poverty in Developing Countries: Some Empirical Evidence. *International Economics* 125 (June).

Márquez, Gustavo. 1996. The Uruguay Pension Reform of 1995: An Assessment. Inter-American Development Bank, Washington, D.C. Unpublished.

—————. 1995. *Reforming the Labor Market in a Liberalized Economy.* Washington, D.C.: Inter-American Development Bank.

Martinelli, C., and M. Tommasi. 1993. *Sequencing of Economic Reforms in the Presence of Political Constraints.* IRIS Report #100, University of Maryland.

McKinnon, Ronald. 1991. *The Order of Economic Liberalization.* Baltimore: Johns Hopkins University Press.

—————. 1973. *Money and Capital in Economic Development.* Washington, D.C.: The Brookings Institution.

McLure, Charles. 1992. *The Political Economy of Tax Reforms and Their Implications for Interdependence: United States. The Political Economy of Tax Reform.* Chicago and London: The University of Chicago Press.

Mondino, F. Sturzenegger, and M. Tommasi. 1993. Recurrent High Inflation and Stabilization: A Dynamic Game. UCLA. Unpublished.

Mouchard Ramirez, Augusto. 1995. Sistema Privado de Pensiones en el Perú, 1995. Características, Evaluación y Posibilidades. Superintendencia de Administradora de Fondos de Pensiones (AFP), Lima. Unpublished.

Mujica, Patricio. 1994. The Chilean Experience. In *Social Security Reforms in Latin America,* ed. Francisco E. Barreto de Oliveira. Washington, D.C.: Inter-American Development Bank.

Mussa, Michael. 1982. Government Policy and the Adjustment Process. In *Import Competition and Response,* Jagdish Bhagwati. Chicago: University of Chicago Press.

Naim, Moises. 1994. Latin America: The Second Stage of Reform. *Journal of Democracy* 5 (no.4, October).

Nitsch, Manfred, and Helmut Scwarzer. 1995. *Recent Development in Financing Social Security in Latin America.* Berlin: Lateinamerika-Institut Freie Universität Berlin.

Perktold, J., and M. Tommasi. 1994. Ideas, State Capacity and Policy Variability: The Shift to Markets as the Outcome of a Learning Process. UCLA. Unpublished.

Perotti, Roberto. 1993. Increasing Returns to Scale. Politics and the Timing of Stabilization. Columbia University. Unpublished.

Perry, Guillermo, and Ana María Herrera. 1994. *Public Finances, Stabilization and Structural Reform in Latin America.* Washington, D.C.: Inter-American Development Bank.

Pita, Claudino. 1993. *La reforma tributaria en América Latina en la década de los años ochenta.* Working Paper Series No. 164, Department of Economic and Social Development, Inter-American Development Bank, Washington, D.C.

Rains, Luisa, Martín, and Jorge Febres. 1996. *Reformas Recientes en la Política Tributaria en América Latina*. VII Seminario Regional de Política Fiscal, CEPAL.

Rodrik, D. 1996. Understanding Economic Policy Reform. *Journal of Economic Literature* 34: 9- 41.

——————.1989. Promises, Promises: Credible Policy Reform via Signalling. *The Economic Journal* 99: 756-72.

Roubini, Nouriel, and Xavier Sala-I-Martin. 1991. *Financial Development, the Trade Regime, and Economic Growth*. National Bureau of Economic Research Working Paper 3876, Cambridge, Mass.

Sachs, Jeffrey. 1994. The Political Challenge of Economic Transition: The Case of Poland. Unpublished.

Sader, Frank. 1993. *Privatizing Public Enterprises and Foreign Investment in Developing Countries, 1988-93*. Foreign Investment Advisory Service Occasional Paper 5, World Bank, Washington, D.C.

Schmidt-Hebbel, Klaus. 1995. *Colombia's Pension Reform: Fiscal and Macroeconomic Effects*. World Bank Discussion Papers 314, World Bank, Washington, D.C.

Shaw, Edward. 1973. *Financial Deepening in Economic Development*. New York: Oxford University Press.

Shome, Parthasarathi. 1992. *Trends and Future Directions in Tax Policy Reform: A Latin American Perspective*. Washington, D.C.: International Monetary Fund.

Tanzi, Vito, and Parthasarathi Shome. 1992. The Role of Taxation in the Development of East Asian Economies. In *The Political Economy of Tax Reform*, eds. Takatoshi Ito and Anne O. Krueger. Chicago and London: The University of Chicago Press.

Tommasi, Mariano, and Andrés Velasco. 1995. Where Are We in the Political Economy of Reform? Unpublished.

Tornell, A. 1995. Are Economic Crises Necessary for Trade Liberalization and Fiscal Reform? The Mexican Experience. In *Reform, Recovery and Growth: Latin America and the Middle East*, R. Dornbusch and S. Edwards. Chicago: University of Chicago Press.

Velasco, Andrés. 1993. A Model of Endogenous Fiscal Deficits, and Delayed Fiscal Reforms. C.V. *Starr Center Report* 93(4). New York University.

——————.1994. The State and Economic Policy: Chile 1952-1992. In *The Chilean Economy: Policy Lessons and Challenges*, eds. B. Bosworth, R. Dornbusch and R. Labán Washington: The Brookings Institution.

Vogel, Robert. 1984. The Effect of Subsidized Agricultural Credit on Income Distribution in Costa Rica. In *Undermining Rural Development with Cheap Credit*, eds. Dale Adams, Douglas Grahmam, and John D. Von Pischke. Boulder: Westview Press.

Wei, Shang-Jin. 1992. Gradualism versus Big Bang: Speed and Sustainability of Reforms. Harvard University. Unpublished.

Westley, Glenn. 1995. *Financial Reforms in Latin America: Where Have We Been, Where Are We Going?* Office of the Chief Economist White Working Paper (January). Inter-American Development Bank, Washington, D.C.

World Bank. 1994. *Averting the Old Age Crisis*. Washington, D.C.: World Bank.

PART THREE

MAKING SOCIAL SERVICES WORK

THE "BUSINESS" OF SOCIAL SERVICES

Latin America and the Caribbean are facing two critical social gaps in education and health. Despite years of effort, public commitments, and billions of dollars, the level of education of the labor force and the health of the whole population are much worse than they should be for the region's level of economic and social development.

The ethical imperative to educate citizens and to ensure their good health has been enshrined in 19 constitutions of Latin American and Caribbean countries. As much as one-third of public sector resources has been committed to education and health, with expenditures on the order of 7 percent of national income. Individuals and families spend another 4 percent of national income out of pocket in the same sectors. As a result, education and health are large sectors of economic activity that significantly affect productivity, income distribution, poverty, and growth. But their outcomes still fall short of expectations.

School buildings with leaking roofs and broken faucets are no surprise to people in the region. Texts and library books are absent from many public schools, and books received are often out of date in content and method. Students spend relatively little time in school, because of short school days, teacher absenteeism, and strikes. Many teachers are unqualified, and entry level salaries are extremely poor.

In public health, many basic problems persist. Patients have come to expect long waiting lines in hospitals and clinics. In public facilities, patients may be given expired medications, or told that the medications they need are not available. Medical staff are often uninformed about recent advances in treatment and prevention of diseases.

Any company managed as poorly as many of these education and health systems are would be out of business quite soon. Businesses operating in competitive markets get information and feedback about their performance through the demand they face and the price they can fetch for their products and services. They can decide what and how much to produce and which combination of inputs will achieve their goals. They have the autonomy and decisionmaking power to take action, and they have incentives to respond. They are held accountable for their financial performance by their shareholders, who delegate managerial tasks to a board or CEO. In order to motivate the firm's management, stock options are offered. The manager, in turn, seeks ways to induce high productivity from workers—paying them by piece rates when possible or with bonuses, promotions, and other prizes. The quality and price of the firm's products or services must attract and retain customers who have other options in the market. Hence, the firm is also interested in seeking out the opinions of its clients, to find out and address their dissatisfactions before it loses them.

It is not possible to provide and finance health and education services solely through private competitive markets because of the difficulty of measuring output and the importance of equi-ty. Because outputs are difficult to measure, it is hard to evaluate the effort and effectiveness of providers. This situation obstructs the possibility for different forms of feedback that characterize standard markets. Also, the market responds to effective demand, and society finds the idea of people's being refused medical care or educational opportunities to be fundamentally unacceptable.

In a sense, the typical business has a rather easy time compared to the difficulties facing the education and health services of the public sector, precisely because of the difficulty with measuring output and the importance of equitable provision. But on top of this, the ways these public systems have been organized make basic feedback, decisionmaking power, and incentives extremely problematic. Often the public has little choice of facilities; schools and hospitals have no say in purchasing the mix of inputs they judge most effective to carry out their functions; and school principals and hospital directors cannot use their knowledge and experience to hire, evaluate, or reward their staff. Doctors and teachers, in turn, have rigid pay schedules that leave few incentives for improving their training and service.

It is true that other factors such as income, public expenditure, the physical and social environment, family backgrounds, and individual behavior influence health and education. Nevertheless, there is a growing recognition that the social service delivery system is severely limited in its ability to respond and adjust to changing circumstances, by certain institutional, organizational, and structural factors. Thinking about the education and health service providers as firms may help demonstrate the need for measures to structure such a "market" with efficient rules and clear roles; to encourage the emergence of numerous providers with greater diversity, autonomy, and accountability; and to give consumers more voice and freedom of choice. In this way the "businesses" of education and health services will face incentives that increase their interest and ability to serve people effectively.

This special report analyzes the rules and roles that combine resources and people in the complex systems of social services. The organization of the systems needs to be viewed in its entirety to the extent possible, since in most countries a centralized structure of incentives and behavior affects not only the efficiency with which a school teaches its students or a clinic cares for its patients, but also the allocation of resources among universities and high schools, hospitals and vaccination campaigns, and social spending and other public expenditures. To assist the analysis, the report will draw examples mainly from the provision of personal health services and primary and secondary education—in part because these two areas represent large shares of public spending, but also because they are central to social welfare. To the degree that these services become more efficient, the serious failures in other important areas, such as public health, can be addressed.

The report also focuses on the context within which services are provided, rather than on particular techniques of providing services. There will be explicit emphasis on organizing the systems in such a way that providers—teachers, educators, doctors, and public health specialists—have the flexibility to exercise their professional judgment, as well as the resources and incentives to serve the interests of their clients. By clarifying the dimensions of the systems' organization and the roles of the public sector, providers, and clients, we can see the implications and opportunities for better policy and better performance.

Chapter 2 of this report demonstrates the urgent need to improve health and education services in Latin America and the Caribbean. Despite gains in life expectancy, infant mortality, and average years of schooling, the region is performing worse than expected for its income level and initial conditions. At a time when educational and health indicators in other regions of the world are improving rapidly, Latin America has remained trapped in a relatively slow pace of improvement.

A better-educated and healthier citizenry has always been an imperative for social well-being. The need is now even more critical—for increasing workforce productivity and economic growth, reducing poverty and inequality, and sustaining the democratic process and modernization of the state.

To satisfy these requirements, the efficiency with which the region's resources are applied and used to deliver social services needs to be improved. Although health status and cognitive abilities are affected by many factors, including the physical and social environment, personal behavior, and genetic inheritance, social services do play a significant role. To accelerate progress in education and health, public policy should aim to improve the efficiency of social service delivery systems, which policy can influence directly. Another reason to focus on improving efficiency is that resources alone do not explain the wide variation in outcomes in the region. Many of the countries already spend large shares of national income on social services, particularly health, to little effect.

Finally, improvements in the efficiency and performance of social service delivery systems are important to mobilizing and maintaining public support from taxpayers and voters. When resources are misspent or performance is lagging, support will wither. Even in those countries that currently spend little, improvements in efficiency will not only increase the effectiveness of the limited resources applied, but also establish a foundation for expanding public action in the future. How the organization of social services affects their efficiency is therefore the specific focus of this report.

Chapter 3 begins by discussing why organizing social services efficiently is so difficult and then outlines a framework for analyzing and improving the systems. Organizing social services is difficult, in both health and education, because service users and governments find it difficult to evaluate the quality of service providers and the effects of their services. It is also difficult because societies are compelled to ensure equitable provision of these services, leading countries to finance services through public resources in rather inflexible ways that discourage close contact with clients or improvements in the provision of services. Hence, it is not surprising to find similarities in the problems of the health and education systems, along with differences that make it possible to derive important lessons.

Organizing social service systems requires clarifying the roles of various agents in the systems, particularly emphasizing the public role in finance and regulation, autonomy for providers and empowerment of consumers. Clarifying roles makes it possible to adopt rules that encourage more efficient behavior by governments, clients, and providers, but the particular rules must be coherent and robust. Coherence requires that various elements of the system be complementary and that they be effective within the context of local institutions, capacities, and environments. The systems must be robust in the sense that they reinforce political processes and groups that are most interested in good performance, and that they adjust over time in ways that improve performance.

Chapter 4 applies the aforementioned framework to the region's education systems, which are rather homogeneous in their organizational features. The education systems typically rely on centralized funding and direct public administration, with services provided by teachers under civil service contracts. Such centralized systems have been criticized for continually underfunding complementary materials, investment in training, and libraries. They are also resistant to innovation, and provide few incentives for tailoring services to the needs of particular population groups.

The constraints on schools leave very little room for directors to exercise professional judgment, let alone creativity, in improving the education of their charges. Directors have little or no

control over the selection or pay of their staff. They are dependent on central offices for materials and maintenance (which are provided irregularly at best); and they have no funds with which to contract support services or experiment with new pedagogical techniques or curriculum. Accountability is diffuse and made more difficult by the absence of standardized examinations—a lacuna that has only recently begun to be filled in several countries.

How government, unions, and teachers interact often frustrates not only their own interests, but also the interests of students and families. The forms that negotiation and representation take, along with the focus on public funding, often divert debate from how the public sector mobilizes its efforts in the education sector. Even so, public funding is compatible with many potential forms of organization that could better serve students, teachers, and the public interest.

For example, there is increasing evidence that greater autonomy for teachers and principals within their schools—under the appropriate accountability mechanisms and public regulation—can improve performance. Giving greater choice to parents and students and increasing their participation in local schools can increase the system's responsiveness. In fact, organizational change is an effective catalyst to expanding accountability, improving resource allocation, encouraging innovation, and generating the resources to improve both equity and quality.

Analysis of the health sector, in Chapter 5, illustrates how the organization of such systems can influence health outcomes. The region's lower-than-expected health outcomes reflect problems common to most of its countries. Public funding for the health sector is volatile, and traditional policies have fragmented and segmented health services among population groups. Information, feedback, and control systems are weak and there are implicit incentives to overspend public resources and undersupply services in the public sector. These problems cause patients to migrate to private providers. In short, the incentive structures facing doctors, clinics, patients and administrators lead to a large waste of resources.

Nevertheless, health standards vary significantly across the region. Many countries have achieved higher life expectancy or lower child mortality than predicted from their income levels. These more successful countries are usually smaller, more densely populated, and more equal in income distribution. They have relatively large amounts of public funding and good public insurance coverage that limits discrimination against groups with less ability to pay. Furthermore, these better cases have more integrated service networks, both public and private, with global incentives toward the integrated care of the patient. The countries with worse performance tend not to have these factors and conditions in place. How organization affects the performance of these systems is an important part of the picture, and one that is responsive to the actions of public policy.

The recommendations in Chapter 6 begin with the recognition that no single organizational system is optimal for every country in every moment. But certain general principles regarding institutions and incentives can help. A system with *clear roles and rules* improves the organization of social services. Differentiating the roles for regulation, financing, purchasing, delivery, and consumer representation would make the systems more effective and the public sector more efficient. *Public finance and regulation, provider autonomy,* and *consumer empowerment* are the cornerstones of improved functioning of the sectors of health and education.

The central authority must play a greater role in establishing the rules of the game, especially where these rules are absent, and in making existing rules coherent. To fulfill this role, the central authority must increasingly distance itself from the direct provision of education and health services. In general, systems will be more efficient when public sources of funding can be allocated according to outcomes, with increased profession-

al and administrative autonomy of schools and health service networks, and payment methods based on capitation—the number of students or affiliated clients served (adjusted for compensating factors of family background, income, or health risk). Equity can be improved when individuals' access to services is guaranteed by the public funding they bring with them to the school or clinic, rather than by proximity to a centrally planned facility. The government can then focus on regulating and monitoring developments in the system, establishing mechanisms to ensure the quality of education and health services, and disseminating information about providers among the population served.

Direct service provision will increasingly be in the hands of autonomous and accountable agencies or units with high professional standards for their management, along with the authority to contract and compensate their staff more flexibly, and in which the distinction between private and public ownership becomes increasingly less important. Consumer decisionmaking powers can be strengthened with greater information regarding the quality of diverse providers, with greater voice in the functioning of these purchasing agencies and providers, and with greater options for choosing among numerous providers.

A general scheme of competition, coordination, and cooperation such as this can be adapted in many different ways across the spectrum of conditions in the region's countries. In smaller countries, centralized service purchasing may be more efficient; in larger countries, purchasing could be delegated to intermediate organizations in provinces or large municipalities. In the health sector, specialized agencies—independent of providers—can be established and made accountable to the public for efficient purchasing of services. Provider autonomy can be delegated to schools and hospitals, or to clusters of these units, which can provide integrated services and capture certain scale economies. Consumer choice, an important element in many future solutions, will be more relevant in urban areas where multiple providers already exist, particularly in the health sector. Consumer voice—the ability to participate, compare providers, and hold them accountable—will be especially important in education, with its more limited options and longer-term relationships between families and providers.

The clear allocation of responsibilities to a set of mutually consistent institutions would remove the main source of inefficiency in the delivery systems of health and education services in the Latin American and Caribbean region. If the myriad social actors committed to and involved in the social services of the region can recognize their shared interest in more efficient systems that generate the feedback, autonomy, and incentives that are common to a simple firm, then perhaps we can get down to the "business" of meeting the urgent educational and health needs of the future.

CHAPTER 2

TOO IMPORTANT TO FAIL, BUT TOO INEFFICIENT TO SUCCEED

The deficiencies of Latin American and Caribbean social service systems are often attributed to the stresses and challenges of development. In this conventional view, the public sector has not yet mobilized enough resources to meet increasing demands resulting from demographic growth and rapid urbanization. Although social services are limited in coverage and of poor quality, it is claimed that this has no major significance for economic growth. In any case, the argument goes, gradual improvements in social indicators are evidence that social progress will eventually follow in the process of development.

We question this conventional wisdom. Most of the region's countries already dedicate substantial shares of national income to education and health. The demographic transitions of the 1980s and 1990s actually reduced the pressures on basic education and health services, rather than increasing them. Even where national resources are relatively meager, it is the slow pace of productivity growth that has limited basic income levels.

Optimism about the pace of social progress is unwarranted by the evidence. While health and education levels in the region have improved, progress has been slow compared to the rest of the developing world. Persistent social gaps in the accumulation of "human capital" have reinforced the region's large proportion of people living in poverty and its highly unequal distribution of incomes. These social gaps continue to limit regional economic productivity and growth, and delay the processes of democratization and modernization of states.

Overall, the contrasts among various countries demonstrate that greater progress is more likely to come from gains in efficiency than from increased spending. Enormous benefits would be realized if the region made better use of the resources now spent on health and education. For example, based on international experience and the region's present income level, it should be possible to prevent about 106,000 infant deaths annually, and to increase the average educational level of the labor force by more than two school years. The failures in social service delivery are principally the result of inefficiencies in the systems themselves.

Social services in the region are thus too important to fail, but at present they are too inefficient to succeed. And the major policy instruments available to improve efficiency are changes in the way health and education services are organized.

DESPITE SIGNIFICANT PROGRESS, GAPS REMAIN

The general health and education standards of the region's population have improved in recent generations. At the beginning of the century, life expectancy at birth in Latin America was not even 40 years. By 1960, it had reached 54 years. Over the last three decades, progress in life expectancy continued, reaching 69.5 years in 1990, while the mortality rate of children under five dropped from

Figure 2.1 Gaps in Human Development for Latin America and the Caribbean, 1995

	Actual	Expected
Education		
Fourth Grade Completed	66%	82%
Average Years of Schooling	5.2	7.0
Health		
Infant Mortality (per 1,000 births)	47	39
Life Expectancy (years)	69.5	72.0
Disability-adjusted Life Years (DALYS)	231.6	200.1

Note: These calculations are based on a sample of 115 countries, with observations between 1950 and 1990. Expected performance is estimated on the basis of per capita income, as well as fixed factors related to time and region. The gap is defined as the difference between observed outcomes in health and education and the outcomes expected based on the calculations.

159 per thousand to 47 per thousand during that same period.

Progress in education has also been remarkable. Illiteracy among adults, 49.9 percent in 1950, had fallen to 14.5 percent by 1990. Between 1960 and 1992, total primary, secondary, and university enrollment rose from 40 million to 122 million. By the early 1980s, more than 50 percent of all students were female. Average years of school for the labor force advanced from 2.3 years in 1950 to 5.2 years in 1990. Despite the gains of recent decades, however, the region's average health and education levels today are lower than would be expected for its level of economic development, especially when compared with other regions of the world.

Although the number of students entering primary school in the region is high, as Figure 2.1 shows, only two of every three children actually complete the primary education cycle. The percentage of children who *fail* to complete primary schooling is almost twice that expected for Latin America's income level. In other words, had the region's primary education system been as effective as the international average for its income levels, some 55 million more children could have completed primary schooling between 1950 and 1990. For secondary education, the limits of coverage and

FIGURE 2.2
The Social Gaps by Regions

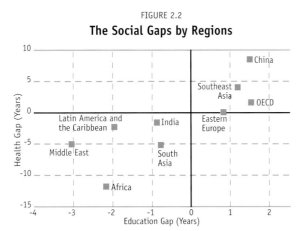

Note: Years of life expectancy and average schooling compared to expected levels based on per capita income.

completion rates are even worse. Considering the region's level of income, the labor force should have at least 7 years of formal schooling—much higher than the actual level of 5.2 years.

Gaps in health care are also large. Today, health services on average cover 78 percent of the population. The 22 percent *not* covered is double what should be expected. Mortality of children under five is 47 for every thousand born; whereas, given the region's per capita income and technological advances, the expected figure would be only 39. For the same conditions of income and available technology, life expectancy should be 72 years, which is higher than the actual figure of 69.5 years.

Social Gaps by Regions

Figure 2.2 indicates the social gaps between the Latin American and Caribbean region and other regions. As noted, the region's workforce has almost two years less education than expected based on income levels; life expectancy of the population is 2.5 years less than the expected level. After making allowance for income differences, Latin America's social achievements are barely above those of Africa and the Middle East, and far below those of China, the former socialist countries, Southeast Asia, and the industrialized nations.

The region's health standards have evolved

very differently from its education levels. In the 1960s, life expectancy in Latin America and the Caribbean was almost seven years *below* what would be expected. Since then, the gap in health standards has narrowed to only 2.5 years below the expected level. Meanwhile, the education gap grew larger. From just after World War II until the late 1960s, the region's education levels were no lower than those of similarly developed nations. In the 1970s, however—when human capital began to accumulate rapidly throughout the world, particularly in Asia—education levels in Latin America and the Caribbean rose more slowly. Thus, while the health gap has been decreasing, the education gap has *increased* considerably during the past two decades, as Figure 2.3 illustrates.

FIGURE 2.3
The Dynamics of Social Gaps in Latin America and the Caribbean

Education

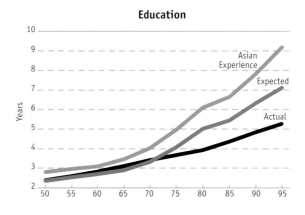

Life Expectancy

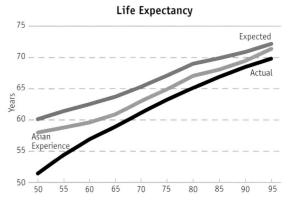

Note: Years of life expectancy and average schooling compared to expected levels based on per capita income.

FIGURE 2.4
The Social Gaps by Country, 1990

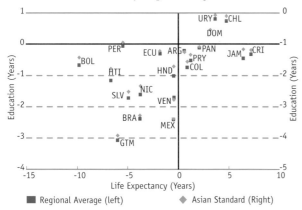

Note: Years of life expectancy and average schooling compared to expected levels based on per capita income.

Social Gaps across Countries in the Region

The regional aggregation of the social gaps obscures the diverse experiences of many countries. Figure 2.4 shows the health and education gaps for 20 countries in the region in 1990. The horizontal axis measures the gap in life expectancy for each country, compared with average life expectancy in countries of similar income levels. The vertical axis measures the gap in education of each country's labor force, compared to the average for the entire sample of countries on the left axis, and for Southeast Asian countries on the right axis.[1]

Most of the region's countries have educational attainment well below the averages of countries with similar income levels—the notable exceptions being Chile and Uruguay. The education gap is particularly severe in the bigger countries—Brazil, Mexico, and Venezuela—and in Central America. None of the region's countries surpasses the average attained by Southeast Asian countries of similar income levels.

---

[1] Southeast Asia and Latin America and the Caribbean do not differ significantly in terms of their life expectancy levels; however, the strong difference in educational attainment is notable, as demonstrated in the graph. The need for two different data points for each country is the result of the nonlinearity of the function.

Box 2.1   Education and Income Inequality

Inequalities in income are closely related to educational levels, according to economic research. In general, income distribution tends to be more unequal in societies where the returns on education are highest. Returns on education also tend to be higher when the workforce is less educated or the demand for skilled labor is very high. Park, Ross and Sabot (1996) find that the impact of growth on the demand for labor accounts for most of the differences between Latin America and Southeast Asia. While Southeast Asia's outward-looking development has resulted in intensive use of labor, Latin American import substitution has probably skewed job demand against unskilled labor.

The connection between educational levels and inequality is somewhat more complex. On the one hand, a shortage of human capital tends to increase returns on education and wage differentials. On the other, human capital distribution in a population changes substantially as education spreads. Inequalities in education tend to be lower when the population as a whole has very little schooling (as in poor countries) or when the entire population is highly educated (as in the developed countries). In the intermediate stage of the spread of education (as in Latin America in the post-war period), inequality increased until the population reached an average of five or six years of schooling, and then tended to decline (Kuznets 1955, Fields 1989, Flug and Spilimbergo 1996).

Given this linkage between education levels and income inequality, the region's relatively slow progress in education prolonged the stage when more education creates greater inequality in human capital. The returns on education therefore declined more slowly than they would have with a dynamic balance in the system.

The income gap in Latin America did not narrow in the last two decades, primarily due to the slow spread of education, which led to sharp inequality in human capital and higher-than-expected returns on education. The pressure of the education gap on inequality could increase in the future, since early evidence suggests that growing globalization of the economy is creating higher than average demand for goods that are more intensive in skilled labor (Grilliches 1969, and Katz and Murphy 1992). In fact, the opening up of Latin American economies appears to have coincided with higher returns on education and a wider gap in the wage structure (Robbins 1995, Flug and Hercovitz 1996).

In terms of life expectancy, half of the region's countries achieve better-than-predicted outcomes—particularly in Costa Rica, some Caribbean countries, and the Southern Cone. Among those with lower-than-predicted life expectancy are Brazil, Mexico, the Andean countries, and most Central American countries.

Consequences for Inequality, Poverty, and Economic Growth

Social gaps are strongly related to the region's high levels of inequality and poverty. Countries with high levels of inequality tend to have poorer education and health services, and people living in poverty are much less able to obtain education and proper health care. Furthermore, ineffective health and education services actually magnify and reproduce poverty levels and unequal income distribution. Economic growth itself depends upon the capacity of social services to increase educational attainment and improve health conditions.

The levels and distribution of education affect income inequality in a variety of ways.[2] In Latin America and the Caribbean, increases in the educational attainment of the labor force are likely to reduce income inequality. On the other hand—given current changes in the global economy that amplify the returns to skilled and educated workers—there is evidence that income inequality will grow much more pronounced without a concerted effort to increase educational attainment (see Box 2.1).

Similarly, education and health have important consequences for poverty.[3] With better education, people earn more and adjust more easily to temporary misfortunes or economic changes. By contrast, families that depend upon workers with little formal education are likely to remain below the poverty level. Moreover, illness that incapacitates a key wage earner can soon drive a family into poverty (see Box 2.2).

Closing the social gaps is also important to sustaining increases in productivity and

Box 2.2 Social Gaps and Poverty

The effects of education and improved health status on poverty are unambiguous—more education and better health always reduce poverty. Education is by far the main factor in determining whether a working individual is poor (Fiszbein and Psacharopoulos 1995). Inadequate primary education has resulted in increasing numbers of uneducated people in the labor market. Over a thirty-year period, the number of uneducated citizens *increased* by more than 15 percent in Latin America. Over the same period, Southeast Asia reduced the absolute number of people without any formal education by 20 percent. Countries with higher primary education completion rates have lower levels of poverty, and countries with higher levels of schooling can reduce poverty over time (Morley 1995; Inter-American Development Bank 1995a). Unemployment, or lack of participation of adults in the labor market, is influenced by disability more than any other factor. When a head of household is disabled—due to injuries, endemic infection or chronic disease—the probability that a family will be poor increases by a factor of five (Castaño 1993). Clearly, the gaps in education and health have severe consequences for the region's poor population.

growth.[4] That investment in human capital promotes economic growth is well recognized. A skilled workforce is essential to modern methods of production and accelerates the development of new and more productive technologies. In turn, improved health status affects productivity directly, through increased capacities and reduced absenteeism, and indirectly through its impact on educational attainment. Both education and health status, then, are significant factors in increasing an economy's capacity to grow (see Box 2.3).

The populations of Latin America and the Caribbean have made advances in health and ed-

---

[2] Ahluwalia (1976); Park, Ross, and Sabot (1996); Bourguignon and Morrison (1990); and Jung (1992).

[3] Morley (1996) and Londoño (1996).

[4] Schultz (1964); Becker (1993); Barro and Sala-i-Martin (1995); and Londoño (1996).

ucation over the last half century, but their progress has been slower than that of other countries. This disparity has left the region with two large social gaps which have negative consequences for income distribution, poverty, and economic growth.

EFFICIENT SOCIAL SERVICES, NOT JUST HIGHER BUDGETS

Today's dynamic global economy poses a challenge to Latin America and the Caribbean. Because of its large proportion of uneducated people, the region must work hard even to stand still. Unfortunately, the significant share of regional resources already being spent on social services does not ensure that adequate social services will be provided. The lagging performance of social services in the region cannot be attributed primarily to demographic pressures and inadequate resources, but is the result of failure to invest efficiently in health and education.

Significant Spending Does Not Guarantee Results

Many would argue that Latin American and Caribbean countries already recognize the importance of education and health. Equitable access to health care and education are goals enshrined in constitutions and political rhetoric. Nineteen constitutions in the region list education and health as basic rights of the population, and all 19 guarantee basic education free of charge. Fifteen constitutions establish financial and institutional commitments to additional levels of education, and 17 establish the government's role in ensuring "access" to health care.

Large sums of public money are spent in the education and health sectors, and armies of workers, professionals, and administrators are employed. The health systems of Latin America and the Caribbean employ a total of more than 3 million people, including 350,000 physicians. The education system has more than 150 million stu-

Box 2.3   Social Gaps and Economic Growth

Education and health both affect growth, and growth provides the resources to improve social well-being and to finance future education and health services. That investment in human capital promotes economic growth has long been recognized (Schultz 1968, Barro 1993). Human capital contributes directly to growth by increasing productivity or boosting investment in physical capital (Lucas 1988), contributing to the invention of new technologies (Romer 1990), and facilitating their adoption (Nelson and Phelps 1966, Jovanovic 1996).

Empirical research has confirmed the importance of investment in human capital for growth. Initial levels of education strongly influence the growth rate of countries, and low-income economies converge faster when their initial stock of human capital is larger (Barro 1993, Barro and Sala-i-Martin 1995). Moreover, human capital affects countries' growth rates by enhancing productivity (Benhabib and Spiegel 1993). Much of this contribution may be related to the impact of nutritional and health status on learning capacity (Knowles and Owen 1995). Birdsall, Ross, and Sabot (1995) and IDB (1995) found that the low rates of growth and high inequality of Latin American countries over the last several decades, compared to East Asian countries, can be attributed to differences in educational performance.

The growing importance of human capital on economic growth in the region is suggested by Graphs a and b. After the crisis of the early 1980s, countries with the strongest rate of growth were precisely those with higher levels of education among younger workers and those with higher life expectancy.

dents and about 4 million teachers. Combined, the two systems employ more than 7 million people—about 5 percent of the region's total employment and more than 12 percent of the employed female labor force.

The social service systems of Latin America and the Caribbean, enormous by world standards, are frequently the largest institutions in their countries. For example, Mexico's Social Security Institute employs more than 300,000 people, and the education ministries of Mexico and Venezue-

Economic Growth and Human Capital in Latin America in the Nineties

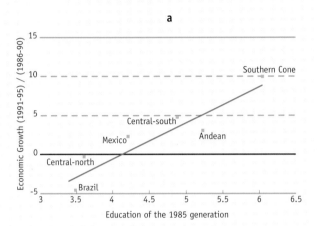

a

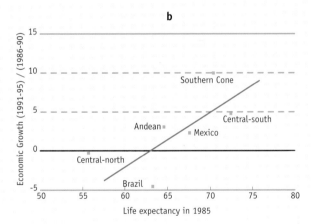

b

FIGURE 2.5

Expenditure per Pupil by Region and Level, 1990
(As percent of GDP)

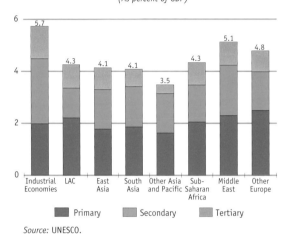

Source: UNESCO.

slightly lower than international levels, with about 4.3 percent of GDP spent on public education in the region in 1992, compared with 4.1 percent in Asia, 4.3 percent in Africa, and 5.7 percent in the more developed countries. However, the regional average of 4 percent is high, considering the relatively small share spent upon secondary education (see Figure 2.5).

In health, the region spends a larger share of its income than do other regions—6.2 percent, compared with 3.7 percent in the fast-growing Asian countries and 4.1 percent in Africa. Only the more developed countries spend more on health, an average of 7.8 percent. One reason for Latin America's relatively high spending on health is the extremely large share of private spending. Recent studies have found that private-sector spending on health in Latin America is almost as large as total public sector spending.[5] *Private* expenditures on health care in Latin America and the Caribbean amount to 2.7 percent of national income: that is higher than in any other region, and even larger than the 1.9 percent of national income that industrial countries spend on private health care (see Figure 2.6).

la each have more than 340,000 employees. All three exceed the average size of the top ten U.S. firms. Even in a small country such as Guatemala, the education ministry employs more than 50,000 people. By contrast, the largest *private* enterprises in these countries rarely have more than a few thousand employees.

Despite the massiveness of these systems, the income share spent on education and health does not seem unusual by international standards. The region's share of spending on education is

---

[5] World Bank (1993), Suárez *et al.* (1994), and Govindaraj *et al.* (1995).

FIGURE 2.6
Health Expenditure by Region, 1990
(As percent of GDP)

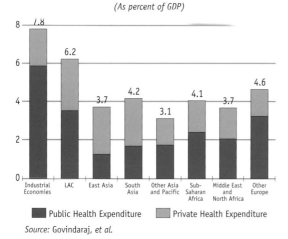

Public Health Expenditure   Private Health Expenditure

Source: Govindaraj, *et al.*

During the past two decades, social expenditures in the region have grown at a faster pace than national income, as is also true for many other regions in the world. In Latin America and the Caribbean, stagnating growth has limited the public sector resources available to invest (see Box 2.4). Nevertheless, the region has increased its efforts, as demonstrated by the rising share of its available income dedicated to public expenditure in education—from 3.6 percent in 1975 to 3.9 percent in 1985, and up to 4.1 percent in 1992. Expenditure on health fluctuated more during the period; the share of GDP spent on health care declined during the 1980s, but recovered substantially during the 1990s. Overall, the region has been increasing its efforts to invest in human capital.

Furthermore, the region's slow progress in education and health cannot be attributed to a rapid expansion in high-risk or school-age populations, since the demographic trends in the region are not unlike those in other parts of the developing world. In fact, the region is facing a window of opportunity over the next decade, because demographic trends are relatively favorable for consolidating and improving the efficiency of social service systems. The student-age population is leveling off, and a rapid expansion of the elder-

Box 2.4 When economic productivity stagnates, there is less to invest in social services

Stagnating productivity has been a major factor limiting the region's capacity to invest in people (see table below). This is especially dramatic in comparison with the fast-growing economies of East Asia. Whereas in 1975, the two regions had roughly comparable ratios of dependents to workers, over the next two decades, East Asian productivity overtook Latin America and the Caribbean. With greater productivity and income, East Asia was able to spend roughly twice as much on education as Latin America and the Caribbean. The region's per capita expenditures in education and health between 1980 and 1995 remained constant because per capita income did not increase.

Limited Resources: Stagnating Economic Productivity

Region	GDP/Worker (US$ 1995)		
	1975	1985	1992
OECD	22,300	25,400	29,600
Latin America and the Caribbean	8,800	8,900	8,900
High Performing Asian Economies	5,300	7,800	11,800
Rest of Asia	3,100	3,900	4,200
Africa	2,900	2,600	2,300
Arab Countries	8,000	8,300	7,300
Rest of Europe	7,600	9,700	10,200

Source: Penn World Tables.
Note: Mexico is included in figures for Latin America and the Caribbean. High-performing Asian economies refer to South Korea, Thailand, Singapore, Hong Kong, and Malaysia.

ly population has not yet affected the region as a whole (see Box 2.5).

The persistence of the social gaps indicates that strong public commitment, high expenditures, and large numbers of personnel are not enough. Erasing the social gaps through investment in human capital requires that the region grow more, spend more, and increase the efficiency of its education and health services. Growing more and spending more are important but difficult goals of public policy. Improving the efficiency of the health and educational systems is critical, however, because increased efficiency contributes to greater economic growth, it mobilizes political support for increased spending, and it releases funds that can be applied to accelerate the pace of social progress.

Efficiency Is Important and Attainable

Measuring the impact of social services is difficult largely because individual health and educational status depends upon many other factors, including social and physical environment, individual behavior, and innate characteristics. Many studies have tried to demonstrate the relative importance of these various factors in "producing" health and educational status. To separate the effect of one factor from all the others, or rank them in terms of importance, is extremely difficult. Therefore, we can only present what we believe is convincing evidence for the importance of efficient delivery of social services. The following analyses adjust for factors that are strongly related to social context, controlling for differences in income and the productivity of the various economies. Nevertheless, after these adjustments large intercountry variations are still apparent in the relation between the level of public spending and the dimension of the social gap.

In education, fourth-grade completion rates are positively affected by overall public spending on education (see Figure 2.7). But a comparison of performance in a sample of 53 countries shows that an additional 1 percent of GDP spent on public education above the current average generates only a 2.4 percent increase in the number of students completing fourth grade. By contrast, the scattering of countries around this average indicates enormous differences in the effectiveness of spending, partly due to the efficiency of education systems and partly due to contextual factors not correlated with income. Countries such as Colombia, El Salvador, and Guatemala spend less than expected and perform worse than

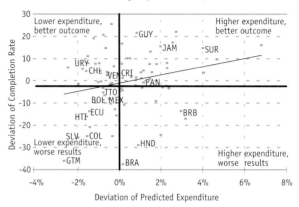

FIGURE 2.7

Fourth Grade Completion Rates and Public Education Expenditures

Deviations from predicted values, 1989

Both axes represent deviations from predicted values. The X-axis shows the deviation of public expenditure in education as a percentage of GNP in the regression on this variable against per capita income. The Y-axis shows the deviation of fourth grade completion rates from the predicted value of this variable in the regression against GDP per capita.

expected. Countries like Guyana, Jamaica, and Suriname achieve more than expected with higher-than-expected spending. In other cases, such as those of Chile and Uruguay, better fourth-grade completion rates are attained at relatively low cost. Meanwhile, in Brazil and Honduras, relatively poor performance is associated with higher-than-expected spending.

Public expenditure on health also has an overall positive impact on reducing child mortality rates: child mortality is lower than expected in countries that make a greater commitment to public spending on health. Even so, very different outcomes emerge from the same level of public effort. For instance, Costa Rica has 10 percent *fewer* deaths of children under five years of age than would be expected on the basis of the country's income, educational level, and income distribution; yet Costa Rica spends much *more* than expected to reach the same relative advantage as Panama. Argentina and Uruguay achieve the expected rates of child mortality for their socioeconomic level, but with higher-than-expected rates of spending. Countries as diverse as Bolivia, Bra-

Box 2.5   A Demographic Window of Opportunity

Demographic and epidemiological changes affect the needs for health and education services. As incomes and education levels rise, populations also become more conscious of these needs and have the means to obtain services. Therefore, demands generally will rise faster than needs.

The demographic structure affects national health service requirements because newborns, young children, and the elderly tend to require more services than young and middle-aged adults. Like most developing regions, Latin America and the Caribbean have had relatively "young" populations compared to the OECD countries. Currently 12 percent of the population is between 0 and 4 years of age, compared to 6 percent in the industrial countries. This translates into relatively high requirements for neonatal and early childhood care, although they are declining as the region's birth rates decline. The region's proportion of older citizens is relatively small: only 7 percent, compared to the industrial countries' average of 18 percent. Although the region as a whole is not yet facing large demands for geriatric care, certain countries, notably Barbados, Trinidad, and Uruguay, are already dealing with the health costs of the elderly (World Bank 1994b).

Moreover, there is a regional change in epidemiology related to the demographic transition, which affects the demand for health services. Infectious diseases are still a major problem, but as the population ages, injuries and non-infectious diseases are rising in relative importance. Currently, infectious and non-infectious diseases each represent approximately 40 percent of the total health burden in Latin America and the Caribbean (as measured by DALYs; see World Bank 1993e). By contrast, in OECD countries more than 80 percent of the health burden is due to non-infectious diseases; and in Africa, less than 14 percent.

The financial burden of health care for the young and old is borne by the working-age population. In Latin America and the Caribbean, the ratio of children to workers peaked in 1965 at 0.5, and will continue to decline through 2050 (see Graph). However, the ratio of elderly to workers has been increasing steadily and will rise fairly sharply after 2015. As a result of these two trends, the ratio of the young and elderly to the population of workers will decline until about 2015, and then start increasing as the currently large cohorts reach old age. The two decades ahead thus present a significant opportunity, while demands for health services are low relative to the size of the working-age population. During this critical period, the region's health systems must be equipped to tackle the accelerat-

Demographics and Public Health Expenditure

Region	Workers per Dependent				Public Health Expenditures (As percent of GDP)
	1950	1980	1990	2000	1990
OECD	3.4	3.2	3.1	2.9	5.7
Latin America and the Caribbean	3.6	3.9	4.1	4.3	3.0
India	3.8	3.9	3.8	4.4	1.2
China	3.7	4.8	4.2	4.2	2.0
Other Asia	3.8	3.9	4.3	4.6	1.4
Africa	3.4	3.4	3.3	3.2	1.7
Arab Countries	3.4	3.7	3.6	3.7	2.0
Rest of Europe	4.1	3.5	3.1	2.9	2.0

Source: Govinadaraj 1995 and World Bank 1993.

Note: Mexico is included in figures for Latin America and the Caribbean. Dependent population is approximated by those under five years of age and those over sixty.

Demographics and Public Education Expenditure

Region	Workers per School-aged Child			Public Education Expenditures (As percent of GNP)		
	1975	1985	1992	1975	1985	1992
OECD	2.7	3.3	3.5	5.3	5.3	5.4
Latin America and the Caribbean	**1.3**	**1.5**	**1.7**	**3.7**	**3.9**	**4.1**
High Performing Asian Economies	1.4	1.9	2.2	3.9	4.1	4.3
Rest of Asia	1.4	1.8	2	2.4	2.6	2.6
Africa	1.2	1.1	1.1	4.6	4.7	4.7
Arab Countries	1.2	1.3	1.3	5.1	5.5	5.2
Rest of Europe	2.2	2.4	2.5	2.7	2.8	4.2

Source: Penn World Tables and UNESCO.

Note: Mexico is included in figures for Latin America and the Caribbean. High-performing Asian economies refer to South Korea, Thailand, Singapore, Hong Kong, and Malaysia.

ing demands of the 21st century.

Demographic trends in education are much simpler to evaluate. The number of young people of school age has been expanding rapidly, particularly during the last two decades, increasing the potential demand for education services. However, this trend is leveling off, so that the student-age population will grow at a slower pace. By the year 2005, the total number of primary school-aged children is expected to level off at about 55 million. Already in countries like Uruguay, Barbados, and the Bahamas, the proportion of the school-age population is stable. In most others it is growing at rates below 1 or 2 percent per year. Consequently, the financial burden of educating children is shared

Ratio of School-aged Children to Labor Force, Actual and Projected

(Ages 5-19)

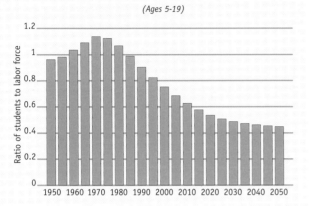

Ratio of Dependents to Labor Force, Actual and Projected

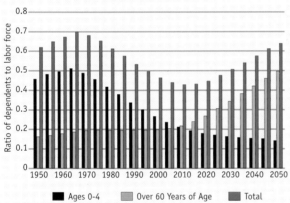

by increasing numbers of adults. In fact, the ratio of school-aged children to workers peaked at about 1.1 in 1970 and has been declining ever since. This favorable demographic situation provides an opportune moment to expand and improve the quality of education in the region.

Latin America and the Caribbean countries now have relatively more school-aged children per worker than most regions of the world (see table below); only Africa and the Arab countries have higher ratios of children to workers. In terms of health needs, however, Latin America has approximately one dependent for every 3.3 workers (combining old and young), a ratio much lower than those of the OECD, former socialist countries, and China. These ratios have been improving over time, and are similar to those of East Asian economies. Evidently the poor performance of the region's health and education systems in the last two decades cannot be attributed to a rapid expansion of demand.

zil, Guatemala, and Mexico have higher-than-expected child mortality, although they are spending at the rate predicted by their socioeconomic characteristics.

These relative differences are significantly affected by the efficiency with which public resources are used to improve educational attainment and health status (although social and environmental factors such as maternal education, poverty, and access to potable water also play a role.) The variation in efficiency is itself a consequence of numerous factors that are linked to the organization of systems. These include such factors as whether resources are allocated to the most effective mix of inputs or most cost-effective actions, whether staff members are adequately motivated, and whether innovation and the use of more effective techniques are rewarded.

Numerous studies have noted the importance of changing the region's social service systems to improve their performance. But the emphasis has been upon particular consequences of the existing ineffective organization, rather than upon its causes. Such studies have tended to demonstrate specific failures—such as inadequate training of personnel, deficiency of management, or misallocation of resources—rather than analyzing how the organization of the systems leads to such inefficiencies. To the extent that these issues were addressed, they were considered largely in terms of specific initiatives to decentralize or privatize services. Nevertheless, there is a growing literature that directly analyzes the issues of payment mechanisms, autonomy of providers, and regulation.[6] The common thread in these studies is a recognition that the roles of the public sector and of social service providers and consumers—and the rules under which they operate—lead to significant differences in the quality, quantity, and effectiveness of the services provided.

[6] Consider the range represented by Goudriann and De Groot (1990), Barnum *et al.* (1995), Israel (1993), and Tirole (1994).

A study in Brazil, for instance, has demonstrated that in the past decade organizational innovations to increase the financial autonomy of schools, to make the school directors themselves accountable, and to create parent councils, have all positively affected the average test scores of students.[7] The introduction of financial autonomy in higher education in São Paulo has also been credited with a dramatic improvement in performance.[8] Some evidence exists that privately managed schools have improved student performance, even after taking into account the differences in spending and student background.[9]

Moreover, when information about the quality and performance of services becomes publicly available, the public can react in powerful ways to bring about change. Introducing consumer choice among autonomous and competitive health plans, rewarded by risk-adjusted capitation, has allowed an expansion of public insurance coverage to more than 10 million Colombians in the last three years, with increasing equity and decreasing average costs.[10] Medical personnel who are paid on the basis of the number of services performed tend to provide more services than do those paid fixed salaries.[11] Other studies suggest that "demand-driven" vocational training programs may be more effective in placing their graduates in employment than are programs for which courses and content are predetermined by government offices.[12]

Setting the Future Course

Despite significant improvements in health and educational status over the last half century, Latin America and the Caribbean have not improved as quickly as other nations of the world, and do not enjoy outcomes at the level predicted by their income levels. The two social gaps are of enormous importance to the region because they interact with and contribute to poverty, income inequality, and slow economic growth. The poor relative performance of the region is not necessarily the

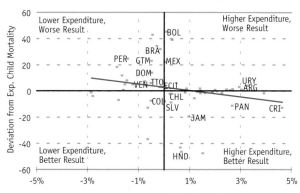

FIGURE 2.8

**Child Mortality Rate
and Public Health Expenditure**

Deviation from Expected Values, 1990

Both axes represent deviations from predicted values. The x-axis shows the deviation of the share of public expenditure of GDP from the predicted value of this variable in the regression of public health expenditures on GDP per capita for 1990. The Y-axis shows the deviation of deaths for children under five years of age per 1000 live births from the predicted value of this variable in a regression on GDP per capita for 1990, primary attainment and inequality.
Source: World Bank (1993), Govindaraj, *et al.* (1995).

result of insufficient spending. In fact, the region spends a much higher share of its national income on health than do other regions of the world. The funds expended on education, although more modest by international standards, are also significant. Instead, the efficiency with which such financial resources are channeled into social services is an important focus of attention. Public policy can strongly influence efficiency levels, and improved efficiency would accelerate progress in education and health. The challenge of bridging the two social gaps calls for public and social commitments to efficient health care and educational systems.

[7] Barros *et al.* (1996).

[8] Castro (1996).

[9] Hanushek (1994), Santana (1996), Aedo (1996), and Navarro (1996).

[10] Londoño (1996).

[11] See Labadie (1996) for the case of Uruguay. This is not always an advantage. Fee-for-service payment systems create incentives for doctors to perform more interventions than may be optimal, or in the case of the Brazilian system, for many doctors to charge for more services than they have actually performed.

[12] Inter-American Development Bank (1985); Castro (1995).

APPROACHES TO ORGANIZING HEALTH AND EDUCATION SERVICES

Organizing public health and education services is no simple task. To organize an education ministry with more than 200,000 employees—twice the size of a typical multinational corporation[1]—is a tricky business under any conditions. Moreover, health and education services have to be provided in multiple locations throughout a country to a diverse clientele—and "production" of these services is not easy to evaluate. For the sake of clarity, we will consider the tales of two hypothetical countries, and then explore the implications of organizational structure, political dynamics, and good intentions.

THE BENEFICENT STATE

In our first country, the beneficent state recognizes that health and education services must be provided equitably to the entire population. Using

---

[1] For comparison, in 1985 the average number of employees in each of the top ten firms in Japan was only 107,000 (Scherer and Ross 1990).

general revenues, this state provides all education and health services directly to the population free of charge. The provision of services is centrally planned, with a government ministry deciding when and where to build schools, clinics, and hospitals. The ministry also determines the required staffing for each facility and decides how many books, medications, and other supplies will be necessary. Students and patients make no choices, for they have none. They go to the local school or clinic that is available to them.

Those who locally administer the school or health facilities think they could do a better job with a different mix of inputs and staff, but they have no role in making such decisions. As long as the required materials and staffing are provided, administrators fill out the required paperwork. When something goes wrong, they petition the central offices, making phone calls and trying to persuade someone in the bureaucracy to take action. A well-connected administrator might get results; otherwise, there is a long wait until the school roof is repaired or the X-ray machine is serviced.

The local administrators have a very small role to play in managing their staffs. The central ministry determines pay scales, standards for promotion, qualifications, and staffing levels. Teachers and doctors realize that the only way they can influence their pay and working conditions is to unionize and negotiate with the ministry. Public unions are formed, and they strike for better wages and job stability. The negotiations are complicated by the fact that the government has a short time horizon because ministers often come and go in a matter of months, while unions and personnel have a long-term perspective.

Bit by bit, the government accedes to wage demands and to demands for additional hiring, until 95 percent of the health and education budgets is spent on personnel. The government resists further wage concessions and instead yields to the union on teachers' and doctors' work conditions—reducing hours and limiting the capacity of su-

pervisors to monitor staff. The union is allowed to eliminate supervisory discretion in promotions, by making promotions a function of seniority. Finally, the government begins to concede larger provider pensions and to shorten the time-of-service requirements for retirement. This concession is of great value to the teachers and doctors and costs the *current* government little; yet over time, the liability balloons, consuming larger and larger shares of public funding.

At this point, teachers and doctors have fixed pay scales, guaranteed employment, larger pensions, and shorter time-of-service requirements than private sector workers. With few incentives to exert themselves within their jobs, they begin to take on other jobs. The doctors show up in the public hospital or clinic for a few hours, but dedicate most of their time to serving clients in the private sector, where each additional service means additional income for the provider. Teachers remain in the public schools for stability and pension benefits, but they dedicate as much time as possible to other work or to training for a second career after they "retire." The lines in hospitals and clinics get longer, and the time spent learning in schools declines.

As the quality of health and education services deteriorates, any consumer with sufficient income flees the public sector for the private sector. Growing numbers of the middle class lose their confidence in the public system and question the expenditure of resources in a system that fails to serve them. As taxpayers, they are angry over wasted money, and attentive politicians shift budgetary resources to activities that have stronger lobbies—infrastructure, the military, and social security pensions. The continued increase in public service employees erodes the wages of education and health personnel, yet the finance minister is loath to expand the education and health budgets when returns in performance are so low. A vicious cycle of deteriorating service quality and middle-class flight continues to sap public education and health systems until they are barely functioning. They become systems in which teachers and doctors pretend to provide services and the poor pretend to be served. In the end, the system is neither equitable nor efficient.

THE SAVAGE MARKET

In our second country, the government plays no role in providing education and health services. Political parties argue that these are social functions that belong not in the public sector, but in churches, charities, and other private organizations. Fees and tuition are the main mechanism for financing these services. As a result, some people obtain an education for their children, and others do not. The rich and upper-middle class establish schools that finance themselves primarily through tuition. Charitable organizations establish schools to serve the middle class and the poor, but they operate with significantly fewer resources and cannot serve the entire population.

As a consequence of this pattern, the distribution of educational attainment is highly unequal. As students grow up and enter the labor market, the income gap between skilled and unskilled workers grows, reinforcing and exacerbating the inequality of opportunities for the next generation of students. The low average level of education also compromises the productivity of the labor force and leads the economy to stagnation.

In the health sector, doctors attend to the needs of the rich and middle class, charging fees for their services. To the degree that they are charitable, they also provide services at reduced or no cost to those who cannot afford them. The poorest people are excluded from health services entirely or are attended by nontraditional practitioners. The medical profession has no pecuniary interest in preventive measures, and few are taken. Little is done to educate people about more healthful behavior, except on a sporadic basis.

Insurance companies emerge, but they accept enrollment only from higher-income people who are at low risk of accidents and major diseases. Because doctors determine which services to provide and at what cost, and because the insurer pays the larger share of health service charges, insurance costs begin to escalate at a rate much faster than inflation. Voluntary consumer cooperatives begin to emerge as individuals and families seek ways to avoid the rising costs of insurance premiums. The cooperatives take prepayments and begin to negotiate contracts with providers. These contracts increasingly use a "capitation" mechanism, by which doctors are paid a fixed fee per enrolled member in return for providing certain basic services when needed. As a result, the cooperatives that bear full risk for their enrollees also try to limit enrollment to low-risk, healthier candidates. Like the insurance companies, they begin to exclude members when the latter reach old age or fall ill with chronic and costly diseases. The doctors try to deny services, and people complain about being put on long waiting lists with a lower priority than private patients.

In the end, the system responds primarily to effective demand—the demand for services by those who can afford them. This system therefore leaves large segments of the population unattended. Furthermore, it is highly inefficient in delivering the services it does provide, and costly for those it serves.

FABLES ALWAYS HAVE A MORAL

Fables always have morals, and these are no exception. Perhaps the two most appropriate ones would be that "good intentions are not enough" and "every silver lining has its cloud."

Good intentions are not enough. Even when all those involved in a social service system are well intentioned, the sum of their actions may be detrimental to performance. Such a result occurs when systems become overburdened relative to available resources; when providers modify, eliminate, or forestall the feedback mechanisms that are crucial to regulate the system; and when strategic choices strengthen certain groups, leading to imbalances in the system's ability to respond to the overall public interest. The teachers, doctors, government officials, and citizens in the "beneficent state" were all motivated by reasonable goals. In the context of difficulty in measuring performance and of unequal income distribution, however, their interaction led to a dysfunctional system.

Teachers and medical personnel—in their effort to eliminate arbitrary and discretionary treatment by supervisors—sought and obtained such rule-bound contracts that it became impossible officially to distinguish the good providers from the bad. It also became impossible to promote or reward good providers for their better performance; only seniority, length of service, and level of formal training could legally be used to determine promotions or pay. Meanwhile, discipline and evaluation were discouraged by the weakness of the position of supervisors in the overall system. Providers also successfully resisted submission to any measurement of their performance—but this lack of performance evaluation isolated the providers from vital information regarding their effectiveness and the needs of those they serve.

The social service delivery systems in the beneficent state fell apart because the choices among mechanisms of funding, resource allocation, control, and planning eventually created incentives that did not respond to the ultimate goals of public policy. This structure made it impossible to adjust to demands and to grant adequate reward for good performance by providers.

In the savage market, the situation was no better. Expansion of nongovernmental services made the system more responsive to citizens' needs, but only for those who could pay. Even then, the system generated incentives to overprovide outputs in some cases and to deny services in others. Even well-intentioned providers discriminated among their patients on the basis of the latters' ability to pay; there also existed plenty of room for the more unscrupulous providers to overcharge and to hide information about the poor quality of the services delivered. Furthermore, the services provided were not always the most necessary or effective, and costs were high for those who received services.

Every silver lining has its cloud. In the beneficent state, centralization of service delivery allowed more equitable funding, but it could not ensure high-quality performance. The efficiencies gained through economies of scale were offset by loss of information regarding consumer needs and the quality of services provided. The layers of norms and supervision that ensured good performance created groups with a vested interest in maintaining civil service benefits, while resisting performance measurement. Increased hiring to serve more people expanded administrative positions, and thus any increase in resources was quickly diverted away from direct service provision. In this case, limited ability to measure performance and assign accountability resulted in deteriorating services.

In the "savage market," efforts to introduce health insurance led to cost explosions and adverse selection of enrollees. The solution of voluntary prepaid cooperatives allowed providers to deny services and forced enrollees to become "secondary citizens" in the practices of private physicians. In regard to education, the unequal provision of educational opportunities reinforced and exacerbated social inequities, so that succeeding generations became increasingly polarized.

Specific effects of organization. The fables also illustrate other phenomena related to different organizational patterns. First, poor performance in public sectors erodes support from taxpayers, service providers, and administrators alike. When public services are poor, people seek alternatives—normally private providers—and begin to resent the taxes they still have to pay to support ineffective systems.

Second, highly centrally administered systems are very poor at choosing the best mix of inputs required in varied local conditions; they are also poor at adjusting to changing requirements over time.

Third, when consumers cannot exercise choice, service providers receive limited feedback about the quality of their services. Even when consumers do have choices, the combination of their lack of information and the relatively greater control and knowledge exercised by providers can make it difficult to censure the poorly performing providers. With little consumer voice in either system, feedback regarding needs, effectiveness, and quality of services does not occur.

Fourth, when supervisors and directors have little discretion in hiring, firing, and wage setting, they cannot adjust for local labor market conditions (such as offering higher wages to attract teachers to rural areas), they cannot adjust their staffing to local and changing needs, and they are restricted in their ability to induce better performance.

Fifth, bilateral monopolies like those between a ministry and a teachers' or physicians' union tend to be conflictual and lead to inefficient contracts, especially when unions focus on the long term, while government ministers have a short-term perspective. Contracts that emerge from negotiations between these two giants tend to become more rigid with regard to discretion in managing employees, less flexible in terms of the mix of inputs provided by the central ministry, and more costly because of the tendency to concede future costs for current cooperation (for instance, ballooning provider pension costs).

A sixth phenomenon relates to the financial incentives for social service employees. Service employees paid on fixed salary have limited incentives to exert themselves. This situation is exacerbated if they are paid on a per-service basis for alternative private sector activities.

A seventh issue is that equity suffers in both kinds of countries. In the first case, public provision of services does not guarantee equity—the poor get little access to low-quality service at high cost, while the rich escape to the private sector or pressure for public programs that satisfy their demands. Similarly, in the market system, when services are funded directly by consumers, only wealthier consumers get services. In this case, under the unregulated market, some consumers are sold more services than they need because of asymmetric information; insurance firms have an incentive to avoid higher-cost clients through adverse selection; and capitation systems provide incentives to deny services or to cut corners on quality.

Fortunately, no countries in the region are quite as bad as our fables depict. The traditional social service systems evolved as adequate solutions to the problems of their times, but are increasingly inadequate to the challenges of today. We have learned more, and through the elements described in the fables we can begin to discern the mechanisms and incentives that are holding back good performance. Already numerous initiatives, large and small, have emerged as countries seek to make adjustments. What is lacking is a more systematic view.

TOWARD A SYSTEMATIC VIEW

To go beyond these fables, we need to systematically distinguish the elements of different structures, and consider their advantages and disadvantages separately. Then we need to consider how coherent the combinations are within a given context. Finally we need to consider the kinds of dynamics, positive or negative, that such combinations may engender.

Table 3.1 presents a typology which seeks to capture the main dimensions of a service system structure.[2] The options presented are neither comprehensive nor the only way of characterizing the

---

[2] There are many schemes for analyzing service-system structures, including those of Rondinelli, Middleton, and Verspoor (1990) and Israel (1986 and 1996).

Table 3.1 Framework for Analyzing Social Service Systems

Agents/Elements	Options					
Finance						
Source	General revenues - national	General revenues - subnational	Mandatory contributions	Private insurance fees	User fees and copayments	
Allocation mechanisms	Installed capacity	"Block grants"	Performance contracts	Full-cost reimbursement	Predefined fees	Capitation
Providers						
Decision-making unit	Hierarchical administration	Autonomous administration				
Ownership	Central government	Subnational political entity	Specific public service entity	Private for-profit or nonprofit entities	Client cooperatives	
Labor regime	Civil service/ public unions	General labor regime/ private unions	Professional codes			
Complementary inputs	Central purchasing	Intermediate purchasing	Autonomous unit purchasing	Individual provider purchasing		
Articulation	Consumer efforts	Fragmented providers	Integrated providers			
Assuring quality	Structured control	Processes	Control by results			
Consumers						
Role of consumers	Excluded	Voice - feedback	Voice - formal decision-making powers	Choice - collective	Choice - individual	

Note: Detailed descriptions provided in text.

Table 3.2 Potential Sources of Finance

Options	*Advantages*	*Disadvantages*	*Complementary Mechanisms*
General revenues - national payroll taxes	Can be allocated progressively across regions Can be the most efficient form of taxation	Limited capacity of taxpayers to hold officials accountable for local services Local contributions to national resources can lead to suboptimal mobilization of tax revenue	Progressive financial allocation mechanisms
General revenues - subnational	Can be accountable to local consumers Sustainability improved because benefits can be captured locally in improved revenues	Inefficient taxation (easier to evade, more distortionary) Can be inequitable across areas/regions	Progressive redistribution mechanisms at national level Coordinated tax policies
Mandatory fees	Assures funding for services Can avoid adverse selection	Can be regressive	Demand-side subsidies can redress inequities
Private insurance payments	Can match consumers preferences to service level	Subject to adverse selection Can have third-party-payer problems of cost containment	Regulation of enrollment and separations Information for consumers
User fees and copayments	Can match consumer preferences to service level Incentives to use services wisely	Consumers need to obtain information which may be costly	Public and private provision of information to consumers

Table 3.3 Financial Allocation Mechanisms			
Options	*Advantages*	*Disadvantages*	*Complementary Mechanisms*
Installed capacity	Can assure supply	Provides no incentives for performance Subject to capture by providers	Strong planning, budget execution, and information systems
		Cannot respond flexibly and quickly to changing and varied demand	External accountability mechanisms
"Block grants"	Provides incentives for cost-effective use of funds by autonomous units	Provides limited incentives for performance	External accountability mechanisms
	Can increase service and quality through efficient mix of inputs	Decisionmakers can divert funds away from service toward perquisites and pay	Performance contracts
Performance contracts	Can relate budgets and payments to performance	Can tolerate low performance because sanctions are "soft"	External accountability mechanisms
	Provides flexibility to negotiate between parties in a "repeat game"	Can concentrate information between institutional purchasers and providers, leaving consumers uninformed	Public information
Fee for defined service	Can provide strong incentives for providing services (outputs)	Can lead to cost increases and overprovision of services	Cost-control measures such as "average" payment per service
	Can respond flexibly and diversely to demand		
Cost reimbursement	Can give providers assurance that their costs of provision will be fully covered	Can lead to cost increases and inefficiency because providers have no incentives to limit costs	Review boards which "allow" or "disallow" costs
Capitation	Can provide strong incentives by linking rewards to outcomes	Can encourage providers to discourage use of services	Quality controls Competition with informed consumers or institutional purchasers
	Can respond flexibly and diversely to demand		

major alternatives, but they begin to demonstrate the range of options available and their particularities. Myriad combinations are possible, and each has numerous nuances which affect its impact.

Financial Sources

Beginning with financial sources, the major options are to finance services with national revenues, local revenues, mandatory contributions, private insurance fees, user fees, and copayments (see Tables 3.1 and 3.2). These options vary in terms of their efficiency, their distributive burden, and the kinds of incentives they create for consumers.

Systems that are financed out of *general revenues at the national level* can be made equitable and progressive.[3] Income, trade, and value-added taxes are easier to implement at the national level.[4] Given their importance in public finance, national taxes are likely to be the most significant aggregate source of taxation revenue. At the na-

[3] In a study of OECD countries, Wagstaff and von Doorslaer (1993) show that of the four ways of financing health care (taxes, social insurance, private insurance, and direct payments), taxes are the most progressive and direct payments the most regressive source of financing.
[4] National taxes are still subject to evasion, however, by corporations and individuals who can hide or shift reported income and expenditures between countries.

Table 3.4 Labor Regime			
Options	*Advantages*	*Disadvantages*	*Complementary Mechanisms*
Civil service/public unions	Stability can assure investment in specific skills	Potential for political interference often responded to by reducing managerial discretion Bilateral monopoly leading to conflictual relationships	Socialization and professionalization to increase commitment to sector and profession Information and accountability of provider pay and performance to the public
General labor regime	May give supervisors more flexibility in staffing, hiring, promotion, and wage-setting Reorients incentives away from pension and stability toward pay and conditions	May reduce attractiveness of career due to uncertainty when public sector is major employer	Adequate grievance procedures Contracts and negotiation processes that encourage resolution of issues
Merit pay	Can create incentives to perform better	When performance measures are subjective, can lead to uncertainty that undermines the performance incentive Can create incentives to work toward what is measured, rather than what is desired	
Fixed wage based on training and seniority	Can encourage investment in sector specific skills by reducing uncertainty of returns	Does not provide incentives to improve performance	Nonpecuniary rewards Recognition based on effective evaluations Career advancement which uses areas of technical competence

tional level it is also possible to promote equity within a country through revenue-sharing formulas that explicitly use provincial or municipal income levels as a criterion for determining the amount of national money transferred. However, national-level taxation also can make authorities less accountable to the local concerned citizens who are actually paying the taxes.

At the other extreme, *private insurance premiums and user fees* have one of the key advantages of market purchases—that of demonstrating demand. But they respond to effective demand rather than to "social" demand, a disadvantage of markets from the public policy perspective. Private insurance can have the additional problem of moral hazard, which restricts the number of people who can get insurance to below the optimal number, or adverse selection, a situation in which only the more-at-risk popula-

tion enters into insurance contracts (see Box 3.1). Charging *user fees* for services can be extremely efficient for discouraging overuse. But user charges can be costly to administer, can discourage the use of cost-effective services, and can become a regressive financial source for sustaining social services.

Local revenues have the advantage of placing resources in the hands of local boards or local politicians, who can be more accountable to citizen demands. Such taxes often enjoy a good level of local support because individuals feel that the resources are more likely to benefit them directly. The main challenge to local taxation is finding an efficient tax base. Income and value added are hard to define at the local level, gross sales taxes tend to cascade through the purchase of intermediate goods, and property taxes are cumbersome and costly to manage. In all cases, the existence of het-

---

Box 3.1 Economic Concepts for Analyzing Social Services

Numerous concepts from the economic literature on institutions and market imperfections are helpful in understanding the behavior of governments, providers, and consumers in social service systems. Some of these concepts are defined below:

Agency Theory is a branch of economics that analyzes the problem of delegated choice, i.e. when a "principal" seeks to achieve his or her goals through assigning a task to an "agent". When the principal has difficulty measuring the agent's output, or attributing the output to the agent's effort, it becomes difficult for the two actors to reach an agreement on a contract that will be "incentive compatible", that is, a contract which leads the agent to behave in a way that is optimal from both the principal's and agent's perspectives. When doctors are hired on fixed salaries, they have less incentive to provide a lot of services of high quality than if they are paid on the basis of the number of quality services performed. When teachers are placed in a classroom with students whose gains in knowledge are not evaluated by test scores, teachers have fewer incentives for good teaching.

Asymmetric information is a condition in which one of the parties to a transaction does not have information that the other has. This is an issue in *"Agency Theory"* because the agent knows more about his or her own abilities and effort, the character of services demanded, and the outcomes than does the principal. This is a key source of inefficiency. Much of institutional economic analysis seeks to determine which kinds of implicit or explicit contracts can offset these inefficiencies.

Adverse selection occurs under asymmetric information, when the person or organization selling the service only knows the average cost, while the individual purchasing the service has more information about his or her specific cost. When the service provider charges average costs, the clients with lower than average costs leave the market and, ultimately,

may lead to the total disappearance of the market. It is especially important in insurance markets where lower than average risk clients will find premia based on average costs to be too expensive, while higher risk clients will find them cheap. Insurance companies, then, have incentives to design their benefits, fees, and marketing strategies to attract only wealthier, healthier, lower risk adults who, for their part, wish to be served by a lower risk pool. As a result, only lower risk individuals may be able to obtain insurance. Adverse selection also occurs in education, when schools can select and accept the most capable students and exclude those who are likely to be more difficult or costly to teach.

Moral hazard occurs when a person changes his or her behavior as a consequence of being insured. This can be manifested by insured individuals undertaking risky activities since they know their health care is assured; or by overusing services for which the individual does not have to pay the full cost.

Externalities are benefits or costs perceived or borne by other individuals in society than the person who consumed the service or commodity. In the case of beneficial externalities, this tends to lead to insufficient investment or consumption of the particular service since the individual only obtains a portion of the total benefits. Individuals have an incentive to immunize themselves against contagious diseases, but not as much as all the individuals in a society collectively. Education also provides benefits to society beyond the benefits obtained by the individual.

Public goods are commodities or services that are "nonexclusive", that is, if one person "consumes" them it does not preclude someone else from enjoying them as well. Some examples of social services which are public goods include mosquito eradication or public radio educational programs.

---

erogeneous local taxes may significantly distort businesses' location decisions.

Mandatory fees are usually indicated in cases where adverse selection creates problems; social security being the most common example. Mandatory fees eliminate adverse selection because higher-risk individuals are automatically pooled with those of lower risk. They effectively

ensure a steady flow of funds into a particular service, and they can be equitable, as occurs when contributions are calculated as a share of income, yet access to services remains the same for all contributors. Users' inability to opt out of the system, however, is a disadvantage of mandatory fees. Even when consumers are dissatisfied with the services they receive, their contributions continue to flow to the providers whether the services are used or not; providers' incomes are protected even when "their" clients leave.

Allocation Mechanisms

Once funds are collected, they must be allocated to service providers. *The allocation mechanism for financial resources* is in many cases the most important dimension of the system (see Tables 3.1 and 3.3). The flow of financial resources provides critical incentives to all of the actors in the system—whether to a hospital director, a teacher, a patient, a union leader, a government minister, or an administrator—affecting the choices they make in purchasing, hiring, and delegating.

The most common allocation mechanisms in the private sector of the region's health systems are *full-cost reimbursement* and *predefined fees*. Under full-cost reimbursement, the provider determines both what services are to be provided and how much they cost, with the individual or insurance company agreeing to pay the full cost retrospectively. Under a predefined fee system, the provider still determines what services are to be provided, but there is a predefined agreement regarding the price per procedure or diagnosis. Both systems provide incentives for technical innovation and provision of services. But as has been demonstrated in many countries, the generalized use of such allocation mechanisms may have costs in terms of equity and allocative efficiency. If fees are paid directly by consumers, such systems tend to discriminate against poorer and sicker groups in the population. If instead a third party insures the clients, particularly under full-cost reimbursement, the systems tend to provide too many services and lead to a dramatic rise in costs.[5]

The most common form of financial resource allocation in the public systems of the region, both for education and health services, is allocation on the basis of inputs or *installed capacity*. In this kind of system, one or more administrative offices determine how many staff positions, materials, investments, and maintenance services will be provided to each unit. The decision regarding inputs automatically translates into financial requirements—wages to be paid, materials to be purchased—that are independent of the number of services being provided at the particular school or health facility. In this regard, the service facility has no "budget," per se. It cannot tell how much it spends on providing services because it does not know.

By contrast, a few systems have chosen to allocate resources on the basis of outputs, transferring funds to the service facilities as a function of the number of services provided. Although full-cost reimbursement and predefined fees also allocate resources on the basis of outputs, they have numerous disadvantages, as discussed earlier. A more promising form of allocation mechanism is *capitation*—in which a prenegotiated payment per person is given to the provider, under which all of the client's educational or health needs are to be covered. In this sense, the capitated payment functions as a per capita budget. Voucher programs like the one used for secondary schools in Colombia or the capitated prepaid health plans of Uruguay are examples of such resource allocation mechanisms. In this case, the allocation mechanism provides a clear message—the providers know how much they receive for each student or each patient in their care and have a clear incentive to find out whether average costs are above or below that level. They also have a strong interest in finding the right mix of inputs, taking into account different inputs' costs and relative effectiveness, so as to provide the service at the least possible cost. These efficiencies liberate funds that—depending on other elements of organization—may be used to expand services,

---

[5] This problem of cost explosion is most apparent in the United States of America, where it has led to a significant public debate on health reform. In Latin America, the experience in Brazil demonstrates that under the *Sistema Unica de Saúde*, doctors and hospitals inflate their bills to ensure adequate compensation under a highly imperfect reimbursement scheme. In Uruguay, Labadie (1996) demonstrates that doctors in IAMCs who are compensated on the basis of services provided, tend to provide more services.

improve service quality, or increase the incomes of the providers.

An intermediate option involves giving provider units a specific block of funds over which they have full discretion. In a *performance contract*, the providers receive funds for a predetermined level of services. Under *block grants*, the level of services to be provided is often less well defined. For this to be effective, the grant must function as a "hard" budget—no additional payments can be allowed for profligate units. Even if the total amount is not directly linked to the quantity and quality of services provided, it still makes the schools or health units aware of the relative costs and benefits of their choices. Knowing its budget, a school might decide to reduce the janitorial staff in order to purchase more texts, or reduce expenditures on photocopying, to pay for more maintenance.

For example, the universities of Campinas and of São Paulo responded to a new system of financial autonomy by internalizing their budget decisions. They gradually reconfigured their staffing profile, concentrated on more productive activities, and managed their costs. The universities increased both the efficiency and quality of their service delivery in a short time, despite their differences in institutional culture and size.[6]

A system of allocation based on installed capacity sends only one message: those who ask and ask repeatedly will get more of the administered resources. By contrast, a budget sends a clear message of responsibility to the managerial functions of the service unit, where most of the information about needs and tradeoffs is located.

Providers: Decision-making Units

The financial resources channeled through allocation mechanisms go eventually to some *decision-*

making unit—an agent or entity responsible for making decisions about the input mix and for delivering the services. These units can be large hierarchically administered systems or autonomous institutions.

When schools and health facilities are components of a large hierarchically administered system, planners can try to optimize the scale and location of investments, and cross-subsidies can be used to ensure a more equitable distribution of services and fees. Despite the economies of scale, however, the planning capacities of centrally administered systems are at a serious disadvantage because information about service needs is highly decentralized and monitoring of personnel and services is costly for a central office. This phenomenon occurs not only in national-level public ministries. Large subnational-level state and municipal governments, serving sizable populations, are subject to the same problem of distance from the information regarding their heterogeneous clients. Hierarchical administration necessarily introduces rules and patterns into its decision-making structure to reduce administrative costs, but these same rules and patterns are sources of inflexibility and inefficiency at the level of the actual school or medical practice.

By contrast, autonomous units have greater flexibility to respond rationally to consumer needs, new opportunities, and changing circumstances. Most important, an autonomous school or health facility can decide how many services to provide and what combination of personnel, materials, and infrastructure is optimal. Autonomous units require information and "signals," along with the capacity to process them. These signals come in the form of budgets, prices for inputs, wages and salaries, the cost of contracting services, student test scores, and the health status of patients. The signals can also include reviews by public agencies or expressions of satisfaction or dissatisfaction from consumers.

An important advantage of autonomous units is that they can be compared with one anoth-

[6] Castro, M.H. de Magalhães (1995) describes this process, begun in 1989, during which the schools themselves unleashed a process of changing their internal allocation mechanisms from ones based upon historical budgets and negotiation to ones based upon performance and transparency.

er and can even offer consumers choices. When there are multiple providers (whether exclusively from the public sector or not), "benchmarking" becomes possible: i.e. decision-making units can compare their performances with an "industry" standard. Service purchasers—public agencies, private insurance companies, or individuals—can also compare performance when many different provider units are making decisions independently. When consumers can choose among providers, then enrollment levels and queue size also provide information regarding the users' perception of service quality. Opening this kind of choice can increase technical efficiency, moderate prices, and create incentives to improve services. With multiple providers, choice by clients is possible but not necessarily sufficient. Additional sources of information (audits, quality checks, sanctions) or institutional checks (by well-informed institutional purchasers) are necessary to ensure that competition in such imperfect markets serves the public interest.

Ownership

The nature of the ownership of service units has an effect on the incentives for managing services. The profit incentive for *privately owned entities* is only the most obvious of the examples within this category. Perhaps more important is the effect of ownership upon investment decisions—decisions to invest in research, expansion, and maintenance (oriented toward improving future services) relative to expenditures on personnel and materials (which affect current services). Thus, when schools or clinics are owned by a distant public agency, local staff and clients have little incentive to preserve them. *Public units* that have some degree of autonomy and that own their facilities have greater incentives to mobilize resources and preserve them. Numerous schools in the region are better preserved because they are owned by local community associations. In Uruguay, consumer health cooperatives invest relatively more in facilities and future services than do doctor-owned cooperatives,

which choose to distribute greater shares of their revenues as salaries.[7] Expansion of infrastructure is particularly poor in systems in which responsibility for assets is diffuse and subject to arbitrary funding decisions, as is the case in most of the centrally administered and centrally owned education systems of the region.

Providers: The Labor Regime

Social services are highly labor intensive, social service personnel have enormous discretion in the quality and quantity of services they provide, and it is difficult to measure performance accurately (see Tables 3.1 and 3.4). Therefore, the labor regime is critically important to the performance of social services. Most teachers, educators, and health professionals are employed in the public sector under a civil service code, and in most cases, their pay and work conditions are negotiated between a strong public union and a public sector ministry.

In some countries and sectors in which public service is not as important a source of employment, however, social service professionals have been able to create independent *professional associations* that acquire almost monopolistic powers. The authority of these associations is frequently ratified or increased through "professional conduct regulations," which give their associates privileged negotiating positions vis-à-vis the government, and their clients—whether private citizens or institutions like insurance companies. The professional associations have the advantage of being able to respond to what professionals know best about their services, and they can serve members' interests so that members are empowered and motivated to maintain high professional standards. Nevertheless, these systems also have a tendency to become inflexible and insulated from the needs of consumers when the corporate interests of the providers expand unchecked.

---

[7] Labadie (1996).

The *civil service codes* in the public sector tend to offer very strong employment guarantees, to establish pay scales based predominantly on formal training and years of service, and to provide large pensions after few years of service relative to the norm in the private sector. Because of the stability they offer, such civil service codes can be effective at inducing individual providers to invest in training. But under such codes, the civil service can also degenerate into a rigid system of entitlements that offers providers few incentives to perform or to increase productivity once they are hired. Particularly in cases in which alternative employment is available, public employees have strong incentives to minimize their effort in their public sector job and to dedicate more hours or more energy to their private sector endeavors. The job guarantees and tenure-linked promotions weaken the ability of supervisors to sanction employees who are unproductive or frequently absent.

Along with the civil service code, most conditions of work are negotiated directly between the government and strong public sector unions. The advantage of strong unions is their ability to give voice to problems of mismanagement and abuse within the system, to represent employees in discussions regarding ways to increase productivity, and to lobby the public for greater resources to the sector. In many cases, however, the effort to control managerial abuse degenerates into rigid rules that eliminate managerial discretion and make effective management all but impossible. In representing employees in discussions of productivity, unions frequently defend the status quo, which is responsible for their strength and privileged position, particularly in the case of union leaders.

The grouping of large numbers of teachers or medical personnel in public service creates conditions of bilateral monopoly between large public unions and the government.[8] The fact that negotiations take place between a single major purchaser (the government) and a single major supplier (the unions) leads to widespread and frequent work stoppages. The structure of bilateral monopoly gives both sides strong incentives to be confrontational because there is a broad range of conditions that each side knows the other can accept. The relations between unions and government are further complicated by the range of goals that union leaders and politicians bring to the negotiating table. In many cases, unions may seek to maximize employment, and membership, in order to assist a political party with which they are affiliated or they may call strikes about issues unrelated to the sector. Politicians also use the negotiations to reward unions that are aligned with them or to score points against unions that are linked to their political opponents.[9]

General labor codes are the main alternative system, and they govern the contracts of many teachers and health care workers who are employed in the private sector. In Latin America and the Caribbean, these general labor codes can also be quite detailed and inflexible—establishing numerous nonwage benefits, as well as restrictions on labor mobility, such as severance payments.[10] Nevertheless, the general labor code does offer more flexibility to the service provider institutions in selecting, hiring, evaluating, monitoring, and rewarding their employees. The disadvantage of the general labor codes is that they may subject doctors and teachers to such a level of uncertainty that able individuals are not attracted to those professions.

In many cases in the region, even private provider institutions are required to follow standard government contract protocols. But several recent initiatives aimed at expanding coverage to rural areas have specifically sought to exempt

---
8 See Nelson (1994), Hausmann (1993 and 1994), and Murillo (1996).
9 See Murillo (1996).
10 The general labor codes in the region have been the subject of several studies, most of which consider them to be quite inflexible by international standards. See Part Two, Chapter 6, "Labor Reform", Márquez (1994) and Cox-Edwards (1993).

teachers from the civil service code as a way of motivating greater effort, allowing higher wages, and increasing flexibility (such as the EDUCO initiative in El Salvador).

Providers: Complementary Inputs

Personnel are a critical input for the provision of efficient social services but they cannot do their jobs without adequate complementary inputs. Such inputs include complementary services as diverse as cleaning, maintenance, and in-service training; they also include complementary materials such as books, audiovisual aids, medicines, and laboratory equipment.

The most common administrative unit for determining the level and kinds of complementary inputs used in social service delivery systems has been the *central purchasing office*. Large centralized systems are frequently at an advantage in the purchase of complementary inputs because of economies of scale and greater bargaining power. Central purchasing, however, is also likely to impose rigid and homogeneous rules upon the provision of complementary inputs, regardless of local need, and it also has difficulties in opportunely contracting complementary services and in quickly distributing needed materials. Furthermore, it is vulnerable to large-scale corruption.

At the other extreme, *individual service providers* can be given their own budgets to spend on complementary inputs, as in the case of medical professionals with a fund for contracting laboratory services or the case of teachers who can access a fund for in-service training.

In between these extremes, *autonomous provider units* such as schools or clinics can be given the power to choose and purchase the complementary inputs they judge are best suited to their own needs. Particularly in the purchasing of materials, however, scale economies tend to make it more efficient for such purchasing to be done by *intermediate purchasers*. These intermediate levels can still be "demand driven" in the sense that au-

tonomous units originate the specific requests and are merely authorizing transfers from their budgets for those inputs they purchase. The intermediate purchasing agency, meanwhile, can take advantage of its larger scale to negotiate better prices.

Providers: Articulated Services

No matter what kinds of units provide the services and no matter how these units are owned, many social services require some kind of articulation, because the range of needs and of the potential services offered makes it difficult to match clients or patients to the providers and services they actually require. This particular element of organization is largely an issue of the health care system.

Consumers themselves can provide an integrated perspective on their needs, but it is very difficult for them to be sufficiently well informed of the range of services available and to be able to evaluate which ones to choose, especially in regard to health care. The most common result is that consumers rely upon service providers, usually doctors, to make the decisions regarding the sources of problems and the best treatments.

When *providers are unintegrated*, they have incentives to provide those services that they are equipped to provide without regard to the client's best overall interest. They also have incentives to refer patients elsewhere when it is too costly for them to provide an indicated service.

A third option involves the organization of providers into units or institutions that have an *integrated perspective* on each client's needs. Such systems have emerged in cases in which a single firm or decision-making unit (such as a health maintenance organization, or HMO) is responsible for all the needs of the consumers which are well specified by regulation or contract. In such a case, any referrals will necessarily be within the same overall unit—whether clinic to hospital, or general practitioner to specialist.

When this integrated approach is combined with a capitated form of financial allocation, providers also have an interest in providing the "right" services, the ones that are most effective at the least cost. This is an option being explored in the health systems of Europe, empowering doctors to act as agents for their affiliated patients, and in which the doctor receives a capitated fund to contract specialized services from hospitals. The General Practitioner Fund Holders in Britain functions this way and has been one of the most interesting innovations in health service delivery of the last decade.

Integrated entities can coordinate the functions of related units either by owning them and using tools of internal management or by subcontracting services through standing arrangements with providers. When the entity owns all of the service providing capabilities, it has the advantages of knowing exactly what is available and of more effectively controlling the relationships among the different providers (as in the case of a local health district with its own clinics and hospital facilities). But it may be at a disadvantage in terms of its flexibility to deal with extraordinary requirements or to adjust the mix of services it provides.

By contrast, subcontracting allows for greater flexibility but limits the control exercised by the contracting agency. In the education sector, municipalities can purchase special education for learning disabled children under contractual terms; but the health care sector's experience with such contracting is much wider and varied. Many of the health institutions that purchase services for their clients (such as the private sector Igualas of the Dominican Republic or the DISSE in Uruguay) establish payments to the hospitals, clinics, and doctors that agree to serve their clients. In the case of private insurers, arrangements to purchase services at prearranged prices are more common. Articulation through contracts is indeed more flexible than articulation through ownership, but it is also subject to the coordination failures that arise in markets with imperfect information and weak enforcement of contracts.

The way providers are articulated has to be consistent with the kinds of demands being placed upon them. The usual approach has been the integration of providers of different services under the same line of command and control. This approach has been dominant in recent years because a premium has been placed upon the system's ability to channel public policy goals uniformly to a variety of providers. In fact, the articulation of service provision has not been the subject of much discussion in the region because this administrative approach has been dominant. But recent efforts to make the systems more responsive to demand will require rethinking the articulation of providers. As consumers are empowered to make choices that affect financial allocation and as providers are given greater leeway to innovate or choose the appropriate interventions, the providers themselves will require additional channels for "horizontal" coordination. Health systems have innovated most strongly in this dimension, with the emergence of institutional purchasers or integrated medical practices that reduce the information requirements for clients, on the one hand, and take on the responsibility of coordinating health services, on the other.

Providers: Ensuring Quality

Ensuring the quality of social services is extremely important because they are difficult to monitor, prices and negotiation are frequently imperfect, and outcomes have strong impacts on life chances. Therefore, effective systems rarely rely upon a single mechanism to ensure quality. Rather, they rely upon a combination of mechanisms in which the incentive structure, the processes for establishing and enforcing standards, and the accountability for results all play roles.

The most common focus of attention for ensuring quality has been on *structured controls*. This option emphasizes the establishment of minimum conditions or standards of treatment or service that public and private providers alike are required to fulfill. This approach can involve certifying the personnel who staff a service unit, either on the basis of completing formal training or recertification through in-service training or exams. Certification is also used to establish minimum qualifications for the institutions that train professionals or that provide complementary services such as laboratories and pharmaceutical companies.

The public sector has a variety of attributes that make it an effective arena for the application of structured controls. Standards are a key mechanism for increasing the efficiency of markets for goods or services; otherwise, consumers and suppliers would have to expend a great deal of time and money in evaluating the quality of the services or products being purchased. The creation of specific grades and qualities for petroleum, wheat, and other commodities is the most obvious example. For services as well, the establishment of norms and standards helps consumers or institutional purchasers to evaluate, negotiate, or choose among the prices and services being offered.

The advantage of using agencies at the level of the executive branch of the central government to establish norms and standards is that such standards can carry the force of law and can take advantage of significant scale economies. For instance, it is common for the public sector to take responsibility for establishing standards for the quality of medications and foods. Standards of medical or educational practice can also be written. In theory, executive agencies can establish standards only for very general issues of practice or infrastructure, because they are usually not agile or subtle enough to be able to establish appropriately tailored protocols or curricula. In practice, however, the public role in ensuring quality has often established detailed standards that are actually beyond the present capabilities of most providers, thus leading to evasion and corruption. Recourse to the judicial system (particularly in health) has also failed to ensure quality but has in fact increased costs and corruption in many countries.

In contrast to structured controls, quality can also be ensured by processes *of negotiation, contracting, and sanction.* Rather than establishing universal minimum standards, the system can rely upon transparent means for consumers and providers to come to agreement about the expected quality of services, predictable sanctions for failure to comply with terms, and mutually acceptable means for arbitration or appeal when the agreement fails. Although private initiative is central to such processes, the public sector still has a role in making contracts more efficient by establishing models, encouraging the formation of arbitration mechanisms and systems of "peer review," and ensuring enforcement—meted out through a variety of institutions including the judicial system and directives from executive or regulatory agencies.

Quality can also be ensured by *measuring results.* The availability of accepted, understood, and widely disseminated information about the performance of different providers makes it easier to allocate resources on the basis of results and outputs; it also makes it possible to compare providers and demonstrate which techniques of pedagogy, treatment, or management are better and which are worse. Student exams and the condition of patients of different health providers are the closest measures of outcome that we can easily obtain and evaluate. Also of use are complementary measures of service quality from consumer surveys, as well as data such as hours of study or waiting times for surgeries.

The public sector can be a vigilant source of such information to increase public accountability of the social service systems, gathering data about the quality of services provided in the systems, and publicizing and disseminating such information.

The Role of Consumers

The role of the consumer has been less emphasized traditionally because the model of social service provision has been oriented "to deliver" services to people rather than "to respond" to their demands. Nevertheless, the consumer's role cannot be ignored if systems are to function better. The simple option of *excluding* consumers from decisionmaking in the system has few advantages in terms of performance; it merely makes life easier for those who wish to take advantage of the system for their own purposes.

Consumers can play a limited or an extensive role in the social service delivery system. In their most limited role, consumers can have *voice in the sense of providing information and feedback* to the provider regarding their needs, satisfactions, and dissatisfactions. These feedback mechanisms can be formal (through surveys, hearings, or evaluation exercises) or informal (when trust between consumer and provider is strong enough to make a conversation or letter have an impact).

Another option is to give clients *voice through formal participation* in decisionmaking through elected representatives on hospital or school boards or through other public forums for reviewing performance and holding providers accountable. Formal participation has the advantage of counterbalancing the interests of providers or politicians in the service systems. It can also increase the transparency of decisionmaking processes and help educate the population regarding important tradeoffs and budget constraints in the provision of services. Nevertheless, elected representatives can also be subject to corruption or capture by special interests, and therefore, complementary mechanisms to ensure good governance are always important. The actual decisionmaking powers of such boards may also be circumscribed by providers who resist their interference.

Consumers can have a significant impact on services by affecting the flow of financial resources. When consumers have *choice* (the ability to select among providers), then they have the capacity to reward the better performers with their business. The advantage of such a mechanism is that con-

sumers already have very strong incentives both to seek out higher-quality services and to express their preferences regarding the services they wish to receive. The disadvantage is that in many cases consumers are poorly informed regarding the full range of options and the nature of their own particular needs, especially in health care. For this reason, and particularly in the health sector, choice is sometimes exercised *collectively* through institutional purchasers, cooperatives, or other forms of association. In such cases, consumers choose from among a relatively smaller set of provider institutions on the basis of broad quality and pricing criteria, leaving it to the purchasing agency to negotiate details on specific aspects of services.

COHERENT AND EFFICIENT SYSTEMS

Until now we have discussed the various elements of the social service system structure as if each one were relatively independent. In fact, however, certain of these options are likely to be more effective in combination, while other combinations of options may be disastrous. In many of these interactions, the disadvantages of a certain mechanism can be offset or reduced by countervailing elements of the organization (see "complementary mechanisms" in Tables 3.2, 3.3, and 3.4). Furthermore, under the varied conditions related to different countries' particular settlement patterns, environments, and social context some options may be infeasible while others may be more likely to bear the desired fruits.

Overall, the experience in the region has concentrated on only a few subsets of these options, with implications for performance and political-economic dynamics. In education, systems that were largely decentralized during the early part of this century became steadily more centralized; teacher unions grew in power; and public "monopolies" eventually became the norm. In health, centralization also proceeded; the more common result in the health sector, however, was a fragmentation of service providers among the ministry of health, the social security system, and a large private sector. Thus, within the region's health sector there is much greater variation. For instance, Brazil's unified health system places a quarter of the region's population under a "fee-for-service" type of allocation mechanism; the cooperatives and mutual associations of Argentina and Uruguay have created capitation schemes with public financing and private provision; meanwhile, Chile, Colombia, and Uruguay have sought to establish systems with structured competition.

Using a scheme developed by Londoño (1995) and Londoño and Frenk (1996), we can distinguish four general models described by particular combinations of the options discussed earlier.

The first of these models, *public monopoly,* is one in which general revenues are used to raise funds for the services, which are administered centrally under a civil service code. In such a system, funds are allocated on the basis of installed capacity, and quality control is purely a public affair, as is ownership of the units providing services. Such systems can be efficient under very particular circumstances. To remain effective, they generally require a strong intrinsic reward system and motivation for those entering service, along with high social status and commensurate pay levels. They also need governance structures that make the service providers accountable to elected officials and that make the elected officials accountable to their constituents. In order to deal with the loss of information between a consumer's needs and the system's centrally planned allocations, the system must either be of a limited scale or provide channels for consumers to voice their concerns and/or participate in local decisions. Such systems typically fail when the country lacks, or loses, these same factors. Most of the education systems in the region bear some resemblance to the public monopoly model. Among health care systems, those of the English-speaking Caribbean, Costa Rica, and Cuba come closest to having the features described by this model.

A second model can be described as *public finance–private provision.* In this kind of system, financial sources consist of general revenues or mandatory contributions such as a payroll tax; these funds are then allocated to providers on the basis of a predefined fee formula. Providers are private entities with staff contracted under general labor codes, and they are regulated by a combination of public supervisory agencies and consumer choice. The providers may have a fragmented perspective on consumer's needs. This public finance/private provision model can function well in cases in which there is a great deal of sophistication regarding payment formulas—establishing prices that are sufficient to induce an effective mix of services but that also encourage productivity gains that lead to lower prices. Another necessary condition for success is that providers must have few opportunities to induce demand and overprovide services. General economic conditions must be stable enough, and compensation high enough, to attract able people into the training programs necessary for providing specialized services. A public regulatory presence is necessary to ensure that the services that are paid for are actually delivered and that quality is maintained. A governance structure that protects the regulatory agency from pressures from providers is also necessary. When these conditions are not present, this model is likely to lead to a situation in which quality is variable, inequities abound, and costs tend to escalate. Certain segments of the health systems in the Southern Cone and Brazil's public financing of health care are cases in the region that begin to approximate this model.

A third model is that of a *free market.* In such a system, user fees and private insurance fees dominate as sources of financing. Providers receive their funding via full-cost reimbursement or predefined fees. Provider units are autonomous and private, with employees contracted under a system of general labor codes. Consumers choose among providers, but the fragmentation of providers means that services are not coordinated.

Such systems can provide relatively good services to small and wealthy segments of the population, but they tend to exclude large numbers of people. When lower-income groups do gain access to services, the services tend to be of much lower quality. Costs in these systems also tend to increase rapidly. No country in the region has such a free-market system in full; however, the large and unregulated private health sectors of the smaller and poorer countries approximate this situation. The increasing share of private provision of education in many countries among poorer groups also demonstrates some of these features.

The fourth model, *structured pluralism,* can also be described as a particular subset of options. In this model, general revenues are the source of financing for services, and they are allocated to providers on the basis of a capitation mechanism. Ownership may be private or public, but the particular institution that gets the capitated payment is responsible for the full range of services to the consumer and therefore has an integrated perspective of consumer needs. The institution may specialize in marketing and evaluating providers, acting as collective agent for its consumers in purchasing services. The employees of the providing units are governed by a general labor code, allowing the units to construct contracts with bonuses and career paths with evaluations and promotions related to performance. Consumers in structured-pluralism systems have choice and voice in the provision of services. The public sector regulators focus on collecting and disseminating information, establishing standards, enforcing contracts, and establishing rules that defend against the problem of adverse selection. To be effective, such a system requires that the various agents and consumers have the capacities to seek out information, to innovate, and to understand and formulate contracts. No system in the region fully fits this model but the Chilean reform of education and the Colombian health reform are both moving in this direction. Other countries have also begun to experiment or to consider

adopting elements of this model in particular segments of their service systems.

When elements of a particular model are adopted without the needed complementary mechanisms, problems can arise that halt the momentum of reform. For instance, studies of the Chilean education reform have recognized the value of the institutional changes but have also remarked upon equally essential complementary factors that were missing. In reviewing this case, Carnoy and Castro (1996), have emphasized that decentralization, although desirable, needed to be accompanied "by a host of other measures focused on capacity building, standard setting, and policy coherence, most of which have usually been the responsibility of central or state governments... rather than of schools or municipalities."[11] Other studies have described how under the Chilean experiment of introducing a form of competition among schools—both private and public—the municipal schools performed less well overall because they have faced more rigid labor codes and "softer" budget constraints than their private counterparts.[12]

Capitation mechanisms are very attractive in terms of providing incentives to serve demand rather than to build up supplies. Nevertheless, introducing capitation in health plans or stipends (*subvenciones*) in education—without establishing standards and rules so that units cannot reduce the amount of services per person or reject applicants—can easily lead to "cream skimming": that is, providers may seek to attract only the healthiest clients or the more easily taught students, to ensure that average costs are below the capitation level. Providers will also have incentives to underserve their clients to the extent possible. A variety of credible information mechanisms, norms, and quality controls can be built into the system to complement a capitation plan and to moderate these disadvantages.

[11] Carnoy and Castro (1996), p. 12.
[12] Aedo (1994 and 1996).

Because service provision has many different characteristics and numerous inputs, any changes that make use of service providers' decision-making power need to be equally sophisticated with regard both to structuring the related budget allocation mechanisms and to obtaining accurate information about provider performance. In many cases, simply moving within the public system to capitated budgets and to local decision-making autonomy will be as sophisticated a change as is currently possible. In other cases, full output-based mechanisms, such as means-tested demand subsidies, may be possible.

In general, the coherence of a system needs to be evaluated by analyzing the incentives and the checks and balances affecting the major actors in the system. This includes evaluating the incentives created for each agent by the particular financial-allocation mechanisms used and by the existing informational and sanction, or reward, mechanisms that hold agents accountable. Such evaluation is needed at all levels, whether in regard to a local school board's power to hire, promote, and fire teachers or a ministry's budgetary decisions regarding the relative priority of different services. In the first case, accountability to parents or local citizens may be required, whereas in the latter case accountability to taxpayers and to a national community of consumers must be ensured. The need for systemwide coherence also means recognizing the political patterns of relationships engendered by the structure of the social service system. Accountability for a local school board in some countries could be achieved simply through allowing parental representation on the school board itself. In other countries, teacher unions may be so strong at the national level that the local school boards would need to be strongly reinforced to counterbalance the unions' leverage.

POLITICAL ECONOMY OF EFFICIENT SYSTEMS

Besides affecting incentives, structural options also have an impact on interests. Consumers, provid-

ers, taxpayers, administrators, and others all have their own interests in how the system functions and the various benefits it confers. Certain options are likely to bolster certain agents and groups—or even to create new ones. Over time, the interaction of these groups may improve or damage the effectiveness of the social service system.

In fact, much of the difficulty currently facing the region's social service systems derives not from poor initial designs; the way they were originally structured was effective and appropriate for that particular time and context. Rather, the difficulties of today emerged when the combination of political and economic interests kept the original systems from adjusting to changing circumstances and needs.[13] The need for adjustment is continual, and reform becomes necessary when adjustments fail to be made.

Whether and how these adjustments occur depends upon the incentives facing different agents in the system. For instance, the use of private sector providers can be promoted in order to introduce competition and increase efficiency in service provision. For better or for worse, strong private sector providers can also exert pressure on public policy (to obtain adequate public funding for services, which would be a positive force, or to obtain overly generous compensation for services rendered, which would be a negative force). For example, Chile's efforts in the last few years to reduce the scale of adverse selection affecting the public health sector have been strongly resisted by private insurers.

When the public is poorly informed about the costs and performance of public systems, it is unable to play a role in holding providers accountable. In most cases, little information is available about the region's centralized public systems, and thus the debates over pay, work conditions, and performance are dominated by educators and health professionals. Without a counterbalance, these groups can effectively capture the resources

---

[13] See Castagnino (1995).

of the sector—with implications that can be positive (esprit de corps, public service) but that are also frequently negative (restrictions on information, constraints on managerial efficiency). Disseminating information about the systems to the public and formally bringing parents, businesses, and community representatives into the decision-making structure of the social service systems can counterbalance the negative dynamics of capture.

The centrally administered systems also weaken the position of mid-level administrators, who are constrained from above by directives and administrative orders and from below by strong civil service codes and union vigilance. A set of options giving the administrator greater decision-making power and comparator information about his or her unit's relative performance could help create a positive lobby for more effective allocation of resources and services from numerous stakeholders.

Dynamic change can also be induced by replacing a hierarchically administered system with one in which public schools or hospitals are given autonomy over established budgets. When administrators are given decision-making power over a fungible budget, they can begin to allocate resources more efficiently among inputs. A typical constraint is administrators' levels of training in administering budgets, but once their scope of decision-making power is increased, the demand for such training or for selecting more capable administrators creates a positive tension in the system. By contrast, a reform that began by simply training administrators in management practices without giving them a greater scope of action would be likely to fail, because those who are well trained would be better able to apply their skills outside the sector. Such a limited reform would fail to create a demand or a lobby group interested in pursuing and extending the new structure.

Capitation is a good example of an organizational change that may induce positive pressures. As indicated earlier, capitation has a tendency to encourage the coverage of more clients because it creates a financial or budgetary incentive to enroll and serve more people. It also promotes greater efficiency by giving providers a direct interest in keeping costs low. The key disadvantage is that, unless checked, capitation also creates an incentive to reduce the quality of those services or even to refuse them when possible. Nevertheless, this flaw is one that is readily and quickly perceived by clients, who have an interest in bringing pressure to bear on the pertinent regulatory structures to address quality control. The dynamic of the political response is then likely to begin focusing on the elements necessary to complement the system. By contrast, a reform that began with quality controls would be much less sustainable, in that it would fail to create a viable constituency for change, because quality controls are easily resisted by existing providers through restricting consumer access to the information that might induce a public response.

Teachers and doctors, school boards and community councils, parents and union leaders, patients and students, government ministers and politicians, all have a common interest in the existence of well-performing education and health sectors. But each constituency also has its own particular interests and its own partial view of what is best for the system. A single institutional design is not possible for every situation, nor is it likely that any reform could introduce an ideal system coherent in every way. The challenge is to find the mix of elements and changes that will set off a positive dynamic of change by first creating the patterns of incentives, public information, and consumer empowerment that will lead to a better system. Ultimately, this dynamic can lead to a system of financial flows and regulatory structures that stimulates collectively efficient behavior.

SUMMARY

Social services are too complex to be delivered through homogeneous or centrally directed systems without some recognition of the differing incentives and interests generated by all the various funding sources, allocation mechanisms, ownership options, and regulatory functions. The advantages and disadvantages of different options and the relationships among these elements should be investigated and considered in the effort to improve the efficiency of the region's social service systems. They are variables that are clearly amenable to policy actions. And when carefully considered, the needed improvements may do more to ensure the sustainability of an action plan than will any political commitment.

The lessons here are not completely new. In recent years, the policy debate in the region has moved toward privatization and decentralization of social services. Nevertheless, these recent trends have not explicitly recognized the full dimensions and implications of such policy changes. If decentralization means delegation without effective financial-allocation mechanisms, then it will not be effective.[14] If privatization occurs without thought to norms, quality controls, and the checks upon the institutional contractors or providers of these services, then it can be a fount of problems.

On the bright side, however, the reforms have created local experiments in increasing the autonomy of local providers, in building mechanisms of accountability through information, in creating groups with interests in good services, and in empowering consumers through choice. In some countries there have also been a few efforts to allocate resources on the basis of outcomes. These experiments show that the need for such changes has been implicitly recognized. It must be borne in mind, however, that reforms that explicitly recognize the full dimensions of organizational change are likely to be more successful than those that are halting and partial. And success is greatly needed.

With limited options for increasing spending in these sectors, the potential gains through greater efficiency—increasing productivity—are required in order to make the urgent improvements in equity and quality now required of the social service systems. We can imagine new fables in which structures reward good outcomes, providers have greater decision-making authority, consumers are empowered, and accountability and information are enhanced, leading to dynamics that favor virtuous cycles of improved social services.

In these future stories, public officials find they can serve more of their citizens more equitably when funds are efficiently used; union leaders pressure for improved conditions and higher pay for their members by collaborating on measures that increase productivity, accepting greater discretion in personnel management in return for better management; and consumers exert their influence on service quality by staying informed, participating in governing councils, exercising choice, and voicing their dissatisfactions.

Succeeding chapters will analyze the particular characteristics of education and health systems in Latin America and the Caribbean. There is great homogeneity in the organizational structure of the various countries' education systems, but considerable organizational heterogeneity within the region's health sector. This organizational variety is associated with significant differences in health outcomes, even after accounting for differences in income and expenditure. By contrast, as Figure 2.4 of the previous chapter shows, the similar organizational structure of the region's education systems is associated with a homogeneous pattern of performance below the international average.

[14] Recent studies of decentralization include Prud'homme (1995), Winkler (1994), Hommes (1995), Carciofi et al. (1996), and La Forgia and González Block (1995).

CHAPTER 4

EDUCATION: THE DYNAMICS OF A PUBLIC MONOPOLY

Latin America and the Caribbean have made gains in education over the last half century, but at a slower pace than other regions. A large part of the resulting education gap is due to the organization of educational systems, which are quite similar throughout the region. Although centralized educational systems may have been appropriate earlier, now this type of organization presents obstacles to improving the quality of education and increasing educational attainment.

Numerous studies of the region's educational systems identify symptoms rather than the root causes of poor educational performance (see Box 4.1). A major source of problems is their form of organization, although other factors like familial context, income, and spending also matter. Because of poor organization, educational systems regularly misallocate resources—underfunding textbooks, maintenance, and teacher training. The lack of evaluation mechanisms and examinations makes it impossible to hold teachers, schools, or administrators accountable for the systems' per-

---

Box 4.1   Problems in Education: Causes or Consequences?

Fifteen sector studies of primary education in the region were made by the World Bank and the IDB between 1991 and 1995. An analysis of these studies demonstrates that the problems identified in each country were remarkably similar. While the studies did not establish causal relationships among various problems, the problems that were diagnosed are consistent with structures of perverse incentives (see diagnostic chart).

High rates of students' repeating grades and dropping out in 11 of the 15 countries were among the problems of internal efficiency in education. Low levels of learning were found in 8 countries. Such poor performance is consistent with systems where results are not measured and resources are not assigned on the basis of performance. In the countries studied, schools receive no reward for reducing grade repetition or for keeping children in school. Likewise, there are no ways to reward teachers for innovations that improve students' learning levels.

Looking into the causes of these poor outcomes, the study found that, while a lack of resources was a problem in 67 percent of the countries, half of these (Argentina, Bolivia, Mexico, Uruguay, and Venezuela) allocate their resources inefficiently. These inefficiencies in budget alloca-

tion are manifest in the distribution of funds among the various levels of education, and between current spending and investment. In Venezuela, for example, over 40 percent of the education budget is set aside for universities; in Bolivia, salaries for teachers and administrators absorb 98 percent of all resources allocated for primary and secondary education.

Inefficiency in resource allocation can explain the existing deficiencies in terms of educational inputs. Low quality of teachers, inadequate educational materials, and defective infrastructure were major problems in 73% of the countries studied.

Finally, in the cases examined there is a clear relationship between countries with problems of resource allocation and those that lack community participation and/or performance evaluation. As the chart shows, these countries overlap in 80 percent of the cases. One possible interpretation of these results is that lack of community participation combined with a low ability to influence decisions has allowed inefficiencies in resource allocation to persist.

Source: Piras (1996).

---

formance. Furthermore, governments and teachers, through the unions that represent them, find themselves locked into a negotiation dynamic that seems to fail both in terms of the system's performance and efficiency, as well as the working conditions of teachers.

This study focuses particularly on primary school organization, and to a lesser extent on secondary schools, with some specific references to higher education systems. It analyzes the current situation of the region's educational systems, many of which are in various stages of reform. Some of these reforms and local initiatives take organizational problems into account. The most promising trends recognize the value of increasing the government's role in financing education, with better mechanisms for allocating resources; increasing the autonomy and accountability of schools; and granting local communities, parents,

and students a more significant role in school management.

EDUCATION GAPS REMAIN

Latin American and Caribbean countries spend heavily on education without achieving what might be expected in terms of coverage and quality. About US$ 50 billion a year is spent on education, approximately 4.3% of GDP, and 4 million teachers are employed to teach a population of approximately 130 million students. Yet, the result of this huge effort is a population with very few years of schooling. In 1960, some 18 million persons had finished high school in Latin America and the Caribbean and the same was true in Southeast Asian countries. By 1990, however, the gap between these two regions was growing, with 45 million and 70 million graduates, respectively.

Summary of Primary Education Assessments in 15 Latin American and Caribbean Countries, 1991-1995

	Argentina	Uruguay	Chile	Bolivia	Brazil	Peru	Mexico	Venezuela	Paraguay	El Salvador	Guatemala	Honduras	Costa Rica	Jamaica	Barbados	Number of countries	Percent of countries
EFFICIENCY PROBLEMS																	
High repetition and drop-out rates		X	X	X	X		X	X	X	X	X	X	X			11	73
Financial constraints	X	X	X		X	X	X	X		X	X			X		10	67
Low educational achievement	X	X					X	X		X	X	X			X	8	53
Bias in favor of higher education	X	X		X			X	X								5	33
Imbalance between investment and recurrent expenditures	X	X		X			X	X				X				5	33
INPUT PROBLEMS																	
Poor teaching quality	X	X	X	X	X	X	X	X	X			X	X			11	73
Lack or inadequate teaching materials	X	X	X	X		X	X	X	X	X	X	X	X			11	73
Insufficient or poor condition of school infrastructure	X		X	X		X	X	X	X	X		X	X	X	X	11	73
Lack or inadequate textbooks	X	X	X	X	X		X	X	X	X			X			10	67
Curriculum deficiencies	X		X	X		X			X	X		X	X	X		9	60
Unsatisfactory teaching training	X	X	X		X					X						5	33
EQUITY PROBLEMS																	
Lack of attention to indigenous languages							X	X	X		X	X		X		6	40
Poor quality and availability of inputs in rural areas				X		X	X					X		X		5	33
Inequity of access among different gender groups				X		X				X		X				4	27
Inequity of access among different age groups			X				X				X	X				4	27
Difficult school access in rural areas				X			X		X			X				4	27
FEEDBACK PROBLEMS																	
Inadequate teachers supervision	X	X	X	X	X		X	X	X	X		X				10	67
Lack of evaluation of academic achievement	X	X	X	X	X		X	X	X	X		X				8	53
Limited capacity of MOE for planning, research and evaluation			X			X				X	X		X		X	6	40
Lack of information systems			X		X	X							X		X	6	40
Lack of community participation	X	X		X			X	X				X				5	33
Concentration of decision-making at national level	X			X							X		X			4	27
Inadequate incentive structure for teachers	X				X					X		X				4	27

Note: These assessments were conducted for projects financed by the IDB and the World Bank.

Sources: IDB Loan Documents and World Bank Staff Appraisal Reports.

Education in Latin America and the Caribbean has advanced in terms of primary education coverage and higher education graduates. The proportion of children receiving pre-school education doubled in one decade, rising from 21% in 1980 to 42% in 1990. In primary education the net enrollment ratio has reached levels of around 90%. The gender gap has been practically eliminated at basic levels, and the percentage of females is even higher than that of males in secondary and university education.

Despite these advances, the region falls far short of what might be expected on the basis of its income level. For example, indicators of enrollment do not show what happens once children enter the system. The rate of primary school *completion* in Latin America and the Caribbean is only 52%. So while more than 90% of children begin school, only 47% finish it (see Figure 4.1). This causes a big gap at the secondary level, where student enrollment is only 23% of the population— as compared with other developing regions such as Southeast Asia, where secondary enrollment rates exceed 80%. Moreover, measuring educational systems by only using the enrollment ratios masks the main weaknesses of Latin American systems, such as poor quality of education, problems of equity in resource allocation, and a low efficiency level.

First, the poor quality of education has been demonstrated through international testing of students. For example, in 1992 examinations of the reading ability of ninth-grade students in 32 countries showed that the only countries with a performance poorer than Venezuela's were Nigeria, Zimbabwe, and Botswana. The Ministry of Education and Culture in Jamaica has determined that approximately 45% of children in grades 7 to 9 have a reading ability more than two grades below their current grade. Many studies in different countries of the region have documented the poor quality of teaching given to primary school children.[1]

FIGURE 4.1
Primary Level Completion Rate, 1988-90
(Percent)

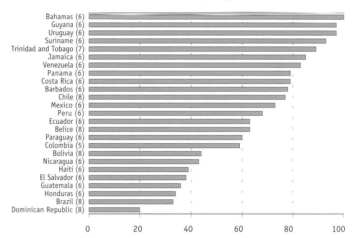

Note: Number in parentheses are the school years used to compute the completion rate because the duration of primary levels varies.
Source: UNESCO, IDB.

Second, inequity is clear in enrollment rates, which differ substantially between countries and regions. In Mexico, even though a net primary enrollment rate of 98% has been maintained during the last five years, in the state of Campeche, 30% of primary schools provide only three or four grades of instruction. In the Northeast of Brazil, where a third of the national population between 10 and 14 years lives, over 20% of this population group does not attend school, and 37% is considered to be illiterate. In rural areas of Bolivia, 55% of the schools only offer the first three grades.

Third, inefficiency in resource allocation partly explains deficiencies in school infrastructure and the lack of teaching materials. In poor areas of Peru, both in the countryside and in urban marginal areas, only 2.4% of the schools have water, drains, and electricity. In three of the poorest provinces in northern Argentina, over 50% of school buildings do not have indoor plumbing and over 30% have no electricity. Textbooks and

---

[1] For Argentina, see Ministry of Education and Culture (1994); for Bolivia, see Woodford (1993); for Uruguay, see Rama (1992). For the region as a whole, see UNESCO (1994).

school supplies are insufficient and inadequate. In secondary public schools in Colombia, it has been calculated that most students have no books or only one or two of the eight required. Even though Trinidad and Tobago spends US$ 380 per student, a third of the children in primary school do not have textbooks. Besides these administrative deficiencies, there are inefficiencies attributable to corruption, as is the case of "phantom teachers" who represent a significant drain on the payroll in some countries.

Finally, systems are inefficient in terms of the time needed to graduate students, that is they have low "internal efficiency." For example, in Nicaragua, Guatemala, Honduras, and El Salvador, students repeat an average of four years before finishing primary school (see Figure 4.2). This is not surprising since students generally spend little time in school. School years and class hours are short; and days are often lost due to strikes and absenteeism by the teachers. During the 1995-96 school year, students in the national public system in Venezuela lost 43 class days because of a teachers' strike. They lost 30 class days in Peru in 1991, and 40 days in Bolivia in 1995. Time actually spent in class in Honduras is around 50% of what the school calendar establishes, primarily as a result of administrative inefficiency.

EDUCATION IS FUNDAMENTALLY PUBLIC

In Latin America and the Caribbean, as elsewhere in the world including the OECD countries, the state has assumed primary responsibility for financing, and in most cases for delivering, education services. It is possible to imagine the state as a very efficient education *provider*, taking advantages of economies of scale, channeling resources into research, and improving the productivity of the system. As a rule, however, such benefits do not materialize in reality.

As a *funder*, the public sector also has the possibility of assuring equity in education. Actual experience, however, has not been very encourag-

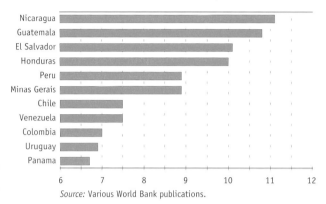

FIGURE 4.2
**Average School Years per
Sixth-Grade Graduate, 1988-92**

Source: Various World Bank publications.

ing in this regard, either. The distribution of spending on education between different regions, between ethnic minorities, and between genders is striking. Rural areas generally tend to be the most disadvantaged. In Honduras, in rural areas the student/teacher ratio is 40, while in urban areas it is 29. The regressive nature of spending per pupil is obvious between states in Brazil, where the rich states spend six times as much as poor states. Inequality in years of enrollment by gender has been practically eliminated in the region, although it persists in some cases, especially among indigenous groups. In Guatemala, the average number of years of study for indigenous boys is quite low, reaching only 1.8 years, but for girls it is only half that much, 0.9 years.

Despite its quasi-monopolistic role, the public sector coexists with a private sector whose share varies by educational level. In most countries, the public sector dominates in primary education, while the private sector is responsible for a higher percentage of secondary, tertiary and preschool education. In Latin America and the Caribbean, the proportion of school enrollment handled by the public sector in 1992 was 86% in primary education and 77% in secondary education.

Obviously there are exceptions. To mention only two, in Haiti 61% of primary school students are in private schools; and 68% of Guatemala's secondary school students attend private schools. Furthermore, although it is not common, some countries accept responsibility for the cost of education without making the state completely responsible for running the schools. For example, Chile introduced a reform in 1980 whereby the state continues to finance primary and secondary education, but the service is now provided in both public and private schools.

Public policies have a great impact on the size and characteristics of the private sector. To the extent that the public sector increases coverage and handles the unsatisfied demand for educational services, the role of the private sector declines.[2] A comparative study using data from fifty developed and developing countries shows that the amount of public spending has a negative impact on private sector participation, by increasing the capacity and in some instances the quality of the public education system.

This process can be seen in the trends of private sector participation in many Latin American countries during the 1980s and early 1990s. For example, in the cases of Argentina, Mexico, Paraguay, and Honduras, the rise in the rate of secondary school enrollment was accompanied by a relative decline of the private sector. By contrast, in those countries where the state was not able to maintain a growing fiscal effort at this level the private sector (both for profit and not for profit) has taken on a growing role. Such was the case in Bolivia, El Salvador, Guatemala, Nicaragua, Jamaica, and the Dominican Republic, countries with a low level of secondary education where the private sector has grown in recent years (see Figure 4.3).

In primary education, declining quality has contributed to increased private sector involvement. The fact that parents who have the alternative of sending their children to public school decide to take on the cost of private education indicates that the latter offers them better service. Participation of the private sector has risen in 14 out of 21 countries of the region during the past decade. People are no longer waiting for the state

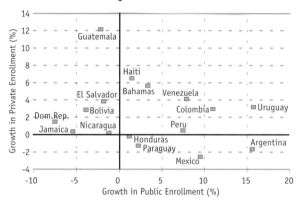

FIGURE 4.3
Private Enrollment and Public Effort in Secondary Education, 1980-1992

Source: UNESCO.

to solve their problems: they take advantage of the existing supply, seek information, and opt for better schools, even when it entails high costs relative to their income.

In higher education, the private sector has gained enrollment in recent years. Argentina, Brazil, and Chile offer clear examples of the benefits and drawbacks in the development of private sector education. Particularly in Chile, the higher education system had been quite small, homogeneous, and financed solely with public funds. After the 1981 reform came a series of structural and regulatory changes, resulting in greater institutional differentiation, more access to the system, and a decline in the proportion of public financing. Enrollment rose by over 100% in ten years, a large number of professional and technical institutes emerged, and allocations of public spending to higher education declined, thereby freeing resources for basic education.[3]

How private sector involvement influences the quality and equity of the educational system depends on adequate regulatory and accreditation mechanisms, cost-recovery systems, and means of financing education for low-in-

---

[2] James (1993).

[3] Brunner and Briones (1994).

come groups. Private participation in Chilean higher education does not seem to have had a negative impact on quality and may have even improved equity in resource allocation ; however, problems have arisen on both of these measures in Argentina and Brazil.

In conclusion, while the public sector could theoretically assure that education is delivered more efficiently and equitably, in practice that has not been achieved. Meanwhile, the expansion of private education in the region in some ways signals the flaws of the public system. Instead of seeing private sector growth as a challenge, it is useful to learn why private schools have expanded and how they respond to public demand and budget restrictions.

EDUCATION SYSTEMS ARE HIGHLY CENTRALIZED

Not only are education systems in Latin America and the Caribbean primarily handled by the public sector, but decision-making structures are also highly centralized. This centralization is evident both in terms of financing and in direct delivery of services by the state.

Central Financing with General Revenues

In the first place, primary and secondary education systems are almost entirely funded through central government revenues. As will be seen, although this structure has some advantages it does not guarantee an adequate spending level nor efficient allocation of resources. These defects have prompted some lower level governments to assume partial responsibility for funding, and it is common to find resources being raised at the school level with community involvement.

In 14 of the 15 countries analyzed in Table 4.1, the main funding source is central government general revenues. Brazil is the only country in the region where the states finance 65% of public spending on primary education, using the

Table 4.1 Sources of Financing of Primary Education in Public Schools

	National	State	Municipal	Earmarked	Fees
Argentina	X	*			
Bolivia	X				*
Brazil	*	X	*	*	
Colombia	X	*	*		*
Costa Rica	X				*
Chile	X		*	*	
Dom. Republic	X				
Ecuador	X				*
Guatemala	X				
Honduras	X				
Jamaica	X				
Mexico	X	*			
Panama	X			*	
Peru	X				
Trinidad	X				
Uruguay	X			*	
Venezuela	X	*			*

Note: X represents 65% - 100% and * represents 1% - 35%.
Sources: Various publications and interviews.

value-added tax.[4] In three countries, Argentina, Colombia, and Mexico, the revenues of the states themselves are an additional but minor source of funding.[5] In Chile, Colombia, and Brazil, municipalities also contribute to a lesser extent to their local education budget with their own resources.

In completely centralized countries the decision on the amount of education spending may be discretionary, it may be established in a constitutionally established law, or mandated in an act that ranks higher than budget legislation. In Bolivia, Costa Rica, Jamaica, and Uruguay, the budget decision is left to the executive branch; in Ecuador, even though the education system is centralized, the government's discretionary power was reduced by a provision in the Constitution that 30% of the budget must be directed to education. Peru had a provision to allot 20% of the central

---

[4] For the purposes of this study revenues deriving from revenue sharing or transfers from the central government are not regarded as revenues from lower levels of government.

[5] In the oil provinces of Argentina, including Neuquen, Tierra del Fuego, Santa Cruz, and Chubut, a significant proportion of resources for education comes from oil royalties. Likewise in Mexico, states like San Luis Potosí and Yucután contribute over 30% of the state's education budget.

government budget to education, but it was eliminated in the 1993 constitutional reform.

In those countries undergoing administrative decentralization, the central government has reserved the right to set a minimum expenditure. In Colombia, according to the 1994 General Education Act, municipalities are obliged to use 30% of the resources transferred for investments in education. Argentina's 1993 Federal Education Law sets goals for the growth of consolidated public spending on education. In Brazil, the 1988 Constitution states that at least 25% of state and municipal revenues must be allocated to education. However, it is important to point out that despite their good intentions these measures have failed in practice. In neither Ecuador, Argentina, nor Brazil have the established spending requirements been met.[6]

Payments by Users

Thus far sources of public financing have been discussed. In practice, there are a number of devices, some formal and others informal, that have enabled schools to complement the meager resources that they receive from the government. Even though primary education is compulsory and free in practically all Latin American and Caribbean countries, there are more and more cases in which fiscal constraints have forced governments to allow, and sometimes to encourage, joint financing with the community, the private sector, and even directly with families.

In Bolivia, Ecuador, and Paraguay, public primary schools charge parents an enrollment fee. In Bolivia those costs are $3 per child, in principle to cover textbook costs. Ecuador charges around $10 a year, plus the costs of uniforms, textbooks, and school supplies. In Paraguay an enrollment fee of $2.70 a year is charged. Even though there is no official provision in this regard, some public schools in Colombia, Costa Rica, and Venezuela have begun to charge enrollment fees. In Costa Rica, this practice has been challenged in the courts.[7]

In addition to charging an annual enrollment fee, in all countries schools to a greater or lesser extent rely on resources coming from parents' voluntary contributions, community labor, NGOs, private sector donations, and donations from religious groups. Certain schools are extremely effective in attracting revenues in addition to public financing, as happens in Trinidad and Tobago's "assisted" schools and in the school cooperatives of Argentina and Paraguay. The fiscal difficulties most countries faced in recent years created greater acceptance for cost recovery. In Jamaica and the Dominican Republic, arrangements for selling or renting textbooks are being proposed.

Even though the state finances most of the costs, education generally entails a set of direct and indirect costs that must be assumed by families. In using the public education system, poor families confront the cost of books, transportation, the enrollment fee (if there is one), school supplies, uniforms, and the opportunity costs of having a child in school who could be generating income. In Ecuador, Jamaica, and Trinidad and Tobago, where the private costs of public education were calculated, they represent a significant obstacle to the education of children in poor families. Financing the direct and indirect costs of the education of poorer children has been a successful device for improving school enrollment in low-income communities.

In conclusion, basic education in all the region's governments except Brazil is financed primarily by the central government. Despite its advantages, such a finance structure does not guarantee an adequate spending level, let alone equitable resource allocation. Lower levels of gov-

---

[6] For the case of Brazil see UNICEF (1995). On expenditures on education in Ecuador, see Fundación Ecuador (1995). Furthermore, there is the problem of defining what constitutes education expenditures. In Brazil the municipalities have used these resources to build urban infrastructure, claiming that it was necessary for transporting children to school.

[7] Revenues from enrollment fees, parents' contributions, community labor, and company donations are only registered at the school level. Hence it is extremely difficult to determine what proportion of total resources invested in education such revenues represent.

ernment and local communities have partially taken on financing, complementing revenues from the central government.

Direct Centralized Delivery of Services

Primary and secondary education in Latin America and the Caribbean has been organized in a centralized manner. This means that schools are directly under the ministries of education or state-level departments. Moreover, centralization means that very specific functions of providing the service, such as the choice of a proper mix of inputs or management of the various inputs, take place at a relatively high level of government.

Some countries in the region are moving toward systems with greater participation by state or municipal governments. Brazil is the only case where the education system took shape under an arrangement in which states provide the service. Chile was the first to begin the decentralization process. Between 1980 and 1987 it transferred management of primary and secondary schools to the municipalities. In Argentina in 1987 the nation ceded to the provinces the delivery of primary education services and in 1994 it completed the transfer of secondary, non-university post-secondary education, and teacher training. In Mexico responsibilities for the provision of pre-school, primary, secondary, and teacher training services was delegated from the federal to the state level in 1992. Finally, Colombia began its process of decentralizing and delegating responsibilities to its departments and municipalities in 1991, a process which is still ongoing.

If "centralization" is defined as the making of decisions relevant to the delivery of educational service at levels higher than that of the school itself or groups of schools, it is clear that delegating functions to lower levels of government does not mean that structures are no longer centralized. In Brazil, Colombia, Mexico, and Chile, the central government retains a considerable de-

Table 4.2 Level of Government Formally Responsible for the Provision of Primary Education

	National	State	Municipal
Argentina		X	
Bolivia	→————————————————→		
Brazil		X	X
Colombia [1]	→————————————→		
Costa Rica	X		
Chile			X
Dom. Republic	X		
Guatemala	X		
Honduras	X		
Jamaica	X		
Mexico		X	
Nicaragua	→————————————————→		
Panama	X		
Peru	→—————→		
Uruguay	X		
Venezuela	→—————→		

Note: X indicates that most major functions are the responsibility of this level of government, including employment, management, investment and maintenance. Where responsibility is at state or municipal level, national governments still retain some functions, such as compensatory programs. Arrow indicates that decentralization is in progress.
[1] Recurrent expenditures go to the departments, while investment resources are transferred to the municipalities.
Sources: Various publications and interviews.

gree of control over budgetary decisions whether through salary negotiations with teachers (Colombia, Mexico, and Chile) or by establishing parameters for resource allocation on the national level (Brazil, Colombia).

Except for Chile, these countries mentioned are the region's largest in population and territory. In terms of scale or number of students, the transfers of budgetary decisions to a province of Argentina, a state in Brazil, or a department in Colombia are not unlike the degree of centralization in countries like Costa Rica, Uruguay, or Jamaica (see Table 4.2).

RESOURCE ALLOCATION ON THE BASIS OF INPUTS, NOT SERVICES PROVIDED

In all countries analyzed except for Chile and a small portion of the Colombian system, allocation of public funds in the education sector is

---

Box 4.2   School and Teacher Incentives in Colombia

In 1995, Colombia's Ministry of Education allotted $144 million to establish a National School and Teacher Incentives Program over three years. This program, which was negotiated with the teacher's union, will reward outstanding schools and teachers for their achievements. The best 40,000 teachers from kindergarten through the third grade level, in all the country's public schools, will receive a bonus of US$600 (about 1-1/2 times the monthly wage). The best school in each of the 2,000 localities will receive an award of US$10,000.

The program is implemented by 2,000 "nucleus directors," local administrators who are responsible for the supervision and support of 20 to 40 schools. These directors, who provide a link between schools and municipal authorities, will apply the evaluation instruments and assist school administrators, teachers, parents, and students during the selection process. Schools will be evaluated in terms of organization, learning opportunities, and climate, as well as results in terms of repetition rates, dropout rates, and number of children above the expected age for their grade level. The questionnaire for the best teachers focuses on pedagogy, relationship with students, and degree of commitment. Mass media, posters, and booklets are used to communicate the program effectively.

The program was launched in March, 1996 among a group of 600 nucleus directors. After reviewing the questionnaires, procedures, and timetables, they held a series of regional meetings that included all 2,000 nucleus directors, and planned visits to more than 40,000 schools. During April and May, discussions about school quality took place in all the schools in Colombia. The nucleus directors visited every school and filled out the questionnaires jointly with each school's Directive Council, composed of the principal, teachers, students, parents and community representatives. A score was given to the school, and a teacher was chosen to receive the bonus. By the beginning of June, most questionnaires had been returned to the Ministry.

While the program's full impact has not yet been measured, certain achievements are clear. Teams visited all of Colombia's schools, many of which had never received a visit before. Communities became involved in examining their schools according to quality criteria. In addition, thousands of schools responded enthusiastically by designing or implementing improvement plans. Schools are being painted or decorated, and libraries organized—all signs that the incentives program is a promising strategy for school improvement.

Source: Colombian Ministry of Education, Directorate of School Organization.

---

based on financing supply. Government resources are allocated based on the preexisting endowment of inputs. The manner in which the budget is distributed is determined by school size, number of classrooms, and the number and classification of teachers.

This procedure for allocating resources based on their historic supply breaks any link between output and income, and hence service providers have no incentives to increase either the quantity or quality of their service. Since inputs are received independently of productivity, there are no incentives for a school principal to strive to increase coverage in his or her zone or to improve the quality of the education imparted. Such efforts would lead only to more students per classroom or more hours devoted to preparing lessons, without bringing in more resources. (See Box 4.2 for an example in which an attempt is made to connect resources to performance.)

An alternative system for resource allocation is financing demand. In education this has been attempted through the use of vouchers. The objective of this device is to link resources directly to the beneficiaries of the service. Rather than allocating the budget in accordance with the way inputs have been assigned in the past, it is distributed based on the number of students. This procedure for financing demand, or capitation, generates better incentives for service providers. This way of allocating resources has been in use in Chile since 1980 for 88% of primary school students and 76% of those in secondary schools. In Colombia, a voucher program was begun in 1992 and it financ-

---

Box 4.3   International Experience with Education Voucher Programs

Vouchers have been widely used in recent years as a public financing mechanism for education, in both developing and industrial countries. The most common objectives of education voucher programs are to increase possibilities of choice for parents, allow low-income families access to private schools, and promote competition among schools.

This tool varies widely in design, depending on regulatory aspects and the target population for the vouchers. There may be special requirements for schools to participate in the program; the vouchers may be selective on the basis of income level or gender; or they may be aimed at the entire student population. Moreover, the amount of subsidy may vary in proportion to family income level; it may give access only to private schools or to any type of school; the funding may be entrusted directly to the schools or it may use the banking sector or the parents themselves as intermediaries.

Three Latin American countries have used education vouchers: Chile, Colombia, and Guatemala. The Chilean system has broad coverage for the entire school population, involving both public and private schools. Since 1980, primary schools and secondary schools have competed with municipal schools to attract and retain students. The schools are all financed by central government transfers based on the actual number of students, so it is necessary to monitor attendance. Initially vouchers were envisioned as the only source of financing, but in order to enhance quality, shared financing was introduced in 1993. Schools may now charge monthly fees, which are then partially offset by a reduction in the education subsidy. Vouchers accordingly serve to guarantee a minimum amount of spending per pupil.

In 1991, Colombia began an experimental voucher program for secondary education. The aim is to lower the cost of educating children of poor families by enabling them to attend private schools. In contrast to the Chilean system, the Colombian program is aimed exclusively at low-income families, whose children have received their primary education in public schools. In addition, only private schools can accept vouchers. The program began with 18,000 vouchers, but in 1995 over 88,000 were given out, a figure that represents approximately 4 percent of secondary school enrollment.

The third country in the region where vouchers are being applied is Guatemala. The basic objective of the program is to encourage a specific population group to remain in school, namely, low-income girls between 7 and 14 years old. The program is being applied in thirteen communities.

The only U.S. experiment with education vouchers is the Milwaukee Plan in Wisconsin, a program aimed at poor children who have not performed well in public school. Any non-sectarian private school chosen by the parents is eligible to receive the subsidy. In 1990 this program began with 300 children, and by 1995 it was serving 832 students in 11 schools. This arrangement restricts the percentage of students with vouchers per school to an upper limit of 49 percent, thereby assuring that most of a private school's clients will have monetary incentives to watch over the quality of service.

In 1981, Great Britain began a financial assistance program whose target population is radically different from that of the Milwaukee Plan. In this instance, the students receiving the subsidy are indeed low income, but they have to display a superior academic record, and the schools must be approved by the Department of Education and Science. By 1992, 27,000 students between 11 and 13 were benefiting from these selective vouchers.

Voucher systems can take many forms, but in all cases resources are allocated on the basis of the number of students served by the program. Even where vouchers represent a fraction of the cost of education, they guarantee a minimum spending level per student.

Reference: West (1996).

---

es 4% of secondary students (Box 4.3).

When voucher programs are introduced in urban areas, where the variety of suppliers is greater, parents have the opportunity to choose the school that they prefer. In such cases the voucher system creates competition between schools, motivating school boards or groups in charge to improve the quality and variety of the services they provide in order to attract more students and hence greater resources. However, even in rural areas where the public school has a local monopoly, this system of resource allocation has advantages over the traditional arrangement of financing supply. In rural areas, financing demand creates incentives for schools to strive to keep students in school and prevent dropping out.

EQUITY IN RESOURCE DISTRIBUTION

To the degree that public funds are poorly distributed, the chance to provide educational opportunities to the population diminishes. Hence, considerations of equity are another important argument for improving efficiency in resource allocation.

Public funds are allocated in response to a political process in which groups less favored in terms of income, ethnicity, or gender are those that have the greatest difficulty having their appeals heard at the central government level. In this sense, centralized systems contribute to inequity in the delivery of educational services, because they reduce accountability and minimize the "voice" of those sectors with greatest needs.

Until now the region's educational systems had based the concept of equity on the same level of spending or of inputs for all children. A new concept of equity seeks to reach equality of results, which is generally associated with different spending levels per child. In order to obtain equal results with populations in different social and economic conditions, resources must be focused on those groups that need them most.

Only recently has the idea of targeting education programs in the region begun to spread. Some countries have already begun to allocate their resources in accordance with this new criterion. In Argentina, even after decentralization the federal government remains responsible for the targeted programs by which books and material for teaching and teacher training are provided to schools attended by the population with greatest needs. In Chile, state aid to each school varies not only based on the educational level, but also takes into account factors such as how rural they are and "allocations by zone."[8] Uruguay also has programs focused on low income populations.

The introduction of targeted programs and increased attention to the actual distribution of public spending offer hope that inequities in the allocation of public resources will over time be reduced.

MANAGEMENT OF THE PUBLIC SECTOR WITHOUT EVALUATION MECHANISMS

Direct delivery of education by the public sector requires the ability to design, administer, and manage the system. But the problems of measurement and evaluation of the results of educational services, particularly by a central body far removed from the school, make it difficult to manage the system effectively.

First, education is a process with many objectives. Thus there is more than one dimension to the end product. In addition to learning basic tools, formal education seeks to develop in the child the skills and values necessary for adequate performance in society.[9] The fact that education has a variety of functions, however, does not mean that the education system does not seek to attain certain objectives in terms of academic knowledge. In fact, such objectives are described in curricular contents along with the minimum standards and requirements that students must meet at each level. Hence, it is possible, although not easy, to measure the results of the education process through examinations. Indeed, this is the traditional way students are evaluated in all countries (See Box 4.4).

Second, even if what children learn can be measured, there are difficulties in identifying the determinants of those results. Countless studies have documented the diversity of factors that

---

[8] "Allocation by zone" is granted to those schools located in isolated locations or where the cost of living justifies an extra contribution. The subsidy for being in a rural area is granted to schools located more than 5 kilometers from a city limit or from another school, and where total enrollment does not exceed 85 students (Aedo 1996).

[9] Fullman (1982).

affect the learning process.[10] The problem lies in identifying to what extent the results are attributable to the effort of the providers (teachers), to the actions of the beneficiaries (students, families), or to external factors (economic situation).[11]

The most common response for assuring that the funds applied to education result in adequate educational services has been through hierarchical control over the service providers. Thus the hope is that controlling inputs would lead to positive results. However, the problems of measurement and evaluation make such control difficult. The creation of complex state bureaucracies to exercise such control can further worsen the situation, by creating a variety of agents with differing functions and degrees of commitment to the system.

Standardized tests in primary school are new in Latin America. Only 7 of the 18 Spanish-speaking countries today have some kind of test for measuring the quality of the education system. Moreover, all the evaluation systems are post-1990, except for the case of Chile where examinations began to be used in 1982 and Costa Rica where they were launched in 1988. By contrast, the English-speaking countries of the Caribbean have a long tradition of standardized tests. In these cases, however, examinations have been used chiefly as a tool for rationing the middle and upper levels of education, rather than as procedures for evaluating system performance (see Table 4.3).

Yet efforts to measure how much students learn have produced resistance on the part of unions and rejection of the use of standardized tests. Standardized tests in mathematics and language were applied in Panama in 1992, prompt-

Table 4.3 System Evaluative Examinations in Primary and Secondary Schooling

	First Year	Frequency	Students Tested	Level of Public Results	Grades Tested	Subjects
Argentina	1993	annual	S	state	3,7,9,12	L,M,N,S
Brazil[1]	1990	annual	S	state	1,3,5,7	L,M,N,S
Colombia	1991	biennial	S	department	3,5	L,M
Costa Rica	1988	annual	U	n.a.	6,11	L,M,N,S
Chile	1982	biennial	U	school	4,8	L,M
Dom. Republic[2]	1992	annual	U	school	4,6,8	L,M,N,S
Jamaica	1975	annual	U	school	6,9,11,13	L,M
Mexico	1993	annual	S	state	prim,sec.	L,M,N,S

S: Sample L: language N: natural science
U: Universe M: mathematics S: social science
[1] Minas Gerais started a parallel system for monitoring student learning in 1992. All students are tested and results are sent to every school.
[2] Exams in the Dominican Republic are used as student evaluative exams.
Sources: Various publications and interviews.

ing resistance on the part of teachers. A similar situation occurred in the Dominican Republic in 1992, when students began to be evaluated.

Instead, education systems have specialized in gathering and processing information on enrollment rates, repetition rates, dropout rates, number of students, number of teachers, and number of schools. The existing information systems have concentrated on measuring the amount of physical inputs. Indeed, in some cases, financial information is not considered among the relevant variables. In many cases there is no way to estimate the cost per student of a school nor to compare the cost-effectiveness of different programs or inputs. To some extent, the priority that governments have given to resolving gaps in coverage makes it possible to justify the emphasis on measuring physical quantities. Nevertheless, problems involved in measuring the results of education have often been used as excuses for avoiding systematic measurements of quality.

Lack of information on the performance of educational systems is a by-product of the problems of organization. The lack of tests and measurements of cost-effectiveness in some sense is convenient for both administrators of the system and teachers. They thereby remain protected from pressures to be accountable for the performance

---

[10] Velez, Schiefelbein and Valenzuela (1993), Fuller (1990), Simmons and Alexander (1978).
[11] IDB (1996).

Box 4.4 Different Exams for Different Purposes

Educational evaluation has multiple objectives, many forms and many effects on educational quality. There are at least three basic functions for student examinations:

a) *Student Evaluative Examinations* are given internally by schools to determine students' success in learning the curriculum. These are broad-based examinations that extensively sample the prescribed syllabus, and their purpose is *certification*. They assess pupils' performance relative to their cohort and select students for promotion or repetition.

b) *Life Chances Examinations* are normed tests usually designed as a *selection* mechanism for the next level of schooling. Although they also have diagnostic implications for the student or the school, the problem with using these exams as evaluative devices of the previous level of education is that the percentage of students who advance to the next highest level is determined by the capacity of the system rather than by academic achievement. Teaching practices are highly responsive to the content of these exams. Therefore, when curriculum planners and test designers work together, these life chances examinations can become a powerful tool to guarantee the implementation of the curriculum and motivate students to learn.

c) *System Evaluative Examinations* are meant to measure pupils or schools performance against some national, state or municipal performance standard. The purpose of these exams is to be *diagnostic* and serve an *accountability* role by offering evidence of standards attained by individual teachers, schools or special programs. They can be used to identify successful and failing schools relative to others with comparable socioeconomic groups, to assess what pedagogical practices seem to be yielding better or worse results than others, and to evaluate the impact of programs intended to raise performance. Since the objective is to assess the system, a sample of schools can be used.

Both student evaluative and life chances examinations are widely used in the region. Student evaluative exams are regularly used within schools to determine whether a student will pass to the next grade level or not. Life chances tests in the region are mainly used to determine whether pupils qualify for entrance to universities. These exams have been in place for many years in the English-speaking Caribbean, but also in Brazil, Chile, Colombia, Costa Rica, Mexico and Venezuela. However, since these kinds of examinations are focused on measuring individual performance, they are not necessarily effective at evaluating schools or the performance of the educational system as a whole.

By contrast, the use of system evaluative examinations is very recent in Latin America, with the exception of Chile and Costa Rica. Nevertheless, during the 1990s an increasing number of countries are moving from in-school individual student evaluation exams, with almost no diagnostic implications, toward system assessment tests that can suggest directions for school improvement. The publication and dissemination of test results is still in very initial stages.

A recent study points out that the use of examinations is widespread among African countries. The study identified 52 public examinations at the primary and secondary levels in the 14 African countries researched. African education systems have been strongly influenced by the British and French systems, which have a long history of formal standard examinations. In addition to using standard examinations, many African countries also publish the results of students on a school-by-school or district-by-district basis; this is common practice in Ethiopia, Kenya, Rwanda and Swaziland.

Reference: Carnoy and Castro (1996), Kellaghan and Greaney (1992).

of the system. Proper management of the education sector thereby becomes less likely.

PERSONNEL MANAGEMENT POLICIES: CENTRALIZED AND CONFLICTIVE

The importance of teachers, both in terms of their impact on learning and because of how heavily they weigh on the cost structure of the education sector, justifies a separate evaluation of human resources policy in education. In the context of education, this includes policies of selection, hiring, dismissal, evaluation, promotion, training and compensation of teachers and administrators. It will be demonstrated that personnel management continues to be very centralized in most cas-

Table 4.4 Level of Personnel Administration in Public Primary Education

	Hiring/Firing Teacher	Hiring/Firing Principals	Teacher Promotions
Argentina	state	state	state
Bolivia	national	national	national
Brazil			
- Minas Gerais	state/school	school	state (e.d.)
- Sao Paulo	state/school	state	state (e.d.)
Colombia	state	state	state
Costa Rica	national	national	n.a.
Chile	municipal	municipal	state (e.d.)
Dom. Republic	national	national	national
Ecuador	national	national	national
Guatemala	national	national	national (e.d.)
Jamaica	school	school/ME [1]	school/ME [1]
Mexico	state	national (u)	state (u)
Peru	state	state	state
Uruguay	national	national	n.a.
Venezuela	state/school (u)	national	national (u, e.d.)

(u) The teachers union participates in the process
(e.d.) According to the *"Estatuto Docente"*
[1] Schools propose the candidates, and the Ministry of Education makes the final decision.
Sources: Various publications and interviews.

es, despite the difficulty of evaluating employees from a centralized location and only with very general criteria that are weakly related to performance. Next, the importance played by salaries is considered, and the section ends with a description of the relationship between teachers' unions and governments.

Teacher Selection Far Removed from Users

Decisionmaking on the selection, hiring, dismissal, and promotion of teachers remains a centralized process in 14 of the 15 countries listed in Table 4.4, even though it is done by different levels of government depending on the country. The particular mechanisms used in these countries vary according to what is established on the national level in the Laws for the Teaching Profession or in the Educational Statutes.[12] Nevertheless, once the

minimum conditions required in existing legislation have been satisfied, the final decision falls to the level of government already indicated (see Table 4.4).

Of the fifteen countries examined, only in Jamaica is the responsibility for selecting teachers and employees, as well as candidates for principal, delegated to the school board. In the remaining countries, the decision is made at some other governmental level. This lack of authority for hiring and firing at the school level causes serious problems of governance between the administration of the school, the community, and teachers. The lack of independence on the part of school administration concerning the future of their teaching staff reduces the incentives for teachers to improve their performance.

Nevertheless, experiments are beginning to appear in which the school and the community have been given responsibility for hiring and monitoring teachers. In Nicaragua's "autonomous centers," the Ministry of Education has transferred to these secondary schools the entire responsibility for paying teachers and other employees. The Administrative Council, presided over by the principal, can use the resources transferred to it from the Ministry and any other revenues from student enrollments or donations to raise teachers' pay. In the case of the EDUCO program aimed at the primary school population in rural areas of El Salvador, the Communal Associations for Education are responsible for hiring and firing teachers. Likewise in rural areas of Mexico where the PARE program is operating, the community is involved in the evaluation and monitoring of teachers, which has brought about a significant reduction in teacher absenteeism.

Salaries and Compensation Arrangements

Another important area in human resource management is the compensation arrangement. Even in social services where there are non-monetary motivational factors, salary structure constitutes

[12] The case of Argentina is different because there is no national Educational Statute, and only a few provinces have such sets of regulations.

an important source of incentives for raising productivity and quality of service. Moreover, salaries are important for attracting to the profession capable people devoted to education. Nevertheless, as is true of promotion, evaluation, and firing, salary arrangements are not used in the region as an incentive for improving performance.

Evidence shows that during the last ten to fifteen years teachers' salaries have declined in a number of countries, but this decline seems to be directly related to changes in the overall job market. Studies in countries as different as Ecuador and Chile show that teachers continue to receive salaries that are similar to those received by professionals with similar characteristics in terms of gender, education, urban or rural area, and age. Another study that compares teachers' salaries with the average of non-farm workers shows a relative rise in teacher's salaries during the 1980s in countries like Colombia, Honduras, and Panama, while the relative salaries of teachers in Argentina and Uruguay seem to have experienced a significant drop. These studies, however, do not have information for incorporating the value of the benefits received by teachers, including pensions and job stability. In this sense, the widespread impression that teachers' salaries are low is not supported in the countries in which studies on the issue have been carried out (see Box 4.5).

Systems of salaried compensation of teachers in the public sector throughout Latin America and the Caribbean tend to be completely centralized at the national level, except in Argentina and Brazil. Negotiations generally take place between education ministries, or in some instances finance ministries, and teachers' unions. In 13 of the 15 countries analyzed, salary scales are negotiated centrally and applied in a uniform and compulsory manner throughout the country. The fact that there are national statutes on education establishes patterns for negotiation.

Centralization of negotiations regarding pay prevents salaries from being adjusted to the local market, reduces the ability to manage personnel at the level where the service is provided, and accordingly, weakens the school's ability to demand better service since pay decisions are beyond its control. This explains why teachers are unavailable for teaching in rural areas of Honduras while there is an oversupply of teachers in many urban schools. Even worse is the case of Bolivia, where the government's obligation to hire graduates from the teacher training schools further weakened the function of salaries as a sign of teacher demand.

Furthermore, pay reflects quantifiable criteria that are ill suited for measuring the quality and quantity of service provided. In all countries salaries are approved at the national level and are established in accordance with scales based on years of service and educational level. In certain cases, additional premiums are paid for training courses, rural locations, and family situation.

This is convenient for unions and teachers insofar as they prefer to reduce the discretionary power of supervisors and stabilize their employment and pay in a predictable way. Under conditions of scarce information, any effort to link the teacher's salary directly to what his or her students learn runs into major problems because of the difficulties of isolating the contribution of teacher's efforts from other factors. Furthermore, approving salaries and imposing rigid schemes based on observable criteria makes the work of system administrators easier, even though the usefulness of pay as a management instrument is thereby lost.

Evaluating the performance of teachers as an input into determining salaries is an innovation that has appeared in the region only recently. It is beginning to be applied in Mexico, and also in the Dominican Republic.[13] Outside the region,

[13] In the Dominican Republic, performance evaluation has been described as a disguised pay raise because all teachers receive the same evaluation. In Mexico an evaluation system has been devised based on the following factors: tests of knowledge, peer evaluation, parents' evaluation, and students' results.

Box 4.5   Are Teachers' Salaries Low?

Teachers' salaries, their levels, and their structure are very important to how education systems function. Salaries influence the system's ability to attract capable and qualified individuals into the teaching profession, as well as motivation and performance, and salaries are the system's largest single category of expenditures. However, little is known about teachers' compensation in Latin America and the Caribbean.

A common assumption is that teachers' salaries are extremely low and have been declining over the past two decades. However, this fails to consider the trends in comparable occupations, differences in hours worked, and the value of benefits—the largest of which is a pension after relatively few years of active service.

Salary conditions and trends vary significantly across countries and regions, and few studies have been made. However, it is important to demonstrate the value of teachers' salaries relative to existing labor market conditions. Only when teachers' incomes are compared to those working in comparable occupations and with comparable education and training is it possible to understand the impact of income on teachers' career choices and motivation.

For example, Psacharopoulos et al. (1993) compared Latin American teachers' salaries to an average of non-agricultural employees, and found that teachers earned above that average in seven countries, and below it in five countries. In Chile, where teachers' wages were higher than the comparison group, they discovered that much of this difference was accounted for by teachers' higher levels of schooling. Mulcahi-Dunn and Arcia (1996) demonstrate that in Ecuador, although entry-level wages are low, the majority of teachers are squarely in the middle class. Furthermore, they found that teachers are compensated as well as other professionals in the labor market with similar characteristics, namely gender, location, education and years of experience. Very few studies have done this kind of comparison to distinguish base pay or entry level pay from the actual salaries received—and no ministry in the region is capable of producing a figure as simple or as critical as the global cost of hiring a new teacher.

The trends over time are also unclear. Barro and Lee (1996), reporting figures aggregated for the entire region, estimate that in 1960 teachers' salaries were 2.6 times the per capita national income, declined to only 2.1 times higher in 1980, and then rose again to 2.6 times by 1990. Psacharopoulos et al. (1993) found that teachers' wages relative to the comparator group fell in five out of eight countries, and rose in the others. Wage reports by Union Bank of Switzerland for seven Latin American cities show that teachers' wages have been declining relative to bank clerks in five of these cities (Bogota, Buenos Aires, Panama City, Rio de Janeiro and Sao Paulo), but were increasing in two (Caracas and Mexico City). Wolff, Schiefelbein and Valenzuela (1993) used primary education unit costs as an imperfect proxy for teachers' salaries. Their analysis suggests that salaries may have declined between 1980 and 1989 in 17 out of the 19 countries for which they had data.

Further research is clearly needed concerning teachers' pay throughout the region. The amount of expenditures and the role played by wages in motivating performance are too large to ignore.

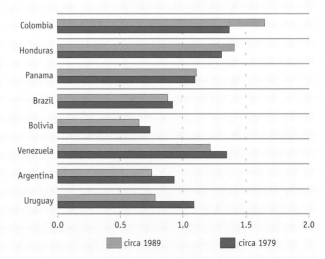

**Mean Earning Ratio
Teachers and Comparator Group**

The comparator group consists of public and private sector employees above fifteen years of age, excluding teachers and agricultural workers.

Source: Psacharopoulos, Valenzuela and Arends.

in the United States, merit pay arrangements for teachers have been used without very positive results.[14] Other instruments, such as promotions, bonuses, and recognition for evaluations seem to be more effective for improving school performance.

THE DYNAMICS OF RELATIONSHIPS BETWEEN GOVERNMENTS, UNIONS, AND TEACHERS

The centralized systems of personnel management with their rigid public employment codes are sustained by the type of relationship existing between teachers, unions, and governments. The incentive structure generated by the system´s current form of organization encourages behavior patterns that lead to situations in which neither learning nor working conditions improve substantially.

Throughout Latin America, except in Argentina and Brazil, one or more unions represent teachers before the centralized public sector agency on the national level. Even where administrative decentralization processes have advanced, as in Chile,[15] Mexico, and Colombia, negotiation over working conditions has remained at the central level. In these countries, the teachers' unions (the College of Teachers in Chile, the National Union of Education Workers in Mexico, and FECODE in Colombia) have opposed transferring this function to states or departments.[16]

On the *government* side, education ministers are quite weak. As a rule, those with political power regard education portfolios not as important positions, but as prizes to award to political allies.[17] Moreover, the ministers have a short horizon for their objectives, because their time in office is quite short (see Figure 4.4). Facing budgetary restrictions, ministers prefer to respond to union demands with concessions whose costs will fall due in the future, such as better pensions or reductions in years-of-service requirements.

On the other side, *unions* have an interest in maintaining negotiations at the national level. That way they can influence salaries, working con-

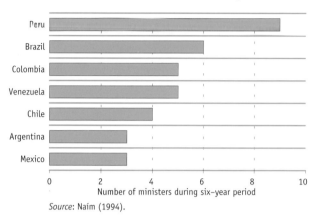

FIGURE 4.4
Turnover of Education Ministers, 1988-93

Source: Naím (1994).

ditions, and promotion opportunities, and reduce the discretionary power of administrators. They can strive for the professionalization of teachers both in order to upgrade their working conditions and to improve their performance . But the unions have many long-term objectives. In addition to teachers' working conditions, they are concerned about total employment and the interests of the political parties associated with them.[18] Their longer time horizon enables them to accept future concessions and a greater degree of participation in the management of the education system.

In this situation, *teachers* have incentives to remain relatively passive. Given their rigid salary scales and promotion possibilities, greater effort on their part has little impact on their pay. Moreover, the size of unions isolates union representatives from the range of teachers' opinions, problems, and interests.

---

[14] Hanushek (1994).

[15] In Chile, salary negotiations took place at the municipal level until the 1991 Education Professionals Act became law.

[16] For a more detailed position on FECODE's position on the educational reform in Colombia, see Montenegro (1995). On the passage of the Education Act in 1991 in Chile, see Espínola (1994). The case of Mexico is described in Prawda (1992).

[17] Naím (1995).

[18] Murillo (1996).

The interplay of these three actors leads to rather conflictual negotiations, resulting in contracts that are unsatisfactory for both parties. Salaries do not improve, the purchase of materials and complementary inputs is put off in the overall budget, and discretionary powers of management are restricted. Neither the system's performance nor working conditions necessarily improve in this process. Eventually, conflicts and poor performance erode social support for providing resources to the sector.

This conflict is evident from the many class days lost each year due to labor problems (see Figure 4.5). At the beginning of the school year, unions have very little to lose by calling a strike; teachers generally do not lose their salaries, and governments often have no way to mobilize further resources to satisfy union demands. Hence, the strike can last until popular pressure to open the schools makes the government grant some concession.

While pay raises are alleged to be the reason for union conflicts in the education sector, the results of negotiations between teachers unions and governments in the region seem to indicate different objectives. Teachers' unions have sought to maximize their political influence by favoring increased employment. Since education budgets are limited, increasing the payroll causes real salaries to decline, or at best remain steady (see Figure 4.6). In many countries the number of teachers has risen faster than school enrollment and student/teacher ratios have decreased despite budget constraints.

Another result is the high and growing proportion of the budget earmarked for salaries. Even as budgets are being cut, the proportion of total expenses devoted to salaries has held steady and even increased at the expense of other inputs. For example in Costa Rica, where salaries fell by 33% during the 1980s, the proportion of educa-

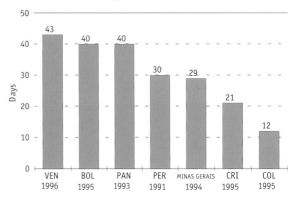

FIGURE 4.5
School Days Lost in Teachers Strikes

Source: Various publications and interviews.

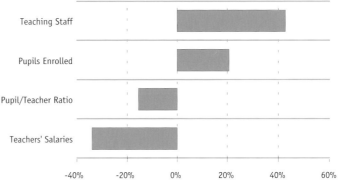

FIGURE 4.6
Increasing Employment and Declining Wages, 1980-92

Source: UNESCO, Wolff, Schiefelbein and Valenzuela.
The graph is the weighted average of 17 countries of the region.
The pattern shown reflects the situation of 11 of the 17 countries:
Argentina, Brazil, Colombia, Ecuador, El Salvador, Mexico, Panama,
Paraguay, Peru, Uruguay and Venezuela.

tion spending allotted to investment fell from 23.4% in 1980 to 1% in 1989.

How union negotiations influence management of the education system is evident in education statutes that create rigidities in personnel management and weaken administrative operations. Unions sometimes participate directly in management decisions: in Bolivia, Colombia, Mexico, and Venezuela, unions have representation at levels where decisions on hiring, firing, and promotions are made. In Bolivia, agreements signed between the teachers' organization and the government guarantee that the national and district education authorities are chosen from lists presented by the Confederation of Education Workers. This ability to interfere in administrative appointments of the ministry enables union leaders to sanction their members administratively if they do not abide by union instructions. The sanctions may be a union fine or even permanent loss of one's job.[19] Finally, the unions clearly have considerable clout over setting classroom norms and standards. The Costa Rican teachers union was able to negotiate a reduction of the number of class days, while in Venezuela they were able to cancel final examinations in secondary schools.

The interplay among government, unions, and teachers demonstrates how the system's organization affects the behavior of the actors. Since the current incentive structure does not fully benefit any of the parties, it is time to begin thinking of more productive forms of organization. Unions, governments and teachers must all redirect their efforts toward measures that will raise the productivity and quality of education. Only then can they demonstrate that the resources devoted to education are well used and yield good results, and that more resources should be channeled into the system.

NOTHING TO DECIDE? LACK OF SCHOOL AUTONOMY

Since the school is where the various inputs into the process interact—principal, teachers, textbooks, school supplies, and school infrastructure—the "management body" of the school would seem the most suitable place for making decisions conducive for achieving the objectives of the system.[20] While acknowledging the importance of external factors on student performance, many studies have investigated the characteristics of schools that are able to teach students from poor families.[21] In some cases research has fo-

cused on aspects of institutional structures, and in others on processes inside schools or classrooms.

Nevertheless, in Latin America school autonomy is quite low, indeed almost non-existent.[22] We understand school autonomy to mean the degree of independence that the school has for making decisions about its operation. In practice, even though the region has highly centralized education systems with almost no autonomy at the school level, decisionmaking regarding the various inputs into the education process has been fragmented by assigning responsibilities to various governmental agencies or levels: ministries of education, ministries of the treasury, ministries of public works, autonomous agencies, and social investment funds.

The initial allocation of resources for financing education is often made in the ministry of education. However, the national budget may contain items preassigned to bodies that are responsible for a particular input. Thus the budget is distributed by items among different government agencies. The main category of teacher salaries is generally controlled in the ministry. Then there are categories for the agency responsible for building schools, for the one responsible for producing textbooks and teaching materials, and yet another for the university to provide teacher training courses.

The fragmentation of decisions among the different levels of government or different agencies on the same level makes it impossible to administer resources efficiently, and prevents teachers and principals from using their training

---

[19] Anaya (1996).

[20] See Caldwell and Spinks (1988), Hargraves and Hopkins (1991), Purkey and Smith (1985), Vignoud (1992).

[21] See Chubb and Hanushek (1991), Cetron and Gayle (1991), and Summers and Wolf (1977) for the United States, Reynolds (1985) in the United Kingdom, Mercado (1989) and Ezpeleta (1988) for the case of Mexico, and Mello (1991) for Brazil.

[22] See Espinola (1994) for a more detailed discussion of school decentralization and local management in Argentina, Brazil, Chile, and Colombia.

and experience to respond to the challenges of their pupils. The existing systems have no single agent capable of internalizing the budgetary restrictions; and those agents who address budgetary issues lack adequate information to allocate resources for those inputs that have the greatest impact on teaching. Moreover, each agency or government level has different incentives and since the results of the education process are not measured, no one is held accountable for the performance of the system as a whole (see Table 4.5).

Various problems arise when countries try to resolve the problem of excessive centralization by delegating functions to other levels of government. Many countries that began administrative decentralization processes did not effect a true transfer of decisionmaking power. The result has been slower processes and increased administrative costs associated with maintaining a new intermediate level of bureaucracy—as happened in Guatemala, Honduras, El Salvador, Peru, Venezuela, Uruguay, and the Dominican Republic. In Honduras, administrative costs per student have more than doubled in the last thirteen years, reaching 36% in 1992.

Difficulties Flowing from Lack of School Autonomy

In practically all countries in the region, public schools have no decisionmaking ability on hiring or firing teachers, choice of textbooks, school maintenance, teacher training, or infrastructure expansion. The school administration not only has no power to make decisions in allocating resources, but the notion of a school budget is utterly unknown because they have never had to administer a budget. Instead of receiving a sum of resources to be administered by the school board, they receive a series of goods and services in kind. This procedure of allocating resources in kind prevents school administrators from efficiently using the resources allotted to them.

Second, because the school is far removed

Table 4.5 Locus of Decisionmaking in Primary and Secondary Public Education

	Salaries	Investment	Maintenance	Textbooks
Argentina	state	state agency	state	state
Bolivia	national	national-SIF	school	household
Brazil				
- Minas Gerais	state	school	school	state
- São Paulo	state	school district	school district	state
Colombia	national	municipal	municipal	municipal
Costa Rica	national	national	national	household
Chile	national	municipal	municipal	national
Dom. Rep.	national	presidency	school	national
Ecuador	national	national	national	national
Guatemala	national	national-SIF	national	national
Jamaica	national	national	national	national
Mexico	national	nat. agency	state	national
Peru	national	nat. agency	state	household
Uruguay	national	national	national	n.a.
Venezuela	national	nat. agency	nat. agency	household

Note: Where precise information regarding responsible unit was unavailable, only level of government is specified. Agency: an autonomous or subsidiary agency that does not have cabinet level status. National-SIF: National Ministry and Social Investment Fund, separate from Ministry of Education

Sources: Various publications and interviews.

from the decisionmaking center, the information on what is happening required for efficient management is lost along the way. A ministry of education cannot know whether the children in a particular school are getting low grades because of their relative poverty, the quality of their teachers, deteriorating conditions of the building, or lack of educational materials. The school administration, however, may be able to evaluate the quality, effort, and the suitability for its first grade students of a particular teacher.

Third, the lack of school autonomy makes it difficult to be accountable to the community. The less power principals have over what happens in their school, the less is the responsibility that can be demanded of them. As the authority of the school in making management decisions increases, so does the possibility and interest of parents and the community in being involved, and hence their governance also improves. Studies in Colombia demonstrate a greater level of community participation in activities of schools in the New

Box 4.6 Three Examples of School Autonomy

The Minas Gerais school system in Brazil introduced a series of innovations in 1991. The five most significant changes are 1) competitive choice of school principals, 2) decentralization of educational, administrative, and financial decisions, including transfer of resources to the school, 3) the establishment of a school council, 4) standardized tests given to students, and 5) preparation of a development plan by each school, as a management tool. Transfers to schools are small (between 5 to 15 percent of the school budget) but significant, because the sum of money is used for purposes other than paying salaries. The school council, headed by the principal, is responsible for handling the resources, which may be used for purchasing equipment, school supplies, maintenance, teacher training, or library and laboratory materials.

In 1991, El Salvador began the EDUCO program to provide preschool and primary education services in rural communities. The distinctive feature of this program emphasizes self-management, which has helped resolve the problem of the activities proper to teachers and to parents. Each EDUCO school is managed by a Community Education Association (ACE, *Asociación Comunal para la Educación*) , which is a committee with legal standing made up of parents and other community members chosen by the community. An ACE's main functions are to hire and fire teachers, monitor teacher attendance, contract maintenance and furnishing of school equipment, and negotiate with other government and international agencies for funds to build and repair schools. Thus far, evaluations of the program have found that students in EDUCO schools perform as well or better than students in traditional schools, even though their social and economic level is lower on average. Furthermore, EDUCO teachers have a lower absentee rate and are more committed to parents to improve student performance.

In 1993, Nicaragua began a pilot program to transfer school administration to local and municipal bodies. The program operates first through decentralization at the local level, delegating responsibilities to the Educational Councils of Autonomous Schools (*Consejos Escolares de las Escuelas Autónomas*), generally larger secondary or primary schools. Second is a municipal level decentralization creating Municipal Education Councils responsible for administering those smaller public schools that have not been granted autonomy. Each school council is made up of the school principal and representatives of teachers and parents. Municipal education councils, presided over by the mayor, are comprised of the municipal delegate from the ministry and representatives of parents, teachers, and the community. Resources were initially transferred on the basis of past budgets, but the government is developing a capitation mechanism based on numbers of students. Under this new model, teachers become employees of the school council or the municipal education council, which hires or fires them in accordance with legislation applicable to teachers. The councils are also responsible for school infrastructure, purchase of educational materials, and paying bonuses to teachers.

Thus far the Nicaraguan experience with autonomous schools has been positive. Although there are no data, principals of primary schools that became autonomous maintain that participation of the educational community in management decisions raised teacher and student morale, led to more rational use of school property, and lowered water and electric power costs. Some principals even claim it improved the academic performance of students and reduced student and teacher absenteeism. Furthermore, as parental influence in school decisions increased, so did their willingness to pay, and hence parents have been more faithful in paying school enrollment fees.

School program, which have greater autonomy than traditional schools.[23]

Despite these advantages of granting school administrations the power to make decisions relevant to the school, the kind of organization prevailing in Latin America has made them extremely weak entities. Except in the cases of Minas Gerais, Nicaragua, and El Salvador (see Box 4.6), the ability to manage at the school level is virtually nonexistent, and that has an effect on the current requirements for the position. In practice, principals are completely restricted in their abilities to maneuver, both by ministries of education

[23] Rojas and Castillo (1988).

or their lower level offices and by the rigidities in teacher hiring that has been negotiated with the unions.

A Guiding Role for the State Remains

Even for a school or a group of schools, optimizing inputs in accordance with the characteristics of pupils is not a trivial task. The school must make a diagnosis, analyze information, and plan the action of the school team. As schools gradually acquire greater initiative and decisionmaking power, they must also prepare teams of administrators and teachers to exercise autonomy capably and responsibly. Where schools have not been involved in decisionmaking, the central level's role is to promote training and establish an adequate strategy for making schools autonomous.

Making the educational service units autonomous entails redefining the roles and functions of the entire system. If schools must assume a more active role in defining both content and process in education, the central level has to assume the more strategic tasks of providing technical support, evaluation, monitoring, and disseminating information. This shift from the previous forms of supervision toward evaluation of results is also a cultural change, the difficulty of which must not be underestimated. Hence, policies for promoting school autonomy must be evaluated within the broader political and institutional context, which involves redefining the roles of the state in delivering social services in general, and education in particular.

The notion of school autonomy has been discussed as if it applied only to management of a single school. However, the optimal management unit depends on a number of factors, including the number of students. Economies of scale in administrative costs may justify the aggregation of schools. In addition, joint management of more than one school facilitates sharing of resources and teaching innovations. Finally, the existence of a level of coordination above the school may stimulate the establishment of standards and encourage comparisons of costs and performance.[24]

SUMMARY

The organization of educational systems in Latin America and the Caribbean is important to understand the region's lagging pace of educational attainment. The systems are generally highly centralized, with the government responsible for both financing and direct provision of services. The distance of central offices from local information, along with rigid employment contracts, limited information regarding performance, and few incentives to perform well, leads to many inefficiencies in resource allocation. The current organization of the system locks teachers, unions and governments into conflictual relationships that reward stubbornness and confrontation more than collaboration and increasing productivity. Furthermore, the resulting labor contracts and centralized administration limit the capacity of local administrators and providers to act upon their knowledge of students' needs.

The particular organization of the educational systems demonstrates how the activities of the public sector, providers, and consumers can lead to poor performance even with the best of intentions. However, recent experiments in the region allocate resources on the basis of the number of students in school, rather than inputs; increase school autonomy, local governance and accountability; increase flexibility and accountability in labor arrangements; and introduce exams and evaluation tools. These are all signs that the organizational issues affecting the sector are beginning to be recognized and addressed.

---

[24] The study carried out by Aedo (1996) on the impact of different organizational structures on the performance of Chilean children in the SIMCE tests points in this direction. Making allowance for the social and economic level of the children and the inputs that the schools make available to students to support their learning, Aedo shows that subsidized private schools where one entity runs several schools provide a better quality of education than private schools in which such an entity is running only one school.

CHAPTER 5

HEALTH SERVICES: A PROFILE OF FOUR SUBREGIONS

Latin America and the Caribbean have enormous health service systems, to which they dedicate substantial resources. Nevertheless, these systems have shown rather poor results in terms of coverage, service quality, and costs. The region's overall health outcomes—as measured by life expectancy and child mortality—are worse than expected given its income and health care spending levels. Nevertheless, there is large variation among and within countries, not only in terms of health outcomes but also in terms of the organizational forms of health service delivery. This chapter will show how the interaction between these diverse organizational forms and the relevant contextual factors contributes to this variation in health outcomes.

Every region in the world is facing problems in the health care sector, and countries as diverse as Britain, Russia, Sweden, and the United States are debating how to reorganize their health systems (see Box 5.1). For the health systems of Latin America and the Caribbean, the major issues are their organizational structure and partic-

Box 5.1 Health Sector Issues beyond the Region

Not only Latin American and Caribbean countries are struggling with rising costs and inefficiencies in their health systems. Many countries are tackling a range of issues related to expanding coverage, improving quality, orienting resources toward public health and preventive care, and containing costs. In Canada and much of Europe, the main issue is not coverage, but cost containment and quality. The former socialist countries are struggling with adapting their centralized and bureaucratized health systems to new forms of financing. Two particular cases demonstrate some of the issues facing other regions.

The United States health system is recognized for its high quality of care, but costs are extremely high and coverage is limited. For decades, payments to providers in the United States were based on "fee-for-service," allowing providers significant latitude to decide on the amounts and kinds of services provided along with their costs. The expansion of public financing for health and the existence of private insurance gave clients and practitioners few incentives to limit costs.

Institutions have responded in various ways to rising costs. Insurance companies began to rely upon predefined fees and average costs per procedure to contain costs. The most dramatic change since the 1970s has been the growth of health maintenance organizations (HMOs), which receive capitated payments in return for assuring a full range of health services. These organizations have been remarkably successful at containing costs, although their impact on the quality of care is still debated.

Along with the problem of rising costs, the U.S. health system now leaves some 34 million people uninsured. These are people whose incomes are too high to qualify for public health insurance, but too low to afford private insurance. The healthcare reform proposed in 1993 sought universal coverage through the creation of regional purchasing organizations, but was defeated by resistance from the medical profession, insurance companies, and a political reaction against government interference.

A very different case can be found in Sweden, where the government's role in public health care is strongly supported. Sweden's health care system is almost entirely publicly funded and publicly provided. Until recent years, the system was highly centralized, and people were restricted in their choice of clinics, hospitals and doctors on the basis of where they lived.

In response to rising costs and dissatisfactions with the quality of care, Sweden undertook a reform of its public health system—allowing citizens to choose among providers, decentralizing decisionmaking authority to local political districts and health boards, and establishing a system of implicit performance contracts between the health boards and the hospitals and clinics they purchase services from. Although Swedes have not switched massively from one place to another, there has been enough movement to affect the system, particularly since budgets vary with the number of services provided and affiliates. A variety of information and accountability mechanisms make the system function well. Not only are health districts and providers evaluated, but the resulting reports are public, and the public takes the information seriously all the way to the polls.

ular forms of allocating resources. These encourage rising costs, discourage effort by providers, bias services toward less cost-effective activities, and result in inequitable coverage across regions and income classes. These problems of coverage, quality, and costs vary from country to country, due to epidemiological characteristics, spending, and particular forms of organization. Even so, the basic dimensions of organization—and particularly the mechanisms for allocating resources—cause inefficiencies that prevent the region from bridging its health gap.

The first of this chapter's four sections briefly reviews the distinctive aspects and problems of the region's health services. The second focuses on complexities of the health sector and the regions' distinct subsystems of health service provision. The third section discusses four categories of health care systems (here characterized as "subregions") distinguished by relatively distinct organizational features that lead to different outcomes and problems. Finally, opportunities are identified for advancing health reforms and using changes in organization to accelerate the region's progress in health.

HEALTH OUTCOMES REMAIN WORSE THAN EXPECTED

Health services in Latin America and the Caribbean are offered by a host of different providers, absorb enormous resources, and employ millions of people. For instance, social security institutions take in payroll taxes of more than $35 billion per year and provide services, frequently in their own hospitals and clinics, to the population of contributing formal sector workers. Ministries of health operate hospitals and clinics, spending $38 billion per year on services that seek to provide universal care. Private medical practices attend growing numbers of rich and poor who are dissatisfied with public services. Prepaid medicine already covers almost 50 million people in the region, mobilizing private resources of about $12 billion per year. Some $16 billion per year is spent out of pocket on medications that are sometimes prescribed by doctors, sometimes by pharmacists, and that are sometimes purchased by the individual simply on the advice of friends and neighbors. The region's more than 22,000 hospitals, 100,000 clinics and health posts, and 150,000 individual practices employ some 3 million people, including 600,000 physicians, 100,000 dentists, and 300,000 formally trained nurses.

The Region's Health Gap Persists

Despite considerable resources dedicated to the sector, the region continues to face a serious gap in its health conditions.[1] Latin America and the Caribbean have clearly experienced improvements in infant mortality, life expectancy, and coverage over the last thirty years. Even so, given its levels of education and income, the region should be enjoying much better health status. Instead, the countries have serious problems of limited coverage, low or declining service quality, and escalating costs.

Approximately 105 million people in the region do not have regular access to the formal health care system. The poorest populations in both urban and rural areas have least access, as low rates of professional birth attendance illustrate: each year more than 2 million women give birth without professional assistance. Coverage is particularly low in eight countries (Bolivia, Ecuador, El Salvador, Guatemala, Haiti, Honduras, Paraguay and Peru), in which more than 40 percent of the population is estimated to have no access even to basic health services. Even in Brazil, which is significantly wealthier, about one-third of the population is unable to obtain basic care. These problems of coverage are exacerbated by the tendency toward geographic concentration of health services. For instance, in Belize, 52 percent of the population lives in rural areas, yet two-thirds of the health centers are in the capital, and in Ecuador, fully 70 percent of the births in rural areas receive no professional attention.

Quality of services is poor or declining in the public health care institutions in most countries, as demonstrated by the flight of clients to private coverage. This shift is especially dramatic in countries where middle-income and upper-income groups obtain coverage with private insurers, despite contributing substantially to social security systems, as happened in Argentina, Colombia, Mexico, and Venezuela, among others. Growing numbers of the poor population are also demonstrating dissatisfaction with health ministry services; the poorest quintile in Latin America spends disproportionate amounts on private medical services and medications—approximately twice as much as the average for the poor in comparable developing countries.[2]

Rising costs are an increasing problem for almost every health system in the world, but even more so where resources are limited and high shares of national income are already allocated to the sector. At 6 percent of GDP, the region's average health care expenditure is among the

---

[1] See Juan Luis Londoño, Is there a health gap in Latin America? The World Bank, Technical Department for Latin America, Working Paper, April 1996.
[2] Londoño and Frenk (1996).

Table 5.1 Health Expenditures and Outcomes by Country

| | Total Health Expenditures, 1990 | | | | | | Health Outcomes, 1991-92 | | | | |
| | as % of GDP | | | | as % of Total | | per capita (Intl. $) | Profes. Birth Attendance (1991) | 1 Year Immunization (1992) | Infant Mortality Rate (1992) | Life Expectancy (1992) |
Country	Public* [1]	Private [2]	Aid flow [3]	Total [4]	Pub+Aid* [5]	Private [6]	[7]	[8]	[9]	[10]	[11]
Argentina	5.85	3.70	0.01	9.56	61.28	38.72	418	95.4	87	24	72.1
Bahamas	2.63	2.20	0.00	4.83	54.41	45.59	580	95.0	n.a	23	73.2
Barbados	3.24	2.90	0.10	6.24	53.26	46.74	636	98.0	90	9	75.3
Belize	2.75	2.41	0.63	5.79	56.26	43.74	205	87.0	80	33	73.7
Bolivia	1.60	3.10	0.82	5.52	37.63	62.37	95	39.5	82	75	59.3
Brazil	2.76	3.64	0.02	6.41	43.20	56.80	296	70.0	78	58	66.3
Chile	3.32	3.90	0.03	7.26	46.08	53.92	433	98.8	93	16	73.8
Colombia	2.91	2.17	0.06	5.14	57.43	42.57	250	80.3	80	37	69.3
Costa Rica	7.50	1.60	0.08	9.18	82.48	17.52	460	96.4	89	14	76.2
Dominican Republic	1.96	3.60	0.15	5.71	35.85	64.15	159	85.0	59	42	69.6
Ecuador	2.31	1.10	0.28	3.70	68.41	31.59	131	22.9	83	50	68.8
El Salvador	1.74	3.26	0.86	5.86	40.37	59.63	100	31.1	66	46	66.3
Guatemala	1.64	2.93	0.46	5.03	37.51	62.49	132	28.0	62	48	64.8
Guyana	4.22	0.85	4.58	9.65	85.74	14.26	123	93.0	82	48	65.1
Haiti	1.84	3.83	1.33	7.00	37.96	62.04	62	40.0	30	86	56.6
Honduras	2.57	2.76	0.35	5.68	50.57	49.43	88	45.6	92	43	67.7
Jamaica	3.10	5.80	0.48	9.38	36.72	63.28	270	73.0	77	14	73.5
Mexico	3.10	2.36	0.03	5.49	56.88	43.12	335	95.4	92	36	70.8
Nicaragua	4.90	1.24	1.77	7.91	80.93	19.07	124	40.3	78	52	66.6
Panama	5.18	3.18	0.31	8.66	62.63	37.37	344	85.0	84	25	72.9
Paraguay	0.98	2.72	0.19	3.88	27.94	72.06	113	27.3	89	38	70.0
Peru	1.06	2.00	0.07	3.13	35.76	64.24	82	45.5	81	64	66.0
Surinam	1.09	2.92	0.12	4.13	28.93	71.07	161	91.0	77	28	70.2
Trinidad & Tobago	2.83	1.94	0.03	4.80	59.48	40.52	411	98.7	85	18	71.6
Uruguay	6.32	1.88	0.06	8.26	77.15	22.85	484	99.0	95	20	72.4
Venezuela	1.96	2.20	0.01	4.16	47.09	52.91	274	99.0	70	23	71.7

Note: * Includes social security systems.

Sources: [1]-[7]: Govindaraj *et al.* (1995).
[8]-[9]-[13]: PAHO (1994).
[10]-[11]: IDB data base.

highest in the world. In at least six countries in the region (Argentina, Costa Rica, Cuba, Guyana, Panama, and Uruguay), health expenditures actually consume more than 8 percent of national income. Furthermore, most countries' health expenditures grew faster than did their GDP during the economic recoveries of the early 1990s.

Experiences Vary Widely Within the Region

Income levels vary enormously across the region as do the shares of resources devoted to health care. It is therefore not surprising to find huge dif-

ferences in health outcomes. The poorer countries devote no more than 2 percent of their national income to public health services, while the more developed countries devote more than 5 percent. The ratio of per capita spending is more than 10 to 1, measured in international dollars, with annual per capita spending of $62 in Haiti and $636 in Barbados. The number of beds per person also differs by a ratio of 10 to 1, while the number of physicians per inhabitant has a range of 20 to 1 (see Table 5.1 and Appendix).

Differences are just as great in terms of outcome or health indicators. The best outcomes are found in Barbados and Costa Rica, while the worst are consistently found in Haiti. The highest infant mortality rates (86 per thousand) are almost 10 times higher than the lowest (9 per thousand). The difference between the highest and lowest life expectancy at birth is almost 20 years, from 57 in Haiti to almost 76 in Costa Rica. A similar diversity exists within countries. In Peru, for example, infant mortality varies between 52 per thousand in Callao to more than 100 per thousand in Inka, a ratio that is also found within other countries. The variation in health conditions among groups with different incomes is huge: it has been estimated that the poorest 40 percent of the population of Latin America and the Caribbean has a disease burden (450 DALYS) four times greater than does the richest 20 percent (110 DALYS).

Regularities Despite Heterogeneity

These differing results are caused largely by intercountry differences in levels of economic development. It is well known that income level exercises a fundamental influence on health indicators, along with other causative factors strongly associated with income, such as maternal education and investment in sewerage infrastructure. Infant mortality, the incidence of transmissible diseases, and the number of years lost because of early death decline substantially with rising per capita income. Average age of death and average life expectancies rise with income (see Table 5.1).

Nevertheless, the organization of health systems also plays a significant role in health outcomes and is itself an important instrument of policy, independent of income. Figure 5.1 groups the countries into four subregions with distinct organizational features (which are later described in detail). Using the data on health gaps reported in Chapter 2, it is possible to see a pattern of differentiation that is independent of income and expenditures. As Table 5.2 shows, the English-speaking Caribbean countries and Costa Rica (integrated public systems) have the best health out-

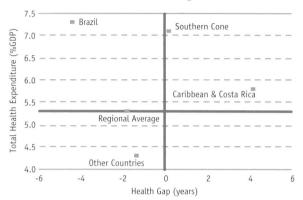

FIGURE 5.1

Expenditures and Health Gaps in Four Subregions

Note: The health gap compares observed life expectancy to the expectation based on per capita income.

comes, although their health care spending consumes a share of income roughly comparable to that of the rest of the region. The countries of the Southern Cone display health outcomes that are close to the levels expected in accordance with their income, but with expenditures higher than 7 percent of GDP. In Brazil, an enormous health gap exists despite very high spending. In the rest of the region, outcomes are worse than expected for the income levels of the countries, with health care spending 50 percent below the regional average. The utilization of resources, then, varies substantially in efficiency from subregion to subregion, reflecting to a certain extent the wide range of health sector organizational structures.

COMPLEX SYSTEMS WITH DISTINCT SUBSYSTEMS

The health of a population depends in general on genetic inheritance, environmental risks, individual behavior patterns, and use of health care services.[3] The use of health care services depends in turn on a whole set of factors related to de-

---

[3] This explanatory model, proposed by Lalonde (1974), has been confirmed empirically many times. The focus on personal health services in the following sections is not meant to undervalue the importance of public health services.

Table No. 5.2 Health Expenditures and Outcomes for Four Subregions				
	Health Expenditures, 1990			Health Outputs
System	Total per capita * [1]	Private as share of Total [1]	Public** as share of GDP [1]	Professional Birth Attendance as % of total [2]	No Access to Health Services % population [2]
Integrated public	399	34.99	3.46	89.1	6.0
Contract-intensive	426	41.81	5.10	96.6	7.5
Public subcontracting	296	56.80	2.76	70.0	28.0
Segmented	231	46.03	2.34	73.2	33.0

* Adjusted for purchasing power parity.
** Includes social security systems.
Sources: [1] Govindaraj *et al.* (1995), [2] PAHO (1994).

Table 5.3 Characteristics of Existing Health Service Subsystems				
	Private	*Private Insured*	*Social Security*	*Health Ministries*
Regulation	Minimal	Some financial	No external regulation	No external regulation
Source of financing	Out-of-pocket	Employers, prepaid, and copayments	Payroll taxes	General taxes
Separation of finance and provision	No financing entity	Separation	No separation	No separation
Cost controls	None	Range of cost controls	Range of cost controls	None
Provider payment mechanism	Fee for service	Range of payment mechanisms	Installed capacity	Installed capacity
Articulation	Little	Contractual	Significant	Some
Consumer options	Many	Many	Limited	Restricted
Ownership	Private	Private	Collective	Public
Criteria for coverage	Ability to pay	Ability to pay	Compulsory affiliation	Last-resort provider, assuring services for the poor
Rationing of services	By service price	By global price	Exclusion	Quality

mand or supply or to the interplay of both in the market. Demand for health services depends on the need for services and on the expression of that need in the market.[4] The need for services depends in turn upon the demographic and epidemiological characteristics of the population, which vary considerably. How these needs are manifested in the market as a demand for services is influenced by the existence of information

and the ability to pay. Although it is difficult to predict the demand for health services by individuals, one can project demand for large population groups.[5] The supply of services in turn depends on the availability of technological capability and the existence of adequate incentives

[4] Musgrove (1995b).
[5] See Phelps (1994).

for serving patients, when and where their needs are expressed.

Demands for health services are largely "derived demands," that is, how patient demands are interpreted by doctors. Users have a limited capacity to define the services they require, so demand is defined by the behavior of the medical professionals who supply those services. A relationship of agency is accordingly established in which patients delegate to their doctor the responsibility to specify their demands. In this way, an interrelationship between supply and demand develops that makes the health services market quite different from other markets in the economy.

The health services market is also distinctive because the demand for services depends on the occurrence of illnesses which are unpredictable for any given individual. Because it is relatively impossible for the population to articulate demands for assured, identifiable, measurable and precise health services, people begin to articulate demands for *contingent* health services (i.e. health plans and insurance) to the extent that they acquire more information and have greater ability to pay.

If demands for health services become increasingly complex, the absence of articulation among providers generates serious problems. Some types of illness require the coordination of numerous procedures and services provided by various specialists and auxiliaries. In the absence of an organizational structure that provides an integrated set of incentives for the patient's care, inefficiencies abound and quality deteriorates. In response to this reality, health services in many countries are increasingly provided by integrated health service delivery organizations.

With regard to supply and demand, a three-tier demand system is usually established in health care markets, involving the participation of patients and doctors, provider institutions, and of financial institutions (third-party payers). Consequently, multiple agency relationships are superimposed on one another, generating complex incentives that are not always compatible.

Coexistence of Multiple Subsystems

In large, heterogeneous developing societies, group action to create an overall rationality in the organization of health care services is usually difficult. Instead, the scattered demands of different groups of users tend to coalesce around various service providers grouped in different manners. In the case of Latin America, the tendency has been for three health subsystems to develop as market niches. Each subsystem is usually associated with certain population types and certain mechanisms of operation and rationing.

For instance, most countries have a huge *private sector* that handles around half of all doctor visits and around one fourth of hospital stays. The system is privately owned, and it tends to be financed directly by users, who have little control over services and who fully assume the risk. Government regulation is minimal. For people with less ability to pay, the supply of services tends to be scattered and is organized around the provision of specific technical interventions. For populations with greater ability to pay, health services tend to be more integrated and to be controlled by independent financing arrangements. In both cases, ability to pay determines the degree of access to services.

The government has increasingly been involved in health services through *public providers.* General taxes usually fund such health services, almost always with poorly defined funding limits and relatively little integration among the services themselves. Because of the close relation between financing and actual service provision, resource allocation tends to be organized around inputs, with little attention to demand; centralization in the management of these various inputs (workers, equipment, medicines) prevents suppliers, hospitals, or clinics from obtaining the mix of inputs that they need on time. Public sector employment generally ensures job stability at a fixed salary, and hence employees have little incentive to satisfy their work responsibilities. In fact, in the case of physicians who can also provide services in private clinics, there is a strong incentive to use their position in the public sector in order to obtain open access to public facilities while providing private services that ensure additional payment for each visit. Government hospitals are normally open to the population, although they are increasingly regarded as intended for poorer people. Since using a price system is prohibited, public facilities are inundated with patients to the point that the quality of care declines and waiting lines become long. Even though they all belong to the same institution, public providers often lack coordination among the services each can supply. For instance, in Paraguay it was discovered that health posts have idle capacity while beds in the main hospitals are overused— primarily as a result of flaws in the referral system.[6]

A third subsystem of health care services is composed of *social security systems*. Organized users, with more or less help from the government, finance entire packages of services through payroll taxes, thereby introducing an explicit degree of solidarity of the wealthier with the poorer and of those who are less sick with those who are more. The insuring institutions take on the user's risk and usually play an active role in health services through their own providers. The system tends to create its own regulations. Although resources are assigned by inputs, there exist overall budget restrictions that have rationalized resource allocation in a number of cases. The user's options are normally limited, and the basic service-rationing mechanism is membership.

Subsystem Coverage and Problems

In Latin America and the Caribbean it is quite common to find that these three subsystems exist side by side serving different population groups. Poorer populations tend to be served with a mix of public hospitals and private professional peo-

---

[6] World Bank project report.

Box 5.2   Public Health System Dynamics and Fragmentation

Health care systems in Latin America and the Caribbean are segmented and fragmented. The public cannot choose freely among them, and the various types of services are not effectively consolidated around users' needs. In societies with sharp inequalities, epidemiology is more varied, and users have different financing arrangements and receive very different amounts of information. Operational rigidities and poor contract design lead to institutional differences among the various health care subsystems. This tends to create natural clients for the different segments of the service market. The poor generally go to the public sector, the middle class to social security, and the upper middle class and the wealthy to the organized private sector. The history of health care systems suggests that the partitioning of the supply of services into a number of niches can result in a certain technical and political equilibrium. The models below illustrate typical health system responses to changes in public spending and formal employment levels.

Diagram A presents the initial distribution of the population among the different health care subsystems. The horizontal axis ranks the population from lower to higher income and the vertical axis indicates population distribution by income group. The segments represent the subsystems chiefly used by each population group. This market equilibrium may be affected by changes in any of the subsystems.

For example, Diagram B shows how the system responds to a crisis in public health care. Cuts in public spending diminish the quantity or quality of the services provided, resulting in longer waiting periods, scarcity of medications, and lower user satisfaction. Some percentage of the consumers served by public suppliers will begin shifting to alternative sources of care, especially those able to pay more. If social security is not available demand tends to move to the private subsystem, through private medical practice or traditional medicine.

Diagram C illustrates the effects of a reduction in income for the social security system. If employment in the formal sector falls, the unemployed will have to be cared for in the public sector or the private sector. If social security enrollment does not fall, but the revenue it receives is reduced owing to declines in real wages or in contributions, the supply of social security services shrinks. Lower-middle-income members will tend to seek more care in public hospitals, generating implicit subsidies for social security. Higher income members will tend to seek care in the mod-

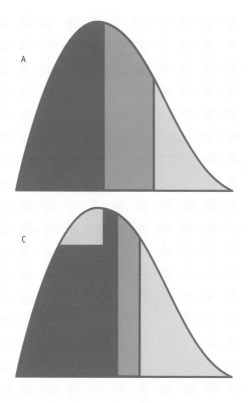

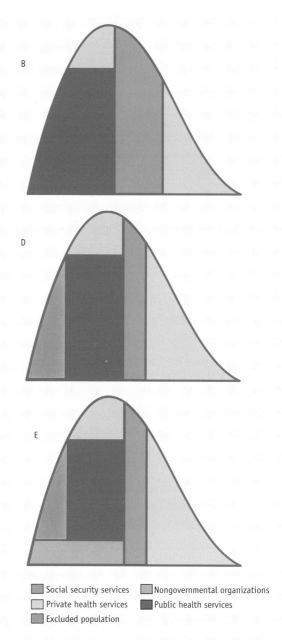

Social security services
Private health services
Excluded population
Nongovernmental organizations
Public health services

ern private sector, creating more demand for health insurance and prepaid medical services through dual enrollment.

Diagram D shows that the combination of cutbacks in public resources and greater demand for services previously provided by social security causes an imbalance that the public system probably cannot solve. The increase in demand, coupled with a reduction in the capacity to provide care, tends to be eliminated through deteriorating quality. Waiting periods lengthen, employee morale drops, and labor conflicts increase. This tends to create a vicious circle, leading to further declines in the prestige of the public services. In this case, part of the poorest group that was previously covered by public hospitals will be left with no access to service. The exodus to the private sector also increases.

The existence of excluded groups and the constraints on response by the modern private sector set the stage for growth in the activities of nongovernmental organizations. As Diagram E shows, they can cover groups not covered by the system, as well as consumers with the ability to pay who have been crowded out of the public sector or social security.

The final configuration is a familiar picture in much of the region. The public health and social security sectors

offer fewer services of poorer quality, narrowing their coverage and increasing their idle capacity, while the private sector, both for-profit and not-for-profit organizations, grows. This exercise shows the interrelationships among the subsystems with regard to both cost and quality, and underscores how consumers affect the system when they react to changes in any of its subsystems.

Source: Maceira (1996).

ple (university trained or traditional). The middle classes, who often work in the public sector and in the formal sector of the economy, tend to be enrolled in the social security system. More affluent populations tend to be served by private health care insurance or comprehensive medical prepayment arrangements.

The fact that these subsystems exist side by side gives rise to problems since the sources of financing and input provision tend to be connected and providers in one subsystem may behave strategically, taking advantage of the behavior of other actors. As explained in Box 5.2, cutbacks in public financing tend to push consumers toward the private sector, and the dynamics of the private sector can undermine the willingness on the part of taxpayers to support public services that they no longer use. Reducing controls over the provision of inputs—of university-trained health professionals or of imported technology—tends to expand private supply, as does greater labor mobility among the various subsystems. The private sector's capacity for technological innovation and marketing and its ability to induce demand challenge the equilibrium of the public systems, by drawing away the latters' resources and financing. Thus, the problems of agency and the incentives generated in a given subsystem not only affect its own performance, but also produce reactions in the other subsystems, and thereby influence the operation of the whole set of structures for health care service delivery.

ORGANIZATIONAL DIVERSITY IN FOUR SUBREGIONS

Within Latin America and the Caribbean today, a wide range of organizational forms can be found. The health systems in the region may be categorized according to the relative importance of different subsystems, their particular internal forms of organization, and the relationships

Organizational Diversity in Health Systems

■ PUBLIC SUBCONTRACTOR
■ CONTRACT INTENSIVE
■ INTEGRATED PUBLIC
■ SEGMENTED

Note: The limits and qualifications to this scheme are discussed in the text.

among them. Using the framework developed in Chapter 3, it is possible to analyze the various health systems in terms of their financial sources, financial-allocation mechanisms, units of service provision, articulation among providers, and options for consumers. While different arrangements often coexist within the same country, four subregions can be distinguished by particular organizational features that lead to distinct problems and generate distinct solutions.

The first category—that of *segmented systems*—is characterized by the coexistence of subsystems of social security insuring the workers of the formal sector, health ministries attending to some public-health interventions and providing personal health care services for the lower and middle classes, and a very large and diverse private sector covering the richest, the poorest, and increasingly the middle classes. This subregion is the largest, covering almost half the population of the region, including all of Central America (with the exception of Costa Rica), Haiti, the Dominican Republic, Suriname, Guyana, the Andean countries, and Paraguay.

Integrated public systems are those where the public system predominates. Financial resources are obtained through general taxes, and resources are allocated to integrated public providers on the basis of installed capacity. These systems are typical of the English-speaking Caribbean and Costa Rica.

In *subcontracting systems*, the government plays an important role in mobilizing resources, while the provision of services is largely private. The main allocation mechanism is on the basis of fee-for-service arrangements, applied with various degrees of sophistication. Brazil, where abundant private resources complement public efforts, is the only country that approximates such a system.

Contract-intensive systems are characterized by the prominence of social security organizations, for which payroll taxes are the major source of financing. There is usually a formal separation between finance and service provision, using a wide range of service-contracting mechanisms. Uruguay and Argentina typify this category, while important parts of the Chilean system fit as well.

Segmented Systems Display Rigidities and Fragmentation

Segmented systems exist in half the countries of the region, and not surprisingly, they are quite diverse. Nevertheless, these countries share certain important health sector organizational features. Their health sectors involve all three subsystems of provision as described earlier: a social security system which ostensibly covers formal sector workers, a public sector that is supposed to provide services to everyone else, and a private sector that serves those who directly pay for services or who purchase private insurance. The range of health outcomes within this subregion is partially a result of diverse income levels and relevant environmental and social factors, but strongly influenced by the interaction of these contextual factors with the particular organizational features of the health service system.

The social security systems are funded through payroll taxes, which rise and fall with wages independently of the quality or quantity of services that the systems provide. The social security systems also have a certain degree of autonomy from the government because of the independence of their income sources and because of their particular governance structures; however, they continue to be public systems, ruled by civil service codes and are subject to extensive government involvement through appointments and other political interventions.

The ministries of health have emerged with a broad mandate to ensure that all citizens have access to adequate health services; in this sense, the ministries seek to compensate for the perceived inequities of the social security systems, which cover only formal-sector workers and their families.[7] The ministries of health tend to be financed from the general revenues of the national government, and their budgets have to be negotiated against those for competing national activities. The ministries also play a direct role in providing services—building, staffing, and operating hospitals, clinics, and other medical facilities and supply networks. Having expanded dramatically between 1950 and 1980, the ministries now em-

---

[7] Families are not covered in the social security systems of the Dominican Republic, Ecuador, El Salvador, Guatemala, and Honduras.

ploy large numbers of doctors, nurses, auxiliaries, and administrators, who receive civil service pensions, job security, and other benefits.

The financial resources allocated to the social security systems or health ministries through payroll taxes or the national budget are used to pay staff, purchase equipment and materials, and build facilities. The decisions over allocating resources among different facilities, programs, and budget categories are usually centrally administered and follow historical patterns and bureaucratic processes.

As a result, the resources that eventually make their way to a particular clinic or physician have probably been allocated in ways that hamper the provision of good services. Hospital directors and physicians possess only limited power to decide how funds are spent in their facilities; they can only request more materials through bureaucratic channels. They do not have the authority to manage a budget, which would give them the necessary scope of action to exploit trade-offs in the financing of different kinds of services, staff, equipment, materials, and maintenance. As a result, it is common to find facilities without personnel, facilities with personnel but no essential medications, and still other facilities with medication overstocks. Various studies and evaluations have noted that supplies are lacking in public and social security systems in countries such as Belize, Guyana, and Venezuela; that a third of public hospital beds in Ecuador are empty because of damaged roofs; and that a third of Peru's publicly operated health posts are not staffed. A study performed in Nicaragua found that health facilities are generally in poor condition there because of years without maintenance and that more than 70 percent of the country's health posts and centers require rehabilitation.[8]

Another consequence of the misallocation of resources is demonstrated by the large number of countries which have built medical facilities which are now underutilized and understaffed. In Belize, occupancy rates in district hospitals averaged 34 percent in 1990 while in the Dominican Republic half of the nation's hospitals had occupancy rates below 30 percent.[9] Evaluations of these systems also regularly demonstrate that the systems are biased toward providing curative rather than preventive care. For instance, in this group of countries, professional birth attendance is quite low, only 73 percent. To address these problems of centralization and misallocation, many countries have sought to decentralize public health care services. Most of these reforms further weakened the service network by municipalizing primary levels of care without expanding the scope of decisionmaking by managers (see Box 5.3).

A high proportion of these countries' medical personnel is contracted by the public sector, to be employed in the ministry or in the social security system or to function as sellers of health services. With a single large employer and only one or a few large unions, negotiations frequently become contests of will and result in excessive hiring. Yet improving the productivity, incomes, and working conditions of smaller numbers of staff might be a better approach. Efforts to reduce excess personnel in Haiti in 1991 were reversed when employees fired during the restructuring were later rehired. In the Dominican Republic, the government has responded to strikes by contracting new staff members, who are then guaranteed employment and who remain relatively free of any supervision that would ensure that they provide the services they were contracted to deliver.[10]

Unlike the situation facing teachers in the education sector, however, key medical staff—that is, doctors—have alternative sources of income through private practice. Therefore, physicians face a very peculiar set of incentives. Additional effort and improved performance in their work for public institutions have little or no effect on their pay

---

[8] IDB and World Bank project evaluations.
[9] La Forgia (1993) and Santana (1996).
[10] Pan-American Health Organization (1992) and Santana (1996).

Box 5.3   Roles and Rules in Decentralizing Public Health Systems

During the past ten years, decentralization has been the most common strategy for reforming public health systems. The experiences vary from country to country, but the dominant trend is toward processes that are incomplete, unbalanced, and have major incentive problems.

Most commonly, decentralization processes are found to be incomplete. The political dynamic has led to the delegation of some functions of health services, typically the maintenance and execution of small investments and the purchase of some inputs. Much slower has been the decentralization of the handling of medications or staffing, which remain quite centralized in many countries. The result has been excessive and wasteful local infrastructure, along with the weakening of the management capability of local bodies.

In decentralization processes there is often little correspondence between responsibilities and resources. The most common strategy is to municipalize primary health care. The scope of responsibilities for local bodies is usually vaguely defined, and the allocation of resources for primary health care is no more precise. Since local bodies have not been subject to an effective budgetary restriction nor to the evaluation of their management, there are few incentives to actually perform their new tasks. Hence, although decentralization has been accompanied by an enormous level of local initiative, it is hard to find very

significant gains in health by such scattered initiatives and structures. Rising local budget deficits then appear in national finances or in the unsustainability of local services, thereby weakening willingness to decentralize.

Finally, the decentralization process has not been accompanied by a restructuring of roles and responsibilities among the various actors in the health system. The prevailing tendency has been to decentralize providers of the ministries toward the incipient local bureaucracies. Then problems of the previous centralized system are often replicated at the local level. Providers have no more autonomy, responsibility, or competency, consumers have no greater voice nor ability to choose, and the mechanisms for allocating resources and incentives do not stimulate improved efficiency and fairness. When local systems fall short in resources or accomplishments, the responsibility tends to be transferred back to the central government.

Decentralization processes now tend to stretch over a long time period, producing considerable political conflict, and bring rather poor results in terms of improving service. Many analysts have identified the difficulties of transferring power during a decentralization process as the major bottleneck. This seems a minor problem, in comparison to the failure to define roles, rules and incentives in decentralization.

---

or promotional opportunities, since these are generally determined by schooling and seniority.[11] But every additional patient served in the private sector adds to income. It is no wonder then that many doctors divert their attention to the private sector, while remaining on the public payroll for its benefits. A situation of low or declining pay in the public sector exacerbates this shift toward private practice and toward reducing actual service in public facilities.

Labor problems in the health sector can be quite severe. In countries as different as Pana-

ma and Haiti, rates of absenteeism in public facilities are extremely high. In Venezuela and Nicaragua, poor incentives for health care staff have led to short hours of attention at public facilities and to such a deterioration in service delivery that people rely on emergency facilities—a practice both costly and inefficient. In the Dominican Republic, despite an official workday of six hours, the excessive number of doctors has led to scheduling three-hour workdays, and even then nothing ensures that doctors are actually present.

The private sector has continued to play a large, and in some cases expanding, role in health services. The people of Latin America and the Caribbean spend almost as much on private health care as on health services from public ministries and social security systems com-

---

[11] During the early 1980s, the Ministry of Health (MOH) of Nicaragua made a huge effort to train nurses and to increase their staffing fivefold, but many have left the MOH to work in other sectors, principally because of limited salary incentives and lack of recognition despite three years of studies in nursing (World Bank 1993).

bined—especially in Brazil and in countries with segmented systems (see Table 5.2). Furthermore, the level of private-sector spending is strongly and inversely related to per capita spending in the public sector (see Table 5.1). In other words, where public systems fail to provide good coverage and high quality, individuals spend large amounts on private services as a share of total health expenditures.

The private sector is quite varied in the countries that have segmented systems. In every country, high percentages of doctors have solo practices, and many hospitals are in the hands of nongovernmental organizations. In the poorer countries and in the poorer areas of almost every country, there are also many forms of traditional medical practice; for instance, in Bolivia some 29 percent of the rural population uses private traditional medical services. Most private services—whether traditional, formal, or nonprofit—are paid for out of pocket under fee-for-service arrangements. In addition, private insurance plans have developed in most of these countries and the growth of private insurance has been particularly strong in the Dominican Republic. In several other countries such as Ecuador, Paraguay, Peru, and Venezuela, prepaid health service companies have also begun to operate.

The fragmentation of health services in this subregion, then, has numerous dimensions. The public systems themselves are fragmented: social security institutes and public ministries duplicate one another's installations and treat one another's patients, with little coordination and no accounting of who pays for what. Financial-allocation decisions are made according to historical patterns and bureaucratic persuasion rather than in response to actual needs and demands. And no single physician, facility, or organization has an integrated perspective on the needs of patients. An individual seeking medical attention at a public facility may be denied access by long lines or by referral to another specialist or to a private-sector physician.

Patients are the only ones with an integrated view of their problems, and their ability to make decisions is limited by their often rudimentary knowledge about their particular conditions and about the available medical treatments. Hence, patients wander—from public or social security systems to private insurance in the Dominican Republic, Mexico, and Venezuela; or from social security coverage to public care, with no established mechanism for coordinating the transfer or effecting payments, in Nicaragua, Peru, and Venezuela. In countries as different as Belize and the Dominican Republic, the public sector attends to a much larger share of inpatient care than outpatient. In itself this distribution could be the result of client preferences and structural coordination but in practice, it demonstrates a segmentation of care and a fragmentation of the providers' incentives to provide the most appropriate and most cost-effective services (see Box 5.2).

This serious fragmentation of the health sector is exacerbated by the absence of clear "rules of the game." Health ministries are formally responsible for defining and establishing the rules, quality standards, and norms to guide the provision of health services. The health ministries are also responsible for monitoring and collecting information on health service providers to ensure compliance with these standards. Nevertheless, the ministries are overburdened with administering their own services, let alone trying to regulate or monitor other subsystems of the health sector—and the regulation that does occur is undermined by its relatively low priority.

Another public-sector function crowded out by attention to the direct administration of health services is public-health interventions. Thus far, we have focused mainly on personal health services—individual preventive or curative care. But also, squarely in the public domain are those specific interventions of a collective nature that either can be undertaken only through collective action—such as eliminating insects or other disease vectors and carrying out educational cam-

| | | | | Private expenditures in drugs as share of | |
| | Traditional medicine | NGOs | Health insurance | Private health expenditures | Total health expenditures |
Country					
Argentina	0	0	3	34.4	13.3
Bahamas	0	1	0	-	-
Barbados	0	0	0	-	-
Belize	2	2	0	23.3	10.2
Bolivia	3	2	0	30.0	18.7
Brazil	1	1	2	36.8	20.9
Chile	0	0	3	-	-
Colombia	1	1	1	45.9	19.5
Costa Rica	0	1	0	40.0	7.0
Dominican Republic	1	2	2	-	-
Ecuador	2	3	0	-	-
El Salvador	2	2	0	46.9	28.0
Guatemala	3	3	0	-	-
Guyana	1	3	0	50.0	7.1
Haiti	3	4	0	-	-
Honduras	2	2	0	-	-
Jamaica	0	1	2	-	-
Mexico	2	0	0	26.9	11.6
Nicaragua	1	2	0	-	-
Panama	1	1	0	-	-
Paraguay	3	2	0	-	-
Peru	2	3	0	43.4	27.9
Suriname	1	2	1	-	-
Trinidad & Tobago	0	0	0	47.0	19.0
Uruguay	0	0	4	13.8	3.2
Venezuela	0	1	1	16.7	8.8

Table No. 5.4   Private Sector Providers and Health Sector Coverage

Rankings reflect the relative importance of the particular category of private sector providers in the health care system as measured

by coverage:	4	3	2	1	0
Traditional medicine	-	above 10%	5-10%	1-5%	below 1%
NGOs	above 20%	10-20%	5-10%	2-5%	below 1%
Health insurance	above 25%	15-25%	10-15%	5-10%	below 5%

Sources: Elaboration based on WB, IDB, PAHO and various health care studies in Latin America.

paigns to modify unhealthy behavior—or that have significant externalities—such as vaccinations and epidemiological tracking. These public-health services are frequently underfunded or squeezed out by the needs of the main hospitals.

The public sector's failure to regulate the whole health system efficiently, combined with the structure of incentives and supply-driven allocation mechanisms for its own facilities, may well explain a significant part of the health gap

Box 5.4   Reforms in Health Systems: Chile and Colombia

As health systems move toward change, most countries have focused reforms on the public health system. To improve its operation, they are mobilizing greater financing and changing the ways government hospitals, health centers and health stations are managed—by decentralizing and by restructuring social security agencies. Some countries have aimed to reform the structure of the overall health system, and to redefine the traditional roles for the public and private sectors in financing, regulation and legislation, coordination, service delivery, and oversight. The most interesting reforms, those of Chile in the 1980s and Colombia in the 1990s, have some similarities, but substantial differences as well.

Reforms in Chile and Colombia share three characteristics. The first is differentiating the roles of the public and private sector. The Ministry of Health is withdrawing from providing services directly, leaving that to local government agencies or private entities. Instead, the central government focusses on regulating and financing the system as a whole. Second, both countries' reforms value competition in the provision of integrated health services and consumer choice as central to reorganizing the system. The ISAPRES in Chile and the EPS in Colombia are the new core institutions. The third similar feature is the creation of a Superintendency of Health as an autonomous government institution for controlling the system.

The reforms differ in substantial ways, such as how they are financed. In Chile, people who pay payroll taxes can freely choose among insurers, whether in the public system (FONASA) or in any of the ISAPRES. When they choose, all the taxes they pay are transferred to the new insurer. The ISAPRES set their own prices, and those wishing to enroll must pay the difference if their tax are not sufficient. Hence those who pay greater taxes have generally opted for the services of the ISAPRES.

In the Colombian system, however, membership is obligatory and universal, while payments to the EPS are based on a capitation premium rather than income or ability to pay. Each worker pays into a Solidarity and Guarantee Fund a fixed percentage of pay for the family's membership; that fund pays to the worker's chosen EPS a capitation premium adjusted for risk (for age, sex, geographical location, and catastrophic illness risk). This fund provides the Colombian approach greater instruments for pursuing fairness.

The systems also vary substantially in organization. Chile has two parallel subsystems for care. Joining ISAPRES is voluntary, and any citizen can receive public health services. ISAPRES plans compete based on the price of their services and on their selection of risks, given that the health plans are weakly regulated. Since ISAPRES are not universal, the public sector plays a substantial role in providing health care. Public hospitals financed by FONASA and the national budget must serve the poorer population as well as more expensive services that ISAPRES do not cover for their members—and that entails an implicit subsidy to ISAPRES.

---

in this subregion. But the existence of a wide range of income-related and other contextual factors leads countries with the segmented systems to manifest the inefficiencies of their health sectors' organizational structures in different ways. These inefficiencies are associated with very poor health outcomes in the countries with lower incomes and less spending—such as the Dominican Republic, Ecuador, Guatemala, Haiti and Peru. In countries in which the context is more propitious and health care spending is higher, the health outcomes are significantly better. In particular, countries that are advanced in the epidemiological transition (having reduced the burden of infectious disease), those with higher general levels of education, and those with high coverage of potable water and other public infrastructure do better. Nevertheless, in such cases the inefficiencies of the organizational structure manifest themselves in high unit costs, as is apparent in Panama and Venezuela.

The declining quality of public services and the flight of middle-class and even poor families to private service providers have not gone entirely unnoticed. Most of the countries have in fact initiated some level of social debate regard-

In Colombia, the EPS system strives for universal coverage since the entire population is obliged to join. The EPS cannot compete on the basis of risk selection because they must follow a Universal Health Plan (the so-called POS) which does not exclude diagnoses but limits less cost-effective procedures. Competition takes place not so much over prices or risks, but over the quality of service delivery. This system does not differentiate over the public or private character of providers, but changes the way public agencies are financed and governed. Public hospitals are granted greater budgetary, hiring, and decisionmaking independence but the financing of inputs is gradually changed into a system whereby user demand is directly subsidized. For the population unable to pay (approximately 30%) there are demand subsidies—vouchers for joining the social security system in the EPS of their choice. In its financing and organization the decentralization system is consistent with the new modality of free choice.

The systems display some differences in their organization and payment mechanisms. The ISAPRES arose primarily as the result of the contracting of independent suppliers, but over time they have gradually reintegrated. Given the lack of upper limits for financing, payment for service modalities have predominated. Colombian EPSs have been integrated more quickly especially in the delivery of outpatient services. In keeping with the overall capitation mechanisms of the EPSs, providers have most frequently used payment through partial capitation.

These two reforms arose in very distinct contexts with different kinds of problems, and have produced different results. Chile introduced the ISAPRES system after a long public health tradition, when the public already had universal access to health care. When the EPS developed in Colombia, social security covered less than 25% of the population, and 25% of the population—the poorest—had no access to any kind of services. Consequently, and in keeping with the type of incentives in each system, after almost fifteen years the ISAPRES have covered somewhat over 20% of the population, while in Colombia in barely three years the new system has expanded its coverage to over 25 percent of the population.

The main problems of the Chilean system arise from the lack of universal coverage under ISAPRES. The system has been plagued by opportunistic behavior (moral hazard and adverse selection) which discriminates against the population and creates imbalances in the risk load that the public subsystem supports. The political economy of the new system did not correct these imbalances early enough, and the resulting pressures created financial problems for public providers, initially due to lack of resources and later because of spiraling costs and low productivity. By contrast, the main problems of the Colombian process result primarily from its rapid pace of expansion. Regulating the transition processes has been technically more difficult than expected, which has led to some conflicts over implementation.

ing reforms for the health sector, and some have even established new mechanisms or entirely new systems. In many countries (including Bolivia, El Salvador, Haiti, Mexico, Paraguay and Venezuela), decentralizing the ministry of health has been the main reform, with the focus on transferring responsibilities to the provinces or states (as in Venezuela), or to municipalities (as in Bolivia). In very few instances thus far, however, has the decentralization been carried out in a way that would give public health care facilities or providers significant autonomy. Furthermore, in many cases decentralization has been pursued without sufficient attention to strengthening the vital central-government functions of regulation and information gathering and dissemination (see Box 5.3).

In 1993, Colombia took an important step, departing from the general characteristics of the typical segmented system by adopting a reform that envisions stronger public financing separate from service provision, as well as payment by capitation, structured competition among integrated public health care service delivery systems, and a gradual transformation of the financial-allocation mechanism from one based on installed capacity to one based on capitation and demand side subsidies (see Box 5.4). To date, the coverage of Colombia's social security system has expanded by five million people, and two million social-security patients are receiving services from a system of newly created integrated health service organizations called EPSs. Through subsidizing demand, almost five million people in the poorest quintile of the population that were previously excluded from the system now appear to be gaining access to services. Public hospitals are being converted to autonomous enterprises, with payments linked to performance.[12] If progress continues, this Colombian reform may demonstrate the role that a change in organizational structure can play in making social services perform more efficiently.

Integrated Public Systems: the English-speaking Caribbean and Costa Rica

Health outcomes in the segmented-systems subregion contrast markedly with health outcomes in the small subregion made up of five countries with small and effective public systems: The Bahamas, Barbados, Costa Rica, Jamaica, and Trinidad and Tobago. Costa Rica is included in this category because despite the formal existence of both a social-security institute and a public ministry, in practice these two are so well coordinated as to constitute a single government health insurance program.[13] The health sectors of the English-speaking countries are structured around "national health insurance" plans, based on a British model with public provision.

These five countries perform relatively well on health outcomes because their delivery systems are integrated and also because they are small, have high income levels, and make signifi-

cant outlays on health care. Size is an issue because most of these countries have populations small enough to be at an efficient scale for administrating integrated health services. The context of high income levels, with their associated positive impact upon health status, is pronounced in the Bahamas, Barbados, and even Trinidad & Tobago.

Nevertheless, these public systems are affected by classical problems generated by the incentives inherent to centralized public administration: financial resources are allocated on the basis of inputs rather than of outputs, and pay schedules and promotion criteria fail to induce high performance. In all of the systems, doctors who are hired by the public sector also provide services privately. Because physicians' public activities are on a fixed salary and their private services are compensated on a fee basis, there exists a strong incentive for them to reduce their hours of "public" service. Even in Costa Rica—with a public health care system among the most effective and equitable in the region—the method used for contracting personnel creates costly problems. Physicians who work from two to four hours in public facilities for full-time wages are known to serve private patients in the public facilities, and some 40 percent of Costa Rica's public-sector nurses are "on leave" at any given time. In Barbados and Jamaica, the law allows doctors to see private patients in public facilities in exchange for channeling part of the resultant fees into the public budget. Though an improvement, this measure fails to address the incentive problem, which results in more favorable treatment of private patients and rising unit costs in public services.

As a consequence of such inefficiencies, these five countries stand out in terms of high expenditures on health, and the burden such expenditures imply in fiscal and tax terms. All five spend at least 2 percent more of their GDP on health services than would be expected based upon their income levels. Partially in response to these cost pressures, Trinidad and Tobago re-

---

[12] Harvard University School of Public Health (1996).

[13] Mexico, Nicaragua, and Panama also have created mechanisms to coordinate the ministry of health with the social security institute; nevertheless, in practice none of these systems achieves the level of *de facto* coordination attained in Costa Rica.

cently initiated a health system reform that includes efforts to increase the autonomy of providers and to improve regulation—seeking to preserve a strong public role in direct provision, but through the creation of more effective structures. These systems must learn how to cope with the erosion of the public monopoly, how to integrate client services more efficiently, and how to introduce organizational structures to use resources more efficiently, so that cost pressures can be stabilized or reversed.

Contracting Private Providers with Public Funds: the Case of Brazil

The organization of the Brazilian health system differs markedly from the organization of the health systems of the other countries of the region. As a result of reforms in the early 1980s, Brazil's public health care services and social security services were unified, national financing of health care services was separated from direct provision, and most public providers were "municipalized." Since then, the national government has largely "purchased" services from public and private entities alike, on the basis of a fee-per-procedure schedule. People can therefore choose among individual providers, who are paid by the Unified Health System.

Although the incentive structure created by the separation of financing from provision holds promise for increasing the system's efficiency, the Brazilian reform lacked certain necessary complementary actions to improve financial mobilization—namely, the articulation of providers and a mechanism to ensure that consumers could exercise informed choice. Unchecked, the excessively complex fee-for-procedure system created incentives for professionals and facilities to provide more services than necessary, especially the more costly services. When the fee schedules failed to keep pace with inflation, many practitioners sought to obtain adequate compensation by billing for services that were never rendered or charg-

ing for an expensive procedure when a cheaper one was actually provided. The absence of effective cost control mechanisms drained public resources. Furthermore, without effective integration mechanisms, the service networks remained atomized, and the poorest of the population remained without access. In addition, instead of increasing the autonomy of providers, municipalization subjected many providers to interference by local politicians.

In sum, the combination of underfunding public health care provision, faulty payment mechanisms, and weak regulatory structures has engendered problems of coverage and quality, along with high unit costs for the services that are actually provided. Through its current reform program, Brazil is seeking to address many of these issues.

Contract-intensive Social Security Systems: Experiences in the Southern Cone

Health systems in the Southern Cone countries, Chile, Argentina, and Uruguay, display a great variety of institutional frameworks in financial allocation mechanisms, decisionmaking units, and articulation. Even so, their health ministries suffer from organizational problems similar to those of the segmented-systems group. Provinces, subnational administrative offices, and hospitals often have considerable autonomy in the Southern Cone, but their budgets are determined on a historical basis related to installed capacity. In all cases, the public system remains the provider of last resort—not only for the poorest, but also for those who have been denied services elsewhere.

The Southern Cone differs most significantly from the other subregions both in terms of the substantial share of the population that is covered by health service institutions that separate financing from provision and in terms of the large number of services provided through prepaid and capitated plans. For these groups, financial re-

Box 5.5   Private Participation in Health Insurance

In Latin America there are numerous ways to link the private sector to insuring health services. Some countries provide social security through the involvement of private insuring and service-providing entities. *Obras Sociales*, Argentina's Social Works Agency, the IAMCs in Uruguay, ISAPRES in Chile, and EPSs in Colombia are examples. In other countries, private companies sell insurance or private health plans. Usually these are insurance companies, or pre-pay medical arrangements, as in Brazil, the Andean region, the Southern Cone, and the Dominican Republic. It is estimated that pre-pay plans cover more than 40 million people throughout the continent, and that the region spends 0.7% of GDP on private health insurance.

The operating structure of private entities in health insurance depends substantially on the regulatory framework adopted. The most regulated entities are those that participate in providing social security. These entities generally have regulations on their capital, liquid assets, and debt; their health plans must offer a minimum package of services and their prices and co-payments are regulated. Private insurance companies are subject to legal and financial controls from banking or insurance superintendencies in most countries, but there are no major regulations on their involvement in the health services market. In most countries medical pre-pay companies operate with no interference in their finances and services.

The operations of insurance companies are determined by the whole body of regulations, the structure of their markets and the form of ownership. The range of regulations can be seen by two extremes in the regions: the Institutions of Group Medical Assistance (IAMCs) in Uruguay and the *Igualas* in the Dominican Republic.

The IAMCs regulate the package of services provided, their premiums, their co-payments and their ownership structure. These complex regulations have not limited their diversity: There are 53 institutions, such as cooperatives of physicians or consumers, with various degrees of vertical integration and different behavior on the markets. Managed-care facilities tend to be more integrated, to pay their physicians better, and to use more services. Consumer cooperatives tend to hire more services, but to consume fewer services. Market behaviors are more competitive in Montevideo and more monopolistic in the country's interior. Greater regulation makes it possible to provide more complete information to users, who have displayed high indices of mobility. The limitations imposed on IAMCs have not prevented the emergence of partial health insurance with less regulation and greater adaptability to the requirements of demand.

The *Igualas* in the Dominican Republic, on the other hand, have practically no regulation on premiums, services, and financial conditions, and hence no useful monitoring. That is why providers dominate the structure of the 25 *Igualas*, which are very diverse: they include large clinics that offer outpatient care, teams of physicians who hire hospital services, and specialized brokers who hire services but do not provide them directly. No *Igualas* have arisen out of consumer cooperatives. Despite the number of institutions, lack of regulation of service packages, pre-existing conditions and limitations, or minimum quality standards reduces competition and effective choice by the consumer. Risk selection and discrimination among consumers are common complaints from users, who find it difficult to assess the efficiency and quality of the various health service providers.

Sources: Labadie (1996) and Santana (1996).

---

sources come from payroll taxes or contributions. There is a redistribution fund that approximates a capitated mechanism in the case of the IAMCs in Uruguay and the *Obras Sociales* in Argentina, and these institutions use a mix of contractual and payment arrangements with providers.[14] These

insurance systems cover more than 20 percent of the population in Chile, about 60 percent in Uruguay, and almost 70 percent in Argentina under the *Obras Sociales* and private health insurers (see Box 5.5).

In general, people in these countries are aware of a large array of health plans, differing in terms of which doctors and hospitals are available to the patient, the amounts of required co-

---

[14] Of the three countries, regulation is quite strong (perhaps excessively so) in Uruguay and weakest in Chile.

payments, and the quality of service. In Argentina's *Obras Sociales*, the insured have little choice of plans, since place of employment determines where their payroll contributions will go. Nevertheless, consumers can choose among the providers, clinics, and hospitals contracted by an *Obra Social*, or use of the services of prepaid companies; a recent survey has shown substantial consumer satisfaction with these services.[15]

In other cases, when consumers have choices among health insurance plans, insurers find ways to screen out higher-risk applicants. In Chile's health system, workers can choose between the public social-security system and private insurers called ISAPRES, but the ISAPRES are not required to insure all applicants and can terminate insurance at any time. As a consequence, the ISAPRES insure working-age, higher-income, and lower-risk citizens with relatively good services leaving poorer, higher-risk, and costlier citizens to the public sector.

In all three countries, the range of contracts between purchasers and providers is quite large. Fee structures, copayments, and capitations are negotiated with public and private providers alike. Complete hospital services are frequently contracted for consumers on a capitated basis, while specialists are usually contracted on a fee schedule. Negotiations take place largely between purchasers and providers, with little direct input from clients. Consumers do exert pressure by seeking out and paying for more and more technologically advanced services out of their relatively high incomes. Doctors, particularly in the private sector, encourage these rising expenditures by investing in equipment and training, the costs of which they then need to recover.

A particular problem facing the Southern Cone countries is an oversupply of personnel and hospital beds, due to the mix of incentives in training doctors. Argentina and Uruguay have the highest concentration of doctors, with one doctor per 330 and per 350 inhabitants as of 1990. These ratios are almost six times higher than the regional average.

The problem of high costs in the public sector due to adverse selection and the problem of high costs in the private sector due to the absence of cost containment and along with oversupply, can be influenced by better forms of regulation which clarify the rules and build in better incentives. The general separation of financing from provision and the existence of numerous payment mechanisms and contractual arrangements create opportunities for better structuring of the sector in these countries. Argentina is now introducing competition among *Obras Sociales*, while Chile is considering regulatory adjustments to diminish the inequities that have emerged in its present system.

THE AGENDA FOR ADVANCING HEALTH REFORMS

In comparison with education services, health services in the region are characterized by a much greater variety of organizational forms, payment mechanisms, and outcomes. The *integrated public systems* prevalent in some countries have contributed to reasonably good services for most of the population. Unfortunately, the cost has been high, and efforts to control these costs have thus far been unsuccessful.

In most of the countries of the region, the failures of public provision have led to the creation of *segmented systems*, in which fragmentation and inefficiency are commonplace. The low standards of provision in the public sectors have delayed the emergence of more efficient and more articulated private solutions, yet the debate in most of these countries remains focused on ways to reform public provision rather than on seeing the opportunities afforded by adopting a systemic perspective and by defining an alternative role for the government.

---

[15] Bitrán (1995).

Brazil has experimented with separating finance from service provision, *contracting private providers* through sophisticated fee-for-procedure methods. Yet coverage remains low, costs are soaring, and the effectiveness of services has not improved.

In the Southern Cone, where *contract-intensive social security* systems predominate, the development of integrated providers with capitated payment mechanisms has had greater success in increasing coverage and improving quality. Even in these cases, however, further advances in efficiency and equity are constrained by ineffective regulation, weak accountability mechanisms, and barriers to consumer choice.

No single formula for reforming health care systems has produced positive outcomes in such diverse countries; in this respect the region's experience parallels that of other countries seeking better and more efficient health care systems. Countries will have to continue experimenting with a variety of approaches, in keeping with the particular characteristics of their own populations and the specific conditions of their own political systems. Nevertheless, some useful general lessons can be drawn from examining the experiences that have already taken place.

A better definition of the complementary roles of different actors, with simpler and more effective rules, is important to improving the health services of the region. In the smaller countries with strong public service traditions, integrated public systems may continue to be the most effective approach, but with greater use of performance contracts or similar measures for increasing the quality and efficiency of services.

In the larger countries, with heterogeneous populations and weaker public sectors, separation of financing, purchasing, and service provision among different actors is likely to yield the best results; in such a case, the central government would play a role in supervising and regulating the system and would simultaneously distance itself from the direct responsibility of providing services. But the pitfalls of such an approach need to be addressed by encouraging the emergence of integrated delivery entities.

Social security institutions can play a greater role in the finance of the system, combining wage taxes and other public funds to ensure equity and efficiency in the allocation of funds. Social security organizations can also play an important role as purchasers of services from independent providers, but this function should be increasingly open to competition and consumer choice. The provision of services can be left to a range of autonomous actors—local health districts, private hospitals, medical group practices—guided by a clear set of incentives and accountability mechanisms, along with sufficient autonomy to exercise their judgment in service delivery for their clients.

Consumers in turn can play a critical role in holding providers accountable for good service provision, through representation on health boards or in the political process, and particularly through exercising the opportunity to choose freely among different plans and providers.

The role of public finances in the financing of the health system must be strengthened. To the extent that the general tax system is efficient and fair, specific resources could be allocated to gradually making the system universal. Should it be necessary, payroll taxes could complement the financing pool. Systems for mobilizing resources through private and prepaid insurance must be efficiently regulated in order to avoid the cost explosions and the inequity with which they have been associated in the past. Just as important as mobilizing these resources is their efficient allocation to the system's providers. Experience has indicated that national financing agencies would gain a great deal in efficiency and equity if instead of extremely complex payment-for-services mechanisms, they would simply concentrate on overall payment mechanisms such as risk-adjusted capitation, accompanied by measures to ensure quality.

Decentralization strategies should be reoriented and become broader in scope in order to make service providers more independent. Continuing to maintain centralized mechanisms for the management of public hospitals and social security makes the system less flexible. But replacing centralized mechanisms with uncoordinated control mechanisms implemented by different agents over different inputs (such as having municipalities handle maintenance and investment, provinces or states handle personnel, and the national government handle the supply of medicines) can make the situation even worse. Local bodies and consumers can play a more active role, as active purchasers of services or as overseers of the quality of results. In turn, providers—whether large individual hospitals or broad service-providing networks—must enjoy full autonomy at the top management level and greater flexibility for administering the areas of budgeting, contracting, and payments. Systems for measuring actual results must be the basis for increasing the accountability of providers. And even in integrated public systems, mechanisms of internal competition among increasingly autonomous providers can be enormously productive.

Empowering consumers with voice and choice holds great promise for improving the region's health service delivery systems. The separation of financing from service provision makes it possible to enhance the role of health service purchasers. Local entities, social security institutions, prepaid companies, and consumer cooperatives can play a more active role in representing the consumer and helping to coordinate and integrate demands. Consumers can play their role more effectively when complex decisions can be simplified through the packaging of services and through educating consumers about service qualities and differences. Consumers can help the system perform better when they can participate in decisions, when demand subsidies give them greater independence, and when they have real choices among alternative plans.

The diversity among the region's health systems demonstrates the richness of experiences with organizational forms native to the region. These systems show that complementary mechanisms and improvements can be implemented, and that governments, providers, and consumers can play distinct roles when they interact within a context of properly structured incentives. Clarifying these roles and efficiently regulating the rules that govern them will require better payment mechanisms, increased autonomy for providers, integration of competitive delivery systems, and consumer choice. In this way, the region's health care service delivery systems can increase coverage and quality and become more cost-effective.

CHAPTER 6

MAKING SOCIAL SERVICES WORK: IMPLICATIONS FOR POLICY

Latin America and the Caribbean must make substantial investments in their populations to bridge the region's social gaps in education and health. There is urgent need to apply more resources more efficiently, and thereby stimulate economic growth and reduce inequality and poverty. Current demographic trends have made the present an opportune moment to accelerate such efforts. As part of this process, the region must consider how to reorganize its various health and education systems, so as to increase their efficiency and mobilize support for further progress.

No single social service delivery structure will be optimal for all countries and contexts, nor is there a single system that will be best in a particular country for all time. Nevertheless, some structures are better than others in particular contexts. Evaluating these structures in terms of their individual elements, overall coherence, and political dynamics will help in the process of design, debate, and implementation (see Table 6.1).

Table 6.1 A Roadmap for Organizational Change	
System Regulation	Roles and Rules
Public Finance	Split finance and provision Stabilize funding Outcome-based allocation mechanisms
Accountable Providers	Split purchaser from provider Autonomy Plurality Responsiveness Labor relations Quality management
Empowered Consumers	Information Voice Choice

ROLES AND RULES

In general, reforms should move in the direction of making social services systems accountable to their clients. They can do this by first clarifying roles and rules. Defining roles will involve clarifying the responsibilities of different actors, taking special care to distinguish financing from provision, and to allocate funds by the number of people served rather than by the amount of inputs used. As the central-level public sector becomes a regulator and financial channel, providers can then become more autonomous and more effective. Providers can begin to exercise greater responsibility and flexibility in teaching students and caring for patients; they can decide the best ways to allocate funds and to integrate service delivery; and they can accept a higher degree of accountability for their performance. In clarifying roles, perhaps the most important change is to empower consumers with more choices and with a voice in the way services are provided. This empowerment involves increasing the amount and quality of information available to consumers, so they can react to their perceptions of these services.

A new framework of rules must complement the new roles. The difficulties of the current education and health systems derive in large part from norms that establish abundant rights, but

only a small range of responsibilities. Public authorities exercise enormous discretion in their administrative powers, but have little effective capacity to judge or enforce compliance with their orders. New rules must be very precise and explicit as to the scope of decisionmaking powers and the resources available under a transparent system of accountability. Above all, the rules must be compatible and cohesive, providing everyone with strong incentives to behave and cooperate in ways that lead to better overall performance.

PUBLIC FINANCE AND CAPITATION

The public sector's role as a funding source for social services is justified to the degree that it promotes greater efficiency and increased equity. To fulfill this role, the public sector first needs to stabilize funding for the long-term requirements of the health and education sectors. It also needs to separate financing from provision to the extent possible, because combining financing with provision leads to rigidities and manipulation that ultimately erode service quality. In the health sector, this separation needs to be complemented by strategies to promote integrated management of service delivery.

The public sector must also allocate financial resources on the basis of outcomes, using capitated systems as much as possible, in tandem with consumer choice among a range of possible providers. One of the strongest ways to empower consumers is in fact to make them responsible for allocating public resources, through their choice of provider for particular educational or health services. When capitation or voucher plans are introduced, consumers determine which providers get the allotted public funds. Such financial-allocation mechanisms reward better providers and signal poorer ones that their quality of care is deficient. By affecting resource allocation, flexibility, and responsiveness, they can establish dynamics for change.

A country's ability to move toward these

kinds of financial-allocation mechanisms will depend on its capacity to administer and monitor such mechanisms. Those governments with weakest capacity can still move away from supply-based subsidies toward using capitation within public budgets—that is, public provision would continue, but the provider units would be given autonomy in the use of funds allocated on the basis of the number of students or patients served. Countries with stronger administrative capacity can consider introducing direct demand subsidies that are means-tested. The possibilities for private provision under public financing are also greater when the public sector has the capacity to oversee and ensure compliance with such contracts or purchases.

In health, the public sector must consider changes that would take all these structural questions into account and that would also attend to three key segments of the health system: personal health services; public health; and investment in equipment, human resources, and research. This section has focused on personal health services, which are more efficient when strong public finance is combined with options for service purchasers to contract with autonomous integrated-delivery organizations. A capitation approach, adjusted by predictable risk, can be the core of a system of incentives to keep people healthy, to improve technical and allocative efficiency, and to improve equity. Such an approach should not discriminate between private and public providers and should also eliminate barriers to mobility for different populations, with a concomitant increase in people's ability to choose among providers. Public action is required in order to introduce the quality checks necessary to complement such a system. Even if the complementary elements cannot be introduced simultaneously, capitation is still a useful engine for change, setting off political dynamics that will lead to the required complementary actions.

By removing itself from the heavy demands of direct provision of personal health services, the public sector can then shift its focus to overall public health and to mobilizing financial resources in order to expand the health system's basic capabilities. Specifically, the central government can finance and actively coordinate the provision of formal public health services, including intervention on risk factors (like vector and sanitary controls) and some other very cost-effective interventions (such as vaccinations or screenings), and it can also finance and actively promote basic investment in equipment, human resource development, and research.

In education, public school budgets that are assigned on a per-student basis can be an important instrument for increasing the autonomy of providers at some local level. The formula for compensating schools has to include contextual adjustments for rural or urban settings and for poor or rich neighborhoods. Compensation should also be structured to give schools incentives to promote or graduate their students, or at least to retain them through the entire school year, rather than simply enrolling them at the beginning of that year. Allocating the public budget this way—if that budget is adequately funded and coupled with greater school autonomy—can expand the role of school directors and teachers in using the school's scarce resources to serve its students; such budgeting can also help planners verify the true costs of educating students. School "governance," in the sense of improved management and increased accountability, should be further enhanced by creating channels for participation by students and their families. Altogether, the capitation of school funding can increase the financial accountability of schools while also expanding providers' knowledge of the marginal value of different inputs to the schooling process.

AUTONOMOUS PROVIDERS

The full value of capitation is felt only when provider units have decisionmaking power regarding allocation of funds to increase technical and allocative efficiency. These gains can be realized when providers choose the mix of inputs, select and evaluate their staff, and even control salaries and promotions. There are reasons to restrict this autonomy, but not with cumbersome bureaucratic controls and certainly not to the degree exercised in the region today. At a minimum, reasonably small administrative units should be able to respond to simple requirements for maintenance and materials. If possible, they should also be able to respond to changing personnel requirements and to modify salaries or other emoluments in order to attract and retain qualified staff. Autonomy would allow them to identify and demand the in-service training or upgrading of skills they require.

In the health sector, autonomy would be most effective if given to integrated health service organizations with prepaid plans. For prepaid plans, the efficient scale for managerial autonomy appears to be in the range of 50,000 to 500,000 affiliates. When clinics, hospitals, and doctors receive autonomy, however, they tend to provide too many curative services. In education, there is far less research concerning this issue, and fewer experiments. All but the smallest schools seem to be appropriate units for a large range of managerial tasks, but schools may perform better with technical and administrative support from a larger entity.

HUMAN RESOURCES

The keystone of any education or health system is its human resources. The systems must attract capable people to the professions of teaching and medicine, and motivate them to care for the well-being of their charges, to invest in professional skills and training throughout their careers, and to remain in their professions. Some of the incentives for carrying out their vocation are imparted during their early professional training, when the intrinsic motivation for providing social services can be instilled, and other incentives are imparted through the recognition providers receive for good service. Incentives are also imparted through

empowerment in the workplace, through giving personnel the scope of decisionmaking power necessary to apply their skills, training, and experience in the service of their clients—an approach that again requires greater autonomy of the service-providing units. Finally, incentives are created by adequate and rational pay schedules, that reward effort to the extent possible.

On this latter point, merit pay schemes should be viewed skeptically vis-á-vis alternative methods of remuneration. There is little evidence that merit pay can be effectively administered in the institutional contexts of educational systems, or that it results in greater provider effort or better performance. There are simpler ways to make pay schedules responsive to provider effort. For instance, experiments with bonuses for all the personnel in a given school can be used to recognize and reward whole teams of teachers and administrators who do exceptional jobs of raising student performance. Teachers' individual opportunities for promotion can be linked to effort, performance, and service to students and the school, rather than strictly to seniority. In the case of health, pay schedules should be mixed and differentiated by type of treatment. For ambulatory care, a mix of partial capitation and individual rewards works best; for hospital care, those payment systems that reward hospitals according to packages of services are most effective, allowing them to pay staff with a mix of salaries and predefined fees.

Public action is critical in holding providers accountable, through establishing standards and providing information about service quality. Certification of schools, qualifying exams, and in-service licensing exams can offer incentives for individual providers to seek and obtain training. In-service licensing requirements would also give incentives for personnel to remain current in their fields.[1]

---

[1] A medical survey in Colombia in 1989 found that 20 percent of general practitioners were unaware of the emergence of AIDS as a public-health threat.

Perhaps the greatest challenge in the improvement of human resources in these sectors is found in the relationship between provider unions and the public sector. The interplay between negotiation and budget constraints has led to contracts that (i) allow real wages to be eroded, (ii) let staffing increase independently of service demand, (iii) provide for very rigid job stability, and (iv) attract personnel through deferred benefits such as pensions.

Personnel should be active in limiting managerial arbitrariness and abuse. But personnel also have a real interest in giving managers and administrators sufficient discretion to allocate resources efficiently and to evaluate staff in ways that can improve both working conditions and performance. Cases in which unions negotiate at the national level with public ministries must be modified so that taxpaying citizens know how much the proposed contracts will cost them now and in the future. Increasing the autonomy given to schools and to local health groups and increasing the flexibility given to school directors and to health administrators should constitute subjects of discussion and conditions for the granting of better pay to teachers and to health care workers. As governments and unions refocus their attention toward raising productivity and wages, and away from increasing employment and union membership, they will better serve teachers and health care workers, students and patients, and the overall public interest. The public debate over the compensation of health and education staff should be elevated above simple issues of wages and arbitrary management to a discussion that recognizes the value of seeking to improve the management and mobilization of human resources in the sectors.

EMPOWERING CONSUMERS: VOICE AND CHOICE

Consumers should be empowered with greater voice in the way systems perform and meaningful choices among providers. Voice can range from the expression of preferences and grievances to full integration into management (through school boards, community associations, and the like), with control over decisions. Such mechanisms of voice create direct feedback from consumers to the service providers and increase efficiency by channeling vital information to those who can best respond to it.

Consumers also need to be empowered with better choices. Many citizens of Latin America and the Caribbean already exercise their preferences by opting for private medical practice and private schools. The region already has the world's highest share of income spent in private medical care. Meanwhile, most private schools in the region are not elite schools for the rich, but marginal schools run by churches and nongovernmental organizations; ironically, the poorest end up paying for services that are provided free to the middle classes.

In basic education, choices can be offered among public-sector providers or between public and private schools. To restrict the emergence of nongovernmental service providers is counterproductive if they can provide quality services at competitive rates. The population already exercises choice in health services, but this can be enhanced through channeling public funds on the basis of the number of clients enrolled in family practices or affiliated with integrated delivery systems. The region should encourage a range of providers with integrated incentives to provide consumers with choices.

Certain isolated or sparsely settled areas of Latin America and the Caribbean obviously cannot provide many service delivery options, and the public sector will remain responsible in such areas. However, creating options for consumers in other areas can provide benchmarks to monitor the efficiency of these more isolated units, and can stimulate innovations in management and technology to make them more effective.

In some cases, consumers may not be capable of evaluating the full range of information that the systems should generate regarding services—particularly in the case of health services, in which the range of services and the multiple dimensions of quality are difficult to monitor and assess in a short time. The emergence of institutional purchasers, insurance agencies, or other kinds of intermediaries can provide consumers with simpler choices of enrollment. In these cases, individuals can choose the plan that they believe best monitors and recruits medical services for them. Reputations and information concerning a small number of plans can be more easily evaluated than data regarding myriad doctors, clinics, and hospitals

Choice allows consumers to take an active role in determining what is best for them; it also provides feedback information and discipline to providers, who ought to be interested in serving these consumers well. When attached to mechanisms that allocate resources on the basis of outputs, this exercise of choice gives providers even stronger motivation for better performance as a way to attract clients.

It is difficult if not impossible to hold social-service systems accountable if consumers lack systematic information regarding their performance. The gap in feedback is partly due to the wide range of potential performance measures and the difficulties of measuring performance. Providers also sometimes resist the introduction of exams or reviews that would monitor their performance. National student exams for the purpose of comparing schools and medical reviews that provide comparative data are both essential for citizens to evaluate the services they fund through taxes. Efforts to collect this kind of information confidentially for use by government offices obviously do not inform the public. Only the people who pay taxes and use the schools and health services are sufficiently numerous to lobby for changes and to hold the systems accountable. There are many efforts to establish or improve information systems that serve government planning and administration purposes but that fail to build a constituency for improvement in services. Public information empowers consumers, since they are the only ones with direct unmediated interest in pressuring for changes in service quality.

THE CASE FOR REAL EQUITY AND COHERENCE

How can the region's social-service systems better respond to the public's health and education needs and allocate resources more rationally? The current systems are so inequitable in assigning resources and priorities to the needs of the poor and marginalized that even modest changes are likely to be progressive. Of course, such changes in resource allocation and autonomy must still be complemented with specific mechanisms to reduce or compensate for inequities. For instance, in health, when consumers are given choices among health providers or plans, the necessary information must be made available and understandable to people of all income classes—an undertaking that requires direct promotional efforts aimed at empowering the poor. Another equity-related issue arises in health because of adverse selection, wherein providers seek ways to attract clients who are healthier than average and therefore less costly to serve. Protecting public sector institutions from becoming insurers of last resort requires safeguards such that neither private nor public actors can exclude applicants or terminate contracts with their affiliates as a result of revealed characteristics. Nevertheless, even without many of these complementary actions to redress inequities, simple changes like capitation and vouchers can make public expenditures much more progressive than is the case in many of the current nontransparent systems of allocation.

In education, financing formulas need to incorporate incentives for providers to serve poorer and more difficult students. These formulas also need to compensate for the higher average cost of schooling in rural or marginalized areas. In some cases, the simplest way of administering such compensatory mechanisms may be through special programs targeted at disadvantaged schools.[2]

Financing health and education services out of progressive and efficient revenues at the national level is preferred, not only because of potential advantages for overall equity but also because of taxation efficiency. If the political economy makes it impossible to provide sufficient resources and allocate them equitably, then dedicated taxes (such as payroll taxes or value-added taxes, which are earmarked and independently administered) are the second-best approach.

The current trend to decentralize health ministries has serious flaws from the perspective of organizational efficiency. Although responsibilities are now delegated to subnational-level (state/province)or municipal governments, wages and employment contracts are still negotiated at the central level, and resources are sometimes transferred without regard to actual service demands. This combination of mechanisms increases autonomy only superficially because those responsible for managing the systems at the decentralized level still do not have sufficient control over inputs or adequate incentives in terms of resources provided. The positive elements of decentralization should be maintained and deepened, but complementary elements such as provider autonomy and flexibility must also be pursued.

The road to closing the two social gaps is not going to be easy. It will require mobilizing and rechanneling enormous amounts of money, addressing and sometimes confronting the inter-ests of strong social groups, and introducing mechanisms and concepts of accountability that are new. Proposals will vary by country, context, and timing, but they should incorporate an incentive structure to affect and shape the actions of government, service providers, and clients alike. In tailoring proposals to specific cases, the selected alternative should pay attention to coherence—that is, to the checks and balances that ameliorate the adverse aspects of change—and to the administrative capacities of the systems themselves.

But too much caution and care in design can also be dangerous. Even if proposals are not perfect or complete, those elements that are feasible and that induce positive dynamics can constitute the first steps. The process of improvement can be reinforced by the imbalances that these first changes induce.[3]

Establishing better rules and roles means reorienting the public role to that of finance and purchasing rather than service provision, introducing capitation, increasing provider autonomy, improving human resource management, and empowering consumers with information, voice, and choice. These measures offer the most promising approach to putting the dynamics of positive change in motion, in order to bridge the region's social gaps in education and health.

---

[2] This is the strategy of the current government in Chile under the "Escuelas 900" program. This program is able to target poorly performing schools on the basis of their student performance because of the existence of regular standardized exams. Otherwise, the targeting would have to rely on socio-economic characteristics, which Carnoy and Castro (1996) argue would be just as effective, noting, however, that the test scores made it possible to evaluate the *effects* of the program and declare it a success.

[3] Hirschman, Albert O. *The Strategy of Economic Development* (Boulder, CO and London: Westview Press, 1988).

A P P E N D I X

Table 1 Public Expenditure in Education as Percentage of GNP

By Region	1980	1990
All countries	4.4	4.6
Industrial Economies	5.9	5.7
Latin America and Caribbean	4.3	4.3
East Asia	3.4	4.1
South Asia	2.2	4.1
Other Asia (including China)	3.5	3.5
Sub-Saharan Africa	4.5	4.3
Middle East and North Africa	4.4	5.1
Other Europe and Central Asia	4.2	4.8

By Income Group	1980	1990
High income	5.2	5.2
Low income excluding LAC	3.8	3.6
Lower-middle income excluding LAC	5.0	5.3
Upper-middle income excluding LAC	4.1	5.5
LAC low income	4.8	3.7
LAC lower-middle income	4.0	3.8
LAC upper-middle income	4.6	5.2

Source: UNESCO and World Bank.

See appendix for country groupings.

Classification according to income follows World Development Report, 1992.

Table 2   Total Public Expenditure on Education

Country	Total Public Educational Expenditures as share of: GNP		Govt. Expenditures		Current Educational Expenditures as share of: Public Educ. Expenditures	
	1980	1990s *	1980	1990s *	1980	1990s *
Argentina	2.70	3.30	15.10	12.40	84.50	96.00
Bahamas	n.a.	3.90	n.a.	16.30	n.a.	n.a.
Barbados	6.50	7.50	20.50	18.60	82.80	81.00
Belize	n.a.	5.70	n.a.	15.50	n.a.	79.90
Bolivia	4.40	2.70	25.30	20.10	96.00	99.50
Brazil	3.60	4.60	n.a.	n.a.	n.a.	n.a.
Chile	4.60	2.70	11.90	12.90	94.90	96.30
Colombia	1.90	3.50	14.30	12.30	93.30	88.20
Costa Rica	7.80	4.60	22.20	20.20	91.30	96.40
Dominican Republic	2.20	1.70	16.00	9.90	75.40	62.50
Ecuador	5.60	3.00	33.30	19.20	94.00	91.10
El Salvador	3.90	1.60	17.10	n.a.	94.10	99.80
Guatemala	1.90	1.60	11.90	12.80	89.40	n.a.
Guyana	9.70	4.70	14.00	n.a.	73.60	80.20
Haiti	1.50	1.80	14.90	20.00	80.10	99.90
Honduras	3.20	4.10	14.20	15.90	91.00	97.70
Jamaica	7.00	6.20	13.10	12.90	99.60	92.10
Mexico	4.70	6.00	n.a.	n.a.	n.a.	63.40
Nicaragua	3.40	3.90	10.40	12.80	87.50	95.80
Panama	4.90	5.50	19.00	18.90	93.70	93.20
Paraguay	1.50	2.80	16.40	16.90	n.a.	92.50
Peru	3.10	1.50	15.20	14.70	94.40	n.a.
Suriname	6.70	8.30	22.50	n.a.	100.00	99.60
Trinidad and Tobago	4.00	3.60	11.50	10.30	76.40	92.20
Uruguay	2.30	2.80	10.00	15.40	94.70	91.10
Venezuela	4.40	5.20	14.70	23.50	95.10	n.a.

* Dates for latest data vary by country from 1989-1993.
Source: UNESCO.

Table 3   Current Expenditure per Pupil by Level of Education (1990 PPP$)

	Primary	Secondary	Tertiary
Argentina [1]	421	562	796
Barbados	2152	2665	7687
Bolivia	172	191	669
Brazil	526	621	5258
Chile	619	557	1795
Colombia	297	495	1782
Costa Rica	438	877	3166
Ecuador	186	341	589
Guatemala [1]	88	146	1110
Haiti	77	115	1382
Honduras	209	370	1658
Jamaica	303	515	4909
Panama	536	659	2142
Paraguay	94	250	998
Peru	163	245	n.a.
Suriname	899	547	2775
Trinidad and Tobago	851	1532	6468
Uruguay	480	600	1680
Median	362	531	1782
Mean [2]	500	661	2864

[1] For Argentina and Guatemala 1992 data is used.
[2] Does not include Argentina and Guatemala.   *Source:* Own calculations based on UNESCO and World Bank.

Table 4   Enrollment Ratios (Percent)

Country	Year	Pre-primary Gross	Primary Gross	Primary Net	Secondary Gross	Secondary Net	Tertiary Gross
Argentina	1992	68	108	95	72	59	43
Bahamas	1992	n.a.	105	100	95	89	n.a.
Barbados	1992	n.a.	105	89	88	81	18
Belize	1992	n.a.	109	96	47	36	n.a.
Bolivia	1992	29	95	91	37	29	22
Brazil	1992	35	111	90	43	19	12
Chile	1992 [8]	70	99	86	69	52	23
Colombia	1992 [9]	44	117	83	61	44	15
Costa Rica	1992	66	103	87	43	37	28
Dominican Republic	1992	14	97	81	37	24	19
Ecuador	1992 [10]	20	123	n.a.	55	n.a.	20
El Salvador	1992 [1]	22	78	70	26	15	16
Guatemala	1992 [2]	16	84	n.a.	24	n.a.	9
Guyana	1988	71	112	n.a.	57	n.a.	5
Haiti	1992 [3]	41	56	26	22	n.a.	1
Honduras	1992	18	112	90	33	21	9
Jamaica	1992 [4]	83	109	100	66	64	9
Mexico	1992 [5]	63	113	100	56	46	14
Nicaragua	1992 [6]	12	103	80	41	26	10
Panama	1992	54	106	91	63	51	22
Paraguay	1992 [11]	32	109	97	34	29	8
Peru	1992 [12]	36	119	88	65	46	39
Suriname	1988 [13]	94	127	100	54	45	9
Trinidad and Tobago	1992 [7]	8	95	88	78	65	7
Uruguay	1992 [14]	34	108	93	83	n.a.	32
Venezuela	1992 [15]	45	96	88	35	20	30

Source: UNESCO.

[1] Data on preprimary level and tertiary level refer to 1991.
[2] Data on preprimary level and tertiary level refer to 1991.
[3] Data on preprimary level and tertiary level refer to 1990.
[4] Data on secondary level (net) refer to 1989 and data on tertiary level refer to 1990.
[5] Data on tertiary level refer to 1986.
[6] Data on tertiary level refer to 1985.
[7] Data on tertiary level refer to 1991.

[8] Data on secondary level (net) refer to 1990.
[9] Data on tertiary level refer to 1991.
[10] Data on tertiary level refer to 1990.
[11] Data on preprimary level refer to 1990 and data on tertiary level refer to 1991.
[12] Data on tertiary level refer to 1990.
[13] Data on preprimary level refer to 1990.
[14] Data on tertiary level refer to 1991.
[15] Data on tertiary level refer to 1990.

Table 5 Private Enrollment as Percentage of Total Enrollment

Country	1980			1990-92		
	Pre-primary	Primary	Secondary	Pre-primary	Primary	Secondary
Argentina	32	18	39	30	20	29
Bahamas	n.d.	21	21	69	n.d.	25
Barbados	20	9	16	n.d.	10	n.d.
Belize	n.d.	n.d.	n.d.	n.d.	n.d.	47
Bolivia	8	8	17	10	10	26
Brazil	46	13	n.d.	26	12	n.d.
Chile	20	20	24	49	40	43
Colombia	64	14	45	58	17	40
Costa Rica	13	3	9	10	5	10
Dominican Republic	87	18	24	55	22	32
Ecuador	42	16	34	40	16	n.d.
El Salvador	20	7	50	33	14	62
Guatemala	21	14	38	32	17	n.d.
Guyana	0	0	0	0	0	0
Haiti	100	57	82	86	61	82
Honduras	16	5	46	21	5	n.d.
Jamaica	85	4	4	86	8	n.d.
Mexico	11	5	19	9	6	12
Nicaragua	43	12	18	28	14	19
Panama	34	6	11	27	8	13
Paraguay	63	15	27	50	14	22
Peru	27	13	15	20	12	16
Suriname	54	55	n.d.	46	52	35
Trinidad & Tobago	n.d.	73	n.d.	n.d.	n.d.	n.d.
Uruguay	25	16	17	29	16	16
Venezuela	17	13	26	17	15	35

Source: UNESCO.

Table 6   Outcome Indicators of the Education System

Country	Adult Literacy Rate as % of age 15+		Mean Years of Schooling population of age 25+		Primary Net Enrollment (Percent)		Primary Completion Rate	
	1980s	1992	1980	1992	1980	1992	1980	1988-90
Argentina	94	96	6.00	9.20	n.a.	95	63	n.a.
Bahamas	n.a.	n.a.	6.20	6.20	n.a.	100	n.a.	100
Barbados	n.a.	n.a.	6.30	9.40	96	89	92	78
Belize	n.a.	n.a.	4.60	4.60	n.a.	96	48	63
Bolivia	n.a.	79	4.00	4.00	79	91	44	44
Brazil	75	82	3.30	4.00	81	90	20	30
Chile	91	94	6.20	7.80	n.a.	86	53	77
Colombia	85	87	5.20	7.50	n.a.	83	n.a.	59
Costa Rica	93	93	5.60	5.70	89	87	75	79
Dominican Republic	74	84	4.30	4.30	73	81	n.a.	20
Ecuador	84	87	5.40	5.60	88	n.a.	67	63
El Salvador	67	75	3.40	4.20	n.a.	70	n.a.	38
Guatemala	n.a.	56	4.00	4.10	58	n.a.	40	36
Guyana	n.a.	97	5.00	5.10	94	n.a.	75	97
Haiti	35	55	1.50	1.70	38	26	14	39
Honduras	60	75	3.00	4.00	78	90	n.a.	34
Jamaica	n.a.	99	5.10	5.30	96	100	80	85
Mexico	83	89	4.00	4.90	n.a.	100	66	73
Nicaragua	n.a.	n.a.	3.50	4.50	73	80	38	43
Panama	86	90	5.90	6.80	89	91	73	79
Paraguay	88	91	4.60	4.90	87	97	53	60
Peru	82	86	5.70	6.50	91	88	75	n.a.
Suriname	90	96	4.00	4.20	n.a.	100	88	93
Trinidad & Tobago	95	n.a.	6.10	8.40	92	88	78	89
Uruguay	95	97	6.10	8.10	n.a.	93	n.a.	97
Venezuela	85	89	5.30	6.50	83	88	70	86

Source: UNESCO.

Note: World Bank data used for completion rates of Brazil and Dominican Republic.

Table 7   Total Health Expenditures in 1990

By Region	Per capita PPP$	As a percentage of GDP		
		Total	Public*	Private
All countries	429	5.14	3.22	1.9
Industrial Economies	1613	7.81	5.88	1.9
Latin America and Caribbean	297	6.24	3.55	2.7
East Asia	152	3.74	1.28	2.5
South Asia	63	4.17	1.71	2.5
Other Asia and Pacific	68	3.12	1.76	1.4
Sub-Saharan Africa	58	4.08	2.42	1.7
Middle East and North Africa	144	3.72	2.08	1.6
Other Europe and Central Asia	284	4.59	3.26	1.4
-Former east bloc nations	269	4.47	3.31	1.3
-Other semi-industrialized nations	305	5.17	3.00	2.2

By Income Group	Per capita PPP$	As a percentage of GDP		
		Total	Public	Private
Low income countries	61	3.84	2.16	1.7
Lower-middle income countries	178	4.22	2.61	1.6
Upper-middle income countries	392	4.82	3.33	1.7
Low income LAC countries	87	7.44	4.96	2.5
Lower-middle income LAC countries	284	6.38	3.53	2.8
Upper-middle income LAC countries	316	5.64	3.10	2.5

Source: Govindaraj, *et al.* 1995.

* Includes social security system.

Table 8   Health Expenditures and Outcomes Ranked by per Capita Health Expenditure (1990)

Country	GDP per capita (US$'93)	Total Health Expenditures per capita		Epidemiological Transition [2]	Access to Health % population	Under 5 Mortality Rate 1993
		US$	Intl. US$[1]			
	[1]	[2]	[2]	[3]	[4]	[5]
Barbados	6,230	400	636	4	97	10
Bahamas	11,420	580	580	4	98	n.a.
Uruguay	3,830	219	484	4	96	21
Costa Rica	2,150	186	460	4	96	16
Chile	3,170	153	433	4	93	17
Argentina	7,220	312	418	4	92	27
Trinidad & Tobago	3,830	190	411	4	97	21
Panama	2,600	173	344	3	79	20
Mexico	3,610	155	335	3	77	32
Brazil	2,930	222	296	3	72	63
Venezuela	2,840	102	274	3	76	24
Jamaica	1,440	154	270	4	89	13
Colombia	1,400	65	250	3	75	19
Belize	2,450	118	205	2	86	22
Surinam	1,180	133	161	2	88	34
Dominican Republic	1,230	59	159	1	71	48
Guatemala	1,100	37	132	1	50	73
Ecuador	1,200	39	131	2	61	57
Nicaragua	340	31	124	2	69	72
Guyana	350	39	123	1	84	63
Paraguay	1,510	49	113	1	54	34
El Salvador	1,320	58	100	1	59	60
Bolivia	760	34	95	1	34	114
Honduras	600	65	88	1	46	56
Peru	1,490	59	82	1	44	62
Haiti	370	27	62	1	n.a.	130

Sources: [1] World Bank (1995).

[2] Govindaraj *et al.* (1995).

[3] Data based on IDB and World Bank reports and Frenk *et al.* (1996).

[4] PAHO (1994).

[5] UNICEF (1995).

[1] International dollars are adjusted for Purchasing Power Parity.

[2] Epidemiological Transition ranked countries from 1 (low) to 4 (high).

[3] GDP per capita belongs to 1991.

Table 9   Relation between the Public Health Care System (PHS) and the Social Security System (SSS)

Country	Public System Provision-Finance	Joint PHS-SSS	Patient Transfers Patients go from	to	Payments	Public Subsidy to SSS
Argentina	same	no (Unions SSS)	SSS	PHS	no	yes
Bahamas	same	no SSS	na	na	-	-
Barbados	same	no SSS	na	na	-	-
Belize	same	no (Brit.SSS)	na	na	-	-
Bolivia	same	no	-	-	-	yes
Brazil	separate	yes	-	-	-	-
Chile	same	no SSS	na	na	-	-
Colombia	same (1)(2)	no	SSS	PHS	yes (1)	yes
Costa Rica	same	yes	PHS	SSS	(3)	-
Dominican Republic	same	no	-	-	-	yes
Ecuador	same	no	PHS	SSS	yes	-
El Salvador	same	no	-	-	-	yes
Guatemala	same	no	-	-	-	yes
Guyana	same	no (Brit.SSS)	na	na	-	-
Haiti	same	no	-	-	-	-
Honduras	same	no	SSS	PHS	yes	-
Jamaica	same	no SSS	na	na	-	-
Mexico	same (4)	no (4)	PHS	SSS	yes (4)	-
Nicaragua	same	yes	SSS	PHS	no (5)	yes
Panama	same (6)	no (6)	PHS	SSS	yes (6)	-
Paraguay	same	no	-	-	-	yes
Peru	same	no	SSS	PHS	no	-
Suriname	same	no	-	-	-	yes
Trinidad & Tobago	same	no SSS	na	na	-	-
Uruguay	same	no	-	-	-	yes
Venezuela	same	no	SSS	PHS	no	-

Notes:

(1) Family Compensation Fund.

(2) The Colombian reform is implementing a public system with separation between finance (public) and provision (cooperatives, *Entidades Promotoras de Salud*) for selected areas.

na: not applicable; A hyphen indicates either no such function, or data was unavailable.

Sources: Elaboration based on WB-IDB-PAHO and Health Care Studies in Latin America.

Country	Population per doctor [1]	Population per nurse [1]	Total Physicians [1]	Total Nurses [1]	Nurse/Doctor Ratio [1]	Hospital Beds per 1000 pop. [2]
Argentina	330	1,650	97,858	59,308	0.00	4.4
Barbados	1,120	220	229	1,043	0.00	8.1
Bolivia	2,080	2,970	3,448	1,161	0.00	1.3
Brazil	670	6,700	224,400	33,493	0.00	3.5
Chile	2,170	2,710	6,071	2,240	0.00	3.2
Colombia	1,150	1,920	11,455	5,966	0.00	1.4
Costa Rica	1,030	490	2,725	5,562	0.00	2.2
Dominican Republic	930	1,330	7,606	5,719	0.00	1.9
Ecuador	960	3,200	10,713	3,348	0.00	1.6
El Salvador	1,560	1,040	3,342	3,213	0.00	1.6
Guatemala	2,270	910	4,052	4,452	0.00	1.6
Guyana	6,220	890	128	144	0.00	1.5
Haiti	7,140	8,930	906	102	0.00	0.8
Honduras	3,130	3,130	1,631	521	0.00	1.1
Jamaica	2,040	490	1,186	2,421	0.00	2.2
Mexico	1,850	2,310	45,489	19,692	0.00	0.8
Nicaragua	1,670	3,340	2,307	691	0.00	1.2
Panama	840	320	2,879	8,996	0.00	2.7
Paraguay	1,610	950	2,680	2,821	0.00	1.2
Peru	970	1,080	22,333	20,679	0.00	1.5
Suriname	1,260	270	355	1,314	0.00	3.2
Trinidad & Tobago	940	250	1,315	5,260	0.00	3.3
Uruguay	350	1,750	8,840	5,051	0.00	4.4
Venezuela	650	1,300	30,366	23,359	0.00	2.6

Table 10   Human Resources of Health Care Systems

Source: [1] UNDP, Human Development Report 1994, [2] PAHO, 1994.

References for General, Education, and Health Topics

General

Aedo, C., and O. Larrañaga. 1994. *Social Service Delivery Systems: An Agenda for Reform*. Washington, D.C.: Inter-American Development Bank.

Ahluwalia, M. 1976. Inequality, Poverty and Development. *Journal of Development Economics*.

Barro, R., and X. Sala i Martin. 1995. *Economic Growth*. New York: McMillan.

Behrman, J. 1993. Investing in Human Resources. In Inter-American Development Bank, *Economic and Social Progress in Latin America*, Washington, D.C.

Benhabib, J., and M. Spiegel. 1994. The Role of Human Capital in Economic Development: Evidence from Cross-National Aggregate Data. *Journal of Monetary Economics*.

Birdsall, N. 1995. Pragmatism, Robin Hood and Other Themes: Good Government and Social Well-being in Developing Countries in L. Chen et al., eds., *Health and Social Science in International Perspective.* Cambridge: Harvard University Press.

Birdsall, N., D. Ross, and R. Sabot. 1995. Inequality and Growth Reconsidered. *The World Bank Economic Review* 9:3 (September).

Bourguignon, F. 1993. Growth, Distribution and Human Resources: a Cross-Country Analysis. Background Paper prepared for the Diaz-Alejandro Memorial Conference, Inter-American Development Bank, Washington, D.C.

Bourguignon, F., and C. Morrison. 1990. Income Distribution, Development, and Foreign Trade: A Cross-Sectional Analysis. *European Economic Review* 34.

Carciofi, R., O. Cetrángolo, and O. Larrañaga. 1996. Descentralización y financiamiento de la educación y la salud. Las experiencias de Argentina y Chile. ECLAC-UNICEF. Mimeo.

Castaño, E. 1993. La probabilidad de ser pobre en Colombia: un análisis estadístico. Santa Fé de Bogotá, Misión Social.

Cox-Edwards, A. 1993. Labor Market Legislation in Latin America and the Caribbean. Regional Studies Program. Report No. 31. The World Bank. Washington, D.C.

Cremer, J., et al. 1994. The Decentralization of Public Services: Lessons from the Theory of the Firm. The World Bank, PRWP No. 1345.

De Groot, H. 1988. Decentralization Decisions in Bureaucracies as a Principal-Agent Problem. *Journal of Public Economics* 36.

ECLAC. 1995. Focalización y pobreza. Cuadernos de la CEPAL. 71. LC/G. Santiago de Chile.

Fields, G. 1989. *Poverty, Inequality and Economic Growth*. Ithaca, New York: Cornell University.

Fiszbein, A., and G. Psacharopoulos. 1995. Income Inequality in Latin America: the Story of the Eighties. Washington, The World Bank, Technical Department for Latin America, Working Paper.

Flug, K., and Z. Hercowitz. 1996. Some International Evidence on Equipment-Skill Complementarity. Inter-American Development Bank, Office of the Chief Economist, Working Paper (forthcoming).

Flug, K., and A. Spilimbergo. 1996. The Importance of Education. Inter-American Development Bank. Office of the Chief Economist. Mimeo.

Grilliches, Z. 1969. Capital-Skill Complementarity. *The Review of Economics and Statistics* (November).

Hausmann, Ricardo. 1993. Frente al colapso de la política social tradicional. Caracas: Ediciones IESA.

⸻. 1994. Sustaining Reform: What Role for Social Policy? In C. Bradford, Jr., ed. *Redefining the State in Latin America*. Paris: OECD.

Hirschman, Alberto O. 1970. *Exit, Voice, and Loyalty.* Cambridge: Harvard University Press.

Hommes, R. 1995. Conflicts and Dilemmas of Decentralization. Prepared for the World Bank's Annual Bank Conference on Development Economics. Washington, D.C.

Infante, T., et al. 1992. La reforma de los sistemas de prestación de servicios sociales en América Latina. Inter-American Development Bank, Working Paper No. 127.

Inter-American Development Bank. 1994a. A la búsqueda del Siglo XXI: nuevos caminos de desarrollo en Costa Rica. Social Agenda Policy Group.

———. 1994b. Social Tensions and Social Reform. Social Agenda Policy Group.

———. 1994c. Technical Cooperation in Support of Public Sector Reform: The IDB Experience. Evaluation Office.

———. 1995a. Economic and Social Progress in Latin America. Overcoming Volatility. Washington, D.C.

———. 1996. Supporting Reform in the Delivery of Social Services: A Strategy. GN-1932. Washington, D.C.

Inter-American Development Bank and United Nations Development Programme. 1993. Social Reform and Poverty—Toward a Comprehensive Agenda for Development.

Israel, A. 1987. Institutional Development: Incentives to Performance. Baltimore: Johns Hopkins University Press.

———. 1996. A Guide to the Perplexed: Institutional Aspects of Social Programs. Inter-American Development Bank. Social Programs Division.

Jaramillo, H. 1994. Reseña de las reformas de políticas sociales en Colombia. ECLAC, Serie Reformas de Política Pública No. 27.

Jovanovic, B. 1996. Research, Schooling, Training, and Learning by Doing in the Theory of Growth. University of Pennsylvania. Mimeo.

Katz, L., and K. Murphy. 1992. Changes in Relative Wages 1963-1987: Supply and Demand Factors. Quarterly Journal of Economics. February.

Kuznets, S. 1955. Economic Growth and Income Inequality. American Economic Review 45:1.

Lau, L. 1995. Human Capital, Physical Capital and Growth in the Southeast Asian Countries. Stanford University Press.

Londoño de la Cuesta, J. 1995a. La estructuración del Estado y el rol de la política social: hacia un modelo horizontal. Technical Department for Latin America, The World Bank, Working Paper.

———. 1995b. Pobreza, desigualdad, política social y democracia. World Bank, Latin American and Caribbean study.

———. 1996a. Brechas sociales en América Latina. Inter-American Development Bank. Office of the Chief Economist, Working Paper (forthcoming).

Lucas, R. 1988. On the Mechanics of Economic Development. Journal of Monetary Economics 22(1).

Mankiw, G. 1995. Economic Growth and Human Capital. Brookings Papers on Economic Activity. Washington D.C.

Márquez, G. 1994. Regulación del mercado de trabajo en América Latina. Ediciones IESA. Caracas.

Morley, S. 1995. Poverty and Inequality in Latin America. Baltimore: Johns Hopkins University Press.

Murillo, M.V. 1996. Latin American Unions and the Reform of Social Service Delivery Systems: Institutional Constraints and Policy Choice. Inter-American Development Bank. Office of the Chief Economist, Working Paper (forthcoming).

Naím, M. 1994. Latin America's Journey to the Market: From Macroeconomic Shocks to Institutional Therapy. The Carnegie Endowment.

Nelson, J.M. 1994. Labor and Business Roles in Dual Transitions: Building Blocks or Stumbling Blocks? In Intricate Links: Democratization and Market Reforms in Latin America and Eastern Europe. Washington, D.C.: Overseas Development Council.

Nelson, R. and E.S. Phelps. 1966. Investment in Humans, Technological Diffusion, and Economic Growth. American Economic Review 56:2.

Papanek, G., and O. Kyn. 1986. The Effect on Income Distribution of Development, the Growth Rate and Economic Strategy. Journal of Development Economics 23.

Paul, S. 1991. Accountability in Public Services: Exit, Voice and Control. *World Development* 20(7).

Poterba, J. 1994. Government Intervention in the Markets for Education and Health Care: How and Why? National Bureau of Economic Research. Working Paper No. 4916. November.

Prud'homme, R. 1995. The Dangers of Decentralization. *The World Bank Research Observer* 10(2).

Robbins, D. 1995. Wage Structures and Trade Liberalization: The Experience of Seven Latin American Countries. Cambridge: Harvard Institute for International Development (December).

Romer, P. 1990. Endogenous Technological Change. *Journal of Political Economy* 98(5).

Rubio, M. 1996. Gasto público en los servicios sociales. Inter-American Development Bank. Office of the Chief Economist, Working Paper (forthcoming).

Schultz, T.W. 1968. Investment in Human Capital. In M. Blaug, ed. *Economics of Education*. Penguin Books.

Thorpe, R. 1994. Challenges of Peace: Towards Sustainable Social Development in Peru. Social Policy Group, Inter-American Development Bank.

Tirole, J. 1994. The Internal Organization of Government. *Oxford Economic Papers* 46(1).

Van Der Gaag, J. 1995. *Private and Public Initiatives. Working Together for Health and Education*. The World Bank. Washington, D.C.

Winkler, D. 1994. The Design and Administration of Intergovernmental Transfers: Fiscal Decentralization in Latin America. The World Bank, Discussion Paper No. 235.

World Bank. 1993a. *The East Asian Miracle: Economic Growth and Public Policy*. New York: Oxford University Press.

Education

Aedo, C. 1996. *Organización Industrial de la Prestación de Servicios Sociales*. ILADES-BID. Proyecto Red de Centros (forthcoming).

Anaya, A. 1996. Educación, sindicatos, y reforma: el caso boliviano. Inter-American Development Bank, Office of the Chief Economist. Mimeo.

Barro, R., and J. Lee. 1993. International Comparisons in Education Attainment. *Journal of Monetary Economics* 32:3.

_____. 1996. International Measures of Schooling Years and Schooling Quality. *American Economic Review* 86(2).

Barros, R., and R.S. Pinto de Mendonça. 1996. O Impacto de Gestão sobre o Desempenho Educacional. Projeto de Pesquisa para Organização Industrial e Serviços Sociais de Desenvolvimento. IPEA-BID. Proyecto Red de Centros.

Becker, G. 1993. *Human Capital: A Theoretical and Empirical Analysis, with Special Reference to Education*. 3d. ed., University of Chicago Press.

Birdsall, N., and R. Sabot, eds. 1996. *Opportunity Foregone: Education in Brazil*. Washington, D.C.: John Hopkins University Press/IDB.

Bruns, B., S. Carlson, E. Cuadra, A. Fiszbein, J. Prawda, L. Wolff, and J.J. Brunner. 1993. *Venezuela 2000. Education for Growth and Social Equity*. Report No. 11130-VE. Vols. I and II. The World Bank. December. Washington, D.C.

Caldwell, B., and J. Spinks. 1988. *The Self Managing School*. London: The Falmer Press.

Carnoy, M., and C. de Moura Castro. 1996. Improving Education in Latin America: Where to Now? A Background Paper for the Inter-American Development Bank. Seminar in Educational Reform. Buenos Aires, Argentina.

Castro, C. de Moura. 1995. *Training Policies for the End of the Century*. Paris. UNESCO: International Institute for Educational Planning.

Castro, C. de Moura, and A. Torkel. 1994. Budget Cuts in Education and Training: Policy or Politics? In Samoff, J., ed. *Coping with Crisis: Austerity, Adjustment and Human Resources*. Cassell-UNESCO.

Castro, M. H. de Magalhaes. 1995. A revolução silenciosa: Autonomia Financeira da USP e UNICAMP. Inter-American Development Bank. Mimeo.

CENPEC. 1993. A democratização do ensino em 15 municípios Brasileiros. Educação e Desenvolvimento Municipal. Documento Síntese.

Cetron, M., and M. Gayle. 1991. *Educational Renaissance: Our Schools at the Turn of the Twenty-First Century.* New York: St. Martin's Press.

Chambers, R., and J. Coleman. 1992. Algunas cuestiones sobre la libre elección de la escuela. *Sociology of Education* 65(4).

Chubb, J. E., and E. Hanushek. 1991. Reforming Educational Reform, in Aaron, H. G., ed. *Setting National Priorities: Policies for the Nineties.* Washington, D.C.: The Brookings Institution.

Corbett, C. 1993. *Bolivia Education Sector: A Proposed Strategy for Sector Development and International Assistance.* Report No. 12042-BO. The World Bank. Washington, D.C. November.

Cox, D., and E. Jiménez. 1990. The Relative Effectiveness of Private and Public Schools. *Journal of Development Economics* 34(1-2).

Crouch, L.A. 1995. *Financing Secondary Expansion in Latin America: An Estimation of Magnitudes Required, and Private and Decentralized Options.* Policy Paper Series. Research Triangle Institute, N.C.

ECLAC. 1995. Calidad y equidad de la educación media en Chile. Santiago, Chile.

Espínola, V. 1994. *La construcción de lo local en los sistemas educativos descentralizados. Los casos de Argentina, Brasil, Chile y Colombia.* CIDE. No. 92.190. Santiago.

_____. 1995. *El impacto de la descentralización sobre la educación gratuita en Chile.* CIDE. 1/95. Santiago.

Ezpeleta, J. 1988. La escuela y los maestros: entre el supuesto y la deducción. *Cuadernos de Investigación.* Mexico: DIE-CINVESTAV del IPN.

Farrell, J., and J. B. Oliveira. 1993. *Teachers in Developing Countries. Improving Effectiveness and Managing Costs.* EDI Seminar Series. The World Bank. Washington, D.C.

Flores, R. 1996. *La escuela básica de la zona marginal de Santo Domingo. Un estudio comparativo de la organización industrial del servicio de educación en la República Dominicana.* ECOCARIBE-BID. Proyecto Red de Centros (forthcoming).

Fuller, B. 1985. Raising School Quality in Developing Countries: What Investments Boost Learning? The World Bank Education and Training Series, No. EDT7. Washington, D.C.

Fullman, M. 1982. *The Meaning of Educational Change.* New York: Teachers College Press.

Fundación Ecuador. 1995. *La crisis educativa: bases para un consenso.* Guayaquil/Quito.

Gomes, C.A. 1993. *Gestão Participativa nas Escolas: Resultados e Incógnitas.* IPEA, Brasilia, Brazil.

Guia Neto, W.S. 1993. *Repasse de Recursos para a Escola: Critérios, Mecanismos e Tendências a Experiência de Minas Gerais.* Brasilia, Brazil: IPEA.

Hanushek, E. 1994. *Making Schools Work, Improving Performance and Controlling Costs.* Washington, D.C.: The Brookings Institution.

Hargraves, D., and D. Hopkins. 1991. *The Empowered School: The Management and Practice of Development Planning.* London: Cassell Educational Press, Ltd.

Hoenack, S. 1994. Economics, Organization and Learning: Research Directions for the Economics of Education. *Economics of Education Review* 13(2).

Horn, R., et al. 1991. Developing Educational Assessment Systems in Latin America: A Review of Issues and Recent Experience. The World Bank. September.

Hoxby, C. 1994. Private Schools Provide Competition for Public Schools? National Bureau of Economic Research, Working Paper No. 4978.

Inter-American Development Bank. 1985. Summary of Evaluation of Secondary Technical-Vocational and University Education Projects. OEO. GN-1543. Washington, D.C.

James, E. 1993. Why Do Different Countries Choose a Different Public-Private Mix of Educational Services? *Journal of Human Resources* 28(3).

Jung, J. 1992. Personal Income Distribution in Korea, 1962-1986: A Human Capital Approach. *Journal of Asian Economics* 3(1).

Kellaghan, T., and V. Greaney. 1992. *Using Examinations to Improve Education: A Study in Fourteen African Countries.* World Bank Technical Paper No. 165. The World Bank, Washington, D.C.

Lau, L. 1995. *Human Capital, Physical Capital and Growth in the Southeast Asian Countries*. Stanford University Press.

Levin, H. 1992. Market Approaches to Education: Vouchers and School Choice. *Economics of Education Review* 11(4).

Lockheed, M., and A. Verspoor. 1991. *Improving Primary Education in Developing Countries*. New York: Oxford University Press.

Lockheed, M., and E. Jiménez. 1994. *Public and Private Secondary Schools in Developing Countries*. HRO Working Papers. The World Bank, Washington, D.C.

Manski, Charles. 1992. Educational Choice (Vouchers) and Social Mobility. *Economics of Education Review* 11(4).

McEwan, P. J. 1996. Evaluating Rural Education Reform: The Case of Colombia´s Escuela Nueva Program. *La Educación*.

Mello, G. 1993a. *Escuelas eficaces: Un tema reactualizado*. Brasilia, Brazil: IPEA.

_____. 1993b. *Autonomia de Escola: Possibilidades, Limites e Condicões*. Cadernos Educação Básica, Brasilia, Brazil.

_____. 1995. *Cidadania e Competitividade. Desafios Educacionais do Terceiro Milênio*. Cortez Editora 4ª. Edição. São Paulo.

Mello, G., and R. N. Silva. 1991. *A Gestão e a Autonomia da Escola nas Novas Propostas de Políticas Educativas para a América Latina*. São Paulo: IEA, Estudos Avançados (12) 5.

Mello, G., and R. Neubauer da Silva. 1993. Competitive selection of school principals: case study of an innovation in Brazil. IIEP. Monograph No. 11. Paris.

Mercado, R. 1989. El trabajo cotidiano del maestro en la escuela. In *La escuela, lugar del trabajo docente*. Cuadernos de Educación. Mexico: DIE-CINVESTAV del IPN.

Miller, E. 1992. *Education for All: Caribbean Perspectives and Imperatives*. Washington, D.C., Inter-American Development Bank.

Ministerio de Cultura y Educación de la Nación. 1994. Sistema Nacional de Evaluación 1er. Operativo Nacional 1993: Resultados Nacionales. Secretaría de Programación y Evaluación Educativa.

_____. 1994. *Censo nacional de docentes y establecimientos educativos*. Secretaría de Programación y Evaluación Educativa. Dirección General Red Federal de Información Educativa. Buenos Aires, Argentina.

_____. 1995. Para trabajar mejor. Manual operativo nivel primario. Plan social educativo. Buenos Aires.

Molina, C.G. 1996. El país, ¿preparado para enfrentar los desafíos del siglo XXI? 1980-1995: Un período de transición de la educación en Colombia. Santa Fé de Bogotá, Colombia. Mimeo.

Montenegro, A. 1995. An Incomplete Educational Reform: The Case of Colombia. HCO Working Papers. The World Bank, Washington, D.C.

Morley, S., and A. Silva. 1994. Problems and Performance in Primary Education: Why Do Systems Differ? Inter-American Development Bank. Mimeo.

Mulcahy-Dunn, A., and G. Arcia. 1996. An Overview of Teacher's Salaries and Living Standards in Ecuador. Center for International Development, Research Triangle Institute, N.C. Mimeo.

Navarro, J.C., et al. 1996. La organización industrial de servicios de educación en Venezuela. IESA-BID. Proyecto Red de Centros (forthcoming).

Ocampo, J.A. 1996. Participación privada en la provisión de servicios sociales: el caso colombiano. Paper presented at World Bank Conference on Latin America and the Caribbean Privatization.

Park, Y., D. Ross, and R. Sabot. 1996. Educational Expansion and the Inequality of Pay in Brazil and Korea. In N. Birdsall and R. Sabot, eds. *Opportunity Foregone: Education in Brazil*. Washington, D.C.: IDB.

Pescador, J. A. 1994. *Aportaciones para la modernización educativa*. Universidad Pedagógica Nacional. 2d ed. México.

Piras, C. 1996. La estructura y los síntomas de la crisis educativa. Inter-American Development Bank. Office of the Chief Economist, Working Paper (forthcoming).

Prawda, J. 1992. Educational Decentralization in Latin America: Lessons Learned. The World Bank, LATHR. No. 27.

Prawda, J., and G. Psacharopoulos. 1993. Educational Development and Costing in Mexico, 1977-1990 - A Cross-State Time-Series Analysis. *International Journal of Educational Development* 13(1).

Psacharopoulos, G., J. Valenzuela and M. Arends. 1993. Teachers' Salaries in Latin America: A Comparative Analysis. Policy Research Working Papers, Education and Employment, The World Bank. Washington, D.C.

Psacharopoulos, G., and Y.C. Ng. 1994. Earnings and Education in Latin America. *Education Economics* 2(2).

Purkey, S., and M. Smith. 1985. Effective Schools: A Review. *The Elementary School Journal.*

Puryear, J.M. 1996. The Public University and Economic Growth. The Inter-American Dialogue. Mimeo.

Puryear, J.M., and J. Brunner. 1994. Una agenda para la reforma educacional en América Latina y el Caribe. Inter-American Dialogue, August.

Puryear, J.M., and A. Olivos. 1995. Putting Education First. Inter-American Dialogue (April).

Rama, G. 1992. Qué aprenden los estudiantes en el ciclo básico de educación media. Montevideo: ECLAC.

Reimers, F. 1995. Education Finance in Latin America: Perils and Opportunities. In Puryear and Brunner, eds. *Education, Equity and Economic Competitiveness in the Americas.*

Reynolds, D. 1985. *Studying School Effectiveness.* London: Falmer.

Rojas, C., and Z. Castillo. 1988. Evaluación del programa escuela nueva. Bogotá: Instituto SER de Investigación.

Rondinelli, D., J. Middleton, and A. Verspoor. 1990. *Planning Educational Reforms in Developing Countries: The Contingency Approach.* Durham, N.C.: Duke University Press.

Rufian, D., and E. Palma. 1992. La descentralización de la educación. Experiencias latinoamericanas: Chile, Colombia y Venezuela. Fundación Friederich Ebert. Mimeo.

SAEB. (Sistema Nacional de Avaliação da Educação Básica). 1995. Avaliação de Matemática e Língua Portuguesa (Leitura) Dos Alunos de 8ª. Série e 3ª. Série do 2º. Grau. Fundação CESGRANRIO.

Sanguinetty, J. 1992. La crisis de la educación en América Latina. U.S. Agency for International Development.

Schiefelbein, E. 1995. Education Reform in Latin America and the Caribbean: An Agenda for Action. Presentation in Rio de Janeiro.

Summers, A., and B. Wolff. 1977. Do Schools Make a Difference? *American Economic Review* (64).

Torres, G., and S. Mathur. 1996. The Third Wave of Privatization: Privatization of Social Sectors in Developing Countries, First Steps. The World Bank. Mimeo.

Tuijman, A.C., and T.N. Postlethwaite. 1994. *Monitoring the Standards of Education.* Oxford: Pergamon Press.

UNESCO. Oficina Regional de Educación para América Latina y el Caribe. 1994. *Medición de la calidad de la educación básica: Resultados de siete países.* Volumen III.

Union Bank of Switzerland. Several Years. Prices and Earnings around the Globe. International Comparison of Purchasing Power.

Vélez, E., E. Schiefelbein, and J. Valenzuela. 1993. Factors Affecting Achievement in Primary Education. HRO Working Papers. The World Bank, Washington, D.C.

West, E. 1996. Educational Vouchers in Practice and Principle: A World Survey. HCD Working Paper No. 64. The World Bank. Washington, D.C.

Wolff, L., E. Schiefelbein, and J. Valenzuela. 1993. Improving the Quality of Primary Education in Latin America: Towards the 21st Century. Regional Studies Program Report No. 28. World Bank, LACTD. Washington, D.C.

Woodford, W. 1993. Sistema de medición de la calidad de la educación. Memoria de investigación.

Woodfurd, P.E., and A. de Zapata. 1995. Estudio de sistemas de pruebas nacionales. Segundo préstamo para el mejoramiento de la calidad de la educación en República Dominicana. Santo Domingo.

World Bank. 1993b. *Caribbean Region: Access, Quality, and Efficiency in Education.* Washington, D.C.

———. 1993c. Brazil Higher Education Reform. Report No. 12366-BR. Washington, D.C.

———. 1993d. Bolivia Education Sector: A Proposed Strategy for Sector Development and International Assistance. Report No. 12042-BO. November 8. Washington, D.C.

———. 1994a. El Salvador Community Education Strategy: Decentralized School Management. Report 13502-ES. Latin America and the Caribbean Regional Office, Washington, D.C.

———. 1995a. *Guatemala Basic Education Strategy: Equity and Efficiency in Education.* Report 13304- GU. Latin America and the Caribbean Regional Office, Washington, D.C.

———. 1995b. *Panama Issues in Basic Education.* Report No. 13701-PAN. Washington, D.C.

———. 1995c. Priorities and Strategies for Education: A World Bank Review. Washington, D.C.

Health

Aedo, C., and O. Larrañaga. 1993. Sistemas de entrega de los servicios sociales: La experiencia chilena. Documento de Trabajo No. 152, Economic and Social Development Department. Inter-American Development Bank.

Akin, J. 1986. Fees for Health Services and the Concern for Equity for the Poor. PHN Technical Note 86-10. The World Bank, Washington, D.C.

Arrow, K. 1963. Uncertainty and the Welfare Economics of Medical Care. *American Economic Review* 53(5).

Baker, L. 1995. HMOs and Fee-for-Service Health Care Expenditures: Evidence from Medicare. National Bureau of Economic Research. Working Paper 5360. November.

Barnum, H., J. Kutzin, and H. Saxenian. 1995. Incentives and Provider Payment Methods. Human Capital Development and Operations Policy Working Paper Series No. 51. The World Bank.

Berman, P., ed. 1995. *Health Sector Reform in Developing Countries: Making Health Development Sustainable.* Harvard Series on Population and International Health. Harvard University Press.

Bicknell, W. 1994. Jamaican Health Sector Assessment: Policy Implications and Recommendations. Mimeo, September.

Birdsall, N., and R. Hecht. 1997. Swimming against the Tide: Strategies for Improving Equity in Health. In Christopher Colclough, ed., *Marketising Education and Health in Developing Countries: Miracle or Mirage?* Oxford: Clarendon Press (forthcoming).

Bitrán, R. 1995a. Barbados: Health Sector Overview. Inter-American Development Bank. Mimeo, March.

———. 1995b. Argentina. Estudio de financiamiento del sector salud. Encuesta urbana de hogares sobre seguros públicos y privados de salud. Inter-American Development Bank. Mimeo (September).

Blomqvist, A. 1991. The Doctor as Double Agent: Information Asymmetry, Health Insurance, and Medical Care. *Journal of Health Economics* 10(4).

Bloom, E. 1995. Health and Health Care in Mexico. Documento de Trabajo, División de Economía, No. 49. Mexico.

Bobadilla, J., P. Cowley, P. Musgrove, and H. Saxenian. 1994. The Essential Package of Health Services in Developing Countries. World Development Report Background Paper No. 1. The World Bank.

Castagnino, E. 1995. Reforma sectorial y financiamiento del sector salud: algunas observaciones sobre experiencias recientes en América Latina y el Caribe. Inter-American Development Bank. Mimeo.

Chen, L., A. Kleiman, and N. Ware. 1994. *Health and Social Change in International Perspective.* Harvard Series on Population and International Health. Harvard University Press.

Chernichovsky, D. 1995. What Can Developing Economies Learn from Health System Reforms of Developed Economies? *Health Policy* 32.

Consejo Nacional de Población. 1995. The Demand for Health Care in Mexico: an Econometric Analysis. Mexico. September.

Dranove, D. 1988. Demand Inducement and the Physician/Patient Relationship. *Economic Inquiry* (April).

Dranove, D., and M. Satterthwaite. 1992. Monopolistic Competition When Price and Quality are Not Perfectly Observable. *RAND Journal of Economics* 23(4).

Dranove, D., and W. White. 1987. Agency and the Organization of Health Care Delivery. *Inquiry* 24(4).

————. 1994. Recent Theory and Evidence on Competition in Hospital Markets. *Journal of Economics and Management Strategy* 3(1).

ECLAC. 1994. El gasto social en América Latina: un examen cuantitativo y cualitativo. Cuadernos de la CEPAL, No. 73.

Ellis, R., and T. McGuire. 1993. Supply-Side and Demand-Side Cost Sharing in Health Care. *Journal of Economic Perspectives* 7(4).

————. 1986. Provider Behavior Under Prospective Reimbursement. *Journal of Health Economics* 5(2).

————. 1988. Insurance Principles and the Design of Prospective Payment Systems. *Journal of Health Economics* 7(3).

————. 1990. Optimal Payment Systems for Health Care. *Journal of Health Economics* 9(4).

Enthoven, A. 1988. *Theory and Practice of Managed Competition in Health Care Finance.* Lectures in Economics 9, North Holland.

————. 1993. Managed Competition: History and Principles. *Health Affairs.* Special Supplement.

Enthoven, A., and S. Singer. 1995. Market-based reform: what to regulate and by whom. *Health Affairs.*

Fielding, J., and R. Thomas. 1993. Can Managed Competition Solve Problems of Market Failure? *Health Affairs* 12.

Flood, C., et al. 1994. Educación y salud: resultados de mediciones sobre acceso y cobertura. Documento de Trabajo GP/04. Ministerio de Economía y Obras y Servicios Públicos. Buenos Aires, Argentina.

Frenk, J. 1994. La salud de la población. Hacia una nueva salud pública. La ciencia desde México No. 133. Secretaría de Educación Pública. Fondo de Cultura Económica. Mexico.

Frenk, J., J.L. Bobadilla, and R. Lozano. 1996. The Epidemiological Transition in Latin America. In Ian M. Timaeus, J. Chaquiel and Ruzinka Lado, eds. *Adult Mortality in Latin America.* Oxford: Clarendon Press.

————. 1995. Comprehensive Policy Analysis for Health System Reform. *Health Policy* 32(1-3).

Fundación Mexicana para la Salud. 1995. Economía y salud: propuestas para el avance del sistema de salud en México. Mexico.

————. 1994. Las cuentas nacionales de salud y el financiamiento de los servicios. Documentos para el análisis y la convergencia no. 7. Mexico.

Gaynor, M. 1994. Issues in the Industrial Organization of the Market of Physician Services. *Journal of Economics and Management Strategy* 3(1).

Gertler, P., L. Locay, and W. Sanderson. 1987. Are User Fees Regressive? The Welfare Implications of Health Care Financing Proposals in Peru. *Journal of Econometrics* 36(1-2).

Govindaraj, R., C. Murray, and G. Chellaraj. 1995. Health Expenditures in Latin America. World Bank Technical Paper No. 274.

Grossman, M. 1972. On the Concept of Health Capital and the Demand for Health. *Journal of Political Economy* 80(2).

Harvard University School of Public Health. 1996. Report on Colombia Health Reform and Proposed Master Implementation Plan. Mimeo (March).

Health Policy Journal. 1995. *Special Issue: Health Sector Reform in Developing Countries: Making Health Development Sustainable* 32(1-3).

Hemenway, D., et al. 1990. Physicians' Responses to Financial Incentives: Evidence from a For-Profit Ambulatory Care Center. *The New England Journal of Medicine* 322(15).

Hoffmeyer, U., and T. McCarthy. 1994. *Financing Health Care,* Vol. I and II. Kluwer Academic Publishers.

Hurst, J. 1991. Reforming Health Care in Seven European Nations. *Health Affairs* (Fall).

Ii, Masako. 1996. The Demand for Medical Care: Evidence from Urban Areas in Bolivia. Living Standards Measurement Study, Working Paper No. 123, The World Bank.

Instituto Centroamericano de Administración Pública. 1995. Ajuste económico, políticas de salud y modelos de atención en Centroamérica. San José de Costa Rica.

Inter-American Development Bank. 1995. Advancing Health Care Reform in Ecuador: Analysis of Current Options. Economic and Sector Study Series. Region 3.

Inter-American Development Bank/Pan-American Health Organization. 1996. Caribbean Regional Health Study, Caribbean Group for Cooperation in Economic Development.

Iunes, R. 1995. Health Care Financing in Paraguay. Mimeo.

Jerome-Forget, M., J. White, and J. Wiener. 1994. *Health Care Reform through Internal Markets: Experience and Proposals.* Montreal: Institute for Research on Public Policy and The Brookings Institute.

Katz, Jorge, and E. Miranda. 1994. Morfología, comportamiento y regulación de los mercados de salud. *Revista de la CEPAL*, No. 54. Santiago de Chile.

Katz, J., and A. Muñoz. 1988. Organización del sector salud. Puja distributiva y equidad. Centro Editor para América Latina, Buenos Aires, Argentina.

Knowles, S., and P. Owen. 1995. Health Capital and Cross-Country Variation in Income per Capita in the Mankiw-Romer-Weil Model. *Economics Letters* 48(1).

Kutzin, J., and H. Barnum. 1992. How Health Insurance Affects the Delivery of Health Care in Developing Countries. Policy Research Working Papers No. 852. The World Bank.

La Forgia, G., R. Levine, L. Brenzel, and B. Couttolenc. 1993. Health Policy Reform in Latin America: Framework and Guidelines for Health Sector Assessment. The Urban Institute. Mimeo.

La Forgia, G., C. Griffin, and R. Bovbjerg. 1993. Extending Coverage and Benefits of Social Financing Systems in Developing Countries, Phase I: Health Financing and Sustainability Project. Washington, D.C.: Abt Associates, Inc.

La Forgia, G. 1993. Belize Health Sector Assessment. Inter-American Development Bank. Mimeo.

_____. 1994. Stepping into Health Sector Reform through Redirecting Financial Flows: A Review of Reform Proposals in Two Latin American Countries. Mimeo.

La Forgia, G., and M.A. González Block. 1995. Descentralización en salud: lecciones de la experiencia. Seminario centroamericano sobre la reforma del sector salud. San José, Costa Rica.

La Forgia, G., and C. Griffin. 1993. Health Insurance in Practice: Fifteen Case Studies from Developing Countries, Health Financing and Sustainability Project. Abt Associates Inc. Small Applied Research Paper No. 4.

Labadie, G. 1996. Regulación y desempeño comparado de dos subsistemas privados de salud en el Uruguay. Regional Research Network Project. Inter-American Development Bank.

Lalonde, M. 1976. *A New Perspective of the Health of Canadians.* Ottawa.

Le Grand, J., C. Propper, and R. Robinson. 1992. *The Economics of Social Problems.* 3d. ed. Macmillan Press.

Lee, H., and J.L. Bobadilla. 1994. Health Statistics for the Americas. World Bank Technical Paper No. 262.

Londoño de la Cuesta, J. 1996b. Is There a Health Gap in Latin America? LATD, Working Paper. The World Bank.

_____. 1996c. Managed Competition in the Tropics: Health Reform in Colombia. Paper presented to the International Health Economics Association, Vancouver (May).

Londoño de la Cuesta, J., and J. Frenk. 1996. Structured Pluralism: A New Model for Health Reform in Latin America. LATD Working Paper. The World Bank, Washington, D.C.

Londoño de la Cuesta, J., and O. Icoechea. 1996. Health Systems in Latin America: A Simple Description of Organization and Finance. LATD, Working Paper, The World Bank.

Ma, C. 1994. Health Care Payment Systems: Cost and Quality Incentives. *Journal of Economics and Management Strategy* 3(1).

Ma, C., and J. Burgess. 1991. Regulation, Quality Competition, and Price in the Hospital Industry. Boston University. Mimeo.

Maceira, D. 1996. Fragmentación y dinámica de los sistemas de salud en América Latina. Inter-American Development Bank. Office of the Chief Economist, Working Paper (forthcoming).

Márquez, P. 1990. Control de costos en salud: una revisión de experiencias de países en las Américas. *Pan-American Health Organization Bulletin* 109(2).

Maynard, A. 1994. Can Competition Enhance Efficiency in Health Care? Lessons from the Reform of the U.K. National Health Service. *Social Science and Medicine* 39(10).

McGuire, T., and M. Pauly. 1991. Physician Response to Fee Changes with Multiple Payers. *Journal of Health Economics* 10(4).

Medici, A. 1994. Economia e Financiamento do Setor Saúde no Brasil AdSAUDE-Série Temática. Facultade de Saúde Pública. Universidade de São Paulo. Brazil.

Mesa-Lago, C. 1989. Financiamiento de la atención a la salud en América Latina y el Caribe, con focalización en el seguro social. Economic Development Institute, The World Bank.

Ministerio de Salud. 1992. La salud en Chile. Informe Nacional del Diagnóstico de la Salud. Documento 1. Programa MINSAL/BID. Serie Herramientas de Trabajo. Santiago de Chile.

Ministerio de Salud Pública. 1994. Programas prioritarios de salud. Dirección General de Salud. Montevideo, Uruguay.

Miranda, Ernesto. 1991. Descentralización y privatización del sistema de salud chileno. Centro de Estudios Públicos, *Estudios Públicos* No. 39.

Murray, C., R. Govindaraj, and P. Musgrove. 1994. National health expenditures: a global analysis. *Bulletin of the World Health Organization* 72(4).

Musgrove, P. 1995b. Mismatch of Need, Demand and Supply of Services: Picturing Different Ways Health Systems can go Wrong. Human Resources Development and Operations Policy Working Papers No. 59, The World Bank.

Musgrove, P., ed. 1988. Crisis económica y salud. La experiencia de cinco países latinoamericanos en los años ochenta. Pan-American Health Organization.

Musgrove, P. 1995a. Cost Effectiveness and Health Sector Reform. Human Resources Development and Operations Policy Working Papers No. 48, The World Bank.

National Economic Research Associates. 1993. A Report on the Economics of Health Care Reform.

Newhouse, J. 1978. *The Economics of Medical Care.* Addison-Wesley Publishing Company.

OECD (Organisation for Economic Cooperation and Development). 1994. *The Reform of Health Care Systems: A Review of Seventeen OECD Countries.* Health Policy Studies No 5. Paris.

———. 1992. *The Reform of Health Care Systems: A Review of Seventeen OECD Countries.* Health Policy Studies No. 2. Paris.

Over, M. 1991. Economics for Health Sector Analysis. Concepts and Cases. Economic Development Institute. The World Bank.

Ovretveit, J. 1995. *Purchasing for Health: Health Services Management.* Open University Press. Buckingham.

Paganini, J. 1993. Calidad y Eficiencia de la Atención Hospitalaria: Desarrollo y Fortalecimiento de los Sistemas Locales de Salud. Pan-American Health Organization, Washington, D.C.

Pan-American Health Organization. 1993. Estructura y Comportamiento del Sector Salud en la Argentina, Chile y el Uruguay. Estudios de casos y modelo histórico-evolutivo de organización y comportamiento sectorial. Cuaderno Técnico No. 36. Washington, D.C.

———. 1994a. Pobreza y salud en Bolivia. Washington, D.C.

———. 1994b. *Health Conditions in the Americas,* Vols. I and II. Washington, D.C.

Pan-American Health Organization/World Health Organization. 1992. Haiti 1992: Health Situation Analysis. Mimeo, Washington, D.C.

Phelps, C. 1992. *Health Economics.* Harper-Collins Publisher.

Piola, S., and S. Magalhaes Vianna. 1995. Economia de saude: Conceitos e contribuição para a gestão da saude. Instituto de Pesquisa Econômica Aplicada, Brazil.

Pope, G. 1989. Hospital Nonprice Competition and Medicare Reimbursement Policy. *Journal of Health Economics* 8(2).

Preker, A., and R. Feachem. 1995. Market Mechanisms and the Health Sector in Central and Eastern Europe. World Bank Technical Paper No. 293.

Programa de Inversión Social. 1994. Diagnóstico Sectorial: Salud. Parte I and II. Montevideo, Uruguay.

Saltman, R. 1995. Applying Planned Market Logic to Developing Countries' Health Systems: An Initial Exploration. World Health Organization, Discussion Paper No. 5.

_____. 1994. A Conceptual Overview of Recent Health Care Reforms. *European Journal of Public Health* 4.

Santana, I. 1996. La Organización Industrial de la Prestación de Servicios de Salud en la República Dominicana. ECOCARIBE-BID. Proyecto Red de Centros.

Santana, I., and M. Rathe. 1993. Sistema de servicios sociales en la República Dominicana: una agenda para la reforma. Inter-American Development Bank. Working Paper No. 150, Economic and Social Development Department.

Schieber, G.J. 1995. Preconditions for Health Reform: Experiences from the OECD Countries. *Health Policy* 32.

Suárez, R., P. Henderson, E. Barillas, and C. Vieira. 1995. Gasto en salud y financiamiento: América Latina y el Caribe. Desafíos para la década de los noventa. Pan-American Health Organization. Washington, D.C.

Van de Ven, W., F. Schut, and F. Rutten. 1994. Forming and Reforming the Market for Third-Party Purchasing of Health Care. *Social Science and Medicine* 39(10).

Van Doorslaer, E., A. Wagstaff, and F. Rutten. 1993. Equity in the Finance and Delivery of Health Care: An International Perspective. Commission of the European Communities, Health Services Research Series No. 8. Oxford Medical Publications.

Walt, G. 1994. *Health Policy: An Introduction to Process and Power.* Witwatersrand University Press. Johannesburg.

Walt, G., and L. Gilson. 1994. Reforming the Health Sector in Developing Countries: the Central Role of Policy Analysis. *Health Policy and Planning* 9(4).

World Bank. 1987. Financing Health Services in Developing Countries. An Agenda for Reform. Washington, D.C.

_____. 1993e. *World Development Report: Investing in Health.* Washington, D.C.

_____. 1994b. *Averting the Old Age Crisis: Policies to Protect the Old and Promote Growth.* Policy Research Reports Series. Oxford University Press.

_____. 1995d. Chile: The Adult Health Policy Challenge. Washington, D.C.

_____. 1995e. *World Development Report: Workers in an Integrating World.* Washington, D.C.

World Health Organization. 1993. Evaluation of Recent Changes in the Financing of Health Services. WHO Technical Report Series 829, Geneva.

PART FOUR

STATISTICAL APPENDIX

The following symbols and conventions have been used in the statistical tables in this Report and its Appendices:

p   Indicates that the data are preliminary estimates.

...   Indicates that the data are not available or not separately reported.

0 or 0.0   Indicates that the amount is nil or negligible.

Dollars   Refers to United States dollars, unless otherwise stated.

In statistical tables, **Latin America** includes only those countries for which data are shown.

TABLE A-1. TOTAL POPULATION

Country	1986	1987	1988	1989	1990	1991	1992	1993	1994	1995p	Average Annual Growth Rates 1970 1980	1980 1990	1990 1995
					Thousands							In Percent	
Argentina	30,737	31,137	31,534	31,929	32,322	32,713	33,101	33,487	33,875	34,267	1.7	1.4	1.2
Bahamas	237	242	246	251	255	259	264	268	272	276	2.1	2.0	1.6
Barbados	254	255	255	256	257	258	258	259	260	261	0.4	0.3	0.3
Belize	170	175	180	185	190	194	200	205	211	217	2.0	2.6	2.7
Bolivia	6,019	6,149	6,283	6,425	6,573	6,729	6,894	7,064	7,238	7,414	2.4	2.1	2.4
Brazil	138,329	141,068	143,771	146,432	149,042	151,598	154,105	156,569	159,000	161,469	2.4	2.1	1.6
Chile	12,327	12,536	12,748	12,961	13,173	13,386	13,599	13,813	14,026	14,242	1.6	1.7	1.6
Colombia	30,054	30,619	31,180	31,739	32,300	32,862	33,425	33,987	34,545	35,101	2.2	2.0	1.7
Costa Rica	2,718	2,797	2,876	2,956	3,035	3,113	3,191	3,269	3,347	3,424	2.8	2.9	2.4
Dominican Republic	6,565	6,716	6,867	7,019	7,170	7,320	7,471	7,620	7,769	7,921	2.6	2.3	2.0
Ecuador	9,330	9,561	9,794	10,029	10,264	10,501	10,741	10,981	11,226	11,476	2.9	2.6	2.3
El Salvador	4,809	4,888	4,976	5,071	5,172	5,279	5,396	5,517	5,641	5,768	2.3	1.3	2.2
Guatemala	8,195	8,434	8,681	8,935	9,197	9,467	9,744	10,030	10,322	10,621	2.8	2.9	2.9
Guyana	792	793	792	793	796	801	808	816	825	834	0.7	0.5	0.9
Haiti	5,981	6,102	6,227	6,355	6,486	6,619	6,754	6,893	7,035	7,180	1.7	1.9	2.1
Honduras	4,319	4,454	4,592	4,734	4,879	5,028	5,180	5,336	5,497	5,663	3.3	3.2	3.0
Jamaica	2,337	2,359	2,378	2,398	2,420	2,444	2,469	2,495	2,521	2,547	1.3	1.3	1.0
Mexico	74,374	76,075	77,789	79,515	81,250	82,997	84,770	86,581	88,431	90,320	2.9	2.3	2.1
Nicaragua	3,312	3,391	3,474	3,567	3,676	3,808	3,957	3,889	4,014	4,140	3.1	2.8	2.4
Panama	2,213	2,259	2,305	2,351	2,398	2,444	2,491	2,538	2,583	2,631	2.6	2.1	1.9
Paraguay	3,807	3,922	4,039	4,157	4,277	4,397	4,520	4,643	4,767	4,894	3.0	3.1	2.7
Peru	19,840	20,261	20,684	21,113	21,550	21,998	22,454	22,916	23,381	23,855	2.7	2.2	2.1
Suriname	388	392	395	399	403	404	404	406	408	409	-0.6	1.1	0.3
Trinidad and Tobago	1,175	1,191	1,206	1,221	1,236	1,250	1,265	1,278	1,292	1,306	1.1	1.3	1.1
Uruguay	3,026	3,043	3,060	3,077	3,094	3,112	3,131	3,149	3,167	3,185	0.4	0.6	0.6
Venezuela	17,595	18,026	18,457	18,889	19,321	19,753	20,187	20,620	21,051	21,491	3.5	2.5	2.2
Latin America	**388,905**	**396,845**	**404,792**	**412,756**	**420,735**	**428,737**	**436,780**	**444,630**	**452,703**	**460,914**	**2.4**	**2.1**	**1.8**

Sources: IDB estimates, based on data from the Latin America Demographic Center and the United Nations Population Division.

TABLE A-2. URBAN AND RURAL POPULATION

(Thousands)

Country	1980 Urban	1980 Rural	1980 %Urban	1990 Urban	1990 Rural	1990 %Urban	1995p Urban	1995p Rural	1995p %Urban	Urban 1970 1980	Urban 1980 1990	Urban 1990 1995	Rural 1990 1995
										In Percent			
Argentina	23,401	4,836	82.9	27,887	4,435	86.3	30,043	4,225	87.7	2.2	1.8	1.5	-1.0
Bahamas	123	87	58.6	161	94	63.3	185	91	66.9	2.3	2.8	2.7	-0.5
Barbados	100	149	40.1	114	143	44.4	121	140	46.2	1.2	1.3	1.1	-0.4
Belize	75	71	51.7	90	99	47.6	103	114	47.5	1.5	1.8	2.7	2.8
Bolivia	2,365	2,990	44.2	3,435	3,137	52.3	4,326	3,088	58.4	3.3	3.8	4.7	-0.3
Brazil	80,334	40,952	66.2	112,643	36,399	75.6	129,184	32,285	80.0	4.1	3.4	2.8	-2.4
Chile	9,054	2,091	81.2	11,314	1,859	85.9	12,470	1,772	87.6	2.3	2.3	2.0	-1.0
Colombia	17,200	9,325	64.8	23,079	9,221	71.5	26,406	8,695	75.2	3.5	3.0	2.7	-1.2
Costa Rica	985	1,299	43.1	1,420	1,615	46.8	1,672	1,752	48.8	3.7	3.7	3.3	1.6
Dominican Republic	2,877	2,820	50.5	4,329	2,841	60.4	5,119	2,802	64.6	4.9	4.2	3.4	-0.3
Ecuador	3,739	4,222	47.0	5,775	4,489	56.3	6,966	4,510	60.7	4.7	4.4	3.8	0.1
El Salvador	1,880	2,645	41.5	2,332	2,840	45.1	2,762	3,006	47.9	2.9	2.2	3.4	1.1
Guatemala	2,587	4,330	37.4	3,628	5,569	39.4	4,393	6,228	41.4	3.3	3.4	3.9	2.3
Guyana	232	527	30.5	261	535	32.8	299	535	35.9	0.7	1.2	2.8	0.0
Haiti	1,272	4,081	23.8	1,840	4,646	28.4	2,243	4,937	31.2	3.6	3.8	4.0	1.2
Honduras	1,281	2,288	35.9	2,132	2,747	43.7	2,704	2,959	47.8	5.5	5.2	4.9	1.5
Jamaica	1,017	1,116	47.7	1,319	1,101	54.5	1,534	1,013	60.2	2.7	2.6	3.1	-1.6
Mexico	42,783	21,695	66.4	58,971	22,279	72.6	67,783	22,537	75.0	4.1	3.3	2.8	0.2
Nicaragua	1,480	1,322	52.8	2,313	1,363	62.9	3,007	1,132	72.6	4.4	4.6	5.4	-3.6
Panama	970	980	49.7	1,281	1,117	53.4	1,452	1,179	55.2	3.1	2.8	2.5	1.1
Paraguay	1,312	1,835	41.7	2,030	2,247	47.5	2,483	2,411	50.7	4.2	4.5	4.1	1.4
Peru	11,153	6,142	64.5	15,132	6,418	70.2	16,740	7,115	70.2	3.9	3.1	2.0	2.1
Suriname	158	203	43.8	173	231	42.8	192	217	46.9	-0.8	0.9	2.2	-1.2
Trinidad and Tobago	616	466	56.9	839	397	67.9	866	440	66.3	5.0	3.1	0.6	2.1
Uruguay	2,442	472	83.8	2,644	450	85.4	2,751	434	86.4	0.6	0.8	0.8	-0.7
Venezuela	12,510	2,514	83.3	17,859	1,462	92.4	20,522	969	95.5	5.0	3.6	2.8	-7.9
Latin America	**221,946**	**119,457**	**65.0**	**303,001**	**117,734**	**72.0**	**346,327**	**114,586**	**75.1**	**3.7**	**3.2**	**2.7**	**-0.5**

Source: IDB estimates based on data from the Latin America Demographic Center and the United Nations Population Division.

TABLE B-1. GROSS DOMESTIC PRODUCT

Country	1986	1987	1988	1989	1990	1991	1992	1993	1994	1995p	1970 1980	1980 1990	1990 1995
					Millions of 1990 Dollars							In Percent	
Argentina	162,118	166,349	163,151	153,207	153,255	166,696	180,960	191,901	206,005	196,949	2.5	-0.9	5.1
Bahamas	2,865	2,974	3,042	3,103	3,134	3,009	2,949	3,005	3,023	3,053	2.8	2.8	-0.5
Barbados	1,590	1,660	1,710	1,797	1,711	1,665	1,584	1,609	1,679	1,717	2.1	1.5	0.1
Belize	265	295	321	362	402	413	446	464	473	491	...	5.0	4.1
Bolivia	4,646	4,766	4,907	5,093	5,330	5,610	5,703	5,969	6,267	6,496	3.9	0.2	4.0
Brazil	372,450	384,839	383,993	395,635	377,896	378,332	376,670	390,098	412,004	432,433	9.4	1.4	2.7
Chile	26,929	28,490	30,528	33,394	34,555	36,968	40,696	43,011	44,780	48,326	2.6	2.8	6.9
Colombia	38,731	40,901	42,703	44,156	45,770	46,553	48,203	50,532	53,320	56,379	5.5	3.7	4.3
Costa Rica	4,824	5,041	5,199	5,470	5,659	5,779	6,201	6,571	6,856	7,027	5.5	2.2	4.4
Dominican Republic	5,360	5,934	6,053	6,331	5,974	6,008	6,499	6,688	6,997	7,341	7.1	2.0	4.2
Ecuador	11,991	11,025	12,351	12,290	12,598	13,234	13,727	14,086	14,764	15,132	9.6	1.8	3.7
El Salvador	4,798	4,919	5,011	5,059	5,304	5,493	5,908	5,961	6,291	6,674	2.3	-0.4	4.7
Guatemala	6,836	7,079	7,354	7,644	7,881	8,170	8,565	8,900	9,257	9,706	5.7	0.9	4.3
Guyana	486	463	420	395	375	413	457	518	566	602	0.9	-3.5	9.9
Haiti	2,151	2,164	2,131	2,099	2,036	1,974	1,682	1,638	1,571	1,642	4.7	-1.0	-4.2
Honduras	2,476	2,625	2,752	2,857	2,853	2,935	3,105	3,309	3,265	3,378	5.7	2.3	3.4
Jamaica	3,159	3,408	3,510	3,751	3,953	3,981	4,046	4,107	4,137	4,171	-0.9	2.3	1.1
Mexico	216,669	220,598	223,507	231,032	241,375	250,296	257,476	259,137	268,892	250,936	6.6	1.7	0.8
Nicaragua	2,753	2,726	2,388	2,372	2,370	2,369	2,391	2,382	2,481	2,590	0.0	-1.4	1.8
Panama	5,534	5,660	4,793	4,780	5,009	5,430	5,896	6,222	6,458	6,570	5.2	0.7	5.6
Paraguay	5,126	5,345	5,682	6,003	6,180	6,326	6,441	6,699	6,890	7,177	8.7	3.0	3.0
Peru	43,467	47,871	43,409	37,804	35,980	37,125	36,853	38,905	44,428	47,618	3.7	-1.2	5.8
Suriname	325	296	317	336	332	342	360	327	312	334	4.7	-1.5	0.1
Trinidad and Tobago	5,781	5,486	5,261	5,210	5,265	5,436	5,357	5,274	5,514	5,707	5.6	-3.0	1.6
Uruguay	8,721	9,420	9,407	9,536	9,590	9,895	10,664	11,006	11,758	11,431	3.1	0.3	3.6
Venezuela	50,081	52,345	55,522	50,955	54,685	59,927	63,424	63,987	62,419	64,980	3.6	1.1	3.5
Latin America	990,131	1022,680	1025,424	1030,671	1029,475	1064,381	1096,262	1132,307	1190,402	1198,860	**5.9**	**1.1**	**3.1**

TABLE B-2. GROSS DOMESTIC PRODUCT PER CAPITA

Country	1986	1987	1988	1989	1990	1991	1992	1993	1994	1995p	1970 1980	1980 1990	1990 1995
					1990 Dollars							In Percent	
Argentina	5,274	5,342	5,174	4,798	4,742	5,096	5,467	5,731	6,081	5,747	0.9	-2.2	3.9
Bahamas	12,065	12,295	12,355	12,382	12,291	11,596	11,169	11,211	11,113	11,059	0.6	0.9	-2.1
Barbados	6,267	6,519	6,695	7,014	6,657	6,459	6,130	6,213	6,457	6,580	1.7	1.2	-0.2
Belize	1,552	1,686	1,786	1,964	2,122	2,127	2,231	2,261	2,243	2,264	...	2.3	1.3
Bolivia	772	775	781	793	811	834	827	845	866	876	1.4	-1.9	1.6
Brazil	2,692	2,728	2,671	2,702	2,536	2,496	2,444	2,492	2,591	2,678	6.8	-0.6	1.1
Chile	2,185	2,273	2,395	2,576	2,623	2,762	2,992	3,114	3,193	3,393	1.0	1.1	5.3
Colombia	1,289	1,336	1,370	1,391	1,417	1,417	1,442	1,487	1,543	1,606	3.2	1.7	2.5
Costa Rica	1,775	1,803	1,807	1,851	1,865	1,857	1,943	2,010	2,049	2,052	2.6	-0.6	1.9
Dominican Republic	817	884	881	902	833	821	870	878	901	927	4.4	-0.4	2.1
Ecuador	1,285	1,153	1,261	1,225	1,227	1,260	1,278	1,283	1,315	1,319	6.5	-0.8	1.4
El Salvador	998	1,006	1,007	998	1,026	1,041	1,095	1,080	1,115	1,157	-0.1	-1.7	2.4
Guatemala	834	839	847	856	857	863	879	887	897	914	2.8	-2.0	1.3
Guyana	613	584	530	498	471	515	566	635	686	722	0.2	-3.9	8.9
Haiti	360	355	342	330	314	298	249	238	223	229	3.0	-2.9	-6.1
Honduras	573	589	599	604	585	584	599	620	594	597	2.4	-0.8	0.4
Jamaica	1,352	1,445	1,476	1,564	1,633	1,629	1,639	1,646	1,641	1,637	-2.2	1.0	0.0
Mexico	2,913	2,900	2,873	2,906	2,971	3,016	3,037	2,993	3,041	2,778	3.6	-0.6	-1.3
Nicaragua	831	804	687	665	645	622	604	613	618	626	-3.0	-4.1	-0.6
Panama	2,501	2,505	2,080	2,033	2,089	2,222	2,367	2,451	2,500	2,497	2.6	-1.3	3.6
Paraguay	1,347	1,363	1,407	1,444	1,445	1,439	1,425	1,443	1,445	1,466	5.6	-0.2	0.3
Peru	2,191	2,363	2,099	1,791	1,670	1,688	1,641	1,698	1,900	1,996	0.9	-3.4	3.6
Suriname	838	755	804	842	824	847	891	806	765	817	5.3	-2.5	-0.2
Trinidad and Tobago	4,918	4,607	4,362	4,266	4,259	4,347	4,236	4,127	4,267	4,369	4.4	-4.3	0.5
Uruguay	2,882	3,096	3,074	3,099	3,099	3,179	3,407	3,495	3,713	3,589	2.7	-0.3	3.0
Venezuela	2,846	2,904	3,008	2,698	2,830	3,034	3,142	3,103	2,965	3,024	0.1	-1.4	1.3
Latin America	2,546	2,577	2,533	2,497	2,447	2,483	2,510	2,547	2,630	2,601	**3.4**	**-1.0**	**1.2**

TABLE B-3. TOTAL CONSUMPTION

Country	1986	1987	1988	1989	1990	1991	1992	1993	1994	1995p	1970 1980	1980 1990	1990 1995
	Millions of 1990 Dollars										In Percent		
Argentina	132,167	133,684	128,234	123,743	123,849	137,564	150,580	158,049	167,662	157,515	2.7	-0.5	4.9
Bahamas	...	...	...	...	...	...	...	...	...	...	...	...	...
Barbados	1,255	1,400	1,405	1,460	1,415	1,436	1,380	1,375	1,404	1,446	1.7	3.0	0.4
Belize	182	220	258	279	292	318	326	334	346	375	...	0.7	5.2
Bolivia	4,216	4,375	4,515	4,632	4,771	4,922	5,078	5,278	5,466	5,603	3.8	0.5	3.3
Brazil[1]	267,920	276,099	275,919	286,709	284,265	287,983	286,914	298,736	321,860	343,512	8.9	2.4	3.9
Chile	20,441	21,186	22,454	24,170	24,397	26,346	28,487	30,200	31,423	34,002	1.9	1.9	6.9
Colombia	30,639	31,945	33,092	34,581	35,460	35,917	36,852	39,562	42,161	43,152	5.6	3.5	4.0
Costa Rica	3,757	3,946	4,082	4,297	4,474	4,549	4,830	5,121	5,376	5,559	4.4	2.1	4.4
Dominican Republic	5,569	6,028	5,960	5,873	4,874	5,572	6,256	6,152	6,381	6,857	7.1	-0.5	7.1
Ecuador	8,810	8,716	9,165	9,202	9,514	9,530	9,741	10,072	10,382	10,577	8.7	1.9	2.1
El Salvador	4,378	4,419	4,490	4,545	5,220	5,378	5,781	5,856	6,265	6,840	2.1	0.7	5.6
Guatemala	5,975	6,417	6,698	6,912	7,053	7,307	7,908	8,296	8,737	9,266	4.9	1.0	5.6
Guyana	418	387	381	310	286	296	285	355	407	494	-0.7	-5.4	11.6
Haiti	2,112	2,116	2,092	2,078	2,040	2,105	1,827	1,946	1,499	1,946	5.2	-1.0	-0.9
Honduras	2,169	2,233	2,260	2,355	2,292	2,345	2,427	2,583	2,508	2,629	5.7	1.9	2.8
Jamaica	2,345	2,464	2,812	3,013	3,024	3,025	2,824	2,909	2,934	3,050	3.2	2.5	0.2
Mexico	163,080	162,395	167,439	179,505	191,642	203,065	213,867	214,627	224,359	196,719	6.5	2.0	0.5
Nicaragua	2,345	2,364	2,439	2,223	2,203	2,328	2,320	2,233	2,196	2,245	2.0	-2.3	0.4
Panama	4,929	4,827	3,017	3,821	4,090	4,728	5,084	5,347	5,484	5,616	3.5	-0.9	6.5
Paraguay	4,181	4,379	4,392	4,460	4,981	5,171	5,565	5,813	6,315	6,400	7.3	3.6	5.1
Peru	34,901	37,971	34,364	29,944	28,320	28,953	29,338	30,337	34,035	36,279	2.4	-0.7	5.1
Suriname	254	134	178	89	243	338	281	279	232	318	17.2	-4.3	5.5
Trinidad and Tobago	4,741	4,206	3,974	3,802	3,739	3,832	3,630	3,479	3,624	3,785	6.6	-2.2	0.2
Uruguay	7,329	8,202	8,134	8,212	8,039	8,296	9,187	9,713	10,629	10,206	1.5	1.1	4.9
Venezuela	38,192	39,604	42,376	38,742	39,742	44,383	48,157	47,829	45,490	47,052	13.7	-0.4	3.4
Latin America	**752,303**	**769,716**	**770,129**	**784,954**	**796,226**	**835,688**	**868,925**	**896,480**	**947,175**	**941,442**	**6.0**	**1.4**	**3.4**

[1] Includes changes in inventories from 1987.

TABLE B-4. GROSS DOMESTIC INVESTMENT

Country	1986	1987	1988	1989	1990	1991	1992	1993	1994	1995p	1970 1980	1980 1990	1990 1995
	Millions of 1990 Dollars										In Percent		
Argentina	27,991	32,145	31,504	23,818	21,452	26,843	35,142	39,957	47,320	41,263	3.7	-7.0	14.0
Bahamas	...	...	...	...	...	...	...	...	...	...	...	...	...
Barbados	247	256	288	339	322	285	142	206	212	227	1.3	-0.2	-6.8
Belize	52	67	86	113	115	124	127	147	113	111	...	6.5	-0.6
Bolivia	795	884	669	568	668	864	909	939	915	1,111	2.2	-1.6	10.7
Brazil[1]	102,722	101,195	96,192	97,338	86,646	83,853	76,219	83,706	85,799	102,959	10.0	-2.8	3.5
Chile	5,038	6,390	7,132	8,731	9,078	9,228	11,625	13,076	13,212	15,718	2.8	0.9	11.6
Colombia	7,857	8,581	9,269	8,590	8,489	7,747	10,766	13,745	15,489	18,866	5.1	1.1	17.3
Costa Rica	1,415	1,464	1,361	1,499	1,569	1,359	1,794	2,067	1,946	1,854	9.3	0.7	3.4
Dominican Republic	1,165	1,478	1,619	1,786	1,502	1,371	1,698	1,823	1,937	2,168	10.2	0.6	7.6
Ecuador	2,709	2,624	2,526	2,600	2,204	2,862	2,828	2,711	2,890	3,134	10.4	-5.0	7.3
El Salvador	613	586	696	877	735	862	1,105	1,209	1,304	1,482	2.7	0.6	15.1
Guatemala	825	1,094	1,082	1,086	1,072	1,315	1,704	1,607	1,602	1,698	5.2	-1.4	9.6
Guyana	116	122	75	127	159	133	131	138	148	155	-0.2	0.5	-0.5
Haiti	258	279	240	246	248	228	60	55	49	90	11.8	-2.2	-18.4
Honduras	388	472	660	635	656	773	869	1,021	1,156	1,222	5.8	0.3	13.3
Jamaica	609	773	903	1,074	1,102	1,168	1,110	1,098	1,113	1,116	-9.4	6.3	0.3
Mexico	38,722	40,846	45,786	47,805	52,843	56,811	64,980	63,023	68,461	50,205	8.6	-2.0	-1.0
Nicaragua	898	885	625	531	457	525	523	498	706	782	0.2	-3.6	11.4
Panama	977	1,001	364	206	859	957	1,352	1,688	1,925	1,988	3.8	-2.8	18.3
Paraguay	1,061	1,131	1,176	1,294	1,413	1,535	1,434	1,467	1,533	1,608	18.2	1.2	2.6
Peru	8,472	10,852	9,836	6,635	7,602	8,460	8,441	9,336	11,388	13,655	8.9	-4.2	12.4
Suriname	68	76	54	71	71	72	83	72	79	99	3.5	-2.5	6.7
Trinidad and Tobago	1,186	944	623	737	663	863	559	563	790	932	16.6	-12.4	7.1
Uruguay	1,051	1,244	1,155	1,050	1,052	1,354	1,512	1,726	1,912	1,944	9.0	-8.5	13.1
Venezuela	9,709	11,091	12,775	6,048	5,588	10,060	13,899	11,309	7,357	9,091	4.6	-7.0	10.2
Latin America	**214,944**	**226,481**	**226,695**	**213,802**	**206,564**	**219,654**	**239,014**	**253,186**	**269,354**	**273,477**	**7.5**	**-3.1**	**5.8**

[1] Excludes changes in inventories from 1987.

TABLE B-5. EXPORTS OF GOODS AND SERVICES[1]

Country	1986	1987	1988	1989	1990	1991	1992	1993	1994	1995p	1970 1980	1980 1990	1990 1995
					Millions of 1990 Dollars							In Percent	
Argentina	10,246	9,898	11,715	12,449	14,800	13,578	13,655	14,337	16,158	20,844	4.8	5.0	7.1
Bahamas	...	...	...	...	...	...	...	...	...	...	...	...	...
Barbados	906	729	809	894	792	760	707	729	797	809	6.1	-0.8	0.4
Belize	178	197	202	230	244	246	293	295	301	284	...	7.9	3.0
Bolivia	706	664	706	879	977	1,048	1,060	1,212	1,448	1,527	2.8	2.7	9.3
Brazil	26,108	31,130	35,202	36,992	35,170	37,498	46,198	51,805	51,805	47,660	9.9	7.1	6.3
Chile	6,782	7,239	8,075	9,376	10,284	11,384	12,924	13,464	14,574	16,242	10.3	6.2	9.6
Colombia	6,341	6,799	6,916	7,323	8,679	9,789	10,305	10,175	10,511	11,814	6.4	6.0	6.4
Costa Rica	1,207	1,460	1,567	1,815	1,963	2,138	2,453	2,752	2,914	3,078	5.9	6.4	9.4
Dominican Republic	1,275	1,528	1,584	1,675	1,832	1,578	1,733	1,862	2,084	2,268	8.1	1.1	4.4
Ecuador	2,731	2,291	3,003	2,953	3,253	3,594	3,939	4,105	4,460	4,682	14.0	5.2	7.6
El Salvador	892	1,001	909	786	973	968	1,031	1,326	1,473	1,725	4.1	-3.5	12.1
Guatemala	1,160	1,230	1,299	1,471	1,567	1,491	1,615	1,771	1,857	2,006	6.5	-2.1	5.1
Guyana	286	278	249	250	251	292	404	418	447	475	-2.4	-4.0	13.6
Haiti	306	291	302	296	300	267	140	190	270	471	10.1	-2.8	9.5
Honduras	963	986	978	1,027	1,032	1,012	1,092	1,080	1,003	1,097	4.6	0.8	1.2
Jamaica	1,852	2,023	1,946	1,952	2,217	2,352	2,470	2,575	2,660	2,851	-0.2	5.0	5.2
Mexico	39,780	43,515	46,039	47,099	48,805	51,043	51,902	53,842	57,795	66,234	8.4	7.3	6.3
Nicaragua	259	253	251	332	392	333	400	415	455	493	1.0	-0.1	4.7
Panama	4,148	4,144	4,254	4,059	4,489	4,874	5,187	5,362	5,657	5,878	7.4	1.9	5.5
Paraguay	981	1,024	1,448	1,571	1,880	2,018	1,936	2,703	3,094	3,385	10.1	8.1	12.5
Peru	4,794	4,446	4,124	4,896	4,165	4,644	4,681	4,869	5,805	6,252	3.0	-2.0	8.5
Suriname	527	466	485	654	489	352	239	200	213	226	2.7	-8.8	-14.3
Trinidad and Tobago	2,033	1,942	2,142	2,071	2,289	2,350	2,379	2,388	2,165	2,554	1.8	0.8	2.2
Uruguay	1,738	1,591	1,736	1,916	2,159	2,215	2,433	2,499	2,703	2,574	7.2	4.7	3.6
Venezuela	14,673	14,418	15,560	16,423	18,806	19,608	19,208	21,517	22,872	23,376	-4.3	2.6	4.4
Latin America	**130,871**	**139,542**	**151,500**	**159,390**	**167,809**	**175,434**	**188,384**	**201,889**	**213,520**	**228,805**	**4.3**	**4.9**	**6.4**

[1] Non-Factor Services.

TABLE B-6. IMPORTS OF GOODS AND SERVICES[1]

Country	1986	1987	1988	1989	1990	1991	1992	1993	1994	1995p	1970 1980	1980 1990	1990 1995
					Millions of 1990 Dollars							In Percent	
Argentina	8,286	9,377	8,301	6,803	6,846	11,289	18,417	20,444	25,136	22,673	10.1	-8.2	27.1
Bahamas	...	...	...	...	...	...	...	...	...	...	...	...	...
Barbados	817	725	792	896	818	817	645	700	735	764	5.3	0.6	-1.4
Belize	147	188	225	259	248	276	301	311	286	279	...	2.2	2.4
Bolivia	1,071	1,156	982	985	1,086	1,223	1,344	1,460	1,562	1,745	1.1	3.0	9.9
Brazil	24,301	23,585	23,320	25,404	28,184	31,002	32,660	44,149	47,460	61,698	8.2	-0.2	17.0
Chile	5,332	6,324	7,133	8,883	9,204	9,990	12,341	13,729	14,430	17,636	5.0	1.5	13.9
Colombia	6,107	6,425	6,573	6,338	6,858	6,900	9,720	12,948	14,840	17,452	6.3	1.7	20.5
Costa Rica	1,555	1,828	1,812	2,141	2,346	2,267	2,876	3,369	3,380	3,465	6.1	3.8	8.1
Dominican Republic	2,649	3,099	3,109	3,003	2,233	2,514	3,188	3,149	3,406	3,952	9.0	-3.7	12.1
Ecuador	2,259	2,605	2,344	2,464	2,373	2,752	2,780	2,801	2,968	3,261	10.4	-2.2	6.6
El Salvador	1,084	1,086	1,083	1,148	1,624	1,715	2,009	2,429	2,750	3,373	3.6	1.2	15.7
Guatemala	1,124	1,662	1,724	1,825	1,812	1,943	2,662	2,774	2,939	3,263	4.2	-2.4	12.5
Guyana	334	324	285	292	320	308	363	393	436	521	-3.2	-4.2	10.2
Haiti	525	522	502	521	551	626	345	553	248	865	13.8	-2.7	9.4
Honduras	1,043	1,066	1,146	1,160	1,127	1,194	1,284	1,374	1,402	1,570	4.9	-0.8	6.9
Jamaica	1,647	1,852	2,152	2,287	2,390	2,565	2,357	2,475	2,570	2,847	-0.7	7.4	3.6
Mexico	24,913	26,158	35,757	43,377	51,915	60,624	73,272	72,356	81,722	62,222	10.9	2.0	3.7
Nicaragua	750	776	927	714	682	817	852	763	876	931	7.2	-4.6	6.4
Panama	4,520	4,312	2,841	3,306	4,429	5,128	5,727	6,175	6,608	6,912	4.6	-0.5	9.3
Paraguay	1,096	1,190	1,334	1,323	2,093	2,397	2,495	3,284	4,052	4,216	13.0	7.7	15.0
Peru	4,700	5,398	4,915	3,672	4,108	4,932	5,607	5,636	6,800	8,568	4.1	-4.1	15.8
Suriname	524	381	399	478	470	420	243	224	212	308	4.6	-9.8	-8.1
Trinidad and Tobago	2,180	1,607	1,477	1,400	1,427	1,608	1,213	1,156	1,065	1,566	13.3	-3.9	1.9
Uruguay	1,397	1,618	1,618	1,641	1,659	1,970	2,468	2,932	3,485	3,293	5.2	-1.0	14.7
Venezuela	12,493	12,767	15,190	10,259	9,451	14,125	17,841	16,668	13,301	14,538	9.9	-6.5	9.0
Latin America	**110,852**	**116,033**	**125,942**	**130,578**	**144,257**	**169,404**	**203,010**	**222,252**	**242,670**	**247,917**	**8.2**	**-0.7**	**11.4**

[1] Non-Factor Services.

TABLE B-7. VALUE ADDED BY AGRICULTURE, FORESTRY AND FISHING

Country	1986	1987	1988	1989	1990	1991	1992	1993	1994	1995p	1970 1980	1980 1990	1990 1995
				Millions of 1990 Dollars							In Percent		
Argentina	11,553	11,208	12,307	11,173	12,449	12,930	12,939	12,810	13,297	13,523	2.1	1.6	1.7
Bahamas	...	...	...	...	...	...	...	...	...	...	...	...	...
Barbados	96	85	80	73	79	76	69	66	65	61	-1.1	-2.4	-5.1
Belize	52	62	62	66	74	76	88	88	91	96	...	3.5	5.5
Bolivia	749	776	794	782	818	899	861	892	951	967	4.1	1.7	3.4
Brazil	32,874	37,796	38,113	39,199	37,741	38,784	40,868	40,365	43,380	45,936	4.7	2.4	4.0
Chile	2,216	2,427	2,706	2,858	3,029	3,112	3,343	3,393	3,679	3,884	2.2	5.7	5.1
Colombia	6,158	6,551	6,732	7,022	7,431	7,740	7,597	7,802	7,916	8,355	4.4	3.0	2.4
Costa Rica	767	799	836	898	921	978	1,018	1,042	1,075	1,107	2.6	3.1	3.8
Dominican Republic	908	935	922	943	871	899	953	960	943	999	3.4	0.5	2.8
Ecuador	1,403	1,439	1,549	1,592	1,689	1,790	1,851	1,819	1,889	1,950	3.0	4.2	2.9
El Salvador	854	865	856	852	907	905	977	952	926	973	2.4	-1.4	1.4
Guatemala	1,751	1,819	1,901	1,959	2,040	2,103	2,166	2,211	2,268	2,334	4.7	1.3	2.7
Guyana	183	174	150	146	126	142	176	187	209	224	1.2	-4.2	12.2
Haiti	718	720	711	703	677	676	669	652	641	594	1.5	-0.9	-2.6
Honduras	475	515	512	563	570	605	626	635	612	641	2.7	2.7	2.4
Jamaica	248	261	252	229	256	255	288	318	341	349	0.9	0.8	6.4
Mexico	19,095	19,330	18,623	18,199	19,274	19,460	19,266	19,539	20,354	19,589	3.4	1.1	0.3
Nicaragua	774	749	673	734	736	707	729	742	822	863	0.0	-0.7	3.2
Panama	501	545	517	536	552	580	619	623	647	641	1.3	2.5	3.0
Paraguay	1,301	1,392	1,560	1,680	1,717	1,706	1,708	1,803	1,793	1,920	6.7	4.0	2.3
Peru	2,590	2,722	2,936	2,795	2,616	2,667	2,538	2,705	3,125	3,356	-0.6	2.2	5.1
Suriname	33	34	34	33	34	40	41	41	37	35	3.7	0.6	0.9
Trinidad and Tobago	109	109	106	113	132	136	134	139	147	148	-1.9	-0.6	2.3
Uruguay	1,018	1,065	1,048	1,084	1,087	1,110	1,244	1,199	1,309	1,344	0.6	0.2	4.3
Venezuela	2,900	3,016	3,154	2,992	2,946	3,016	3,078	3,166	3,235	3,212	3.0	2.0	1.7
Latin America	**89,325**	**95,392**	**97,135**	**97,225**	**98,771**	**101,389**	**103,844**	**104,146**	**109,751**	**113,101**	**3.5**	**2.0**	**2.7**

Average Annual Growth Rates

TABLE B-8. VALUE ADDED BY INDUSTRY

Country	1986	1987	1988	1989	1990	1991	1992	1993	1994	1995p	1970 1980	1980 1990	1990 1995
				Millions of 1990 Dollars							In Percent		
Argentina	60,808	63,368	60,881	55,189	55,208	61,370	67,034	70,968	75,643	71,061	2.1	-1.9	5.2
Bahamas	...	...	...	...	...	...	...	...	...	...	...	...	...
Barbados	252	251	268	283	270	257	240	242	252	269	4.8	0.6	0.0
Belize	61	68	70	81	90	94	102	111	106	110	...	4.1	4.0
Bolivia	1,313	1,332	1,469	1,587	1,699	1,771	1,803	1,923	2,026	2,114	3.7	-0.7	4.5
Brazil	148,369	149,837	145,892	150,088	137,649	134,985	129,741	138,427	148,128	150,890	9.5	0.1	1.9
Chile	11,181	11,581	12,531	13,812	14,201	15,152	16,453	17,232	17,716	18,936	1.8	3.4	5.9
Colombia	14,148	15,097	15,791	16,501	16,811	16,900	17,443	17,854	18,205	19,202	5.0	5.1	2.7
Costa Rica	1,258	1,323	1,349	1,412	1,446	1,463	1,593	1,711	1,784	1,808	7.9	1.9	4.6
Dominican Republic	1,679	2,019	2,010	2,131	1,986	1,929	2,182	2,231	2,426	2,482	9.3	2.5	4.6
Ecuador	5,223	4,109	5,187	4,879	4,792	5,021	5,227	5,505	5,900	6,056	14.5	1.1	4.8
El Salvador	1,246	1,299	1,351	1,388	1,418	1,475	1,612	1,605	1,737	1,855	1.0	-0.8	5.5
Guatemala	1,374	1,425	1,485	1,537	1,560	1,599	1,714	1,770	1,814	1,895	7.4	-0.2	4.0
Guyana	102	100	95	82	82	93	96	116	125	127	-0.9	-5.9	9.1
Haiti	513	514	508	505	468	413	284	280	193	218	8.2	-2.8	-14.2
Honduras	562	579	633	675	669	675	749	821	768	801	6.1	2.9	3.6
Jamaica	1,215	1,311	1,386	1,596	1,707	1,674	1,681	1,670	1,664	1,665	-3.4	3.1	-0.5
Mexico	62,527	64,493	66,165	69,989	74,052	76,626	78,903	78,961	82,149	75,824	6.6	1.8	0.5
Nicaragua	683	681	532	518	506	526	512	514	529	558	0.6	-2.4	2.0
Panama	889	915	667	649	723	843	979	1,117	1,160	1,175	5.3	-2.2	10.2
Paraguay	1,342	1,389	1,464	1,539	1,581	1,619	1,660	1,717	1,791	1,873	10.8	2.3	3.4
Peru	16,653	18,735	16,775	14,319	13,729	14,406	14,274	15,194	18,064	19,470	3.8	-1.7	7.2
Suriname	94	76	85	84	82	81	87	79	80	85	4.6	-2.1	0.6
Trinidad and Tobago	2,620	2,401	2,361	2,338	2,377	2,461	2,400	2,261	2,453	2,543	5.7	-3.9	1.4
Uruguay	2,829	3,154	3,166	3,148	3,074	3,116	3,248	3,102	3,217	3,077	4.0	-1.6	0.0
Venezuela	24,413	25,406	27,009	24,726	27,459	30,478	32,212	33,158	32,501	33,839	3.0	1.8	4.3
Latin America	**361,355**	**371,461**	**369,131**	**369,057**	**363,639**	**375,028**	**382,229**	**398,569**	**420,432**	**417,931**	**5.7**	**0.4**	**2.8**

Average Annual Growth Rates

TABLE B-9. INDUSTRY: VALUE ADDED BY MINING AND QUARRYING

Country	1986	1987	1988	1989	1990	1991	1992	1993	1994	1995p	1970 1980	1980 1990	1990 1995
	Millions of 1990 Dollars										In Percent		
Argentina	3,516	3,747	4,010	4,151	4,384	4,132	4,469	4,737	5,291	5,519	3.3	0.9	4.7
Bahamas	...	...	...	...	...	...	...	...	...	...	...	...	...
Barbados	12	11	10	9	10	9	9	9	10	11	19.8	4.3	2.6
Belize	1	1	1	2	2	3	3	3	3	3	...	16.0	7.1
Bolivia	364	370	443	507	546	558	566	601	643	665	3.0	-0.6	4.0
Brazil	5,555	5,513	5,534	5,753	5,910	5,966	6,012	6,045	6,329	6,525	7.3	6.8	2.0
Chile	4,282	4,267	4,602	5,039	5,316	5,563	5,675	5,728	5,881	6,306	3.4	4.4	3.5
Colombia	2,780	3,449	3,606	4,025	4,264	4,236	4,119	4,004	3,934	4,618	-2.0	17.8	1.6
Costa Rica[1]	...	...	...	...	...	...	...	...	...	...	...	...	...
Dominican Republic	230	289	269	267	224	222	183	117	220	241	18.6	-0.7	1.5
Ecuador	2,138	969	2,090	1,888	1,870	2,028	2,146	2,381	2,634	2,734	9.5	3.6	7.9
El Salvador	16	18	19	20	20	22	23	26	29	31	0.7	2.3	8.9
Guatemala	20	20	20	21	20	21	28	31	32	36	24.2	-5.4	12.8
Guyana	39	40	38	28	33	40	36	53	57	50	-5.5	-5.8	8.6
Haiti	3	3	3	3	3	3	2	2	2	3	-0.7	-22.9	-0.6
Honduras	50	31	42	47	43	45	50	52	53	55	2.4	0.9	4.8
Jamaica	218	231	220	299	367	388	378	379	405	379	1.5	0.5	0.7
Mexico	5,758	6,056	6,089	6,056	6,223	6,271	6,384	6,441	6,544	6,497	8.9	2.7	0.9
Nicaragua	14	13	12	16	13	13	15	15	14	15	-14.1	-3.7	3.4
Panama	5	6	4	3	4	6	9	11	12	11	5.0	-4.3	21.0
Paraguay	18	19	20	21	22	23	24	24	25	26	29.7	4.8	3.1
Peru	1,214	1,178	1,001	953	870	889	865	934	968	993	7.4	-4.0	2.7
Suriname	8	7	9	10	10	10	11	12	14	14	-2.9	2.9	7.8
Trinidad and Tobago	1,262	1,157	1,126	1,113	1,119	1,084	1,030	938	995	988	4.5	-3.6	-2.5
Uruguay	23	27	21	21	17	20	23	26	28	24	...	...	7.2
Venezuela	9,779	10,366	10,895	10,865	12,730	13,802	14,053	15,329	16,181	16,959	0.1	2.1	5.9
Latin America	**37,303**	**37,786**	**40,085**	**41,119**	**44,020**	**45,355**	**46,113**	**47,898**	**50,304**	**52,703**	**3.2**	**3.2**	**3.7**

[1] Included in Manufacturing.

TABLE B-10. INDUSTRY: VALUE ADDED BY MANUFACTURING

Country	1986	1987	1988	1989	1990	1991	1992	1993	1994	1995p	1970 1980	1980 1990	1990 1995
	Millions of 1990 Dollars										In Percent		
Argentina	44,752	45,539	43,322	40,234	41,056	45,949	49,320	51,540	53,704	50,213	1.6	-1.4	4.1
Bahamas	...	...	...	...	...	...	...	...	...	...	...	...	...
Barbados	116	108	115	121	118	112	102	99	106	114	6.2	-0.8	-0.7
Belize	41	44	43	48	53	53	57	60	63	65	...	2.3	4.2
Bolivia	739	758	799	839	904	948	948	1,004	1,049	1,093	4.8	-0.7	3.9
Brazil	104,711	105,706	102,103	105,044	95,106	92,859	89,062	96,138	103,841	105,503	9.2	-0.2	2.1
Chile	4,882	5,140	5,593	6,204	6,273	6,684	7,420	7,796	8,021	8,543	1.1	2.6	6.4
Colombia	7,664	8,140	8,295	8,760	9,131	9,206	9,748	9,972	10,061	10,147	6.0	2.9	2.1
Costa Rica[1]	953	1,006	1,028	1,063	1,091	1,113	1,228	1,307	1,352	1,393	7.4	2.2	5.0
Dominican Republic	904	1,020	1,013	1,060	1,016	1,041	1,167	1,192	1,226	1,218	7.0	2.1	3.7
Ecuador	2,455	2,497	2,548	2,421	2,438	2,516	2,606	2,671	2,789	2,850	9.5	0.5	3.2
El Salvador	1,004	1,034	1,070	1,098	1,152	1,220	1,340	1,320	1,424	1,524	0.2	-0.9	5.8
Guatemala	1,088	1,110	1,134	1,161	1,186	1,214	1,254	1,290	1,329	1,372	6.2	-0.1	3.0
Guyana[2]	48	45	42	39	34	38	45	47	49	56	5.2	-7.4	10.3
Haiti	364	361	352	344	320	263	207	205	137	135	8.4	-3.3	-15.9
Honduras	355	378	397	412	415	422	448	476	466	485	6.3	3.0	3.2
Jamaica	620	655	690	742	771	713	722	708	704	697	-2.1	3.0	-2.0
Mexico	45,436	46,804	48,310	51,777	54,921	57,125	58,421	57,980	60,081	56,223	6.3	2.0	0.5
Nicaragua	562	553	413	406	399	425	403	403	407	420	2.4	-2.8	1.0
Panama	431	447	346	365	407	442	478	512	534	535	3.6	-0.5	5.6
Paraguay	898	929	984	1,042	1,068	1,080	1,084	1,106	1,121	1,150	8.3	2.2	1.5
Peru	12,192	13,755	12,213	10,300	9,702	10,301	10,058	10,457	12,123	12,668	3.3	-1.9	5.5
Suriname	45	35	39	40	40	39	39	37	37	39	3.6	-3.1	-0.8
Trinidad and Tobago	702	650	655	688	707	766	783	759	819	840	1.7	-1.4	3.5
Uruguay	2,352	2,585	2,562	2,557	2,520	2,507	2,545	2,316	2,410	2,342	3.3	-1.1	-1.5
Venezuela	10,953	11,224	12,004	10,584	11,224	12,318	12,631	12,502	12,058	12,924	5.2	3.3	2.9
Latin America	**244,268**	**250,521**	**246,068**	**247,349**	**242,052**	**249,354**	**252,118**	**261,896**	**275,912**	**272,548**	**5.6**	**0.3**	**2.4**

[1] Includes Mining and Quarrying.
[2] Includes Electricity, Gas and Water.

TABLE B-11. INDUSTRY: VALUE ADDED BY CONSTRUCTION

Country	1986	1987	1988	1989	1990	1991	1992	1993	1994	1995p	Average Annual Growth Rates 1970 1980	1980 1990	1990 1995
					Millions of 1990 Dollars						In Percent		
Argentina	9,624	11,019	10,695	8,088	6,814	8,267	10,060	11,156	12,896	11,465	2.6	-6.7	11.0
Bahamas	...	...	...	...	...	...	...	...	...	...	...	...	...
Barbados	86	91	99	107	96	89	82	86	86	92	2.0	0.6	-0.9
Belize	13	17	19	24	27	29	32	37	30	30	...	7.2	2.1
Bolivia	133	132	151	160	164	173	193	214	217	228	0.7	-3.2	6.8
Brazil	28,983	29,197	28,289	29,163	26,320	25,407	23,740	24,911	26,369	26,405	10.4	-1.3	0.1
Chile	1,254	1,369	1,487	1,742	1,820	1,889	2,132	2,430	2,478	2,660	-0.9	4.3	7.9
Colombia	2,786	2,506	2,837	2,606	2,265	2,271	2,460	2,633	2,887	3,041	5.2	2.2	6.1
Costa Rica	163	164	165	185	181	167	172	200	212	187	10.2	-1.8	0.7
Dominican Republic	459	616	636	720	670	587	730	803	857	906	10.5	5.1	6.2
Ecuador	648	664	571	593	505	500	498	477	502	495	5.8	-2.6	-0.4
El Salvador	170	189	204	211	184	203	216	224	247	262	5.7	-0.9	7.2
Guatemala	119	136	158	170	157	159	200	193	184	199	13.2	-3.7	4.8
Guyana	15	16	15	15	15	15	15	16	19	21	0.9	-1.5	7.2
Haiti	127	130	131	135	123	127	59	57	42	68	12.6	0.3	-11.2
Honduras	106	110	126	145	131	127	170	206	167	169	6.2	0.8	5.3
Jamaica	296	338	388	457	465	468	470	467	438	467	-9.3	5.5	0.1
Mexico	8,580	8,795	8,759	8,938	9,575	9,807	10,552	10,868	11,568	9,027	7.0	-0.7	-1.2
Nicaragua	84	90	84	71	67	62	67	68	80	93	-1.7	-0.9	6.7
Panama	234	228	89	59	83	180	280	368	377	382	6.2	-12.3	35.7
Paraguay	317	323	332	340	337	347	364	374	388	403	20.3	0.7	3.6
Peru	3,047	3,588	3,345	2,854	2,944	2,995	3,125	3,552	4,717	5,547	4.3	-0.5	13.5
Suriname	33	27	27	24	21	20	24	17	17	19	8.8	-4.0	-1.7
Trinidad and Tobago	595	530	517	474	485	542	515	492	564	637	13.8	-7.7	5.6
Uruguay	280	346	369	377	323	355	411	496	524	447	8.5	-6.8	6.7
Venezuela	2,824	2,908	3,138	2,291	2,469	3,232	4,352	4,111	3,034	2,688	8.6	-4.1	1.7
Latin America	**60,979**	**63,532**	**62,631**	**59,951**	**56,241**	**58,019**	**60,939**	**64,457**	**68,898**	**65,937**	**6.8**	**-2.0**	**3.2**

TABLE B-12. INDUSTRY: VALUE ADDED BY ELECTRICITY, GAS AND WATER

Country	1986	1987	1988	1989	1990	1991	1992	1993	1994	1995p	Average Annual Growth Rates 1970 1980	1980 1990	1990 1995
					Millions of 1990 Dollars						In Percent		
Argentina	2,915	3,063	2,854	2,717	2,954	3,023	3,185	3,536	3,752	3,864	6.9	2.7	5.5
Bahamas	...	...	...	...	...	...	...	...	...	...	...	...	...
Barbados	39	41	44	45	46	47	48	48	49	52	7.8	4.6	2.8
Belize	6	6	7	7	8	9	10	11	11	12	...	7.5	7.7
Bolivia	77	73	77	81	86	92	96	104	118	128	7.3	3.9	8.4
Brazil	9,120	9,421	9,966	10,128	10,312	10,753	10,927	11,333	11,589	12,457	12.4	6.0	3.9
Chile	763	805	850	827	791	1,015	1,225	1,278	1,336	1,427	5.0	2.6	12.5
Colombia	919	1,002	1,054	1,110	1,152	1,187	1,115	1,245	1,322	1,395	8.7	4.5	3.9
Costa Rica	141	152	156	164	175	183	194	204	219	228	7.8	5.4	5.5
Dominican Republic	85	95	92	84	76	79	102	118	123	118	10.8	-1.0	9.2
Ecuador	-18	-21	-22	-23	-22	-23	-23	-24	-25	-24	8.9	9.6	1.2
El Salvador	56	57	58	59	62	31	32	35	38	40	8.9	1.9	-8.6
Guatemala	147	158	172	186	197	205	232	255	269	288	9.4	4.7	7.9
Guyana[1]	...	...	...	...	...	...	...	...	...	...	...	...	...
Haiti	19	20	22	23	22	20	16	17	12	13	13.8	4.3	-10.5
Honduras	51	60	68	71	80	81	82	87	82	92	10.6	9.4	2.7
Jamaica	81	88	88	98	105	107	111	116	117	122	3.7	5.5	3.1
Mexico	2,753	2,837	3,007	3,219	3,333	3,423	3,525	3,673	3,956	4,077	9.1	6.0	4.1
Nicaragua	23	25	23	24	26	26	27	28	29	30	3.4	2.0	2.8
Panama	219	234	228	222	229	214	212	227	238	247	9.4	3.6	1.6
Paraguay	109	118	128	136	154	169	187	213	257	294	17.5	7.9	13.7
Peru	199	214	215	212	213	221	226	251	256	261	10.0	2.7	4.2
Suriname	8	7	10	10	12	12	13	12	11	13	10.1	3.6	2.3
Trinidad and Tobago	60	64	63	63	66	69	73	72	76	77	7.2	6.1	3.3
Uruguay	174	197	213	192	214	233	269	265	255	265	3.8	3.7	4.3
Venezuela	857	909	972	985	1,036	1,126	1,176	1,216	1,229	1,267	8.5	5.8	4.1
Latin America	**18,805**	**19,623**	**20,347**	**20,638**	**21,327**	**22,301**	**23,059**	**24,318**	**25,318**	**26,743**	**9.5**	**5.1**	**4.6**

[1] Included in Manufacturing.

TABLE B-13. VALUE ADDED BY SERVICES

											1970 1980	1980 1990	1990 1995
	1986	1987	1988	1989	1990	1991	1992	1993	1994	1995p			
Country					Millions of 1990 Dollars							In Percent	
Argentina	89,757	91,774	89,964	86,844	85,598	92,396	100,987	108,123	117,065	112,366	3.0	-0.5	5.6
Bahamas	...	...	...	...	...	...	...	...	...	...	...	...	...
Barbados	1,030	1,086	1,122	1,168	1,125	1,086	1,031	1,047	1,087	1,110	2.4	1.5	-0.3
Belize	116	127	139	160	175	179	193	201	208	214	...	5.3	4.1
Bolivia	2,192	2,259	2,231	2,303	2,370	2,468	2,556	2,644	2,749	2,839	4.0	0.4	3.7
Brazil	140,832	145,090	147,879	152,583	151,087	152,959	151,283	158,080	163,733	167,508	11.3	2.4	2.1
Chile	12,047	12,814	13,457	14,588	15,163	16,338	18,119	19,321	20,175	21,795	3.3	1.6	7.5
Colombia	18,424	19,253	20,180	20,633	21,528	21,914	23,163	24,876	27,200	28,822	6.2	3.1	6.0
Costa Rica	2,800	2,919	3,014	3,160	3,293	3,338	3,590	3,819	3,997	4,112	5.4	2.1	4.5
Dominican Republic	2,774	2,980	3,122	3,257	3,117	3,180	3,363	3,497	3,628	3,860	7.3	2.1	4.4
Ecuador	5,364	5,477	5,615	5,819	6,118	6,423	6,650	6,762	6,974	7,126	8.5	1.8	3.1
El Salvador	2,698	2,755	2,804	2,820	2,979	3,113	3,319	3,404	3,628	3,846	3.0	0.1	5.2
Guatemala	3,712	3,835	3,968	4,148	4,282	4,468	4,686	4,918	5,175	5,478	5.5	1.1	5.0
Guyana	118	123	121	120	122	123	125	130	138	147	2.8	-0.5	3.7
Haiti	921	930	913	891	891	885	729	706	737	829	6.0	0.0	-1.4
Honduras	1,172	1,228	1,282	1,318	1,300	1,309	1,377	1,480	1,492	1,554	7.1	2.0	3.6
Jamaica	1,696	1,837	1,872	1,926	1,990	2,051	2,077	2,119	2,132	2,157	1.2	1.7	1.6
Mexico	135,047	136,775	138,719	142,843	148,049	154,211	159,307	160,637	166,388	155,521	7.1	1.7	1.0
Nicaragua	1,296	1,296	1,183	1,119	1,129	1,137	1,150	1,126	1,129	1,169	-0.3	-1.5	0.7
Panama	4,144	4,200	3,610	3,595	3,734	4,007	4,298	4,482	4,651	4,754	5.9	1.2	4.9
Paraguay	2,484	2,564	2,658	2,784	2,882	3,002	3,073	3,179	3,306	3,384	8.8	2.7	3.3
Peru	24,224	26,414	23,698	20,690	19,635	20,052	20,041	21,006	23,239	24,791	4.1	-1.3	4.8
Suriname	174	165	171	188	186	192	204	182	168	186	6.7	-0.2	0.1
Trinidad and Tobago	3,052	2,976	2,794	2,760	2,756	2,839	2,823	2,874	2,914	3,017	5.9	-2.3	1.8
Uruguay	4,873	5,201	5,194	5,304	5,430	5,669	6,172	6,705	7,233	7,010	3.0	1.7	5.2
Venezuela	22,768	23,923	25,358	23,236	24,280	26,433	28,133	27,663	26,682	27,929	4.4	0.2	2.8
Latin America	**483,714**	**498,001**	**501,067**	**504,257**	**509,218**	**529,771**	**548,450**	**568,982**	**595,828**	**591,525**	**6.3**	**1.3**	**3.0**

TABLE B-14. SERVICES: VALUE ADDED BY WHOLESALE AND RETAIL TRADE

											1970 1980	1980 1990	1990 1995
	1986	1987	1988	1989	1990	1991	1992	1993	1994	1995p			
Country					Millions of 1990 Dollars							In Percent	
Argentina	26,550	26,733	26,113	23,472	23,904	27,843	30,410	31,778	34,321	32,347	3.2	-2.3	6.2
Bahamas	...	...	...	...	...	...	...	...	...	...	...	...	...
Barbados	278	293	301	308	293	275	253	259	272	281	2.5	0.9	-0.9
Belize	34	40	46	56	63	62	66	69	72	74	...	3.9	3.0
Bolivia	557	602	578	613	647	689	702	729	762	801	2.9	2.6	4.4
Brazil	27,809	28,331	27,569	28,314	26,340	26,119	25,493	27,288	28,892	31,039	8.3	0.3	3.3
Chile	3,743	4,151	4,372	4,987	5,179	5,776	6,828	7,417	7,702	8,518	3.7	2.0	10.5
Colombia	5,637	5,886	6,181	6,295	6,473	6,500	6,789	7,130	7,520	7,884	5.7	2.4	4.0
Costa Rica	972	1,011	1,024	1,078	1,131	1,133	1,275	1,370	1,439	1,482	4.6	1.7	5.6
Dominican Republic	884	985	1,027	1,045	902	945	1,025	1,088	1,149	1,278	7.1	-0.5	7.2
Ecuador	2,407	2,466	2,517	2,570	2,667	2,773	2,856	2,905	3,010	3,076	8.7	1.0	2.9
El Salvador	743	754	757	783	807	858	958	1,024	1,112	1,203	1.0	-1.6	8.3
Guatemala	1,699	1,750	1,805	1,868	1,898	1,977	2,066	2,150	2,263	2,411	4.9	-0.3	4.9
Guyana	21	22	22	21	22	23	24	26	27	29	1.9	-3.6	5.6
Haiti	356	359	355	355	351	341	204	175	131	135	6.2	-1.3	-17.4
Honduras	296	301	310	296	293	300	308	334	334	349	6.2	-1.1	3.5
Jamaica	686	761	769	795	831	850	895	931	946	1,000	-2.9	1.7	3.8
Mexico	56,924	57,249	58,223	60,404	62,869	65,582	67,935	67,024	68,914	58,997	8.2	0.8	-1.3
Nicaragua	647	644	563	547	549	576	584	571	580	608	-0.9	-2.3	2.0
Panama	737	702	531	554	628	696	752	793	830	821	4.8	-1.6	5.5
Paraguay[1]	1,337	1,384	1,440	1,507	1,562	1,630	1,640	1,703	1,776	1,803	9.0	2.8	2.9
Peru	8,403	9,231	8,218	6,907	6,711	6,936	6,729	7,021	8,175	9,230	4.3	-1.5	6.6
Suriname	62	44	50	66	62	61	65	41	36	54	4.0	-4.6	-2.5
Trinidad and Tobago	1,038	1,036	939	884	812	847	847	818	827	879	4.6	-3.7	1.6
Uruguay	1,150	1,238	1,218	1,207	1,209	1,311	1,488	1,736	1,951	1,734	4.1	-0.8	7.5
Venezuela	10,012	10,435	11,003	9,269	9,618	10,391	11,432	10,974	10,318	12,868	2.5	1.0	6.0
Latin America	**152,982**	**156,410**	**155,932**	**154,201**	**155,822**	**164,494**	**171,625**	**175,352**	**183,359**	**178,899**	**5.9**	**0.1**	**2.8**

[1] Includes Financial Services except property rents.

TABLE B-15. SERVICES: VALUE ADDED BY TRANSPORT AND COMMUNICATION

Country	1986	1987	1988	1989	1990	1991	1992	1993	1994	1995p	1970 1980	1980 1990	1990 1995
					Millions of 1990 Dollars							In Percent	
Argentina	7,898	8,184	8,146	8,393	8,035	8,386	9,324	9,967	10,745	10,662	1.9	1.4	5.8
Bahamas	...	...	...	...	...	...	...	...	...	...	...	...	...
Barbados	119	125	125	133	122	131	126	128	131	135	1.1	2.4	2.2
Belize	19	21	26	33	37	40	48	51	51	53	...	12.5	7.6
Bolivia	414	436	437	471	497	529	554	588	627	654	9.7	4.3	5.7
Brazil	14,704	15,658	16,645	17,993	18,260	19,987	20,761	22,157	23,672	25,737	13.5	5.8	7.1
Chile	1,651	1,809	1,968	2,216	2,363	2,595	2,952	3,184	3,458	3,884	4.0	3.9	10.5
Colombia	3,644	3,765	3,895	4,020	4,170	4,313	4,539	4,722	5,032	5,326	7.5	2.7	5.0
Costa Rica	207	225	244	267	285	293	334	370	399	423	10.6	4.6	8.2
Dominican Republic	369	461	465	496	464	496	571	607	638	702	7.2	3.0	8.6
Ecuador	890	908	964	1,040	1,087	1,153	1,219	1,273	1,327	1,367	10.3	4.3	4.7
El Salvador	348	354	362	366	389	408	446	476	500	535	4.2	0.4	6.6
Guatemala	490	513	536	591	628	665	715	749	789	838	8.2	2.3	6.0
Guyana	26	29	26	25	25	25	26	28	30	33	3.1	-0.3	5.3
Haiti	37	41	43	45	45	42	37	32	19	20	5.3	0.9	-15.2
Honduras	130	135	145	154	160	165	172	177	185	193	4.0	5.1	3.8
Jamaica	272	304	318	331	342	356	376	405	428	472	1.3	4.5	6.6
Mexico	16,965	17,480	17,882	18,627	19,870	21,031	22,631	23,382	25,211	24,734	9.5	1.9	4.5
Nicaragua	109	111	94	91	91	96	97	94	93	98	0.9	-3.0	1.3
Panama	1,167	1,218	1,102	1,044	1,048	1,191	1,286	1,320	1,362	1,467	20.1	2.1	7.0
Paraguay	197	207	219	230	239	250	257	265	276	285	9.7	3.7	3.7
Peru	2,098	2,308	2,182	1,978	1,870	1,909	1,966	2,062	2,232	2,366	6.1	-0.3	4.8
Suriname	18	21	21	20	19	23	24	22	22	24	4.1	0.6	4.0
Trinidad and Tobago	413	417	413	423	425	437	431	432	449	476	6.4	1.0	2.3
Uruguay	517	545	573	621	625	683	766	855	992	1,022	3.2	1.4	10.4
Venezuela	2,292	2,480	2,679	2,510	2,500	2,619	2,763	2,788	2,688	2,798	6.5	-0.7	2.3
Latin America	54,994	57,756	59,508	62,117	63,595	67,822	72,419	76,134	81,357	84,302	7.7	2.8	5.8

Average Annual Growth Rates columns: 1970–1980, 1980–1990, 1990–1995.

TABLE B-16. SERVICES: VALUE ADDED BY FINANCIAL SERVICES

Country	1986	1987	1988	1989	1990	1991	1992	1993	1994	1995p	1970 1980	1980 1990	1990 1995
					Millions of 1990 Dollars							In Percent	
Argentina	23,480	24,214	23,464	22,360	21,020	23,996	28,762	31,639	35,689	33,729	4.2	-1.1	9.9
Bahamas	...	...	...	...	...	...	...	...	...	...	...	...	...
Barbados[1]	...	...	...	...	...	...	...	...	...	...	...	...	...
Belize	12	13	14	15	16	16	17	18	19	20	...	3.3	4.5
Bolivia	477	469	461	446	454	464	482	488	501	513	2.2	-2.0	2.5
Brazil[2]	58,448	60,459	62,273	64,152	63,650	63,325	60,825	63,777	65,672	63,326	9.1[a]	2.9	-0.1
Chile	2,973	3,130	3,288	3,469	3,609	3,837	4,066	4,304	4,483	4,750	4.0	0.6	5.6
Colombia	4,183	4,327	4,555	4,605	5,016	5,160	5,679	6,483	7,327	7,734	5.4	3.5	9.0
Costa Rica	560	589	623	659	693	704	750	807	847	859	5.8	3.6	4.4
Dominican Republic	525	553	595	648	671	675	679	679	684	692	7.8	5.3	0.6
Ecuador[3]	1,014	1,031	1,037	1,095	1,233	1,345	1,406	1,420	1,467	1,501	7.3	1.0	4.0
El Salvador[4]	...	...	696	698	724	745	790	759	812	839	...	...	3.0
Guatemala	626	642	664	690	722	754	787	826	868	920	3.9	2.4	5.0
Guyana	36	37	37	39	40	40	40	42	45	49	2.9	1.8	4.2
Haiti	116	115	117	118	123	125	119	111	100	102	8.0	1.8	-3.8
Honduras	287	304	333	355	368	392	418	452	473	497	5.7	4.5	6.2
Jamaica	248	263	268	281	295	332	293	264	245	170	...	...	-10.4
Mexico	23,020	23,908	24,221	24,952	25,819	26,650	27,531	28,528	29,759	30,297	4.8	3.9	3.3
Nicaragua	138	142	136	135	132	131	132	131	132	137	-0.5	-0.9	0.7
Panama	917	932	793	793	877	885	960	1,064	1,129	1,141	3.4	1.8	5.4
Paraguay[5]	322	328	335	343	351	363	388	398	412	428	7.2	1.1	4.1
Peru[1]	...	...	...	...	...	...	...	...	...	...	...	...	...
Suriname	39	41	41	43	44	46	49	52	48	48	...	2.5	2.0
Trinidad and Tobago	503	447	393	378	423	456	479	490	503	517	8.4	-8.3	4.1
Uruguay	1,545	1,641	1,653	1,694	1,768	1,843	2,040	2,213	2,392	2,355	2.3	1.7	5.9
Venezuela	5,066	5,287	5,594	5,185	5,458	6,199	5,751	6,524	6,135	6,121	4.1	0.5	2.3
Latin America	124,534	128,870	131,591	133,150	133,505	138,485	142,441	151,470	159,742	156,745	6.4	2.1	3.3

[1] Included in Other services.
[2] Includes Government until 1979 and Other Services until 1994.
[3] Includes Value Added Tax from 1990.
[4] Included in Other Services before 1988.
[5] Property rents only.
[a] 1970-1979.

TABLE B-17. SERVICES: VALUE ADDED BY GOVERNMENT

Country	1986	1987	1988	1989	1990	1991	1992	1993	1994	1995p	Average Annual Growth Rates 1970 1980	Average Annual Growth Rates 1980 1990	Average Annual Growth Rates 1990 1995
					Millions of 1990 Dollars							In Percent	
Argentina[1]	...	...	...	...	...	...	...	...	...	...	...	...	...
Bahamas	...	...	...	...	...	...	...	...	...	...	...	...	...
Barbados	253	263	266	269	273	267	254	254	254	256	1.7	1.7	-1.2
Belize	30	32	32	33	35	36	38	38	40	40	...	5.3	2.7
Bolivia	530	543	535	542	536	540	562	574	589	595	7.3	-2.3	2.1
Brazil[2]	39,871	40,640	41,392	42,125	42,837	43,527	44,205	44,859	45,496	47,407	...	2.0	2.0
Chile[1]	...	...	...	...	...	...	...	...	...	...	...	...	...
Colombia	2,968	3,178	3,400	3,535	3,636	3,624	3,794	4,085	4,782	5,175	6.8	4.6	7.3
Costa Rica	775	794	810	826	839	847	855	873	894	917	5.8	0.9	1.8
Dominican Republic	461	437	471	484	497	491	501	517	536	538	6.3	2.5	1.6
Ecuador	552	556	579	580	594	599	597	584	576	578	8.6	1.6	-0.6
El Salvador	362	377	390	385	391	394	380	381	391	405	6.5	3.1	0.7
Guatemala	464	489	508	532	552	578	610	668	711	741	6.5	3.8	6.1
Guyana	28	28	28	28	28	27	26	26	27	28	...	-1.0	-0.4
Haiti	308	313	291	255	246	243	248	272	286	304	12.5	-0.8	4.4
Honduras	200	209	211	217	185	178	185	204	188	182	20.7	1.1	-0.3
Jamaica	332	338	350	343	334	332	332	331	327	326	6.9	-0.8	-0.5
Mexico[1]	...	...	...	...	...	...	...	...	...	...	...	...	...
Nicaragua	247	246	263	220	228	199	200	196	185	182	5.9	2.5	-4.4
Panama	805	826	801	789	741	759	785	771	776	802	5.5	2.0	1.6
Paraguay	169	173	175	199	204	210	227	237	252	260	4.2	5.0	4.9
Peru	3,003	3,146	2,864	2,457	2,159	2,012	2,050	2,100	2,167	2,174	4.9	-0.7	0.1
Suriname	51	55	55	56	57	59	63	66	61	59	7.9	5.4	0.6
Trinidad and Tobago	556	562	538	537	562	551	535	536	525	518	4.9	1.3	-1.6
Uruguay	...	...	...	...	...	...	...	...	...	...	...	...	...
Venezuela	2,807	2,876	3,007	3,130	3,368	3,630	3,670	3,571	3,600	3,607	7.5	2.0	1.4
Latin America	**54,772**	**56,082**	**56,966**	**57,543**	**58,303**	**59,103**	**60,117**	**61,142**	**62,663**	**65,094**	**6.3**	**2.0**	**2.2**

[1] Included in Other services.
[2] Included in Financial Services before 1980.

TABLE B-18. SERVICES: VALUE ADDED BY OTHER SERVICES

Country	1986	1987	1988	1989	1990	1991	1992	1993	1994	1995p	Average Annual Growth Rates 1970 1980	Average Annual Growth Rates 1980 1990	Average Annual Growth Rates 1990 1995
					Millions of 1990 Dollars							In Percent	
Argentina[1]	31,829	32,643	32,240	32,619	32,640	32,170	32,490	34,738	36,311	35,627	2.2	1.0	1.8
Bahamas	...	...	...	...	...	...	...	...	...	...	...	...	...
Barbados[2]	380	404	429	457	438	414	398	407	430	438	3.1	1.5	0.0
Belize	21	21	22	23	23	24	24	25	26	26	...	2.7	2.7
Bolivia	215	210	220	230	237	245	256	265	271	276	-1.2	0.5	3.1
Brazil[3]	...	...	...	...	...	...	...	...	...	...	...	...	...
Chile[1]	3,679	3,724	3,829	3,916	4,012	4,131	4,273	4,416	4,532	4,644	2.1	0.9	3.0
Colombia	1,992	2,097	2,149	2,178	2,234	2,316	2,362	2,457	2,538	2,704	6.4	2.5	3.9
Costa Rica	286	300	313	330	346	361	376	398	418	431	3.7	2.4	4.5
Dominican Republic	536	545	564	585	583	573	587	606	622	650	8.3	2.6	2.2
Ecuador	501	516	518	534	537	553	571	579	594	605	7.3	3.1	2.4
El Salvador[4]	1,245	1,270	599	588	667	709	745	765	812	863	3.5	-6.6	5.3
Guatemala	433	441	456	467	483	494	509	525	545	567	6.8	0.9	3.3
Guyana	7	7	7	7	7	8	8	8	9	9	-12.7	0.3	5.0
Haiti	104	102	107	119	126	134	122	115	201	268	-4.4	4.7	16.3
Honduras	260	278	284	296	294	275	294	313	313	333	6.1	1.9	2.6
Jamaica	158	170	166	176	188	182	182	188	185	189	9.1	-7.0	0.1
Mexico[1]	38,138	38,138	38,393	38,861	39,491	40,948	41,210	41,703	42,504	41,494	5.7	1.9	1.0
Nicaragua	154	154	127	126	128	134	137	135	139	146	-2.9	-2.9	2.6
Panama	518	521	383	416	440	476	516	535	553	522	-0.3	1.5	3.5
Paraguay	459	473	489	505	526	547	561	575	591	608	11.3	2.5	2.9
Peru[2]	10,720	11,729	10,434	9,348	8,894	9,197	9,295	9,823	10,664	11,022	3.4	-1.5	4.4
Suriname	4	4	4	4	4	3	3	3	1	1	0.5	-0.9	-18.0
Trinidad and Tobago	541	514	511	537	534	548	532	600	610	627	5.7	2.9	3.3
Uruguay[1]	1,661	1,777	1,749	1,782	1,828	1,832	1,878	1,900	1,898	1,898	2.9	3.9	0.8
Venezuela	2,592	2,845	3,075	3,142	3,335	3,595	4,518	3,807	3,942	2,535	6.4	-3.1	-5.3
Latin America	**96,431**	**98,883**	**97,069**	**97,246**	**97,993**	**99,867**	**101,848**	**104,885**	**108,707**	**106,485**	**3.9**	**0.9**	**1.7**

[1] Includes Government.
[2] Includes Financial Services.
[3] Included in Financial Services.
[4] Includes Financial Services before 1988 and Value Added Tax from 1993

NATIONAL ACCOUNTS
METHODOLOGICAL NOTE

In order to permit comparisons of gross domestic product and its major aggregates among countries and calculate values for Latin America, Statistics and Quantitative Analysis computes a consistent set of National Accounts estimates in constant 1990 dollars.

The estimates presented in this section of the Statistical Appendix cover 10 sectors of origin for value added, *their aggregates for the sectors of Industry and Services,* and four main components of expenditure on gross domestic product.

The preparation of the estimates is done as follows:

1. Rebasing each country's national accounts in constant local currency to a common base year; and

2. Conversion of the estimates obtained in step one into U.S. dollars.

The first step is necessitated by the fact that countries use different base years for the calculation of constant price series in their own national accounts.[1]

While the rebasing is only partial and therefore imperfect, it nonetheless allows for more meaningful comparisons of national accounts aggregates across countries by using the relative price systems of a common base year.[2]

1. The *rebasing* was done in a series of steps:

1.1. On the origin side, each of the 10 sectors was rebased (rescaled) to 1990 using the implicit price deflator calculated for the sector:

$$S_t^{90} = S_t^b \times PS_{90}$$

Where
S_t^{90} = constant value added of sector S in prices of 1990
S_t^b = constant value added of sector S in prices of national base year b
PS_{90} = value of the implicit price deflator of sector S in 1990

Gross domestic product was obtained as the sum of the ten[3] sectors.[4]

1.2. On the expenditure side, the same exercise (i.e., taking the main components, rebasing them, and summing them) could generate a series for gross domestic product that is different from that calculated on the sector side.

Therefore, to ensure consistency between the two measures, the rebasing procedure on the expenditure side is carried out for each component except for consumption, which is treated as a residual category. The adjustment is made on the expenditure side because in

most countries of the region, gross domestic product is first calculated on the origin side. Private consumption, or total consumption when the former is not available, is taken as the residual category because, in most Latin American countries, it is derived as a residual in the elaboration of the National Accounts by the local authorities[5].

2. The *conversion* of the rebased expenditure and sector of origin estimates from local currency into U.S. dollars was also done in a series of steps:

2.1. Exports and imports of goods and non-factor services were each converted into 1990 dollars[6] such that their values in 1990 coincided with the "equivalent" concepts in the Balance of Payments.

2.2. The remaining elements (gross domestic product, investment and each of the sectors of origin)[7] were converted by using the conversion factor calculated for 1990 according to the following method:

The conversion factor cf_t^j is estimated as a function of the ratio of the implicit price deflator of GDP for country "j" over the implicit price deflator of the United States. The use of alternative price indicators does not significantly change the results. However, for Trinidad and Tobago the consumer price index is preferred.

$$cf_t^j = a^j \left(IPD_t^j / IPD_t^{us}\right)^{b^j} \qquad (1)$$

Where
cf_t^j = conversion factor for year t for country j
IPD_t^j = implicit price deflator for year t for country j
j = country for which estimate is being carried out
US = United States
t = year

The estimation of the parameters aj and bj were carried out through a least squares regression for annual data for the period 1960-94. The exchange rate observed is the principal rate published in *International Financial Statistics* by the International Monetary Fund. The use of alternative exchange rates in the case of multiple exchange rate systems or parallel rates does not significantly modify the estimate of the coefficients over this period of time. The regression was performed for each country where exchange rates varied sufficiently to allow reasonable estimates. There were 17 such cases. Of the remaining countries, several had only recently experienced exchange rate variations (e.g., Guatemala and the Dominican Republic), while others have not modified their exchange rates (Bahamas, Panama). In these cases GDP-weighted averages of three years around 1990 were used to estimate the conversion factor in 1990:

$$cf_t^j = \left(\sum_{k=1987}^{1989} GDP_k^j \cdot EX_k^j\right) \Big/ \left(\sum_{k=1987}^{1989} GDP_k^j\right) \qquad (2)$$

Where

EX^j = market exchange rate of country j

GDP^j = nominal gross domestic product of country j

If the assumption is that in the long run the exchange rate moves in line with the relative prices of the country vis-à-vis the United States, the coefficient bj should be equal to 1.

The classification by economic activity corresponds to the major divisions of the *International Standard Industrial Classification of all Economic Activities* (ISIC), Series M, No. 4, Rev. 2, United Nations (1968), as published in *A System of National Accounts,* Studies in Methods, Series F, No. 2, Rev. 3, United Nations, New York, 1968.

Each activity has been briefly identified in each table. The complete description under each heading for those which are incomplete is as follows:

Agriculture, Forestry and Fishing: Agriculture, Hunting, Forestry and Fishing.

Wholesale and Retail Trade: Wholesale and Retail Trade, Restaurants and Hotels.

Transport and Communications: Transport, Storage and Communications.

Financial services: Financing, Insurance, Real Estate, and Services to Enterprises including adjustments for banking services, and in those cases where series are presented at market prices, payments of import duties less subsidies on imports.

Other services: Community, Social and Personal Services.

The aggregation of activities into major sectors is as follows:

Industry: includes Mining and Quarrying, Manufacturing, Electricity, Gas and Water, and Construction.

Services: includes Wholesale and Retail Trade, Transport and Communications, Financial, Government and Other Services.

Growth Rate Calculations:

Growth rates for any period (e.g., 1970-80) are based on a geometric average formula between 1970 and 1980. The growth rate for the Latin American region is calculated over the set of countries for which data are available both for the beginning and the end of the period.

Source:

The original National Account data used for this presentation come from official sources in the member countries. For each country, the source is identified under the heading "Total GDP" in the list of sources accompanying the Statistical Profile for each country chapter.

---

[1] Argentina, 1986; Barbados, 1974; Bolivia, 1990; Brazil, 1980; Chile, 1986; Colombia, 1975; Costa Rica, 1966; Dominican Republic, 1970; Ecuador, 1975; El Salvador, 1990; Guatemala, 1958; Guyana, 1988; Haiti, 1976; Honduras, 1978; Jamaica, 1986; Mexico, 1980; Nicaragua, 1980; Panama, 1970; Paraguay, 1982; Peru, 1979; Suriname, 1980; Trinidad and Tobago, 1985; Uruguay, 1983; and Venezuela, 1984.

[2] The determination of a common base year across a group of countries is not without its problems given the different economic situations affecting individual countries and the difficulty of evaluating the degree of "normality" of a system of relative prices.

[3] For those countries that measure value added by sector at factor cost or basic prices rather than market prices (see the note to Table B-3), an adjustment has been made for net indirect taxes (the difference between the two).

[4] As Gross Domestic Product is calculated as the sum of the rebased sectors, the growth rate for it may differ in some years from that calculated using a country's constant price series on its original base year. However, the observed differences between the two series over the period 1960 to 1994 were, on average, less than 1 percent.

[5] Since consumption is a residual item, its annual growth rate in 1990 prices may be different from the growth rate obtained from the original series for a few countries in some years, but the trend remains the same.

[6] Converting local currencies into dollars remains a difficult operation due to the large and sometimes erratic movements in relative prices and exchange rates in the countries of the region, not to mention the difficulty of arriving at a correct statistical estimation of these movements. If available, conversion factors based on the Purchasing Power Parity methodology of the International Comparison Project would have been preferred. This option will be pursued in the future. For the time being, it was decided to temporarily adopt a method of smoothing out the market-based exchange rate. This last method is based on the idea that an underlying real long-run exchange rate, or fundamental equilibrium exchange rate, exists. However, it is realized that this method is imperfect because the market exchange rate bears little reference to the relative prices of nontradable goods and services.

The intensity of the bias depends on the importance of the nontradable sector in the country, and on the situation of the relative prices between tradable and nontradable goods. In extreme low-income countries where the agriculture and services sectors are important, the bias may be higher and the estimate of per capita GDP will probably be underestimated. Smoothing out the exchange rate helps to avoid sharp swings due to variable supply and demand conditions for foreign currency.

[7] Consumption is directly available as a residual component in dollars. The implicit conversion factor for consumption changes slightly over time, and is somewhat different from the conversion factor (calculated in step two). For this reason, the growth rate of consumption in 1990 dollars may differ slightly from the growth rate in local currency. In general the difference is small, and the trend is the same.

TABLE C-1. CURRENT REVENUES

(As a Percent of GDP)

Country	1986	1987	1988	1989	1990	1991	1992	1993	1994	1995p
Argentina	15.6	14.7	13.1	14.0	13.4	15.4	17.7	17.5	16.8	...
Bahamas	17.0	16.9	14.8	15.2	15.9	15.9	17.5	16.8	18.7	19.6
Barbados	25.8	25.3	28.9	29.2	27.4	30.2	31.0	30.8	29.0	29.9
Belize[1]	24.5	24.0	25.5	26.1	26.1	24.8	25.2	23.8	24.4	22.5
Bolivia[2]	14.7	13.8	13.5	7.1	7.2	7.4	9.0	9.1	10.3	16.9
Brazil	23.3	35.5	21.4	21.5	24.2	22.1	24.3	...	...	...
Chile	30.9	30.6	31.4	29.6	25.7	27.1	26.3	25.8	25.5	25.9
Colombia	9.7	10.6	10.1	10.1	10.1	12.0	12.2	13.7	14.0	13.9
Costa Rica	15.4	15.7	15.5	15.3	14.5	14.8	15.5	15.7	15.1	16.7
Dominican Republic	12.0	12.7	14.9	15.7	12.5	13.6	15.3	15.9	15.1	15.0
Ecuador	14.3	14.0	15.1	16.6	18.3	15.5	15.9	16.0	15.7	17.9
El Salvador	16.0	12.8	11.4	9.4	9.5	10.3	11.0	11.1	11.8	12.7
Guatemala	8.9	9.4	10.1	9.5	8.1	9.1	10.6	9.1	7.6	8.4
Guyana	45.9	36.3	41.6	31.1	34.2	36.5	38.0	37.9	32.7	35.3
Haiti	...	...	...	...	7.3	7.6	5.5	5.5	3.3	7.0
Honduras	15.5	16.0	15.6	14.8	16.5	17.7	17.3	16.9	16.4	18.8
Jamaica	31.9	28.7	28.5	29.9	27.6	28.8	28.7	31.4	31.6	34.2
Mexico	16.0	17.1	16.8	17.8	17.1	20.5	20.6	17.1	16.8	17.3
Nicaragua	32.0	27.7	20.3	23.0	14.6	19.3	20.4	19.5	20.1	21.4
Panama	20.0	20.2	13.1	12.2	25.8	19.6	21.0	20.2	19.8	19.8
Paraguay	7.8	8.9	8.9	12.3	12.6	11.8	12.5	12.5	14.5	15.5
Peru	12.1	9.0	8.2	6.5	8.8	9.1	11.0	11.1	13.1	13.7
Suriname	31.0	29.0	29.3	31.2	31.5	27.2	22.4	11.0	19.4	31.6
Trinidad and Tobago	31.6	30.7	28.6	26.3	25.7	29.9	26.3	27.4	26.1	26.9
Uruguay	16.8	16.3	16.8	15.6	17.8	18.3	18.9	18.5	18.7	18.9
Venezuela	20.6	22.3	18.1	19.8	22.4	22.8	17.2	16.5	17.7	15.9

[1] 1995 data derived from calendar year (January - December); in previous years, fiscal year (April - March) used.
[2] Due to changes in methodology and coverage, data from 1989 are not comparable with those of earlier years.

TABLE C-2. TOTAL EXPENDITURES

(As a Percent of GDP)

Country	1986	1987	1988	1989	1990	1991	1992	1993	1994	1995p
Argentina	19.5	19.5	17.5	16.8	15.6	17.5	18.8	17.9	17.0	...
Bahamas	17.5	17.5	17.8	19.3	18.3	20.2	19.8	17.5	19.4	20.7
Barbados	31.1	30.5	31.2	30.0	34.2	32.3	32.1	31.0	30.8	27.7
Belize[1]	30.0	25.5	18.8	27.7	27.1	29.7	30.0	31.9	32.8	28.0
Bolivia[2]	17.4	17.8	19.3	13.5	14.4	13.4	15.4	15.9	17.1	19.0
Brazil	37.6	48.6	37.9	41.7	39.6	27.8	31.9	...	...	...
Chile	31.6	28.5	28.1	24.9	24.5	25.1	23.6	23.8	23.6	22.6
Colombia	11.0	11.1	11.8	11.8	11.2	12.8	14.5	14.8	15.7	16.8
Costa Rica	18.8	17.7	18.0	19.4	18.9	17.9	17.5	17.6	21.9	21.3
Dominican Republic	13.6	14.5	15.5	15.3	12.5	10.8	12.5	16.3	16.3	14.5
Ecuador	16.4	20.2	17.1	16.2	14.8	14.1	16.2	15.6	15.8	19.6
El Salvador	21.4	17.0	16.3	14.9	13.4	15.5	16.2	14.6	14.2	14.1
Guatemala	10.8	11.8	12.9	13.2	10.2	9.1	10.7	10.5	9.2	9.1
Guyana	105.9	80.9	74.9	48.6	71.7	50.8	58.8	47.5	46.7	46.6
Haiti	...	...	...	...	9.1	8.3	8.6	9.6	7.7	12.8
Honduras	23.7	23.4	22.4	21.3	23.0	21.9	24.8	27.4	21.6	22.5
Jamaica	33.3	32.1	34.9	32.2	26.8	27.8	26.7	29.2	31.3	34.7
Mexico	29.1	31.3	26.5	22.8	20.0	17.3	16.1	16.7	17.4	18.0
Nicaragua	48.0	44.2	45.9	29.9	34.8	27.0	28.1	27.4	30.0	29.4
Panama	24.7	24.6	18.4	19.2	19.1	19.9	25.3	20.2	20.6	19.7
Paraguay	7.9	8.6	8.4	10.0	9.5	12.1	13.6	13.1	13.8	16.1
Peru	16.5	15.9	12.0	12.8	12.3	10.7	12.7	13.0	14.9	15.9
Suriname	57.3	54.2	51.5	48.6	41.7	46.5	41.8	37.3	36.1	36.3
Trinidad and Tobago	37.5	36.5	34.3	30.7	27.4	30.2	29.2	27.7	26.3	26.6
Uruguay	18.1	17.6	18.7	19.0	17.8	17.9	18.6	19.6	20.8	21.1
Venezuela	21.0	23.9	25.6	20.8	24.5	24.2	21.0	19.0	24.0	20.7

[1] 1995 data derived from calendar year (January - December); in previous years, fiscal year (April - March) used.
[2] Due to changes in methodology and coverage, data from 1989 are not comparable with those of earlier years.

TABLE C-3. CURRENT SAVINGS

(As a Percent of GDP)

Country	1986	1987	1988	1989	1990	1991	1992	1993	1994	1995p
Argentina	-1.0	-1.8	-2.3	-0.2	-0.8	-0.8	-0.3	0.6	0.7	...
Bahamas	1.4	1.5	-0.2	-0.6	0.2	-1.1	0.7	1.5	2.0	1.6
Barbados	1.6	1.2	4.5	4.5	0.2	2.7	2.3	3.3	2.3	4.5
Belize[1]	2.0	3.8	7.3	8.6	9.3	7.3	5.7	2.9	2.6	1.7
Bolivia[2]	-0.4	-2.6	-2.3	-0.7	0.4	1.9	0.0	-0.8	-1.8	0.3
Brazil	-5.2	8.7	-13.3	-21.7	-24.7	-5.5	-8.6	...	...	...
Chile	4.8	7.6	10.4	8.9	6.4	6.5	7.1	6.4	6.6	7.7
Colombia	1.3	1.9	1.1	0.7	1.1	2.7	2.0	1.8	1.0	0.1
Costa Rica	0.5	0.4	-0.1	-1.1	-2.3	-1.6	-0.2	0.0	-4.6	-2.6
Dominican Republic	1.9	5.0	7.0	9.0	6.0	8.2	9.4	7.7	7.4	7.1
Ecuador	1.1	-3.4	0.1	2.7	6.3	3.2	2.5	3.2	3.3	2.6
El Salvador	1.0	-0.8	-1.4	-2.6	-1.9	-1.8	-0.6	-0.2	0.3	1.8
Guatemala	0.0	-0.3	-0.2	-0.6	-0.3	1.5	2.9	1.7	0.8	1.9
Guyana	-5.0	-27.2	-10.3	-4.9	-14.5	-8.6	-11.3	2.9	0.2	2.9
Haiti	...	...	...	...	-1.5	-0.6	-2.9	-3.7	-4.0	-4.6
Honduras	-3.0	-2.0	-1.9	-2.7	-0.7	1.5	0.0	-1.5	0.1	3.3
Jamaica	5.1	3.6	2.3	4.1	4.9	6.1	7.3	6.7	5.2	5.3
Mexico	-9.5	-11.0	-7.8	-3.1	-0.2	5.5	7.0	2.6	1.7	1.2
Nicaragua	-9.4	-11.8	-19.5	-3.6	-18.6	-4.2	-1.8	-1.1	-0.9	2.5
Panama	-2.8	-3.3	-4.8	-6.1	7.1	2.8	-2.4	2.3	1.8	2.3
Paraguay	1.2	2.2	2.7	3.7	4.7	2.3	0.9	1.3	3.1	3.7
Peru	-1.4	-4.5	-2.5	-4.2	-2.2	-0.1	1.0	1.1	1.9	1.5
Suriname	-24.2	-23.9	-19.7	-13.5	-6.3	-17.8	-17.1	-23.2	-13.3	-1.4
Trinidad and Tobago	-0.8	1.3	-2.3	-2.0	-0.1	3.1	-1.2	1.4	1.4	2.0
Uruguay	0.3	0.5	0.1	-1.1	1.9	2.1	2.0	1.1	0.6	0.2
Venezuela	6.1	5.7	-0.4	2.3	3.4	5.0	1.6	2.2	0.4	-0.4

[1] 1995 data derived from calendar year (January - December); in previous years, fiscal year (April - March) used.
[2] Due to changes in methodology and coverage, data from 1989 are not comparable with those of earlier years.

TABLE C-4. OVERALL SURPLUS OR DEFICIT

(As a Percent of GDP)

Country	1986	1987	1988	1989	1990	1991	1992	1993	1994	1995p
Argentina	-3.2	-4.4	-3.8	-2.6	-1.7	-1.2	-0.1	0.3	0.1	...
Bahamas	-0.5	-0.6	-3.0	-4.1	-2.4	-4.3	-2.3	-0.7	-0.6	-0.8
Barbados	-5.3	-5.3	-2.3	-0.8	-6.7	-2.1	-1.1	-0.1	-1.8	2.3
Belize[1]	-4.5	0.4	7.1	-0.8	0.7	-3.2	-3.4	-6.7	-7.4	-4.1
Bolivia[2]	-1.7	-3.7	-5.0	-2.0	-1.3	0.7	-1.0	-3.7	-3.4	-0.6
Brazil	-14.0	-12.6	-16.3	-17.5	-6.2	-0.5	-3.9	...	...	...
Chile	-0.5	2.3	3.6	5.0	1.4	2.2	2.8	2.0	2.0	3.5
Colombia	-1.3	-0.5	-1.4	-1.7	-0.1	-0.8	-2.2	-0.9	0.9	-2.9
Costa Rica	-3.3	-2.0	-2.5	-4.1	-4.4	-3.1	-1.9	-1.9	-6.9	-4.6
Dominican Republic	-0.4	-1.3	0.0	0.7	0.5	3.6	3.8	0.5	-0.1	1.2
Ecuador	-2.2	-6.2	-2.0	0.4	3.5	1.4	-0.3	0.4	-0.1	-1.7
El Salvador	-3.6	-0.9	-3.0	-3.7	-1.5	-3.2	-3.3	-1.3	-0.8	-0.5
Guatemala	-1.5	-1.3	-1.7	-2.9	-1.8	0.0	0.5	-1.3	-1.4	-0.7
Guyana	-58.8	-42.4	-31.6	-6.6	-22.9	-15.6	-17.1	-6.0	-6.8	-7.9
Haiti	...	...	...	...	-1.3	-0.5	-2.8	-3.8	-4.3	-1.9
Honduras	-6.0	-5.8	-4.1	-6.0	-4.1	-3.2	-5.4	-7.8	-4.7	-3.2
Jamaica	0.7	1.5	-1.5	-0.2	3.0	4.4	4.2	3.5	1.9	1.0
Mexico	-13.1	-14.2	-9.7	-5.0	-2.8	3.2	4.5	0.4	-0.6	-0.6
Nicaragua	-14.5	-16.0	-25.1	-3.5	-18.7	4.1	-3.3	0.0	-4.9	-0.1
Panama	-4.5	-4.2	-5.2	-6.9	6.8	-0.1	-4.0	0.1	0.0	0.3
Paraguay	0.0	0.4	0.6	2.4	3.2	-0.2	-1.0	-0.6	1.0	-0.3
Peru	-4.3	-6.9	-3.9	-6.3	-3.5	-1.5	-1.5	-1.6	2.9	-0.6
Suriname	-26.0	-24.8	-21.3	-14.0	-6.3	-17.4	-11.2	-8.3	-2.3	3.5
Trinidad and Tobago	-5.9	-5.9	-5.7	-4.2	-1.2	-0.2	-2.8	-0.2	0.0	0.4
Uruguay	-1.3	-1.3	-2.0	-3.4	-0.1	0.4	0.3	-1.1	-2.1	-2.2
Venezuela	-0.4	-1.6	-7.4	-1.0	-2.1	-0.1	-3.7	-2.4	-6.2	-4.7

[1] 1995 data derived from calendar year (January - December); in previous years, fiscal year (April - March) used.
[2] Due to changes in methodology and coverage, data from 1989 are not comparable with those of earlier years.

TABLE C-5. DOMESTIC BORROWING

(As a Percent of GDP)

Country	1986	1987	1988	1989	1990	1991	1992	1993	1994	1995p
Argentina	-0.7	0.3	0.2	1.5	-0.7	0.3	-0.8	...	...	...
Bahamas	4.1	2.7	3.4	4.3	3.9	4.0	3.8	5.3	3.7	2.4
Barbados	1.3	2.0	0.8	0.2	7.4	2.1	4.8	1.5	0.5	-0.8
Belize[1]	0.9	-1.8	...	...	...	...	...	4.0	4.5	2.9
Bolivia	...	...	...	1.2	1.6	-0.6	1.1	1.9	2.1	...
Brazil	13.9	...	...	...	...	...	...	...	...	...
Chile	-1.5	-2.4	-5.8	-5.8	-1.3	-0.9	-0.4	-0.2	-0.2	-0.4
Colombia	-0.2	0.8	0.2	1.0	0.3	0.7	1.9	1.0	0.4	0.4
Costa Rica	2.0	1.4	2.3	3.7	3.4	4.2	2.5	2.8	7.0	5.7
Dominican Republic	0.0	-1.2	-0.3	0.9	-0.1	-3.9	-1.9	-0.3	0.3	-0.8
Ecuador	...	1.6	1.5	0.8	-0.1	...	...	...	...	...
El Salvador	1.9	-0.2	2.3	3.0	-0.1	1.5	0.6	-0.3	-1.2	-0.6
Guatemala	1.7	1.3	1.5	2.4	1.5	0.9	0.1	1.3	-0.4	-0.9
Guyana	80.6	42.9	33.5	25.2	5.4	2.2	5.3	-10.8	-2.2	5.0
Haiti	...	...	...	...	1.1	0.4	2.5	3.2	3.8	-0.7
Honduras	3.5	3.9	3.4	4.6	-0.9	-1.2	-0.4	1.5	1.1	0.0
Jamaica	2.5	-2.3	-0.6	-2.8	-5.1	-8.2	-3.4	-4.3	-2.4	0.5
Mexico	...	...	...	...	...	...	...	...	...	...
Nicaragua	13.0	17.3	24.7	-0.1	10.7	-4.6	-6.1	0.0	-1.5	1.1
Panama	2.1	2.9	0.4	0.2	0.0	0.0	0.0	0.0	0.0	...
Paraguay	0.3	-0.7	-0.4	-1.6	-1.2	0.1	0.0	0.3	-1.2	-0.4
Peru	2.0	4.8	0.5	3.4	1.7	-0.5	0.6	0.1	-4.1	-0.4
Suriname	25.6	24.5	20.9	16.7	2.2	19.0	8.5	7.4	-2.2	-4.4
Trinidad and Tobago	7.4	6.0	5.8	5.0	3.3	1.9	3.6	-1.9	-1.1	2.6
Uruguay	1.5	1.3	1.9	3.3	0.1	-0.3	-0.3	0.7	1.6	...
Venezuela	3.3	-0.3	2.2	2.8	0.9	0.2	3.0	1.7	6.5	4.5

[1] 1995 data derived from calendar year (January - December); in previous years, fiscal year (April - March) used.

TABLE C-6. FOREIGN BORROWING

(As a Percent of GDP)

Country	1986	1987	1988	1989	1990	1991	1992	1993	1994	1995p
Argentina	0.7	2.1	1.2	1.0	1.4	-0.2	-0.1	...	...	...
Bahamas	3.8	0.2	0.2	1.0	0.8	0.8	0.9	0.4	0.5	0.0
Barbados	4.1	4.8	2.6	0.8	-0.2	0.2	-2.7	-1.4	1.3	3.1
Belize[1]	3.6	1.4	...	...	...	...	...	2.7	3.0	0.3
Bolivia	...	...	...	0.8	-0.2	0.0	0.8	2.4	1.7	...
Brazil	0.1	...	...	...	...	...	...	...	...	...
Chile	3.0	1.7	2.0	0.4	0.4	0.6	0.2	-1.3	0.0	-2.0
Colombia	1.5	-0.3	1.2	0.7	0.3	-0.3	-0.7	-0.6	0.2	2.6
Costa Rica	1.4	0.6	0.2	1.2	0.9	1.7	1.5	-0.9	-0.1	-1.1
Dominican Republic	0.8	0.6	0.3	-0.1	-0.1	-0.8	-1.4	-1.6	-1.3	-1.1
Ecuador	...	0.7	-0.7	-1.8	-1.9	...	...	...	...	...
El Salvador	1.7	1.1	0.7	0.7	1.3	1.6	2.6	1.7	2.0	1.2
Guatemala	0.6	0.5	0.7	0.4	0.4	0.2	-0.1	0.0	1.4	0.2
Guyana	5.5	2.9	-4.0	5.9	-11.3	4.6	7.6	8.0	4.9	5.6
Haiti	...	...	...	...	0.2	0.1	0.3	0.6	0.5	2.6
Honduras	4.7	2.8	3.7	1.9	7.1	1.4	5.3	6.8	3.4	3.2
Jamaica	-1.1	2.3	3.5	1.6	1.2	3.0	-0.7	0.8	0.5	-0.1
Mexico	...	...	...	...	...	...	...	...	...	...
Nicaragua	1.1	0.0	0.4	3.6	8.0	0.5	9.4	0.0	6.3	-1.0
Panama	1.8	0.4	0.0	0.0	0.0	2.8	1.5	0.3	0.8	...
Paraguay	-0.2	0.3	-0.1	-0.8	-1.9	0.1	1.0	0.3	0.3	0.7
Peru	2.3	2.1	3.4	2.9	1.8	2.0	0.9	1.5	1.2	0.9
Suriname	0.5	0.3	0.8	0.4	0.1	0.5	0.0	0.8	-1.1	-0.3
Trinidad and Tobago	-1.5	-0.1	-0.1	-0.8	-2.0	-1.7	-0.8	2.1	1.2	-3.0
Uruguay	-0.2	0.1	0.1	0.1	0.0	-0.1	-0.1	0.4	0.5	...
Venezuela	0.0	0.3	0.1	0.1	1.2	-0.1	0.7	0.7	-0.2	0.3

[1] 1995 data derived from calendar year (January - December); in previous years, fiscal year (April - March) used.

TABLE C-7. TAX REVENUES

(As a Percent of Current Revenue)

Country	1986	1987	1988	1989	1990	1991	1992	1993	1994	1995p
Argentina	89.4	91.2	92.1	93.2	92.1	92.3	95.0	94.0	94.0	...
Bahamas	85.0	87.1	88.7	88.0	88.0	86.5	90.0	89.6	90.4	91.3
Barbados	88.6	85.8	85.6	92.1	92.4	93.4	93.0	92.7	93.6	93.8
Belize[1]	86.9	90.3	89.4	84.7	84.3	86.1	85.2	87.7	89.6	89.3
Bolivia[2]	...	...	...	93.3	93.9	94.7	96.7	96.7	95.4	...
Brazil	76.0	46.1	73.3	73.2	83.6	75.9	70.0	...	...	...
Chile	62.0	62.2	57.7	58.6	63.2	64.8	67.4	68.9	69.6	67.7
Colombia	92.7	89.7	92.6	91.5	90.1	87.9	90.4	87.4	87.7	85.9
Costa Rica	88.9	92.2	93.0	94.4	96.3	97.0	97.2	98.1	97.6	98.2
Dominican Republic	95.3	89.6	78.3	78.7	83.6	86.9	90.3	92.9	93.4	93.3
Ecuador	58.8	61.0	51.2	50.6	43.0	49.2	46.1	47.9	50.3	44.4
El Salvador	91.2	94.5	89.9	92.4	93.2	92.4	87.7	93.2	92.1	93.3
Guatemala	79.7	87.2	87.0	83.2	84.4	81.0	78.4	87.4	88.9	90.7
Guyana	90.7	84.8	92.1	89.4	89.2	94.3	96.0	95.4	96.0	96.5
Haiti	...	...	...	...	100.0	100.0	100.0	100.0	100.0	100.0
Honduras	84.5	84.6	82.2	84.8	89.8	87.4	92.6	92.4	92.7	89.6
Jamaica	87.5	90.2	88.9	89.4	87.1	85.0	87.0	89.9	89.4	95.6
Mexico	70.4	62.9	72.2	67.5	67.2	58.4	60.1	72.7	75.0	60.5
Nicaragua	87.5	91.1	92.2	94.2	89.8	92.0	94.6	95.4	95.4	95.7
Panama	72.5	73.0	73.5	72.4	48.2	67.8	65.4	65.0	66.8	67.3
Paraguay	87.2	84.3	82.2	75.9	75.1	79.0	76.5	74.9	73.5	79.3
Peru	90.3	93.3	92.7	95.5	95.7	94.0	88.0	85.8	85.6	84.5
Suriname	68.7	63.3	66.1	62.9	64.8	74.4	72.4	67.7	86.5	86.3
Trinidad and Tobago	77.2	79.9	80.9	82.7	86.7	84.6	86.8	84.8	83.6	85.3
Uruguay	94.1	91.6	90.7	92.0	90.5	87.7	88.3	87.2	84.6	84.1
Venezuela	82.5	82.0	80.5	74.5	76.9	77.5	76.3	78.4	79.9	78.5

[1] 1995 data derived from calendar year (January - December); in previous years, fiscal year (April - March) used.
[2] Due to changes in methodology and coverage, data from 1989 are not comparable with those of earlier years.

TABLE C-8. DIRECT TAXES

(As a Percent of Current Revenue)

Country	1986	1987	1988	1989	1990	1991	1992	1993	1994	1995p
Argentina	...	...	...	...	...	...	...	...	...	...
Bahamas	3.4	3.1	3.3	3.3	3.9	4.1	3.2	3.7	3.1	2.6
Barbados	33.9	27.5	34.0	38.7	40.2	43.2	44.4	40.9	36.8	39.2
Belize[1]	20.6	22.4	21.5	19.7	20.4	22.1	25.9	24.6	27.2	22.7
Bolivia	...	...	...	...	...	...	...	...	...	...
Brazil	53.4	30.9	49.6	53.1	57.3	52.4	50.6	...	...	...
Chile	10.0	11.7	19.0	16.7	17.4	19.3	17.7	18.2	18.8	19.7
Colombia	33.3	33.3	34.5	35.4	34.9	41.6	43.9	35.3	37.3	35.3
Costa Rica	17.4	15.9	17.4	17.4	18.3	16.7	16.7	20.3	22.2	22.3
Dominican Republic	21.3	18.5	17.9	19.9	21.9	18.6	16.5	16.6	16.3	17.9
Ecuador	11.6	11.8	9.2	11.1	7.3	9.6	9.3	8.7	10.1	11.4
El Salvador	18.3	26.9	26.5	28.5	26.7	27.9	25.2	24.2	25.2	26.1
Guatemala	13.4	16.6	21.7	20.2	19.7	25.3	18.5	20.9	15.9	19.3
Guyana	40.6	36.2	36.6	34.2	36.0	41.7	33.6	32.7	34.5	36.4
Haiti	...	...	...	...	15.4	16.4	19.0	15.9	18.1	...
Honduras	21.9	23.2	24.5	24.9	21.6	22.2	27.3	28.3	20.8	24.4
Jamaica	35.5	37.2	38.5	38.4	41.5	36.4	36.4	34.6	35.5	...
Mexico	27.2	23.8	30.4	29.4	28.7	24.9	28.2	35.0	33.6	26.6
Nicaragua	22.3	22.9	18.6	23.5	24.9	17.6	16.6	13.2	10.8	13.2
Panama	37.0	37.1	38.5	31.5	21.1	31.3	29.9	29.1	29.5	31.2
Paraguay	27.3	24.4	21.7	17.0	14.7	16.8	18.9	18.7	19.9	21.2
Peru	27.1	24.1	27.4	23.6	14.3	14.2	16.5	18.7	18.3	19.3
Suriname	31.4	30.3	34.7	35.1	37.4	42.1	38.5	38.2	46.8	49.3
Trinidad and Tobago	55.5	58.4	55.8	54.7	48.6	52.0	47.8	43.5	46.4	52.8
Uruguay	19.6	19.2	19.8	15.2	14.0	11.8	14.7	16.2	15.6	16.4
Venezuela	46.9	47.6	58.3	62.3	67.6	65.5	56.5	53.9	41.8	42.0

[1] 1995 data derived from calendar year (January - December); in previous years, fiscal year (April - March) used.

TABLE C-9. INDIRECT TAXES

(As a Percent of Current Revenue)

Country	1986	1987	1988	1989	1990	1991	1992	1993	1994	1995p
Argentina	...	...	...	...	...	...	...	...	...	...
Bahamas	81.6	84.1	86.4	84.6	84.1	82.4	86.8	85.9	87.2	88.7
Barbados	54.8	58.3	51.7	53.5	52.3	50.2	48.7	51.8	56.8	54.6
Belize[1]	66.3	67.9	67.9	65.0	64.0	64.0	59.3	63.2	62.4	66.6
Bolivia	...	...	...	...	...	...	...	...	...	...
Brazil	22.6	15.2	23.7	20.1	26.3	23.5	19.4	...	...	...
Chile	52.0	50.5	38.7	41.8	45.8	45.5	49.7	50.7	50.7	48.0
Colombia	59.4	56.4	58.1	56.0	55.2	46.4	46.4	51.6	50.2	50.5
Costa Rica	71.5	76.3	75.6	77.0	78.1	80.2	80.5	77.8	75.4	75.9
Dominican Republic	74.0	71.0	60.4	58.7	61.6	68.3	73.8	76.2	77.1	75.3
Ecuador	47.2	49.2	42.0	39.5	35.8	39.5	36.8	39.2	40.1	33.0
El Salvador	73.9	71.0	64.5	63.9	69.7	64.3	62.4	67.1	65.4	66.3
Guatemala	66.3	70.6	65.3	63.0	64.7	55.7	59.9	66.5	73.0	71.5
Guyana	50.2	48.6	55.5	55.2	53.2	52.6	62.3	62.7	61.6	60.1
Haiti	...	...	...	...	84.6	83.6	81.0	84.1	81.9	...
Honduras	62.6	61.3	57.7	59.9	68.2	65.1	65.4	64.2	59.4	55.5
Jamaica	52.1	52.9	50.4	51.0	45.6	48.6	50.6	55.2	53.9	...
Mexico	43.2	39.0	41.8	38.1	38.5	33.4	31.9	37.7	41.4	33.9
Nicaragua	65.2	68.1	73.6	70.5	64.7	74.4	77.9	82.2	84.6	82.5
Panama	35.4	35.8	35.0	40.9	27.1	36.5	35.6	35.9	37.3	36.0
Paraguay	60.0	59.9	60.5	58.9	60.4	62.1	57.6	56.2	53.6	58.1
Peru	63.2	69.2	65.3	71.9	81.4	79.9	71.5	67.0	67.2	65.2
Suriname	37.3	32.9	31.4	27.8	27.4	32.3	33.9	29.5	39.7	37.0
Trinidad and Tobago	21.7	21.5	25.1	28.0	38.0	32.5	39.0	41.3	37.2	32.4
Uruguay	74.5	72.4	70.9	76.9	76.5	75.8	73.6	71.0	68.9	67.8
Venezuela	35.6	34.5	22.2	12.3	9.3	12.0	19.9	24.5	38.1	36.5

[1] 1995 data derived from calendar year (January - December); in previous years, fiscal year (April - March) used.

TABLE C-10. NON-TAX REVENUES

(As a Percent of Current Revenue)

Country	1986	1987	1988	1989	1990	1991	1992	1993	1994	1995p
Argentina	10.6	8.8	7.9	6.8	7.9	7.7	5.0	6.0	6.0	...
Bahamas	15.0	12.9	11.3	12.0	12.0	13.5	10.0	10.4	9.6	8.7
Barbados	11.4	14.2	14.4	7.9	7.6	6.6	7.0	7.3	6.4	6.2
Belize[1]	13.1	9.7	10.6	15.3	15.7	13.9	14.8	12.3	10.4	10.7
Bolivia	...	...	...	2.4	2.4	2.2	1.9	2.1	1.9	...
Brazil	24.0	53.9	26.7	26.8	16.4	24.1	30.0	...	...	...
Chile	38.0	37.8	42.3	41.4	36.8	35.2	32.6	31.1	30.4	32.3
Colombia	7.3	10.3	7.4	8.5	9.9	12.1	9.6	12.6	12.3	14.1
Costa Rica	11.1	7.8	7.0	5.6	3.7	3.0	2.8	1.9	2.4	1.8
Dominican Republic	4.7	10.4	21.7	21.3	16.4	13.1	9.7	7.1	6.6	6.7
Ecuador	41.2	39.0	48.8	49.4	57.0	50.8	53.9	52.1	49.7	55.6
El Salvador	8.8	5.5	10.1	7.6	6.8	7.6	12.3	6.8	7.9	6.7
Guatemala	20.3	12.8	13.0	16.8	15.6	19.0	21.6	12.6	11.1	9.3
Guyana	9.3	15.2	7.9	10.6	10.8	5.7	4.0	4.6	4.0	3.5
Haiti	...	...	...	...	...	...	...	...	...	...
Honduras	15.5	15.4	17.8	15.2	10.2	12.6	7.4	7.6	4.2	7.8
Jamaica	12.5	9.8	11.1	10.6	12.9	15.0	13.0	10.1	10.6	4.4
Mexico	29.6	37.1	27.8	32.5	32.8	41.6	39.9	27.3	25.0	39.5
Nicaragua	12.5	8.9	7.8	5.8	10.2	8.0	5.4	4.6	4.6	4.3
Panama	27.5	27.0	26.5	27.6	51.8	32.2	34.6	35.0	33.2	32.7
Paraguay	12.8	15.7	17.8	24.1	24.9	21.0	23.5	25.1	26.5	20.7
Peru	9.7	6.7	7.3	4.5	4.3	6.0	12.0	14.2	14.4	15.5
Suriname	31.3	36.7	33.9	37.1	35.2	25.6	27.6	32.3	13.5	13.7
Trinidad and Tobago	22.8	20.1	19.1	17.3	13.3	15.4	13.2	15.2	16.4	14.7
Uruguay	5.9	8.4	9.3	8.0	9.5	12.3	11.7	12.8	15.4	15.9
Venezuela	17.5	18.0	19.5	25.5	23.1	22.5	23.7	21.6	20.1	21.5

[1] 1995 data derived from calendar year (January - December); in previous years, fiscal year (April - March) used.

TABLE C-11. CURRENT EXPENDITURES

(As a Percent of Total Expenditures)

Country	1986	1987	1988	1989	1990	1991	1992	1993	1994	1995p
Argentina	85.4	84.6	87.9	84.2	90.7	92.6	95.7	94.6	95.0	...
Bahamas	88.9	88.2	84.2	82.0	85.9	84.1	85.0	87.5	85.8	87.2
Barbados	78.1	78.8	78.4	82.5	79.8	85.2	89.4	88.6	86.5	91.6
Belize[1]	75.3	79.5	97.2	62.8	61.9	58.7	65.1	65.4	66.7	74.2
Bolivia[2]	86.8	92.3	82.0	83.6	82.9	83.8	83.3	82.5	80.6	87.2
Brazil	75.9	55.1	91.6	103.6	123.5	99.3	103.1	...	...	...
Chile	82.6	80.6	74.6	83.2	78.7	82.2	81.3	81.2	79.9	80.8
Colombia	75.8	78.6	77.1	79.3	80.5	72.7	71.0	80.7	83.1	82.4
Costa Rica	79.6	86.6	86.6	84.5	88.7	92.0	90.0	88.8	89.5	90.8
Dominican Republic	74.4	53.5	51.5	43.8	52.2	50.6	47.8	50.1	47.2	54.7
Ecuador	80.2	85.8	88.2	86.0	81.1	86.8	83.2	82.4	78.1	78.3
El Salvador	70.0	79.7	78.8	80.3	85.0	78.1	71.6	77.2	80.9	77.7
Guatemala	82.5	81.9	80.7	76.2	83.0	83.0	72.8	70.9	74.8	71.3
Guyana	48.1	78.5	69.4	74.0	67.8	88.7	84.0	73.7	69.7	69.6
Haiti	70.2	67.1	67.7	69.6	97.0	98.0	98.0	96.6	95.4	91.4
Honduras	78.3	76.8	78.0	81.9	74.6	74.3	69.6	67.1	75.7	69.0
Jamaica	80.3	78.3	74.9	80.0	84.5	81.7	80.1	84.6	84.4	83.3
Mexico	87.8	89.7	92.7	91.4	86.7	86.9	84.8	86.7	86.5	89.5
Nicaragua	86.3	89.3	86.7	88.9	95.5	87.0	78.7	75.2	69.9	64.1
Panama	92.5	95.5	97.2	95.2	97.6	84.6	92.7	88.7	87.5	89.0
Paraguay	83.8	77.9	73.6	86.1	83.1	78.9	85.5	84.7	82.6	73.0
Peru	82.2	85.2	88.5	83.5	89.5	86.4	79.2	76.8	75.3	77.1
Suriname	96.2	97.6	95.1	92.2	90.6	96.7	94.5	91.6	90.6	90.9
Trinidad and Tobago	86.4	80.3	89.9	92.2	94.2	88.7	94.4	94.2	93.6	93.3
Uruguay	91.1	89.4	88.9	87.9	89.1	90.6	90.9	88.7	87.0	88.7
Venezuela	68.9	69.2	72.3	84.3	77.7	73.4	74.6	75.2	72.4	78.9

[1] 1995 data derived from calendar year (January - December); in previous years, fiscal year (April - March) used.
[2] Due to changes in methodology and coverage, data from 1989 are not comparable with those of earlier years.

TABLE C-12. PURCHASE OF GOODS AND SERVICES

(As a Percent of Total Expenditures)

Country	1986	1987	1988	1989	1990	1991	1992	1993	1994	1995p
Argentina	20.0	21.4	22.4	21.2	21.5	20.0	18.9	17.1	17.2	...
Bahamas	71.3	73.5	68.4	67.4	69.6	67.3	67.3	67.4	66.5	67.2
Barbados	46.1	47.2	45.2	49.1	47.1	49.3	48.0	49.2	48.2	50.8
Belize[1]	56.5	60.7	78.7	51.6	52.4	49.0	55.6	53.2	53.5	58.8
Bolivia[2]	39.3	45.5	46.8	54.8	52.6	54.6	52.0	49.6	47.4	...
Brazil	10.1	10.8	15.4	15.5	14.7	18.3	12.2	...	...	...
Chile	30.2	30.1	27.6	28.8	28.4	30.2	31.5	32.4	32.9	32.2
Colombia	24.8	24.3	23.2	24.4	27.1	22.3	21.8	24.9	25.9	23.9
Costa Rica	33.8	35.7	35.6	34.0	35.3	34.9	33.1	34.8	29.8	31.0
Dominican Republic	37.0	28.6	24.8	23.9	27.4	25.1	26.4	24.6	25.8	29.6
Ecuador	43.7	51.8	39.0	37.8	42.6	47.2	43.8	45.5	45.3	36.4
El Salvador	50.9	62.2	59.3	60.5	61.1	49.1	45.4	45.9	46.9	49.3
Guatemala	53.0	51.6	51.0	47.0	56.0	47.8	47.9	46.3	47.9	41.3
Guyana	24.8	30.7	30.0	28.0	15.9	20.4	20.5	25.2	26.4	26.2
Haiti	...	...	...	...	84.5	89.2	81.9	78.0	83.3	71.6
Honduras	57.7	54.4	56.0	60.7	53.6	47.9	43.1	37.3	44.3	40.9
Jamaica	40.2	38.9	35.6	37.2	40.4	39.6	34.3	50.0	46.4	45.6
Mexico	13.8	12.6	13.5	16.6	17.0	22.1	17.2	18.6	19.1	16.3
Nicaragua	73.3	78.8	66.2	76.5	81.2	58.3	50.4	46.9	38.0	31.8
Panama	55.5	60.6	71.0	66.6	63.3	53.4	55.0	50.7	46.6	45.2
Paraguay	45.5	44.5	39.9	40.1	49.2	47.5	50.0	56.2	54.0	49.8
Peru	46.6	49.9	39.1	38.4	35.5	34.8	38.5	36.6	36.3	39.3
Suriname	72.0	71.5	67.9	63.5	60.5	58.1	65.3	65.6	65.2	74.8
Trinidad and Tobago	47.9	45.7	47.0	43.6	43.6	42.1	45.1	45.6	44.0	44.3
Uruguay	73.6	72.4	71.6	69.5	69.6	72.4	73.8	74.1	74.1	74.9
Venezuela	28.2	23.0	21.8	24.5	20.3	22.1	26.4	24.6	21.4	21.9

[1] 1995 data derived from calendar year (January - December); in previous years, fiscal year (April - March) used.
[2] Due to changes in methodology and coverage, data from 1989 are not comparable with those of earlier years.

TABLE C-13. INTEREST PAYMENTS

(As a Percent of Total Expenditures)

Country	1986	1987	1988	1989	1990	1991	1992	1993	1994	1995p
Argentina	8.8	7.3	4.9	5.1	4.1	8.2	8.6	5.5	6.6	...
Bahamas	11.4	9.1	10.6	9.3	10.8	11.7	11.0	13.4	11.6	11.8
Barbados	8.9	11.1	11.3	10.9	11.4	13.8	18.4	14.7	14.3	14.3
Belize[1]	10.3	10.0	11.3	6.7	5.0	4.2	4.4	6.2	6.5	7.4
Bolivia[2]	...	...	...	7.2	8.3	10.0	9.7	11.4	12.5	...
Brazil	33.7	20.7	45.9	58.0	72.5	31.2	45.2	...	...	...
Chile	4.9	6.2	7.9	11.4	8.2	7.3	6.0	5.2	4.1	3.2
Colombia	9.1	11.8	11.5	11.5	11.9	10.9	8.4	9.3	9.1	9.0
Costa Rica	12.9	15.3	15.2	15.2	17.6	23.2	20.8	17.7	18.6	27.0
Dominican Republic	8.5	8.4	9.1	4.5	3.3	6.5	4.2	7.8	5.4	6.4
Ecuador	15.9	19.3	26.2	30.2	22.5	23.0	22.8	23.3	21.7	17.6
El Salvador	6.9	6.9	6.1	6.8	9.1	16.5	13.3	13.7	11.2	9.5
Guatemala	12.2	11.7	11.4	10.4	11.1	17.5	9.2	8.6	9.7	11.0
Guyana	16.3	35.6	27.2	23.0	37.3	43.8	41.5	35.0	34.6	31.9
Haiti	...	...	...	...	8.3	6.6	7.3	9.9	9.5	5.2
Honduras	10.8	12.9	13.5	14.3	11.4	14.2	18.6	17.2	21.9	19.9
Jamaica	32.4	30.1	26.1	30.6	33.1	31.8	33.7	32.9	36.0	37.0
Mexico	46.7	56.2	57.4	49.5	41.9	28.4	21.7	15.0	12.2	23.9
Nicaragua	2.6	0.7	0.2	0.0	0.0	4.2	10.2	14.0	17.2	13.3
Panama	28.3	24.4	13.2	15.6	17.2	13.1	17.4	15.0	18.2	15.4
Paraguay	6.7	9.5	9.5	16.1	10.7	8.4	6.8	6.0	4.8	4.5
Peru	20.1	17.5	28.2	23.4	27.6	25.1	16.4	17.5	14.0	11.6
Suriname	5.9	7.9	9.2	10.5	10.9	10.0	9.5	9.3	5.7	5.1
Trinidad and Tobago	6.8	7.4	11.3	16.0	16.7	15.9	18.3	21.3	20.8	19.5
Uruguay	10.4	8.7	8.7	10.3	10.4	9.5	7.7	7.2	6.1	7.1
Venezuela	11.4	15.3	10.5	16.6	16.0	14.3	16.6	15.9	16.8	22.1

[1] 1995 data derived from calendar year (January - December); in previous years, fiscal year (April - March) used.
[2] Due to changes in methodology and coverage, data from 1989 are not comparable with those of earlier years.

TABLE C-14. CURRENT TRANSFERS AND SUBSIDIES

(As a Percent of Total Expenditures)

Country	1986	1987	1988	1989	1990	1991	1992	1993	1994	1995p
Argentina	56.5	55.9	60.7	58.0	64.4	63.7	68.2	72.1	37.6	...
Bahamas	6.2	5.6	5.2	5.2	5.6	5.1	6.7	6.8	7.7	8.2
Barbados	23.0	20.6	21.9	22.5	21.3	22.1	22.9	24.6	24.1	26.5
Belize[1]	8.4	8.9	7.2	4.5	4.5	5.5	5.0	6.0	6.7	8.0
Bolivia[2]	22.1	27.0	16.3	11.4	13.5	9.7	8.0	7.2	10.9	...
Brazil	32.2	23.6	30.3	30.1	36.3	49.8	45.7	...	...	...
Chile	47.6	44.3	39.1	43.0	42.2	44.7	43.9	43.6	43.0	45.5
Colombia	41.9	42.5	42.0	43.2	41.0	39.4	38.8	46.5	48.1	49.5
Costa Rica	32.9	35.6	35.8	35.2	35.9	33.9	36.1	36.3	41.0	32.9
Dominican Republic	23.9	13.8	15.3	12.2	17.1	14.7	11.5	11.0	8.7	12.7
Ecuador	14.3	12.7	21.5	17.3	14.7	14.3	12.1	12.0	8.2	7.2
El Salvador	12.1	10.6	13.3	13.0	14.8	12.5	12.9	17.6	22.8	18.9
Guatemala	17.3	18.6	18.3	18.8	15.8	17.8	15.7	16.0	17.2	19.0
Guyana	2.9	5.3	6.9	15.6	11.5	20.0	18.2	13.0	5.3	5.8
Haiti	...	...	...	...	1.3	1.0	0.6	1.9	0.0	15.3
Honduras	9.8	9.5	8.5	6.8	9.6	12.2	7.8	12.6	8.7	7.7
Jamaica	7.7	9.3	13.2	12.3	11.0	10.3	12.1	1.6	2.0	0.7
Mexico	23.2	19.0	21.5	23.4	25.1	31.9	43.8	49.9	53.7	49.3
Nicaragua	10.4	9.8	20.3	12.4	14.4	24.5	18.1	14.3	14.6	18.9
Panama	8.7	10.4	13.0	13.0	17.1	18.1	20.2	23.1	22.6	28.5
Paraguay	19.8	17.0	15.5	19.9	18.9	19.9	24.4	21.2	18.7	18.1
Peru	15.4	17.8	21.1	21.7	26.5	26.5	24.3	22.6	25.0	26.3
Suriname	18.3	18.2	18.0	18.2	19.2	28.6	19.8	16.8	19.7	11.1
Trinidad and Tobago	31.7	27.2	31.6	32.6	33.9	30.8	30.9	27.3	28.8	29.5
Uruguay	6.2	5.7	6.0	5.6	9.0	8.7	9.4	7.4	6.9	6.7
Venezuela	29.3	31.0	33.1	40.4	30.7	29.3	31.3	32.6	22.5	28.7

[1] 1995 data derived from calendar year (January - December); in previous years, fiscal year (April - March) used.
[2] Due to changes in methodology and coverage, data from 1989 are not comparable with those of earlier years.

TABLE C-15. CAPITAL EXPENDITURES[1]

(As a Percent of Total Expenditures)

Country	1986	1987	1988	1989	1990	1991	1992	1993	1994	1995p
Argentina	14.6	15.4	12.1	15.8	9.3	7.4	4.3	5.4	5.0	...
Bahamas	11.1	11.8	15.8	18.0	14.1	15.9	15.0	12.5	14.2	12.8
Barbados	21.9	21.2	21.6	17.5	20.2	14.8	10.6	9.8	10.9	8.4
Belize[2]	24.7	20.5	2.8	37.2	38.1	41.3	34.9	34.6	33.3	25.8
Bolivia[3]	13.2	7.7	18.0	16.4	17.1	16.2	16.7	17.5	19.4	12.8
Brazil	24.1	44.9	8.4	-3.6	-23.5	0.7	-3.1	...	...	...
Chile	17.4	19.4	25.4	16.8	21.3	17.8	18.7	18.8	20.1	19.2
Colombia	24.2	21.4	22.9	20.7	19.5	27.3	29.0	19.3	16.9	17.6
Costa Rica	20.4	13.4	13.4	15.5	11.3	8.0	10.0	11.2	10.5	9.2
Dominican Republic	25.6	46.5	48.5	56.2	47.8	49.4	52.2	49.9	52.8	45.3
Ecuador	19.8	14.2	11.8	14.0	18.9	13.2	16.8	17.6	21.9	21.7
El Salvador	30.0	20.3	21.2	19.7	15.0	21.9	28.4	22.8	19.1	22.3
Guatemala	17.5	18.1	19.3	23.8	17.0	17.0	27.2	29.1	25.2	28.7
Guyana	51.9	21.5	30.6	26.0	32.2	11.3	16.0	26.3	30.3	30.4
Haiti	29.8	32.9	32.3	30.4	3.0	2.0	2.0	3.4	4.6	8.6
Honduras	21.7	23.2	22.0	18.1	25.4	25.7	30.4	32.9	24.3	31.0
Jamaica	19.7	21.7	25.1	20.0	15.5	18.3	19.9	15.4	15.6	16.7
Mexico	12.2	10.3	7.3	8.6	13.3	13.1	15.2	13.3	13.5	10.5
Nicaragua	13.7	10.7	13.3	11.1	4.5	13.0	21.3	24.8	30.1	35.9
Panama	7.5	4.5	2.8	4.8	2.4	15.4	7.3	11.3	12.5	11.0
Paraguay	16.2	22.1	26.4	13.9	16.9	21.1	14.5	15.3	17.4	27.0
Peru	17.8	14.8	11.5	16.5	10.5	13.6	20.8	23.2	24.7	22.9
Suriname	3.8	2.4	4.9	7.8	9.4	3.3	5.5	8.4	9.4	9.1
Trinidad and Tobago	13.6	19.7	10.1	7.8	5.8	11.3	5.6	5.8	6.4	6.7
Uruguay	8.9	10.6	11.1	12.1	10.9	9.4	9.1	11.3	13.0	11.3
Venezuela	31.1	30.8	27.7	15.7	22.3	26.6	25.4	24.8	27.6	21.1

[1] Includes net lending.
[2] 1995 data derived from calendar year (January - December); in previous years, fiscal year (April - March) used.
[3] Due to changes in methodology and coverage, data from 1989 are not comparable with those of earlier years.

TABLE C-16. TOTAL INVESTMENT

(As a Percent of Total Expenditures)

Country	1986	1987	1988	1989	1990	1991	1992	1993	1994	1995p
Argentina	4.7	5.1	4.9	3.8	2.2	1.6	1.8	2.0	1.6	...
Bahamas	10.2	9.3	7.5	10.5	5.1	3.4	4.4	5.6	7.2	11.6
Barbados	16.6	13.7	12.2	11.4	13.2	9.1	6.8	6.3	8.4	6.8
Belize[1]	20.1	15.1	31.8	36.0	40.3	48.0	44.6	32.6	...	...
Bolivia[2]	11.0	7.1	15.5	...	...	...	...	...	...	...
Brazil	5.0	2.6	3.0	2.4	1.6	2.7	2.0	...	...	...
Chile	9.5	9.6	10.1	10.1	9.0	10.3	12.0	13.2	13.5	13.0
Colombia	1.7	1.6	2.3	1.9	12.5	13.2	12.4	15.5	15.6	16.0
Costa Rica	6.1	4.8	4.1	3.7	3.9	3.3	3.6	3.5	3.4	4.0
Dominican Republic	9.4	27.4	33.8	40.5	26.9	21.1	27.9	30.6	34.6	32.0
Ecuador	9.1	5.6	7.9	4.5	5.2	3.5	4.2	5.6	13.9	11.7
El Salvador	21.6	11.9	18.0	15.2	8.4	13.2	19.5	18.4	14.4	16.2
Guatemala	7.8	8.2	10.3	10.2	9.7	9.6	10.0	9.3	9.6	12.5
Guyana	11.7	18.2	13.1	15.9	16.0	10.1	12.6	16.4	24.3	26.3
Haiti	...	...	...	...	...	...	...	...	...	...
Honduras	10.7	14.1	14.9	13.9	8.4	12.8	17.6	21.4	22.9	23.7
Jamaica	15.4	13.7	16.3	14.3	9.3	11.3	15.6	10.5	...	...
Mexico	3.4	2.9	2.0	2.2	4.2	6.0	6.5	6.4	7.7	5.2
Nicaragua	12.0	7.9	8.0	4.4	2.8	7.8	12.0	9.1	15.5	17.1
Panama	5.6	3.2	2.2	3.7	1.2	3.1	4.1	8.1	12.5	8.2
Paraguay	12.4	13.0	22.3	9.9	10.4	11.8	8.7	10.8	12.6	17.9
Peru	13.5	9.5	7.8	11.5	9.3	11.4	12.8	13.2	15.4	15.9
Suriname	3.8	1.9	3.5	6.6	7.5	2.2	5.1	8.2	9.4	9.1
Trinidad and Tobago	15.1	20.9	12.2	10.2	6.8	5.3	6.4	5.8	6.7	7.6
Uruguay	7.7	7.9	8.8	9.0	8.8	8.1	7.7	7.8	8.7	7.9
Venezuela	9.2	7.6	12.3	2.5	2.8	5.0	5.8	5.2	2.8	3.0

[1] 1995 data derived from calendar year (January - December); in previous years, fiscal year (April - March) used.
[2] Due to changes in methodology and coverage, data from 1989 are not comparable with those of earlier years.

TABLE C-17. FINANCIAL INVESTMENT AND NET LENDING

(As a Percent of Total Expenditures)

Country	1986	1987	1988	1989	1990	1991	1992	1993	1994	1995p
Argentina	0.6	0.5	0.6	0.8	0.5	0.3	0.4	0.4	0.3	...
Bahamas	-2.2	-2.5	1.0	-0.1	3.4	6.1	3.7	5.4	5.9	0.1
Barbados	0.4	0.8	3.5	0.3	-0.2	0.7	1.7	1.6	2.5	-0.7
Belize[1]	0.0	0.0	-29.0	-0.5	-4.9	-8.6	-11.4	-0.2	...	...
Bolivia[2]	2.2	0.5	0.4	...	...	...	...	...	...	...
Brazil	22.5	46.8	11.5	9.6	6.5	7.4	5.5	...	...	...
Chile	6.3	7.5	5.7	4.0	3.8	4.3	5.4	4.7	5.3	4.6
Colombia	4.2	0.3	2.0	3.3	1.1	8.0	13.8	3.8	1.3	1.7
Costa Rica	0.0	0.0	0.0	0.0	0.0	0.0	0.0	0.0	0.0	0.0
Dominican Republic	2.5	2.8	3.9	1.6	0.8	0.6	0.3	0.5	1.1	1.1
Ecuador	2.9	1.9	0.0	0.1	1.1	0.0	0.0	0.1	5.2	3.0
El Salvador	5.4	3.6	1.4	2.1	-0.4	5.0	3.1	1.2	0.8	1.1
Guatemala	0.8	0.4	1.9	2.2	2.2	2.3	1.2	4.4	4.2	5.5
Guyana	0.0	0.0	0.0	0.0	0.0	0.0	0.0	0.1	1.4	0.0
Haiti	...	...	...	...	...	...	...	...	...	...
Honduras	5.0	4.8	1.8	0.9	1.4	2.7	1.1	1.3	1.3	7.3
Jamaica	0.0	0.0	2.6	1.7	4.7	1.6	3.2	1.9	...	...
Mexico	0.3	0.2	0.2	0.3	0.0	0.0	0.0	0.0	...	...
Nicaragua	0.9	0.2	0.0	0.0	0.0	3.4	0.8	0.9	2.1	3.8
Panama	1.1	0.8	0.3	0.2	0.2	0.1	0.8	0.4	...	...
Paraguay	1.8	2.2	2.1	3.1	0.4	0.8	...	...	...	0.9
Peru	...	...	...	...	...	...	...	...	...	...
Suriname	0.0	0.4	1.4	1.2	1.9	1.1	0.4	0.1	...	...
Trinidad and Tobago	-1.6	-1.2	-2.2	-2.4	-2.2	-0.6	-2.0	-1.4	-0.3	-0.9
Uruguay	...	...	...	...	...	...	...	...	...	...
Venezuela	12.6	16.3	9.1	8.3	11.8	12.4	10.3	10.2	17.3	7.2

[1] 1995 data derived from calendar year (January - December); in previous years, fiscal year (April - March) used.

[2] Due to changes in methodology and coverage, data from 1989 are not comparable with those of earlier years.

GOVERNMENT FINANCE NOTES

The statistical tables refer generally to the central government. The data do not cover extra-budgetary revenues and expenditures of the central government, or the transactions of state and local governments, decentralized agencies or other entities comprising the general government, except for Chile, where the data reflect the general government concept. The data for Argentina refer to "National Administration" and includes decentralized agencies in addition to central government.

Total Revenues:

Include current and capital revenues.

Current Revenue: Includes all nonrepayable receipts raised by the government in the form of tax and nontax revenue, but excludes the sale of fixed government capital assets. Current revenue excludes the proceeds from government borrowings and from the issuance of government bonds and the sale of other financial assets.

> *Tax Revenue*—Direct Taxes:
>
> *Income Taxes:* Include taxes imposed on the actual or presumptive income and profits of individuals and corporations in the form of dividends, rents, royalties, interest, wages, pensions, and other income; and on capital gains on land, financial securities, equity or other assets.
>
> *Property Taxes:* Include taxes on the use or ownership of wealth and tangible property such as real estate holdings, land, and other fixed assets. Included also are betterment levies and special levies on improvements of immovable property.
>
> *Other Direct Taxes:* Include taxes on inheritances, gifts, and property transfers.
>
> *Tax Revenue*—Indirect Taxes:
>
> *Production and Sales Taxes:* Include all general sales, value-added and turnover taxes, and all other taxes and duties levied on the production, extraction, sale, leasing or delivery of goods and rendering of services.
>
> *International Trade Taxes:* Include all taxes on international trade and commercial transactions in the form of both specific and *ad-valorem* import and export duties raised for purposes of revenue mobilization and for protectionism. Also included are taxes that are levied on foreign exchange transactions.
>
> *Other Indirect Taxes:* Include revenue from fiscal monopolies, business and professional licenses, motor vehicle registrations, poll and stamp taxes, and excise duties.

Nontax Revenue: Comprises noncompulsory current revenue arising from government ownership of property, enterprises, financial assets, land, or intangible holdings, in the form of dividends, interest, rents, royalties, and entrepreneurial income. Also included are administrative fees, charges, fines, and forfeits levied by the government.

Capital Revenue: Includes sales of fixed assets, stocks (strategic materials, stabilization stocks, grains), land, and intangible assets.

Total Expenditures and Net Lending:

Include all payments by the government in the form of current and capital expenditures and financial investment and net lending, but exclude amortization payments on domestic and external government debt.

Current Expenditures: Include expenditures for goods and services, interest payments and transfers and subsidies:

> *Goods and Services:* Include wages and salaries to government employees and the purchases of goods and services for the operation of the administration other than fixed assets and land.
>
> *Interest Payments:* Include domestic and external interest payments on government debt outstanding in the form of bonds and other financial liabilities.
>
> *Current Transfers:* Include transfers and subsidies intended to support the current expenditures of state and local governments, decentralized agencies, and public enterprises.

Capital Expenditures: Is comprised of fixed investment, capital transfers and financial investment and net lending:

> *Fixed Investment:* Includes government outlays for investment in capital equipment, public works, and construction and the acquisition of any other fixed assets for nonmilitary productive purposes. Also included is the purchase of inventories and of land, subsoil deposits, and nonfinancial intangible assets such as patents, copyrights, and trademarks.
>
> *Capital Transfers:* Include unrequited transfers with the purpose of permitting the acquisition of fixed assets by the beneficiary, compensation for damages or destruction of fixed assets or capital gains. Includes transfers for the construction of bridges, highways, hospitals, schools and other buildings. However, transfers for military construction or the purchase of military equipment are classified as current transfers. Also included is the amortization by the government of debts contracted by third parties, only if the government does not assume the debt. Includes transfers to those enterprises that have accumulated large losses in various years or suffered losses beyond their control. The nonreimbursable unrequited

transfers of irregular character for both parties to the transaction are also considered as capital transfers.

Financial Investment and Net Lending: This category comprises government transactions in financial claims undertaken for purposes of public policy rather than for management of government liquidity. It covers government net loans to, and the acquisition of financial assets issued by other government levels, financial and nonfinancial public enterprises and government participation in the equity capital and debt of private enterprises. Net lending to financial institutions includes the provision of funds for their capitalization and the financing of any government lending activity considered to be part of the financial sector.

Current Savings:

Represent current revenue less current expenditures. By disbursing only part of its current receipts for current expenditures, the government generates a current account surplus available for the financing of real investment, financial investment and capital transfers, thereby contributing to domestic capital formation.

Surplus (+) or Deficit (-):

Total revenues plus grants less total expenditures and net lending.

Source:

Official statistics of member countries and IDB estimates. All calculations use current values in local currency.

TABLE D-1. BALANCE OF PAYMENTS SUMMARY[1]

(Millions of Dollars)

Item	1986	1987	1988	1989	1990	1991	1992	1993	1994	1995p
Current Account Balance	-17,180	-8,740	-9,779	-8,518	-1,522	-17,093	-35,086	-44,466	-47,536	-32,116
Trade Balance	17,762	21,452	24,904	29,445	30,380	12,278	-6,075	-9,860	-15,454	-706
Exports of Goods (fob)	87,389	99,868	115,443	128,510	141,675	141,754	150,743	161,956	187,692	227,047
Imports of Goods (fob)	-69,627	-78,415	-90,539	-99,065	-111,295	-129,475	-156,818	-171,815	-203,146	-227,753
Service Balance	-39,257	-35,791	-41,044	-44,759	-42,007	-40,315	-41,520	-45,741	-44,637	-46,370
Freight and Insurance	-3,039	-3,348	-3,475	-3,552	-4,329	-5,878	-7,029	-8,983	...	...
Travel	2,072	2,755	2,095	3,309	2,280	2,112	1,419	1,725	388	3,454
Transportation	-1,438	-1,467	-1,637	-1,811	-1,620	-1,618	-1,414	-1,502	-1,495	-644
Investment Income	-33,318	-31,138	-35,292	-40,087	-35,224	-32,469	-32,452	-34,846	-34,532	-36,256
Other Services	-3,533	-2,593	-2,736	-2,618	-3,114	-2,461	-2,044	-2,135	...	...
Unrequited Transfers	4,396	5,599	6,362	6,796	10,105	10,944	12,510	11,135	12,555	14,961
Private	3,141	3,739	4,540	4,764	6,834	8,822	10,089	8,166	9,289	6,555
Official	1,254	1,859	1,822	2,032	3,271	2,122	2,421	1,831	1,863	1,306
Capital Account Balance	12,072	14,092	7,972	7,029	16,099	29,414	59,032	66,864	44,103[a]	52,726[a]
Non-Monetary Sectors	16,065	15,975	11,197	10,045	12,727	27,945	54,625	69,351	49,743	57,212
Private Sector	-6,237	-6,861	-4,012	-7,724	8,431	25,619	44,500	51,730	45,633	30,772
Direct Investment	4,176	4,696	8,374	8,336	6,657	11,103	13,747	13,661	18,173	17,692
Portfolio Investment[2]	-128	-131	-427	446	3,728	12,409	18,991	29,496	...	...
Other Long-Term	-12,912	-10,741	-11,286	-5,898	1,952	432	-824	-7,427	...	...
Other Short-Term	2,658	-635	-730	-10,426	-3,905	1,758	12,650	16,005	...	...
Government Sector[3]	22,302	22,836	15,209	17,769	4,296	2,326	10,126	17,621	5,126	21,925
Long-Term[4]	20,123	13,384	8,437	6,143	-9,330	2,840	20,983	25,810	6,335	-8,551
Short-Term	2,180	9,451	6,772	11,626	13,626	-514	-10,857	-8,190	...	...
Monetary Sector	-3,993	-1,883	-3,225	-3,016	3,373	1,469	4,406	-2,487	...	...
Long-Term	-3,416	-2,797	-3,707	-2,774	3,343	4,036	69	-1,893	...	...
Short-Term	-578	914	482	-242	30	-2,567	4,337	-593	...	...
Change in Reserves	7,949	-4,047	5,951	-2,678	-13,746	-19,173	-25,524	-21,458	2,833	-20,895
Errors and Omissions	-2,920	-1,306	-4,146	4,168	-830	6,852	1,578	-940	...	...

[1] The totals in this table are those shown for Latin America in the following Appendix D tables. For 1994 and 1995, particularly in the capital account, these totals are often incomplete because of missing country data. Furthermore, countries may provide estimates for aggregates and not their components. Therefore, in earlier years, components do not always correspond with the totals.

[2] Excludes, by definition of the private sector, government portfolio investment.

[3] Includes change in arrears financed by Paris Club debt rescheduling, refinancing, and debt relief.

[4] Includes Government Sector portfolio investment.

[a] Includes for 1994, Errors and Omissions for Argentina; for 1995, Argentina, Dominican Republic, El Salvador and Haiti.

TABLE D-2. CURRENT ACCOUNT BALANCE

(Millions of Dollars)

Country	1986	1987	1988	1989	1990	1991	1992	1993	1994	1995p
Argentina	-2,859	-4,235	-1,572	-1,305	4,552	-647	-6,546	-7,452	-9,311	-2,195
Bahamas	21	-58	-61	-92	-96	-99	-39	12	-113	-309
Barbados	8	-23	42	24	-16	-25	144	65	123	43
Belize	12	9	-3	-19	15	-26	-29	-49	-31	-30
Bolivia	-389	-432	-304	-270	-199	-263	-534	-506	-114	-308
Brazil	-5,311	-1,452	4,156	1,002	-3,823	-1,450	6,089	19	-1,153	-17,784
Chile	-1,192	-736	-235	-705	-537	112	-708	-2,096	-757	160
Colombia	383	336	-216	-201	542	2,349	912	-2,115	-3,045	-4,208
Costa Rica	-161	-256	-179	-415	-424	-75	-370	-619	-463	-152
Dominican Republic	-183	-364	-19	-327	-280	-157	-708	-425	-159	210
Ecuador	-596	-1,187	-683	-716	-366	-707	-215	-682	-807	-822
El Salvador	117	136	26	-194	-152	-167	-109	-77	-18	-276
Guatemala	-18	-443	-414	-367	-213	-184	-706	-702	-625	-595
Guyana	-141	-110	-94	-113	-150	-119	-147	-138	-101	-95
Haiti	-45	-31	-40	-63	-88	-123	-41	-78	4	-60
Honduras	-117	-182	-131	-196	-93	-217	-311	-271	-355	-270
Jamaica	-16	-125	48	-282	-312	-240	29	-184	48	-210
Mexico	-1,377	4,247	-2,374	-5,825	-7,451	-14,888	-24,442	-23,400	-28,784	-654
Nicaragua	-688	-679	-715	-362	-305	-5	-769	-604	-694	-529
Panama	-396	803	345	-899	-238	-723	-724	-576	-519	-587
Paraguay	-365	-490	-210	256	-172	-324	-600	-834	-749	-1,184
Peru	-1,233	-1,790	-1,334	132	-678	-813	-1,657	-1,676	-2,250	-3,748
Suriname	-21	76	64	165	37	-75	14	44	59	80
Trinidad and Tobago	-412	-225	-89	-39	459	-5	139	113	218	174
Uruguay	42	-141	22	134	186	42	-9	-244	-390	-338
Venezuela	-2,245	-1,390	-5,809	2,161	8,279	1,736	-3,749	-1,993	2,450	1,572
Latin America	**-17,180**	**-8,740**	**-9,779**	**-8,518**	**-1,522**	**-17,093**	**-35,086**	**-44,466**	**-47,536**	**-32,116**

TABLE D-3. TRADE BALANCE (FOB)

(Millions of Dollars)

Country	1986	1987	1988	1989	1990	1991	1992	1993	1994	1995p
Argentina	2,446	1,017	4,242	5,709	8,628	4,419	-1,450	-2,428	-4,239	2,342
Bahamas[1]	-607	-676	-666	-835	-815	-677	-712	-728	-782	-1,102
Barbados	-244	-297	-343	-415	-411	-414	-274	-330	-355	-491
Belize	-16	-24	-42	-64	-59	-98	-104	-119	-88	-74
Bolivia	-51	-128	-48	-6	55	-44	-432	-396	-79	-222
Brazil	8,304	11,158	19,168	16,112	10,747	10,578	15,239	14,329	10,861	-3,157
Chile	1,092	1,309	2,209	1,578	1,335	1,588	772	-982	659	1,384
Colombia	1,922	1,868	827	1,474	1,971	2,959	1,233	-1,657	-2,284	-2,404
Costa Rica	40	-139	-98	-239	-443	-200	-472	-760	-686	-512
Dominican Republic	-630	-880	-718	-1,039	-1,058	-1,071	-1,612	-1,607	-1,632	-1,964
Ecuador	543	-33	619	661	1,003	644	925	588	435	267
El Salvador	-124	-349	-356	-663	-666	-705	-962	-1,035	-1,155	-1,359
Guatemala	168	-355	-340	-358	-217	-443	-1,044	-1,021	-997	-1,055
Guyana	-26	2	19	12	-23	17	-21	-26	5	15
Haiti	-113	-101	-104	-111	-177	-247	-139	-185	-84	-317
Honduras	23	-41	-34	-45	-12	-72	-151	-91	-429	-364
Jamaica	-248	-352	-357	-590	-502	-392	-425	-815	-644	-588
Mexico[2]	5,019	8,786	2,611	405	-881	-7,279	-15,934	-13,481	-18,465	7,088
Nicaragua	-420	-439	-483	-229	-237	-420	-548	-392	-434	-361
Panama[3]	-247	-256	93	-200	-236	-509	-506	-462	-537	-925
Paraguay	-288	-321	-159	164	-254	-747	-869	-1,211	-1,277	-1,675
Peru	-55	-514	-90	1,242	394	-137	-555	-571	-1,108	-2,116
Suriname	33	65	119	218	92	-1	69	84	99	110
Trinidad and Tobago	169	357	405	506	1,013	564	696	547	741	690
Uruguay	273	102	292	463	426	61	-122	-387	-672	-566
Venezuela	798	1,694	-1,863	5,694	10,706	4,900	1,322	3,275	7,691	6,647
Latin America	**17,762**	**21,452**	**24,903**	**29,445**	**30,380**	**12,278**	**-6,075**	**-9,860**	**-15,454**	**-706**

[1] Includes goods for processing in Free Trade Zone.
[2] Includes maquiladoras.
[3] Includes activity within the Colón Free Zone.

TABLE D-4. EXPORTS OF GOODS (FOB)

(Millions of Dollars)

Country	1986	1987	1988	1989	1990	1991	1992	1993	1994	1995p
Argentina	6,852	6,360	9,134	9,573	12,354	11,978	12,235	13,117	15,839	20,830
Bahamas[1]	866	785	678	1,106	1,226	756	714	662	734	697
Barbados	280	162	176	186	213	204	191	182	189	176
Belize	93	103	119	124	129	126	141	132	144	156
Bolivia	546	519	543	724	831	760	608	716	985	1,041
Brazil	22,348	26,210	33,773	34,375	31,408	31,619	35,793	39,630	44,102	46,506
Chile	4,191	5,303	7,053	8,080	8,372	8,942	10,008	9,199	11,538	16,039
Colombia	5,331	5,661	5,343	6,031	7,079	7,507	7,263	7,429	8,756	10,406
Costa Rica	1,085	1,107	1,181	1,333	1,354	1,498	1,739	1,867	2,102	2,442
Dominican Republic	722	711	890	924	735	658	563	511	644	743
Ecuador	2,186	2,021	2,202	2,354	2,714	2,851	3,008	3,062	3,717	4,362
El Salvador	778	590	611	558	644	587	598	732	1,252	1,661
Guatemala	1,044	978	1,073	1,126	1,211	1,230	1,284	1,363	1,550	1,995
Guyana	210	241	215	205	204	239	382	414	463	496
Haiti	191	210	180	148	266	202	76	82	57	85
Honduras	902	831	889	911	895	841	839	853	922	1,137
Jamaica	590	725	898	1,029	1,191	1,197	1,117	1,105	1,248	1,463
Mexico[2]	21,803	27,599	30,692	35,171	40,711	42,687	46,196	51,885	60,882	79,542
Nicaragua	258	295	236	319	332	268	223	267	351	497
Panama[3]	2,500	2,661	2,505	2,741	3,358	4,207	5,115	5,428	5,917	5,972
Paraguay	576	597	871	1,180	1,382	1,121	1,082	1,500	1,871	1,992
Peru	2,572	2,701	2,732	3,555	3,324	3,392	3,535	3,513	4,554	5,572
Suriname	337	339	358	549	466	346	341	298	294	416
Trinidad and Tobago	1,378	1,414	1,470	1,551	1,960	1,775	1,691	1,500	1,778	2,428
Uruguay	1,088	1,182	1,405	1,599	1,693	1,605	1,801	1,732	1,913	2,117
Venezuela	8,664	10,564	10,217	13,059	17,623	15,159	14,202	14,779	15,890	18,278
Latin America	**87,389**	**99,868**	**115,443**	**128,510**	**141,675**	**141,754**	**150,743**	**161,956**	**187,692**	**227,047**

[1] Includes goods for processing in Free Trade Zone.
[2] Includes maquiladoras.
[3] Includes activity within the Colón Free Zone.

TABLE D-5. IMPORTS OF GOODS (FOB)

(Millions of Dollars)

Country	1986	1987	1988	1989	1990	1991	1992	1993	1994	1995p
Argentina	4,406	5,343	4,892	3,864	3,726	7,559	13,685	15,545	20,078	18,488
Bahamas[1]	1,474	1,461	1,344	1,940	2,041	1,433	1,426	1,391	1,516	1,799
Barbados	523	459	519	600	624	617	465	511	544	667
Belize	108	127	161	189	188	224	245	251	232	230
Bolivia	597	646	591	730	776	804	1,041	1,112	1,064	1,263
Brazil	14,044	15,052	14,605	18,263	20,661	21,041	20,554	25,301	33,241	49,663
Chile	3,099	3,994	4,844	6,502	7,037	7,354	9,236	10,181	10,879	14,655
Colombia	3,409	3,793	4,516	4,557	5,108	4,548	6,030	9,086	11,040	12,810
Costa Rica	1,045	1,245	1,279	1,572	1,797	1,698	2,211	2,627	2,789	2,954
Dominican Republic	1,352	1,592	1,608	1,964	1,793	1,729	2,174	2,118	2,276	2,707
Ecuador	1,643	2,054	1,583	1,693	1,711	2,207	2,083	2,474	3,282	4,095
El Salvador	902	939	967	1,220	1,310	1,291	1,561	1,766	2,407	3,020
Guatemala	876	1,333	1,413	1,484	1,428	1,673	2,328	2,384	2,547	3,049
Guyana	236	238	196	193	227	222	403	440	458	481
Haiti	303	311	284	259	443	449	214	267	141	401
Honduras	880	871	923	956	907	913	990	944	1,351	1,501
Jamaica	837	1,077	1,255	1,619	1,693	1,588	1,541	1,921	1,892	2,050
Mexico[2]	16,784	18,813	28,081	34,766	41,592	49,966	62,130	65,366	79,347	72,453
Nicaragua	677	734	718	547	570	688	771	659	785	858
Panama[3]	2,747	2,917	2,412	2,941	3,593	4,715	5,620	5,889	6,453	6,897
Paraguay	864	919	1,030	1,016	1,636	1,868	1,951	2,711	3,148	3,667
Peru	2,627	3,215	2,822	2,313	2,930	3,529	4,090	4,084	5,662	7,688
Suriname	304	274	239	331	374	347	273	214	194	306
Trinidad and Tobago	1,209	1,058	1,064	1,045	948	1,210	996	953	1,037	1,738
Uruguay	815	1,080	1,112	1,136	1,267	1,544	1,923	2,118	2,585	2,682
Venezuela	7,866	8,870	12,080	7,365	6,917	10,259	12,880	11,504	8,199	11,631
Latin America	**69,627**	**78,415**	**90,539**	**99,065**	**111,295**	**129,475**	**156,818**	**171,815**	**203,146**	**227,753**

[1] Includes goods for processing in Free Trade Zone.
[2] Includes maquiladoras.
[3] Includes activity within the Colón Free Zone.

TABLE D-6. SERVICE BALANCE

(Millions of Dollars)

Country	1986	1987	1988	1989	1990	1991	1992	1993	1994	1995p
Argentina	-5,307	-5,244	-5,814	-7,022	-5,074	-5,859	-5,845	-5,470	-5,392	-4,992
Bahamas	627	620	617	739	705	556	656	722	645	748
Barbados	241	269	369	434	352	355	378	374	451	505
Belize	0	3	13	14	45	44	45	41	29	12
Bolivia	-433	-416	-391	-414	-413	-401	-344	-346	-320	-320
Brazil	-13,695	-12,678	-15,103	-15,331	-15,369	-13,542	-11,339	-15,913	-14,437	-18,600
Chile	-2,368	-2,183	-2,626	-2,498	-2,072	-1,817	-1,911	-1,500	-1,754	-1,579
Colombia	-2,324	-2,533	-2,007	-2,573	-2,455	-2,308	-2,055	-1,595	-1,624	-2,499
Costa Rica	-272	-344	-336	-368	-173	-17	-72	-3	81	206
Dominican Republic	160	186	346	328	408	527	472	741	980	1,611
Ecuador	-1,184	-1,286	-1,399	-1,474	-1,476	-1,461	-1,260	-1,400	-1,387	-1,320
El Salvador	-142	-54	-119	-142	-117	-133	-85	-87	-151	-306
Guatemala	-261	-281	-298	-259	-223	0	-52	-44	-77	-6
Guyana	-131	-133	-132	-147	-155	-157	-156	-141	-138	-149
Haiti	-84	-101	-130	-126	-104	-111	-58	-66	-68	-201
Honduras	-298	-316	-312	-318	-319	-298	-323	-299	-147	-137
Jamaica	61	39	-118	-195	-101	-117	96	241	212	-196
Mexico	-7,970	-6,458	-7,240	-8,773	-10,545	-10,355	-11,893	-13,559	-14,334	-11,708
Nicaragua	-383	-375	-363	-302	-270	-429	-557	-486	-536	-368
Panama	-340	883	127	-797	-280	-502	-614	-385	-203	111
Paraguay	-88	-195	-86	68	26	350	235	335	486	449
Peru	-1,282	-1,399	-1,405	-1,306	-1,391	-1,122	-1,584	-1,589	-1,581	-2,054
Suriname	-54	8	-62	-73	-84	-87	-84	-61	-45	-56
Trinidad and Tobago	-553	-559	-485	-537	-547	-571	-557	-439	-524	-499
Uruguay	-257	-251	-291	-337	-248	-59	84	90	222	195
Venezuela	-2,922	-2,993	-3,799	-3,350	-2,125	-2,800	-4,697	-4,900	-5,025	-5,218
Latin America	**-39,257**	**-35,791**	**-41,044**	**-44,759**	**-42,007**	**-40,315**	**-41,520**	**-45,741**	**-44,637**	**-46,370**

TABLE D-7. SERVICE TRANSACTIONS: FREIGHT AND INSURANCE

(Millions of Dollars)

Country	1986	1987	1988	1989	1990	1991	1992	1993	1994	1995p
Argentina	136	108	137	193	142	-224	-619	-695	...	...
Bahamas	-73	-76	-76	-87	-88	-79	-82	-86	-88	-87
Barbados	-50	-52	-63	-57	-75	-77	-54	-81	9	...
Belize	-14	-16	-20	-24	-23	-28	-30	-31	-29	-28
Bolivia	-97	-110	-102	-130	-138	-127	-116	-117	-111	-136
Brazil	-69	-30	394	71	-72	-230	-152	-998	-411	-1,122
Chile	16	13	7	-55	139	47	110	65	149	...
Colombia	-230	-211	-246	-171	-86	-126	-161	-300	-307	-352
Costa Rica	-119	-146	-146	-176	-195	-154	-243	-291	-312	-295
Dominican Republic	-92	-149	-149	-188	-156	-157	-216	-204	-218	-259
Ecuador	-22	-48	-29	5	0	-31	-30	-66	-74	...
El Salvador	-55	-41	-74	-94	-96	-116	-146	-152	-179	-339
Guatemala	-89	-120	-148	-158	-135	-171	-198	-222	-242	-247
Guyana	-22	-21	-19	-19	-22	-22	-40	-44	-46	-56
Haiti	-43	-56	-53	-52	-61	-63	-48	-60	-31	...
Honduras	-80	-82	-85	-87	-85	-85	-93	-100	-118	-132
Jamaica	-132	-173	-202	-260	-252	-250	-249	-322	-322	-690
Mexico	-514	-654	-862	-1,184	-1,664	-1,725	-2,050	-2,577	-3,041	...
Nicaragua	-70	-77	-75	-49	-51	-42	-63	-49	-65	497
Panama	-355	-305	-210	-302	-432	-577	-638	-700	-772	-763
Paraguay	-123	-136	-151	-140	-209	-252	-271	-322	-391	-531
Peru	-84	-51	-59	-20	-154	-225	-344	-410	-467	...
Suriname	-13	-16	-21	-24	-22	-17	-20	-23	-14	-25
Trinidad and Tobago	-168	-146	-124	-155	-162	-232	-212	-192	-164	-178
Uruguay	-33	-24	-21	-24	-8	20	44	22	31	49
Venezuela	-643	-730	-1,079	-368	-423	-937	-1,108	-1,028	-758	-846
Latin America	**-3,039**	**-3,348**	**-3,475**	**-3,552**	**-4,329**	**-5,878**	**-7,029**	**-8,983**	**...**	**...**

TABLE D-8. SERVICE TRANSACTIONS: TRAVEL

(Millions of Dollars)

Country	1986	1987	1988	1989	1990	1991	1992	1993	1994	1995p
Argentina	-326	-275	-341	-224	-268	-957	-1,429	-1,608	-1,640	-1,010
Bahamas	968	988	972	1,119	1,128	986	1,051	1,126	1,136	1,172
Barbados	297	345	423	484	453	417	424	476	541	548
Belize	12	14	16	21	32	38	46	49	53	55
Bolivia	9	-2	-2	-2	-2	-1	-2	0	4	-7
Brazil	-509	-184	-588	474	-122	-212	-319	-801	-1,212	-2,419
Chile	-151	-168	-243	12	105	243	174	275	224	...
Colombia	-193	-317	-77	-159	-48	-41	64	61	45	29
Costa Rica	71	68	105	94	130	186	213	318	387	356
Dominican Republic	417	476	641	571	582	602	682	906	976	1,519
Ecuador	14	-3	6	18	13	12	14	40	49	20
El Salvador	-32	-33	-20	-46	15	14	15	18	16	13
Guatemala	14	18	-33	-15	18	45	83	87	54	64
Guyana	-7	-5	-6	-14	-8	-15	-1	5	7	8
Haiti	46	48	40	37	-3	5	19	13	-9	...
Honduras	-4	-8	-10	-10	-9	-6	-6	-7	-1,921	23
Jamaica	452	517	432	490	638	704	777	863	842	1,380
Mexico	848	1,175	847	574	7	147	-23	605	957	3,011
Nicaragua	4	3	4	3	-3	-11	-7	10	10	-1,356
Panama	122	102	78	75	73	94	95	103	112	183
Paraguay	100	70	55	52	25	366	338	412	540	698
Peru	23	9	30	-16	-37	5	-67	-3	79	...
Suriname	-6	-5	-4	-6	-12	-15	-9	5	8	15
Trinidad and Tobago	-82	-64	-77	-34	-28	-9	-4	-25	-3	20
Uruguay	84	78	64	61	127	233	277	318	456	374
Venezuela	-99	-93	-218	-251	-527	-717	-984	-1,521	-1,321	-1,241
Latin America	**2,072**	**2,755**	**2,095**	**3,309**	**2,280**	**2,112**	**1,419**	**1,725**	**388**	**3,454**

TABLE D-9. SERVICE TRANSACTIONS: INVESTMENT INCOME

(Millions of Dollars)

Country	1986	1987	1988	1989	1990	1991	1992	1993	1994	1995p
Argentina	-4,404	-4,472	-5,127	-6,422	-4,400	-4,260	-3,656	-2,989	-2,547	-2,950
Bahamas	-184	-183	-167	-173	-169	-214	-176	-171	-213	-180
Barbados	-17	-18	-19	-14	-33	-31	-17	-29	-41	-48
Belize	-2	-7	-8	-9	-10	-11	-16	-18	-22	-22
Bolivia	-309	-278	-265	-259	-249	-247	-198	-206	-188	-203
Brazil	-11,122	-10,314	-12,080	-12,546	-11,608	-9,651	-7,997	-10,323	-9,091	-10,948
Chile	-1,904	-1,726	-1,933	-1,942	-1,817	-1,810	-1,860	-1,505	-1,773	...
Colombia	-1,748	-1,990	-1,745	-2,299	-2,305	-2,090	-1,996	-1,575	-1,707	-2,367
Costa Rica	-271	-290	-343	-370	-233	-174	-203	-225	-207	-194
Dominican Republic	-250	-306	-271	-249	-249	-193	-321	-395	-319	-343
Ecuador	-1,007	-1,045	-1,220	-1,352	-1,353	-1,300	-1,135	-1,255	-1,210	...
El Salvador	-102	-92	-106	-101	-132	-121	-97	-112	-95	-96
Guatemala	-214	-179	-176	-179	-196	-103	-141	-118	-130	-169
Guyana	-85	-89	-94	-103	-109	-109	-110	-94	-83	-86
Haiti	-15	-21	-27	-26	-18	-18	-12	-11	-11	-19
Honduras	-209	-233	-231	-238	-237	-246	-282	-256	-263	-269
Jamaica	-281	-343	-335	-350	-430	-439	-294	-196	-205	-306
Mexico	-7,367	-6,585	-7,043	-8,101	-8,316	-8,265	-9,209	-11,030	-11,745	-12,948
Nicaragua	-254	-244	-262	-205	-217	-363	-495	-429	-466	-1,043
Panama	-469	616	-275	-1,042	-576	-727	-813	-620	-556	-453
Paraguay	-47	-111	-81	-23	-14	-6	-49	-44	-34	-67
Peru	-951	-1,026	-1,079	-984	-1,054	-807	-987	-1,006	-1,064	-1,166
Suriname	-3	-5	-9	-6	-9	-11	-8	-6	-4	-2
Trinidad and Tobago	-211	-275	-302	-378	-397	-442	-448	-326	-412	-443
Uruguay	-292	-302	-324	-349	-321	-232	-187	-192	-206	-173
Venezuela	-1,602	-1,619	-1,771	-2,368	-774	-598	-1,746	-1,715	-1,943	-1,761
Latin America	**-33,318**	**-31,138**	**-35,292**	**-40,087**	**-35,224**	**-32,469**	**-32,452**	**-34,846**	**-34,532**	**-36,256**

TABLE D-10. SERVICE TRANSACTIONS: OTHER GOODS, SERVICES AND INCOME

(Millions of Dollars)

Country	1986	1987	1988	1989	1990	1991	1992	1993	1994	1995p
Argentina	-576	-415	-390	-536	-626	-484	-175	-77	...	...
Bahamas	-67	-80	-79	-96	-151	-131	-134	-136	-194	-199
Barbados	23	17	49	46	29	67	45	30	25	68
Belize	3	8	22	21	40	42	41	37	26	12
Bolivia	-15	-16	-17	-14	-15	-18	-17	-15	-20	30
Brazil	-1,121	-1,180	-1,532	-1,695	-1,927	-1,892	-1,605	-2,327	-1,924	-1,911
Chile	-73	-40	-145	-181	-200	-57	-6	8	-16	...
Colombia	-162	-130	-11	33	-32	-90	-32	-119	-99	-315
Costa Rica	42	18	22	52	90	91	104	149	154	267
Dominican Republic	72	152	108	175	203	241	293	384	492	627
Ecuador	-64	-85	-75	-53	-48	-28	-4	11	-20	...
El Salvador	23	87	24	46	70	70	122	140	84	94
Guatemala	28	1	59	87	86	226	197	207	240	339
Guyana	-9	-7	-3	-5	-10	-9	-14	0	-3	-1
Haiti	-45	-41	-53	-52	9	-1	6	10	0	...
Honduras	-29	-7	-1	2	-3	20	36	41	0	241
Jamaica	-36	-46	-93	-131	-134	-182	-173	-152	-204	-650
Mexico	-669	-259	-130	161	-331	-142	-241	-132	-82	...
Nicaragua	-63	-57	-29	-51	1	-19	16	-9	-8	0
Panama	-7	87	126	81	238	257	309	357	418	421
Paraguay	13	14	123	206	240	221	207	288	421	396
Peru	-159	-195	-186	-198	-112	-52	-150	-135	-149	...
Suriname	-19	40	-20	-26	-26	-28	-37	-27	-26	-57
Trinidad and Tobago	-156	-54	5	10	-3	60	36	12	-6	1
Uruguay	-23	-9	-14	-47	-48	-42	-60	-28	-28	-56
Venezuela	-446	-394	-496	-453	-454	-583	-806	-652	-1,061	-1,370
Latin America	**-3,533**	**-2,593**	**-2,736**	**-2,618**	**-3,114**	**-2,461**	**-2,043**	**-2,135**	**...**	**...**

TABLE D-11. UNREQUITED TRANSFERS

(Millions of Dollars)

Country	1986	1987	1988	1989	1990	1991	1992	1993	1994	1995p
Argentina	2	-8	0	8	998	793	749	446	320	455
Bahamas	1	-2	-12	4	15	23	18	19	24	45
Barbados	11	6	16	5	43	33	40	21	27	28
Belize	27	31	26	31	29	28	30	30	29	32
Bolivia	96	112	135	150	159	183	243	237	285	234
Brazil	80	68	91	221	799	1,514	2,189	1,603	2,423	3,973
Chile	84	138	182	215	200	341	431	386	338	355
Colombia	785	1,001	964	898	1,026	1,698	1,734	1,138	862	694
Costa Rica	152	226	255	191	192	142	173	143	142	154
Dominican Republic	286	331	354	384	371	387	432	442	493	563
Ecuador	45	132	97	97	107	110	120	130	145	231
El Salvador	383	539	501	611	631	670	938	1,045	1,289	1,390
Guatemala	75	193	224	250	227	260	391	363	449	465
Guyana	16	21	20	22	28	21	30	29	32	39
Haiti	152	171	193	174	193	234	155	173	156	458
Honduras	158	174	216	167	238	152	163	119	221	231
Jamaica	170	188	522	502	291	269	357	390	481	574
Mexico	1,574	1,919	2,255	2,543	3,975	2,746	3,385	3,640	4,015	3,965
Nicaragua	115	135	130	169	202	844	336	274	275	200
Panama	190	176	125	98	278	288	395	271	221	227
Paraguay	11	27	35	24	56	72	34	42	42	42
Peru	104	123	161	196	319	446	482	484	439	422
Suriname	1	3	7	20	30	13	29	21	4	26
Trinidad and Tobago	-28	-23	-9	-8	-6	2	0	5	0	-17
Uruguay	25	8	21	8	8	40	29	53	59	32
Venezuela	-121	-91	-147	-183	-302	-364	-374	-368	-216	143
Latin America	**4,396**	**5,599**	**6,362**	**6,796**	**10,105**	**10,944**	**12,510**	**11,135**	**12,555**	**14,961**

TABLE D-12. CAPITAL ACCOUNT BALANCE, EXCLUDING RESERVES

(Millions of Dollars)

Country	1986	1987	1988	1989	1990	1991	1992	1993	1994	1995p
Argentina	1,666	2,430	3,595	206	-1,888	3,618	10,959	9,912	9,868[a]	176[a]
Bahamas	25	-17	70	92	53	174	9	5	79	291
Barbados	70	83	45	-27	43	10	-98	-9	9	-4
Belize	1	3	27	25	25	22	22	33	18	24
Bolivia	362	200	141	170	205	204	468	92	456	767
Brazil	2,014	4,422	-1,618	1,518	5,365	795	10,373	10,008	8,943	29,306
Chile	716	1,013	1,177	1,394	3,011	834	2,931	2,611	4,432	1,168
Colombia	1,160	-1	939	478	-2	-783	166	2,661	3,063	4,468
Costa Rica	77	163	196	352	209	324	344	262	-80	201
Dominican Republic	145	-32	93	399	408	-50	166	90	280	-91[a]
Ecuador	821	1,338	687	788	430	701	414	1,266	1,016	-591
El Salvador	69	-61	62	169	22	-28	135	99	84	422[a]
Guatemala	63	462	275	384	147	655	604	768	669	438
Guyana	78	37	51	88	165	159	198	173	113	103
Haiti	55	53	51	75	36	38	-3	-2	-5	248[a]
Honduras	174	280	238	307	225	131	293	246	220	186
Jamaica	39	206	134	319	401	175	243	249	352	370
Mexico	1,998	-1,617	-1,071	1,499	8,526	25,159	27,039	33,760	12,754	15,311
Nicaragua	660	764	707	495	447	6	709	397	595	402
Panama	122	-84	181	278	84	-131	-294	-951	92	...
Paraguay	181	189	-156	-20	29	151	-205	220	401	443
Peru	2,480	2,954	3,227	1,780	2,555	-4,510	1,364	2,076	3,605	2,609
Suriname	1	-51	-66	-173	-15	33	-49	-73	-84	-50
Trinidad and Tobago	-218	64	-75	60	-250	-120	-101	87	-39	-67
Uruguay	18	333	241	24	-70	-356	-41	228	386	372
Venezuela	-707	960	-1,180	-3,650	-4,061	2,204	3,386	2,656	-3,124	-3,776
Latin America	**12,072**	**14,092**	**7,972**	**7,029**	**16,099**	**29,414**	**59,032**	**66,864**	**44,103**	**52,726**

[a] Includes Errors and Omissions.

TABLE D-13. NON-MONETARY SECTORS

(Millions of Dollars)

Country	1986	1987	1988	1989	1990	1991	1992	1993	1994	1995p
Argentina	1,689	2,463	3,572	150	-1,988	3,649	11,019	12,411	9,868	176
Bahamas	-2	-29	31	48	20	162	47	4	63	306
Barbados	61	82	36	-24	32	6	-104	-17	-93	...
Belize	6	3	26	34	27	16	10	26	15	-4
Bolivia	388	205	189	225	173	176	396	99	317	617
Brazil	4,968	6,199	496	4,224	8,352	3,766	9,243	11,258	14,459	29,306
Chile	999	1,886	1,747	1,955	3,462	1,455	1,380	2,549	4,223	1,952
Colombia	2,472	234	738	398	-29	-149	-346	2,681	4,384	4,303
Costa Rica	88	156	195	347	210	332	336	234	-61	314
Dominican Republic	66	-6	129	320	368	-38	178	102	240	...
Ecuador	828	1,288	699	823	455	712	440	1,298	...	...
El Salvador	31	-66	41	156	65	-50	135	80	9	212
Guatemala	50	424	258	398	164	658	590	768	669	516
Guyana	74	49	51	103	176	143	201	166	115	...
Haiti	65	62	46	45	59	54	10	29	22	270
Honduras	174	251	250	328	302	166	337	258	223	198
Jamaica	30	202	138	320	418	213	278	252	389	391
Mexico	1,515	-1,358	-1,053	1,538	214	18,411	25,391	31,821	11,242	19,416
Nicaragua	660	757	718	494	442	10	710	412	588	...
Panama	221	-458	-94	338	650	387	50	-723	496	...
Paraguay	225	182	-153	0	59	103	-182	243	329	358
Peru	2,521	3,021	3,232	1,956	2,580	-3,985	1,131	1,958	4,007	2,609
Suriname	-10	-54	-87	-185	-20	33	-22	-35	-23	-54
Trinidad and Tobago	-178	43	1	83	-265	-130	-112	172	81	-143
Uruguay	88	342	67	-31	-21	-204	115	231	332	401
Venezuela	-964	97	-75	-3,998	-3,176	2,050	3,394	3,074	-2,150	-3,930
Latin America	**16,065**	**15,975**	**11,197**	**10,045**	**12,727**	**27,945**	**54,625**	**69,351**	**49,743**	**57,212**

TABLE D-14. PRIVATE SECTOR

(Millions of Dollars)

Country	1986	1987	1988	1989	1990	1991	1992	1993	1994	1995p
Argentina	508	-332	633	-5,117	-2,991	326	11,727	6,783	4,616	-6,294
Bahamas	-12	-8	39	43	7	156	50	20	69	306
Barbados	17	25	-6	-30	25	41	-58	21	16	...
Belize	2	2	16	23	19	6	4	9	8	0
Bolivia	135	-47	-87	-158	38	83	211	79	100	383
Brazil	-3,977	-6,512	-6,129	-3,658	1,091	3,648	5,504	11,773	16,706	29,505
Chile	716	1,449	1,782	2,531	3,581	1,264	1,045	3,197	4,439	...
Colombia	1,915	391	372	37	-11	-115	160	2,713	3,884	2,723
Costa Rica	-23	64	74	142	121	279	348	279	221	349
Dominican Republic	50	89	106	48	280	4	314	133	206	...
Ecuador	-20	1,028	546	808	1,140	1,306	1,043	1,924	1,623	...
El Salvador	12	5	7	20	-2	42	46	33	-2	16
Guatemala	192	428	460	241	182	849	627	872	611	490
Guyana	22	13	-4	26	-62	46	138	70	43	46
Haiti	39	40	28	28	8	14	0	0	0	6
Honduras	-18	2	25	19	-4	-6	135	22	96	90
Jamaica	20	129	42	-107	341	245	377	247	508	400
Mexico	-5,827	-3,909	-7	1,846	5,635	15,398	20,394	21,636	10,747	5,847
Nicaragua	-16	-5	-11	25	20	-153	18	38	72	...
Panama	144	-487	-375	9	403	147	-20	-915	277	...
Paraguay	108	143	-100	62	181	76	-120	110	129	208
Peru	-5	-17	-35	-57	-135	14	187	518	3,087	...
Suriname	-12	-57	-94	-191	-19	30	-29	-37	-25	-56
Trinidad and Tobago	-112	12	-139	128	-191	-31	-73	153	144	13
Uruguay	-48	105	-73	-125	-143	-156	15	105	119	129
Venezuela	-46	589	-1,082	-4,315	-1,083	2,105	2,459	1,948	-2,061	-3,387
Latin America	**-6,237**	**-6,861**	**-4,012**	**-7,724**	**8,431**	**25,619**	**44,500**	**51,730**	**45,633**	**30,772**

TABLE D-15. PRIVATE SECTOR: DIRECT INVESTMENT

(Millions of Dollars)

Country	1986	1987	1988	1989	1990	1991	1992	1993	1994	1995p
Argentina	574	-19	1,147	1,028	1,836	2,439	4,179	6,305	1,215	872
Bahamas	-13	11	37	25	-17	0	7	27	27	171
Barbados	5	5	11	5	10	6	14	7	12	...
Belize	5	7	14	19	17	14	16	9	9	3
Bolivia	10	36	-36	-46	10	23	33	27	128	372
Brazil	202	1,031	2,629	608	324	89	1,924	801	2,035	2,576
Chile	313	885	952	1,279	582	400	321	410	870	1,008
Colombia	642	293	159	547	484	433	740	710	1,516	2,051
Costa Rica	57	76	121	95	160	173	222	244	82	...
Dominican Republic	50	89	106	110	133	145	180	183	190	199
Ecuador	81	123	155	160	126	160	178	469	531	470
El Salvador	24	18	17	14	2	25	15	16	0	...
Guatemala	69	150	330	76	48	91	94	143	38	70
Guyana	0	4	6	9	7	24	152	25	17	15
Haiti	5	5	10	9	8	14	0	0	0	6
Honduras	30	39	48	51	44	52	48	35	55	60
Jamaica	-5	53	-12	57	138	133	142	78	117	200
Mexico	2,400	2,634	2,879	3,174	2,634	4,762	4,393	4,389	7,978	6,964
Nicaragua	0	0	0	0	0	0	15	39	40	44
Panama	172	-782	-265	1,028	-147	138	173	-658	-85	...
Paraguay	1	5	8	13	76	84	137	111	180	207
Peru	22	32	26	59	41	-7	145	371	2,326	1,691
Suriname	-34	-73	-96	-168	-43	10	-30	-47	-30	-61
Trinidad and Tobago	-22	35	63	149	109	169	178	379	516	286
Uruguay	33	55	45	0	0	0	0	102	170	124
Venezuela	-444	-16	21	34	76	1,728	473	-514	239	364
Latin America	**4,176**	**4,696**	**8,374**	**8,336**	**6,657**	**11,103**	**13,747**	**13,661**	**18,173**	**17,692**

TABLE D-16. PRIVATE SECTOR: PORTFOLIO INVESTMENT[1]

(Millions of Dollars)

Country	1986	1987	1988	1989	1990	1991	1992	1993	1994	1995p
Argentina	0	0	0	0	3	472	1,919	3,156	...	3,875
Bahamas	0	0	0	0	0	0	0	0	0	...
Barbados	-6	-2	-1	-5	-6	-8	-4	-10	1	...
Belize	0	0	0	0	0	0	0	7	6	4
Bolivia	0	0	0	0	0	0	0	0	0	...
Brazil	-203	-105	-148	-215	584	3,816	7,366	8,394	11,575	10,011
Chile	0	0	0	87	359	25	332	1,067	1,022	22
Colombia	30	48	0	179	-4	81	60	203	-65	-313
Costa Rica	-3	0	0	0	0	0	0	0	0	...
Dominican Republic	0	0	0	0	0	0	0	0	0	...
Ecuador	0	0	0	0	0	0	0	0	...	...
El Salvador	0	0	0	0	0	0	0	0	0	...
Guatemala	-1	0	0	0	0	93	27	0	0	...
Guyana	0	0	0	0	0	0	0	0	1	...
Haiti	0	0	0	0	0	0	0	0	...	...
Honduras	-1	1	0	0	0	0	0	0	0	...
Jamaica	0	0	0	0	0	0	0	0	0	...
Mexico	0	-69	-389	502	3,093	7,671	8,342	17,034	6,150	450
Nicaragua	0	0	0	0	0	0	0	0	0	...
Panama	55	-4	171	-102	-301	31	15	-617	-6	...
Paraguay	0	0	0	0	0	0	0	0	0	...
Peru	0	0	0	0	0	0	0	222	550	199
Suriname	0	0	0	0	0	0	0	0	0	0
Trinidad and Tobago	0	0	0	0	0	0	0	0	0	0
Uruguay	0	0	-60	0	0	0	0	0	0	...
Venezuela	0	0	0	0	0	229	934	40	562	314
Latin America	**-128**	**-131**	**-427**	**446**	**3,728**	**12,409**	**18,991**	**29,496**	**...**	**...**

[1] Excludes, by definition of the private sector, government portfolio investment.

TABLE D-17. PRIVATE SECTOR: OTHER LONG-TERM

(Millions of Dollars)

Country	1986	1987	1988	1989	1990	1991	1992	1993	1994	1995p
Argentina	-390	37	-111	-344	246	1	-271	-8,744	...	...
Bahamas	2	-17	5	20	29	159	47	-3	46	135
Barbados	4	4	-15	-24	16	36	16	3	28	10
Belize	0	0	0	0	4	2	3	3	6	5
Bolivia	0	13	22	9	55	64	170	52	-28	11
Brazil	-4,160	-7,415	-7,107	-3,534	-320	-1,208	-2,916	-2,393	-3,762	-1,677
Chile	-204	77	5	322	1,215	77	3	645	1,385	...
Colombia	1,324	61	309	-150	-315	-371	-370	796	1,759	512
Costa Rica	-57	-53	-1	13	17	26	14	6	113	...
Dominican Republic	0	0	0	65	-17	14	-23	-22	-29	...
Ecuador	-70	-2	-2	43	11	3	103	348	225	...
El Salvador	-1	0	-11	1	-4	17	31	17	-2	...
Guatemala	38	10	3	21	18	123	96	164	302	163
Guyana	22	9	-11	14	-68	23	-18	-22	-20	...
Haiti	35	35	18	18	0	0	0	0	0	...
Honduras	-48	-66	-49	-48	-61	-200	72	-45	-42	-16
Jamaica	-37	-4	-6	-6	61	30	9	1	17	0
Mexico	-8,873	-2,293	-3,220	-1,394	307	1,573	1,648	201	724	...
Nicaragua	-3	7	2	-5	-16	-37	2	-58	41	...
Panama	30	-82	-152	-916	596	197	-173	-44	-69	...
Paraguay	34	-74	-53	-36	8	-50	-61	-36	-34	1
Peru	-60	-29	-22	-10	4	117	80	52	284	177
Suriname	19	12	-2	10	9	16	-2	0	-7	-3
Trinidad and Tobago	28	-57	-181	-4	-282	-184	-234	-215	-366	-273
Uruguay	12	7	-21	20	9	-93	-35	4	6	...
Venezuela	-555	-922	-686	17	430	97	986	1,861	-971	-1,312
Latin America	**-12,912**	**-10,741**	**-11,286**	**-5,898**	**1,952**	**432**	**-824**	**-7,427**	**...**	**...**

TABLE D-18. PRIVATE SECTOR: OTHER SHORT-TERM

(Millions of Dollars)

Country	1986	1987	1988	1989	1990	1991	1992	1993	1994	1995p
Argentina	324	-350	-403	-5,801	-5,076	-2,586	5,900	6,066	...	...
Bahamas	...	...	...	...	...	...	...	...	...	...
Barbados	14	18	-1	-7	6	7	-84	21	-24	...
Belize	-3	-5	2	5	-2	-9	-15	-9	-13	-12
Bolivia	125	-96	-72	-121	-28	-4	8	0	0	0
Brazil	184	-23	-1,503	-517	503	951	-870	4,971	6,858	18,595
Chile	607	487	825	843	1,425	762	389	1,075	1,162	...
Colombia	-51	37	-96	-360	-180	-177	-210	1,003	675	473
Costa Rica	-22	40	-46	34	-56	80	112	29	27	...
Dominican Republic	0	0	0	-127	164	-155	157	-28	46	...
Ecuador	-31	907	393	605	1,003	1,143	762	1,107	867	...
El Salvador	-11	-13	0	5	0	0	0	0	0	...
Guatemala	86	269	128	144	116	543	411	566	271	258
Guyana	0	0	0	3	0	0	4	66	45	7
Haiti	0	0	0	0	0	0	0	0	...	...
Honduras	0	29	26	16	14	142	16	32	84	46
Jamaica	62	79	60	-158	143	82	225	169	373	200
Mexico	646	-4,181	723	-436	-399	1,392	6,011	12	-4,105	...
Nicaragua	-13	-13	-13	30	36	-115	1	57	-10	...
Panama	-113	381	-129	-2	255	-219	-34	404	437	...
Paraguay	74	211	-55	85	97	43	-196	35	-17	...
Peru	33	-20	-39	-106	-180	-96	-38	-127	-73	...
Suriname	3	4	3	-33	16	3	4	9	12	8
Trinidad and Tobago	-118	34	-20	-17	-19	-16	-17	-12	-6	...
Uruguay	-92	43	-96	-145	-152	-64	50	-1	-56	5
Venezuela	953	1,527	-417	-4,366	-1,589	51	66	561	-1,891	-2,753
Latin America	**2,658**	**-635**	**-730**	**-10,426**	**-3,905**	**1,758**	**12,650**	**16,005**	**...**	**...**

TABLE D-19. GOVERNMENT SECTOR

(Millions of Dollars)

Country	1986	1987	1988	1989	1990	1991	1992	1993	1994	1995p
Argentina	1,181	2,795	2,939	5,267	1,003	3,323	-708	5,628	5,252	6,470
Bahamas	10	-21	-8	5	13	6	-3	-16	-6	0
Barbados	44	58	42	7	6	-35	-46	-38	-109	...
Belize	4	1	10	11	8	10	6	16	7	-3
Bolivia	253	252	275	382	136	92	184	20	217	234
Brazil	8,945	12,711	6,625	7,882	7,261	118	3,739	-515	-2,247	-199
Chile	283	437	-35	-576	-119	191	335	-648	-216	...
Colombia	557	-157	366	361	-18	-34	-506	-32	500	1,580
Costa Rica	111	93	121	205	89	53	-11	-46	-282	-35
Dominican Republic	16	-95	23	272	88	-43	-134	-31	34	...
Ecuador	848	260	153	15	-685	-594	-603	-626	-607	...
El Salvador	19	-71	34	136	66	-92	89	47	11	197
Guatemala	-142	-5	-202	157	-18	-191	-38	-104	58	25
Guyana	53	36	56	78	238	96	63	97	72	...
Haiti	26	23	18	17	51	40	10	29	22	263
Honduras	192	249	225	309	305	172	202	236	127	108
Jamaica	11	73	96	427	77	-33	-99	5	-119	-10
Mexico	7,342	2,551	-1,046	-308	-5,421	3,013	4,997	10,185	495	13,569
Nicaragua	675	762	729	469	422	162	692	374	517	...
Panama	77	29	281	330	247	240	70	192	219	...
Paraguay	117	40	-53	-62	-122	28	-61	133	200	150
Peru	2,526	3,038	3,267	2,013	2,715	-3,999	944	1,440	920	...
Suriname	2	3	8	7	-1	3	8	2	2	2
Trinidad and Tobago	-66	30	140	-45	-73	-98	-39	20	-63	-155
Uruguay	136	236	139	94	122	-48	100	126	212	273
Venezuela	-918	-492	1,007	317	-2,093	-55	935	1,126	-89	-543
Latin America	**22,302**	**22,836**	**15,209**	**17,769**	**4,296**	**2,326**	**10,126**	**17,621**	**5,126**	**21,925**

TABLE D-20. GOVERNMENT SECTOR: LONG-TERM[1]

(Millions of Dollars)

Country	1986	1987	1988	1989	1990	1991	1992	1993	1994	1995p
Argentina	2,094	2,490	169	4,007	-979	1,177	-1,983	14,863	2,220	759
Bahamas	10	-21	-8	5	13	6	-3	-16	-6	0
Barbados	48	75	43	9	6	-45	-49	-35	-16	-11
Belize	4	1	10	11	8	10	6	16	7	-3
Bolivia	-52	-28	271	243	223	191	231	155	83	49
Brazil	8,570	7,672	7,597	2,531	-3,593	-3,424	16,635	-1,360	3,951	311
Chile	640	121	-99	-748	-50	203	288	-489	-130	...
Colombia	503	-163	366	256	27	81	-33	-126	345	1,236
Costa Rica	-40	-378	-208	-46	411	267	-14	11	-286	...
Dominican Republic	92	-20	137	-30	-209	749	-8	-35	-46	...
Ecuador	651	285	81	232	-518	-597	-688	-697	-489	...
El Salvador	42	-54	23	202	32	20	57	79	41	...
Guatemala	-61	-23	-224	29	-33	-82	61	8	74	25
Guyana	-15	-20	-15	234	503	96	155	92	61	...
Haiti	0	18	-5	2	49	29	-11	-15	-12	112
Honduras	49	107	66	37	158	108	63	187	112	66
Jamaica	-141	206	30	198	87	93	-7	53	-87	-12
Mexico	7,116	2,780	-1,051	-305	-5,393	3,000	5,426	10,156	530	-11,221
Nicaragua	391	73	202	-88	-135	240	-417	-215	-526	...
Panama	88	-377	-502	-362	-191	-202	55	-178	223	...
Paraguay	111	-13	-41	59	-140	17	-54	95	154	175
Peru	940	1,184	1,151	1,053	832	649	549	2,612	541	-197
Suriname	1	1	7	6	-1	3	7	2	2	2
Trinidad and Tobago	-66	30	140	2	-73	-98	-39	20	-63	-155
Uruguay	136	232	124	100	45	-94	211	133	225	315
Venezuela	-986	-794	174	-1,494	-407	445	545	495	-572	-1
Latin America	**20,123**	**13,384**	**8,437**	**6,143**	**-9,330**	**2,840**	**20,983**	**25,810**	**6,335**	**-8,551**

[1] Includes Government Sector portfolio investment.

TABLE D-21. GOVERNMENT SECTOR: SHORT-TERM

(Millions of Dollars)

Country	1986	1987	1988	1989	1990	1991	1992	1993	1994	1995p
Argentina	-913	305	2,770	1,260	1,982	2,146	1,275	-9,235	...	...
Bahamas	...	...	...	...	...	...	...	...	...	...
Barbados	-4	-17	-1	-3	1	10	3	-3	-93	...
Belize	0	0	0	0	0	0	0	0	0	0
Bolivia	306	279	5	140	-87	-99	-46	-135	134	185
Brazil	375	5,039	-972	5,351	10,854	3,542	-12,896	845	-6,198	-510
Chile	-357	316	64	172	-69	-12	47	-159	-86	...
Colombia	54	6	0	105	-45	-115	-473	95	155	344
Costa Rica	151	471	329	251	-323	-214	2	-57	4	...
Dominican Republic	-76	-75	-113	302	297	-792	-126	4	81	...
Ecuador	197	-25	72	-217	-167	3	85	71	-118	...
El Salvador	-23	-17	11	-66	35	-112	32	-32	-30	...
Guatemala	-81	18	22	128	15	-108	-99	-112	-16	...
Guyana	68	56	70	-156	-265	0	-92	4	10	...
Haiti	26	5	23	15	3	12	21	44	35	151
Honduras	143	142	159	272	147	64	140	49	15	42
Jamaica	152	-133	66	229	-10	-126	-92	-48	-31	3
Mexico	226	-229	5	-3	-28	13	-429	29	-35	...
Nicaragua	285	689	527	557	557	-78	1,109	590	1,042	...
Panama	-11	407	784	692	439	442	15	370	-4	...
Paraguay	7	52	-12	-121	18	11	-8	38	46	-25
Peru	1,586	1,854	2,116	960	1,883	-4,648	395	-1,172	379	...
Suriname	1	2	0	0	0	0	0	0	0	0
Trinidad and Tobago	0	0	0	-47	0	0	0	0	0	...
Uruguay	0	4	15	-5	77	47	-112	-7	-13	-43
Venezuela	68	302	833	1,811	-1,686	-500	390	631	483	-542
Latin America	**2,180**	**9,451**	**6,772**	**11,626**	**13,626**	**-514**	**-10,857**	**-8,190**	**...**	**...**

TABLE D-22. MONETARY SECTOR

(Millions of Dollars)

Country	1986	1987	1988	1989	1990	1991	1992	1993	1994	1995p
Argentina	-23	-33	23	56	100	-31	-60	-2,499	...	...
Bahamas	27	12	39	45	33	12	-38	1	16	-15
Barbados	10	1	10	-4	11	3	6	8	102	...
Belize	-5	0	2	-9	-2	6	13	7	4	27
Bolivia	-26	-5	-47	-54	32	29	72	-8	139	150
Brazil	-2,954	-1,777	-2,114	-2,706	-2,987	-2,971	1,130	-1,250	-5,516	...
Chile	-283	-873	-570	-561	-451	-621	1,551	62	209	-784
Colombia	-1,312	-235	201	80	27	-634	512	-20	-1,321	166
Costa Rica	-11	6	1	4	-1	-8	7	28	-19	-113
Dominican Republic	79	-26	-36	79	41	-11	-14	-11	39	...
Ecuador	-7	50	-12	-35	-25	-11	-26	-32	...	...
El Salvador	38	5	21	13	-43	22	0	19	75	210
Guatemala	13	39	17	-14	-17	-4	14	0	0	-78
Guyana	4	-12	0	-15	-11	16	-3	7	-1	...
Haiti	-10	-9	5	31	-23	-16	-13	-31	-27	-22
Honduras	0	29	-11	-21	-77	-35	-44	-12	-3	-12
Jamaica	8	4	-5	-2	-17	-38	-35	-4	-37	-21
Mexico	483	-259	-18	-39	8,312	6,748	1,648	1,939	1,512	-4,104
Nicaragua	1	7	-10	1	6	-3	-1	-15	7	...
Panama	-99	374	275	-60	-567	-518	-344	-228	-404	...
Paraguay	-44	7	-4	-20	-30	48	-23	-23	72	85
Peru	-41	-67	-5	-176	-25	-525	233	118	-402	...
Suriname	12	3	21	12	5	0	-27	-38	-61	4
Trinidad and Tobago	-40	22	-77	-23	14	10	11	-85	-120	76
Uruguay	-70	-8	175	55	-49	-153	-156	-3	54	-29
Venezuela	257	863	-1,105	348	-885	154	-8	-418	-974	154
Latin America	**-3,993**	**-1,883**	**-3,225**	**-3,016**	**3,372**	**1,469**	**4,406**	**-2,487**	**...**	**...**

TABLE D-23. CHANGE IN RESERVES

(Millions of Dollars)

Country	1986	1987	1988	1989	1990	1991	1992	1993	1994	1995p
Argentina	891	1,917	-1,858	1,348	-3,378	-2,630	-4,550	-2,547	-558	2,019
Bahamas	31	60	1	27	-9	-13	29	-19	-9	-17
Barbados	-20	-6	-38	43	38	40	-28	-21	-88	-44
Belize	-12	-12	-22	-16	-16	16	0	14	4	-4
Bolivia	-115	48	43	105	-18	-22	-27	71	-139	-150
Brazil	3,231	-2,165	-1,712	-1,701	-1,245	-197	-15,069	-9,213	-7,348	-12,966
Chile	252	-136	-826	-570	-2,331	-1,249	-2,547	-420	-3,127	-1,061
Colombia	-1,292	-402	-193	-434	-610	-1,836	-1,092	-206	-167	-350
Costa Rica	-94	-37	-242	-146	172	-348	-175	60	45	-185
Dominican Republic	-44	147	-110	2	-8	-342	-26	-90	377	-119
Ecuador	207	116	-32	-187	-280	-157	-99	-528	-331	155
El Salvador	-44	-82	20	-115	-170	70	-92	-112	-113	-147
Guatemala	-113	53	141	-72	30	-554	20	-152	-53	157
Guyana	62	77	32	30	-18	-41	-35	-38	-28	24
Haiti	-25	-9	-23	1	31	-22	-11	-19	-16	-188
Honduras	-60	-65	-14	29	-24	-66	-11	106	-17	-118
Jamaica	-103	-166	-135	-46	-119	86	-212	-114	-369	-20
Mexico	117	-5,585	6,637	-178	-2,303	-7,993	-1,745	-7,232	17,665	-9,593
Nicaragua	211	-6	-44	-64	39	-86	-1	79	-55	-4
Panama	-60	38	5	-49	-298	-199	-116	-90	-93	-215
Paraguay	140	-38	168	-145	-219	-299	347	-86	-338	-7
Peru	425	1,094	149	-265	-275	-950	-603	-413	-3,070	-103
Suriname	40	9	5	0	-10	44	12	-13	-34	-102
Trinidad and Tobago	722	256	143	-67	-97	153	35	-159	-186	-41
Uruguay	-282	-88	-17	-95	-152	-155	-189	-193	-90	-209
Venezuela	3,882	935	3,872	-113	-2,476	-2,424	662	-124	972	2,391
Latin America	**7,949**	**-4,047**	**5,951**	**-2,678**	**-13,746**	**-19,173**	**-25,524**	**-21,458**	**2,833**	**-20,895**

TABLE D-24. ERRORS AND OMISSIONS

(Millions of Dollars)

Country	1986	1987	1988	1989	1990	1991	1992	1993	1994	1995p
Argentina	302	-112	-165	-249	715	-341	137	87	...[a]	...[a]
Bahamas	-77	15	-10	-27	52	-62	1	2	43	36
Barbados	-59	-54	-50	-39	-65	-24	-17	-35	-44	5
Belize	-1	0	-3	9	-25	-13	6	2	9	10
Bolivia	141	184	120	-5	12	81	93	343	-203	-309
Brazil	66	-805	-827	-819	-296	852	-1,393	-814	-442	1,444
Chile	224	-141	-116	-119	-143	303	324	-95	-548	-267
Colombia	-251	67	-530	157	70	270	14	-340	150	90
Costa Rica	98	131	225	209	43	100	202	298	498	136
Dominican Republic	82	249	36	-74	-121	548	569	424	-498	...[a]
Ecuador	-432	-268	28	115	216	163	-99	-56	122	1,258
El Salvador	-142	7	-107	141	299	126	66	90	47	...[a]
Guatemala	67	-73	-2	55	36	83	82	85	9	...[a]
Guyana	1	-4	11	-4	3	1	-16	3	15	-32
Haiti	15	-14	12	-14	22	108	56	99	29	...[a]
Honduras	3	-33	-93	-139	-107	152	29	-82	152	202
Jamaica	80	85	-46	10	29	-20	-60	50	-31	-140
Mexico	-738	2,955	-3,192	4,504	1,228	-2,278	-852	-3,128	-1,635	-5,064
Nicaragua	-184	-79	52	-69	-181	85	60	128	154	130
Panama	333	-757	-531	670	452	1,052	1,134	1,616	520	...
Paraguay	44	338	198	-91	362	472	458	700	687	748
Peru	-1,672	-2,258	-2,042	-1,647	-1,602	6,273	896	13	1,715	1,242
Suriname	-21	-35	-4	8	-12	-2	22	42	60	72
Trinidad and Tobago	-92	-95	21	45	-112	-29	-73	-42	6	-67
Uruguay	221	-105	-247	-63	36	469	238	209	94	176
Venezuela	-930	-505	3,117	1,603	-1,742	-1,516	-299	-539	-298	-187
Latin America	**-2,920**	**-1,306**	**-4,146**	**4,168**	**-830**	**6,852**	**1,578**	**-940**	**...**	**...**

[a] Included in Capital Account.

BALANCE OF PAYMENTS NOTES

The concepts and definitions underlying the Balance of Payments statistics are described in the IMF Balance of Payments Manual, Fifth Edition (1991). For analytical purposes, the tables follow a summarized uniform presentation of the balance of payments for the Latin American countries.

Current Account Balance

This account is the sum of the trade, services and unrequited transfers balances. It is also the sum of exports of goods and services, imports of goods and services, and the unrequited transfers balance.

Trade Balance: This records the difference between merchandise exports and imports, both expressed as "free on board" (f.o.b.) values.

Exports of Goods: Merchandise exports (including non-monetary gold), valued f.o.b.

Imports of Goods: Merchandise imports (including non-monetary gold), valued f.o.b.

Service Balance: This is the net result of income and expenditure under the categories of freight and insurance on international shipments, travel, transportation, investment income, and other services.

Freight and Insurance: The entries cover net transactions in connection with all forms of transportation used for international shipments, including ocean and inland waterway shipping, and air, rail, and road transportation. This account also includes insurance claims paid by foreigners to residents (credit) and by residents to foreigners (debit) with respect to international shipments.

Travel: This category includes all receipts for goods and services provided to foreigners visiting the reporting country (credit), and all payments for goods and services provided by foreigners to the residents of the reporting country traveling abroad (debit).

Investment Income: The entries in this account cover net income derived from holdings of external financial assets by residents, and from liabilities to nonresidents, respectively. These holdings constitute approximately all Nonfactor Services (NFS), and are composed of two elements: income on direct investments, and other investment income. Direct Investment Income is derived from dividends on shares and profits of enterprises. Other Investment Income is derived from interest on loans and deposits; as well as interest and dividends on bonds, securities, and other instruments classified under portfolio investment. The credits of Investment Income are income received by residents of the reporting country from assets invested abroad; the debits are income paid to nonresidents on their assets invested in the reporting country.

The concept of capital income used is accrued income. Therefore, the income that is in arrears is included in this item. In compensation, income in arrears is also included in the capital account: as a credit if the entity in arrears is nonresident; as a debit if it is resident.

Other Services: This category refers to receipts and payments of the following items: (1) payments for transportation services other than freight, such as ship repairs, harbor and airport fees, mail transportation fees, and passenger fares and shipboard expenses arising from international travel; (2) expenditures by diplomats and military personnel; and (3) services related to assistance programs, professional and technical services, motion picture rentals, authors' royalties, and all other expenses not included in the other categories of the services account.

Unrequited Transfers: This account refers to receipts and payments without a quid pro quo. They may be in cash or in kind and include both private and official (government) transactions.

Private Unrequited Transfers: Include remittances of migrants to their families and contributions for missionary, educational, charitable, and similar purposes.

Official Unrequited Transfers: The main component is economic aid in the form of grants.

Capital Account Balance:

This is the net result of capital inflows and outflows of the monetary and nonmonetary sectors. Capital movements in the following categories are entered on a net basis. Detail of gross recordings may be either unavailable, or incomplete for all categories.

Nonmonetary Sectors: This is made up of the Private and Government Sectors.

Private Sector: This is the sum of private direct investment, private portfolio investment, other private long-term capital, and other private short-term capital. This item also includes public enterprises or enterprises where the public sector shares its ownership. The components of the public sector excluded are the general government, the central bank, and public commercial banks.

Direct Investment: The flow of international capital where the investor (either foreign or domestic) has a permanent and effective share in the management or control of firms outside of the country in which he or she resides.

Portfolio Investment: This covers transactions in equity securities and debt securities (bonds), short-term money market instruments, and derivative instruments such as options (when they generate financial claims and liabilities) of the private sector. This includes all participations in the capital of private firms. In this category, the investor does not participate in a permanent or effective manner in the management or control of firms.

Other Long-Term: This is a residual category that includes all private, long-term capital transactions in assets or liabilities (not covered under direct or portfolio investment), with an original contractual maturity of more than one year, or with no stated maturity, as, for example, with equity securities.

Other Short-Term: This account is a residual category that includes all private, short-term capital transactions in assets or liabilities (not covered under direct or portfolio investment), with an original maturity of 12 months or less, on which the domestic private sector is creditor or debtor. Outstanding liabilities and assets in this category are adjusted to exclude valuation changes. Liabilities mainly cover commercial short-term obligations and debts to banks. Assets include foreign notes and coin, deposits in foreign banks, holdings of foreign government and corporate short-term obligations, and commercial claims. Commercial obligations and claims include trade bills, acceptances, and other short-term claims arising from the financing of trade.

Government Sector: This category covers foreign transactions in assets and liabilities of the general government and the central bank. Transactions by local governments (states and provinces) are usually in securities or in loans. The principal types of transactions by central governmental institutions are official lending and borrowing, repayments on official loans, and transactions with international nonmonetary institutions.

Portfolio Investment: This account includes transactions in government sector bonds.

Long-Term: This is a residual category that includes all official, long-term capital transactions in assets or liabilities (not covered under official portfolio investment).

Short-Term: This account is a residual category that includes all official, short-term capital transactions in assets or liabilities (not covered under official portfolio investment), with an original maturity of 12 months or less, on which the domestic public sector is creditor or debtor.

Monetary Sector: The entries cover the net foreign transactions of commercial banks, savings banks and similar institutions. Central bank transactions are not included in this account.

Change in International Reserves: Shows the change in the net position in actual assets and liabilities available to an economy's monetary authorities to use in meeting Balance of Payments needs. Thus, this category includes changes in monetary gold, Special Drawing Rights (SDRs), reserve position in the International Monetary Fund (IMF), foreign exchange, and the use of IMF credit.

Errors and Omissions: This item is an offset to the over or under statement of the recorded components in the Balance of Payments. Hence, if the balance of those components is a credit, the item for net errors and omissions will be shown as a debit of equal value, and vice versa.

Sources:

The historical data are from the International Monetary Fund Balance of Payments magnetic tapes, various dates. The Balance of Payments of Mexico, however, is the exception. Unlike the IMF method, the IDB includes maquiladora exports with Exports of Goods, f.o.b., and registers maquiladora imports under Imports of Goods, f.o.b. The source for the latest year(s) is IDB estimates based on official information in the countries.

TABLE E-1. DISBURSED TOTAL EXTERNAL DEBT OUTSTANDING [1]

(Millions of Dollars)

Country	1986	1987	1988	1989	1990	1991	1992	1993	1994	1995p
Argentina	52,450	58,458	58,741	65,257	62,233	65,396	68,339	70,566	77,387	85,098
Bahamas	216	193	171	221	266	412	440	453	411	392
Barbados	580	577	703	644	683	652	610	569	575	562
Belize	121	137	139	144	152	169	172	184	177	183
Bolivia	5,575	5,836	4,902	4,136	4,278	4,076	4,223	4,220	4,749	4,938
Brazil	111,020	122,324	119,344	115,905	121,465	122,445	130,546	145,438	151,104	157,397
Chile	21,145	21,489	19,582	18,032	19,227	17,947	19,134	20,637	22,939	22,569
Colombia	15,362	17,008	16,995	16,878	17,232	17,334	17,197	17,177	19,416	19,784
Costa Rica	4,576	4,721	4,531	4,589	3,756	4,026	3,938	3,850	3,843	3,672
Dominican Republic	3,687	3,923	3,999	4,061	4,396	4,494	4,612	4,833	4,293	4,171
Ecuador	9,334	10,473	10,745	11,317	12,109	12,468	12,280	14,110	14,954	14,366
El Salvador	1,858	1,982	1,994	2,078	2,147	2,180	2,261	2,012	2,188	2,264
Guatemala	2,794	2,796	2,639	2,637	2,840	2,825	2,753	2,891	3,017	3,083
Guyana	1,634	1,738	1,866	1,633	1,946	1,960	1,897	1,954	2,000	2,058
Haiti	710	844	818	803	884	747	773	773	712	778
Honduras	2,974	3,299	3,307	3,385	3,722	3,395	3,614	4,075	4,418	4,480
Jamaica	4,221	4,724	4,553	4,560	4,671	4,410	4,264	4,112	4,318	4,229
Mexico	100,889	109,469	99,213	93,838	104,450	114,064	112,227	118,469	128,302	158,298
Nicaragua	6,821	7,976	8,741	9,743	10,692	10,654	11,145	10,541	11,019	9,614
Panama	4,859	5,630	6,066	6,318	6,679	6,733	6,486	6,958	7,107	8,053
Paraguay	2,087	2,520	2,352	2,383	2,106	2,067	1,634	1,597	1,979	2,112
Peru	14,888	17,490	18,245	18,583	20,070	20,719	20,339	20,449	22,623	23,097
Suriname	67	76	97	118	126	194	205	206	198	193
Trinidad and Tobago	1,855	1,802	2,061	2,117	2,508	2,475	2,374	2,133	...	...
Uruguay	3,906	4,299	3,821	4,449	4,415	4,189	4,570	4,848	5,099	5,080
Venezuela	34,340	34,570	34,738	32,377	33,170	34,122	37,848	37,539	36,850	37,434
Latin America	**407,970**	**444,353**	**430,360**	**426,205**	**446,221**	**460,154**	**473,883**	**500,594**	**529,676**	**573,905**

[1] Sum of long-term and short-term external debt and use of IMF credit.

TABLE E-2. DISBURSED TOTAL EXTERNAL DEBT OUTSTANDING: LONG-TERM

(Millions of Dollars)

Country	1986	1987	1988	1989	1990	1991	1992	1993	1994	1995p
Argentina	45,299	51,074	49,346	53,632	48,706	49,368	49,849	58,393	66,005	72,483
Bahamas	216	193	171	221	266	412	440	453	411	392
Barbados	426	448	529	480	504	483	401	347	330	319
Belize	97	111	126	136	146	159	162	166	161	167
Bolivia	4,625	4,821	4,340	3,629	3,867	3,686	3,798	3,792	4,185	4,358
Brazil	97,061	104,959	105,497	95,434	95,858	94,202	105,168	113,884	119,213	118,659
Chile	18,124	18,008	16,058	13,789	14,689	14,790	15,181	16,031	17,618	16,714
Colombia	13,765	15,352	15,384	15,261	15,793	15,583	14,361	13,945	14,615	14,452
Costa Rica	3,932	4,010	3,863	3,849	3,367	3,601	3,514	3,398	3,383	3,193
Dominican Republic	3,076	3,353	3,407	3,446	3,541	3,834	3,790	3,813	3,716	3,606
Ecuador	8,345	9,089	9,147	9,585	10,030	10,093	9,932	10,176	10,608	12,172
El Salvador	1,669	1,745	1,740	1,865	1,938	2,078	2,159	1,905	2,002	2,065
Guatemala	2,413	2,454	2,255	2,243	2,368	2,362	2,250	2,420	2,529	2,564
Guyana	868	968	995	1,261	1,757	1,760	1,673	1,731	1,788	1,836
Haiti	576	674	683	684	746	610	626	618	627	712
Honduras	2,504	2,815	2,858	2,950	3,491	3,170	3,322	3,738	3,984	4,048
Jamaica	3,354	3,808	3,774	3,786	3,968	3,737	3,595	3,488	3,518	3,459
Mexico	90,929	98,506	86,529	80,085	81,816	85,442	81,743	86,401	92,843	109,560
Nicaragua	5,807	6,447	7,020	7,661	8,245	8,771	8,999	8,770	9,006	8,104
Panama	3,495	4,027	4,005	3,935	3,988	3,918	3,771	3,799	3,923	4,773
Paraguay	1,912	2,252	2,121	2,123	1,733	1,706	1,386	1,309	1,370	1,485
Peru	11,375	13,022	12,723	13,001	13,965	15,662	15,809	16,624	18,149	18,155
Suriname	...	...	...	...	...	...	...	...	...	...
Trinidad and Tobago	1,582	1,636	1,816	1,785	2,052	1,963	1,894	1,849	1,800	1,886
Uruguay	2,938	3,270	3,037	3,113	3,114	2,926	3,174	3,436	3,836	3,826
Venezuela	32,763	30,484	29,464	29,089	28,159	28,589	29,628	30,177	30,475	30,974
Latin America	**357,151**	**383,526**	**366,890**	**353,043**	**354,105**	**358,902**	**366,623**	**390,664**	**416,096**	**439,920**

TABLE E-3. DISBURSED TOTAL EXTERNAL DEBT OUTSTANDING: SHORT-TERM [1]

(Millions of Dollars)

Country	1986	1987	1988	1989	1990	1991	1992	1993	1994	1995p
Argentina	4,410	3,531	5,717	8,525	10,445	13,546	16,176	8,653	7,171	6,571
Bahamas	...	...	...	...	...	...	...	...	...	...
Barbados	114	107	163	159	178	169	158	171	190	206
Belize	12	14	5	5	6	10	11	19	16	16
Bolivia	757	829	353	255	154	145	176	207	300	286
Brazil	9,457	13,389	10,514	18,049	23,787	27,006	24,579	31,250	31,705	38,596
Chile	1,689	2,017	2,202	2,973	3,382	2,199	3,231	4,130	5,029	5,658
Colombia	1,597	1,656	1,610	1,617	1,438	1,751	2,836	3,233	4,800	5,332
Costa Rica	472	579	596	705	377	343	342	371	393	407
Dominican Republic	307	287	374	492	783	571	698	834	388	404
Ecuador	503	895	1,194	1,407	1,814	2,192	2,249	3,863	4,148	2,015
El Salvador	127	214	243	208	209	102	102	107	185	199
Guatemala	311	283	296	321	406	399	473	470	488	519
Guyana	666	654	761	266	75	50	56	46	72	52
Haiti	56	90	88	77	101	105	112	122	50	35
Honduras	361	407	412	400	199	192	180	219	325	342
Jamaica	189	237	295	391	346	281	311	289	483	509
Mexico	5,900	5,800	7,879	8,662	16,082	21,857	24,535	27,281	31,599	32,899
Nicaragua	1,014	1,529	1,721	2,083	2,447	1,859	2,123	1,748	1,962	1,469
Panama	1,012	1,258	1,733	2,063	2,418	2,599	2,605	3,046	3,051	3,144
Paraguay	175	268	230	261	373	361	248	289	608	627
Peru	2,785	3,624	4,721	4,824	5,350	4,351	3,900	2,942	3,537	3,663
Suriname	...	...	...	...	...	...	...	...	...	...
Trinidad and Tobago	273	166	131	127	127	127	198	129	327	348
Uruguay	573	636	475	1,134	1,201	1,205	1,344	1,374	1,233	1,233
Venezuela	1,577	4,085	5,274	2,290	2,000	2,284	5,275	4,682	3,732	4,221
Latin America	**34,336**	**42,553**	**46,986**	**57,292**	**73,698**	**83,705**	**91,918**	**95,472**	**101,792**	**108,826**

[1] Includes arrears on long-term debt.

TABLE E-4. DISBURSED TOTAL EXTERNAL DEBT OUTSTANDING: USE OF IMF CREDIT

(Millions of Dollars)

Country	1986	1987	1988	1989	1990	1991	1992	1993	1994	1995p
Argentina	2,741	3,853	3,678	3,100	3,083	2,483	2,314	3,520	4,211	6,044
Bahamas	...	...	...	...	...	...	...	...	...	...
Barbados	40	22	10	4	1	0	51	51	54	37
Belize	12	11	8	3	0	0	0	0	0	0
Bolivia	192	186	209	252	257	245	249	221	264	294
Brazil	4,501	3,976	3,333	2,423	1,821	1,238	799	304	186	142
Chile	1,331	1,465	1,322	1,270	1,157	958	722	476	291	197
Colombia	0	0	0	0	0	0	0	0	0	0
Costa Rica	172	132	71	35	11	83	82	81	66	72
Dominican Republic	304	284	218	123	72	89	123	186	190	161
Ecuador	486	490	405	325	265	182	100	71	198	179
El Salvador	62	22	11	5	0	0	0	0	0	0
Guatemala	70	59	88	73	67	64	31	0	0	0
Guyana	101	116	110	106	113	149	168	177	179	170
Haiti	79	80	47	41	38	33	35	34	35	31
Honduras	110	77	37	35	32	34	112	118	109	90
Jamaica	678	679	483	383	357	391	357	335	318	261
Mexico	4,060	5,163	4,805	5,091	6,551	6,766	5,950	4,787	3,860	15,839
Nicaragua	0	0	0	0	0	0	24	23	51	41
Panama	353	346	328	320	272	216	110	113	133	136
Paraguay	0	0	0	0	0	0	0	0	0	0
Peru	728	845	801	758	755	706	631	883	938	1,279
Suriname	...	...	...	...	...	...	...	...	...	...
Trinidad and Tobago	0	0	115	205	329	385	282	155	91	52
Uruguay	395	392	309	202	101	58	52	38	30	21
Venezuela	0	0	0	998	3,012	3,249	2,946	2,680	2,643	2,239
Latin America	**16,416**	**18,198**	**16,387**	**15,752**	**18,292**	**17,352**	**15,137**	**14,252**	**13,847**	**27,301**

TABLE E-5. DISBURSED EXTERNAL PUBLIC DEBT OUTSTANDING: LONG-TERM

(Millions of Dollars)

Country	1986	1987	1988	1989	1990	1991	1992	1993	1994	1995p
Argentina	40,958	49,221	47,546	51,832	46,906	47,568	47,605	52,024	55,785	61,218
Bahamas	216	193	171	221	266	412	440	453	411	392
Barbados	426	448	529	480	504	483	401	347	330	319
Belize	97	111	119	128	135	150	155	162	160	167
Bolivia	4,070	4,621	4,140	3,429	3,690	3,534	3,674	3,695	4,113	4,311
Brazil	82,420	90,525	93,983	89,426	89,187	86,365	91,988	92,968	94,512	93,781
Chile	14,689	15,542	13,696	10,866	10,426	10,071	9,578	8,868	8,947	8,498
Colombia	12,181	13,828	13,846	13,989	14,671	14,469	13,239	12,865	13,604	13,003
Costa Rica	3,625	3,709	3,547	3,545	3,063	3,297	3,180	3,118	3,155	3,013
Dominican Republic	2,930	3,220	3,290	3,342	3,442	3,751	3,724	3,763	3,681	3,587
Ecuador	8,260	8,991	9,028	9,427	9,867	9,951	9,831	9,935	10,384	11,958
El Salvador	1,586	1,675	1,685	1,826	1,912	2,057	2,147	1,897	1,994	2,060
Guatemala	2,294	2,338	2,142	2,120	2,241	2,235	2,108	2,237	2,368	2,422
Guyana	868	968	995	1,261	1,757	1,760	1,673	1,731	1,788	1,836
Haiti	576	674	683	684	746	610	626	618	627	712
Honduras	2,379	2,701	2,757	2,866	3,424	3,095	3,232	3,650	3,884	3,963
Jamaica	3,291	3,750	3,724	3,744	3,934	3,709	3,567	3,460	3,440	3,386
Mexico	75,826	84,358	80,598	76,114	75,981	77,822	71,068	74,892	79,097	93,188
Nicaragua	5,807	6,447	7,020	7,661	8,245	8,771	8,999	8,770	9,006	8,104
Panama	3,495	4,027	4,005	3,935	3,988	3,918	3,771	3,799	3,923	3,971
Paraguay	1,826	2,224	2,093	2,095	1,714	1,685	1,365	1,283	1,352	1,469
Peru	11,000	12,635	12,337	12,617	13,635	15,444	15,581	16,384	17,890	17,661
Suriname	...	...	...	...	...	...	...	...	...	...
Trinidad and Tobago	1,582	1,636	1,816	1,785	1,779	1,737	1,708	1,699	1,682	1,796
Uruguay	2,895	3,126	2,951	3,008	3,045	2,897	3,139	3,369	3,774	3,655
Venezuela	25,329	25,008	25,181	25,166	24,509	24,939	25,830	26,855	28,039	28,960
Latin America	**308,624**	**341,974**	**337,880**	**331,567**	**329,066**	**330,728**	**328,630**	**338,842**	**353,945**	**373,388**

TABLE E-6. DISBURSED MULTILATERAL PUBLIC DEBT OUTSTANDING

(As a Percent of Total Debt)

Country	1986	1987	1988	1989	1990	1991	1992	1993	1994	1995p
Argentina	5.1	7.2	6.9	6.7	8.0	8.3	7.4	10.1	9.9	10.3
Bahamas	...	...	...	...	...	...	...	...	...	...
Barbados	23.3	28.0	23.8	25.7	26.5	27.5	28.2	28.6	26.6	28.1
Belize	30.9	29.8	29.4	35.7	37.6	35.7	34.2	31.7	36.1	35.5
Bolivia	16.9	18.9	26.3	34.8	37.2	42.2	43.4	47.4	47.9	48.0
Brazil	9.0	10.0	9.6	9.6	9.4	9.0	7.7	6.5	6.1	5.5
Chile	10.8	15.0	17.3	19.7	21.5	24.0	22.6	21.0	19.0	16.4
Colombia	29.7	33.9	33.0	33.5	35.4	35.5	34.2	33.1	27.7	26.3
Costa Rica	20.7	23.2	23.1	23.4	30.4	29.4	29.9	31.7	33.6	34.7
Dominican Republic	17.6	19.2	18.6	19.2	19.5	19.6	18.8	18.4	21.8	22.8
Ecuador	15.1	17.6	18.1	17.4	17.6	17.9	18.3	16.6	16.1	19.2
El Salvador	35.9	36.9	36.3	37.3	36.5	38.3	40.7	52.4	57.2	59.2
Guatemala	29.4	31.9	33.8	34.3	34.8	33.6	32.2	28.9	28.3	26.9
Guyana	19.0	20.8	19.2	22.6	24.0	27.0	28.3	29.4	30.4	32.9
Haiti	48.3	49.7	52.8	55.7	54.9	67.5	67.1	66.3	73.2	75.7
Honduras	40.1	40.9	41.2	43.8	42.5	48.8	49.8	47.9	46.7	46.2
Jamaica	21.3	24.4	23.8	23.9	25.0	26.8	26.2	28.0	27.4	28.3
Mexico	8.1	9.5	10.4	11.5	13.7	13.6	13.8	13.6	13.3	11.4
Nicaragua	11.5	10.8	10.5	9.5	9.1	9.3	10.1	11.0	11.9	14.6
Panama	19.6	19.2	16.8	15.8	15.3	14.2	10.7	9.0	8.2	7.1
Paraguay	32.1	32.9	33.1	30.8	34.9	35.0	42.5	43.1	36.0	36.7
Peru	11.2	12.2	11.2	10.9	11.0	9.1	10.2	13.4	14.8	16.1
Suriname	...	...	...	...	...	...	...	...	...	...
Trinidad and Tobago	3.5	4.0	3.2	3.3	4.1	6.4	8.8	14.0	...	...
Uruguay	10.1	12.8	14.8	14.1	15.8	20.5	21.3	22.5	23.9	24.4
Venezuela	0.3	0.5	0.9	1.7	4.9	6.5	7.2	7.7	8.5	9.0
Latin America	**10.0**	**11.6**	**11.7**	**12.2**	**13.4**	**13.5**	**13.0**	**13.0**	**12.8**	**12.2**

TABLE E-7. SERVICE PAYMENTS ON THE TOTAL EXTERNAL DEBT

(Millions of Dollars)

Country	1986	1987	1988	1989	1990	1991	1992	1993	1994	1995p
Argentina	7,323	6,244	5,023	4,357	6,161	5,545	5,003	6,562	6,692	9,569
Bahamas	142	53	68	56	45	73	79	82	94	84
Barbados	82	104	94	102	141	140	102	113	94	114
Belize	17	16	17	19	20	20	20	21	29	33
Bolivia	251	224	372	292	385	320	310	349	343	382
Brazil	11,627	12,019	16,875	14,132	8,134	8,303	8,484	11,111	16,114	21,199
Chile	2,220	2,367	2,148	2,668	2,772	2,700	2,693	2,842	2,909	4,093
Colombia	2,268	2,680	3,099	3,719	3,654	3,645	3,763	3,163	3,685	3,431
Costa Rica	500	334	403	345	501	418	544	552	497	694
Dominican Republic	374	307	340	322	239	270	329	333	504	540
Ecuador	1,152	838	1,059	1,029	1,084	1,106	981	920	986	1,234
El Salvador	286	260	203	171	208	248	233	293	341	260
Guatemala	383	344	374	304	212	289	517	302	282	282
Guyana	75	72	66	88	296	102	102	92	99	108
Haiti	47	61	59	52	33	27	5	5	1	13
Honduras	299	341	369	142	389	307	377	362	433	438
Jamaica	675	750	735	643	661	719	711	542	595	642
Mexico	12,946	12,088	15,473	15,563	11,316	13,545	20,821	21,147	19,049	20,194
Nicaragua	40	44	21	11	16	530	106	125	183	278
Panama	515	461	28	13	228	250	911	233	312	299
Paraguay	223	239	316	152	325	258	626	286	259	257
Peru	718	482	348	407	476	1,152	1,005	2,758	1,057	1,653
Suriname	6	6	...	...	...	...	...	...	45	41
Trinidad and Tobago	328	407	339	247	453	425	572	620	674	444
Uruguay	509	618	729	660	987	806	524	586	508	968
Venezuela	5,103	4,872	5,552	3,831	4,990	3,322	3,331	3,945	3,691	4,651
Latin America	**48,107**	**46,233**	**54,109**	**49,326**	**43,725**	**44,518**	**52,149**	**57,344**	**59,475**	**71,900**

TABLE E-8. SERVICE PAYMENTS ON THE TOTAL EXTERNAL DEBT: INTEREST

(Millions of Dollars)

Country	1986	1987	1988	1989	1990	1991	1992	1993	1994	1995p
Argentina	4,489	4,056	3,103	2,129	2,717	2,927	2,825	3,301	4,111	5,746
Bahamas	...	...	...	...	...	...	...	...	...	...
Barbados	41	39	45	48	49	46	43	41	41	43
Belize	6	6	5	7	7	6	7	7	8	8
Bolivia	109	101	121	126	144	138	119	132	150	153
Brazil	7,789	7,399	12,662	5,220	2,232	3,494	3,828	4,371	6,560	9,671
Chile	1,681	1,659	1,262	1,636	1,792	1,556	1,340	1,121	1,207	1,417
Colombia	1,147	1,268	1,374	1,568	1,484	1,430	1,266	1,085	1,224	1,352
Costa Rica	262	189	229	170	206	234	242	209	210	230
Dominican Republic	227	145	182	121	86	106	134	147	215	232
Ecuador	771	373	372	494	474	504	420	404	489	750
El Salvador	92	89	79	69	84	81	84	122	99	109
Guatemala	171	169	126	132	111	132	171	112	117	118
Guyana	61	60	55	59	120	53	49	42	36	33
Haiti	17	18	17	17	15	16	5	5	1	3
Honduras	142	126	158	72	178	160	174	152	179	183
Jamaica	290	283	251	230	260	240	212	204	215	225
Mexico	8,375	8,326	8,712	9,310	7,304	8,186	7,548	6,989	8,013	10,335
Nicaragua	24	15	12	5	11	201	64	72	118	124
Panama	346	256	13	5	107	122	309	88	147	135
Paraguay	91	109	133	75	90	107	246	88	96	101
Peru	352	290	219	239	247	525	465	1,138	536	571
Suriname	...	...	...	...	...	...	...	...	...	...
Trinidad and Tobago	137	143	156	177	214	210	176	136	271	189
Uruguay	347	358	354	369	428	255	262	263	304	367
Venezuela	3,085	2,747	3,123	3,086	3,242	2,425	2,137	2,162	2,118	2,516
Latin America	**30,050**	**28,222**	**32,764**	**25,363**	**21,602**	**23,153**	**22,125**	**22,388**	**26,462**	**34,601**

TABLE E-9. SERVICE PAYMENTS ON THE TOTAL EXTERNAL DEBT: AMORTIZATION

(Millions of Dollars)

Country	1986	1987	1988	1989	1990	1991	1992	1993	1994	1995p
Argentina	2,834	2,188	1,920	2,228	3,444	2,618	2,178	3,261	2,581	3,823
Bahamas	...	...	...	...	...	...	...	...	...	...
Barbados	41	64	49	54	92	94	59	72	53	71
Belize	10	10	12	11	13	13	13	14	21	25
Bolivia	142	122	251	166	241	182	191	216	193	229
Brazil	3,839	4,621	4,213	8,913	5,902	4,809	4,656	6,740	9,555	11,528
Chile	539	709	885	1,032	980	1,144	1,353	1,722	1,702	2,676
Colombia	1,121	1,412	1,725	2,151	2,171	2,215	2,497	2,078	2,462	2,079
Costa Rica	238	146	174	176	295	184	303	343	287	464
Dominican Republic	147	162	158	201	152	165	195	186	289	308
Ecuador	382	465	686	535	611	602	561	517	497	484
El Salvador	194	171	124	102	124	167	149	170	242	151
Guatemala	212	175	247	172	102	157	346	190	166	164
Guyana	14	12	12	30	175	49	53	51	61	47
Haiti	30	43	42	35	18	10	0	0	0	10
Honduras	157	215	211	70	211	147	203	210	254	255
Jamaica	385	468	484	412	401	479	499	338	381	417
Mexico	4,570	3,762	6,761	6,253	4,012	5,359	13,274	14,158	11,036	9,859
Nicaragua	16	29	9	7	4	329	43	54	65	154
Panama	169	206	15	8	121	129	603	146	165	164
Paraguay	132	131	183	77	235	151	380	197	163	156
Peru	366	191	129	169	229	627	540	1,620	521	1,082
Suriname	...	...	...	...	...	...	...	...	...	...
Trinidad and Tobago	191	265	183	71	239	215	396	484	403	255
Uruguay	162	260	376	291	559	551	262	324	204	601
Venezuela	2,018	2,125	2,429	745	1,748	897	1,194	1,783	1,573	2,135
Latin America	**17,909**	**17,952**	**21,277**	**23,907**	**22,078**	**21,293**	**29,945**	**34,874**	**32,872**	**37,136**

TABLE E-10. TOTAL EXTERNAL DEBT TO GROSS DOMESTIC PRODUCT

(In Percent)

Country	1986	1987	1988	1989	1990	1991	1992	1993	1994	1995p
Argentina	39.9	42.0	41.1	45.5	40.6	37.1	35.0	33.0	33.1	37.2
Bahamas	9.2	7.5	5.9	7.4	8.5	13.3	14.4	14.8	13.1	11.8
Barbados	44.1	39.8	45.6	37.8	39.9	38.7	38.6	34.6	33.3	30.0
Belize	53.0	49.4	44.2	39.5	37.9	39.1	35.9	35.1	32.5	31.7
Bolivia	125.6	124.8	107.5	84.7	80.3	69.5	69.5	52.3	54.3	62.3
Brazil	33.4	34.8	33.1	30.2	32.1	31.0	32.9	34.9	35.8	33.3
Chile	90.2	84.2	69.5	56.1	55.6	46.3	43.8	43.6	45.5	40.7
Colombia	42.0	43.8	41.7	39.2	37.6	36.1	34.2	32.3	34.0	33.7
Costa Rica	105.2	101.8	92.8	86.4	66.4	67.8	61.6	55.9	52.9	49.2
Dominican Republic	69.2	80.9	69.7	70.3	73.6	54.8	52.0	51.1	41.6	35.4
Ecuador	79.2	94.7	88.2	93.2	96.1	92.5	89.6	101.6	102.7	96.7
El Salvador	47.2	47.8	44.9	43.9	40.5	37.4	35.1	28.0	27.0	23.5
Guatemala	36.2	38.7	34.2	38.9	36.0	29.5	27.1	25.0	23.2	20.9
Guyana	245.9	294.1	354.0	397.6	518.8	558.2	502.0	458.4	431.2	423.4
Haiti	...	...	...	...	43.4	35.8	46.5	44.2	42.1	35.3
Honduras	78.1	84.3	88.3	107.7	130.5	109.7	120.5	133.2	131.4	117.2
Jamaica	139.4	143.6	133.1	121.9	118.2	112.2	117.8	115.3	121.7	129.4
Mexico	51.7	54.5	47.9	42.2	43.3	43.6	41.1	42.0	41.7	56.4
Nicaragua	267.7	319.5	431.2	510.6	451.1	606.2	623.0	579.5	574.7	503.9
Panama	93.6	105.0	131.7	136.2	133.3	122.5	107.8	106.0	103.0	108.6
Paraguay	43.9	50.4	43.5	40.7	34.1	31.5	24.3	22.5	26.2	27.2
Peru	46.1	48.2	51.6	54.3	55.8	52.2	51.2	47.4	45.0	41.7
Suriname	16.1	18.7	25.9	32.9	37.8	62.5	126.8	258.2	117.8	40.7
Trinidad and Tobago	37.0	37.9	44.6	45.2	47.6	44.8	43.0	38.6	...	...
Uruguay	51.3	51.1	44.0	48.7	46.0	40.5	39.7	39.3	38.2	38.9
Venezuela	55.0	55.4	53.1	60.4	60.7	56.5	61.9	64.7	69.5	69.0
Latin America	**45.9**	**47.8**	**44.9**	**43.0**	**43.3**	**41.3**	**40.9**	**41.1**	**41.2**	**43.3**

TABLE E-11. DEBT SERVICE RATIO [1]

(In Percent)

Country	1986	1987	1988	1989	1990	1991	1992	1993	1994	1995p
Argentina	82.8	74.3	44.2	36.2	37.0	34.4	31.0	38.0	31.3	34.4
Bahamas	6.7	2.6	3.4	2.2	1.7	3.5	3.8	3.9	4.2	4.6
Barbados	10.9	15.1	12.0	11.5	16.8	16.8	12.4	12.8	9.0	...
Belize	11.5	9.7	8.5	8.4	7.9	7.6	6.8	7.3	10.0	11.4
Bolivia	36.6	33.5	54.0	32.8	38.7	34.0	39.2	38.5	28.6	30.0
Brazil	46.3	41.8	45.8	36.4	22.4	23.2	20.7	24.7	31.5	37.8
Chile	40.6	36.3	25.8	27.2	26.0	23.3	20.9	23.1	19.5	21.3
Colombia	34.3	38.1	44.2	48.9	40.5	38.4	38.8	30.1	28.9	23.4
Costa Rica	34.7	22.4	24.3	17.7	23.9	18.1	20.2	18.3	14.6	17.6
Dominican Republic	26.1	19.5	17.8	15.6	12.4	13.9	16.7	14.7	19.4	16.1
Ecuador	43.3	33.9	39.8	35.6	33.1	32.2	26.8	24.6	21.8	23.3
El Salvador	27.1	27.3	21.1	18.3	20.8	26.8	23.1	25.0	20.3	12.4
Guatemala	31.8	29.5	28.7	20.9	13.4	16.5	26.3	14.5	12.2	9.9
Guyana	30.2	25.5	25.2	35.1	117.1	34.6	22.4	18.5	18.6	18.4
Haiti	15.7	18.8	21.1	21.5	10.1	10.2	4.3	3.8	1.2	...
Honduras	29.1	35.4	35.2	13.1	36.9	29.1	34.2	31.7	32.2	27.3
Jamaica	47.9	45.9	41.5	32.0	28.4	32.0	31.0	21.8	22.2	17.9
Mexico	45.7	34.1	38.9	34.2	21.7	24.6	35.7	33.0	25.7	21.6
Nicaragua	13.8	13.4	7.4	3.3	3.9	152.2	33.5	33.6	39.9	44.3
Panama	7.9	7.3	0.6	0.2	3.9	3.8	11.6	2.8	3.5	3.1
Paraguay	26.9	29.2	25.8	9.1	16.4	12.1	30.7	11.1	8.0	7.3
Peru	21.1	13.3	9.4	8.9	10.9	25.7	21.8	59.7	17.6	...
Suriname	1.6	1.5	...	...	...	...	...	...	12.3	7.9
Trinidad and Tobago	18.8	24.8	19.3	13.3	19.5	19.1	26.3	32.7	31.2	...
Uruguay	31.7	36.5	39.1	29.5	40.8	33.1	18.3	19.5	14.7	26.2
Venezuela	45.3	37.8	43.7	24.6	23.2	17.9	19.5	22.3	19.6	21.4
Latin America	**41.9**	**36.0**	**37.2**	**30.2**	**23.9**	**24.2**	**26.8**	**27.5**	**24.6**	**25.9**

[1] Debt service to exports of goods and services.

EXTERNAL DEBT NOTES

Unless otherwise specified, the concept used in the tables is disbursed debt (i.e., the credit effectively used by the country).

Principal repayments and interest payments are recorded on a "cash" basis. The difference with the Balance of Payments approach of what was "due" is equal to the amount due but fallen in arrears and/or the payment of old arrears and/or the part which has been rescheduled.

Total External Debt:

The sum of long- and short-term external debt and the use of International Monetary Fund (IMF) credit:

Long-term Debt: Debt with an original or extended maturity of more than one year, repayable in foreign currency, goods or services. This is divided into public or publicly guaranteed debt and private nonguaranteed debt:

Public or Publicly Guaranteed: includes all external long-term debt contracted directly by public bodies or by private entities with a guarantee of payment by any of the following public institutions: central governments or their departments; political subdivisions (such as states, provinces, departments or municipalities); central banks; autonomous institutions (such as corporations, development banks, railways, utilities, etc.) where (a) the budget of the institution is subject to the approval of the government of the reporting country; or where (b) the government owns more than 50 percent of the voting stock or more than half of the members of the Board of Directors are government representatives; or where (c) in the case of default the state would become liable for the debt of the institution.

Consequently, long-term public or publicly guaranteed debt excludes: obligations with a maturity of less than one year; loans contracted with the option of repayment in local currency; the debt of the private sector without the guarantee of the public sector; the "purchases" and "repurchases" operations with the International Monetary Fund and the "swap" transactions between central banks.

Private Nonguaranteed: is the external obligation of a private resident of the country with a nonresident that is not guaranteed by a public institution of that country.

Short-term Debt: Debt with an original maturity of one year or less. It could be public or private, but there is no available data for this distinction.

Use of IMF Credit: Net credit (purchases, repurchases and charges) transactions with respect to all uses of IMF resources, excluding those resulting from drawings in the reserve tranche and the IMF Trust Fund. The use of IMF credit is a special item and is not included in either short- or long-term debt.

Data are also presented on a regional level, by types of credits and creditors. For this purpose, the latter are defined as follows:

Suppliers: include credits from manufacturers, exporters or other suppliers of goods to finance the purchase of their products;

Private Banks: consist of credits extended by commercial banks, whether their ownership is private or public, as well as credits from private financial institutions other than commercial banks;

Bond Issues: consist of securities offered to the general public, which are traded in the stock exchanges, as well as securities privately placed with a limited number of investors, usually banking institutions, that could trade them on the stock exchanges at a later date;

Other: consists of debts that arise from a settlement for compensation to nonnationals for property owned by them, which has been acquired by the public authorities by means of expropriation or by common consent and other nonclassified debt;

Official Multilateral: includes loans and credits extended by international, regional or subregional financial organizations, such as the World Bank, the International Development Association, the Inter-American Development Bank (IDB) and the Central American Bank for Economic Integration. However, this category does not include the loans made out of the funds administered by the IDB on behalf of a government. Loans from the Canadian Fund, for example, are registered with the Canadian Government as official bilateral loans; and

Official Bilateral: includes direct loans from governments or public entities, and government loans administered by the IDB as explained above.

Sources:

The World Bank Debtor Reporting System (DRS) is the source for most of the data in the tables, supplemented where necessary by IDB estimates using official information from the countries.

TABLE F-1. MARKET EXCHANGE RATES [1]

(Local Currency per Dollar)

Country	1986	1987	1988	1989	1990	1991	1992	1993	1994	1995p
Argentina[2]	-	-	-	-	0.5	1.0	1.0	1.0	1.0	1.0
Bahamas	1.0	1.0	1.0	1.0	1.0	1.0	1.0	1.0	1.0	1.0
Barbados	2.0	2.0	2.0	2.0	2.0	2.0	2.0	2.0	2.0	2.0
Belize	2.0	2.0	2.0	2.0	2.0	2.0	2.0	2.0	2.0	2.0
Bolivia	1.9	2.1	2.4	2.7	3.2	3.6	3.9	4.3	4.6	4.8
Brazil[2]	-	-	-	-	-	-	-	-	0.6	0.9
Chile	193.0	219.5	245.0	267.2	305.1	349.4	362.6	404.3	420.1	396.8
Colombia[3]	194.3	242.6	299.2	382.6	502.3	627.1	680.1	786.6	826.5	912.8
Costa Rica	56.0	62.8	75.8	81.5	91.6	122.4	134.5	142.2	157.1	179.7
Dominican Republic	2.9	3.8	6.1	6.3	8.5	12.7	12.8	12.7	13.2	13.6
Ecuador	122.8	170.5	301.6	526.4	767.8	1,046.3	1,534.0	1,919.1	2,196.7	2,564.5
El Salvador	4.9	5.0	5.0	5.0	6.8	8.0	8.4	8.7	8.7	8.8
Guatemala	1.9	2.5	2.6	2.8	4.5	5.0	5.2	5.6	5.8	5.8
Guyana	4.3	9.8	10.0	27.2	39.5	111.8	125.0	126.7	138.3	142.0
Haiti[4]	5.0	5.6	6.0	6.6	7.5	7.7	9.1	12.4	14.7	14.5
Honduras	2.0	2.0	2.0	2.0	4.1	5.3	5.5	6.5	8.4	9.5
Jamaica	5.5	5.5	5.5	5.7	7.2	12.1	23.0	24.9	33.1	35.1
Mexico	0.6	1.4	2.3	2.5	2.8	3.0	3.1	3.1	3.4	6.4
Nicaragua[2]	-	-	-	-	0.1	4.3	5.0	5.6	6.7	7.5
Panama	1.0	1.0	1.0	1.0	1.0	1.0	1.0	1.0	1.0	1.0
Paraguay	339.2	550.0	550.0	1,056.2	1,229.8	1,325.2	1,500.3	1,744.4	1,911.5	1,970.4
Peru[2]	-	-	-	-	0.2	0.8	1.2	2.0	2.2	2.3
Suriname[5]	5.3	8.6	6.6	7.8	9.8	10.2	14.8	48.9	195.3	451.9
Trinidad and Tobago	3.6	3.6	3.8	4.3	4.3	4.3	4.3	5.4	5.9	5.9
Uruguay	0.2	0.2	0.4	0.6	1.2	2.0	3.0	3.9	5.1	6.3
Venezuela	8.1	14.5	14.5	34.7	46.9	56.8	68.4	90.8	148.5	180.0

Source: International Monetary Fund, International Financial Statistics, various issues.

[1] Period average.

[2] (-) Indicates that the exchange rate is less than half of a significant digit, given the magnitude of the depreciations experienced.

[3] Refers to annual average until 1990; representative market rate from 1991.

[4] Official rate for 1986; reference rate for 1987-1995.

[5] Average exchange rate taking into account parallel rate.

TABLE F-2. AVERAGE ANNUAL GROWTH OF CONSUMER PRICES

(In Percent)

Country	1986	1987	1988	1989	1990	1991	1992	1993	1994	1995p
Argentina	85.7	123.1	348.3	3,086.9	2,313.7	171.7	24.9	10.6	4.2	3.4
Bahamas	5.4	5.8	4.4	5.4	4.7	7.1	5.8	2.6	1.5	2.0
Barbados	1.3	3.3	4.9	6.2	3.1	6.3	6.0	1.2	0.1	1.8
Belize	0.8	2.0	5.3	0.0	3.0	2.2	2.4	1.5	2.3	3.2
Bolivia	276.3	14.6	16.0	15.2	17.1	21.4	12.1	8.5	7.9	10.2
Brazil	125.0	233.3	690.0	1,289.0	2,937.7	440.9	1,008.7	2,148.5	2,668.6	84.4
Chile	19.5	19.9	14.7	17.0	26.0	22.0	15.4	12.7	11.4	8.2
Colombia	18.9	23.3	28.1	25.8	29.1	30.4	27.0	22.6	23.8	21.0
Costa Rica	11.8	16.8	20.8	16.5	19.0	28.7	21.8	9.8	13.5	23.2
Dominican Republic	9.7	15.9	44.4	45.4	59.4	53.9	4.5	5.3	8.3	12.5
Ecuador	23.0	29.5	58.2	75.6	48.5	48.7	54.6	45.0	27.3	22.9
El Salvador	31.9	24.9	19.8	17.6	24.0	14.4	11.2	18.6	10.5	10.1
Guatemala	36.9	12.3	10.8	11.4	41.2	33.2	10.0	13.4	12.5	8.7
Guyana	7.9	28.7	39.9	89.7	63.6	101.5	28.2	10.0	16.1	8.1
Haiti	3.3	-11.5	4.1	7.9	20.4	18.2	17.9	18.9	36.1	27.1
Honduras	4.4	2.5	4.5	9.9	23.3	34.0	8.7	10.8	21.7	29.5
Jamaica	15.1	6.7	8.3	14.3	22.0	51.1	77.3	22.1	35.1	19.9
Mexico	86.2	131.8	114.2	20.0	26.6	22.7	15.5	9.7	6.9	35.0
Nicaragua	681.4	911.9	10,215.2	4,770.3	7,485.2	2,742.3	20.3	20.4	7.8	11.0
Panama	-0.1	1.0	0.4	0.1	0.8	1.3	1.8	0.5	1.3	1.0
Paraguay	31.7	21.8	22.6	26.4	38.2	24.3	15.1	18.4	20.4	15.4
Peru	200.0	66.7	660.0	3,371.1	7,481.5	409.5	73.6	48.6	23.7	11.1
Suriname	18.7	53.4	7.3	0.8	21.7	26.0	43.7	143.5	368.5	235.9
Trinidad and Tobago	7.7	10.7	7.8	11.3	11.1	3.8	6.6	10.7	8.8	5.3
Uruguay	76.4	63.6	62.2	80.5	112.5	102.0	68.4	54.1	44.7	42.2
Venezuela	11.5	28.1	29.5	84.5	40.6	34.2	31.4	38.1	60.8	59.9

Source: Official statistics, IDB estimates and International Monetary Fund, International Financial Statistics, various issues.

ARGENTINA
Statistical Profile[1]

	1986	1987	1988	1989	1990	1991	1992	1993	1994	1995p
Real Gross Domestic Product (GDP)[2]					(Average Annual Growth Rates)					
Total GDP	7.3	2.6	-1.9	-6.2	0.1	8.9	8.7	6.0	7.4	-4.4
Agriculture, Forestry and Fishing .	0.1	-3.0	9.8	-9.2	11.4	3.9	0.1	-1.0	3.8	1.7
Manufacturing	11.4	1.8	-4.9	-7.1	2.0	11.9	7.3	4.5	4.2	-6.5
Construction	20.0	14.5	-2.9	-24.4	-15.7	21.3	21.7	10.9	15.6	-11.1
Non-Financial Public Sector[3]					(As a Percent of GDP)					
Current Revenue	24.6	23.5	22.1	24.0	20.4	20.3	20.9	19.4	17.8	16.9
Current Expenditures	25.2	25.0	24.8	25.2	20.9	20.8	20.3	17.2	16.9	16.7
Current Saving	-0.6	-1.5	-2.7	-1.2	-0.5	-0.5	0.6	2.3	1.0	0.2
Capital Expenditures[4]	3.2	3.9	4.2	3.1	1.4	1.0	0.8	1.5	1.4	1.1
Overall Balance (- Deficit)	-3.1	-5.0	-6.0	-3.8	-1.5	-0.5	0.6	1.1	-0.1	-0.5
Domestic Financing	-0.7	0.3	0.2	1.4	-0.1	-0.6	-0.4	-0.6	...	...
Money and Credit[5]					(As a Percent of GDP)					
Domestic Credit	15.0	19.7	18.9	13.6	21.1	20.9	20.4	22.0	23.0	21.6
Public Sector	10.0	9.6	10.4	7.5	12.1	10.7	7.8	6.9	6.4	6.2
Private Sector	5.0	10.2	8.6	6.1	9.0	10.2	12.6	15.1	16.6	16.3
Money Supply (M1)	4.0	3.4	2.2	0.9	1.9	2.8	4.2	4.7	5.7	6.0
					(Annual Percentage Rate)					
Interest Rate[6]	95.0	176.0	372.0	17,236.0	1,517.9	61.7	16.8	11.3	8.1	11.9
Prices and Salaries					(Average Annual Growth Rates)					
Consumer Prices	85.7	123.1	348.3	3,086.9	2,313.7	171.7	24.9	10.6	4.2	3.4
Real Wages[7]	-0.7	-5.4	-5.5	0.1	-8.9	-11.2	-5.0	-1.6	0.7	-1.3
Exchange Rates					(Pesos per Dollar)					
Market Rate[8]	-	-	-	-	0.5	1.0	1.0	1.0	1.0	1.0
					(Index 1990 = 100)					
Real Effective[9]	108.2	119.1	130.3	148.7	100.0	73.4	64.6	59.0	58.1	57.7
					(Index 1980 = 100)					
Terms of Trade	73.2	63.8	67.3	68.6	65.4	60.1	59.9	62.0	61.9	62.8
Balance of Payments					(Millions of Dollars)					
Current Account Balance	-2,859.0	-4,235.0	-1,572.0	-1,305.0	4,552.0	-647.0	-6,546.0	-7,452.0	-9,310.0	-2,277.0
Trade Balance	2,446.0	1,017.0	4,242.0	5,709.0	8,628.0	4,419.0	-1,450.0	-2,428.0	-4,239.0	2,272.0
Exports of Goods (FOB)	6,852.0	6,360.0	9,134.0	9,573.0	12,354.0	11,978.0	12,235.0	13,117.0	15,839.0	20,968.0
Imports of Goods (FOB)	4,406.0	5,343.0	4,892.0	3,864.0	3,726.0	7,559.0	13,685.0	15,545.0	20,078.0	18,696.0
Service Balance	-5,307.0	-5,244.0	-5,814.0	-7,022.0	-5,074.0	-5,859.0	-5,845.0	-5,470.0	-5,392.0	-4,981.0
Unrequited Transfers	2.0	-8.0	0.0	8.0	998.0	793.0	749.0	446.0	320.0	432.0
Capital Account Balance[10]	1,666.0	2,430.0	3,595.0	206.0	-1,888.0	3,618.0	10,959.0	9,912.0	9,868.0	2,208.0
Non-Monetary Sector	1,689.0	2,463.0	3,572.0	150.0	-1,988.0	3,649.0	11,019.0	12,411.0	4,866.0	6,955.0
Private	508.0	-332.0	633.0	-5,117.0	-2,991.0	326.0	11,727.0	6,783.0	1,698.0	1,677.0
Government	1,181.0	2,795.0	2,939.0	5,267.0	1,003.0	3,323.0	-708.0	5,628.0	3,168.0	5,278.0
Monetary Sector	-23.0	-33.0	23.0	56.0	100.0	-31.0	-60.0	-2,499.0	2,084.0	4,186.0
Change in Reserves (- Increase)	891.0	1,917.0	-1,858.0	1,348.0	-3,378.0	-2,630.0	-4,550.0	-2,547.0	-558.0	69.0
Errors and Omissions	302.0	-112.0	-165.0	-249.0	715.0	-341.0	137.0	87.0	-	-
Total External Debt					(Millions of Dollars)					
Disbursed Debt	52,450.0	58,458.0	58,740.8	65,256.7	62,233.3	65,396.4	68,339.0	70,565.6	77,387.4	85,098.0
Debt Service Actually Paid	7,323.2	6,244.2	5,023.1	4,357.4	6,160.9	5,544.6	5,003.1	6,562.4	6,691.9	9,569.0
					(In Percent)					
Interest Payments Due/Exports of Goods and Non-factor Services	51.0	51.1	42.0	51.2	38.0	36.1	28.3	22.5	22.6	23.5

[1] Data sources are listed at the end.
[2] At market prices.
[3] Corresponds to the National Non-Financial Public Sector, excluding the provinces.
[4] Includes net lending.
[5] Mid-year values.
[6] Average nominal rate offered on 30-day time deposits.

[7] In Manufacturing.
[8] (-) Indicates that the exchange rate is less than half of a significant digit, given the magnitude of the depreciations experienced.
[9] Trade-weighted.
[10] For 1994 and 1995, includes capital movements pending classification by resident.

BAHAMAS
Statistical Profile[1]

	1986	1987	1988	1989	1990	1991	1992	1993	1994	1995p
Real Gross Domestic Product (GDP)[2]					(Average Annual Growth Rates)					
Total GDP	2.5	3.8	2.3	2.0	1.0	-4.0	-2.0	1.9	0.6	0.8
Agriculture, Forestry and Fishing	...	...	...	...	...	...	...	...	...	...
Manufacturing	...	...	...	...	...	...	...	...	...	...
Construction	...	...	...	...	...	...	...	...	...	...
Central Government					(As a Percent of GDP)					
Current Revenue	17.0	16.9	14.8	15.2	15.9	15.9	17.5	16.8	18.7	19.6
Current Expenditures	15.5	15.4	15.0	15.8	15.7	16.9	16.8	15.3	16.7	18.1
Current Saving	1.4	1.5	-0.2	-0.6	0.2	-1.1	0.7	1.5	2.0	1.6
Fixed Investment	1.8	1.6	1.3	2.0	0.9	0.7	0.9	1.0	1.4	2.4
Deficit or Surplus	-0.5	-0.6	-3.0	-4.1	-2.4	-4.3	-2.3	-0.7	-0.6	-0.8
Domestic Financing	4.1	2.7	3.4	4.3	3.9	4.0	3.8	5.3	3.7	2.4
Money and Credit[3]					(As a Percent of GDP)					
Domestic Credit	28.6	29.3	34.5	37.1	44.3	48.8	50.5	51.5	59.1	63.5
Public Sector	2.2	2.6	5.8	8.3	10.7	11.9	12.4	12.9	14.0	13.0
Private Sector	26.4	26.7	28.7	28.8	33.6	36.8	38.1	38.6	45.0	50.5
Money Supply (M1)	9.8	10.4	9.4	9.8	10.1	11.0	11.2	11.8	12.3	13.6
					(Annual Percentage Rate)					
Interest Rate[4]	5.6	5.5	6.0	6.5	6.6	6.9	6.1	5.2	4.3	4.2
Prices and Salaries					(Average Annual Growth Rates)					
Consumer Prices	5.4	5.8	4.4	5.4	4.7	7.1	5.8	2.6	1.5	2.0
Real Wages	...	...	...	...	...	...	...	...	...	...
Exchange Rates					(Bahamas Dollars per Dollar)					
Market Rate	1.0	1.0	1.0	1.0	1.0	1.0	1.0	1.0	1.0	1.0
					(Index 1990 = 100)					
Real Effective[5]	94.9	96.9	98.3	96.4	100.0	97.0	94.9	92.9	94.3	97.3
					(Index 1980 = 100)					
Terms of Trade	...	...	...	...	...	...	...	...	...	...
Balance of Payments					(Millions of Dollars)					
Current Account Balance	21.2	-57.9	-60.8	-91.6	-95.5	-98.9	-38.6	12.0	-112.8	-309.1
Trade Balance[6]	-607.4	-676.4	-666.4	-834.6	-814.9	-677.1	-711.8	-728.3	-781.5	-1,101.9
Exports of Goods (FOB)[6]	866.4	784.6	678.0	1,105.6	1,226.3	756.0	714.4	662.2	734.0	697.3
Imports of Goods (FOB)[6]	1,473.8	1,461.0	1,344.4	1,940.2	2,041.2	1,433.1	1,426.2	1,390.5	1,515.5	1,799.2
Service Balance	627.4	620.4	617.1	739.3	704.6	555.7	655.6	721.7	645.2	747.7
Unrequited Transfers	1.2	-1.9	-11.5	3.7	14.8	22.5	17.6	18.6	23.5	45.1
Capital Account Balance	24.7	-16.6	70.2	92.1	52.9	174.0	8.7	5.1	79.2	290.5
Non-Monetary Sector	-2.3	-28.5	30.9	47.5	20.0	162.1	46.6	3.9	63.2	305.7
Private	-12.4	-7.8	39.0	42.6	7.3	156.2	49.9	20.2	69.1	306.0
Government	10.1	-20.7	-8.1	4.9	12.7	5.9	-3.3	-16.3	-5.9	-0.3
Monetary Sector	27.0	11.9	39.3	44.6	32.9	11.9	-37.9	1.2	16.0	-15.2
Change in Reserves (- Increase)	30.8	59.9	0.7	26.6	-9.3	-13.0	28.7	-19.0	-9.3	-17.0
Errors and Omissions	-76.7	14.6	-10.1	-27.1	51.9	-62.1	1.2	1.9	42.9	35.6
External Public Debt					(Millions of Dollars)					
Disbursed Debt	215.5	192.7	171.3	221.0	266.2	412.4	440.4	453.3	411.4	392.2
Debt Service Actually Paid	141.9	53.2	67.5	56.1	45.2	73.1	78.7	81.9	94.0	83.6
					(In Percent)					
Interest Payments Due/Exports of Goods and Non-factor Services	1.1	0.7	1.3	0.7	0.7	1.1	1.2	1.3	1.4	...

[1] Data sources are listed at the end.
[2] At market prices.
[3] Mid-year values.
[4] Average of nominal rates quoted by commercial banks for 3-month time deposits.
[5] Trade-weighted.
[6] Include Goods for Processing in Free Trade Zone.

BARBADOS
Statistical Profile[1]

	1986	1987	1988	1989	1990	1991	1992	1993	1994	1995p
Real Gross Domestic Product (GDP)[2]					(Average Annual Growth Rates)					
Total GDP	5.1	2.6	3.5	3.6	-3.1	-4.2	-5.7	1.0	3.8	2.7
Agriculture, Forestry and Fishing .	4.5	-11.2	-5.9	-9.0	8.5	-4.6	-9.2	-4.6	-0.7	-6.0
Manufacturing	5.1	-6.6	6.7	5.4	-2.7	-5.6	-8.4	-2.9	6.8	7.5
Construction	7.2	6.2	9.0	8.1	-10.2	-7.5	-8.1	5.1	0.4	6.5
Tourism	6.7	15.2	10.5	10.1	-6.1	-9.0	-2.0	3.7	9.4	1.5
Central Government					(As a Percent of GDP)					
Current Revenue	25.8	25.3	28.9	29.2	27.4	30.2	31.0	30.8	29.0	29.9
Current Expenditures	24.2	24.1	24.4	24.7	27.3	27.5	28.7	27.5	26.7	25.4
Current Saving	1.6	1.2	4.5	4.5	0.2	2.7	2.3	3.3	2.3	4.5
Fixed Investment	5.2	4.2	3.8	3.4	4.5	2.9	2.2	2.0	2.6	1.9
Deficit or Surplus	-5.3	-5.3	-2.3	-0.8	-6.7	-2.1	-1.1	-0.1	-1.8	2.3
Domestic Financing	1.3	2.0	0.8	0.2	7.4	2.1	4.8	1.5	0.5	-0.8
Money and Credit[3]					(As a Percent of GDP)					
Domestic Credit	42.6	37.8	41.1	43.0	44.0	52.9	56.1	56.2	53.0	52.3
Public Sector	7.8	4.6	9.7	8.2	8.0	13.0	17.3	16.9	16.4	15.7
Private Sector	34.8	33.2	31.5	34.8	35.9	40.0	38.8	39.3	36.6	36.6
Money Supply (M1)	15.2	14.0	15.3	14.8	13.9	15.0	13.6	14.8	15.6	13.7
					(Annual Percentage Rate)					
Interest Rate[4]	3.0	3.0	4.0	6.0	5.5	7.0	5.5	4.4	4.3	5.0
Prices and Salaries					(Average Annual Growth Rates)					
Consumer Prices	1.3	3.3	4.9	6.2	3.1	6.3	6.0	1.2	0.1	1.8
Real Wages	2.8	-1.5	2.4	-3.3	1.7	-2.1	-7.4	0.4	-1.7	-1.7
Exchange Rates					(Barbados Dollars per Dollar)					
Market Rate	2.0	2.0	2.0	2.0	2.0	2.0	2.0	2.0	2.0	2.0
					(Index 1990 = 100)					
Real Effective[5]	92.3	98.7	101.3	97.8	100.0	98.2	95.4	94.5	93.1	91.7
					(Index 1980 = 100)					
Terms of Trade	...	...	...	...	...	...	...	...	...	...
Balance of Payments					(Millions of Dollars)					
Current Account Balance	8.4	-22.9	42.2	23.8	-16.4	-25.3	143.8	64.5	123.2	42.6
Trade Balance	-243.7	-297.3	-342.9	-414.6	-411.0	-413.5	-274.2	-329.8	-355.4	-490.7
Exports of Goods (FOB)	279.6	161.7	175.8	185.7	213.1	203.9	190.5	181.5	188.8	176.0
Imports of Goods (FOB)	523.3	459.0	518.7	600.3	624.1	617.4	464.7	511.3	544.2	666.7
Service Balance	240.9	268.6	368.7	433.6	352.1	355.2	377.7	373.5	451.2	505.1
Unrequited Transfers	11.2	5.8	16.4	4.8	42.5	33.0	40.3	20.8	27.4	28.3
Capital Account Balance	70.4	83.1	45.3	-27.4	42.6	9.5	-98.2	-8.5	9.1	-3.5
Non-Monetary Sector	60.9	82.4	35.7	-23.6	31.6	6.2	-103.9	-16.9	-92.6	...
Private	17.1	24.8	-5.9	-30.4	25.3	41.2	-58.4	21.0	16.3	...
Government	43.8	57.6	41.6	6.8	6.3	-35.0	-45.5	-37.9	-108.9	...
Monetary Sector	9.5	0.7	9.6	-3.8	11.0	3.3	5.7	8.4	101.6	...
Change in Reserves (- Increase)	-20.1	-6.3	-38.0	42.8	38.3	39.9	-28.3	-20.9	-88.0	-44.3
Errors and Omissions	-58.7	-54.1	-49.7	-39.1	-64.6	-24.2	-17.2	-34.9	-44.3	5.2
Total External Debt					(Millions of Dollars)					
Disbursed Debt	579.5	576.8	702.8	643.6	683.0	652.1	609.7	568.5	574.5	562.0
Debt Service Actually Paid	81.8	103.5	94.1	101.9	140.6	140.0	101.6	113.0	93.5	114.0
					(In Percent)					
Interest Payments Due/Exports of Goods and Non-factor Services	7.6	8.5	8.4	6.5	8.6	9.0	7.6	8.7	8.5	...

[1] Data sources are listed at the end.
[2] At factor cost.
[3] Mid-year values.
[4] Minimum nominal rate on savings deposits.
[5] Trade-weighted.

BELIZE
Statistical Profile[1]

	1986	1987	1988	1989	1990	1991	1992	1993	1994	1995p[2]
Real Gross Domestic Product (GDP)[2]					(Average Annual Growth Rates)					
Total GDP	4.6	11.2	9.2	13.1	11.0	2.7	7.7	4.2	2.2	3.7
Agriculture, Forestry and Fishing .	-4.5	20.3	0.2	6.0	11.8	3.9	15.1	0.1	2.9	6.3
Manufacturing	2.6	6.8	-0.6	11.0	10.2	-0.2	7.6	4.7	4.8	4.4
Construction	3.9	32.2	8.9	28.4	10.1	7.7	12.1	14.3	-20.5	1.1
Central Government[3]					(As a Percent of GDP)					
Current Revenue	24.5	24.0	25.5	26.1	26.1	24.8	25.2	23.8	24.4	22.5
Current Expenditures	22.6	20.3	18.3	17.4	16.8	17.5	19.5	20.9	21.9	20.8
Current Saving	2.0	3.8	7.3	8.6	9.3	7.3	5.7	2.9	2.6	1.7
Fixed Investment[4]	6.0	3.9	6.0	10.0	10.9	14.3	13.4	10.4	...	...
Deficit or Surplus	-4.5	0.4	7.1	-0.8	0.7	-3.2	-3.4	-6.7	-7.4	-4.1
Domestic Financing	0.9	-1.8	...	...	...	...	...	4.0	4.5	2.9
Money and Credit[5]					(As a Percent of GDP)					
Domestic Credit	44.2	36.4	32.2	28.5	24.9	27.6	32.3	37.7	40.3	43.9
Public Sector	19.3	14.7	5.9	-1.2	-4.8	-5.4	-3.2	2.2	5.2	8.1
Private Sector	24.8	21.7	26.3	29.7	29.8	33.0	35.5	35.4	35.1	35.9
Money Supply (M1)	15.5	14.2	15.0	13.3	12.6	14.6	13.7	14.1	14.2	14.0
					(Annual Percentage Rate)					
Interest Rate[6]	8.3	7.2	5.7	6.0	6.3	6.4	6.0	6.0	6.1	7.2
Prices and Salaries					(Average Annual Growth Rates)					
Consumer Prices	0.8	2.0	5.3	0.0	3.0	2.3	2.4	1.5	2.3	3.2
Real Wages	...	...	...	...	...	...	...	...	...	...
Exchange Rates					(Belize Dollars per Dollar)					
Market Rate	2.0	2.0	2.0	2.0	2.0	2.0	2.0	2.0	2.0	2.0
					(Index 1990 = 100)					
Real Effective[7]	86.2	92.8	94.0	95.3	100.0	99.9	101.2	98.3	103.9	108.2
					(Index 1980 = 100)					
Terms of Trade	...	...	...	...	...	...	...	...	...	...
Balance of Payments					(Millions of Dollars)					
Current Account Balance	11.9	9.4	-2.6	-19.0	15.4	-25.8	-28.6	-48.5	-30.5	-29.7
Trade Balance	-15.7	-24.1	-41.8	-64.1	-59.2	-97.5	-103.9	-118.5	-88.4	-73.8
Exports of Goods (FOB)	92.6	102.8	119.4	124.4	129.2	126.1	140.6	132.0	143.5	155.9
Imports of Goods (FOB)	108.3	126.9	161.2	188.5	188.4	223.6	244.5	250.5	231.9	229.7
Service Balance	0.3	2.6	13.4	14.0	45.2	43.7	44.9	40.5	28.7	12.2
Unrequited Transfers	27.4	30.9	25.8	31.1	29.4	28.0	30.4	29.5	29.3	32.0
Capital Account Balance	0.8	2.7	27.2	25.4	25.1	22.2	22.3	32.8	18.0	23.5
Non-Monetary Sector	5.8	2.8	25.6	34.4	27.1	16.3	9.7	25.7	14.5	-3.6
Private	2.1	2.2	16.1	23.2	19.2	6.1	3.6	9.4	7.5	-0.4
Government	3.7	0.6	9.5	11.2	7.9	10.2	6.1	16.3	7.0	-3.2
Monetary Sector	-5.0	-0.1	1.6	-9.0	-2.0	5.9	12.6	7.1	3.6	27.1
Change in Reserves (- Increase)	-11.8	-11.9	-21.7	-15.5	-15.5	16.4	-0.1	14.2	3.7	-4.0
Errors and Omissions	-0.9	-0.2	-2.9	9.1	-25.0	-12.8	6.3	1.5	8.7	10.3
Total External Debt					(Millions of Dollars)					
Disbursed Debt	120.7	136.7	139.2	143.6	152.3	168.9	172.3	184.4	176.8	183.0
Debt Service Actually Paid	16.6	16.0	17.1	18.5	20.2	19.6	19.6	21.0	28.9	33.0
					(In Percent)					
Interest Payments Due/Exports of Goods and Non-factor Services	6.7	6.5	5.7	6.9	5.5	4.1	3.7	3.9	2.0	2.2

[1] Data sources are listed at the end.
[2] GDP at market prices, Sector of Origin at factor cost.
[3] 1995 data derived from Calendar Year (January–December); in previous years, Fiscal Year (April–March) used.
[4] Development Expenditure.
[5] Mid-year values.
[6] Weighted nominal average deposit rate.
[7] Trade-weighted.

BOLIVIA
Statistical Profile[1]

	1986	1987	1988	1989	1990	1991	1992	1993	1994	1995p
Real Gross Domestic Product (GDP)[2]					(Average Annual Growth Rates)					
Total GDP	-2.5	2.6	3.0	3.8	4.6	5.3	1.6	4.7	5.0	3.7
Agriculture, Forestry and Fishing .	-3.5	3.5	2.4	-1.5	4.6	9.9	-4.2	3.6	6.7	1.7
Mining and Quarrying	-14.4	1.5	19.9	14.5	7.6	2.2	1.3	6.3	6.9	3.4
Manufacturing	1.9	2.5	5.4	5.0	7.8	4.8	0.1	5.9	4.4	4.2
Construction	-21.5	-0.9	14.5	5.8	2.5	6.0	11.2	11.1	1.3	5.0
Non-Financial Public Sector					(As a Percent of GDP)					
Current Revenue	25.4	22.9	25.4	26.5	27.3	29.0	28.9	26.8	29.2	28.9
Current Expenditures	24.1	24.5	24.2	25.2	25.3	26.2	26.1	25.5	26.1	25.1
Current Saving	1.3	-1.6	1.2	1.4	2.0	2.8	2.8	1.4	3.1	3.8
Capital Expenditures[3]	4.8	5.6	7.9	8.4	8.3	8.7	10.0	8.8	8.5	7.9
Overall Balance (- Deficit)	-2.4	-7.0	-5.9	-5.5	-4.4	-4.3	-4.5	-5.8	-2.8	-1.7
Domestic Financing	-3.3	4.7	1.3	3.5	1.9	1.0	0.7	1.0	-0.6	-1.6
Money and Credit[4]					(As a Percent of GDP)					
Domestic Credit	0.7	7.2	13.2	19.2	24.5	28.2	31.9	45.8	52.8	48.4
Public Sector[5]	-5.7	-4.9	-0.5	2.7	4.0	4.8	3.7	10.6	11.0	4.6
Private Sector	6.3	12.1	13.7	16.5	20.5	23.4	28.2	35.2	41.7	43.8
Money Supply (M1)	2.8	4.0	4.7	5.0	4.9	5.9	7.2	8.2	9.0	9.7
					(Annual Percentage Rate)					
Interest Rate[6]	...	17.8	15.8	16.1	14.4	11.4	11.7	10.2	9.6	10.4
Prices and Salaries					(Average Annual Growth Rates)					
Consumer Prices	276.3	14.6	16.0	15.2	17.1	21.4	12.1	8.5	7.9	10.2
Real Wages[7]	-13.5	29.3	23.9	8.6	2.4	-6.6	4.0	6.7	7.9	1.1
Exchange Rates					(Bolivianos per Dollar)					
Market Rate	1.9	2.1	2.4	2.7	3.2	3.6	3.9	4.3	4.6	4.8
					(Index 1990 = 100)					
Real Effective[8]	74.1	76.9	81.1	84.3	100.0	96.3	98.8	102.4	111.3	115.4
					(Index 1980 = 100)					
Terms of Trade	81.8	83.4	75.2	77.5	74.1	66.1	52.6	48.6	52.6	52.2
Balance of Payments					(Millions of Dollars)					
Current Account Balance	-388.9	-432.3	-304.4	-270.1	-198.9	-262.6	-533.9	-505.5	-114.3	-308.2
Trade Balance	-51.0	-127.6	-48.4	-6.0	55.2	-43.9	-432.4	-396.2	-79.3	-221.8
Exports of Goods (FOB)	545.5	518.7	542.5	723.5	830.8	760.3	608.4	715.5	985.1	1,041.4
Imports of Goods (FOB)	596.5	646.3	590.9	729.5	775.6	804.2	1,040.8	1,111.7	1,064.4	1,263.2
Service Balance	-433.2	-416.4	-391.3	-414.0	-413.3	-401.2	-344.1	-346.2	-320.0	-320.0
Unrequited Transfers	95.6	111.8	135.3	149.9	159.2	182.5	242.6	236.9	285.0	233.6
Capital Account Balance	362.4	199.7	141.2	170.4	204.8	204.0	467.8	91.7	456.3	766.6
Non-Monetary Sector	388.1	204.7	188.5	224.5	173.0	175.5	395.7	99.3	316.9	616.6
Private	134.8	-46.8	-86.8	-157.9	37.5	83.3	211.3	79.2	99.9	383.0
Government	253.3	251.5	275.3	382.4	135.5	92.2	184.4	20.1	217.0	233.6
Monetary Sector	-25.7	-5.0	-47.3	-54.1	31.8	28.5	72.1	-7.6	139.4	150.0
Change in Reserves (- Increase)	-114.7	48.4	43.4	104.8	-18.2	-22.3	-26.5	71.0	-139.0	-149.9
Errors and Omissions	141.2	184.2	119.8	-5.1	12.3	80.9	92.6	342.8	-203.0	-308.5
Total External Debt					(Millions of Dollars)					
Disbursed Debt	5,574.9	5,836.2	4,901.6	4,135.5	4,278.2	4,076.0	4,223.3	4,220.1	4,748.8	4,938.0
Debt Service Actually Paid	250.7	223.5	372.2	292.0	385.4	320.0	309.9	348.6	342.9	382.0
					(In Percent)					
Interest Payments Due/Exports of Goods and Non-factor Services	42.9	38.9	41.4	30.9	25.6	27.6	25.3	21.2	15.7	16.4

[1] Data sources are listed at the end.
[2] At market prices.
[3] Includes net lending.
[4] Mid-year values.
[5] Decrease between 1994–1995 due mainly to methodological change in January 1995.

[6] Average nominal time deposit rate.
[7] 1995 value through September.
[8] Trade-weighted.

BRAZIL
Statistical Profile[1]

	1986	1987	1988	1989	1990	1991	1992	1993	1994	1995p
Real Gross Domestic Product (GDP)[2]					(Average Annual Growth Rates)					
Total GDP	7.5	3.5	-0.1	3.2	-4.4	0.2	-0.8	4.1	5.7	4.2
Agriculture, Forestry and Fishing	-8.0	15.0	0.8	2.9	-3.7	2.8	5.4	-1.2	7.5	5.9
Manufacturing	11.3	1.0	-3.4	2.9	-9.5	-2.4	-4.1	7.9	8.0	1.6
Construction	17.8	0.7	-3.1	3.1	-9.7	-3.5	-6.6	4.9	5.9	0.1
Wholesale and Retail Trade	7.5	1.9	-2.7	2.7	-7.0	-0.8	-2.4	7.0	5.9	7.4
Non-Financial Public Sector					(As a Percent of GDP)					
Borrowing Requirements	11.8	24.8	57.9	89.8	32.0	28.5	48.4	65.7	26.5	6.5
Operational Balance (- Deficit)[3]	-3.8	-5.9	-5.1	-7.4	1.4	-0.5	-2.0	-1.4	2.0	-4.6
Money and Credit[4]					(As a Percent of GDP)					
Domestic Credit	0.0	0.0	34.0	14.1	32.3	33.3	30.1	24.2	43.0	38.4
Public Sector	0.0	0.0	0.0	4.7	18.4	21.0	16.5	12.2	14.0	7.2
Private Sector	0.0	0.0	34.0	11.7	14.0	12.3	13.7	11.9	29.0	31.2
Money Supply (M1)	9.5	4.3	2.3	1.4	4.0	2.8	2.0	1.2	2.5	3.1
					(Annual Percentage Rate)					
Interest Rate[5]	58.2	357.0	955.6	2,622.9	1,412.1	558.0	1,547.6	3,019.3	1,327.5	53.3
Prices and Salaries					(Average Annual Growth Rates)					
Consumer Prices	125.0	233.3	690.0	1,289.0	2,937.7	440.9	1,008.7	2,148.5	2,668.6	84.4
Real Wages[6]	-0.3	-23.4	-1.6	30.6	-42.7	14.9	5.3	-1.4	-16.0	8.5
Exchange Rates					(Reals per Dollar)					
Market Rate[7]	...	...	...	...	...	...	...	...	0.6	0.9
					(Index 1990 = 100)					
Real Effective[8]	158.0	158.0	146.4	117.4	100.0	124.6	134.9	120.3	101.8	88.6
					(Index 1980 = 100)					
Terms of Trade	101.9	90.5	101.6	87.3	82.3	86.8	84.8	86.3	89.5	89.9
Balance of Payments					(Millions of Dollars)					
Current Account Balance	-5,311.0	-1,452.0	4,156.0	1,002.0	-3,823.0	-1,450.0	6,089.0	19.0	-1,153.0	-17,784.0
Trade Balance	8,304.0	11,158.0	19,168.0	16,112.0	10,747.0	10,578.0	15,239.0	14,329.0	10,861.0	-3,157.0
Exports of Goods (FOB)	22,348.0	26,210.0	33,773.0	34,375.0	31,408.0	31,619.0	35,793.0	39,630.0	44,102.0	46,506.0
Imports of Goods (FOB)	14,044.0	15,052.0	14,605.0	18,263.0	20,661.0	21,041.0	20,554.0	25,301.0	33,241.0	49,663.0
Service Balance	-13,695.0	-12,678.0	-15,103.0	-15,331.0	-15,369.0	-13,542.0	-11,339.0	-15,913.0	-14,437.0	-18,600.0
Unrequited Transfers	80.0	68.0	91.0	221.0	799.0	1,514.0	2,189.0	1,603.0	2,423.0	3,973.0
Capital Account Balance	2,014.0	4,422.0	-1,618.0	1,518.0	5,365.0	795.0	10,373.0	10,008.0	8,943.0	29,306.0
Non-Monetary Sector	4,968.0	6,199.0	496.0	4,224.0	8,352.0	3,766.0	9,243.0	11,258.0	14,459.0	29,306.0
Private	-3,977.0	-6,512.0	-6,129.0	-3,658.0	1,091.0	3,648.0	5,504.0	11,773.0	16,706.0	29,505.0
Government	8,945.0	12,711.0	6,625.0	7,882.0	7,261.0	118.0	3,739.0	-515.0	-2,247.0	-199.0
Monetary Sector	-2,954.0	-1,777.0	-2,114.0	-2,706.0	-2,987.0	-2,971.0	1,130.0	-1,250.0	-5,516.0	...
Change in Reserves (- Increase)	3,231.0	-2,165.0	-1,712.0	-1,701.0	-1,245.0	-197.0	-15,069.0	-9,213.0	-7,348.0	-12,966.0
Errors and Omissions	66.0	-805.0	-827.0	-819.0	-296.0	852.0	-1,393.0	-814.0	-442.0	1,444.0
Total External Debt					(Millions of Dollars)					
Disbursed Debt	111,019.7	122,323.7	119,343.7	115,905.4	121,465.4	122,445.2	130,546.4	145,437.8	151,103.9	157,397.0
Debt Service Actually Paid	11,627.2	12,019.0	16,874.9	14,132.4	8,133.5	8,303.0	8,484.0	11,111.3	16,114.4	21,199.0
					(In Percent)					
Interest Payments Due/Exports of Goods and Non-factor Services	42.4	33.1	29.4	29.2	30.9	27.2	20.8	22.1	18.3	21.1

[1] Data sources are listed at the end.
[2] GDP at market prices, Sector of Origin at factor cost.
[3] Excludes monetary and exchange correction.
[4] Mid-year values.

[5] Annualized nominal monthly overnight market rate.
[6] Minimum wages.
[7] (-) Indicates that the exchange rate is less than half of a significant digit, given the magnitude of the depreciations experienced.
[8] Trade-weighted.

CHILE
Statistical Profile[1]

	1986	1987	1988	1989	1990	1991	1992	1993	1994	1995p
Real Gross Domestic Product (GDP)[2]					(Average Annual Growth Rates)					
Total GDP	5.6	6.6	7.3	9.9	3.3	7.3	11.0	6.3	4.2	8.5
Agriculture, Forestry and Fishing	7.6	9.5	11.5	5.6	6.0	2.7	7.4	1.5	8.5	5.5
Mining and Quarrying	0.9	-0.3	7.8	9.5	5.5	4.6	2.0	0.9	2.7	7.2
Manufacturing	7.6	5.3	8.8	10.9	1.1	6.6	11.0	5.1	2.9	6.5
Construction	9.7	9.1	8.6	17.2	4.5	3.8	12.8	14.0	2.0	7.4
General Government[3]					(As a Percent of GDP)					
Current Revenue	30.9	30.6	31.4	29.6	25.7	27.1	26.3	25.8	25.5	25.9
Current Expenditures	26.1	22.9	21.0	20.7	19.3	20.6	19.2	19.4	18.9	18.3
Current Saving	4.8	7.6	10.4	8.9	6.4	6.5	7.1	6.4	6.6	7.7
Fixed Investment	3.0	2.7	2.8	2.5	2.2	2.6	2.8	3.1	3.2	2.9
Deficit or Surplus	-0.5	2.3	3.6	5.0	1.4	2.2	2.8	2.0	2.0	3.5
Domestic Financing	-1.5	-2.4	-5.8	-5.8	-1.3	-0.9	-0.4	-0.2	-0.2	-0.4
Money and Credit[4]					(As a Percent of GDP)					
Domestic Credit	96.2	90.1	76.4	68.8	65.3	54.5	50.5	54.1	53.9	48.2
Public Sector	38.2	37.2	28.3	23.7	23.4	17.1	12.5	10.8	9.7	5.0
Private Sector	57.9	52.9	48.1	45.0	41.9	37.4	38.0	43.3	44.2	43.2
Money Supply (M1)	4.9	4.2	4.3	3.9	4.4	4.4	4.6	3.7	3.7	3.2
					(Annual Percentage Rate)					
Interest Rate[5]	19.0	25.2	15.1	27.7	40.3	22.3	18.3	18.2	15.1	13.7
Prices and Salaries					(Average Annual Growth Rates)					
Consumer Prices	19.5	19.9	14.7	17.0	26.0	22.0	15.4	12.7	11.4	8.2
Real Wages	2.0	-0.2	6.5	1.9	1.8	4.9	4.5	3.5	4.5	4.1
Exchange Rates					(Pesos per Dollar)					
Market Rate	193.0	219.5	245.0	267.2	305.1	349.4	362.6	404.3	420.1	396.8
					(Index 1990 = 100)					
Real Effective[6]	86.6	93.3	99.3	97.3	100.0	96.9	91.6	90.6	89.4	84.9
					(Index 1980 = 100)					
Terms of Trade	88.3	93.5	105.7	99.2	86.2	88.1	82.4	75.2	83.9	93.8
Balance of Payments					(Millions of Dollars)					
Current Account Balance	-1,192.0	-736.0	-235.0	-705.0	-537.0	112.0	-708.0	-2,096.0	-757.0	160.0
Trade Balance	1,092.0	1,309.0	2,209.0	1,578.0	1,335.0	1,588.0	772.0	-982.0	659.0	1,383.5
Exports of Goods (FOB)	4,191.0	5,303.0	7,053.0	8,080.0	8,372.0	8,942.0	10,008.0	9,199.0	11,538.0	16,038.6
Imports of Goods (FOB)	3,099.0	3,994.0	4,844.0	6,502.0	7,037.0	7,354.0	9,236.0	10,181.0	10,879.0	14,655.1
Service Balance	-2,368.0	-2,183.0	-2,626.0	-2,498.0	-2,072.0	-1,817.0	-1,911.0	-1,500.0	-1,754.0	-1,578.6
Unrequited Transfers	84.0	138.0	182.0	215.0	200.0	341.0	431.0	386.0	338.0	355.1
Capital Account Balance	716.0	1,013.0	1,177.0	1,394.0	3,011.0	834.0	2,931.0	2,611.0	4,432.0	1,168.1
Non-Monetary Sector	999.0	1,886.0	1,747.0	1,955.0	3,462.0	1,455.0	1,380.0	2,549.0	4,223.0	1,951.7
Private	716.0	1,449.0	1,782.0	2,531.0	3,581.0	1,264.0	1,045.0	3,197.0	4,439.0	...
Government	283.0	437.0	-35.0	-576.0	-119.0	191.0	335.0	-648.0	-216.0	...
Monetary Sector	-283.0	-873.0	-570.0	-561.0	-451.0	-621.0	1,551.0	62.0	209.0	-783.6
Change in Reserves (- Increase)	252.0	-136.0	-826.0	-570.0	-2,331.0	-1,249.0	-2,547.0	-420.0	-3,127.0	-1,060.8
Errors and Omissions	224.0	-141.0	-116.0	-119.0	-143.0	303.0	324.0	-95.0	-548.0	-267.3
Total External Debt					(Millions of Dollars)					
Disbursed Debt	21,144.5	21,489.4	19,581.9	18,032.3	19,227.2	17,946.9	19,133.9	20,637.2	22,938.6	22,569.0
Debt Service Actually Paid	2,219.6	2,367.4	2,147.5	2,667.8	2,771.7	2,699.5	2,693.4	2,842.3	2,908.8	4,093.0
					(In Percent)					
Interest Payments Due/Exports of Goods and Non-factor Services	37.3	26.5	22.2	18.8	17.9	14.7	11.3	10.2	8.2	...

[1] Data sources are listed at the end.
[2] GDP at market prices, Sector of Origin at factor cost.
[3] Central government, decentralized entities and municipalities.
[4] Mid-year values.

[5] Weighted average rate offered by banks on nominal deposits of 30 to 89 days.
[6] Trade-weighted.

COLOMBIA
Statistical Profile[1]

	1986	1987	1988	1989	1990	1991	1992	1993	1994	1995p
Real Gross Domestic Product (GDP)[2]					(Average Annual Growth Rates)					
Total GDP	5.8	5.4	4.1	3.4	4.3	2.0	3.8	5.3	5.9	5.3
Agriculture, Forestry and Fishing .	3.4	6.4	2.8	4.3	5.8	4.2	-1.9	2.7	1.5	5.6
Mining and Quarrying	62.1	24.1	4.5	11.6	5.9	-0.6	-2.8	-2.8	-1.8	17.4
Manufacturing	5.9	6.2	1.9	5.6	4.2	0.8	5.9	2.3	0.9	0.9
Construction	4.9	-10.0	13.2	-8.1	-13.1	0.2	8.4	7.0	9.7	5.3
Wholesale and Retail Trade	3.6	4.4	5.0	1.8	2.8	0.4	4.4	5.0	5.5	4.8
Non-Financial Public Sector					(As a Percent of GDP)					
Current Revenue	23.3	22.4	21.6	22.4	23.6	25.2	25.5	28.0	28.2	30.2
Current Expenditures	15.3	16.0	16.2	16.3	16.8	18.2	18.7	19.7	21.3	23.2
Current Saving	8.1	6.4	5.4	6.1	6.8	7.0	6.8	8.3	6.9	7.0
Capital Expenditures[3]	8.5	8.0	7.4	7.9	7.2	6.9	8.7	9.7	7.5	9.0
Overall Balance (- Deficit)	-0.5	-1.8	-2.1	-1.9	-0.3	0.2	-0.2	0.2	2.8	-0.5
Domestic Financing	...	2.4	0.9	1.1	0.8	0.9	0.2	-0.4	0.0	0.7
Money and Credit[4]					(As a Percent of GDP)					
Domestic Credit	20.5	18.4	20.4	...	20.5	16.9	14.8	15.7	18.0	...
Public Sector	4.4	4.3	5.9	...	4.9	3.6	0.7	-0.4	0.5	...
Private Sector	16.1	14.1	14.5	...	...	...	14.0	16.2	17.5	...
Money Supply (M1)	9.3	9.4	8.9	9.0	8.5	8.3	9.6	9.7	9.3	8.9
					(Annual Percentage Rate)					
Interest Rate[5]	31.4	30.8	33.5	33.7	36.4	37.2	26.7	25.8	29.4	32.3
Prices and Salaries					(Average Annual Growth Rates)					
Consumer Prices	18.9	23.3	28.1	25.8	29.1	30.4	27.0	22.6	23.8	21.0
Real Wages[6]	3.9	-0.4	-0.5	1.9	0.4	-1.8	2.3	6.2	3.0	0.1
Exchange Rates					(Pesos per Dollar)					
Market Rate[7]	194.3	242.6	299.2	382.6	502.3	627.1	680.1	786.6	826.5	912.8
					(Index 1990 = 100)					
Real Effective[8]	73.2	82.1	85.2	88.3	100.0	96.7	88.6	84.4	75.4	74.6
					(Index 1980 = 100)					
Terms of Trade	122.8	114.8	107.0	101.2	89.1	83.8	74.3	71.9	81.6	90.7
Balance of Payments					(Millions of Dollars)					
Current Account Balance	383.0	336.0	-216.0	-201.0	542.0	2,349.0	912.0	-2,114.5	-3,045.4	-4,208.4
Trade Balance	1,922.0	1,868.0	827.0	1,474.0	1,971.0	2,959.0	1,233.0	-1,657.2	-2,284.1	-2,403.8
Exports of Goods (FOB)	5,331.0	5,661.0	5,343.0	6,031.0	7,079.0	7,507.0	7,263.0	7,428.5	8,755.9	10,406.4
Imports of Goods (FOB)	3,409.0	3,793.0	4,516.0	4,557.0	5,108.0	4,548.0	6,030.0	9,085.7	11,040.0	12,810.2
Service Balance	-2,324.0	-2,533.0	-2,007.0	-2,573.0	-2,455.0	-2,308.0	-2,055.0	-1,595.3	-1,623.7	-2,498.8
Unrequited Transfers	785.0	1,001.0	964.0	898.0	1,026.0	1,698.0	1,734.0	1,138.0	862.4	694.2
Capital Account Balance	1,160.0	-1.0	939.0	478.0	-2.0	-783.0	166.0	2,661.1	3,062.6	4,468.2
Non-Monetary Sector	2,472.0	234.0	738.0	398.0	-29.0	-149.0	-346.0	2,680.7	4,383.9	4,302.5
Private	1,915.0	391.0	372.0	37.0	-11.0	-115.0	160.0	2,712.5	3,884.3	2,722.6
Government	557.0	-157.0	366.0	361.0	-18.0	-34.0	-506.0	-31.8	499.6	1,579.9
Monetary Sector	-1,312.0	-235.0	201.0	80.0	27.0	-634.0	512.0	-19.6	-1,321.2	165.8
Change in Reserves (- Increase)	-1,292.0	-402.0	-193.0	-434.0	-610.0	-1,836.0	-1,092.0	-206.4	-167.3	-349.6
Errors and Omissions	-251.0	67.0	-530.0	157.0	70.0	270.0	14.0	-340.2	150.1	89.8
Total External Debt					(Millions of Dollars)					
Disbursed Debt	15,362.4	17,007.9	16,994.7	16,877.9	17,231.7	17,334.2	17,197.0	17,177.4	19,415.8	19,784.0
Debt Service Actually Paid	2,268.3	2,680.0	3,099.3	3,718.9	3,654.2	3,645.1	3,763.1	3,162.6	3,685.4	3,431.0
					(In Percent)					
Interest Payments Due/Exports of Goods and Non-factor Services	20.9	20.9	20.9	21.9	19.4	17.5	15.2	12.2	11.6	13.7

[1] Data sources are listed at the end.
[2] At market prices.
[3] Includes net lending.
[4] Mid-year values.
[5] Weighted average nominal deposit rate paid by commercial banks, financial corporations, and commercial finance companies on all certificates of deposit.

[6] In Industry, excluding the coffee-husking process.
[7] Refers to annual average until 1990; representative market rate from 1991–1995.
[8] Trade-weighted.

COSTA RICA
Statistical Profile[1]

	1986	1987	1988	1989	1990	1991	1992	1993	1994	1995p
Real Gross Domestic Product (GDP)[2]					(Average Annual Growth Rates)					
Total GDP	5.5	4.8	3.4	5.7	3.6	2.3	7.7	6.3	4.5	2.5
Agriculture, Forestry and Fishing .	4.8	4.2	4.6	7.4	2.5	6.3	4.0	2.4	3.2	3.0
Manufacturing	7.3	5.5	2.2	3.4	2.6	2.1	10.3	6.4	3.5	3.0
Construction	3.1	1.1	0.0	12.4	-2.3	-7.5	2.6	16.5	6.2	-12.0
Non-Financial Public Sector					(As a Percent of GDP)					
Current Revenue	26.4	27.2	28.2	27.4	27.6	27.6	28.2	28.4	26.0	29.3
Current Expenditures	23.5	24.4	24.2	26.1	26.5	23.7	22.2	22.4	26.6	26.6
Current Saving	2.9	2.9	4.0	1.3	1.1	3.8	6.0	6.0	-0.6	2.8
Capital Expenditures[3]	6.6	5.5	5.3	6.3	5.2	4.1	5.3	5.5	6.0	5.0
Overall Balance (- Deficit)	-1.7	-0.3	-0.3	-2.9	-2.9	-0.1	0.7	0.6	-6.6	-2.1
Domestic Financing	0.0	-0.4	0.7	2.0	2.6	-1.6	-1.1	0.5	5.7	3.1
Money and Credit[4]					(As a Percent of GDP)					
Domestic Credit	31.0	33.0	32.3	28.8	27.8	25.6	19.5	22.0	22.3	18.7
Public Sector	15.3	16.3	15.2	12.9	13.0	11.9	7.8	6.0	5.8	5.7
Private Sector	15.7	16.7	17.0	15.9	14.8	13.7	11.7	16.0	16.4	12.9
Money Supply (M1)	14.1	13.6	10.8	11.8	12.3	8.4	8.6	8.3	7.4	7.6
					(Annual Percentage Rate)					
Interest Rate[5]	16.7	14.1	15.2	15.6	21.2	27.3	15.8	16.9	17.7	23.9
Prices and Salaries					(Average Annual Growth Rates)					
Consumer Prices	11.8	16.8	20.8	16.5	19.0	28.7	21.8	9.8	13.5	23.2
Real Wages	5.9	-0.9	-1.4	4.1	2.4	-2.4	0.8	8.7	1.9	-2.1
Exchange Rates					(Colones per Dollar)					
Market Rate	56.0	62.8	75.8	81.5	91.6	122.4	134.5	142.2	157.1	179.7
					(Index 1990 = 100)					
Real Effective[6]	84.6	93.2	101.8	98.1	100.0	109.6	107.5	109.2	111.8	106.9
					(Index 1980 = 100)					
Terms of Trade	130.6	107.5	106.0	100.9	101.6	90.5	89.0	90.6	94.0	98.7
Balance of Payments					(Millions of Dollars)					
Current Account Balance	-160.6	-256.4	-178.5	-414.9	-424.0	-75.2	-370.4	-619.2	-463.2	-152.2
Trade Balance	39.6	-138.5	-97.9	-238.6	-442.5	-199.5	-471.8	-759.8	-686.3	-512.0
Exports of Goods (FOB)	1,084.8	1,106.7	1,180.7	1,333.4	1,354.2	1,498.1	1,739.1	1,866.8	2,102.3	2,441.7
Imports of Goods (FOB)	1,045.2	1,245.2	1,278.6	1,572.0	1,796.7	1,697.6	2,210.9	2,626.6	2,788.6	2,953.7
Service Balance	-271.5	-343.9	-336.0	-367.7	-173.4	-17.3	-71.9	-2.5	80.8	206.3
Unrequited Transfers	151.9	226.0	255.4	191.4	191.9	141.6	173.3	143.1	142.3	153.5
Capital Account Balance	77.0	162.5	196.1	351.6	209.0	323.7	343.6	261.6	-79.5	200.7
Non-Monetary Sector	87.9	156.2	194.9	347.4	209.6	332.0	336.4	233.7	-61.0	314.1
Private	-23.3	63.5	74.0	142.2	120.9	278.8	347.8	279.2	221.4	348.6
Government	111.2	92.7	120.9	205.2	88.7	53.2	-11.4	-45.5	-282.4	-34.5
Monetary Sector	-10.9	6.3	1.2	4.2	-0.6	-8.3	7.2	27.9	-18.5	-113.4
Change in Reserves (- Increase)	-94.4	-37.3	-242.1	-145.7	171.6	-348.4	-175.1	59.6	44.7	-184.8
Errors and Omissions	97.5	131.2	224.6	208.9	43.4	99.9	201.9	298.0	498.0	136.3
Total External Debt					(Millions of Dollars)					
Disbursed Debt	4,576.3	4,721.4	4,530.5	4,589.4	3,755.5	4,026.4	3,937.8	3,850.4	3,842.6	3,672.0
Debt Service Actually Paid	500.0	334.4	402.5	345.4	501.2	417.6	544.4	551.8	496.6	694.0
					(In Percent)					
Interest Payments Due/Exports of Goods and Non-factor Services	21.9	21.4	22.1	23.7	15.5	10.1	8.7	8.1	6.6	6.2

[1] Data sources are listed at the end.
[2] At market prices. Mining and Quarrying included in Manufacturing.
[3] Includes net lending.

[4] Mid-year values.
[5] Average official bank rate for nominal time deposits of more than 30 days and less than 90 days. Beginning 1991, average rate offered by state-owned commercial banks on time deposits of one month.
[6] Trade-weighted.

DOMINICAN REPUBLIC
Statistical Profile[1]

	1986	1987	1988	1989	1990	1991	1992	1993	1994	1995p
Real Gross Domestic Product (GDP)[2]					(Average Annual Growth Rates)					
Total GDP	3.5	10.1	2.2	4.4	-5.5	1.0	8.0	3.0	4.3	4.8
Agriculture, Forestry and Fishing	-0.5	2.9	-1.3	2.3	-7.6	3.1	6.0	0.7	-1.8	6.0
Mining and Quarrying	-11.1	25.9	-7.0	-0.6	-16.3	-0.9	-17.5	-36.0	88.2	9.4
Manufacturing	9.1	12.7	-0.7	4.6	-4.2	2.5	12.1	2.1	2.9	-0.7
Construction	15.5	34.1	3.2	13.2	-6.9	-12.5	24.4	10.1	6.6	5.7
Central Government					(As a Percent of GDP)					
Current Revenue	12.0	12.7	14.9	15.7	12.5	13.6	15.3	15.9	15.1	15.0
Current Expenditures	10.1	7.7	8.0	6.7	6.5	5.5	6.0	8.2	7.7	7.9
Current Saving	1.9	5.0	7.0	9.0	6.0	8.2	9.4	7.7	7.4	7.1
Fixed Investment	1.3	4.0	5.2	6.2	3.4	2.3	3.5	5.0	5.6	4.6
Deficit or Surplus	-0.4	-1.3	0.0	0.7	0.5	3.6	3.8	0.5	-0.1	1.2
Domestic Financing	0.0	-1.2	-0.3	0.9	-0.1	-3.9	-1.9	-0.3	0.3	-0.8
Money and Credit[3]					(As a Percent of GDP)					
Domestic Credit	24.6	23.6	18.0	22.2	18.9	11.3	13.2	15.1	17.1	17.0
Public Sector	10.6	6.7	4.7	6.0	4.3	0.9	0.4	-0.6	0.3	1.0
Private Sector	14.0	16.9	13.3	16.2	14.6	10.4	12.7	15.7	16.9	16.0
Money Supply (M1)	9.0	10.8	10.3	10.3	10.2	7.5	8.7	9.2	9.5	8.5
					(Annual Percentage Rate)					
Interest Rate	...	...	...	...	...	...	...	...	...	...
Prices and Salaries					(Average Annual Growth Rates)					
Consumer Prices	9.7	15.9	44.4	45.4	59.4	53.9	4.5	5.3	8.3	12.5
Real Wages	7.0	-2.3	4.0	-11.0	-4.6	6.0	15.0	5.0	-12.5	9.9
Exchange Rates					(Pesos per Dollar)					
Market Rate	2.9	3.8	6.1	6.3	8.5	12.7	12.8	12.7	13.2	13.6
					(Index 1990 = 100)					
Real Effective[4]	85.0	99.2	118.8	98.2	100.0	98.7	98.5	94.7	92.2	90.6
					(Index 1980 = 100)					
Terms of Trade	90.3	82.1	89.6	77.2	62.6	61.5	56.2	53.7	57.8	66.1
Balance of Payments					(Millions of Dollars)					
Current Account Balance	-183.4	-364.1	-18.9	-327.3	-279.6	-157.3	-707.9	-425.1	-158.7	209.9
Trade Balance	-629.6	-880.2	-718.3	-1,039.4	-1,058.3	-1,070.5	-1,611.8	-1,607.4	-1,631.8	-1,964.0
Exports of Goods (FOB)	722.1	711.3	889.7	924.4	734.5	658.3	562.5	511.0	644.0	742.7
Imports of Goods (FOB)	1,351.7	1,591.5	1,608.0	1,963.8	1,792.8	1,728.8	2,174.3	2,118.4	2,275.8	2,706.7
Service Balance	160.1	185.5	345.8	327.7	408.1	526.7	472.1	740.7	979.9	1,610.9
Unrequited Transfers	286.1	330.6	353.6	384.4	370.6	386.5	431.8	441.6	493.2	563.0
Capital Account Balance[5]	145.2	-31.6	93.4	398.9	408.2	-49.5	165.6	90.4	279.6	-90.7
Non-Monetary Sector	66.3	-5.9	129.3	320.0	367.7	-38.4	177.6	101.6	240.4	...
Private	50.0	89.0	106.1	48.0	279.8	4.2	313.6	132.9	206.1	...
Government	16.3	-94.9	23.2	272.0	87.9	-42.6	-134.0	-31.1	34.3	...
Monetary Sector	78.9	-25.7	-35.9	78.9	40.5	-11.1	-14.0	-11.2	39.2	...
Change in Reserves (- Increase)	-44.1	146.8	-110.1	2.0	-7.9	-341.5	-26.2	-89.6	376.6	-119.2
Errors and Omissions	82.3	248.9	35.6	-73.6	-120.7	548.3	568.5	424.3	-497.5	...
Total External Debt					(Millions of Dollars)					
Disbursed Debt	3,687.4	3,923.2	3,998.5	4,060.5	4,395.5	4,493.8	4,611.8	4,833.0	4,293.1	4,171.0
Debt Service Actually Paid	374.1	307.1	339.7	322.4	238.6	270.4	329.1	333.0	503.7	540.0
					(In Percent)					
Interest Payments Due/Exports of Goods and Non-factor Services	18.8	20.3	14.7	11.8	13.4	8.6	9.1	10.5	5.9	5.2

[1] Data sources are listed at the end.
[2] At market prices.
[3] Mid-year values.
[4] Trade-weighted.
[5] Includes Errors and Omissions for 1995.

ECUADOR
Statistical Profile[1]

	1986	1987	1988	1989	1990	1991	1992	1993	1994	1995p
Real Gross Domestic Product (GDP)[2]					(Average Annual Growth Rates)					
Total GDP	3.1	-6.0	10.5	0.3	3.0	5.0	3.6	2.0	4.3	2.3
Agriculture, Forestry and Fishing .	10.2	2.5	7.7	2.8	6.1	5.9	3.4	-1.7	3.9	3.2
Mining and Quarrying	2.7	-54.7	115.8	-9.7	-0.9	8.4	5.8	11.0	10.6	3.8
Manufacturing	-1.6	1.7	2.0	-5.0	0.7	3.2	3.6	2.5	4.4	2.2
Construction	1.5	2.5	-14.1	4.0	-14.9	-1.1	-0.3	-4.3	5.3	-1.4
Non-Financial Public Sector					(As a Percent of GDP)					
Current Revenue	24.6	21.9	21.5	26.2	27.1	25.4	25.8	26.1	24.1	24.9
Current Expenditures	21.5	24.5	21.4	20.1	19.5	18.5	19.6	19.1	17.4	20.6
Current Saving	3.1	-2.6	0.1	6.1	7.6	6.9	6.2	7.0	6.7	4.3
Capital Expenditures[3]	8.1	7.1	6.0	7.5	7.5	7.9	7.9	7.4	6.9	5.2
Overall Balance (- Deficit)	-5.1	-9.6	-5.9	-1.4	0.1	-1.0	-1.7	-0.4	-0.2	-0.9
Domestic Financing	-0.4	1.8	2.8	-2.9	-3.6	-1.0	0.5	...	...	...
Money and Credit[4]					(As a Percent of GDP)					
Domestic Credit	29.3	25.4	21.1	19.2	15.6	14.1	14.0	13.5	37.0	...
Public Sector	4.6	3.3	4.8	8.0	4.6	3.1	2.4	1.0	19.4	...
Private Sector	25.0	22.5	16.9	11.9	10.9	11.0	11.6	12.5	17.6	...
Money Supply (M1)	10.3	10.1	8.9	7.8	7.4	8.2	6.9	8.4	8.9	6.5
					(Annual Percentage Rate)					
Interest Rate[5]	...	...	...	40.2	43.6	41.5	46.8	32.0	33.7	43.3
Prices and Salaries					(Average Annual Growth Rates)					
Consumer Prices	23.0	29.5	58.2	75.6	48.5	48.7	54.6	45.0	27.3	22.9
Real Wages[6]	3.0	-7.4	-15.9	-17.1	-16.0	-8.7	15.7	5.9	24.4	11.5
Exchange Rates					(Sucres per Dollar)					
Market Rate	122.8	170.5	301.6	526.4	767.8	1,046.3	1,534.0	1,919.1	2,196.7	2,564.5
					(Index 1990 = 100)					
Real Effective	61.5	80.0	106.5	92.1	100.0	95.3	94.7	82.3	77.7	79.1
					(Index 1980 = 100)					
Terms of Trade	82.2	88.9	79.2	86.0	81.7	71.0	70.2	68.5	72.9	70.6
Balance of Payments					(Millions of Dollars)					
Current Account Balance	-596.0	-1,187.0	-683.0	-716.0	-366.0	-707.0	-215.0	-682.0	-807.0	-822.0
Trade Balance	543.0	-33.0	619.0	661.0	1,003.0	644.0	925.0	588.0	435.0	267.0
Exports of Goods (FOB)	2,186.0	2,021.0	2,202.0	2,354.0	2,714.0	2,851.0	3,008.0	3,062.0	3,717.0	4,362.0
Imports of Goods (FOB)	1,643.0	2,054.0	1,583.0	1,693.0	1,711.0	2,207.0	2,083.0	2,474.0	3,282.0	4,095.0
Service Balance	-1,184.0	-1,286.0	-1,399.0	-1,474.0	-1,476.0	-1,461.0	-1,260.0	-1,400.0	-1,387.0	-1,320.0
Unrequited Transfers	45.0	132.0	97.0	97.0	107.0	110.0	120.0	130.0	145.0	231.0
Capital Account Balance[5]	821.0	1,338.0	687.0	788.0	430.0	701.0	414.0	1,266.0	1,016.0	-591.0
Non-Monetary Sector	828.0	1,288.0	699.0	823.0	455.0	712.0	440.0	1,298.0	...	...
Private	-20.0	1,028.0	546.0	808.0	1,140.0	1,306.0	1,043.0	1,924.0	1,623.0	...
Government	848.0	260.0	153.0	15.0	-685.0	-594.0	-603.0	-626.0	-607.0	...
Monetary Sector	-7.0	50.0	-12.0	-35.0	-25.0	-11.0	-26.0	-32.0	...	...
Change in Reserves (- Increase)	207.0	116.0	-32.0	-187.0	-280.0	-157.0	-99.0	-528.0	-331.0	155.0
Errors and Omissions	-432.0	-268.0	28.0	115.0	216.0	163.0	-99.0	-56.0	122.0	1,258.0
Total External Debt					(Millions of Dollars)					
Disbursed Debt	9,334.4	10,473.4	10,745.1	11,317.4	12,109.3	12,468.1	12,279.9	14,109.8	14,954.4	14,366.0
Debt Service Actually Paid	1,152.4	838.2	1,058.6	1,029.2	1,084.4	1,106.0	981.2	920.4	986.3	1,234.0
					(In Percent)					
Interest Payments Due/Exports of Goods and Non-factor Services	34.6	38.4	41.8	43.6	38.5	35.3	28.5	30.5	24.2	...

[1] Data sources are listed at the end.
[2] At market prices.
[3] Includes net lending.

[4] Mid-year values.
[5] Average of nominal free market rates offered by deposit money banks on 30- to 89-day time deposits. Beginning 1992, weighted average.
[6] Minimum wages.

EL SALVADOR
Statistical Profile[1]

	1986	1987	1988	1989	1990	1991	1992	1993	1994	1995p
Real Gross Domestic Product (GDP)[2]					(Average Annual Growth Rates)					
Total GDP	0.2	2.5	1.9	1.0	4.8	3.6	7.5	7.4	6.0	6.1
Agriculture, Forestry and Fishing	-4.3	1.3	-1.0	-0.6	6.5	-0.3	8.0	-2.6	-2.7	5.1
Mining and Quarrying	2.8	12.6	7.2	3.7	-0.7	9.4	5.3	10.7	11.9	7.1
Manufacturing	1.3	3.0	3.4	2.7	4.9	5.9	9.9	-1.5	7.9	7.0
Construction	2.6	11.5	7.8	3.6	-12.8	10.3	6.4	3.6	10.1	6.0
Non-Financial Public Sector					(As a Percent of GDP)					
Current Revenue	17.5	15.2	13.5	11.6	12.4	13.0	13.6	13.7	15.2	16.1
Current Expenditures	16.0	15.4	14.0	13.4	12.8	13.8	13.4	13.0	13.3	12.9
Current Saving	1.5	-0.2	-0.6	-1.8	-0.4	-0.8	0.2	0.8	2.0	3.2
Capital Expenditures[3]	6.5	3.1	4.3	4.9	2.5	4.1	6.7	4.6	4.3	4.1
Overall Balance (- Deficit)	-2.6	0.3	-2.9	-4.7	-0.4	-2.8	-4.6	-1.6	-0.6	-0.1
Domestic Financing	1.2	-1.2	1.7	2.9	-1.1	0.8	0.6	-0.3	-1.5	-1.2
Money and Credit[4]					(As a Percent of GDP)					
Domestic Credit	37.8	36.7	34.1	33.6	31.1	28.6	30.3	28.5	30.7	33.8
Public Sector	9.1	8.6	6.7	7.2	8.6	8.9	9.1	8.7	6.5	4.6
Private Sector	28.7	28.1	27.4	26.4	22.5	19.7	21.1	19.8	24.2	29.2
Money Supply (M1)	12.2	12.5	10.1	9.8	9.1	8.5	10.1	9.9	9.8	9.1
					(Annual Percentage Rate)					
Interest Rate[5]	15.0	15.0	15.0	16.3	18.0	16.1	11.5	15.3	13.6	14.4
Prices and Salaries					(Average Annual Growth Rates)					
Consumer Prices	31.9	24.9	19.8	17.6	24.0	14.4	11.2	18.6	10.5	10.1
Real Wages[6]	-9.2	10.1	-9.8	-4.7	-5.6	-7.4	-1.1	-5.3	1.2	-0.5
Exchange Rates					(Colones per Dollar)					
Market Rate	4.9	5.0	5.0	5.0	6.8	8.0	8.4	8.7	8.7	8.8
					(Index 1990 = 100)					
Real Effective[7]	114.1	100.4	88.0	89.2	100.0	97.3	96.3	87.5	83.2	77.3
					(Index 1980 = 100)					
Terms of Trade	108.3	71.1	76.5	64.9	51.9	51.1	48.3	50.7	58.7	67.9
Balance of Payments					(Millions of Dollars)					
Current Account Balance	116.9	135.9	25.7	-194.4	-151.7	-167.4	-108.9	-77.2	-18.1	-275.6
Trade Balance	-124.4	-349.1	-355.9	-662.7	-665.6	-704.6	-962.3	-1,034.9	-1,155.3	-1,358.9
Exports of Goods (FOB)	777.9	589.6	610.6	557.5	643.9	586.8	598.1	731.5	1,252.2	1,661.3
Imports of Goods (FOB)	902.3	938.7	966.5	1,220.2	1,309.5	1,291.4	1,560.5	1,766.4	2,407.4	3,020.2
Service Balance	-142.1	-54.0	-118.9	-142.4	-117.1	-132.8	-84.8	-87.4	-151.3	-306.2
Unrequited Transfers	383.3	538.9	500.5	610.7	631.0	669.9	938.2	1,045.0	1,288.5	1,389.5
Capital Account Balance[8]	68.8	-60.7	61.8	168.5	22.0	-27.9	135.0	99.0	83.9	422.2
Non-Monetary Sector	31.1	-66.1	40.9	155.7	64.5	-49.9	135.0	80.2	8.6	212.3
Private	12.0	4.7	6.8	20.1	-1.9	42.2	46.3	33.1	-2.3	15.6
Government	19.1	-70.8	34.1	135.6	66.4	-92.1	88.7	47.1	10.9	196.7
Monetary Sector	37.7	5.4	20.9	12.8	-42.5	22.0	0.0	18.8	75.3	209.9
Change in Reserves (- Increase)	-43.8	-81.8	19.6	-115.0	-169.8	69.8	-91.6	-112.0	-113.0	-146.6
Errors and Omissions	-141.8	6.9	-107.1	140.9	299.4	125.6	65.6	90.3	47.3	...
Total External Debt					(Millions of Dollars)					
Disbursed Debt	1,858.4	1,981.8	1,994.0	2,077.9	2,146.8	2,180.3	2,261.2	2,011.7	2,187.6	2,264.0
Debt Service Actually Paid	286.0	260.0	202.9	170.6	208.3	248.3	232.8	292.5	340.6	260.0
					(In Percent)					
Interest Payments Due/Exports of Goods and Non-factor Services	10.2	11.0	9.9	9.3	13.3	12.8	10.5	10.3	6.3	...

[1] Data sources are listed at the end.
[2] At market prices.
[3] Includes net lending.
[4] Mid-year values.
[5] Rate offered by banks and savings and loans associations on nominal time deposits of 180 days.
[6] For formal private sector employment only.
[7] Trade-weighted.
[8] Includes Errors and Omissions for 1995.

GUATEMALA
Statistical Profile[1]

	1986	1987	1988	1989	1990	1991	1992	1993	1994	1995p
Real Gross Domestic Product (GDP)[2]					(Average Annual Growth Rates)					
Total GDP	0.1	3.5	3.9	3.9	3.1	3.7	4.8	3.9	4.0	4.9
Agriculture, Forestry and Fishing .	-0.8	3.9	4.5	3.1	4.1	3.1	3.0	2.1	2.5	2.9
Mining and Quarrying	29.6	-0.1	2.6	3.5	-5.2	8.4	30.2	10.8	3.8	12.3
Manufacturing	0.7	2.0	2.2	2.3	2.2	2.4	3.3	2.9	3.0	3.3
Construction	3.1	14.5	15.7	7.8	-7.9	1.4	25.5	-3.0	-4.9	8.0
Central Government					(As a Percent of GDP)					
Current Revenue	8.9	9.4	10.1	9.5	8.1	9.1	10.6	9.1	7.6	8.4
Current Expenditures	8.9	9.7	10.4	10.1	8.5	7.6	7.8	7.4	6.9	6.5
Current Saving	0.0	-0.3	-0.2	-0.6	-0.3	1.5	2.9	1.7	0.8	1.9
Fixed Investment	0.8	1.0	1.3	1.4	1.0	0.9	1.1	1.0	0.9	1.1
Deficit or Surplus	-1.5	-1.3	-1.7	-2.9	-1.8	0.0	0.5	-1.3	-1.4	-0.7
Domestic Financing	1.7	1.3	1.5	2.4	1.5	0.9	0.1	1.3	-0.4	-0.9
Money and Credit[3]					(As a Percent of GDP)					
Domestic Credit	23.0	19.7	18.2	18.3	15.1	10.5	10.8	12.0	11.4	...
Public Sector	8.7	5.6	3.6	4.1	3.3	0.8	0.8	1.1	0.8	...
Private Sector	14.3	14.1	14.6	14.2	11.8	9.7	10.0	11.0	10.5	...
Money Supply (M1)	8.4	8.6	8.1	7.7	7.3	6.0	6.3	6.4	7.2	6.4
					(Annual Percentage Rate)					
Interest Rate[4]	13.2	14.0	15.2	16.0	23.3	34.1	19.5	24.7	22.9	...
Prices and Salaries					(Average Annual Growth Rates)					
Consumer Prices	36.9	12.3	10.8	11.4	41.2	33.2	10.0	11.9	10.9	11.8
Real Wages	-18.3	6.7	5.2	6.5	-14.8	-6.3	16.3	10.8	7.2	...
Exchange Rates					(Quetzales per Dollar)					
Market Rate	1.9	2.5	2.6	2.8	4.5	5.0	5.2	5.6	5.8	5.8
					(Index 1990 = 100)					
Real Effective[5]	71.8	74.0	79.8	82.6	100.0	85.0	80.5	79.3	75.8	77.0
					(Index 1980 = 100)					
Terms of Trade	105.1	90.1	92.3	93.9	94.2	90.8	84.4	86.2	90.7	97.8
Balance of Payments					(Millions of Dollars)					
Current Account Balance	-17.6	-442.5	-414.0	-367.1	-212.9	-183.7	-705.9	-701.7	-625.3	-595.0
Trade Balance	168.1	-355.3	-339.9	-358.3	-216.6	-443.0	-1,044.1	-1,020.8	-996.5	-1,054.6
Exports of Goods (FOB)	1,043.8	977.9	1,073.3	1,126.1	1,211.4	1,230.0	1,283.7	1,363.2	1,550.1	1,994.5
Imports of Goods (FOB)	875.7	1,333.2	1,413.2	1,484.4	1,428.0	1,673.0	2,327.8	2,384.0	2,546.6	3,049.1
Service Balance	-260.8	-280.5	-298.4	-258.6	-223.3	-0.4	-52.3	-44.1	-77.4	-5.7
Unrequited Transfers	75.1	193.3	224.3	249.8	227.0	259.7	390.5	363.2	448.6	465.3
Capital Account Balance	63.4	462.2	275.0	384.1	146.8	654.5	604.1	768.3	669.0	437.8
Non-Monetary Sector	50.4	423.5	258.1	398.4	163.8	658.4	589.7	768.3	669.0	515.6
Private	192.1	428.3	460.1	241.1	181.7	849.0	627.2	872.1	611.1	490.4
Government	-141.7	-4.8	-202.0	157.3	-17.9	-190.6	-37.5	-103.8	57.9	25.2
Monetary Sector	13.0	38.7	16.9	-14.3	-17.0	-3.9	14.4	0.0	0.0	-77.8
Change in Reserves (- Increase)	-112.9	53.1	141.4	-71.7	29.9	-554.1	19.9	-151.8	-52.9	156.9
Errors and Omissions	67.3	-72.7	-2.4	54.7	36.2	83.3	81.8	85.2	9.2	0.3
Total External Debt					(Millions of Dollars)					
Disbursed Debt	2,794.1	2,795.6	2,638.9	2,636.9	2,840.2	2,824.9	2,753.2	2,890.5	3,017.0	3,083.0
Debt Service Actually Paid	382.6	344.4	373.5	303.7	212.3	288.8	517.2	302.4	282.3	282.0
					(In Percent)					
Interest Payments Due/Exports of Goods and Non-factor Services	17.9	14.3	14.1	11.7	11.5	7.3	9.2	6.3	6.0	4.0

[1] Data sources are listed at the end.
[2] At market prices.

[3] Mid-year values.
[4] Maximum nominal commercial bank lending rate.
[5] Trade-weighted.

GUYANA
Statistical Profile[1]

	1986	1987	1988	1989	1990	1991	1992	1993	1994	1995p
Real Gross Domestic Product (GDP)[2]					(Average Annual Growth Rates)					
Total GDP	-0.2	-0.2	-6.0	-4.9	-3.0	6.0	7.8	8.2	8.5	5.1
Agriculture, Forestry and Fishing	1.5	-4.7	-13.7	-2.9	-13.8	12.4	24.3	6.2	11.8	7.2
Mining and Quarrying	-7.8	3.0	-4.5	-26.1	18.0	21.3	-11.5	49.0	6.6	-11.4
Manufacturing	-1.1	-6.9	-5.5	-7.4	-13.1	10.5	19.3	3.5	5.9	12.7
Construction	-1.6	4.9	-4.7	-2.0	2.1	2.0	2.0	3.5	20.0	9.7
Central Government					(As a Percent of GDP)					
Current Revenue	45.9	36.3	41.6	31.1	34.2	36.5	38.0	37.9	32.7	35.3
Current Expenditures	50.9	63.5	51.9	35.9	48.7	45.1	49.4	35.0	32.5	32.4
Current Saving	-5.0	-27.2	-10.3	-4.9	-14.5	-8.6	-11.3	2.9	0.2	2.9
Fixed Investment	12.4	14.7	9.8	7.7	11.5	5.1	7.4	7.8	11.3	12.3
Deficit or Surplus	-58.8	-42.4	-31.6	-6.6	-22.9	-15.6	-17.1	-6.0	-6.8	-7.9
Domestic Financing	80.6	42.9	33.5	25.2	5.4	2.2	5.3	-10.8	-2.2	5.0
Money and Credit[3]					(As a Percent of GDP)					
Domestic Credit	258.3	209.4	278.9	138.1	90.7	26.5	24.2	16.0	5.1	5.8
Public Sector	230.7	185.1	248.9	118.5	78.1	19.0	14.4	8.3	-6.5	-11.3
Private Sector	27.5	24.2	30.0	19.6	12.7	7.4	9.8	7.7	11.6	17.2
Money Supply (M1)	35.2	31.7	33.2	22.5	14.8	10.8	13.1	13.4	13.3	13.1
					(Annual Percentage Rate)					
Interest Rate[4]	12.0	11.1	12.2	15.8	29.2	29.5	22.5	12.3	11.4	12.9
Prices and Salaries					(Average Annual Growth Rates)					
Consumer Prices	7.9	28.7	39.9	89.7	63.6	101.5	28.2	10.0	16.1	8.1
Real Wages	...	...	...	...	...	...	...	...	...	...
Exchange Rates					(Guyana Dollars per Dollar)					
Market Rate	4.3	9.8	10.0	27.2	39.5	111.8	125.0	126.7	138.3	142.0
					(Index 1990 = 100)					
Real Effective[5]	36.2	70.3	55.8	70.6	100.0	116.0	104.7	95.6	95.8	95.6
					(Index 1990 = 100)					
Terms of Trade	102.4	105.0	109.8	97.4	100.0	128.7	125.6	103.2	102.7	73.2
Balance of Payments					(Guyana Dollars per Dollar)					
Current Account Balance	-141.1	-109.5	-93.6	-113.3	-149.6	-119.0	-146.7	-137.9	-100.8	-94.9
Trade Balance	-25.9	2.4	18.6	11.6	-22.9	17.2	-20.8	-25.8	5.2	15.2
Exports of Goods (FOB)	210.0	240.5	214.6	204.7	203.9	239.0	381.7	414.0	463.4	495.7
Imports of Goods (FOB)	235.9	238.1	196.0	193.1	226.8	221.8	402.5	439.8	458.2	480.5
Service Balance	-131.4	-132.6	-131.7	-146.5	-155.0	-157.2	-155.9	-141.1	-138.0	-149.1
Unrequited Transfers	16.2	20.7	19.5	21.6	28.3	21.0	30.0	29.0	32.0	39.0
Capital Account Balance	78.2	36.6	50.9	88.2	164.5	158.6	198.0	172.9	113.4	102.8
Non-Monetary Sector	74.4	48.9	51.2	103.2	175.8	142.6	201.0	166.2	114.6	...
Private	21.7	12.7	-4.3	25.5	-61.9	46.2	137.9	69.7	43.0	46.3
Government	52.7	36.2	55.5	77.7	237.7	96.4	63.1	96.5	71.6	...
Monetary Sector	3.8	-12.3	-0.3	-15.0	-11.3	16.0	-3.0	6.7	-1.2	...
Change in Reserves (- Increase)	62.4	77.0	32.2	29.5	-18.1	-40.5	-35.1	-38.4	-27.8	24.3
Errors and Omissions	0.5	-4.1	10.5	-4.4	3.2	0.9	-16.2	3.4	15.2	-32.2
External Public Debt					(Millions of Dollars)					
Disbursed Debt	1,633.8	1,737.6	1,865.9	1,633.1	1,945.5	1,960.0	1,896.8	1,954.1	2,039.0	2,058.0
Debt Service Actually Paid	74.6	72.1	66.3	88.3	295.5	102.0	101.6	92.4	97.0	107.8
					(In Percent)					
Interest Payments Due/Exports of Goods and Non-factor Services	33.0	28.7	32.3	37.3	40.5	34.1	22.8	17.6	14.7	14.3

[1] Data sources are listed at the end.
[2] At factor cost.
[3] Mid-year values.

[4] Rate on 3-month nominal deposits at commercial banks.
[5] Trade-weighted.

HAITI
Statistical Profile[1]

	1986	1987	1988	1989	1990	1991	1992	1993	1994	1995p
Real Gross Domestic Product (GDP)[2]					(Average Annual Growth Rates)					
Total GDP	0.6	0.6	-1.5	-1.5	-3.0	-3.0	-14.8	-2.6	-4.1	4.5
Agriculture, Forestry and Fishing .	2.4	0.3	-1.3	-1.1	-3.7	-0.1	-1.1	-2.6	-1.7	-7.2
Manufacturing	-2.8	-0.8	-2.6	-2.1	-7.0	-17.7	-21.5	-0.8	-33.3	-1.4
Construction	-6.1	2.3	1.0	3.1	-9.1	3.5	-54.0	-3.5	-25.0	60.0
Non-Financial Public Sector					(As a Percent of GDP)					
Current Revenue	...	...	...	...	7.7	8.2	6.5	7.8	4.7	8.9
Current Expenditures	...	...	...	...	8.8	8.2	8.4	9.2	7.4	11.7
Current Saving	...	...	...	...	-1.1	0.0	-1.9	-1.5	-2.7	-2.8
Capital Expenditures[3]	...	...	...	...	5.1	4.5	0.4	1.0	0.4	5.9
Overall Balance (- Deficit)	...	...	...	...	-3.7	-1.8	-2.3	-2.5	-3.1	-3.1
Domestic Financing	...	...	...	...	1.6	0.7	2.0	1.8	2.6	-1.5
Money and Credit[4]					(As a Percent of GDP)					
Domestic Credit	...	...	...	...	31.3	30.1	37.6	42.9	41.2	29.1
Public Sector	...	...	...	...	19.4	18.2	23.8	27.0	27.2	14.3
Private Sector	...	...	...	...	11.9	11.9	13.7	15.9	13.9	14.8
Money Supply (M1)	...	...	...	...	14.0	13.6	16.8	19.3	18.5	10.8
					(Annual Percentage Rate)					
Interest Rate[5]	...	...	...	...	10.2	10.2	6.0	5.7	5.2	6.2
Prices and Salaries					(Average Annual Growth Rates)					
Consumer Prices	3.3	-11.5	4.1	7.9	20.4	18.2	17.9	18.9	36.1	27.1
Real Wages[6]	-7.8	5.2	-2.7	-9.9	-17.0	-15.4	-15.2	-16.0	-26.5	197.0
Exchange Rates					(Gourdes per Dollar)					
Market Rate	5.0	5.6	6.0	6.6	7.5	7.7	9.1	12.4	14.7	14.5
					(Index 1990 = 100)					
Real Effective[7]	72.2	82.1	87.6	89.5	100.0	129.7	131.3	124.7	124.7	125.0
					(Index 1980 = 100)					
Terms of Trade	77.5	84.2	77.2	65.1	65.2	67.9	63.8	65.7	66.7	69.2
Balance of Payments					(Millions of Dollars)					
Current Account Balance	-44.9	-31.1	-40.4	-62.7	-88.3	-123.3	-41.4	-77.9	4.1	-59.6
Trade Balance	-112.5	-101.1	-103.5	-111.0	-176.8	-246.6	-138.5	-185.0	-83.8	-316.9
Exports of Goods (FOB)	190.8	210.1	180.4	148.3	265.8	202.0	75.6	81.6	57.4	84.5
Imports of Goods (FOB)	303.2	311.2	283.9	259.3	442.6	448.6	214.1	266.6	141.2	401.4
Service Balance	-84.3	-101.1	-129.7	-126.0	-104.4	-110.9	-57.9	-66.3	-68.4	-200.9
Unrequited Transfers	151.9	171.1	192.9	174.3	192.9	234.2	155.0	173.4	156.2	458.2
Capital Account Balance[8]	54.6	53.4	51.3	75.1	36.2	37.7	-3.0	-1.6	-4.5	247.7
Non-Monetary Sector	65.0	62.4	46.3	44.5	59.3	53.9	9.6	29.0	22.1	269.6
Private	39.4	39.6	28.0	27.7	8.0	13.6	0.0	0.0	0.0	6.2
Government	25.6	22.8	18.3	16.8	51.3	40.3	9.6	29.0	22.1	263.4
Monetary Sector	-10.4	-9.0	5.0	30.6	-23.1	-16.2	-12.6	-30.6	-26.6	-22.0
Change in Reserves (- Increase)	-24.9	-8.8	-22.8	1.3	30.6	-22.2	-11.3	-19.1	-16.3	-188.1
Errors and Omissions	15.2	-13.5	11.8	-13.7	21.5	107.8	55.7	98.6	29.1	...
Total External Debt					(Millions of Dollars)					
Disbursed Debt	710.4	844.1	818.2	802.5	884.0	747.1	772.8	773.0	712.1	778.0
Debt Service Actually Paid	46.6	61.2	59.2	51.8	32.7	26.6	4.9	4.5	0.8	13.0
					(In Percent)					
Interest Payments Due/Exports of Goods and Non-factor Services	5.1	6.0	8.3	9.5	7.9	7.7	11.3	10.7	17.5	...

[1] Data sources are listed at the end.
[2] At market prices.
[3] Includes net lending.
[4] Mid-year values.

[5] Six-month nominal deposit rate (December of each year).
[6] Real minimum wages (Nominal minimum wages increased from 15 Gourdes to 36 Gourdes in 1995).
[7] Trade-weighted.
[8] Includes Errors and Omissions for 1995.

HONDURAS
Statistical Profile[1]

	1986	1987	1988	1989	1990	1991	1992	1993	1994	1995p
Real Gross Domestic Product (GDP)[2]					(Average Annual Growth Rates)					
Total GDP	0.7	6.0	4.6	4.3	0.1	3.3	5.6	6.1	-1.3	3.6
Agriculture, Forestry and Fishing .	-0.7	8.3	-0.5	10.0	1.1	6.1	3.6	1.3	-3.6	4.7
Mining and Quarrying	-6.7	-38.6	35.3	13.0	-7.7	4.2	10.7	3.6	2.3	3.4
Manufacturing	4.1	6.6	5.0	3.8	0.7	1.7	6.1	6.3	-2.0	4.0
Construction	-19.9	4.0	14.7	14.7	-9.9	-2.8	34.0	21.1	-19.2	1.4
Non-Financial Public Sector					(As a Percent of GDP)					
Current Revenue	25.3	26.0	25.1	24.6	27.3	29.7	29.3	27.3	27.1	31.5
Current Expenditures[3]	24.4	25.0	24.6	25.1	25.8	23.1	22.1	23.4	22.5	23.6
Current Saving	0.8	1.0	0.5	-0.4	1.5	6.6	7.2	3.8	4.6	7.9
Capital Expenditures[4]	7.0	7.4	7.2	7.2	7.5	9.1	11.6	14.5	12.5	10.1
Overall Balance (- Deficit)	-5.8	-6.2	-6.6	-7.4	-5.9	-2.2	-3.7	-10.0	-7.3	-2.0
Domestic Financing	1.3	2.2	2.5	5.3	-0.6	-4.3	-1.8	2.5	0.8	0.1
Money and Credit[5]					(As a Percent of GDP)					
Domestic Credit	38.0	39.0	41.7	40.8	39.6	28.2	25.9	26.9	26.1	23.5
Public Sector	11.3	12.4	12.2	12.7	12.8	5.7	3.3	3.6	3.8	1.8
Private Sector	26.7	26.6	29.4	28.1	26.8	22.5	22.7	23.3	22.3	21.7
Money Supply (M1)	9.6	10.4	11.5	11.1	12.4	10.3	10.7	10.6	10.3	11.2
					(Annual Percentage Rate)					
Interest Rate[6]	15.8	15.2	15.3	15.3	17.5	22.0	21.5	22.0	25.0	28.4
Prices and Salaries					(Average Annual Growth Rates)					
Consumer Prices	4.4	2.5	4.5	9.9	23.3	34.0	8.7	10.8	21.7	29.5
Real Wages[7]	-4.2	-2.3	-4.4	-9.0	16.8	0.1	13.3	1.8	-10.0	-2.0
Exchange Rates					(Lempiras per Dollar)					
Market Rate	2.0	2.0	2.0	2.0	4.1	5.3	5.5	6.5	8.4	9.5
					(Index 1990 = 100)					
Real Effective[8]	66.4	69.1	68.8	64.0	100.0	108.9	109.0	114.5	120.2	108.0
					(Index 1980 = 100)					
Terms of Trade	104.8	97.5	109.2	107.0	106.2	111.0	108.1	108.8	112.6	125.2
Balance of Payments					(Millions of Dollars)					
Current Account Balance	-117.1	-182.0	-130.8	-196.3	-92.9	-217.4	-310.8	-270.6	-354.9	-270.0
Trade Balance	22.6	-40.9	-34.0	-44.5	-11.8	-71.9	-150.9	-90.9	-429.0	-364.1
Exports of Goods (FOB)	902.1	830.5	889.4	911.2	895.2	840.6	839.3	853.0	922.1	1,136.9
Imports of Goods (FOB)	879.5	871.4	923.4	955.7	907.0	912.5	990.2	943.9	1,351.1	1,501.0
Service Balance	-298.1	-315.5	-312.4	-318.4	-319.3	-297.8	-323.2	-298.8	-146.8	-136.7
Unrequited Transfers	158.3	174.4	215.6	166.6	238.2	152.3	163.3	119.1	220.9	230.8
Capital Account Balance	173.9	280.1	238.3	306.7	224.6	131.2	292.9	246.4	219.6	185.8
Non-Monetary Sector	173.5	251.0	249.6	327.6	301.5	165.7	337.3	258.1	223.0	198.0
Private	-18.3	1.6	24.7	18.7	-3.7	-6.0	134.9	22.2	95.9	90.1
Government	191.8	249.4	224.9	308.9	305.2	171.7	202.4	235.9	127.1	107.9
Monetary Sector	0.4	29.1	-11.3	-20.9	-76.9	-34.5	-44.4	-11.7	-3.4	-12.2
Change in Reserves (- Increase)	-59.8	-64.9	-14.4	28.5	-24.3	-65.8	-11.3	106.0	-17.0	-118.2
Errors and Omissions	3.2	-33.4	-93.1	-138.9	-107.4	152.0	29.2	-81.8	152.3	202.4
Total External Debt					(Millions of Dollars)					
Disbursed Debt	2,974.2	3,299.2	3,306.8	3,385.2	3,722.0	3,395.0	3,614.1	4,075.1	4,417.9	4,480.0
Debt Service Actually Paid	298.7	341.4	369.0	142.3	388.9	307.3	377.0	362.0	433.2	438.0
					(In Percent)					
Interest Payments Due/Exports of Goods and Non-factor Services	15.3	18.7	17.6	17.6	18.0	21.1	25.9	23.7	15.0	13.3

[1] Data sources are listed at the end.
[2] GDP at market prices. Sector of Origin at factor cost.
[3] On a cash basis.
[4] Includes net lending.

[5] Mid-year values.
[6] Weighted nominal lending rate.
[7] Minimum wages.
[8] Trade-weighted.

JAMAICA
Statistical Profile[1]

	1986	1987	1988	1989	1990	1991	1992	1993	1994	1995p
Real Gross Domestic Product (GDP)[2]					(Average Annual Growth Rates)					
Total GDP	1.6	7.8	2.9	6.8	5.5	0.7	1.5	1.4	0.8	0.5
Agriculture, Forestry and Fishing .	-2.1	5.2	-3.4	-9.1	11.5	-0.2	13.1	10.1	7.5	2.2
Mining and Quarrying	6.5	6.0	-4.5	35.6	22.8	5.7	-2.5	0.3	6.9	-6.4
Manufacturing	2.2	5.5	5.4	7.5	3.9	-7.5	1.3	-1.9	-0.5	-1.0
Construction	3.0	14.2	14.8	18.0	1.6	0.6	0.4	-0.5	-6.3	6.7
Central Government[3]					(As a Percent of GDP)					
Current Revenue	31.9	28.7	28.5	29.9	27.6	28.8	28.7	31.4	31.6	34.2
Current Expenditures	26.7	25.1	26.2	25.8	22.7	22.7	21.4	24.7	26.5	28.9
Current Saving	5.1	3.6	2.3	4.1	4.9	6.1	7.3	6.7	5.2	5.3
Fixed Investment	5.1	4.4	5.7	4.6	2.5	3.1	4.2	3.1	...	...
Deficit or Surplus	0.7	1.5	-1.5	-0.2	3.0	4.4	4.2	3.5	1.9	1.0
Domestic Financing	2.5	-2.3	-0.6	-2.8	-5.1	-8.2	-3.4	-4.3	-2.4	0.5
Money and Credit[4]					(As a Percent of GDP)					
Domestic Credit	50.8	40.6	32.5	26.5	24.2	15.0	9.8	11.9	15.7	19.9
Public Sector	31.3	19.1	6.2	-2.3	-2.6	-6.6	-6.7	-6.8	-7.0	-3.4
Private Sector	19.6	21.5	26.3	28.9	26.7	21.7	16.5	18.7	22.7	23.3
Money Supply (M1)	11.9	13.7	13.6	11.2	11.0	11.2	13.1	15.0	15.0	13.9
					(Annual Percentage Rate)					
Interest Rate[5]	14.6	15.5	14.3	20.2	24.5	27.5	23.0	39.8	34.0	26.2
Prices and Salaries					(Average Annual Growth Rates)					
Consumer Prices	15.1	6.7	8.3	14.3	22.0	51.1	77.3	22.1	35.1	19.9
Real Wages	...	...	...	...	...	...	...	...	...	...
Exchange Rates					(Jamaica Dollars per Dollar)					
Market Rate	5.5	5.5	5.5	5.7	7.2	12.1	23.0	24.9	33.1	35.1
					(Index 1990 = 100)					
Real Effective[6]	94.8	95.7	95.5	89.2	100.0	111.1	127.8	111.8	95.0	94.6
					(Index 1980 = 100)					
Terms of Trade	76.5	85.2	92.3	89.2	86.0	83.0	79.6	78.5	78.4	...
Balance of Payments					(Millions of Dollars)					
Current Account Balance	-16.1	-124.8	47.5	-282.4	-312.1	-240.1	28.5	-184.0	48.4	-210.1
Trade Balance	-247.9	-352.1	-356.9	-589.8	-502.1	-391.6	-424.6	-815.1	-644.4	-587.5
Exports of Goods (FOB)	589.5	725.2	898.4	1,028.9	1,190.6	1,196.7	1,116.5	1,105.4	1,247.7	1,462.5
Imports of Goods (FOB)	837.4	1,077.3	1,255.3	1,618.7	1,692.7	1,588.3	1,541.1	1,920.5	1,892.1	2,050.0
Service Balance	61.4	39.2	-117.5	-194.8	-100.9	-117.0	95.7	241.3	212.3	-196.3
Unrequited Transfers	170.4	188.1	521.9	502.2	290.9	268.5	357.4	389.8	480.5	573.6
Capital Account Balance	38.8	206.0	133.5	318.5	401.3	175.0	243.0	248.5	352.2	370.0
Non-Monetary Sector	30.4	202.3	138.1	320.3	418.1	212.6	278.2	252.0	389.1	390.5
Private	19.8	129.1	41.7	-106.8	341.4	245.2	376.7	247.1	507.6	400.0
Government	10.6	73.2	96.4	427.1	76.7	-32.6	-98.5	4.9	-118.5	-9.5
Monetary Sector	8.4	3.7	-4.6	-1.8	-16.8	-37.6	-35.2	-3.5	-36.9	-20.5
Change in Reserves (- Increase)	-102.7	-165.8	-135.0	-46.1	-118.5	85.5	-211.6	-114.2	-369.2	-20.0
Errors and Omissions	80.0	84.6	-46.0	10.0	29.3	-20.4	-59.9	49.7	-31.4	-139.9
Total External Debt					(Millions of Dollars)					
Disbursed Debt	4,221.2	4,723.9	4,552.6	4,560.2	4,670.6	4,409.7	4,263.6	4,111.8	4,317.9	4,229.0
Debt Service Actually Paid	675.3	750.0	735.4	642.5	661.3	719.3	710.6	541.5	595.1	642.0
					(In Percent)					
Interest Payments Due/Exports of Goods and Non-factor Services	23.4	20.6	18.6	18.1	15.7	15.5	14.1	13.0	10.7	7.1

[1] Data sources are listed at the end.
[2] At market prices.
[3] Fiscal year ends March 31.

[4] Mid-year values.
[5] Weighted nominal deposit rate.
[6] Trade-weighted.

MEXICO
Statistical Profile[1]

	1986	1987	1988	1989	1990	1991	1992	1993	1994	1995p
Real Gross Domestic Product (GDP)[2]					(Average Annual Growth Rates)					
Total GDP	-3.6	1.8	1.3	3.3	4.5	3.6	2.8	0.7	3.5	-6.9
Agriculture, Forestry and Fishing	-2.7	1.4	-3.8	-2.3	5.9	1.0	-1.0	1.4	4.2	-3.8
Mining and Quarrying	-4.1	5.3	0.4	-0.6	2.8	0.8	1.8	0.9	1.6	-0.7
Manufacturing	-5.3	3.0	3.2	7.2	6.1	4.0	2.3	-0.8	3.6	-6.4
Construction	-10.3	2.8	-0.4	2.1	7.0	2.4	7.8	2.8	6.4	-22.0
Non-Financial Public Sector					(As a Percent of GDP)					
Current Revenue	30.4	30.6	30.4	29.4	29.6	26.6	26.3	26.1	25.6	25.8
Current Expenditures	38.1	39.2	35.2	30.4	27.0	22.4	20.6	21.2	21.9	22.1
Current Saving	-7.7	-8.6	-4.8	-1.0	2.6	4.2	5.7	4.8	3.7	3.7
Capital Expenditures[3]	6.0	5.6	4.4	4.0	5.0	4.5	4.0	3.3	3.9	0.4
Financial Balance (- Deficit)	-16.0	-16.0	-12.5	-5.6	-3.9	1.8	3.4	0.7	-0.3	0.0
Domestic Financing[4]	15.8	13.8	14.1	6.1	2.7	-1.5	-3.1	-0.2	0.6	...
Money and Credit[5]					(As a Percent of GDP)					
Domestic Credit	29.3	21.3	21.7	25.3	27.7	30.6	33.9	35.5	39.5	39.2
Public Sector	20.3	14.1	13.6	13.8	12.5	9.9	6.4	1.6	1.1	0.6
Private Sector	9.0	7.2	8.1	11.5	15.2	20.7	27.5	33.9	38.5	38.6
Money Supply (M1)	4.6	3.7	4.5	4.1	4.5	5.8	10.1	10.8	10.4	7.0
					(Annual Percentage Rate)					
Interest Rate[6]	87.9	96.0	68.2	44.9	34.8	19.3	15.7	15.0	13.9	48.6
Prices and Salaries					(Average Annual Growth Rates)					
Consumer Prices	86.2	131.8	114.2	20.0	26.6	22.7	15.5	9.7	6.9	35.0
Real Wages[7]	-5.9	-1.9	-1.3	9.0	2.9	6.5	8.8	7.1	4.1	-14.8
Exchange Rates					(New Pesos per Dollar)					
Market Rate	0.6	1.4	2.3	2.5	2.8	3.0	3.1	3.1	3.4	6.4
					(Index 1990 = 100)					
Real Effective[8]	121.8	132.7	109.6	100.2	100.0	90.9	85.6	80.5	85.7	115.0
					(Index 1980 = 100)					
Terms of Trade	65.1	72.9	63.2	66.9	69.8	61.8	60.9	62.0	62.9	62.0
Balance of Payments					(Millions of Dollars)					
Current Account Balance	-1,377.0	4,247.0	-2,374.0	-5,825.0	-7,451.0	-14,888.0	-24,442.0	-23,400.0	-28,784.0	-654.4
Trade Balance[9]	5,019.0	8,786.0	2,611.0	405.0	-881.0	-7,279.0	-15,934.0	-13,481.0	-18,465.0	7,088.4
Exports of Goods (FOB)[9]	21,803.0	27,599.0	30,692.0	35,171.0	40,711.0	42,687.0	46,196.0	51,885.0	60,882.0	79,541.5
Imports of Goods (FOB)[9]	16,784.0	18,813.0	28,081.0	34,766.0	41,592.0	49,966.0	62,130.0	65,366.0	79,347.0	72,453.1
Service Balance	-7,970.0	-6,458.0	-7,240.0	-8,773.0	-10,545.0	-10,355.0	-11,893.0	-13,559.0	-14,334.0	-11,707.7
Unrequited Transfers	1,574.0	1,919.0	2,255.0	2,543.0	3,975.0	2,746.0	3,385.0	3,640.0	4,015.0	3,964.9
Capital Account Balance	1,998.0	-1,617.0	-1,071.0	1,499.0	8,526.0	25,159.0	27,039.0	33,760.0	12,754.0	15,311.2
Non-Monetary Sector	1,515.0	-1,358.0	-1,053.0	1,538.0	214.0	18,411.0	25,391.0	31,821.0	11,242.0	19,415.5
Private	-5,827.0	-3,909.0	-7.0	1,846.0	5,635.0	15,398.0	20,394.0	21,636.0	10,747.0	5,846.6
Government	7,342.0	2,551.0	-1,046.0	-308.0	-5,421.0	3,013.0	4,997.0	10,185.0	495.0	13,568.9
Monetary Sector	483.0	-259.0	-18.0	-39.0	8,312.0	6,748.0	1,648.0	1,939.0	1,512.0	-4,104.3
Change in Reserves (- Increase)	117.0	-5,585.0	6,637.0	-178.0	-2,303.0	-7,993.0	-1,745.0	-7,232.0	17,665.0	-9,592.8
Errors and Omissions	-738.0	2,955.0	-3,192.0	4,504.0	1,228.0	-2,278.0	-852.0	-3,128.0	-1,635.0	-5,064.0
Total External Debt					(Millions of Dollars)					
Disbursed Debt	100,889.3	109,468.7	99,212.7	93,837.6	104,449.5	114,064.4	112,227.1	118,469.2	128,301.9	158,298.0
Debt Service Actually Paid	12,945.5	12,088.0	15,473.0	15,563.4	11,315.6	13,544.9	20,821.4	21,147.2	19,048.9	20,194.0
					(In Percent)					
Interest Payments Due/Exports of Goods and Non-factor Services	31.7	24.8	23.6	22.0	19.0	18.0	17.5	18.3	17.4	16.6

[1] Data sources are listed at the end.
[2] At market prices.
[3] Includes net lending.
[4] Includes deficit of non-controlled public sector and financial intermediaries.
[5] Mid-year values.

[6] Nominal average yield on one-month treasury bills, calculated from the weighted average rate of discount on daily transactions among dealers on the Mexican Securities Exchange.
[7] Wages, salaries and benefits in Manufacturing.
[8] Trade-weighted.
[9] Include *maquiladoras*.

NICARAGUA
Statistical Profile[1]

	1986	1987	1988	1989	1990	1991	1992	1993	1994	1995p
Real Gross Domestic Product (GDP)[2]					(Average Annual Growth Rates)					
Total GDP	-1.0	-0.7	-12.4	-1.7	0.0	-0.2	0.4	-0.4	3.3	4.2
Agriculture, Forestry and Fishing .	-8.8	-3.2	-10.2	9.2	0.2	-3.9	3.1	1.8	10.8	5.0
Mining and Quarrying	31.5	-7.9	-8.7	41.0	-22.1	-1.4	17.1	2.7	-10.1	10.9
Manufacturing	2.1	-1.6	-25.3	-1.9	-1.5	6.4	-5.1	0.0	1.0	3.0
Construction	0.0	7.0	-7.0	-15.0	-5.9	-8.1	8.3	1.5	17.8	16.3
Non-Financial Public Sector					(As a Percent of GDP)					
Current Revenue	35.2	29.0	21.6	27.5	17.6	24.3	27.7	28.4	28.7	30.8
Current Expenditures	44.7	41.7	40.0	29.4	35.7	26.8	26.3	25.2	26.1	24.6
Current Saving	-9.5	-12.8	-18.4	-1.9	-18.1	-2.5	1.4	3.2	2.7	6.2
Capital Expenditures[3]	7.0	5.0	9.6	6.2	2.3	5.5	9.9	12.4	15.1	16.4
Overall Balance (- Deficit)	-14.9	-17.2	-27.4	-4.5	-18.4	4.1	-3.4	-0.2	-5.6	-1.8
Domestic Financing	14.9	17.2	25.0	-0.2	10.3	-4.5	-6.8	-1.2	-1.6	-0.1
Money and Credit[4]					(As a Percent of GDP)					
Domestic Credit	32.3	19.1	6.5	9.4	8.2	39.4	36.1	37.7	38.1	35.5
Public Sector[5]	16.9	7.7	1.2	-1.0	3.6	10.1	3.5	2.8	6.4	6.4
Private Sector	15.3	11.3	5.3	10.4	4.6	29.3	32.6	34.9	31.7	29.1
Money Supply (M1)	23.6	19.4	4.5	4.4	1.7	7.5	8.4	7.4	6.8	7.2
					(Annual Percentage Rate)					
Interest Rate[6]	...	...	...	1,585.9	9.5	11.6	12.0	11.6	11.7	11.1
Prices and Salaries					(Average Annual Growth Rates)					
Consumer Prices	681.4	911.9	10,215.2	4,770.3	7,485.2	2,742.3	20.3	20.4	7.8	10.0
Real Wages	...	-32.9	-42.6	35.6	64.9	-4.5	11.4	-6.4	-0.1	0.6
Exchange Rates					(Gold Cordobas per Dollar)					
Market Rate[7]	...	...	...	...	0.1	4.3	5.0	5.6	6.7	7.5
					(Index 1990 = 100)					
Real Effective[8]	133.6	91.7	91.3	149.2	100.0	104.5	107.2	110.2	118.1	132.4
					(Index 1980 = 100)					
Terms of Trade	93.2	97.9	89.1	97.3	80.9	69.6	48.1	52.3	61.2	65.7
Balance of Payments					(Millions of Dollars)					
Current Account Balance	-687.7	-678.8	-715.4	-361.7	-305.2	-4.8	-769.0	-604.3	-694.4	-528.7
Trade Balance	-419.6	-439.3	-482.6	-228.6	-237.3	-419.9	-547.7	-392.4	-433.5	-360.9
Exports of Goods (FOB)	257.8	295.1	235.7	318.7	332.4	268.1	223.1	267.0	351.2	497.3
Imports of Goods (FOB)	677.4	734.4	718.3	547.3	569.7	688.0	770.8	659.4	784.7	858.2
Service Balance	-383.2	-374.9	-362.8	-302.0	-269.5	-429.3	-556.9	-485.5	-536.3	-367.8
Unrequited Transfers	115.1	135.4	130.0	168.9	201.6	844.4	335.6	273.6	275.4	200.0
Capital Account Balance	660.0	763.9	707.4	495.0	447.1	6.2	709.2	396.8	594.8	402.1
Non-Monetary Sector	659.5	757.1	717.6	493.7	441.6	9.5	709.9	412.0	588.2	...
Private	-15.9	-5.3	-11.1	24.8	19.8	-152.5	17.8	37.7	71.5	...
Government	675.4	762.4	728.7	468.9	421.8	162.0	692.1	374.3	516.7	...
Monetary Sector	0.5	6.8	-10.2	1.3	5.5	-3.3	-0.7	-15.2	6.6	...
Change in Reserves (- Increase)	211.3	-6.2	-43.9	-64.1	39.3	-86.1	-0.5	79.4	-54.7	-3.7
Errors and Omissions	-183.6	-78.9	51.9	-69.2	-181.2	84.7	60.2	128.1	154.3	130.3
Total External Debt					(Millions of Dollars)					
Disbursed Debt	6,820.9	7,975.9	8,740.9	9,743.0	10,691.9	10,653.7	11,145.3	10,541.3	11,019.0	9,614.0
Debt Service Actually Paid	39.6	43.8	20.5	11.3	15.8	529.8	106.2	125.3	183.3	278.0
					(In Percent)					
Interest Payments Due/Exports of Goods and Non-factor Services	88.5	75.6	96.7	62.1	58.3	110.3	158.5	115.6	102.1	48.1

[1] Data sources are listed at the end.
[2] At market prices.
[3] Includes net lending.
[4] Mid-year values.
[5] Includes Area de Propiedad del Pueblo (APP).

[6] Average rate offered by commercial banks on one-month nominal deposits.
[7] (-) Indicates that the exchange rate is less than half of a significant digit, given the magnitude of the depreciations experienced.
[8] Trade-weighted.

PANAMA
Statistical Profile[1]

	1986	1987	1988	1989	1990	1991	1992	1993	1994	1995p
Real Gross Domestic Product (GDP)[2]					(Average Annual Growth Rates)					
Total GDP	3.3	2.4	-15.6	-0.4	4.6	9.6	8.5	5.4	3.7	1.9
Agriculture, Forestry and Fishing	-2.8	8.9	-5.2	3.7	3.0	5.0	6.7	0.6	3.9	-0.9
Manufacturing	2.2	3.7	-22.6	5.5	11.6	8.7	8.1	7.0	4.3	0.2
Construction	7.5	-2.8	-60.7	-33.8	40.2	117.0	55.4	31.5	2.3	1.3
Transportation and Communications	2.4	4.3	-9.6	-5.2	0.4	13.7	7.9	2.7	3.2	7.7
Non-Financial Public Sector					(As a Percent of GDP)					
Current Revenue	31.0	30.9	22.9	23.3	28.4	30.2	32.2	31.4	32.0	30.7
Current Expenditures	26.8	27.9	32.2	33.4	30.4	29.6	27.8	25.8	24.4	24.3
Current Saving	4.2	3.0	-9.3	-10.1	-2.0	0.6	4.4	5.7	7.6	6.3
Capital Expenditures[3]	4.7	3.9	1.3	1.2	0.8	2.2	3.5	4.4	3.9	3.6
Overall Balance (- Deficit)	-0.4	-0.9	-10.5	-11.3	-2.6	-1.3	1.6	1.5	4.0	3.0
Domestic Financing	-1.0	-0.8	-0.3	1.8	-4.6	-1.4	-1.8	...	...	...
Money and Credit[4]					(As a Percent of GDP)					
Domestic Credit	69.4	72.6	75.0	67.9	52.6	52.2	58.4	60.8	67.0	71.0
Public Sector	16.3	13.5	14.4	14.1	5.0	2.2	-0.5	-5.5	-5.9	-9.0
Private Sector	53.1	59.1	60.7	53.8	47.6	50.0	58.9	66.3	72.9	80.0
Money Supply (M1)	8.0	8.4	6.5	5.6	6.9	7.4	8.7	9.3	10.0	9.3
					(Annual Percentage Rate)					
Interest Rate[5]	6.5	6.6	7.5	8.5	8.4	7.7	5.7	5.9	6.1	...
Prices and Salaries					(Average Annual Growth Rates)					
Consumer Prices	-0.1	1.0	0.4	0.1	0.8	1.3	1.8	0.5	1.3	1.0
Real Wages	-0.3	5.2	0.3	0.0	0.9	0.3	1.3	4.1	...	...
Exchange Rates					(Balboas per Dollar)					
Market Rate	1.0	1.0	1.0	1.0	1.0	1.0	1.0	1.0	1.0	1.0
					(Index 1990 = 100)					
Real Effective[6]	78.8	84.0	90.6	94.6	100.0	102.7	105.1	108.2	112.3	115.8
					(Index 1980 = 100)					
Terms of Trade	116.6	111.6	94.7	98.2	114.0	111.4	110.8	104.6	99.7	98.2
Balance of Payments					(Millions of Dollars)					
Current Account Balance	-395.9	803.2	344.8	-899.4	-238.1	-722.8	-724.2	-575.7	-519.0	-586.9
Trade Balance[7]	-246.6	-255.6	92.9	-199.9	-235.5	-508.5	-505.6	-461.7	-536.5	-924.9
Exports of Goods (FOB)[7]	2,500.0	2,661.2	2,504.7	2,740.8	3,357.6	4,206.9	5,114.6	5,427.6	5,916.5	5,972.4
Imports of Goods (FOB)[7]	2,746.6	2,916.8	2,411.8	2,940.7	3,593.1	4,715.4	5,620.2	5,889.3	6,453.0	6,897.3
Service Balance	-339.6	882.7	126.6	-797.2	-280.4	-502.0	-614.0	-385.3	-203.1	110.7
Unrequited Transfers	190.3	176.1	125.3	97.7	277.8	287.7	395.4	271.3	220.5	227.4
Capital Account Balance	122.4	-83.9	180.6	278.0	83.6	-130.8	-293.8	-951.1	91.8	...
Non-Monetary Sector	221.0	-458.0	-94.0	338.4	650.1	386.8	50.2	-723.0	495.7	...
Private	143.8	-487.4	-375.3	8.5	402.7	146.8	-19.8	-915.2	276.9	...
Government	77.2	29.4	281.3	329.9	247.4	240.0	70.0	192.2	218.8	...
Monetary Sector	-98.6	374.1	274.6	-60.4	-566.5	-517.6	-344.0	-228.1	-403.9	...
Change in Reserves (- Increase)	-59.6	37.6	5.4	-48.7	-297.7	-198.8	-116.4	-89.6	-93.1	-215.0
Errors and Omissions	333.1	-756.9	-530.8	670.1	452.2	1,052.4	1,134.4	1,616.4	520.3	...
Total External Debt					(Millions of Dollars)					
Disbursed Debt	4,859.3	5,630.3	6,066.4	6,318.1	6,678.6	6,732.9	6,486.4	6,958.3	7,106.9	8,053.0
Debt Service Actually Paid	515.0	461.2	28.1	13.3	228.2	250.4	911.4	233.4	312.0	299.0
					(In Percent)					
Interest Payments Due/Exports of Goods and Non-factor Services	19.1	17.9	21.9	12.3	11.1	7.2	4.9	3.3	1.2	...

[1] Data sources are listed at the end.
[2] At market prices.
[3] Includes net lending.
[4] Mid-year values.
[5] Average rate offered by deposit money banks on 6-month nominal time deposits. Beginning December 1992, weighted average rate.
[6] Trade-weighted.
[7] Include activity within the Colón Free Zone.

PARAGUAY
Statistical Profile[1]

	1986	1987	1988	1989	1990	1991	1992	1993	1994	1995p
Real Gross Domestic Product (GDP)[2]					(Average Annual Growth Rates)					
Total GDP	0.0	4.3	6.4	5.8	3.1	2.5	1.8	4.1	3.1	4.2
Agriculture, Forestry and Fishing .	-6.1	7.0	12.1	7.7	2.2	-0.6	0.1	5.6	-0.6	7.1
Manufacturing	-1.4	3.5	5.8	5.9	2.5	1.1	0.4	2.0	1.4	2.6
Construction	1.0	2.0	2.6	2.5	-0.9	3.0	5.0	2.7	3.6	4.0
Wholesale and Retail Trade	3.3	3.5	4.1	4.7	3.6	4.4	0.6	3.8	4.3	1.5
Central Government					(As a Percent of GDP)					
Current Revenue	7.8	8.9	8.9	12.3	12.6	11.8	12.5	12.5	14.5	15.5
Current Expenditures	6.6	6.7	6.2	8.6	7.9	9.6	11.6	11.1	11.4	11.8
Current Saving	1.2	2.2	2.7	3.7	4.7	2.3	0.9	1.3	3.1	3.7
Fixed Investment	1.0	1.1	1.9	1.0	1.0	1.4	1.2	1.4	1.7	2.9
Deficit or Surplus	0.0	0.4	0.6	2.4	3.2	-0.2	-1.0	-0.6	1.0	-0.3
Domestic Financing	0.3	-0.7	-0.4	-1.6	-1.2	0.1	0.0	0.3	-1.2	-0.4
Money and Credit[3]					(As a Percent of GDP)					
Domestic Credit	12.5	11.3	11.5	10.8	11.0	9.6	15.1	22.8	20.9	19.1
Public Sector	2.9	2.5	3.0	1.0	0.6	-1.9	-0.3	6.1	3.5	0.5
Private Sector	9.6	8.7	8.6	9.9	10.4	11.5	15.4	16.7	17.4	18.6
Money Supply (M1)	7.9	8.3	9.0	8.9	6.9	7.6	7.6	7.4	7.3	8.0
					(Annual Percentage Rate)					
Interest Rate[4]	11.0	11.0	14.0	14.0	12.0	12.0	10.4	10.6	12.0	12.1
Prices and Salaries					(Average Annual Growth Rates)					
Consumer Prices	31.7	21.8	22.6	26.4	38.2	24.3	15.1	18.4	20.4	15.4
Real Wages[5]	10.1	10.1	13.4	0.7	-3.7	-4.8	-8.8	-3.9	2.7	1.8
Exchange Rates					(Guaranies per Dollar)					
Market Rate	339.2	550.0	550.0	1,056.2	1,229.8	1,325.2	1,500.3	1,744.4	1,911.5	1,970.4
					(Index 1990 = 100)					
Real Effective[6]	62.1	77.3	74.5	97.4	100.0	85.9	87.7	90.6	91.5	93.9
					(Index 1980 = 100)					
Terms of Trade	118.7	123.6	136.3	157.1	158.6	155.2	149.3	156.8	166.0	173.0
Balance of Payments					(Millions of Dollars)					
Current Account Balance	-364.9	-489.8	-210.2	255.6	-172.3	-324.1	-600.1	-834.0	-748.8	-1,183.9
Trade Balance	-288.4	-321.3	-159.1	164.1	-253.5	-746.8	-869.1	-1,210.7	-1,276.7	-1,674.6
Exports of Goods (FOB)	575.8	597.4	871.0	1,180.0	1,382.3	1,120.8	1,081.5	1,500.0	1,871.3	1,992.4
Imports of Goods (FOB)	864.2	918.7	1,030.1	1,015.9	1,635.8	1,867.6	1,950.6	2,710.7	3,148.0	3,667.0
Service Balance	-87.6	-195.4	-86.2	68.0	25.6	350.4	235.1	334.7	485.9	448.7
Unrequited Transfers	11.1	26.9	35.1	23.5	55.6	72.3	33.9	42.0	42.0	42.0
Capital Account Balance	181.3	189.3	-156.3	-19.8	29.2	151.0	-204.5	219.9	400.6	442.8
Non-Monetary Sector..................	225.3	182.3	-152.8	0.4	58.8	103.4	-181.5	243.2	328.7	357.8
Private	108.3	142.8	-99.7	62.1	180.9	75.9	-120.2	110.0	129.0	208.0
Government	117.0	39.5	-53.1	-61.7	-122.1	27.5	-61.3	133.2	199.7	149.8
Monetary Sector	-44.0	7.0	-3.5	-20.2	-29.6	47.6	-23.0	-23.3	71.9	85.0
Change in Reserves (- Increase)	139.8	-37.8	168.2	-145.2	-219.3	-298.9	346.9	-86.3	-338.3	-6.7
Errors and Omissions	43.8	338.3	198.3	-90.6	362.4	472.0	457.7	700.4	686.5	747.8
Total External Debt					(Millions of Dollars)					
Disbursed Debt	2,086.8	2,519.9	2,351.5	2,383.2	2,105.5	2,066.9	1,634.2	1,597.4	1,978.6	2,112.0
Debt Service Actually Paid	223.2	239.3	316.3	151.7	324.9	257.6	625.8	285.6	258.8	257.0
					(In Percent)					
Interest Payments Due/Exports of Goods and Non-factor Services	15.4	21.0	11.8	7.1	5.3	4.7	8.3	3.6	2.7	2.6

[1] Data sources are listed at the end.
[2] At market prices.
[3] Mid-year values.

[4] Short-term nominal deposit rate.
[5] Real minimum wages.
[6] Trade-weighted.

PERU
Statistical Profile[1]

	1986	1987	1988	1989	1990	1991	1992	1993	1994	1995p
Real Gross Domestic Product (GDP)[2]					(Average Annual Growth Rates)					
Total GDP	9.2	8.5	-8.3	-11.7	-5.4	2.8	-1.4	6.4	13.1	7.0
Agriculture, Forestry and Fishing	6.2	5.1	7.9	-4.8	-6.4	1.9	-6.1	10.4	14.7	5.6
Mining and Quarrying	-4.5	-3.0	-15.0	-4.9	-8.7	2.2	-2.6	8.1	4.0	2.4
Manufacturing	15.6	12.8	-11.2	-15.7	-5.8	6.2	-2.4	4.9	15.8	4.5
Construction	21.4	17.7	-6.8	-14.7	3.2	1.7	4.4	14.3	32.1	17.2
Non-Financial Public Sector					(As a Percent of GDP)					
Current Revenue	15.9	13.3	10.9	9.0	10.0	10.3	11.3	13.3	15.0	16.7
Current Expenditures	16.6	17.0	15.7	14.3	11.8	9.0	9.8	10.5	11.3	13.3
Current Saving	-0.7	-3.7	-4.7	-5.3	-1.8	1.2	1.5	2.8	3.6	3.4
Capital Expenditures[3]	5.8	4.9	3.7	4.4	2.8	2.8	3.5	4.5	5.1	5.1
Overall Balance (- Deficit)	-5.7	-7.9	-8.1	-8.5	-4.5	-1.5	-1.7	-1.3	3.1	-0.1
Domestic Financing	2.3	5.2	4.1	4.9	2.0	-0.6	0.8	-0.3	-4.2	-1.0
Money and Credit[4]					(As a Percent of GDP)					
Domestic Credit	9.3	11.0	3.6	3.5	1.6	5.6	6.3	8.8	7.2	8.7
Public Sector	0.0	2.7	1.4	1.4	0.8	2.0	0.7	0.8	-2.6	-3.6
Private Sector	9.3	8.3	2.2	2.1	0.8	3.5	5.5	7.9	9.8	12.3
Money Supply (M1)	8.0	6.8	3.0	2.2	0.7	3.5	3.8	4.4	4.2	4.9
					(Annual Percentage Rate)					
Interest Rate[5]	...	...	161.8	1,135.6	2,439.6	170.5	59.7	44.1	22.3	16.0
Prices and Salaries					(Average Annual Growth Rates)					
Consumer Prices	200.0	66.7	660.0	3,371.1	7,481.5	409.5	73.6	48.6	23.7	11.1
Real Wages	26.6	6.1	-23.6	-46.7	-14.4	15.2	-3.6	-0.8	14.9	13.3
Exchange Rates					(New Soles per Dollar)					
Market Rate[6]	...	...	...	...	0.2	0.8	1.2	2.0	2.2	2.3
					(Index 1990 = 100)					
Real Effective[7]	219.8	186.0	212.6	120.2	100.0	80.8	78.9	91.4	84.3	82.0
					(Index 1980 = 100)					
Terms of Trade	73.3	78.1	87.5	76.7	80.0	75.4	74.2	68.4	76.1	83.8
Balance of Payments					(Millions of Dollars)					
Current Account Balance	-1,233.0	-1,790.0	-1,334.0	132.0	-678.0	-813.0	-1,657.0	-1,676.0	-2,250.0	-3,748.0
Trade Balance	-55.0	-514.0	-90.0	1,242.0	394.0	-137.0	-555.0	-571.0	-1,108.0	-2,116.0
Exports of Goods (FOB)	2,572.0	2,701.0	2,732.0	3,555.0	3,324.0	3,392.0	3,535.0	3,513.0	4,554.0	5,572.0
Imports of Goods (FOB)	2,627.0	3,215.0	2,822.0	2,313.0	2,930.0	3,529.0	4,090.0	4,084.0	5,662.0	7,688.0
Service Balance	-1,282.0	-1,399.0	-1,405.0	-1,306.0	-1,391.0	-1,122.0	-1,584.0	-1,589.0	-1,581.0	-2,054.0
Unrequited Transfers	104.0	123.0	161.0	196.0	319.0	446.0	482.0	484.0	439.0	422.0
Capital Account Balance	2,480.0	2,954.0	3,227.0	1,780.0	2,555.0	-4,510.0	1,364.0	2,076.0	3,605.0	2,609.0
Non-Monetary Sector	2,521.0	3,021.0	3,232.0	1,956.0	2,580.0	-3,985.0	1,131.0	1,958.0	4,007.0	2,609.0
Private	-5.0	-17.0	-35.0	-57.0	-135.0	14.0	187.0	518.0	3,087.0	...
Government	2,526.0	3,038.0	3,267.0	2,013.0	2,715.0	-3,999.0	944.0	1,440.0	920.0	...
Monetary Sector	-41.0	-67.0	-5.0	-176.0	-25.0	-525.0	233.0	118.0	-402.0	...
Change in Reserves (- Increase)	425.0	1,094.0	149.0	-265.0	-275.0	-950.0	-603.0	-413.0	-3,070.0	-103.0
Errors and Omissions	-1,672.0	-2,258.0	-2,042.0	-1,647.0	-1,602.0	6,273.0	896.0	13.0	1,715.0	1,242.0
Total External Debt					(Millions of Dollars)					
Disbursed Debt	14,887.7	17,490.3	18,245.3	18,583.3	20,069.5	20,718.8	20,339.2	20,448.5	22,623.4	23,097.0
Debt Service Actually Paid	718.3	481.8	348.0	407.2	476.0	1,152.2	1,004.6	2,758.4	1,057.0	1,653.0
					(In Percent)					
Interest Payments Due/Exports of Goods and Non-factor Services	33.0	31.6	32.6	26.4	29.6	23.4	25.8	26.2	22.9	...

[1] Data sources are listed at the end.
[2] At market prices.
[3] Includes net lending.
[4] Mid-year values.
[5] Average rate offered by commercial banks on 31- to 179-day nominal time deposits; converted to percent per annum by compounding monthly interest rates.

[6] (-) Indicates that the exchange rate is less than half of a significant digit, given the magnitude of the depreciations experienced.
[7] Trade-weighted.

SURINAME
Statistical Profile[1]

	1986	1987	1988	1989	1990	1991	1992	1993	1994	1995p
Real Gross Domestic Product (GDP)[2]					(Average Annual Growth Rates)					
Total GDP	0.8	-6.2	7.8	4.2	0.1	3.5	5.8	-4.4	-4.2	5.2
Agriculture, Forestry and Fishing .	-2.6	5.5	-0.5	-2.4	0.9	18.6	1.1	2.2	-9.6	-5.5
Mining and Quarrying	13.4	-17.7	43.8	6.6	-1.9	1.4	5.5	10.5	16.6	5.6
Manufacturing	2.7	-22.3	11.9	1.5	0.9	-3.2	0.9	-4.1	-0.7	3.5
Construction	7.3	-17.3	-1.7	-10.3	-13.7	-2.2	18.9	-28.1	0.0	9.6
Central Government					(As a Percent of GDP)					
Current Revenue	31.0	29.0	29.3	31.2	31.5	27.2	22.4	11.0	19.4	31.6
Current Expenditures	55.2	53.0	49.0	44.8	37.8	45.0	39.5	34.2	32.7	33.0
Current Saving	-24.2	-23.9	-19.7	-13.5	-6.3	-17.8	-17.1	-23.2	-13.3	-1.4
Fixed Investment	2.2	1.1	1.8	3.2	3.1	1.0	2.1	3.1	3.4	3.3
Deficit or Surplus	-26.0	-24.8	-21.3	-14.0	-6.3	-17.4	-11.2	-8.3	-2.3	3.5
Domestic Financing	25.6	24.5	20.9	16.7	2.2	19.0	8.5	7.4	-2.2	-4.4
Money and Credit[3]					(As a Percent of GDP)					
Domestic Credit	115.9	132.1	137.1	142.0	126.8	126.7	113.1	58.0	14.0	5.7
Public Sector	75.5	94.7	101.8	102.8	86.2	84.3	71.9	34.7	7.6	-0.5
Private Sector	40.4	37.4	35.3	39.2	40.6	42.4	41.2	23.3	6.4	6.2
Money Supply (M1)	60.3	68.0	74.2	75.3	69.8	67.8	57.9	32.5	14.7	16.0
					(Annual Percentage Rate)					
Interest Rate[4]	2.7	2.4	2.2	2.3	2.6	2.5	2.7	2.7	4.9	8.6
Prices and Salaries					(Average Annual Growth Rates)					
Consumer Prices	18.7	53.4	7.3	0.8	21.7	26.0	43.7	143.5	368.5	235.9
Real Wages	-10.9	-32.2	-3.2	8.0	-15.9	-7.5	-14.7	-37.3	-28.2	...
Exchange Rates					(Guilders per Dollar)					
Market Rate[5]	5.3	8.6	6.6	7.8	9.8	10.2	14.8	48.9	195.3	451.9
					(Index 1990 = 100)					
Real Effective[6]	76.4	93.0	68.6	85.1	100.0	84.7	90.6	115.8	101.3	69.8
					(Index 1980 = 100)					
Terms of Trade	81.3	78.5	84.7	122.0	99.1	84.1	80.9	76.3	81.2	88.3
Balance of Payments					(Millions of Dollars)					
Current Account Balance	-20.6	76.0	64.2	164.5	37.3	-74.8	14.2	44.0	58.6	79.6
Trade Balance	33.0	64.5	119.0	218.3	91.5	-1.2	68.5	84.4	99.3	109.5
Exports of Goods (FOB)	337.1	338.8	358.4	549.2	465.9	345.9	341.0	298.3	293.6	415.6
Imports of Goods (FOB)	304.1	274.3	239.4	330.9	374.4	347.1	272.5	213.9	194.3	306.1
Service Balance	-54.3	8.3	-62.1	-73.3	-83.9	-86.6	-83.6	-61.3	-44.7	-56.2
Unrequited Transfers	0.7	3.2	7.3	19.5	29.7	13.0	29.3	20.9	4.0	26.3
Capital Account Balance	1.2	-50.8	-65.8	-172.9	-14.7	32.5	-48.6	-73.1	-84.1	-49.5
Non-Monetary Sector	-10.4	-53.9	-86.6	-184.9	-20.0	32.6	-21.5	-34.9	-23.2	-53.8
Private	-12.1	-56.5	-94.1	-191.4	-18.8	29.8	-29.2	-36.9	-25.3	-55.8
Government	1.7	2.6	7.5	6.5	-1.2	2.8	7.7	2.0	2.1	2.0
Monetary Sector	11.6	3.1	20.8	12.0	5.3	-0.1	-27.1	-38.2	-60.9	4.3
Change in Reserves (- Increase)	40.0	9.4	5.2	0.1	-10.3	43.9	12.0	-12.7	-34.3	-101.6
Errors and Omissions	-20.6	-34.6	-3.6	8.3	-12.3	-1.6	22.4	41.8	59.8	71.5
External Public Debt					(Millions of Dollars)					
Disbursed Debt	67.1	75.9	96.6	117.7	125.5	194.2	204.9	206.1	198.1	192.8
Debt Service Actually Paid	5.9	6.4	...	...	...	...	...	...	45.2	41.0
					(In Percent)					
Interest Payments Due/Exports of Goods and Non-factor Services	0.9	1.0	1.2	0.8	1.9	2.5	1.9	1.8	1.3	...

---

[1] Data sources are listed at the end.
[2] GDP at market prices. Sector of Origin at factor cost.
[3] Mid-year values.

[4] Average nominal deposit rate.
[5] Average exchange rate taking into account parallel rate.
[6] Trade-weighted.

TRINIDAD AND TOBAGO
Statistical Profile[1]

	1986	1987	1988	1989	1990	1991	1992	1993	1994	1995p
Real Gross Domestic Product (GDP)[2]					(Average Annual Growth Rates)					
Total GDP	-3.3	-4.6	-3.9	-0.8	1.5	2.7	-1.7	-1.6	4.2	3.2
Agriculture, Forestry and Fishing	0.8	0.2	-2.8	6.0	17.0	3.0	-1.1	3.5	5.7	0.6
Mining and Quarrying	-4.5	-8.4	-2.6	-1.2	0.6	-3.2	-5.0	-8.9	6.1	-0.6
Manufacturing	4.9	-7.4	0.7	5.1	2.7	8.4	2.2	-3.1	7.9	2.5
Construction	-21.0	-10.9	-2.5	-8.2	2.2	11.8	-5.0	-4.4	14.6	13.0
Central Government					(As a Percent of GDP)					
Current Revenue	31.6	30.7	28.6	26.3	25.7	29.9	26.3	27.4	26.1	26.9
Current Expenditures	32.4	29.3	30.9	28.3	25.8	26.8	27.5	26.1	24.7	24.9
Current Saving	-0.8	1.3	-2.3	-2.0	-0.1	3.1	-1.2	1.4	1.4	2.0
Fixed Investment	5.7	7.6	4.2	3.1	1.9	1.6	1.9	1.6	1.8	2.0
Deficit or Surplus	-5.9	-5.9	-5.7	-4.2	-1.2	-0.2	-2.8	-0.2	0.0	0.4
Domestic Financing	7.4	6.0	5.8	5.0	3.3	1.9	3.6	-1.9	-1.1	2.6
Money and Credit[3]					(As a Percent of GDP)					
Domestic Credit	40.6	47.9	53.5	52.2	44.6	43.2	47.8	48.6	38.8	33.0
Public Sector	6.3	14.7	19.0	18.9	15.7	11.7	15.9	16.5	11.8	7.5
Private Sector	34.4	33.3	34.5	33.4	28.9	31.4	31.9	32.1	26.9	25.5
Money Supply (M1)	12.4	12.1	11.0	11.0	10.4	11.2	11.4	12.1	10.9	11.4
					(Annual Percentage Rate)					
Interest Rate[4]	6.0	5.5	5.8	5.9	5.5	6.5	6.3	6.7	6.5	6.0
Prices and Salaries					(Average Annual Growth Rates)					
Consumer Prices	7.7	10.7	7.8	11.3	11.1	3.8	6.6	10.7	8.8	5.3
Real Wages[5]	-3.5	-11.6	-6.8	-12.8	-9.2	-0.7	-1.6	-6.9	-7.6	-3.2
Exchange Rates					(Trinidad and Tobago Dollars per Dollar)					
Market Rate	3.6	3.6	3.8	4.3	4.3	4.3	4.3	5.4	5.9	5.9
					(Index 1990 = 100)					
Real Effective[6]	87.7	94.7	100.9	102.3	100.0	100.7	98.2	108.8	117.7	118.2
					(Index 1980 = 100)					
Terms of Trade	59.6	59.0	68.5	66.5	71.1	71.6	69.6	72.5	88.2	103.4
Balance of Payments					(Millions of Dollars)					
Current Account Balance	-411.9	-225.0	-88.6	-38.5	459.0	-4.7	138.9	113.1	217.8	174.1
Trade Balance	168.9	356.7	405.3	505.5	1,012.5	564.2	695.7	547.2	741.1	690.0
Exports of Goods (FOB)	1,378.4	1,414.3	1,469.5	1,550.8	1,960.1	1,774.5	1,691.4	1,500.1	1,777.6	2,427.9
Imports of Goods (FOB)	1,209.4	1,057.6	1,064.2	1,045.2	947.6	1,210.3	995.6	952.9	1,036.6	1,737.9
Service Balance	-552.5	-559.1	-484.7	-536.5	-547.4	-571.2	-557.2	-438.7	-523.6	-499.1
Unrequited Transfers	-28.4	-22.6	-9.2	-7.5	-6.2	2.4	0.4	4.7	0.3	-16.8
Capital Account Balance	-217.9	64.2	-75.2	60.1	-250.2	-119.8	-100.8	87.2	-38.6	-66.5
Non-Monetary Sector	-177.8	42.5	1.4	82.7	-264.5	-129.6	-112.0	172.4	80.9	-142.8
Private	-111.9	12.1	-138.5	128.1	-191.4	-31.2	-72.9	152.6	144.2	12.5
Government	-65.9	30.4	139.9	-45.4	-73.1	-98.4	-39.1	19.8	-63.3	-155.3
Monetary Sector	-40.1	21.7	-76.6	-22.6	14.3	9.8	11.2	-85.2	-119.5	76.3
Change in Reserves (- Increase)	721.6	255.6	142.8	-67.1	-96.8	153.4	34.6	-158.6	-185.5	-40.7
Errors and Omissions	-91.8	-94.8	21.1	45.4	-112.0	-29.0	-72.6	-41.8	6.3	-66.8
Total External Debt					(Millions of Dollars)					
Disbursed Debt	1,855.0	1,802.3	2,061.4	2,117.2	2,508.4	2,475.3	2,374.0	2,132.6	...	...
Debt Service Actually Paid	328.4	407.4	339.2	247.3	452.9	425.0	571.8	619.9	673.7	444.0
					(In Percent)					
Interest Payments Due/Exports of Goods and Non-factor Services	11.3	10.9	11.0	12.8	10.5	11.7	10.6	11.5	9.5	...

[1] Data sources are listed at the end.
[2] At market prices.
[3] Mid-year values.

[4] Weighted nominal average deposit rate.
[5] Minimum wages.
[6] Trade-weighted.

URUGUAY
Statistical Profile[1]

	1986	1987	1988	1989	1990	1991	1992	1993	1994	1995e
Real Gross Domestic Product (GDP)[2]					(Average Annual Growth Rates)					
Total GDP	8.9	7.9	0.0	1.3	0.9	3.2	7.9	3.0	6.8	-2.4
Agriculture, Forestry and Fishing .	-2.5	4.6	-1.6	3.5	0.3	2.2	12.1	-3.7	9.2	2.7
Manufacturing	11.7	9.9	-0.9	-0.2	-1.5	-0.5	1.5	-9.0	4.0	-2.8
Construction	3.5	23.5	6.7	2.2	-14.5	10.1	15.7	20.5	5.7	-14.7
Wholesale and Retail Trade	9.2	7.7	-1.6	-0.9	0.2	8.4	13.5	16.7	12.3	-11.1
Non-Financial Public Sector					(As a Percent of GDP)					
Current Revenue	25.4	23.8	24.9	23.8	28.9	31.1	31.7	30.8	30.6	32.2
Current Expenditures	22.6	21.7	22.6	23.5	24.5	25.7	26.4	26.9	27.4	29.2
Current Saving	2.8	2.1	2.3	0.3	4.4	5.3	5.3	3.9	3.2	3.0
Capital Expenditures[3]	4.2	3.5	4.2	3.8	4.0	4.1	3.9	4.7	5.7	4.4
Overall Balance (- Deficit)	-1.3	-1.5	-1.9	-3.5	0.4	1.3	1.4	-0.8	-2.4	-1.4
Domestic Financing	-1.3	-1.9	-1.3	-4.0	-2.0	-2.5	-2.5	...	...	...
Money and Credit[4]					(As a Percent of GDP)					
Domestic Credit	58.2	48.3	47.6	47.1	46.0	34.1	29.0	31.9	29.0	34.2
Public Sector	13.2	10.3	12.2	11.6	13.5	8.4	5.7	7.3	5.5	5.2
Private Sector	45.0	37.9	35.4	35.5	32.5	25.7	23.3	24.6	23.5	29.0
Money Supply (M1)	5.7	5.6	6.0	5.1	4.9	4.7	5.4	6.1	5.2	4.7
					(Annual Percentage Rate)					
Interest Rate[5]	61.7	60.8	67.8	84.7	97.8	75.2	54.5	39.4	37.0	38.2
Prices and Salaries					(Average Annual Growth Rates)					
Consumer Prices	76.4	63.6	62.2	80.5	112.5	102.0	68.4	54.1	44.7	42.2
Real Wages	6.7	4.7	1.5	-0.4	-7.3	3.8	2.2	4.8	0.9	-2.9
Exchange Rates					(Pesos per Dollar)					
Market Rate	0.2	0.2	0.4	0.6	1.2	2.0	3.0	3.9	5.1	6.3
					(Index 1990 = 100)					
Real Effective[6]	87.0	89.2	94.6	90.4	100.0	87.7	81.9	69.9	66.3	64.8
					(Index 1980 = 100)					
Terms of Trade	103.2	106.5	114.0	114.4	99.9	93.7	93.2	95.0	99.4	99.8
Balance of Payments					(Millions of Dollars)					
Current Account Balance	41.9	-140.8	22.2	133.5	185.9	42.4	-8.8	-243.7	-389.8	-338.3
Trade Balance	273.3	102.4	292.3	462.8	426.0	61.0	-121.8	-386.7	-671.5	-565.6
Exports of Goods (FOB)	1,087.8	1,182.3	1,404.5	1,599.0	1,692.9	1,604.7	1,801.4	1,731.6	1,913.4	2,116.6
Imports of Goods (FOB)	814.5	1,079.9	1,112.2	1,136.2	1,266.9	1,543.7	1,923.2	2,118.3	2,584.9	2,682.2
Service Balance	-256.7	-251.2	-291.4	-337.3	-248.2	-58.7	84.4	89.6	222.3	195.3
Unrequited Transfers	25.3	8.0	21.3	8.0	8.1	40.1	28.6	53.4	59.4	32.0
Capital Account Balance	18.4	333.4	241.4	23.9	-69.9	-356.4	-40.8	228.0	385.8	372.2
Non-Monetary Sector	88.0	341.5	66.8	-30.7	-21.4	-203.9	114.8	230.6	331.8	401.2
Private	-47.9	105.4	-72.5	-125.1	-143.0	-156.0	15.0	104.7	119.4	128.6
Government	135.9	236.1	139.3	94.4	121.6	-47.9	99.8	125.9	212.4	272.6
Monetary Sector	-69.6	-8.1	174.6	54.6	-48.5	-152.5	-155.6	-2.6	54.0	-29.0
Change in Reserves (- Increase)	-281.5	-88.0	-16.5	-94.8	-151.7	-154.8	-188.7	-193.0	-89.8	-209.4
Errors and Omissions	221.3	-104.6	-247.1	-62.6	35.7	468.8	238.3	208.6	93.8	175.5
Total External Debt					(Millions of Dollars)					
Disbursed Debt	3,906.1	4,298.8	3,820.8	4,448.6	4,415.1	4,188.7	4,570.2	4,847.7	5,098.9	5,080.0
Debt Service Actually Paid	508.8	618.0	729.4	659.9	986.7	805.9	524.0	586.1	507.5	968.0
					(In Percent)					
Interest Payments Due/Exports of Goods and Non-factor Services	24.6	24.2	24.0	27.2	26.9	21.2	15.7	14.4	14.0	15.0

[1] Data sources are listed at the end.
[2] At market prices. Mining and Quarrying included in Manufacturing. For 1995, total GDP reflects entire year; the components reflect only January–September.
[3] Includes net lending.

[4] Mid-year values.
[5] Rates on 1- to 6-month domestic currency fixed nominal deposits at deposit money banks; average rate for five most representative private banks at end of month.
[6] Trade-weighted.

VENEZUELA
Statistical Profile[1]

	1986	1987	1988	1989	1990	1991	1992	1993	1994	1995p
Real Gross Domestic Product (GDP)[2]					(Average Annual Growth Rates)					
Total GDP	6.3	4.5	6.2	-7.8	6.9	9.7	6.1	0.3	-2.8	2.2
Agriculture, Forestry and Fishing .	7.7	4.0	4.6	-5.1	-1.5	2.4	2.1	2.9	2.2	-0.7
Petroleum	8.7	5.2	4.1	0.0	17.9	9.5	1.4	9.0	5.4	5.2
Manufacturing	7.1	2.5	6.9	-11.8	6.0	9.7	2.5	-1.0	-3.6	7.2
Construction	6.3	3.0	7.9	-27.0	7.8	30.9	34.6	-5.5	-26.2	-11.4
Non-Financial Public Sector[3]					(As a Percent of GDP)					
Current Revenue	25.4	26.5	23.9	29.0	32.7	29.4	24.0	25.6	27.8	24.8
Current Expenditures	19.7	20.5	19.4	18.6	20.4	19.4	18.1	17.2	19.3	18.7
Current Saving	5.7	6.0	4.5	10.4	12.3	10.0	6.0	8.4	8.4	6.1
Capital Expenditures[4]	13.3	12.0	13.9	11.5	12.4	13.9	12.1	10.0	22.2	12.7
Overall Balance (- Deficit)	-7.4	-6.0	-9.4	-1.1	0.1	-2.2	-5.9	-1.3	-13.3	-5.9
Domestic Financing	0.0	5.9	7.4	0.5	...	...	...	...	...	...
Money and Credit[5]					(As a Percent of GDP)					
Domestic Credit	27.2	28.6	30.6	24.1	18.5	27.6	22.8	21.2	30.5	20.2
Public Sector	-2.0	0.5	1.0	1.2	2.5	10.6	6.4	6.7	8.1	7.3
Private Sector	29.2	28.1	29.7	22.9	16.0	17.0	16.5	14.5	22.3	12.9
Money Supply (M1)	21.4	19.2	15.3	10.5	8.2	9.8	11.2	7.2	7.8	8.9
					(Annual Percentage Rate)					
Interest Rate[6]	8.9	9.0	9.0	33.1	29.1	31.3	35.6	53.9	39.0	25.1
Prices and Salaries					(Average Annual Growth Rates)					
Consumer Prices	11.5	28.1	29.5	84.5	40.6	34.2	31.4	38.1	60.8	59.9
Real Wages	-4.3	-15.1	-8.8	-15.8	-7.9	-8.2	3.8	-6.8	-11.0	-7.0
Exchange Rates					(Bolivares per Dollar)					
Market Rate	8.1	14.5	14.5	34.7	46.9	56.8	68.4	90.8	148.5	180.0
					(Index 1990 = 100)					
Real Effective[7]	61.2	85.4	76.5	89.8	100.0	93.6	89.6	86.6	89.9	71.9
					(Index 1980 = 100)					
Terms of Trade	57.3	69.5	56.7	70.8	83.9	66.2	63.6	60.5	59.0	59.9
Balance of Payments					(Millions of Dollars)					
Current Account Balance	-2,245.0	-1,390.0	-5,809.0	2,161.0	8,279.0	1,736.0	-3,749.0	-1,993.0	2,450.0	1,572.0
Trade Balance	798.0	1,694.0	-1,863.0	5,694.0	10,706.0	4,900.0	1,322.0	3,275.0	7,691.0	6,647.0
Exports of Goods (FOB)	8,664.0	10,564.0	10,217.0	13,059.0	17,623.0	15,159.0	14,202.0	14,779.0	15,890.0	18,278.0
Imports of Goods (FOB)	7,866.0	8,870.0	12,080.0	7,365.0	6,917.0	10,259.0	12,880.0	11,504.0	8,199.0	11,631.0
Service Balance	-2,922.0	-2,993.0	-3,799.0	-3,350.0	-2,125.0	-2,800.0	-4,697.0	-4,900.0	-5,025.0	-5,218.0
Unrequited Transfers	-121.0	-91.0	-147.0	-183.0	-302.0	-364.0	-374.0	-368.0	-216.0	143.0
Capital Account Balance	-707.0	960.0	-1,180.0	-3,650.0	-4,061.0	2,204.0	3,386.0	2,656.0	-3,124.0	-3,776.0
Non-Monetary Sector	-964.0	97.0	-75.0	-3,998.0	-3,176.0	2,050.0	3,394.0	3,074.0	-2,150.0	-3,930.0
Private	-46.0	589.0	-1,082.0	-4,315.0	-1,083.0	2,105.0	2,459.0	1,948.0	-2,061.0	-3,387.0
Government	-918.0	-492.0	1,007.0	317.0	-2,093.0	-55.0	935.0	1,126.0	-89.0	-543.0
Monetary Sector	257.0	863.0	-1,105.0	348.0	-885.0	154.0	-8.0	-418.0	-974.0	154.0
Change in Reserves (- Increase)	3,882.0	935.0	3,872.0	-113.0	-2,476.0	-2,424.0	662.0	-124.0	972.0	2,391.0
Errors and Omissions	-930.0	-505.0	3,117.0	1,603.0	-1,742.0	-1,516.0	-299.0	-539.0	-298.0	-187.0
Total External Debt					(Millions of Dollars)					
Disbursed Debt	34,340.3	34,569.8	34,737.6	32,376.9	33,170.4	34,121.6	37,848.3	37,539.2	36,849.6	37,434.0
Debt Service Actually Paid	5,103.1	4,871.9	5,551.6	3,830.8	4,989.8	3,321.5	3,331.4	3,944.8	3,690.9	4,651.0
					(In Percent)					
Interest Payments Due/Exports of Goods and Non-factor Services	34.3	25.9	29.1	26.6	17.1	15.5	18.3	17.0	17.5	15.6

[1] Data sources are listed at the end.
[2] At market prices.
[3] On a cash basis.
[4] Includes net lending.

[5] Mid-year values.
[6] Nominal average annual time deposit rate.
[7] Trade-weighted.

SOURCES OF THE STATISTICAL PROFILES

Real Gross Domestic Product:

Argentina: Ministerio de Economía y Obras y Servicios Públicos, Secretaría de Programación Económica.

Bahamas: IDB estimates based on information furnished by the Department of Statistics and the Central Bank of the Bahamas.

Barbados: Barbados Statistical Service and the Central Bank of Barbados.

Belize: Central Statistical Office, Ministry of Finance.

Bolivia: Instituto Nacional de Estadística, Departamento de Cuentas Nacionales.

Brazil: Fundação Instituto Brasileiro de Geografía e Estatística, Departamento de Contas Nacionais.

Chile: Banco Central de Chile, Departamento de Cuentas Nacionales.

Colombia: Departamento Administrativo Nacional de Estadística.

Costa Rica: Banco Central de Costa Rica, Departamento de Contabilidad Social.

Dominican Republic: Banco Central de la República Dominicana, División de Cuentas Nacionales.

Ecuador: Banco Central del Ecuador, Subgerencia de Cuentas Nacionales.

El Salvador: Banco Central de Reserva de El Salvador, Departamento de Cuentas Económicas.

Guatemala: Banco de Guatemala, Departamento de Estudios Económicos.

Guyana: Statistical Bureau and Bank of Guyana.

Haiti: Institut Haïtien de Statistiques et d'Informatique, Banque de la République d'Haïti and International Monetary Fund estimates.

Honduras: Banco Central de Honduras, Departamento de Estudios Económicos.

Jamaica: Statistical Institute of Jamaica.

Mexico: Instituto Nacional de Estadística, Geografía e Informática.

Nicaragua: Banco Central de Nicaragua, Gerencia de Estudios Económicos.

Panama: Contraloría General de la República, Dirección de Estadística y Censo.

Paraguay: Banco Central del Paraguay, Departamento de Cuentas Nacionales y Mercado Interno.

Peru: Instituto Nacional de Estadística and Banco Central de Reserva del Perú.

Suriname: Algemeen Bureau Voor de Statistiek and IDB estimates.

Trinidad and Tobago: Central Statistical Office of Trinidad and Tobago.

Uruguay: Banco Central del Uruguay, Departamento de Estadísticas Económicas.

Venezuela: Banco Central de Venezuela, Departamento de Cuentas Nacionales.

Non-Financial Public Sector:

Argentina: Ministerio de Economía y Obras y Servicios Públicos and Secretaría de Hacienda.

Bolivia: Banco Central de Bolivia, Gerencia de Estudios Económicos and Ministerio de Finanzas.

Brazil: Banco Central do Brasil, Departamento Econômico.

Colombia: Departamento Nacional de Planeación.

Costa Rica: Ministerio de Hacienda, Autoridad Presupuestaria.

Ecuador: Ministerio de Finanzas, Banco Central del Ecuador and International Monetary Fund estimates.

El Salvador: Ministerio de Hacienda and Banco Central de Reserva de El Salvador.

Haiti: Ministère de l'Economie et des Finances and International Monetary Fund.

Honduras: Banco Central de Honduras, Departamento de Estudios Económicos and International Monetary Fund.

Mexico: Dirección General de Planeación Hacendaria. Secretaría de Hacienda y Crédito Público.

Nicaragua: Ministerio de Finanzas y Banco Central de Nicaragua

Panama: Contraloría General de la República, Ministerio de Planificación y Política Económica, International Monetary Fund and IDB estimates.

Peru: Banco Central de Reserva del Perú and Ministerio de Economía.

Uruguay: Banco Central del Uruguay.

Venezuela: Banco Central de Venezuela and International Monetary Fund.

Central Government:

Bahamas: Central Bank of the Bahamas, *Quarterly Statistical Digest*.

Barbados: Central Government of Barbados and Ministry of Finance.

Belize: Ministry of Finance.

Chile: Contraloría General de la República, División de Contabilidad.

Dominican Republic: Tesorería Nacional, Contraloría General de la República and Banco Central de la República Dominicana.

Guatemala: Ministerio de Finanzas.

Guyana: Ministry of Finance and Bank of Guyana.

Jamaica: Ministry of Finance, Fiscal Policy Management Unit.

Paraguay: Ministerio de Finanzas.

Suriname: International Monetary Fund based on data furnished by the Ministerie van Financiën en Planning and Planbureau.

Trinidad and Tobago: Central Statistical Office of Trinidad and Tobago and the Ministry of Finance and the Economy.

Money and Credit (mid-year observations):

International Monetary Fund, *International Financial Statistics* and the following national sources:

Brazil: Domestic Credit: Banco Central do Brasil, Departamento Econômico.

Ecuador: International Monetary Fund, *International Financial Statistics* and IDB estimates based on information furnished by the Banco Central del Ecuador.

Guyana: International Monetary Fund, *International Financial Statistics* and Bank of Guyana.

Haiti: Banque de la République d'Haïti and International Monetary Fund estimates.

Nicaragua: Banco Central de Nicaragua (annual average).

Peru: International Monetary Fund, *International Financial Statistics*, and Banco Central de Reserva del Perú.

Suriname: Centrale Bank van Suriname and International
             Monetary Fund, *International Financial Statistics*.

Prices and Salaries:
Consumer Prices: International Monetary Fund, *International Financial Statistics*.

Real Wages:

Argentina:	Fundación de Investigaciones Económicas Latinoamericanas.
Barbados:	Central Bank of Barbados.
Brazil:	Fundação Getúlio Vargas, *Conjuntura Econômica*.
Chile:	Banco Central de Chile, *Boletín Mensual*, various issues.
Colombia:	Departamento Administrativo Nacional de Estadística, *Encuesta mensual manufacturera*.
Costa Rica:	Banco Central de Costa Rica, Departamento de Contabilidad Social based on data furnished by the Caja Costarricense de Seguro Social.
Dominican Republic:	Oficina Nacional de Planeación.
Ecuador:	Consejo Nacional de Desarrollo (CONADE) and Banco Central de Ecuador.
El Salvador:	Instituto Salvadoreño del Seguro Social.
Guatemala:	Instituto Guatemalteco de Seguridad Social and Banco de Guatemala, Sección de Cuentas Nacionales.
Haiti:	Ministère des Affaires Sociales, and the Institut Haïtien de Statistiques et d'Informatique.
Honduras:	Banco Central de Honduras, Departamento de Estudios Económicos.
Mexico:	Banco de México.
Nicaragua:	IDB estimates based on data furnished by the Ministerio de Trabajo.
Panama:	Contraloría General de la República, Dirección de Estadística y Censo, and IDB estimates.
Paraguay:	Banco Central de Paraguay.
Peru:	Banco Central de Reserva del Perú.
Suriname:	Algemeen Bureau Voor de Statistiek and IDB estimates.
Trinidad and Tobago:	Central Statistical Office of Trinidad and Tobago.
Uruguay:	Dirección General de Estudios y Censos, *Boletín Mensual*.
Venezuela:	Oficina Central de Coordinación y Planificación (CORDIPLAN), Dirección de Planificación de Empleo, Producción y Precios.

Exchange Rates:
Market Rate: International Monetary Fund, *International Financial Statistics* and the following national sources:
Haiti: Banque de la République d'Haïti.

Real Effective:
IDB estimates based on data from the International Monetary Fund, *International Financial Statistics*, and the following national sources:

Guatemala:	Banco de Guatemala, Departamento de Estudios Económicos.
Mexico:	Banco de México, Dirección de Operaciones Internacionales.
Peru:	Banco Central de Reserva del Perú.

Terms of Trade:
ECLAC, *Balance preliminar de la economía de América Latina y el Caribe*, various issues, and IDB estimates for Guyana, Jamaica, Suriname and Trinidad and Tobago.

Balance of Payments:
International Monetary Fund, *Balance of Payments Statistics* (magnetic tapes) and the following national sources:

Argentina:	Ministerio de Economía.
Bahamas:	Central Bank of the Bahamas.
Barbados:	Central Bank of Barbados.
Belize:	Central Bank of Belize.
Bolivia:	Banco Central de Bolivia.
Brazil:	Banco Central do Brasil.
Chile:	Banco Central de Chile.
Colombia:	Banco de la República, Subgerencia de Estudios Económicos.
Costa Rica:	Banco Central de Costa Rica.
Dominican Republic:	Banco Central de la República Dominicana, División de Balanza de Pagos.
Ecuador:	Banco Central del Ecuador, Subgerencia de Balanza de Pagos.
El Salvador:	Banco Central de Reserva de El Salvador.
Guatemala:	Banco de Guatemala, Departamento de Estudios Económicos.
Guyana:	Ministry of Finance.
Haiti:	Banque de la République d'Haïti.
Honduras:	Banco Central de Honduras.
Jamaica:	Bank of Jamaica.
Mexico:	Banco de México.
Nicaragua:	Banco Central de Nicaragua.
Paraguay:	Banco Central del Paraguay.
Peru:	Banco Central de Reserva del Perú.
Suriname:	Centrale Bank van Suriname.
Trinidad and Tobago:	Central Bank of Trinidad and Tobago.
Uruguay:	Banco Central del Uruguay.
Venezuela:	Banco Central de Venezuela.

External Debt:
World Bank, *World Debt Tables* (magnetic tapes) and the following national sources:

Bahamas:	Treasury Accounts, Treasury Statistical Printout and Quarterly Reports from Public Corporations, and estimates.
Suriname:	IDB estimates based on information from the Centrale Bank van Suriname.
All countries:	Interest Payments Due/Exports of Goods and Non-Factor Services: Ibidem and see also Balance of Payments above.